Listen then of Woden
He of the one eye
He is the young man
He is the old man
Friend of the ravens
Feeder of wolves

Tell then of Woden
Lord of the battle
Seated in Valhalla
Seated in your hall
Watches he all things
Writing in Runes

Watch then for Woden
He of the white hair
Shape change traveller
Stalks by dark night
Seeking out sword clash
Foul father of death

Woden's Wolf

by Geoff Boxell

Library of Congress Catalog Card Number: 98-87886

ISBN 1-892977-00-1

© 1998 Geoff Boxell

HT Communications
PO Box 1401; Arvada, Colorado 80001

THE YOUNG MAN

At the knock of the door,
Beware the stranger,
Young man with white hair,
Old man with one eye,
Speaking with wolves,
Talking in riddles,
Woden the traveller,
Comes in the night.

The Fosse

he bite of the early morning had given way to a gentle warmth as the autumn day progressed. The sun shining in the cloudless sky had turned the silver of the frost to warm droplets on the lush grass of the water mead. The couple held hands as they sat on the bridge that crossed the water mill's weir. The young man ran his thumb over the girl's small hand. She looked at him and smiled. His thoughts, however, were elsewhere and the caress was almost absent minded.

Eventually, he pulled himself around and turned his attention to the maid by his side. He squeezed her hand and stood, pulling her up with him. Together, they crossed the bridge and followed the path toward the hedged holding on the other bank of the river, leaving the rushing sound of the fast flowing water behind, as it both crashed over the weir and fell from the turning water wheel.

On impulse, the young man stopped and turned back to look at the river. His tall, gangling build contrasted with the small and tidy frame of the girl holding his hand. He bent and kissed her head, his golden hair mingling with her chestnut brown. She snuggled to his side and leaned against him.

Time hung.

"Come, we should go. My mother will be upset if I am late for this last meal at home before I leave." He let go of her hand and put his arm around her slim shoulder. As one unit, they left the peace and sanctity of the river Wandle and headed toward the noise and bustle of the farm yard.

* * *

"Don't look now, but your mother is watching." The girl tossed her head slightly, causing her shiny, chestnut hair to dance over her shoulders. The young man tried not to look, but after a few moments of hesitation, he snuck a quick glance.

Woden's Wolf

"She'll notice," he whispered, as he dipped his spoon back into the bowl of thick broth. "Eve, please." The girl looked quizzically at the young man. "She'll notice," he added.

"She never has in the past." The girl smiled serenely at the older woman sitting at the other end of the table in the hall. She blew on the steaming broth before she sucked the contents into her mouth. Closing her eyes dreamily, she let out a pleasurable sigh as she eased the now empty spoon out. "Wonderful, so creamy."

The young man gave a slight gasp and his eyes opened wide.

"Godfrew? Are you all right?" the older woman asked.

"Ah, it's just a bit hot, mother." Godfrew blinked, then lowered his face to the dish and its steamy contents. Eve removed her left hand from Godfrew's britches and let it rejoin her right hand in her lap.

"Eve. Have you finished already, child?" Godfrew's mother asked, already stretching across the waxed wooden table toward the ladle sitting in the earthenware dish containing the broth. "For such a wee thing, you have a good appetite."

"Thank you, mother-in-law, but I have finished at present." Eve gently put her hand on Godfrew's. "I am sure you have finished, Frew. Come, let's go outside. With you soon leaving to join King Harold's gathering, we should spend as much time together as we can."

"Mother?"

"Yes, go Godfrew. Your wife is right. Enjoy each other's company while you may. It could be some time before the problems are over and you are with each other again." The woman re-filled her own bowl whilst the youngsters left the hall.

"Rosemund, you spoil the boy. He won't get that well fed on campaign, as well I know." The older man pursed his lips disapprovingly. "Now ... when I was with Harold in Wales ..."

"You spent your time organising the storage train and getting fat on its contents, Alfred ... and well you know it!" Rosemund ate some of the broth, then looked at the spoon. "Funny, it's not that hot ... certainly not hot enough to have got that sort of reaction out of the boy."

"Boy? He is a man now, woman. In fact, he is a warrior—the thane for our holding—with his own shield bearer and five men to back him." Alfred used his toes to stir the big deer hound asleep at his foot. As the animal rolled over, he caressed its belly with his foot. "Too protective by far, you are. Would you have been so if his younger twin brothers had lived?"

"Don't, Alfred. Just don't go there. You know it hurts. Even after all these years, it still hurts." Rosemund blinked away a small tear and busied herself eating the now cold broth.

"Yes ... well, sorry my love, but the boy has to perform his duties for the holding. We have the five hides. We must put up a sword thane." The hound rolled onto its back and started kicking Alfred with its front paw to ensure that the foot rubbing continued.

"You could have hired someone. He is all we have. If anything happens to him, I would die. So would your line, Alfred. Did you think of that when you gave him the long axe and helmet to go and play soldier?"

"It had to be done. You women just do not understand the value of pride. My father was given this land by ..."

"Knute. I know the story." Rosemund put her bowl down and stood up. She sighed sadly before leaning across and lifting the earthenware dish of broth off of its iron stand in the middle of the table. "Pride, Alfred? Of pride, I know ... but if Godfrew does not come back from these campaigns of the king's ... what then? Of what value is pride when you have no son ... when you, Alfred of Garrat, have no heir?"

"I am sure that the king knows what he is about. He is a brilliant general." Alfred had stopped stroking the hound. It stood up and shook, shaking the table as it did so. "But you are right. We need to secure the holding. The boy should look for a wife. That young hand-fast maid of his is sweet. I like the child, but he will have to look for better stock to breed with ... something with a better pedigree."

"The way our son and his little maid carry on, I wouldn't be surprised if she isn't with child by the time Godfrew leaves for the north."

"With child? Pregnant?" Alfred flicked the ears of his deer hound. It had sat down and started shuffling toward it master, crowding him from the edge of the table. "Stop it, Grendal. Stop it now and I'll fuss over you in a moment." The hound lowered its enormous head and gazed sadly at the plump, bald man on the stool in front of him. "I know the boy has declared himself hand-fast bound to the girl, but she is just a child ... and so innocent."

* * *

"I wish you wouldn't do that." Godfrew settled himself comfortably on the straw on the barn floor.

"But you like it." Eve, sitting in front of him, unpinned the head cover that declared her a wife and laid it on the floor beside her.

"I do, but not whilst my parents are watching." Godfrew propped himself on his elbow and observed the play of the filtered light coming in through the cracks in the barn door. The light turned Eve's long hair into burnished metal as it glinted off the shine. "You know that the nail marks take a week to go. At least, don't be so rough when you do it."

"It's to brand you as mine." Eve undid the lacing of her bodice and exposed her small breasts. The nipples were relaxed and smooth. Godfrew leaned across to tweak them, but she slapped his hands away. "If anyone else ever tried to have you, they would see the marks, and know that someone else owned you."

"And I would want someone else? In fact, with my weapon scarred with nail marks, would anyone else want me?"

"You soldiers have a reputation." Eve removed the kirtle pin from her skirt and placed it on top of her head covering before laying the skirt on the ground around her.

"Soldier? I am not a soldier. I am a warrior ... a long axeman ... a thane." Godfrew's mock pomposity was emphasised by the bobbing of his head. Each movement made his golden hair slide across his face.

"Soldier or warrior. Once out of here, all you will think of is rape and pillage ... rape and pillage ... then you will come back here covered in scars and useless to me in the hay." Eve got up and let her underskirt join the rest of her clothing on the floor. Slowly, she walked the few steps to Godfrew and stood over him.

The Fosse

"I already have the scars, thanks to you, my young minx." Godfrew rolled onto his back and gazed up at the small, fine female form that stood naked above him.

"Rape and pillage ... rape and pillage ... rape and pillage." Eve knelt over both sides of Godfrew's knees and rolled his britches back. Grasping his penis with both hands, she moved forward to straddle him. "And what poor innocent soul is this weapon going to stab and thrust, pray?"

"Eve." Godfrew's voice was quiet and serious. "All joking apart, I will not betray you. You would never betray me, would you?" He went to sit up, but the young maid—still holding him firmly—leaned forward and sought his lips with hers. Her warm tongue teased the tip of his, then rolled around his mouth before stretching toward the back of his throat. Just as Godfrew started to feel uncomfortable, Eve broke away from the kiss and sat up again. She sank her fingernails in and rocked Godfrew's penis, each time making it more vertical and closer to her sparse bush.

"Eve, you look so beautiful. Promise me you are for my eyes only. Just for me?"

"Oh, my brave, upright warrior. I promise! No man will ever see me naked, except you." She rubbed the head against herself, smearing her wetness into her pubic hair. "Only you, my brave warrior, shall know the full beauty of my body." Her breath started to come in short pants as the rubbing became more frantic. At last, she let go—threw herself forward, smothered Godfrew's chest in kisses and slid down onto him. Slowly and rhythmically, she ground her hips until Godfrew was a groaning and writhing mess beneath her. With a high-pitched gasp, she pushed down hard—again and again—before making a final thrust that caused Godfrew considerable pain. As he yelped, Eve sank her teeth into his chest and bit till she tasted blood.

She sat up, pulled herself off of Godfrew and lay alongside him. "Do you think your friend Godwine will come in here, like last time, to find out what all the noise is about? And will I have to throw things at him whilst you just lie there and laugh—like last time?" She picked up a piece of straw and tickled Godfrew's cheek. "Oh, it wasn't a tumble in the hay after all. It was only straw. We shall have to do it all over again," she giggled.

"Eve." Godfrew turned his face toward Eve and opened his eyes. In the darkened light of the barn, the white of the cataract on his left eye stood out. "Godwine is my friend and my shield bearer. I need him, Eve. He is my protector. What if something happens to him? What if something happens to me? What if we loose against the Norse? What if the Normans also invade? What if ..."

Eve stopped the flow of words with a deep kiss. She cupped Godfrew's chin with her tiny hand. "What can go wrong? English warriors are the best in middle earth, Frew. What can go wrong when you are led by ..." She gave him another long kiss. "... King Harold Godwinson, the Golden Warrior? With Harold at the front, what can go wrong?"

* * *

"The king is dead."

Godfrew glanced at Godwine, his shield bearer, then back at the man in front of him. "How?"

"Nay enough of buggers like ye there, mon. How come ye take sae long tae get here, eh?" The Geordie wiped his forehead with his tattered sleeve, leaving a smeared streak.

"Defending English-Norse like you at Stamford Bridge and getting injured in the process." Godfrew shifted his weight stiffly onto his good leg, emphasising his injury. In fact, the leg was not the problem. It was his back. The big Norwegian berserker[1] had held the bridge by screaming insults, surrounded by dead English. Godfrew had not wanted to be next, but there had been no one in front of him. As he advanced, with Godwine covering his vulnerable side, the naked berserker ran toward him, swinging a massive long axe. The man's chest muscles and private parts flopped up and

---

[1] Berserker: literally *bear-skin*. The true nature and meaning of the berserker is subject to much debate. Some authorities maintain that berserkers were individual warriors of a violent nature—given to *blood lust* —that were used as storm troopers. Others believe them to be members of an organised religious warrior group dedicated to Woden, whilst still others think of them as warrior shamen. The wearing of bear and wolf skins by certain warriors is well recorded in literature and art. In literature, there is often a strong implication of the animal's nature being adopted or absorbed by the wearer. It is sometimes alluded that even that the warer was, in fact, a *shape changer*. It is also a recorded fact that some berserkers fought either naked or naked under their animal cloak, thus the pun *bare-skin*. In earlier times, the berserker was admired for his blood lust and insensibility to injury. As warrior bands became more disciplined and enlarged to become armies, the unpredictability and irrational behaviour of the beserker was no longer needed by the military.

The Fosse

down as he closed the gap between them. Godfrew had timed his axe swing and missed. He slipped in a pool of blood and went sprawling, taking his shield bearer with him.

The berserker had leaped over them both and turned around. Just as he steadied himself to strike Godfrew and his companion down, a spear came up between the planks on the bridge. It slit his crotch from anus to penis and reappeared through his navel. The man was still staring at it when a house carl[2] beheaded him with his long axe.

Godfrew had almost been trampled to death as the exultant English swept over the bridge to get at the Vikings on the other side of the river bank. He did not know whether it was the fall or the feet trampling all over him, but a savage pain hit Godfrew every time he tried to move his legs.

"Nothing is broken," the old wise-woman had later told him. "Maybe the bridge troll struck him." But it was not the bridge troll that struck down the berserker. It was an Englishman. Some say it was the king himself—Harold Godwinson—and now the King was dead.

Godwine grabbed the Geordie by the shoulder and shook him. "How did the King die? Was he attacking and heading his Danish house carls in a charge? Was he defending when the wall of shields broke? How, man? How?"

"Arrows, mon, arrows. Mail protects the body ... nay the face. The battle is lost! The House carls and earls are dying tae a mon o'er his body. Nae, all is lost ... and now... what of us?"

"We fight." Godfrew pushed his hand into his side and massaged his back as the healing monk had told him to. That old monk surely had an evil streak in him. He had really seemed to enjoy the pain he caused when he put a foot to Godfrew's spine. The old monk had yanked Godfrew's legs and head in the opposite direction at the same time. The treatment was harsh, but it had allowed Godfrew to walk again.

---

[2] House carl: armed retainer, literally house-freeman. The bond between a lord and his house carl was close and personal. The house carl was expected to die for his lord, even if his lord was already dead, and the actions of King Harold's house carls at Hastings exemplifies this. House carls were not bound for life, the usual term being Christmas to Christmas, nor were they always permanent residents at the lord's hall. The personal bodyguard of a lord was usually referred to as being his *hearth troop*.

"The Godwinson gave me an arm band when I became his thane.[3] You do not leave a ring giver," Godfrew said.

"Oh, aye ... well ... I've got a long way tae gang home, mon ... an' I a wif and bairns tae protect. English-Norse, ye called me? It's the French-Norse ye'll have tae look oot frae now. Harold nay gave me a ring, sae I'll nay be obliged tae die frae him."

"But others will." A group of Fyrdmen[4] came into the clearing bearing farm tools and wooden clubs. The lead man stood in front of Godfrew. "It was to stop the Norman Bastard burning our villages that the King rushed back here after crushing the Vikings at Stamford. We just wish we could have got here sooner. Maybe if we had got here sooner ..."

"God holds man's fate. We all have to die one day. Today it was the King's turn. Are there many others?" Godfrew scanned the trees in the fosse and up the valley leading to it.

"If you are after blood vengeance, thane, you had better get your mail coat on, because the Bastard's men are heading this way." More men pushed out of the trees onto the valley floor. Some were thanes and their house carls, but most were farm labourers—late arriving members of the local Fyrd.

"Hmm." Godfrew cast his eye over the band. "Fyrdmen, those with slings or bows to the trees along the fosse! The rest to the top of the fosse and be ready to block the entrance with stones and logs! Thanes, are you with me? Make a wall of shields across the valley. We flee when the Normans charge and draw them in. Then the Fyrdmen can put the stop in the bottle."

"Quite the battle marshal, young thane." Godfrew turned. The speaker was a bear of a man, already dressed in his mail coat and conical helmet. It was hard to tell his age, but the scars on his face told of many battles fought. A stray lock of

---

[3] Thane: (thegn, thain) originally a man holding five hides of land and able to equip himself for the select Fyrd, but by the 11th century many thanes held less than five hides and many never performed military duties; this is explained, in part, by the fact that elevation to thanehood was one way—upwards—and hereditary.

[4] Fyrd: it is now widely accepted that there were two types of Fyrd. 1) The general Fyrd which was basically the *Home Guard,* as it were, of Old England. The actual composition of the general Fyrd is subject to much debate, but is normally thought to have consisted of all freemen within the shire. The general Fyrd would only serve in its own location, normally the Earldom. 2) The select Fyrd which consisted of one thane or nominated freemen per 5 hides of land. The hide was an artificial unit whose acreage could vary considerably. It was the normal unit of assessment for Fyrd service and Danegeld assessment in Saxon England. In the Danelaw, its equivalent was the *carucates.*

The Fosse

faded yellow hair that had escaped the helmet contrasted with the dark brown of the man's beard. "But what if it is the Bastard's whole army and not just a troop?"

"Then we die quicker, my Lord Waltheof." Godfrew turned to face the Earl.

"You know me." There was humour in the big man's voice.

"You hold land at Balham, my Lord. I saw you once at a Michaelmas Fair—at Tooting with the King, when he was still the Earl of Wessex. My father recognised him as his lord and was in attendance on him. I tagged along." Godfrew seemed a bit embarrassed at having to recall the event.

"Balham? That was a long time ago. I leased that land to ... to ..." Waltheof's forehead creased as he struggled to remember: "... Alnod ... yes, Alnod of London. That was quite a few years ago." He looked closely at Godfrew, particularly his face. "Ah, now I remember you there ... the eye ... the elf-smitten eye. You were a lot smaller then, young thane. You got under everybody's feet and you almost tripped our Harold up." Waltheof broke away to take in what was going on around him.

Godfrew started to kneel and went down quickly in a crumpled heap. Godwine, his shield bearer, helped him stand again. Waltheof looked down, "Carry on doing that, my young friend, and you won't get up again. Then you really will die quicker." A smile split Earl Waltheof's face, allowing his white teeth to contrast with his beard. "Now it all comes back. I saw you again at the Stamford fight—on the bridge. Then I saw you again ... I was with the King ... visiting the wounded. You were lucky that old monk was able to put your back into line again. I've seen others with the same injury who have never walked afterwards."

"Will you lead us, my Lord?" Godfrew begged.

"Like you, an injury from the battle up north against my Viking kin has delayed my arrival, but I've not come all this way just to watch." Waltheof sighed. "And now, England's golden warrior is fallen, they say. I will have Norman blood for that."

The Earl turned and called out in a loud voice, "Come on, you men! You heard what the young thane said! Get to your places and be ready to make food for the ravens."

Godfrew helped Godwine undo the bag that contained the mail coats and helmets. His motion was stiff, as he had to bend over with a straight back. He had chosen to sit on his arse rather than squat. Old women sat when they shucked peas and topped turnips—not young warriors. Warriors squatted—keeping the weight on the balls of their feet, ready to spring up, should danger arise.

Having a dusty arse did not sit well with Godfrew. His family may not have that big a holding, but they were masters of good land and had a reputation for being shrewd farmers as well as warriors. Godwine helped him to his feet and pulled on the heavy mail coat. The leather underlay struck cold as it slid over his linen shirt. Godfrew took the proffered helmet. It was not one of the fashionable, conical ones with a nasal-guard, the kind worn by most of the English, Vikings and Normans alike. This had been his grandfather's helmet when he had fought first against—and then for—King Knute the Mighty. It was very old—even then. The helmet's origins were obscure.

Godfrew ran his thumb over the gilt dragons that arched over the eye holes in the face-guard. The artwork distinguished it from modern armour that was mass produced. Although the new armour was efficient, it was also very plain. He patted the golden boar on the crest, as he would do his favourite hound, ducked his head forward and put the helmet on from the back. This ensured that his long golden hair was trapped in the top of the helmet to give his head some additional padding. He settled the face-guard, giving his good eye a clear view, then tilted his head and focused his eye, using the rim of the eye hole as a guide. As his vision sharpened, he could see the men at the valley mouth using their axes to cut halfway through trees alongside the road. Godfrew picked up his own axe, Neckbiter, and stroked it fondly. Some warriors trimmed their moustaches and shaved their chins with their long axe—increasing the intimacy between them. Despite his twenty summers, Godfrew had nothing but downy fluff on his face.

"Are you ready to join the others at the road's head, Master?" Godwine asked. He had been Godfrew's shield bearer, back protector, and boon companion since childhood, being

The Fosse

the son of Godfrew's father's reeve.[5] The only time he used the term "Master" was when they were in high company. With them both about to die, the term grated.

"With you, my friend? I am with you. Just don't expect me to run." The companions walked to where Earl Waltheof was standing, surrounded by thanes and house carls.

"There are no rings or arm bands to be won today ... just word fame." Waltheof leaned on his long axe, using it to give him support. His Stamford injury had been a cut to the thigh bone. It was still weeping, both staining and matting his fine linen trousers.

A house carl at the back chanted:

*"Wealth dies, kinsmen die;
a man himself must die, but word fame never dies
for him who achieves it well."* [6]

"Well said." Waltheof used his free hand to pinch his nose and stifle a sneeze. "English—for though you be Saxon, Norse, Dane, or a mix of all ... today ... today we are all English! We cannot save King Harold, the golden warrior ... giver of rings! We may not be able to save our land from those half-Norse Frenchmen ... those scavenging wolves ... those thieving crows! But we can have blood vengeance! Give food to the ravens ... life blood to the earth." He gestured with his hand. "Make a wall of shields made here ... across the road head! Wait till you see the whites of their horse's eyes! Run ... run to draw them into the valley! With luck, they will not see the fosse till it is too late."

Waltheof turned to Godfrew. "I wouldn't try the running, if I were you. Take the end position and melt into the trees," he added quietly.

A group of armed men jogged along the path toward them. "God's peace." They halted in front of Waltheof, panting. "My Lord! Earl Ansgar has withdrawn from the King's camp and is headed to London with the treasure hoard. The battle is lost! All are leaving." The house carl took a couple of deep

---

[5] Reeve: land owner's representative or manager (village/manor). The role of the Shire Reeve is not fully understood but is thought to have been that of geld (tax) assessment and collection and Fyrd assessment and marshalling.
[6] Free translation of part of the poem by Haramal.

breaths before continuing: "Do you stand or flee, my Lord Waltheof?"

"We stand! How far behind are the Norman wolves?" Waltheof's eyes burnt into the house carl.

"Not far! You would hear them, but for the trees. Many are wrecking the camp! Others are heading this way, looking for Ansgar and the hoard."

"Then we should be ready for them. We will teach them not to be so greedy." Waltheof straightened his posture. "The wall!" he cried.

"The wall!" the warriors echoed back. Shield bearers moved to the front and locked their linden-board shields together. The axe and spear men made up the row behind. As the muffled sound of horsemen started to fill the valley, the warriors started a war chant—a chant their forefathers brought from the homeland:

> See how we stand here, bold feeders of wolves.
> Come taste the kiss of iron maiden's tongue.
> Come ragged foam wave, break on our wood wall!
> Come test your own skills 'gainst us shavers of heads.
> Come claim your own land, make up the worm food.
> Come on the luckless! Ride back with the Valkries.

As the horsemen came into sight, they shouted. The English broke and ran. The Normans let out an exultant yell and plunged after them while Godfrew moved back to the trees at the side of the path. The air became thick with dust and the pungent smell of horses. Many of the horsemen had foot soldiers running with them and holding the horseman's stirrups—Celtic style. Godfrew tried to count how many there were as they came through four or five abreast, but found the numbers too great. The earth shook with their passing. Godfrew pulled his mail shirt up and plunged his nose inside the neck hole. The smell of sweaty leather was better than the choking dust. He looked at his companion. Godwine was doing the same.

How long they took to pass, Godfrew did not know. In battle, time was different—sometimes fast, sometimes slow—and so he waited. At last, the press of Normans eased to a trickle and stopped. A lone Norman horseman trotted along the path. His tired arms held a drooping and bloodstained spear. The companions stepped out.

Godfrew faced the horseman, planted his feet securely, then swung his axe back. His left hand was at the base of the haft, his right hand at the top. Godwine stood to his left, facing the horseman, an exact axe length away. The shield covered them both. Just as Godfrew swung the axe, the Norman pulled back on the horse's reins, causing the animal to rear. Godfrew's right hand slid along the smooth wooden haft until it met the left, just prior to the axe head making contact. The horse's head flew over Godwine's shoulder and the creature crashed to the ground, spraying crimson blood over men and trees alike. The rider tried to pull himself free of the fallen animal, but Godwine stepped forward and smashed the enemy's face with his broad sword. The companions looked at each other and nodded. Ahead, they could hear the sound of trees falling and rocks rolling. Quickly, they headed toward the source of the noise.

It was chaos. Boulders and fallen trees blocked the narrow entrance to the fosse. Fyrdmen were brutally smashing anyone that was trying to clamber over the barricade and escape. Beyond was a hell of screams, noise and dust. The air thrummed with arrows and whistled with slung stones. The companions watched in amazement as a lone Norman tried to leap his horse over the blockage, only to have the animal land on a fallen tree trunk and skewer itself on a branch. A Fyrdman pulled the Norman's head back and slit his throat, leaving the man to gurgle his life into his own frantic hands, trying to piece his own windpipe and artery back together again.

"The trees, Frew." Godwine nodded to the side of the fosse. They stepped across the trickling stream that ran alongside the road and forced their way through the scrubby trees. As they kept to the side of the stream, the valley deepened into a fosse. All along the edge of the fosse, the English were throwing everything they could onto the hapless Normans below—insults as well as weapons.

"Master." Godwine slipped from familiar name to high name. "See? Earl Waltheof is over there." They eased past busy slingers to reach the Earl.

"It worked well, my Lord? The trap?" Godfrew leaned against a tree to take the pressure off of his left leg, as it was starting to ache again.

"It worked very well, young thane." Waltheof turned behind and yelled, "Hey, you men. Take more time over your aim. Don't waste your shots. There is plenty of time to finish this business. The light will hold for a while yet." He turned back to face Godfrew. "The first rank plunged into the fosse, trapping themselves. When they stopped, the others ran them down. Goddamn them, they are the masters of their own confusion."

A cheer went up as a huge boulder rolled down the hill toward the fosse. Fyrdmen and warriors alike scattered out of its way. The rock hit the lip of the fosse and seemed to hang suspended for an eternity before falling onto the Normans beneath. Fyrdmen started to slide down the fosse walls, clubs and knives tucked into their belts. "Thanes and house carls hold back," Waltheof called. Most armoured men did hold back, but not all could hear over the yells and cries of the doomed Normans and the screams of their terrified, crippled horses. "I'd not want to try and work in that tight space in armour, nor with anything longer than a saxe[7] knife." The Earl closed his eyes and rocked his head gently. He called his shield bearer forward. "Tell the warriors on this side to go to the head of the valley. Try to get word to those on the other side ... they are to go to the end of the fosse. When in sufficient strength, they are to work toward each other and finish off all the flies in the trap." He turned to Godfrew. "They won't need us. We will gather a small band and visit King Harold's camp. There may yet be some flies there that are still feasting on the corpse."

* * *

The distance to the camp was further than they thought. The light was starting to fade before they reached it. Plunder-

---

[7] Saxe (sÊx): a long-bladed, single-edged knife similar to a machete. The saxe was normally carried in a horizontal scabbard, either at the front or back of the waist. Most saxe have a point. English saxe were typically of the "broken back" variety: that is, the blade widened from the tang end before tapering to the point. The length could vary from that of a small knife to that of a sword. The weapon was traditional among the Saxons. They even took their name from it.

ers—most unarmed camp followers—were still picking over the remains of the campsite. Waltheof called the band to a halt. "Quietly now ... don't frighten them off! Fyrdmen, hide your weapons and make your way around the camp! Wait for the warriors to move. Warriors, two shield lengths apart ... and in at the jog ... only when I give the signal! Young thane ..." he made eye contact with Godfrew, "... you and your shield bearer can be my body guard. The rest of you, off now."

The Fyrdmen moved along the edge of the campsite. When the end had been reached, they drifted in, joining the plunderers in turning over the increasingly grubby spoils. The scavenging proved too interesting for the Normans to notice the warriors lining up at the end of the clearing until the line was ready and the shield bearers started to beat their sword hilts against their shields and cry: "Out, out, out ..." Startled heads popped up like so many disturbed hares. The Fyrdmen pulled out their weapons to stab and club the plunderers alongside them.

"To me! To me," a Breton sergeant cried, as soon as he realised just what was happening. "If you want to save your miserable hairy hides—to me." Twenty or thirty men-at-arms—who had been rummaging through a gilded wagon—grabbed at the swords and shields they had cast aside. They ran to join the sergeant. "Lock shields, form a circle, and pray—for only God and a strong right arm will save us from these barking dogs."

"Out, out, out ..." the warriors attacked the Bretons. The circle shrank, but it did not break. The ground turned soft as the feet of attackers and defenders trod the flowing blood into the earth. The Fyrdmen—their task completed—joined the band.

"Pull back." Waltheof waved with his axe. "Pull back." The band regrouped around the Earl. "Wogs![8] What are wogs doing fighting for the Normans?"

"Bretons, my Lord. French wogs."

---

[8] Wogs: foreigners from the Saxon—*wealas,* hence Wales, Welsh. The use of the word is best exemplified in the phrase: "Wogs begin at Watford—Watford being where the Danelaw began and Saxon England ended. Alternatively, *wog* or *woh* could mean wrong or crooked. Interestingly, the French-speaking population of Belgium (southern part) are today called "Waalen" (singular Waal—High Dutch). In High German this is rendered *welsch,* and purportedly indicates someone who speaks one of the Latin tongues.

"Our wogs or the Frenchmen's wogs, either way, they die! Form a swine-snout wedge! Thorkel, take the place of honour at the head! Fyrdmen ... in the middle! Keep there till the wall of shields is breached. Young thane, take the right wing! That is best for your one eye? Yes? Good! I will take the left wing."

The band charged the wall. At first they were a crowd—until they got close—then they formed a flying wedge. "Out, out, out, wogs, out, out ..." Thorkel smashed his shield into the wall and the wedge plunged in. The wings enfolded the circle to prevent Thorkel and the head group from being cut off. Godwine locked shield to shield with a Breton and pushed him slightly off balance, exposing the man's side. Godfrew removed the Breton's head and right arm with one blow, but had to release Neckbiter when it jammed in the man's shield on the follow through. Alongside, a Breton stepped forward to disembowel a Fyrdman, but the gap the Breton left in the wall was enough to let the lightly-clad Fyrdmen slip through. Once in the centre, they struck from behind. Opposite Godfrew, a Fyrdman buried his bill hook into a Breton's back, splitting the man's boiled-leather jerkin as if it were cheap linen. As he tried to free his weapon, another Breton turned and spiked the Fyrdman through the ribs with his short sword, then all dissolved into a mess of individual fights as the circle broke up and the wall of shields was no more. Godfrew found himself facing the Breton sergeant.

"Saxon bastard! Make your move! Come on now! Don't be shy." The Breton weaved his body slowly, moving the weight from one foot to the other. "Come to me! Come on! I won't hurt you. Not much." The Breton was getting impatient. He knew that there was fighting going on behind him, but did not know who was at his back. "Oh! That's it, is it? Got a sore leg and can't move too quick, eh?"

The sergeant feinted to the left—drew Godfrew's attention—then struck. Godwine stepped between them and took the full blow on his collar bone, the sword graunching down through his ribs. Godfrew stepped back and swung Neckbiter. The blade smashed across the sergeant's face and took off most of his right hand, leaving only the thumb. Neckbiter's flow was stopped by a rock. The haft snapped in twain. God-

The Fosse

frew glanced at his boon companion and then at the crippled sergeant. He took two steps forward and jammed the remains of Neckbiter's handle in the Breton's left eye. The man screamed and fell to the ground twitching. Godfrew slowly eased himself down alongside his shield bearer.   "Frew, it hurts." Godwine coughed blood, groaned and died.

 "Godwine! God's friend! God's peace! No, no, no, no, no! No more peace! And friendship only with Woden now."Godfrew slid himself down on his arse and leaned against a tree at the edge of the clearing. He slowly started to strip himself of his armour.

Woden's Wolf

The Homecoming

he day was hot for late autumn.

The dust on the road hung like a cloud around the ox cart as it trundled across the ruts. Sunlight dully reflected off the patches of sweat on the oxen's backs.

"That's it, Master. From here, I head to Southwark by way of Balham. I trust you find things well at the homestead. There have been some bad things happening here since the King was slain at Hoar Apple Hill." The carter hawked and spat. The gob lay on the dust as a silver ball, the road too dry to soak it up.

"I trust so, too, Cerdic. It took me longer to get home than I thought. With no horse to ride, I am lost." Godfrew squinted, his blind eye closed to keep out the sunlight.

"And Godwine lost. So many lost. These are sad times, Master Godfrew, sad times." Cerdic gave the lead ox a flick on the back with his whip. "Ho, away William, my beauty."

"You'll have to change your beast's name, my friend, if you want to keep out of trouble," Godfrew called out after him.

"We shall see ... we shall see. They'll have to understand what I'm saying first." Cerdic cackled, coughed and spat again into the all-enclosing dust.

Godfrew slung his bag over his shoulder and headed toward the path that crossed the heath toward Wandsworth. The trees near the crossroad area soon gave way to hawthorn, furze and blackberry. It was all that the gravel-topped plateau seemed capable of sustaining. The heavy crop of berries on the hawthorn promised a harsh winter. Flocks of small birds were feasting on the blackberries and rose in a cloud as Godfrew approached, only to resettle once he had passed. Midges hung in a crown around his sweaty head, ignoring any attempt to make them go away. Getting tired, he stopped by a hawthorn bush, glad of its shade and the chance to put the bag down. Mail-coats and helmets—so vital in battle—were a curse the rest of the time. Now, it was only Godfrew's mail and helmet. Godwine's was ...

Godfrew scratched his head and tried to remember. Where was it? Buried? Stolen? He gave up. The departure from the battle of the fosse had been hurried. The light had all but gone by the time the last Norman had died. So much death, so much noise, so much confusion. Then there were the weeks of searching—looking for the enemy forces, picking off the stragglers, seeking out the main army, the despair as the remains of the English force melted away. The common purpose was lost. Every man seemed to be thinking about home and worrying about tomorrow.

Godfrew eased his aching back and shouldered his load. The heath was quiet: no cattle or sheep with their herders, no flocks of geese with their attendant maids—only the wild birds and the annoying gnats.

The path narrowed as he came near to where the track from his homestead of Garrat joined it at right angles. Trees grew here, as at most of the cross roads. On this east hill of the Wandle valley, the trees grew down the slope of the hill before becoming cleared fields, then water meads. The west hill, opposite, was steeper. It rose almost straight away from water meads to wooded hills. Between the hills ran the sparkling, rushing Wandle with its abundant fish.

As he turned off toward Garrat, Godfrew noticed the smell of damp, burnt wood. Not the sharp acrid smell from the charcoal burners' mounds that he was familiar with, but something more sinister, smelling of destruction and decay. As the descent into the valley increased, he saw the cause. At first, it was burnt grass under the trees, then the burnt trees. By the time he came nearer to the clearing of the spring field, the whole wood was burnt to charred stands of oak, elm, and ash.

He kicked a mound of ash. It was cold. The motes hung in the still air, imitating smoke. Godfrew squinted with his good eye and tried to see his home. A wisp of smoke came from behind the high hedge that surrounded the low homestead. Hearth fire or house fire? With his bag banging painfully against his back, Godfrew ran down the hill.

No one came to meet him. No dogs ran out to greet him. The only sound was his pounding feet and beating heart. The hedge was there, but the roof of the main hall did not show above it. He reached the hedge and walked, panting,

The Homecoming

toward the gate. He stopped, not wanting to see what was on the other side. Fighting panic, he swallowed hard and stepped through the gap.

It reeked of desolation. The main hall was all but ashes. Remains of the end wall drunkenly leaned against the stump of one of the centre posts. Cattle stalls were burnt, leaving only a black stain on the ground to show where they had been. The woven-wattle sheep cote had been pulled down and its battered remains spread across the green. The green itself was torn and gouged with hoof prints. The smell of earth mingled with that of the burnt homestead. Godfrew felt a knot in his stomach. A physical numbness spread throughout his body. A hand tugged at his sleeve and Godfrew half-heartedly reached for his saxe.

"Easy, Master ... easy! It's only me." Godfrew looked down into the weathered face of Wryneck, an old bonded serf. At his side hung his equally old skeleton of a wife. "It's all gone, Master! All gone. They killed what they didn't take. All gone!" The words whistled through broken and missing teeth. "Such a to do—and without warning. One day we hear of victory for the King against the Norse ... and the next ... this. At first I thought they were Icelanders, or Dublin Norsemen belonging to the King ... all that quick talk, I couldn't follow. But then, I thought, when they speak, at least I can understand some of what they say ... but not this lot. All yelling at once, like a flock of magpies. Cackle, cackle, cackle ... " The skeleton wife nodded in agreement. "Only one could speak properly ... hard to catch, but he could speak ... something about food for the King. Your father, the Master, he told him ... gave food and me son to the King months back ... been sending food for the last month. This speaker yelled something at him ... couldn't catch what ... and then yelled even louder for food for the King. You know the Master, your father ... he tried to be nice and ... 'wouldn't you and your men like to come into the hall and have something to drink while we talk this over' ... and 'shouldn't the need for more supplies be taken to the Hundred Thing Moot' ... and he hit him ... this speaker ... just leaned down from his saddle and hit him. That's when your mother, the Lady ... she went berserk. A real fury, she was."

At the mention of his mother, Godfrew snapped out of his

trance. "My mother? Where is she? Where is she?" He found himself shaking the old serf.

"Steady, Master! I means no harm. I'm trying me best! Please!" The whine of the man's voice got through to Godfrew and he let him go. "Come, Master, to our little fire over here ... we've some goose stew. Not that we killed the bird ... them strangers killed it ... but Gurtude, me wife—you know Gurtrude, Master ... well, she pulled it from under their noses when they started to fire the hall." Godfrew resigned himself to the old man's prattling and followed him toward the smoking fire. "Well, Master, as I said ... all gone!"

"All gone? All gone? What do you mean, Wryneck, all gone? Cut the noise and tell me. Where are my parents?" Godfrew lowered himself to the trampled grass by the fire.

"Gone!" Wryneck assured him earnestly.

"To the little priory above Tooting. They sent them to the monks," added Gurtrude.

"I came past there this morning. If I had known, I would have stopped and comforted them."

"How can you do that, young Master ... when they be dead?" asked the puzzled Wryneck.

"Dead?"

"Why, yes! These foreigners ... they killed them. Though not till after your mother, the Lady, had done for two of them."

"And crippled two more," added Gurtrude.

"It was her what twigged who they were and what king they were talking about ... 'no men bastards', she called them."

"Norman," corrected Godfrew.

"Just so ... 'no men'. Told them they wouldn't get nothing ... and what with the one who could speak hitting the Master ... she had a go at them. At first they thought it funny, jumping off their horses and pulling her about ... till she stuck one of them with her eating knife. That shook them. And by the time they had realised what she had done, she had got three more ... two of them dead. That's when the one who could speak rode her over with his horse. There was all sorts of goings on, Master ... the hounds barking and fighting ... the bondsmen having a go. Not me, though, Master ... I'm too old. You know that, Master! You understand." His face took on a pleading look as Godfrew got up and walked back to the ashes of the hall. "But they were everywhere ...

The Homecoming

the 'no men'. So many of the hearth folk fell. When they started the burning ... that's when we ran ... those that were left. There are others about, Master. They still gather here in the evenings, Master. Master?"

Godfrew stood where the hall door had been. At his feet lay the charred remains of two great hounds. The tips of their rib bones were white ash that drifted into motes as the air moved with his arrival. "Grendal."

"And his mother, Master. They got Grendal before he did much more than chew a few arms and legs. His mother killed one and gelded another before they got her ... shot her through with arrows. Mind, she hadn't let go of his bollocks ... had to cut them off they did ... " Wryneck smiled at the remembrance.

"And what happened to my parents?" Godfrew's voice was almost a whisper.

"As I told you, young Master ... meaning no disrespect ... you being the Master now ... what with your dear old father dead and all ... as I told you ... they took them up to the monks at Tooting." Wryneck looked to his wife for confirmation and then to the figure who had slipped in through the gate and joined them.

A young, strong voice belonging to Ake the Swineherd took over the conversation. "The one who could speak our language said something about them fighting well and deserving a Christian burial. He left the dead folk for us to look after. Though, in truth, Master, he just left them ... for I think he thought only old Wryneck and his missus were left alive." Ake had one cross eye on Godfrew and the other on the gap in the hedge. No one knew which one he was looking with. "They put the Master and the Lady in the cart with their own dead and their three wounded. I followed them to the monk's house on the top of the hill above Tooting. We did our best, Master, but what could we do against armed men. All our best men had gone to join the King under the banner of the Wessex Dragon at the Hoar Apple Tree. Ake's young daughter was at his side, arms and legs entwined around her father's, her crossed eyes staring unblinkingly at Godfrew. "Will you stay and rebuild, Master? They do say that all who fought against the Bastard will lose their land. They also say we must stop calling him William the Bastard and call him King

Woden's Wolf

William."

"No, Ake. I won't stay. You must expect a new master now." Godfrew closed his eyes, breathed deeply and let out a sigh. This land was now lost—land given to his grandfather by Knute the Mighty, land given to him for unspoken service in Denmark when King Knute had some problems with his Danish relations—a service his father would not name and his grandfather would only wink and laugh about—land that had enabled the youngest son from a big brood to move from the family holding at Boxhulle in Sussex and become a land holder in his own right ... land that was now lost.

"What of my wife, Eve?" Godfrew asked.

"Your hand-fast, Master? She is with the Normans." Ake cocked his head and tensed. He had heard a sound that no one else had picked up. A small piglet came through the gate and ambled toward him, stopping to snuffle at the remains of Grendal before coming and sitting at Ake's feet. The pig rubbed its back contentedly on the daughter's leg, but Ake's daughter took no notice and continued to stare at Godfrew.

"They have her prisoner?" An edge slipped into Godfrew's quiet voice.

"Er ... not really a prisoner ... she sort of just went with them." Ake's voice started to become as wheedling as Wryneck's. "She and our animals."

"So my hand-fast wife is with the Normans and my parents with the monks. I should visit them." Godfrew bent his knees and went to pat Grendal's mother farewell, but the stench of the bits of putrid flesh still sticking to her back bone and between her teeth stopped him. The sunlight glinted on the arrowheads in the chest cavity. Godfrew picked up a handful of ash and sprinkled it over them.

* * *

The moonlight made the low stone wall in front of the small priory at Tooting appear white and very sharp in relief. In the graveyard, a freshly dug grave had been decorated with hand-scattered, bright wind flowers.

At the foot of the grave lay three Norman heads with blank, staring eyes.

The Homecoming

* * *

"Whose men? Drogo de Dunkirk? Oh, the Fleming! He's the only one we can understand, this Drogo." The landlord of the inn wiped his wet hands on the sack apron around his waist. "Flemish isn't that bad. You just have to get him to speak slowly. He and his boys are stopping up at Wimbledon manor. The Normans have taken it over, it seems. Æthelstan never came back from the battle. Now, Drogo is shacked up with his widow. I heard that she wasn't happy at first, but ... well ... you have to live, don't you. Now that's what I have to keep reminding my missus when she complains about the uncouth manners of the Normans. Do you know, they have worse manners than serfs? And before all this trouble I never allowed serfs in here. Well ... apart from their bad manners that the wife objected to—her family are all carls, high freemen—you never knew where the money they spent had come from. That's what worried me. What's a serf doing with money?" He spat into the wooden mug and wiped the inside with his apron.

"Do these Drogo's men come into Wandsworth village at all, or do they just stay at the manor?" Godfrew leaned forward, resting his chin on the beer mug. The hood of his blue wool cloak fell over his face.

"Oh, they get out and about all right. Mainly stealing honest Englishmen's goods and chattels ... though not from me. They always pay when they get in here. I think it's more fear of my wife's tongue than anything else. Holy Rood, even I am terrified of that!" Realising that he had spoken in a loud voice, the landlord suddenly went silent, listening for his wife's voice. Hearing her in the yard, he relaxed. "In fact, two of them were here earlier. Had a young wench with them. I'm sure I've seen her somewhere before ... can't think where ... tiny young thing ... a waist you could encompass with your two hands and a crown of long hazelnut-coloured hair ... pretty ... pert manners ... sticks in your mind, if you know what I mean. I do know her from somewhere, I'm sure! Though this young miss had her hair free, whereas I seem to remember the other having a wife's head cover."

Woden's Wolf

"Are they still here?" Godfrew asked quietly.

"Drogo's boys? I think they went to the ostler's looking for horses ... though whether they will pay for them is another matter. If you ask me ... sorry ... what was your name?" He turned around to find himself alone in the smoke-filled room. The leather door was askew, letting in a shaft of weak autumn sunshine that reflected off a small puddle of beer which slowly soaked into the earthen floor. "Charming! Almost as polite as those Norman barbarians."

Godfrew slowly moved from cottage to cottage through the muddy village toward the ostler's. The smell of pig dung rose pungently as he skirted the holding pens near the village slaughter house. The eyes of the condemned animals watched him pass, relieved for the stay of execution. In a village of wattle and daub buildings, only the church and the ostler's stables were of stone. The church had been built out of love, the ostler's out of a combination of greed and shrewdness. Godfrew's father knew the ostler, Snorrie the Icelander, quite well. In summer, Snorrie pastured his horses on the Garrat water meads. It was Snorrie who had taught Godfrew to read and write the Runes: Norse Runes, rather than Saxon ones. But the teaching had mainly been at Garrat, whiling away long summer evenings—while Snorrie and his father drank dark ale and told old stories in between the lessons. Godfrew knew the stone stable, but not that well, as he rarely visited Wandsworth, preferring to go to the market at Tooting for his needs. He quietly moved toward the stable, then stopped when he heard voices. He recognised his handfast wife Eve's voice and its teasing tone.

"What is your want, my bold soldier?" she giggled and pulled at the Norman's belt.

"What did she say?" the shorter Norman asked his companion.

"Who knows? Who cares? Do you think that she will take us both on at once like she indicated earlier?" The taller Norman ran his fingers through his thick brown hair, then rubbed his hands together. He smiled at Eve: "Come on, my lovely. A promise is a promise. Don't be shy."

Eve kept pulling at the shorter one's belt, letting the back of her hand touch his belly. "Ooh, I do believe this soldier

The Homecoming

knows how to stand to attention."

"Oh, Lord, I think all my dreams are about to come true," the short one's voice was thick and his face started to flush. "Oh, my little beauty, don't just let it be a tease, not after me keeping you safe from my rough friends."

"What about me?" the tall one's voice had an edge to it.

"Oh soldier, soldier, won't you marry me, with your mail shirt, sword, and drum," Eve sang. She looked at the tall one and winked.

"Your dreams and mine are both going to come true, I think." The tall one gave a lop-sided smile.

"But I put the rabbit in the warren first. It was me that found her—me that kept the others off." The short one kept watch on Eve, his eyes widening with the arousal of his body.

"Fine! I have plans for my own amusement that won't interfere with yours. Besides we have the afternoon to fill." The taller one held out his hand to Eve and she took it. "Where we go?" he asked her, his English pronunciation mangled.

"We go in here, my bold soldiers. Come." Eve led them to the stable door and pulled them through. She fell backwards into a mound of hay, taking them with her. The short one sat up and pulled Eve into a sitting position, the tall one leaned forward from behind her and undid the tie belt around her waist. He then lifted her upper garment, pulled it over her uplifted arms and over her head. Eve shook her head, making the sunlight dance and bring out the highlights in her hair. She smiled beguilingly at first one, then at the other Norman.

"Breasts like autumn apples. Nipples like little cherries. Oh, Lord. You beautiful."

The short one leaned forward and tried to pull Eve's skirt off. She stopped him, so he rolled it up to her waist instead. Meanwhile, the tall one fondled her breasts with his rough, red hands, tweaking her nipples between forefinger and thumb. "Come, my beauty. Grant me my wish."

The short one eased her legs apart and breathed deep, inhaling her smell. The pulse on his temple beat rapidly. He could taste the adrenaline in his mouth. A pleasant numbness spread through his body. He pulled back, yanked off his shirt, lowered his breeches and shuffled across the hay toward his target. The tall one lay back, taking Eve with him. He gently ran his thumb over the silken skin of her cheek. As the short one entered Eve, the tall one leaned forward and put his lips to Eve's. He lips parted and the Norman probed gently with his tongue, his right hand still teasing her nipple. His companion cupped both her breasts and gently squeezed them each time he pushed in. The short one's breath now came in short pants and his thrusts became more forceful. Suddenly, they stopped. The tall one felt a sticky wetness enter his mouth and he pulled away coughing. He opened his eyes, tears running down his cheeks from the coughing. He wiped his mouth and found the spittle flecked with blood. Surprised, he looked to his companion. The man's head rested on the girl's breasts. His eyes were wide open and a trickle of blood came from the side of his mouth. A hayfork protruded from the short Norman's back, pinning both him and Eve to the earth floor. The tall Norman barely had time to take in a startled breath before he felt the sharp sting of Godfrew's saxe as it cut his throat.

* * *

"Well, Norman, as I said ... this is rich land if you know how to make it work. The common land on the hill top is poor gravel stuff, but fine grazing for sheep and with several ponds for their watering. The slope toward Kingston is well wooded with lots of oak trees, so there is plenty of pannage for the swine ... enough for the lord of the manor and those of the bondsmen and freemen. They pay the manor quite a reasonable rate for the privilege, by the way. There are also harts and hinds in there, too. And wild boar! They are for the lord of the manor only, of course. The Thames is not far, but the monks from Canterbury and Westminster have the fishing rights. Myself, I can't see why, as it is far from their Minsters. King Harold himself has a fishery west of Putney." Realising his slip of the tongue, Ranulf the Reeve quickly looked at the Norman on the horse alongside him on the ride through the lands of Wimbledon manor.

"Sheep, swine, no fish? Is that right, Saxon?" The Norman looked anxiously at Ranulf, seeking confirmation that he had understood what had been said. Without his mail coat

The Homecoming

and helmet, he was not easy to distinguish from his English riding partner—only his short hair and shaven neck made him different.

"Sheep... swine... no fish! That is right." Ranulf snorted in relief that the Norman had grasped something of what he had said. "Now our fish come from the river Wandle, down the other side of the hill ... trout, mainly. There is a big mill near Duntshill Ho, that is held, or was held, by a thane called Stanleigh who owed allegiance to my late Lord Æthelstan. Part of his annual payment was in fish. Now, myself, I wanted to get the miller to stock his mill pond with quality fish and net the entrances. That way, we would have had a regular supply, as opposed to a once a year crop of smoked and dried fish from Stanleigh. The miller would have had to pass over a percentage to the manor, of course. But my Lord Æthelstan never let me do it. Always putting it off. Not very progressive, my Lord Æthelstan. You understand, Norman?" Ranulf glanced at the Norman, and nodded his head up and down slowly.

"Fish ... mill," the Norman agreed.

"Just so. Closer to the Thames, there is another mill on the Wandle ... something to do with processing cloth. I'm not sure what. The problem is, it does something to the water they use, so you must make sure that if you buy any fish from the villagers in Wandsworth that they have caught it upstream of the cloth mill. They shouldn't be allowed to do that to the water, but they are freemen, so they take no notice of what my Lord Æthelstan says, or should I say said." Ranulf became aware that he was prattling on. "Look, I'm sorry if you can't understand all I say. If I'm talking too fast. Just tell me and I will ..." He was shocked to find the horse next to him had no rider. "Norman! Where are you Norman?" He looked back up the track and saw the man lying in the dust. "I thought you and your people were supposed to be good horsemen?" Ranulf trotted back and looked down. "What's up?"

A figure emerged from the bushes, slipped under Ranulf's horse and cut the girth strap. With a heave, saddle and rider joined the dead Norman in the dust. Godfrew put his knee into the reeve's back and pulled his head back by his hair. The saxe rested on Ranulf's neck. "So, Normans' friend, how goes it at Wimbledon with the new lord of the manor?"

"Ill, sir ... ill ... but we have to live ... don't we?" Ranulf gulped.

"It seems to me that you do little to curb the Normans' thieving, my friend. What of the new master, Drogo, whom you must love so much—seeing as you are doing your best to help him and his boys settle in." Godfrew gave the hair a sharp tug. "Is Drogo often at the hall?"

"Often, sir ... often ... even on this day, he is there."

"Alone? Or are his boys always with him?" The saxe caressed the tight skin on Ranulf's plump neck. Godfrew twisted it slightly and caressed the neck again. The sharp edge left an unbleeding cut.

"They are always with him, sir, except on Sunday morning. The lady Leofhearta—who he says is now his wife—she goes to the little abbey at Mortlake for mass. My Lord Drogo's men escort her." Ranulf tried to turn his head to see if Godfrew was pleased with the information, but the movement only cost him another light cut. The first cut had now started to bleed. "Though whether they go to protect her or to stop her running away, I wouldn't like to say, sir. Please, sir! Let me go!"

"And on Sunday morns—he is alone?" The knee pushed forward more heavily.

"Except for his priest. He brought his own from France. He never goes near our local priest. He takes his own private mass in the hall." Ranulf's voice was even more pleading. "Please, sir! Please! I am an Englishman ... like you ... I only want to live ... that is all. Surely, you understand?"

"You are not an Englishman, you are a nothing—and nothing is all your life will ever be." Godfrew put the saxe to the reeve's cheek and carved the Runic letter "N" in the soft flesh. He turned Ranulf's head and did the same the other side. "'N' ... for nothing ... for that is what you are, Norman lover."

"Sir! Sir! Master Godfrew, let me go!" The voice was hysterical now. Blood was streaming down the marked face and soaking into the soft wool top garment—red blood on bright yellow cloth.

"So you do know me, Ranulf the Nothing. In your own interest, forget me, or forget your life." Godfrew pushed the man

The Homecoming

forward into the dirt of the road and went back into the enshrouding bushes.

* * *

The band rode out of the manor through the gate in the hedge and started up the hill toward the common. A shaft of sun broke through the clouds. It briefly glinted on the helmets and mail coats of the armed men. Godfrew caught a glimpse of some riders in softer garments in the middle of the escort—the lady Leofhearta and her attendants. Steam puffed from the horse's nostrils like dragon's breath and a light smoke of fog rose from their backs. Some of the beasts were fidgety, still settling to the saddle and bridle, remonstrating against having to carry a rider when they would have preferred to roll in the straw of the warm stables. The chink of horse fittings and the clump of hooves died as the band entered the trees that covered the slope of the hill. Godfrew drew back and listened to the birds going about their business, hopping from branch to branch, looking curiously at the hooded figure beneath them. The early morning mist condensed on the remaining leaves and dripped onto the watcher's thick, wool-hooded cloak with gentle plops. Godfrew pulled the garment closer and watched the gate into the manor. He strained his ears to try and get inside the enclosed area without being physically present. Occasionally, the sound of Leofhearta and her escort drifted back down into the valley.

A dull, flat, clanging sound came from the small village—down the path, south of the manor—calling the faithful to celebrate mass. In one's and two's, then in three's and four's, the folk of the manor trickled through the gate. Some strode purposefully, eager to celebrate. Others drifted idly, unwilling to complete another chore that they resented having to perform. Godfrew watched and listened. Despite the progression of the day, there was still no warmth in it. He shrunk further into his cloak's warm confines.

The clanging stopped as all were gathered in. Godfrew stood up from the squat, keeping his back straight. A woman with two shrieking children rushed out of the gate and headed toward the village. The woman's stride broke only when she stopped to cuff the taller and noisier of her brats. Slowly, the silence engulfed Godfrew and the trees. Still, he waited.

Once certain that all had gone, Godfrew moved from the cover of the small trees and briars and stealthfully walked to the gate, approaching it obliquely. He kept to the shadow of the hedge, the faded dark blue of his cloak merging with the shadows, hiding him. The manor green and yard was empty, but for the geese and a stray pig that had escaped from its pen. It was revelling in its freedom by rolling and wallowing in the mud at the side of the stinking midden heap. Godfrew squinted his eye and watched the hall door. There was no movement.

For the first time he wondered if Ranulf the Nothing had been telling the truth about Drogo and his taking a private mass. Moving from hedge to sty, sty to stable, stable to barn, barn to privy, Godfrew kept his eye on the hall entrance. The privy stank, so he breathed through his mouth in short breaths. Dampness dripped from the rotting thatch. Then, at last, he heard a voice.

"I have set the chessmen up, my Lord, so when you have finished your business, all is ready." The priest held an elaborately carved white bishop in his hand, lifting it to eye level, holding it at arm's length, appreciating the workmanship of the walrus-ivory piece. The priest mused as to whether one day he might play the bishop in reality. He did not hear Godfrew come behind him, but he did hear the thud as the pommel of the saxe took him behind the ear.

Godfrew looped a walrus hide rope around the priest's ankles and tied them. Running the rope up to the priest's wrists, he did the same, then looped it around the neck, finishing in a slip knot.

Godfrew moved from the hall proper and approached the curtained area where the lord and lady slept. As he got near the heavy drapes, a young boy—his blond hair, damp with sweat and stuck to his face—came from behind. He looked through Godfrew with dull-blue eyes and walked slowly, even stiffly, out of the hall. The priest was coming to and tried to get the boy's attention. As he struggled, the movements of his hands and feet tightened the slip knot around his neck. With bulging eyes and a purple face, he subsided into a whistling, wheezing silence.

The Homecoming

Godfrew moved the curtain aside and stepped into the private quarters. Drogo was naked, washing his private parts in a silver bowl that contained water warm enough to make a drift of steam. He looked up. "It had better be urgent for you to barge in like this." He observed the man in front of him. When next he spoke, he did so slowly, in Flemish "Ah, by your dress, you are Saxon. I know of your curt manners. Well, man, what's to do?"

"It is personal, Lord Drogo, for you alone. May I approach?" Godfrew pulled his hood back, the edges of his hair dull with damp.

Drogo grabbed a rag and started rubbing himself dry. "Aye, you can, but it had best be good." He spoke slowly so that his Flemish would be better understood.

Godfrew came face to face and bent to whisper in Drogo's ear: "Garrat." Drogo looked puzzled and Godfrew grabbed him by his chest hair and pulled him close. "I said, 'Garrat.'"

Drogo's puzzlement increased. He opened his mouth to speak. Instead, he vomited blood, huge volumes of it, bright and glistening blood. Godfrew twisted the saxe and withdrew it at a different angle from that with which it had gone in.

Drogo doubled over, still spewing a crimson torrent. Godfrew watched, then took a well-aimed kick at the Fleming's chest, sending him sprawling across the herb-strewn floor. Drogo was making strange gurgling sounds now. His body went into spasms, knocking over a table and scattering the wooden platter with the remains of his breakfast bread and a half-empty wooden mug of small beer.

Godfrew looked at his clothes. They were sodden with blood. He started to strip them off, casting them onto the floor. The water in the bowl was still warm, so he used it to wash the half-congealing blood off of his hands and face. It was too chill to remain naked long, so he went to a carved chest against the wall to look for clean clothing. As he opened the lid, he took a quick step back. There was a wolf in the box! Nothing moved, so Godfrew went back to the chest again and looked in. The wolf-skin cloak had risen once the pressure of the box lid had been removed. The animal's mask sat above the carved edge, its empty eye holes showing the white hood lining.

Godfrew pulled the cloak out. It was cunningly made of

three pelts—the largest pelt providing the main body and mask, the others attached to the sides to provide a good width. The fur of all three matched perfectly. The lining was thick, white wool cloth—fine, but not coarse. Godfrew had never seen its like before. He put it to one side and rummaged in the depths of the chest. Discarding the better and finer items, he selected baggy breeches—undershirt and over mantle in plain colours—and an overshirt that had been carefully patched in several places.

He quickly put them on, glad to keep some warmth in his body. Of his own clothes, he kept only his leg bindings and belt. On the top of the carved wooden chest there had been a small ivory casket with the crucifixion scene engraved on it. Godfrew picked it up and looked inside. The contents were English in design. It obviously belonged to the lady of the manor. He closed the casket and put it back on the floor.

Picking up his discarded saxe, he rolled the now dead Drogo over onto his back. There were some gold rings on his fingers. Godfrew recognised a red-gold one with carved Runes as his mother's. He broke the top off of the breakfast table, put the piece of wood under the Fleming's hand and proceeded to chop off the fingers to retrieve the rings. Pocketing the jewellery, he washed the blade of the saxe in the now cold water of the silver bowl and bent to wipe it on Drogo's rag.

The wolf cloak smiled at him—beckoning. He pulled it toward him and stroked the fur on the mask. It reminded him of Grendal. Looping his fingers under the masked hood, he stood up and swung the cloak over his back, wolf skin outwards. He fastened it with the thick, red-gold chain. The clasps were moulded in the form of Woden's ravens. He pulled the masked hood over his head and cautiously went back into the hall. The priest no longer struggled, but lay there watching him balefully.

"Will you absolve me, father?" The priest looked from man's face to wolf's face. Neither looked friendly. "It is lucky for you that I am English and not Norse, Master Priest, or you would be with your master by now. And I mean the Devil. Not Jesus!" Godfrew whispered into his ear in only slightly accented Latin. The sound of voices in the yard terminated the conversation.

The Homecoming

The folk had started to return from the village. Rather than wait, Godfrew strode out toward the gate. The folk made way for him. One saw the young face that belied the stiff, old-man's walk. Then he noticed the screwed-up eye. "Woden!" he gasped. The folk ran and Godfrew went back into the woods.

* * *

Ranulf the Reeve moved in the saddle to relieve the ache in his buttock. He was not surprised that Drogo was dead, nor was he surprised at who had killed him. He knew it hadn't been Woden—rather that bad-tempered, nasty Godfrew of Garrat with his whitened eye always screwed up in the light and his stiff walk. Guessing why the young man had wanted to know about Drogo's movements had been easy. All around had heard what the Fleming and his men had done at the stead of Garrat. Vengeance was easy to understand. He felt the need for it now himself, with his face marked for life. The scabs were stiffening and making it painful to talk. The wise woman had recommended pig's fat to ease the problem, but his wife had objected to the smell. Ranulf was not sad that Godfrew had stuck the Fleming. The man's arrogance was enough to make anyone wince—taking over the manor as if it was his by right, forcing himself upon Æthelstan's widow, if that was what she was. There had been no proof of his death. The body of her husband had not been brought back. There was just no return from the battle. Æthelstan had not been an easy man either—stern, fixed in his ways, never letting his reeve get on with making the manor as profitable as it could have been. But he was fair. He would listen to advise, even if he rarely took it. There were no fines or physical punishment for freemen, bondsmen or serfs—except with the vote of the Manor Moot. Drogo and his men treated the folk as cattle, forcing them to do more work than tradition said was their due, beating them when it took their fancy. Often, it seemed, the beatings were just for sport. Not all the foreigners were as bad. Gilbert the Breton, who was now lord at Half-Fathing manor, had called the Manor Moot as soon as he arrived. He swore to uphold all traditional rights, even sought their voiced assent before he took his English widow to wife—her and her brood of daughters. Daughters: these could be a liability, Ranulf mused. At least he only had sons. But the eldest ... now there was a problem ... and one seemingly of Drogo's making. At first, the interest of the new lord of the manor toward the boy had been flattering. The offer of having the boy taught Latin and to read and write had filled him and his wife with joy. Then, after a couple of weeks, the boy's manner had changed. He had become sullen and withdrawn. His behaviour had become worse. He stopped joining the rest of the folk when they went to mass in the village. Instead, he stayed behind with Lord Drogo for his private mass in the hall with that French priest of his. He was learning French manners, no doubt. No, Ranulf the Reeve was not sad that Drogo was dead. And he would not be sad when young Godfrew was dead either. Ranulf again fidgeted in the saddle. "Shall we move, Norman?"

"You say, Saxon go here, my scar-faced friend?" The Norman had a well-dented helmet with a deep gouge on the nasal guard. He also had the flattened, broken nose that went with it.

"What I said," replied Ranulf in a bored voice, "was that he is likely to have gone along here. The folk saw him head along this road toward Wandsworth, rather than Merton. He wouldn't have tried to go up the hill toward the Kingston—Putney road—as the undergrowth is too thick and he probably knew that would increase his chances of getting caught. You can see for yourself! He isn't in sight across the water meads. Besides, with all this rain we've had this last couple of weeks, he wouldn't have been able to walk across that land anyway. That cuts out his trying to get back to his own homestead of Garrat and its hearth folk. All of which means, my dearly beloved Norman master, that he is likely to have gone this way—to Wandsworth village, Duntsford manor or to the Duntshill homestead. Either way, we will find him. The hue and cry has already been raised in the village. Your dearly beloved soldiers have gone ahead to raise it all along the road. So, he will be caught."

"You say, scar face, he go here. Yes?" The Norman waved to the gathered folk behind him with his drawn sword. "Find, my smelly ferrets. Raise hue and cry. Find him, you Saxon filth! I want his hide! Drogo saved my life once. I owe him this." He trotted off with Ranulf beside him. "Search bushes, Ranulf?"

"Bushes, sergeant," the reeve confirmed. "B-U-S-H-E-S." Talking had made the scabs on Ranulf's scared cheeks start to bleed again.

Another mounted Norman joined the horsemen."Yes, you folk, all search the B-U-S-H-E-S." He turned to the sergeant, "The hue and cry has been raised in that stinking cesspit that they call Wandsworth. They are making their way along the road and searching the west hill. They didn't seem very enthusiastic about it—at least, not until I gee'd a couple of them up with the flat of my sword. I had to go there, as when I tried the manor over at Dunsthill, I got no help. The place is still held by a Dane, Swien or Svend, something like that. Wouldn't help at all. Pretended he couldn't understand. He understood all right. I spoke to him slowly in Flemish." He pulled off his helmet and wiped the sweat from his brow. He looked at the wet hand and then ran it over his hair to dry it. "Obviously, you have had no luck. What does the scar face here say?"

"Oh, who knows. Trying to understand his dog barkings wears me out. I sometimes wonder why we ever came to this God-forsaken country."

"To get rich, that's why. This sort of thing ..." the newcomer gesticulated toward the folk prodding and poking the roadside bushes with their hay forks and bill hooks, "was bound to happen. It's always the same, even at home. You kill them, they kill you. As for the language, we will learn, or our children will. My old grandfather still only spoke Norse ... hardly knew a French word. Came out with the original Duke: Hrolf Ganger. You know, one of the originals, so to speak."

"I suppose so. It just annoys me that having survived that hell hole outside Hastings, Lord Drogo should end up naked and stuck like a pig in his own hall. He was a good captain. He looked after the boys." He rode up to some of the folk: "You smelly Saxon dogs. Saxon bastard! Murderer! He there?"

A serf with tatty clothes and broken front teeth was looking straight into Godfrew's eyes. "There is no one of that ilk here, Norman sergeant," he called out without breaking eye con-

Woden's Wolf

tact with Godfrew. "No Saxon bastard or murderer here." He ran his tongue over his jagged fangs. "Only us honest English," he continued in a whisper.

"What you say? Speak slow man. Curse you for your dog-barking tongue."

"No here, sergeant." The serf winked at Godfrew and moved on. Godfrew sunk deeper into his cloak, the wolf's dark gray pelt hiding him amongst the brambles.

"Well, Charles, it looks as if you may have to get the hounds out, if you are to find him," the Norman told his sergeant.

"Yes, let's go. Hey, Ranulf. You look still, here. I go back. Big hound. Find Saxon bastard." The Normans rode off up the Merton road toward Wimbledon.

"You know, Charles, every time I think of the hounds, I can't help laughing at poor old Robert ... you know ... at that funny little place the other side of the river here. My life ... poor old Robert ... one day he looses his balls to a big dog ... the next, his skull to a Saxon Wolfshead."

Charles, the sergeant, looked puzzled. "Wolfshead? What is that?"

"It is what the Saxons call a rebel. It has something to do with the price paid for proof of killing a rebel being the same as that for proof of killing a wolf. Honestly, Charles, you really are going to have to try and spend more time learning the Saxon tongue. Mind, if you go up north, you will have to learn the Norse-Saxon mix that they use there."

"It all sounds the same dog barking to me. Let's get the hounds."

* * *

"I want a horse, Snorrie," the voice said from the darkness. Snorrie kept on grooming the mare with long deliberate strokes. The horse's coat was shining as the light from the burning torch caught it. "Snorrie, I want a horse!" the voice insisted.

"It's a good thrashing I should be giving you, young Godfrew, not a horse!" The old man's speech had a tinge of an Icelandic accent. He carried on grooming, refusing to look at the speaker.

The Homecoming

"Snorrie, the horse!" the voice was curt now.

"It's funny ... when you were but a boy I always commented on how polite you were ... and thoughtful too. I used to tell your father that I thought you would be better suited to be a churchman than a warrior. And here you are, rudely demanding I sell you—and I did say sell—sell you a horse." He turned quickly and pointed the horse brush straight at Godfrew, despite the fact that the warrior believed himself invisible in the dark stable corner. Anger blazed in the Icelander's eyes. "You left bodies in my stable—dead bodies! One was but a small wench, little more than a child, but the other two ... the other two, my short-tempered friend ... were Norman soldiers." He lowered the brush, then thrust it toward Godfrew again. "And don't tell me you didn't do it! Oh, I knew it was you that did it! When you hear of a young man enquiring about Drogo's boys—men who had been killing folk at Garrat—and then find two of them in a compromising state with a certain young warrior's hand-fast wife ... and them all dead to boot, you can easily put two and two together. You nearly got me hanged!"

"I never meant to put you at risk, Snorrie. It was fate that I found them in your stable." Godfrew's voice had softened. "Besides, I had the right. Killing her and those committing adultery with her was lawful. No wergeld either!"

"Well, the legality of your acts may or may not be lawful under English law. Your arrangement with the maid was somewhat informal. Then of course there is the fact that in English eyes you were the Thane." Snorrie paused and rested his chin on the mare's back whilst he thought. "Married or not, Thane or not, one thing is certain, you were not a bondsman and thereby you may well be liable for wergild for your actions. All arguable points of law, of course. But do the Norman's have the will to understand the our laws?"

"Forget that. Snorrie. The horse! I need a horse!"

The old Icelander suddenly realised that he had been sidetracked and moodily returned to brushing the mare. "Yes, they wanted to hang me, the Normans did. There and then, in my own stable, from my own roof beam." Snorrie's voice was now a shout. He waved the brush at Godfrew. "Would have done it, too, if it weren't for one of their masters being present ... reminding them that 'King' William insisted that they followed the English laws. And they still held me! I spent a week chained to the tail of a cart at Brixton awaiting the gathering of the Hundred Moot. Have you ever laid in your own piss and shit, boy? All inside your breeches, sticking, stinging, burning? Nor had I, till then! It is not a nice experience."

The voice dropped in volume and Snorrie went back to grooming the horse. "Naturally, when they brought me before the Hundred Moot, I was let off. In addition to my twelve sworn men, I had witnesses that told the Moot I was with Abbot Helm at Mortlake all that morning ... now there is a shrewd buyer and seller of horse flesh." He glanced back at Godfrew, who had now moved into the light being given off by the torch. "My still being alive is no thanks to you. And you want a horse from me"I forgot."

"You forgot?" A note of resignation entered Snorrie's voice. "You haven't changed much. Always forgetting things, the important things ... like not killing people in someone else's stable." The brush stokes became firmer than the voice and the mare jittered. Snorrie stopped brushing and turned again to Godfrew. "You want a horse? For your dead father's sake, I will sell you one. Just never come back here again!"

"I want a fast one with good lungs and plenty of stamina."

"You will get what I sell you. You do not want a fast one. You want a plain horse—one that has no distinguishing features, does not stand out. You are very distinctive Godfrew ... one eye with a white lens, always screwed up in the light, your long legs, your stiff walk. People remember you. You were named at the Hundred Moot in relation to an incident at Tooting. No doubt people will link you with what happened here and at Wimbledon. Only the simple folk think it's all down to Woden. You will be called to the Shire Moot. You won't go, but you will be called. There, no doubt, you will be made outlaw and declared a Wolfshead [9] ... probably." Snorrie glanced at the wolf cloak and pointed. "Very appropriate, but it will get you hanged. If you must wear it, turn it inside out. If you wish to avoid being hanged, you will need to be

---

[9] Wolfshead: Old English term for an outlaw or rebel. The term is thought to be either related to the cult of Woden (and hence war like activities) or the fact that the financial reward for a proven slaying of an outlaw and that of a wolf were the same—5 silver pennies.

very discrete in all things." The ostler walked further into the stable and brought out a small dark pony to the waiting Godfrew. "What are you going to pay for her with?"

"A gold ring." Godfrew pulled out a simple band.

"And the rest?" Snorrie tilted his head and raised his eyebrows.

"That nag is not worth even this."

"That plain, unnoticeable, but very strong nag is worth whatever I ask for to someone in your position. And don't even think about trying to steal her from me. I may not be young, but I can still drop you, boy. I need no weapons." Snorrie folded his still muscular arms across his barrel chest.

"How much?"

"Any more rings?"

Godfrew rummaged in his purse and pulled out another. This one was embossed in a heavy Flemish pattern. He proffered it to Snorrie. The older man took it and went to stand under the torch. First, he held it to the light, then he bit it to gauge its softness. The torchlight glinted off of his bald head. "This one and half the other."

"I have a choice?"

"No! Try and haggle and I'll take the other half as well."

"A saddle comes with it, of course?"

"It's an extra that will cost you the other half of the plain ring. It would be a pity to cut it up." The ostler pocketed both rings. "I must admit though, boy ... it was funny ... them three all stuck together." He glanced across, but Godfrew wasn't laughing. "Come on, lad! It was funny! The look on those Normans' faces." He shook his head from side to side and then snuck another glance at Godfrew. "Still not smiling? No... well ... I suppose ... it was your hand-fast wife. It was funny, though." He looked at Godfrew again. "Don't try and work out why she did it, boy. You'll be at it for years and still end up with the wrong answer. I came here ... oh ... many summers ago in mighty Knute's time—years before the sainted Edward had come to the throne, so that will tell how long ago it was. I only stopped to water my horse ... saw this young girl—a skinny thing about fourteen or fifteen years of age. And I've been here ever since. You wouldn't think my missus was skinny once, would you? All those years we've been together and I still don't understand her—let alone her logic. She broke down crying when they took me away after finding your little piece of work. She didn't stop till I got home again. Go, boy, before I change my mind about letting you have the horse."

The Kentish Maid

"**Nephew,** I never thought to see you again!"

The rotund man pulled Godfrew into the inn out of the rain. "It's as if the heavens themselves are crying for the land. Your poor mother and my brother ... sad happenings ... but come, get your wet clothes off and join us by the fire. You must tell us all!"

He turned to a maid with long golden hair: "Elfgifu, get some of my old clothes for my nephew here. And don't think you can hover while he changes either."

The maid pulled a face behind his back and disappeared into the back room. "A pleasant maid—but saucy—from Kent ... near where my wife, your aunt, is from. That's right, isn't it, beloved?"

A big square built woman with a huge chest nodded in agreement and continued with her task of slicing slivers off of a roast goose. "But tell us, where have you been? What has happened?" he continued. "Much has happened here, I can tell you." He poured three large mugs of ale and passed one to his wife. Another, he put on the trestle next to Godfrew who had stripped to the waist and was rubbing himself down. He held his own mug to his bulbous nose and inhaled the fumes, savouring the smell. His first taste was but a half mouthful, which he swilled around his mouth; the second went straight down his gullet. "First the stories: King Harold has won ... King Harold has lost ... Harold of Norway is to be King ... William of Normandy is to be King. Armed men back and forth ... many staying long enough to taste my fine ales, of course." He glanced at Godrew's mug. "You haven't touched yours yet? Would you like it mulled to take the chill from your body? No? Where was I ... yes, so much coming and going ... even here in the Battersea marshes. Do you know it took almost a month before we found out just who was king? And another before we heard about your poor mother and my brother? Your hair ... is that silver I see amongst the gold? A young man getting old, eh? Still, with what you have seen of late..." he shook his head into his beer mug. "Of course, all this trouble has done terrible things to the price of barley. Do you know what I paid for the last load? I paid ..."

"Uncle Edwin! The Normans, do you see many of them?" Godfrew's voice was low and intended for his uncle's ears only.

"Normans? Oh, not really. A group came the other day, looking at the fishery by the church of Saint Mary. Old Albert was with them. You remember him ... the underreeve. They all crawled in here ... wanted wine! Wine, I ask you! So I said to them, we don't have that watery stuff here. Sold them barley wine ... my finest ... four summers old ... as golden as a dragon's egg and thick as honey. My brother loved his barley wine, God rest his soul!" Edwin looked mournfully into his mug, hiccuped and took another mouthful.

"Yes, but do they call here often?" Godfrew had stripped to his linen breeches and was unwinding his leg bindings. The maid came in and smiled at him through the golden veil of her hair. He took the proffered clothes and smiled back.

"Out, wench, out! That's an English warrior you are teasing. Beware he doesn't grab you!" Edwin laughed.

"Edwin, no talk of warriors. Not in here." His wife brandished the carving knife. Goose fat dulled its steely gleam. "I'll not have our livelihood put at risk by your idle prattle."

"It's only fun, my beloved. She does get worried ... my wife, your aunt. Normans, eh? Well, if we are to cater to their trade, I suppose I will have to start stocking wine. Maybe they will take cider. That would suit your Kentish relations, wouldn't it, my love ... a good strong Kentish cider. I once had a pint in an inn near Bromley ... it was as black as a dark ale and tasted like nectar. Now if I could get hold of some of that ... maybe water it down with clear water from the Falcon brook ... from nearer to the hill, of course ... it's too muddied near here ... maybe that would be to their taste."

"Uncle Edwin, the clothes are very ... shall we say ... generous? I thank you. None the less, I am tired to the bone. May I find a place to sleep?" The maid had returned and was watching from the corner. Godfrew sneaked a look and smiled to her.

"Yes, of course. There is fresh straw in the lean-to out the back ... a bit draughty, but dry, none the less. I am glad we had this chat. It's good to catch up with what you have been doing. Elfgifu, where are you, wench? Ah, there you are hiding in the corner. Take my nephew to the lean-to and come back here when you have finished. Don't tarry! He may look scrawny, but he has the strength to wield a long axe and cut Norsemen and Normans in twain." Edwin's wife caught his eye. "Sorry, my beloved," Edwin replied.

Godfrew followed the maid out, just far enough behind her to appreciate the movement of her body.

"Edwin, I don't want him to stay long. He's been up to mischief. He has that look in his eye. And don't spoil him! I've heard about what you used to give him before we wed. As an only child, he got more than enough from your brother without you having to give him more."

"My poor brother. Dear God, how I miss my poor brother. We were always arguing, but ... oh, how I miss him." Edwin poured himself another mug of ale and settled by the fire.

"Don't go getting morbid on me. And don't think you can sit there getting all mellow, either. There may not be any paying customers here at present, but when the rain stops ..."

The maid Elfgifu took Godfrew to the lean-to. "How did you get here?"

"My horse is in Uncle Edwin's store barn, though he has yet to know it. A strong horse, but not fast. I will get a better one soon. A white one, I think, with perhaps a yellow mane." Godfrew started to heap up some straw up against the tavern wall and Elfgifu helped him. "Your accent, Elfgifu. It does not sound Kentish."

"I have worked here a while. I have found it doesn't pay to be different. Your uncle's wife's family and mine are connected. I came to see the big wide world, but this island in the Battersea marshes is all I have seen. Perhaps later I will travel." Although talking to Godfrew, she did not look up from her task of heaping straw.

"I will be travelling soon, but I don't know where to, at present." Godfrew sat on the straw pile. He nodded his head for Elfgifu to join him, but she stood back.

"That will be nice for you." She looked at his face this time. When she first caught sight of the white cataract covering the lens of his left eye, she frowned, but unlike most people, she did not look away. Rather, she smiled at him. The sight of the smile and her bright, green eyes made Godfrew return the intimacy. "Does your uncle know of your plans?" She broke eye contact.

"Not yet, but his wife will not be happy with me being here. She will force my leave, I am sure. It was always that way with her, even when I was a boy and came to stay with Uncle Edwin. He always wanted a son—and until he married, I was it. The fact that she has never produced has, I think, made her resentment of me all the greater. But that is her problem, not mine. Recently I have only seen my uncle when he came to us at the homestead." Godfrew stretched himself luxuriously. "I will need something to cover me in this draughty place tonight. My cloak is too wet. I left it by the fire in the tavern to dry."

Elfgifu smiled at him saucily. "I am sorry, but you will have to make do with this old horse blanket in the corner, complete with fleas. But your cloak is here." She turned and picked up the wolf skin from the floor by the entrance. "If I had left it by the fire, it would have been ruined. The wool lining would have scorched and the leather hide cracked. It needs to be laid out here on the straw. The straw will absorb the wet and the draft will help it dry. Do you know nothing about looking after yourself, or have you always had a body servant looking after you?"

"At one time, but he is gone now." Godfrew hooded his eyes and his happy mood seemed in danger of going. When the maid sat down beside him, he turned and smiled at her wanely. Her returned smile brought back the happiness. "Thank you, Elfgifu. What would I do without you?"

"Get by, no doubt, Edwin's nephew." She played with the damp fur of the cloak. "You know my given name, but what is yours? Edwin only calls you nephew."

"My gift of the elves, that is for me to know and you to find out." Godfrew got up and offered her his hand. Elfgifu took it and led the way back into the tavern proper.

"Your cloak tells me that I should call you Wulf."

* * *

The Kentish Maid

"Uncle Edwin, I must visit London. I have some business to attend to. Is there anything you want while I am there?" Godfrew tightened up his horse's girth strap and checked the saddle for adjustment. "I know that most of your trade is local, but perhaps you have something I can do for you?"

"Well, I have a surplus of smoked fish. The monks at the priory on the next island trade them for my ale, you know. They used to brew their own till they tasted mine. They have no money, of course ... or so they will tell you! They always say that ... even the ones from the rich houses ... but smoked fish ... there is only so much smoked fish that you want. Of course, many of the local folk buy their ale with the same currency ... what, not smoked fish again, I say to them ... can't you catch anything else in the river ... what about catching some silver pennies[10]... and they laugh." Edwin turned and called to the maid hovering by the tavern door. "Elfgifu, get my wife to give you a pack of the fish and bring them here ... oh ... and make sure that they are wrapped properly."

"Uncle, what do I do with the smoked fish?" Godfrew picked his cloak up and reversed it, keeping the fur on the inside, displaying the dirty, white wool lining.

"Sell it, of course! Well ... not sell it, as such ... go and see Aldred at the sign of The Bush near the horse ferry on the Westminster bank. He will give you silver in exchange. We have a standard rate, so you won't need to haggle. He has a nice place ... Aldred ... a bit smelly in summer ... but then ... I suppose it is smelly here in summer, come to think of it."

Edwin pulled his plump bottom lip. "He gets a lot of his trade from the ferry, of course. There has been a lot of coming and going of late ... what with one thing and another. He does these wonderful duck pies. I'm sure that he makes more on the pies than he does on the ale ... I've spoken to my wife, your aunt ... tried to get her to make duck pies, but she says it is all a waste ... we would have to pay more for the ducks than the fish. And we always have smoked fish coming out of our ears ..."

---

[10] Silver penny: standard coin in Old England. The term "pound" was often used, but there was no actual pound coin. Rather, it referred to the weight of the silver pennies.

Godfrew took the proffered pack of fish and tied them to the back of the pony. "Aldred at The Bush ... Westminster bank ... across the horse ferry." He mounted the small dark pony, wishing it were faster and better looking. "I must be on my way, Uncle Edwin. I have a lot to do." As he looked over his uncle's head, he saw Elfgifu watching him. She smiled at him. "Till I return," Godfrew smiled.

"Till then," said Edwin.

"Till then," whispered Elfgifu.

* * *

The dark pony stood still on the flat-bottomed ferry as it crossed the Thames. The animal's eyes were on the far bank and she whinnied softly at the thought of the soft green grass she could see there. Despite the pony's placid behaviour, Godfrew held the reins tight in his left hand. With his right arm across her neck, he stroked her absently with his free hand. The pony turned her head and nuzzled him, her soft muzzle on his cheek, her breath stirring his silver-streaked, golden hair. The sky was a leaden grey, but the threatened rain had yet to fall. A faint spin drift came back from the front of the ferry as it made its way across the river. Godfrew could just see the Westminster on Thorney Island surrounded by burned houses. The ferryman told Godfrew that the Normans had burnt these houses during William the Bastard's coronation on Christmas Day. The English had made their traditional shout of affirmation, but the Normans did not understand. They had panicked and burned the houses.

"Are you stopping at The Bush, young Master?" the ferryman asked. "If you are, be sure to have one of their duck pies. Best there is, Aldred's duck pies. Keep away from his smoked fish pies, though. I don't know where he gets the fish from, but they are so old, I reckon you could sole your shoes with them. In fact, perhaps that's where in fact he does get the fillings from!" The ferryman laughed and made his way back to the steersman. "Just warning the lad there about Aldred's smoked fish pies. Last one I had gave me the squirts for a week."

The Kentish Maid

The ferry grounded on the soft mud of the Westminster bank. Godfrew led his pony off and made for the small tavern. The animal's hoofs made a sucking sound as they made their way up the slight slope.

The tavern was much larger than the one at Battersea. It had benches set up on the grass in front of it. Godfrew hobbled the pony and left it to graze. As he lifted the pack off of her back, he caught a whiff of the fish and screwed his eyes up. Taking a deep breath, he carried the bundle inside.

"Yes, young man, what can I do for you?" A taller version of his uncle came toward him. "Oh, I see... or should I say... smell ... that you have brought some smoked fish from my friend Edwin of Battersea." He took the pack and put it by a leather curtain. "Maud, my dear, some of Edwin's fish has arrived. It is by the door." He turned back to Godfrew: "I'll get the money."

Aldred disappeared behind another curtain and returned a moment later with some silver pennies which he counted into Godfrew's hand. "Beautiful fish your uncle gets. I can't seem to get enough of them. The guild of shoemakers sent a man over here the other day and bought up all up my stock, so your arrival today is most welcome. Do you work for Edwin?"

"Yes, I am Wulf, his journeyman."

"Oh! Things must be looking up for Edwin, having someone working for him full time. When I first visited him on that island of his ... it was in summer ... and did it stink! I wondered how he managed to make a living with hardly anyone living there ... and them that did as poor as church mice ... I mean ... most evenings, hardly anyone is in the place except him and his fat wife... oh, and that shy maid he has there. It took a while to work out that most of his trade is making house ales. He tailors his ale to the taste of the family ordering it ... that and the fact that he is flexible with payment. You realise that the poor families pay him with fish? Of course you do! That's why you are here. But the cunning bit is that he allows them to pay part of it with labour ... letting them send their children to help steep the malt and then prepare the wort ... cheap price ... custom made to your pallet ... very shrewd. Yes, he's not from Battersea himself ... and with his wife ... a real outsider ... a Kentish maid ... it is very shrewd! You know what some folk are like about outsiders ... won't talk to them ... let alone buy from them ... yes, very shrewd and profitable. I hear that some of the local gentry are getting their ales from him now. That will upset our friend Walter at the sign of The Ram in Wandsworth."

Aldred gestured to a table and bench, "Join me, pray." He brought two earthenware mugs of frothy ale and returned for two platters, each with a large slice of pie on it. "The last of Edwin's smoked fish pie. "Aldred took a bite and washed it down with the ale. "What do you think of the ale? Not bad is it? But not as good as your Master Edwin's. At least, not as good as the special double brew he keeps for himself and friends. That's my trouble ... see, such a quick turnover, I can't afford to make special ales." He returned to munching the pie. "Ah, Maud, my dear!" Pieces of pastry flew as he spoke: "Meet Edwin's new journeyman: Wulf, isn't it?" Godfrew nodded his assent. "Brought us some more fish." Aldred's wife was even bigger and more dominating than Uncle Edwin's. Godfrew then realised why the two men got on so well.

* * *

The peep-hole in the solid oak door slid open. "Yes?"

"I have business with Teodoric the goldsmith." Godfrew bent to catch the eye of the speaker.

"So 'ave many people. 'oo should I tell the Master is without?" the high voice hinted that the speaker was a young apprentice.

"Wulf, Aldred at The Bush's journeyman. It concerns a deposit he wishes to make. Please hurry, I don't feel safe on the street."

The peep hole closed abruptly and Godfrew could hear retreating footsteps. The rain kept up its persistent downpour. Yellow puddles formed around the horse dung in the street and little foul rivers ran through the cobbles to meet at a large, smelly midden heap at the end of a row of half-timbered stone houses that adjoined the wall of Teodoric's house. There was no cover at the wall, so Godfrew turned his back to the rain and pressed his face against the door. The rain dripped off the end of his cloak, ran down the back of

The Kentish Maid

his leg wrappings and into his shoes. He wriggled his cold wet feet and felt most miserable. The peep-hole opened again. "For mercy's sake let me in out of this weather."

"The Master will see you, but stand well back from the door." Godfrew stood back and the door opened outwards. In the yard stood the apprentice and two archers, bows drawn. "Can't be too sure these days, Master Wulf. Please ter follow me." The apprentice turned and ran toward the house. The archers unnotched their arrows and went about closing the door. Godfrew followed the boy, dodging puddles and muck as he went. "Your cloak, Master Wulf?" asked the boy, once they were inside.

Godfrew pulled back the hood of the sodden garment. "No, I doubt I'll be long. Now Teodoric?"

"Follow me, though yer really should let me look after your cloak, as Master Teodoric won't like yer dripping all over 'is polished wooden floor."

The apprentice climbed up a broad sweep of stairs, two at a time. Godfrew's back was all right at the present, but he took the stairs only one at a time, just in case. The boy knocked at a door. "Master Teodoric, Master Wulf of The Bush is 'ere." At the grunted response, the boy flicked the latch and open the door.

Inside sat Teodoric the goldsmith. At his feet—and either side of him—were ornate charcoal braziers. The heat eddied across the room. Teodoric was examining a gold arm band that had been damaged by what looked like a sword cut. "Come in, I'll not be long." Teodoric did not look up from his task, rolling the piece in his hands, first this way and then that. "Hmm." He put the piece on the table and looked up. "Now, Master Wulf, how much does our good friend Aldred want to deposit this time?"

"I don't know," replied Godfrew. "I want to make a withdrawal on behalf of someone else."

"A what? Now if you ... I know you, don't I? Your name is not Wulf at all, it's, it's ... ah, yes, I know now ... it's young Godfrew from Garrat. You have aged, boy, and not for the better." Teodoric moved his thin rump on the plump cushion that graced his stool. "What's all this Aldred nonsense?"

"I needed to get in. I thought you might be reluctant to open the door to the son of a dead man whose treasure you were holding."

"I see. That's the withdrawal part then?" Teodoric played with some nasal hair, tweaking it this way and that, then he leaned back and crossed his hands over his stomach. "Your father is dead. I am duty bound to hand the treasure, what little there is, to his heir. You, my friend, have been declared outlaw and a Wolfshead. You cannot inherit. There are, of course, other's who may now inherit. And they will no doubt put their cases to the Shire Moot, which, in the fullness of time, will come up with a decision. Until then, the treasure stays here."

Godfrew put his right hand inside the cloak and pulled his saxe from its hiding place behind his back. "I would like to take it with me now. I am sure you wish to keep your life."

"And if I say no and you kill me, do you think you will get out of here alive?" Teodoric's snake-like eyes were glued on the blade of the saxe.

"I'm sure it won't come to that. We are both reasonable men."

"Yes, you are a man now. Six months ago, you were a youth. All right, Master 'Wulf,' let's say that we talk about the problem."

"There is no problem. I want to withdraw what gold and coin you hold of my father's. The jewels can be kept for my relatives, if they want them. The coin will need to be in bags, the gold in travelling bars." Godfrew drew nearer to the goldsmith and felt the warmth from the braziers.

"Did you say bags of coin? Bag, singular. I will show you the books if you have the time. You can calculate and read can't you? Oh, yes, you can! I remember how proud your father was of the fact. But the gold travelling bars, there is a worry. Your father is due two and a half at standard weight. I have only one and a half at present. You can either take that or return later tonight for the full payment." Teodoric had not moved nor taken his eyes off of the saxe.

"I'm not sure that I can trust your figures. With interest, there should be more." Steam drifted from the edges of Godfrew's cloak and the fumes from the charcoal was starting to make his eyes water.

The Kentish Maid

"Interest is usury and usury is forbidden by Mother Church."

"Yet popular."

"True. Well what are you going to do?"

"I'll take what you have ready."

"Not the gold. I keep it in another place. Safe." Teodoric smiled, not very pleasantly.

"Then I shall be back for it later. Now the silver pennies." Godfrew brought the blade of the saxe to the end of Teodoric's nose and nicked it. Teodoric moved his stool back and got out of range. He knocked twice on the floor with the heel of his foot. A long minute passed, then the apprentice came in. "Twenty seven silver pennies, Tork, in a soft leather purse, if you please." Godfrew leaned forward menacingly. "No, make that a round thirty ... to cover interest. Master Wulf will come with you."

"A pleasure doing business with you. I'll return later to finish the matter."

"I'll look forward to that."

"I'm sure you will." Godfrew followed the boy, collected the purse and left.

* * *

Godfrew sat at the upstairs window in the house across the street and occasionally watched the street below. A Norman guarded the door to Teodoric's yard now. There were others inside. Getting lodging so close had been fortunate, though not deliberate. Soon after leaving, he had been stricken by stomach cramps and a strong need to use the privy. A serving maid had seen his distress and brought him into the house where he now lodged.

With so much uncertainty around, many were glad of an extra source of income and his host was amongst them. The room was small and musty, but it was dry. Only one leak in the thatch was troubling and even that was not a problem now he had moved his cot.

The rain had ceased after two days, together with Godfrew's need to constantly visit the privy. He had been able to get out and about the city of London ... watching, talking, buying things he needed. All was a-bustle with much coming and going to the king's hall by both English and Norman. The former were in their best clothes, the latter in mail-coats.

Godfrew had his cloak draped over his knees. He had purchased some thread and a needle and was making an adjustment to the hood. He had cut out the lining behind the wolf's eyes and was stitching the hide around the cut. The stitches were large, but tidy. The workmanship was not up to his mother's standards, but it was serviceable. His time with the army had convinced him that stitching leather was an essential skill. His time as a child watching his mother had not been a waste.

Hearing voices outside, he looked out. As he watched, Teodoric's door opened. A fresh Norman guard came out and, after a chat, the old one went in. The guard was changed thrice a day. The one who was on now would be there all night. The lack of cover made it a very uncomfortable job, standing in all weather. It also made it difficult to sleep, as the door into Teodoric's yard was in view of the whole street, but Godfrew had learnt the man's pattern: he would wait until the apprentice brought him food and drink prior to the house lights going out. The Norman would then eat, piss, and afterwards sit on the roadside with his back to the door. Godfrew was unsure whether the man slept or not. If he did, he didn't snore.

Godfrew looked at his handiwork and then tried the cloak on. It took a bit of pushing and pulling, but he got the eye-holes to line up with his own. He then pinched the wolf's mask and took the cloak off. Using the creases in the mask, he put in some more stitches to hold the shape, so that next time the eye-holes would line up automatically.

At sunset, the lights opposite came on and Godfrew went downstairs to eat with his hosts. The couple were both Londoners, though the man, like many Londoners, bore a Danish name. The man made his living as a hammer smith for the London monier. The dinner conversation, as it had every night Godfrew had been there, centred around the fact that there was a new and foreign king. As a result, there was much uncertainty as to whether he would continue the English practice of having a monier in each shire, or centralise it. If it was centralised, where would the mint be? In fact, where would the capital be? Winchester? London? Salisbury? York?

York would not have been a likely choice, as the north was still more Viking than English and more English than Norman. So where? The conversation had no end. As per every other night, it went around and around in a circle. Godfrew nodded his head at the appropriate times whilst his hosts continued to worry about the location of the mint.

Godfrew looked at the comfort of the house and appreciated that its standards told of happy and profitable times in the past. The double story suggested that perhaps some of the realm's silver coins had been diverted. There were five or six children. Godfrew wasn't sure if there was a set of twins or a set of triplets, as they all looked alike and never seemed to keep still. Either way, the good wife looked and acted as if she was permanently exhausted. Having a serving maid helped her. The maid was helpful—too helpful for Godfrew's liking in his present situation. The housewife made it clear that she found having a lodger just another burden that she would rather not have had. Not that she was rude. It was just in her tone and manner when she spoke to him.

After the meal, Godfrew returned to his room and watched the house opposite and its guard. As the evening lengthened, the lights went out one by one until only the kitchen and Teodoric's room remained lit. Godfrew eased the leather curtain to his room and listened. The host and his wife were getting ready to retire for the night, but he could not hear the maid. A clink, followed by a splash of water, told that she was in the yard—probably washing a bowl or dish.

He went back to the window. The Norman was still awaiting his supper. The host and his wife climbed the stairs and went to their chamber. Soon snores filled the upper story and the Norman still awaited his supper.

Godfrew picked up his cloak and gear and moved silently down the stairs. He stopped before he got to the main room and looked for the maid. She was asleep, curled up like a cat by the fire. Godfrew left, checked to see if the pony was ready, then made his way to the street.

"Dog's shit, cat's balls and snails, your worship." The apprentice proffered a steaming plate to the Norman guard: "Good appetite."

"More pig's swill, I suppose, you Saxon dog. Thank you." The Norman took the plate and used a piece of hard acorn bread to shovel the stew into his mouth. Regardless of the quality of the food, it was hot. It took a while for the Norman to eat the meal, accompanying his mouthfuls with much sucking in of cold air. There was a small jug of watery ale. He took a swig of it between each mouthful. Eventually, he finished. Putting his utensils down, he walked a little way from the door in the wall, slackened his breeches, and started to piss against the stones. The walrus rope flicked over his neck and Godfrew pulled his victim close as he tightened the rope. His wrists crossed and locked. The Norman fought, kicking and struggling. Godfrew pushed him against the wall and the man's helmet tipped forward, levered by the nasal guard, then came off as his face rolled sideways. The struggles became less coordinated now and the man's efforts concentrated on a vain attempt to get some fingers under the rope to relieve the pressure on his windpipe. Blood flicked onto the stone wall as the Norman's fingernails cut and scratched his own throat. Slowly, the struggling ceased and the Norman shat himself. Godfrew checked the street and saw that nothing moved. He pulled the dead man to the front of the door and propped him up. The man squelched in his own excreta. Godfrew replaced the missing helmet and looked at his handiwork. The Norman looked no different tonight than he did at on any other night about this time. He just smelled a bit more.

Godfrew unwound more of the walrus hide rope and attached a small grappling hook. With two swings the hook caught on the top of the stone wall, Godfrew pulled the hood of his cloak back onto his head and quickly climbed the wall. It was only the height of two men, so it did not take much effort. Before letting himself down the other side, he flattened himself on the top and looked into the yard. The lights were still burning in the kitchens and he could see at least two men working in there. Otherwise, all was still. He lowered himself into the yard, leaving the rope in place.

"I just saw a wolf climb down the wall." The balding man in grease covered clothing picked up a piece of firewood and strode into the yard.

The Kentish Maid

His companion continued his task of raking out the oven's fire box. "What was that, Erik? I've got me 'ead in the oven. For a minute there, I thought you said there was a wolf climbing down the wall. Erik?" The second scullion emerged from the oven's fire box with a face like a Black-a-Moor. He looked around the kitchen and then glimpsed his mate lying in the yard with a wolf worrying him. "ERIK!" He charged out, grabbing a cleaver as he ran. The wolf stood up and hit the scullion with Erik's firewood. Godfrew dragged Erik into the kitchen and trussed him up with strips cut from the man's own shirt. As it was cold, he left him near the fire. When he started to drag the second man, Godfrew's back gave a twinge – so, in spite of the cold, Godfrew trussed him up and left him where he had fallen in the yard.

The lamp in Teodoric's room was still alight and Godfrew made his way up there cautiously, sniffing the air like the wolf he had become. Outside Teodoric's door stood another Norman. He had a scored nasal guard on his helmet and a badly broken nose. Godfrew recognised him as the sergeant from Wimbledon.

Teodoric sat in his room counting out money. The silver pennies winked at him in the lamp light, returning the affection that Teodoric obviously felt for them. There was a knock at the door. "What is it, Charles-Who-Once-Was-a-Sergeant? Oh, blast! I forgot." He switched to French. "What do you want Charles?" There was no response. "Come in! Come in!" The door swung open and Charles the ex-Sergeant stood there. "Well ... WELL? Oh, goodness me ... well."

A wolf peered over Charles' shoulder. "Good evening, Teodoric," said the wolf.

Charles the ex-sergeant bowed his knees, then slowly lay prone as a priest before the altar. Teodoric screamed and piddled himself. In the dim glimmering light of the doorway, the wolf stepped forward and changed into a man—a man with one eye, a young face, silver-streaked hair, and the stance of an old man. "Wolf ... shape-changer ... Woden." Teodoric stood up sharply, catching the edge of the bench with his knees and setting the coins jangling and dancing onto the floor.

"You owe someone some money, I believe, Teodoric."

"A few outstanding debits, all accounted for ..." He waived his hand over the bench and the books piled on one side.

"I am thinking of one person in particular," said the one-eyed man. "Someone you feared enough to bring in the Normans."

"I am acting as banker for the new king. He set the guard. I owe no one. See here!" He pointed to a chest against the wall behind him, "I have the gold ready for your friend ... both travelling bars." A look of disbelief crossed the shape-changer's face. "Oh, dear God, was it you, Lord Woden. Was it you yourself?" Teodoric sank to his knees. The urine was dripping from his breeches onto the polished wooden floor of which he was so proud.

"It was I. You needed to be put to the test ..." the man's voice rose in pitch, "... and you failed. The gold, Teodoric."

"You are welcome to it—and more besides. Take it! Please!" Teodoric's voice took on a whining edge. He lowered his head and started to cry.

"I asked for what was owed. You offered two and a half bars. How much do you really owe? And remember, I know all."

"Four. And another ten silver pennies. Oh, Lord Woden, take it and leave ... leave!" Teodoric's voice had thickened from the crying and snot ran down his nose, mixing with the tears.

"And what shall I do with you, my greedy friend?"

"Master! Woden! What ever. I just don't want to die! Please, don't kill me." Teodoric grovelled and fawned. He started to shuffle on his knees toward the one-eyed man.

"Stay put, you smelly thief. Lay on your belly like the snake that you are!" As Teodoric rolled over, Godfrew stepped forward and laced ankles, wrists, and neck together. He finished his work off with a rag gag, then went to the chest and took out the four travelling bars of gold that were due to him. As he collected the silver coins from the floor, he said, "I have my reward, but what reward shall I find for you? Perhaps a reminder that you should always lend a sympathetic ear to those in need."

Godfrew pulled out his saxe and sliced off one of Teodoric's ears.

Teodoric opened his eyes in shock and saw the man turn back into a wolf as he left. Teodoric started crying again, though whether from relief, fear, pain, frustration, or anger, not even he knew.

Godfrew made his way downstairs as quietly as he could, keeping his ears well open for any sound of movement, but all he could catch was the laboured breathing of the trussed and gagged men in the kitchen. As he drew near them, they averted their eyes and rolled out of his way. As best he could with his restricted right hand, Erik made a sign to ward off the evil one. Erik rolled back and watched through the open doorway. He saw the wolf silently climb the wall and disappear, then breathed easier.

Godfrew went around the rear of his host's house and found the dark pony. He slipped the gold travelling bars into the narrow pouches he had sewn under the saddle skirt. As he looked and listened, there was no movement and no sounds.

Taking a chance, he entered the house. The fire had died down and the maid had curled into a tighter ball. She snuffled in her sleep, but did not wake, so Godfrew made his way up the stairs. The host and his wife were still snoring. Godfrew left the monies he owed on the cot in his own room and made his way downstairs again. The maid had thrown an arm out. Godfrew bent down, put a cut half silver penny in the palm of her hand and folded her fingers over it. She had been helpful and kind when he had been unwell and in need of a roof.

If Godfrew had wanted, she would have been helpful and kind in other ways, too. That thought amused Godfrew. He left and rode out of the small yard on the dark pony, his mind again on a maid, but this time he was thinking of the one from Kent.

* * *

The crust of ice on the puddles cracked loudly as the small pony walked on them. Patches of fog hung at saddle height and the pony's breath hung around both horse and rider in clouds. Hoar frost twinkled on tufts of coarse marsh grass and lowering clouds crushed all beneath. The rider bowed over the pony's neck for warmth. His off-white hooded cloak made him all but disappear into the scene. Only the dark pony stood out. In the distance, an island in the marsh could be seen. Billows of smoke and steam rose from it, merging with the fog and low cloud.

The rider lifted his head and watched, looking for any activity. He nudged the pony's ribs and the creature quickened its pace on the pot-holed causeway. The cold air cut into the rider's face, making his cheeks sting and his eyes water. The fog now came in higher patches that covered him and his mount. Damp at first—then cold—it froze on any surface it came into contact with. Both horse and rider began to shiver. As the island got closer, the rider came into an area clear of fog and was able to see that the hamlet and outlying buildings were still intact. The smoke and steam came from a shed on a small rise on the other side of the tavern. Uncle Edwin was brewing. The Normans had not come raiding. Godfrew relaxed and loosened his grip on the reins. The pony caught the change in mood and slackened its pace.

"Welcome back, Wulf," Elfgifu, the Kentish Maid, encased in a large sheep-skin cloak, took hold of the dark pony's bridle and stood at the saddle looking up at Godfrew. "Let's get the pony put away and you indoors. You look frozen. Your face is all pink with blue blotches." She laughed. "You really do look funny."

"My elven gift, I can't get off the horse. My knees won't move." Godfrew gesticulated with a cramped claw of a hand toward the small tavern. "See if Uncle Edwin can come and help me get off. Quickly, before I freeze to death."

"Then don't run away." The maid giggled all the way to the dripping eaves of the tavern, pulled the door open and called inside: "Master Edwin, your help, if you please. Your nephew is back and needs you."

"Yes, yes, all right, girl. I hope he hasn't brought those fish back. We've so many more brought in since he's been away. I don't know what we are going to do with them all." Edwin emerged looking even larger than usual with all his extra clothing. A thick, purple wool felt cap covered his head and most of his face. "Oh good, you got rid of the fish, nephew. You have another bundle, I see, but it smells of cloth. You had no problem with Aldred? No, of course, you wouldn't

The Kentish Maid

have had ... I must find a way of getting the fish to him more regularly ... I would ask you but ..." He looked to the open door where his voluminous wife stood, "... I'm sure you won't be here that long. Now come, nephew, let's help you off that horse."

He freed Godfrew's foot from the stirrup on his side whilst the maid did the same the other side, then he reached up and rolled Godfrew out of the saddle. They both landed in a heap, Godfrew's fall softened by his uncle's stomach. "Nephew, nephew, get off me, please." Godfrew rolled off onto his still bent knees and assumed an attitude of prayer. Edwin caught his breath and came over to catch Godfrew's elbow. "Can you move your knees yet? No? Elfgifu! Come here, girl! Grab his other elbow and lift when I give the word." The stubble on Edwin's unshaven chin mimicked the hoar frost that hung on everything around him. "Ready now, one, two, three!"

"Hold, hold." Godfrew was in a crouching position and endeavouring to straighten his legs. "Gently now, ahhhh, gently." The ice on his cloak, breeches and leg wrappings cracked as he tried to straighten, then slid to join the ice on the frozen ground. He stood upright. "Right ... now slowly ... "With his uncle on one side and Elfgifu the other he made toward the door. Each step was painful, as his still numb and cramped legs were forced to move. The dark pony followed them to the door of the tavern The horse was worried at Godfrew's distress, nuzzling his cloak from behind. "Please, when you can, the pony ... the saddle ... I will need the saddle."

"All in good time, nephew. All in good time. Now ... sit here by the fire ... Elfgifu, get his cloak off, girl! Put it somewhere to dry, then see to the pony before the poor creature freezes to the spot. Get one of Stain the Mute's boys to help you." The maid unfastened the cloak with difficulty, the clips being frozen together. "Now sit down on the stool. See ... my wife, your aunt ... has brought some ale she has mulled with a poker ... drink it nephew ... thaw your blood."

Slowly, the feeling returned to Godfrew's body. At first, the feeling was pleasant. Then, when his fingers and toes regained their feeling, the pain hit him in waves. Despite wanting to be brave in front of his Kentish maid, Godfrew moaned with the pain.

"Suck your fingers, Wulf. It will warm them more slowly." Elfgifu had unlaced Godfrew's leg bindings and removed his coverings and shoes. She commenced to chafe his purple and white feet with her warm hands. "Slowly, my love, suck your fingers slowly. There is no hurry and it will hurt less." Godfrew smiled at her.

"The pony, girl. See to the pony. My nephew doesn't want you fussing around him. Hurry!" Edwin put another log on the fire and poked the embers with an old bent iron rod. Godfrew touched Elfgifu's hand as she passed. "Things are looking up for us here, nephew. The Normans are to build a new castle at the edge of the city. Courtesy of my monkish friends, I learnt of their need for supplies. I have a contract to supply them with small ale for the workers they are bringing in to build it. From what I can gather, it will go on for years. Maybe I can even persuade them to buy some of my surplus smoked fish." Edwin continued to poke the fire, sending up whirls of sparks. "So what have you in the package you brought back?"

"A present for your wife and other bits," Godfrew replied between sucking his still frozen fingers. "I trust she likes ribbons still."

"Oh, yes, nephew. There is no end to her liking for ribbons, especially bright ones. I rarely go to the city myself. You can't trust the boys to brew properly. Too young, you see. Always playing about ... irresponsible ... unlike I was at their age. Besides, the brewing needs my special touch. But if I do go, I durst not come home without some special ribbons or a broach for my wife, your aunt. Ah, here she comes now, so hush a while ... more mulled ale for my nephew, my love? So thoughtful! He is still half ice at present." Edwin took the proffered mug from her and held it for his nephew to drink from. "I don't know why you travelled so early. You should have stayed a few more days till the weather improved ... still, this time of year, you could have been there weeks waiting for that, I suppose. It affects the brewing to no end, this cold weather ... stops the fermenting, you see. You will remember when you were a boy and stayed here that I stopped at late autumn, but demand is up and with this new contract, I

The Kentish Maid

durst not stop at all. Do you know how I get over the problem? Cunning ... I bryer the neighbour's cows in the brewing shed ... their warmth raises the temperature, you see ... keeps the fermentation going. In fact, with you so cold, it will be best for you to sleep in there too while you are here, rather than in the lean-to. It smells a bit, but it is nice and warm."

"Thank you, Uncle. I won't be staying here for long. In fact, if I can get myself thawed out, I will go in the next day or so."

Edwin looked to see if his wife was around, but she had retired to the kitchen again. "You could stay for as long as you like, of course, but if you wish, you are free to go." He looked relieved that the potential for disagreement with his wife over his nephew's stay was being removed. "I shall tell my wife, your aunt, of your decision. I am sure she will be disappointed, but she will not stay in your way, I'm sure." Edwin crossed paths with Elfgifu as she came back in.

"Wulf, I haven something for thee." Elfgifu slipped back into her native Kentish dialect.[11] "For thy feet." She proffered sheep-skin shoes with hard, bullock hide soles. "I maden them myself whilst thou were away." Godfrew tried to put on the new shoes, but his hands were still not functioning properly. The maid helped him. "Thou art thawing out now, but thy face is still mottled pink!" she giggled. "And now I see thy feet be the same colour." She looked at Godfrew, her face serious. "Wulf, thou dost not mind me making a gift for thee?"

"Never, my elven gift. In fact ..." Godfrew waved his still clawed hand at the parcel and saddle being brought in by three dirty and extraordinarily scruffy boys, "... I have something for you too, but you will have to open the parcel, for my fingers still refuse to obey me." Elfgifu open the parcel and laid out its contents before the fire. "The gaudy ribbons are for my uncle's wife, but the fine linen, needles and thread are for you."

"And what is this?" Elfgifu held up an orange. "It smells strange, nice, but strange."

---

[11] Kentish dialect: Kentish was a very distinct dialect in the 11th century and for long afterwards. The people of attributed this to their descent from the Jutes, rather than from the Angles or Saxons who traditionally made up the Teutonic conquers of England.

Woden's Wolf

"A fruit of the orient. Take care, for it cost me a whole silver penny." Godfrew gave a sheepish grin. "They say it makes lovers true."

"Then I shall keep it forever." Elfgifu sat back on her heels alternatively smelling and looking at the fruit.

"No, you must eat it, then the true love becomes part of you, never to go away. Besides, it will not keep and will rot," he added off-handedly.

"If I am to eat it, so shall you." The maid went to bite the orange.

"Hold on! I was told that you have to skin it, like flesh. Get your eating knife and hurry before my uncle or his wife come back in."

Elfgifu cut the orange into segments and peeled them, sharing the fruit with Godfrew. They had just finished their secret banquet when Edwin and his wife came back in. "Ah, Elfgifu, you are back." The maid scuttled off with her gifts, away to her sleeping place. "Now, nephew, I have brought my wife, your aunt, for the gift you have so kindly bought her." Edwin's wife was smiling, though whether it was from the thought of the gift, or from the thought of his leaving Godfrew was not sure. "Oh, see the ribbons, my love. So bright, they go with your smile." Edwin's wife took the ribbons and nodded to Godfrew before going back to the kitchen. "Well, nephew, I see you have treated yourself to some nice sheepskin shoes. They will keep you warm. You should have spoken to the maid Elfgifu. She has talents in that area and I am sure she would have made you a pair if you had but asked her."

* * *

"It's your turn," the first of Stain the Mute's scruffy sons pushed his younger brother. "I did it last time."

"It's not fair. You're only picking on me 'cos I'm younger. Get Snot to do it! He's youngest." The second of Stain's sons moved to the other side of the brewing vat. "Besides, I can't. It's too cold."

"Can't find it?" Snot, the littlest of the brood, strode forward. "I may be shortest, but I'm biggest." The urchin climbed the short ladder and leaned over the top of the open vat.

The Kentish Maid

"Smells strong already, this lot. You sure it needs it?" he enquired of his brothers.

"Better had, just in case. Go on, Snot, get on with it before old fat Edwin comes in. If he catches you, he'll feed you to his big fat wife or put you in the fish pie."

"Make you stink like you should," added the middle brother, knowingly.

"What?" asked the elder. "That doesn't make sense, you dunderhead. You are stupid."

"Look, shall I, or shan't I?" asked Snot, swaying his body over and back from the vat's edge. "Do I, or don't I?"

"Oh, do it and get on with it." Snot's brothers watched as he dropped the front of his breeches and urinated into the vat.

"Oi, what are you up to, you filthy little rats?" Godfrew stood at the entrance of the brewing shed, the cold air coming in with him and causing steam to rise from vat and incumbent cows alike.

"We have to, Master's nephew! We have to!" shouted the eldest. His brother's shout gave Snot such a fright that he piddled down the front of his breeches before he managed to recover.

"He started it," the middle one pointed at the eldest.

"No, no. It was Snot. I only copied him, 'cos he said to."

"Never mind who started it." The cows looked at Godfrew, begging him to close the door and keep the cold out. "Why are you doing it? You will ruin Uncle Edwin's ale, he'll never sell it now."

"Yes, he will, " insisted the eldest in a defiant voice.

"No, he won't, you impudent rat." Godfrew closed the door and put his saddle down by his feet. "Now get here and explain yourselves."

"Won't."

"Why?"

"I've finished. Can I come down now?" asked Snot.

"Yes! Why? Because I will beat the living daylights out of you if you don't! That's why! Now, get over here—now!" Stain the Mute's sons lined up in front of Godfrew, still nudging and squabbling amongst themselves. Their flickering eyes showed as the only bright spots in faces of uniform dirt. As Godfrew watched, a flea jumped from the head of the eldest

Woden's Wolf

to the head of the middle, then to the head of the youngest son. Snot lifted his right hand and skillfully squashed the flea with his thumb nail, without even looking. "Now why do you piddle in the ale and why would no one notice?" Godfrew had a horrible idea as to what the answer would be. As a drinker of the ale himself, he felt his stomach tighten.

"'cos we needed to go one day and it was raining outside?" tried the eldest, but Godfrew appeared unimpressed.

"'cos fat Edwin told us to?" ventured the middle one. Godfrew's black look made him lower his eyes to the ground and start kicking a dried cow pat on the floor.

"'cos it was funny. And our mum says the Normans are evil and our dad nods it, too. And we have to keep doing it 'cos they tasted the ale and told your uncle that they wanted to buy it and more too, but it had to taste the same. Now we durst not piddle in the vat in case it doesn't taste the same. And they make me." He looked resentfully at his now mute brothers. "They can't piddle as far as me. I can get it into the middle of the vat." Snot smiled victoriously at his crestfallen brothers.

"If my uncle ever catches you, he will kill you and use your bodies to ferment his barley wine. Now get out of here, I'm expecting someone."

"So the maid comes here, does she, Edwin's nephew? Don't let him catch you two together or he will kill you and use your bodies to ferment his barley wine." Snot laughed and raced his brothers to the door. Godfrew picked up a piece of the dried cow pat and shied it after them. He was just wiping his hands when Elfgifu came in.

"I can't stay long, Wulf. There are visitors at the tavern and I will be needed to serve their meal shortly." Elfgifu came and stood in front of Godfrew, her eyes searching his to try and find out what he wanted her to do or say next.

"Over here, Kentish Maid." Godfrew led her over to his saddle and indicated for her to sit down. "I have another gift for you, if you will have it." He put his hand into his purse and produced a red gold band with Runes cut into its face. "It was my mother's. My father gave it to her when he asked her to be his."

The Kentish Maid

Elfgifu took the ring wonderingly and fingered the Runes. "I thought your mother was dead and buried when you returned from the Sussex battle?"

"Another was looking after the ring for me, keeping it warm till I was able to claim it back. Will you take the ring?" Godfrew arched his brows, his heart beating fast.

"Can I? I don't know. We have only just met. Is this right?"

Godfrew stepped forward, lifted her chin and gently kissed her lips. "It is right. I know this."

"But I don't. I'm sorry, Wulf, I am all confusion. I must go back and help with the food." Elfgifu ran out of the shed, but she took the ring with her.

Godfrew grabbed his blanket and lay down alongside his pony. A curious cow investigated the pair, then decided to join them. In the warm and strange smells of the shed, they all drifted into sleep.

* * *

"You say these customers last night were from London, Uncle Edwin?" Godfrew remained tucked into the pony's underbelly, his head resting on her ribs.

"Oh, indeed, nephew ... and strange tales they told, too. Not just of the happenings of Christmas and the coronation, but of murder and robbery. You may not know this, but your father had treasure in store with a certain goldsmith called Teodoric. I doubt anyone will see that again, for he is a tight-fisted thief, given the chance. The goldsmith is now a banker for the Norman king. Well, two of his guards were killed, one inside the house. The goldsmith and his men were trussed up like swine awaiting slaughter. It appears that he had ten gold bars and a hundred silver pennies stolen. Teodoric and his men claim that it was a wolf that did it ... or even Woden himself ... but wolves don't strangle men ... and Woden is only a nightmare that old people use to frighten children with. The Norman king won't believe them ... of that I'm sure. If you ask me ..."

"Strange things are afoot in London, Uncle. I think it best to keep away from the place. In fact, I think I will travel to the south and go today."

"If you think it best, nephew, but I will miss you." Edwin looked to see if his wife was nearby, but she was not. "Of course, my wife, your aunt, will miss you too. Do you have to go? Yes, yes, I'm sure you know what you want to do. Come here." Edwin moved to the wall and levered a piece of mud from it. Behind was a small cavity from which he removed a couple of pieces of broken gold jewellery. "Take this and journey safely. I would that I had great treasure that I could give you, nephew. I regret that I have but little treasure."

"Uncle, the treasure you have given me is more valuable than you know."

The dark pony

slowly climbed the hill out of the Falcon Brook valley and made toward the common of Wandsworth. Godfrew kept the hood of his off-white cloak over his face in case he met any who knew him. The danger would not pass till he neared the hamlet of Mitcham. Despite the mid-winter chill, there were many people on the roads. None had stopped to talk. All seemed to be too busy with their own thoughts and worries. Even the shepherds bringing a flock down the hill, headed toward London by way of Clapham and Lambeth, had done no more than nod. In the past they had always been only too keen to stop and gossip whilst their charges ate and enjoyed their last days of freedom.

Everyone was uncertain and closed. The weather mimicked the people. Lowering clouds threatened snow, but were not delivering it. A chill wind blew cold enough to make the travellers shrink into their clothes for comfort.

"Are you warm enough, little elf's gift?" Godfrew looked back from the pony's bridle he held as he walked.

"Why do you call me little? We must weigh the same, though you are four hands taller ... I am hardly little." Elfgifu's voice came from within her hooded cloak, floating on her visible breath.

"Uncle Edwin said he had but "little" treasure to give me. It is he you must take that point up with."

Godfrew slipped on the icy grass and was held up only by the pony. Elfgifu giggled. "I know," he said. "Clumsy me again. Once we reach the crest, it gets better ... though the wind will still be cutting. There are very few trees across the common land that covers the ridge of the East Hill from here to Streatham. We won't go that far, but will cut down to Mitcham. I wish to pass the grave of my parents. The place is on the way."

Elfgifu leaned forward, "Your holding was near there, wasn't it? Will we see it?"

"Not this time ... not now ... one day, perhaps, but not now."

Godfrew lapsed into the silence that seemed to bind all

others they passed on the road. Once on the common, they met few others. The couple and their pony all bent their heads to the oncoming wind and trudged forward. Their pace was set and unchanging until they reached the burnt wood lane where Godfrew halted the pony. Elfgifu slid down from the saddle and stood at his side.

"It's down there, then? Your Garrat?"

"It was. My Garrat no longer exists." Godfrew's eyes watered from the chill wind. "We must move on, or like Lot's wife we will be turned to pillars, though of ice rather than salt."

Elfgifu linked her arm into Godfrew's. "I will walk with you for a while, Wulf." The pony caught the word and started off toward the small priory on the road above Tooting.

* * *

At last, the end of the first stage of the journey was in sight. Ahead stood the manor of Croydon, held by the Archbishop of Canterbury. It was an island with meres and artificial fish ponds, formed by cuting off the river Wandle.

With bodies convulsed by shivering and limbs that did not want to function, the travellers waited in a grove of trees wondering how to get across to the nearby village. Godfrew had been here in summer with his father, buying cattle to fatten on the water meads at Garrat. At that time of year, the ground was firm. Knowledge of the paths across the boggy fields was irrelevant. Now, the area was impassable to all but those with local knowledge. Snow started to fall and the dark pony fidgeted. At last a goose girl with her charges came by and Godfrew left the trees to speak to her.

"Greetings, maid. Can I ask a favour?" The girl gave out a scream that sent the geese scattering, then joined them in running across what appeared to be marsh.

Godfrew returned to Elfgifu and the pony. "We must follow her! Quick ... on the pony!" The girl was way ahead now, but her foot prints showed where she had trod. Despite the surface water, the ground beneath was firm enough for Godfrew and the pony. In the gathering gloom they made their way to the village. As they got near the village church, a priest came out and walked toward them.

"So you are the marsh pixie that frightened Greta. The poor

girl is frightened out of her wits. It was all I could do to persuade her to take her geese home rather than seek sanctuary in the church. If you want to get help, my son, it pays to wear a dark cloak, not a white one that blends in with the snow!" He took hold of the pony's bridle on the opposite side of Godfrew. "Are you after shelter?" Godfrew nodded his assent. "Then come with me. The manor is held by the church and has guest rooms up at the priory. I will take you there, if you wish. It won't take long to get one ready for you."

"We are not yet wed, Father," Elfgifu added in a quiet voice.

"In that case, I had better get two ready. Unless you want me to perform the honours for you?" the priest added with a twinkle in his eye.

"I have yet to get the approval of the maid's father. It is to see him that we are on the road." Godfrew matched the pony's slow walk, keeping as close to it as possible to be near the animal's warmth.

"Well, to travel at this time of year to get a father's permission for his daughter ... it must be love, my son. You have a keen man after your hand, young woman." The priest looked up at Elfgifu and was rewarded by a smile. "Either that, or he is moon struck!" he added and laughed. "See, we are here. Let me help you down from the saddle, my child." Two men servants ran out to meet them. "Toft, Ulf. Take our guest's pony and put it in the stables and feed it."

"Bring the saddle to me, please," Godfrew called after them. It was then that he slipped on a patch of ice and crashed heavily to the ground. Searing pain bit into his back and an agonising pain leapt through his hip. Too cold to scream, he let out short, pained breaths. "I ... I ... I can't move." Together, the priest and Elfgifu dragged him to the door of the guest house. The priest banged heavily on the door and it was opened by a thin monk.

"Brother, help me get him in." The priest was out of breath from his efforts, the sharp cold air cutting into his lungs. "Quickly now ... stand him up." The two men put their arms under Godfrew's arm pits and heaved. He gave a muffled scream as his left foot took the weight of his body. "No good, brother. Get others quickly. Young man, lean on me!" The priest braced himself against the stone wall and took Godfrew's full weight on himself. Other monks silently gathered

Woden's Wolf

and brought a wooden stretcher. Together, they got the moaning Godfrew onto it and carried him into a small cell-like room.

"My child," the priest turned to Elfgifu. "Firstly, your name and your young man's. Then come with me and I will show you your room. Don't worry about your swain. We will return, but first you must warm yourself or you too will need the help of our healer. So ... what are you called?"

"Elfgifu, Father. My name is Elfgifu and he is called Wulf. He sometimes says he is Wulfsbane, but I call him Wulf. He will be all right? I shouldn't leave him."

"With God's blessing and the help of our healer, he will be all right. But first, you must warm yourself."

In his cell, Godfrew passed quickly from swoon into darkness.

* * *

The days became weeks and Godfrew could still not travel. The monks had put his back straight again, but the pain in his hip could not be cured by herbal infusion, poultice or bleeding. Sometimes the pain was just a nudging ache as in a loose tooth. Other times, it was so intense that Godfrew could not move. Even getting up from cot to privy took the help of three others and sometimes took up to an hour. Godfrew spent most of his time reading whilst Elfgifu spent her time making and repairing clothes, thereby paying back for the food they ate. Despite being a monkery, the rooms were warm and comfortable—though a trifle small. Each guest room had a cot with sheep skins, a small table for food and a stool. Lit by a rush, the room was comfortable. The thick stone walls kept the cold out and the warmth in. In the evening, once the light had faded, Elfgifu would join Godfrew. They sat and talked—always of the future and never of the past. One evening, as Elfgifu left the cell for her own, the priest and two monks whom Godfrew did not recognise, came in.

The priest motioned toward the visitors. "Wulf, I have brought these brothers in to see you. They are from Lewisham. Brother John and Brother Marcus are from the mother church of St. Pieters of Ghent." They inclined their heads toward Godfrew as they were introduced.

"From Ghent? You are a Flem, then. My last meeting with a Flem was not pleasant." Godfrew eased himself up on his elbows to see his visitors more clearly.

"A Flem, Master Wulf? Well, I suppose many years ago I was, but I have been in this country for most of my long life, as the rheumatism in my poor old joints remind me. I know that the new Norman king brought many of my countrymen with him when he invaded. We have always been a popular source of mercenaries. But we monks of Lewisham have been here since the time of Alfred the Great. It was his niece, Ethelrude, who granted us the manor at Lewisham. We have always tried to repay our hosts for their tolerance of us. Perhaps, my prickly friend, that is why I am here now to see you. Father Olaf says that you have the pain of a broken limb without the break. I have a few skills in these things. I might be able to help you, provided you don't object to a Flem touching you?"

Godfrew softened his face and acknowledged his bad manners. "If I bite you, brother, it will be because of the pain, not because you have some unpleasant countrymen." He lay back and waited to see what the monks had in mind for him. Brother Marcus pulled back the sheep-skin cover and just looked. After some time, he turned to Brother John and spoke to him in Latin.

"It is as I suspected ... no inflammation, no bruising, no protrusions ... nothing is broken. Poultices are ineffective, so it's not muscular. I suspect that he has the same complaint as Jacob." He bent down and spoke to Godfrew. "Your problem is not a simple one, and it may be that we cannot cure it."

"Brother Marcus, what was Jacob's complaint?" Godfrew asked anxiously.

"So you understand Latin? Father Olaf, you never told us this. Your young man is educated!" Marcus beamed to the priest.

"I never knew, till now. I knew he was educated ... as he could read ... but I have only seen him reading books in English. You have many secrets, my son." Godfrew glanced away sheepishly. "If I had known your Latin skills, I would have found something more positive for you to do with your time than reading old history chronicles."

"Reading history is never a waste of time, father, but yes, I will help you more in the future. I warn you, though, that my Latin is limited. Mostly, I can only insult people. I can read more than I can understand and understand more than I can speak. Latin is a foreign language and things foreign do not sit well with me."

Brother Marcus started to warm his hands on a stone bottle filled with hot water that he had brought in with him. "And does Flemish sit well with you, young Wulf? It seems to me that you should be spending more time reading the Scriptures and what our precious Lord Jesus taught than reading history. It seems that your reading is only feeding your prejudices." Brother Marcus pulled the stool over and sat down, his attention now on Godfrew's face.

"Provided you speak slowly, I can understand your Flemish. It is the same with Norse. Latin and French are foreign. They are not of our folk."

"We are all God's children, Wulf. It was not long ago that the Danes and their other Norse cousins were doing the same as these half-breed Norman relations are doing now."

"At least we could understand them when they spoke to us. It was not long before they settled and worked alongside us. Their children spoke more English than Norse. The Normans come to rule us."

"And Knute the Mighty did not? You have much to learn, young man. Now I will warn you that the examination will get painful from now on. You may have wondered why Brother John is here." Marcus looked at the burly monk with a smile. "Do you think that he is another healer? Go to him with a headache and he is as likely to give you soapwort as feverfew, so instead of having a clear head, you could end up with a lathery mouth. He is here to hang on to you and make sure that you don't bite me as you threatened." Brother John came forward, held Godfrew's arms down and put his not inconsiderable weight across Godfrew's chest. "You asked me earlier what Jacob's complaint was. Jacob wrestled with an angel of the Lord, as you will recall. As a sign, he was given the new name of Israel — "the Lord fights." He was also struck with sciatica. That is an inflammation of the sciatic nerve that sits in the hip joint. The Jews still refuse to eat

The Cray

that part of an animal ... you know ... in remembrance. In your case, it may be inflamed because of the way your body is made, or it may be trapped from your back injury. From what Father Olaf has told me, the latter seems the more likely. If so, I may be able to cure you, but I can't promise. Now be prepared to be hurt."

Marcus stood up, took Godfrew's injured leg and pulled it upright, Godfrew screamed in agony. Marcus then twisted it sideways and leaned with it across Godfrew's body, moving the young man's back in the opposite direction at the same time. Godfrew tried to resist, but Brother John held him down. There was an audible crack and Godfrew passed out.

* * *

Brother Marcus was sitting on a rock at the side of a fish pond, seemingly more intent on watching the ducks swimming than on his fishing. Godfrew, accompanied by Elfgifu, limped slowly over. Marcus cocked his head slightly as he heard them approach, but did not otherwise move, unwilling to break the serenity of the moment. The lovers came and sat beside him, one on either side. All remained quiet.

The fishing line bobbed, but Marcus did not see it. Godfrew nudged him. "What? Oh, yes, a fish." Marcus pulled the line in and wound it around the end of his pole. As the line shortened, the surface of the pond became agitated as a large trout fought for its life. The monk stood up and brought the fish to land with a pull and a swing. "It seems a pity to eat such a beautiful example of God's creation ..." he turned to the maid, "... but then, we do have to live, don't we? And he did give all creatures into our care, for our own use, in Noah's time. If we just sat and admired what the Lord has given us, instead of making it work, then what bad stewards we would be." Then he turned to Godfrew: "So young, Wulf. He of the old head on young shoulders." Godfrew looked puzzled. "The silver streaks in your hair lad. It was a jest."

"Is it that noticeable? With no mirrors in the monkery, I have not seen my reflection lately ... at least not clearly. The change started only months back. I can't get used to the idea of it happening. I wonder what Elfgifu's father will make of me?"

"You are feeling well enough to travel then, Wulf?" Marcus looked up from unhooking the trout.

"If I walk on my toes, I can manage. It will be slow, but I will not let this curse of Jacob rule my life."

"You are in good company with the problem. In his letters, Paul the apostle talks of being given a constant pain that God would not relieve him of, despite his prayers and pleading. Many think that he, as well as Jacob, suffered from sciatica. I am just sorry that I could not give you the complete cure I had hoped for. I have done what I can. The rest is in God's hands now."

"You could try drinking from a healing spring," the monk continued. "Your pain is eased by the willow bark infusions I make for you. Perhaps, if you combined that with the curing waters, you would gain the complete relief I pray for. Elfgifu," Marcus turned to the maid, "you are from Kent, they say? Do you know Sandling near the chapel of St. Mary by the river Cray? There is a healing spring there. It is a genuine one. The manor belongs to the See of Canterbury. Despite what some would tell you, Archbishop Stigand will not allow falsehood to flourish on any of his holdings. Well, do you know it?"

"Oh, yes, Brother Marcus, I know it quite well. I can get us accommodation there while Wulf takes the waters." She took Godfrew's hand and squeezed it. "I just wish that the hermit guarding it would wash in his own healing waters a bit more."

"Ah, yes, he does smell a bit. Still, hermits are supposed to be lonely creatures. He could be using his lack of hygiene to keep others away." Marcus turned back to Godfrew. "But try it, please, I have known it to work for others. However, I fear that much of your problem lies in your soul. Become God's friend and seek his peace. Leave your bitterness behind. You have your maid—your future wife—to think of."

Godfrew sighed. "Brother, God's friend is dead and God's peace has gone. Some time later, I may seek him again, but not now."

Father Olaf joined them and bent to admire the trout. "Good fishing, brother. It will improve tonight's dinner to no end. Now, Wulf, you asked for your pony to be readied. I'm sorry, but you will have to stay with us a few days longer and help us to eat Brother Marcus' fine fish."

The Cray

"There is trouble? The Norman wolves are on the scavenge again?"

"No, not the Normans. It is not always the Normans, Wulf. The bournes are flowing and the land is flooded at present."

"Bournes, father? You mean the woe waters?" queried Godfrew.

"If you like, the woe waters. Carlshalton, Caterham, and Coulsdon, as well as Smitham Bottom, south of us here in Croydon, are flooded—despite there being no rain for a week. Yes, I know they are called woe waters, though I am sure it has more to do with heavy autumn and winter rains than with foretelling of disaster." The priest wiped his hands on his rough cassock and looked resignedly at Godfrew, waiting for the inevitable reply.

"They flowed last year, too, despite not flowing for many years. You know as well as I, Father, what happened last year. You may scoff at my reading history, but the flow of the Wandle's woe waters before disasters is well recorded, particularly in your own chronicle."

"And the previous time they flowed was in 1051, the year our pious king, Edward the Confessor, made the mistake of exiling Earl Godwin and his sons—including the late king—from this troubled kingdom," acknowledged Olaf.

"They flowed in 1048—the year of the severe winter and the earthquake that shook the whole country. Before that, in 1041—when King Hardaknute died and the terrible storms came ... doing more damage than had ever been know before ... and more cattle died that year of moraine than ever before recorded," Godfrew reminded the priest.

"Before that, they flowed in 1035—the year Knute died and Alfred the Aetheling came back to England, only to be murdered ... I know. Perhaps God does sometimes use natural happenings to warn us of what is to come. But don't accuse me of writing the chronicles. The local monks do that ... and some of them are more superstitious than a good Christian should be ... but enough of this. Your departure is, at present, delayed. With your leg still not strong, it is perhaps no bad thing. So, let us rejoice in this beautiful spring day that the good Lord has given us and catch some more of the fish."

He took the fishing pole and cast the line into the pond.

Woden's Wolf

* * *

Godfrew leaned down from the saddle and spoke to Elfgifu as she walked alongside. "You should change places. What will your father think when he sees us? A fine son-in-law I would make, riding whilst his would be wife walks."

Elfgifu kept looking ahead as they approached the small bridge across the river Cray. "And what, my beloved one, would he think if he saw you hobbling or even crawling alongside?"

"Hmm. At least, let me dismount before we enter the hamlet. Which begs the question, elven one ... when Brother Marcus mentioned Sandling, why did you say you knew it, rather than that was where your family lived? Have you a secret?"

Elfgifu still did not look at Godfrew. "I thought it wise not to." She then looked at him. "It is you, Wulf, I think who has the secrets! No, in these times it is best not to say too much. What folk don't know they can't pass on." She grabbed the pony's bridle as they came to the bridge and led the creature across.

On the right, contrasting with the ever present orchards, was an open field where the chewed and trampled grass showed the scars of the recent market. On the other bank of the river was the small stone chapel of ease that was dedicated to St. Mary. The paths met one another at right angles and they turned right toward the hamlet of Sandling.

A bondsman—coming toward them—looked at them. Seeing who it was walking alongside the pony, he called out. "Be it thou, young Elfgifu? And thou hast a man in tow! A captive from far London? They sayen they have tails. Hasen thou a tail, young man?" The man gave a broken-toothed smile. "I'm sure thou hast, though maybe at the front, rather than the rear!" He burst into laughter. "Welcome home, maid. Thy father and mother thought thee gone with no news for months. Best hurry." He continued on his way, pruning saw in his hand, still laughing at his own joke.

"Daft Gryth. But he is right. My parents will be worried."

"Parents is it now? I have only heard you speak of your father. Can I get off the pony? The cottages are only a short way ahead. I can walk the rest."

"Not yet. My family lives a way outside the hamlet—up the lane near the blacksmith's forge. My father has a small garden there. He says it reminds him of home."

"Home? I thought your family was long established here." Godfrew was fidgeting in the saddle, longing to stop being the invalid.

"My mother's family are all from here ... and have been since Hengest's time—or at least that is what they would have you believe. My father has been here only since just before I was born. He was brought in by the landholder Elfgat to help run the cloth mill."

"So your river has mills on it, as does mine. It did not look strong enough. Please, elf's gift. When can I get down?"

As they went through the hamlet, housewives and children called out greetings to Elfgifu and stared curiously at Godfrew. "Quickly, let us pass behind these cottages and make through the orchard to the blacksmith's lane. I want you to meet my parents first rather than my grandmother, aunts and cousins. There is plenty of time for meeting them later. They would crow it over my father if they could say that they had met you first."

The apple trees had been pruned low, so that the fruit was easily picked, but the paths between the rows were wide enough to allow Godfrew to remain mounted. Soon they reached a lane and Elfgifu led them along it. The orchards thinned. To the left was a large field with a grassy mound. "That is where the Hundred Moot meets. It is also where the healing spring is. But now is not the time for you to meet the smelly hermit that lives there. It is not much further to our cottage, so you can dismount, if you wish."

Godfrew eased himself out of the saddle and lowered himself to the ground, taking the weight on his good leg.

"I still think you would have been better off riding all the way, but if you want to be the hero ..." Godfrew smiled and Elfgifu kissed him on the cheek. The path was soft and the pony made sucking sounds as it walked, Godfrew kept to the right side of the creature, leaning into it's side for support.

"Wulf, is it hurting?"

Godfrew shook his head. "I'm all right, once I get moving. It's the starting that's the hard part. What will your father think of me?"

"You will get your chance now. That's him working in the garden in front of the cottage ahead." Elfgifu nodded toward a square built man grubbing the soil in a small cleared patch. Behind it stood a small but substantial thatched cottage—its sides made of split timber. The man had black hair and his skin was a dark brown. As he worked, he sang to himself in a strange lyrical tongue.

"That is your father?"

"My dear Da, yes."

"He's a wog, isn't he?"

"He is of the Cymry,[12] yes. He is my beloved father and he is my best secret." Elfgifu left Godfrew and the pony and ran toward her father. "Da, Da, it's me. I'm home!"

"Her father is a wog! Just what sort of family am I getting involved in?" Godfrew watched as the man stopped what he was doing, dropped his gardening tool, ran toward Elfgifu and swept her off her feet. As he watched, Godfrew asked himself: "Do you love her, Godfrew Wulfsbane? Yes, I do. Then that's what matters, not who her father is or where he is from." Godfrew resolved the matter and headed toward the couple entwined together. Their tears flowed freely, mixing as they embraced. They pulled apart to look at each other's faces, then embraced again. At the sound of the pony shaking its head and rattling its bit and bridle, they turned.

"Da, this is Wulf, the nephew of Edwin of Boxshulle, whom I worken for." Elfgifu held her father's hand and led him toward the young man.

"Elfgifu's father, peace." Godfrew quieted the dark pony with his hand.

"Oh, aye, peace. So is this a visit then—or is there more purpose to this visit, boy?" Hywel, Elfgifu's father, looked Godfrew up and down intensely. "More perhaps of that a bit later, eh? Now, Cariad, see thy mother and the childer."

Elfgifu walked to the cottage and called inside. Upon hearing a muffled response, she went in. "Well, Wulf," the lilt of Hywel's voice sounded beautiful, yet strange. The Welsh accent was well mixed with Kentish overtones. "Is there more to this than just the gallant escort?"

"Yes, Elfgifu's father. I would have her for my wife." Godfrew

---

[12] Cymry, Cymru: native names for Welsh, Wales.

eased the weight off of his sore leg.

"Oh, there's interesting. Is this for the chapel or for the hand-fast then? By your dress and manner, I would guess that you be more than a bondsman. But, boy, I warn you, freeman, or even thane, I'll not see her tied only by the hand-fast marriage!" Hywel stood squarely and folded his arms across his chest, inviting only one answer to his question.

"I love the maid. Only a God blessed marriage will do." Godfrew permitted himself a wane smile.

"Oh, aye ... well ... we shall talk later, then. Now come and meet my Cariad's mam. Tie your pony up, boy. Don't let him eat my vegetables, whatever you do."

Inside the cottage, Elfgifu's mother was busy putting wooden platters on a wooden table. Hanging onto one side of her apron was a small blond girl of about nine summers. On the other side was a small, dark boy about two years older. "Well, Elfgifu, it's very nice to haven thee home again ... with us being so worried abouten thee. But what is to be done for the young man thou hast broughten with thee? I mean there hardly be enough space for us now." She carried on preparing the table, the children turning this way and that as their mother did.

"If it be hard, mother, perhaps mine aunts may helpen. If 'tis inconvenient, we will not stay long." Elfgifu kept looking to the door for her father. "But mother, dost thou meeten him first. He is my love. We have but comen here to get your permission to be wed."

"That's another worry. Where will the money comen for the wedding? 'Tis as well thy father be a freeman, or we wouldst haven to buy thy freedom from the landholder." Elfgifu's mother twittered. Having set the table, she retreated to the far end of the cottage to get cheese and bread to set on the table. The children still hung to her apron.

"Mother, may I helpen thee?" Elfgifu was getting anxious about her father's lack of appearance. "At least let me see'n to the childer. Here Maud, Siward. 'Tis I, your sister, come home. Come." The children looked at their sister, but did not leave the protection of their mother's apron.

"No, no. I'll manage." Elfgifu's mother gave a twittering giggle that sounded like startled birds. "I've managed all these years. I can managen again now." She put the food on the table and returned for a flask of small ale, the children in tow.

"Oh, Da," Elfgifu went to her father as he came through the door. "'Tis good to see thee."

"And to see thee, Cariad. Now sit thee down, girl. Your man will be here in a moment. Come, child, stop this crying. 'Tis only your old da ... and pleased to see thee he is, too." Hywel pulled a clean cloth from the back of his cord belt and wiped Elfgifu's eyes. "There's pretty. Now, here is the new man you want in your life. Tidda," he called to his wife, "come meet this man our daughter has brought to us from afar."

"When I have finished this, Hywel. You are so impatient." She put earthenware beakers on the table and arranged them in a pattern around the flask. "Now, did you sayen Elfgifu's man is here?"

"Elfgifu's mother ... peace." Godfrew stood in the doorway, silhouetted against the light outside. His off-white cloak engulfed him, the hood thrown back.

"Come in, boy ... sit you down." Hywel watched as Godfrew limped to one of two stools in front of the table and gratefully sat down. "A beautiful repast, Tidda. Always lays a good table, your mam. Best bread this side of the Medway," he said to Elfgifu. "Tuck in, boy. We may not have much compared to some, but we always eat well. Tidda, Cariad, come and join in. I'll not eat till thou hasen joined us. No ... stay seated, boy. I have the feeling you need that seat more than we do." Hywel sat on the floor, gathered his younger children to him and started to share his food with them.

"You have much that others desire, Elfgifu's father. I desire your daughter for my wife." Godfrew put a piece of the soft blue-streaked cheese into his mouth and squashed it against his pallet with his tongue, savouring the strong nutty taste.

"Well, she takes after her mam. My Tidda, still as beautiful now as when I first saw her ... eh, my love." Hywel winked at his wife, who blushed and went coy.

"Oh, Hywel, why dost thou sayen these things in front of strangers. I find it so embarrassing." responded his wife without meaning it.

"Well, there's sharp for you. 'Cos I mean it, that's why. You think I would still be here instead of back in my own country if it were false?" At last, Hywel stopped feeding the children

The Cray

and took a bite himself. Godfrew became aware that he was the only one not seated on the floor and shifted uncomfortably. Hywel became aware of Godfrew's discomfort: "Stay where thou be, Wulf. Best all stay where they feel most comfortable. There's sense now, isn't it?"

Once the meal was finished, Elfgifu's mother, with her children hanging on to her skirt, took the crockery out to wash in the trough. Elfgifu went with her, offering unwanted help. At last, Hywel got off the floor and sat on the other stool, opposite Godfrew.

"Is it time to talk, Elfgifu's father?"

"Well ..." Hywel dragged the word to twice its normal length, "... as good as anytime, I suppose."

"As I keep reassuring you, I want to wed your daughter. If it is a matter of money, I can find some. But I will marry her." Godfrew insisted.

"There's determined. What if I said no?" the twinkle in Hywel's eyes betrayed the answer.

"I would steal her from you as quickly as I stole her from my Uncle Edwin."

"And as you English stole the land from the Cymry."

"And as the Normans are stealing it from us."

"Now, there's ironic. You steal it from us ... the Vikings steal it from you ... you steal it back ... only to have the Normans steal from you. I'm not sure that I feel any sympathy for the English, really. Thieves born of thieves, complaining about the thieving of more thieves."

"If you found us so detestable, why did you come here?" the question was genuine and Godfrew's tone told this.

"Ah, well ..." again the word was drawn out, "... there's a long story. Thou hast heard of the raid into south Wales made by the late King Harold's elder brother, Earl Swein and that power mad Prince Griffith from the North? Must be twenty or more years ago now. Asken my daughter her age and add a year. Terrible damage they did. Some got hurt in exchange. Mind, we haven't survived this long without picking up a trick or two. Two who did get a bit damaged were the landholder of this place, Elfgat, and Godwine Clubfoot—the landholder from further up the valley. Well, they got left behind in our village ... to recuperate, see ... them and their men. Asked my old mam if they could stay with her—and us lot—at the old manor house that Lloyd the Timid had fled from ... me mam being his cook, see. Did I say 'ask'? Well t'was more: 'let us stay or we will burn the place down and ravish your daughters in the bargain' ... and her on her own since the Vikings had carried me Da off. Shrewd men, old Elfgat and Godwine. Saw how we prepared the cloth ... using the mill and all ... wanted to do the same back here. Well, it seemed all adventure then ... and with me mam hard pressed to feed twelve mouths—me, my twin Caradog and my younger brother Dai sort of volunteered to come here and set things up. Volunteered? Hard bargainers, these Saxons: 'Come back with us and we won't kill you.' Well, not so pointed ... but the meaning was there, boy. Still, it's a strange old world! Met my Tidda and never been back home. Caradog's still around these parts too ... found himself some plump Kentish maid. Dai went back ... or started back ... never got further than Hereford or thereabouts. Women, boy, they have a lot to answer for. Is my daughter with child?" His eyes were serious now.

"We have spent the last three months in a small priory chaperoned by very observant monks. Your maid is still a maid. I said I wanted the marriage God blessed—not handfast—and I meant it."

"That's good, boy. Having to marry 'cos thy sweetheart is with child is not the best. Childer are a blessing ... don't get me wrong ... but not straight away. You need to get to know each other a bit first. No, having to get married is not the best start." Hywel's voice left Godfrew, unsure if the man was speaking from experience or not. "Do you love her, boy ... really love her?"

"Yes. Do you love your wife?"

"If you love my Cariad only half as much as I love my Tidda, then all will be well." Finally Hywel seemed to relax "Where do you live?"

"At present, nowhere. My holding was taken for my being in arms against William the Bastard. I am unsure where to go. I have some money, but not enough to buy land. That's if men can still buy land under the Normans."

"I can find you work here for a while. You will have to do something till the wedding." Hywel took a handful of soil and ran it through his fingers. "Do you garden, boy?"

The Cray

"No. I know about cattle and horses. The gardening was done by serfs or bondsmen."

"Well, you may have to learn, then!"

* * *

"Well, Da?"

"Well, what Cariad?"

"Did he ask?"

"He asked."

"And?"

"And what, Cariad?"

"And didst thou sayen yes?"

"And did I have a choice with him telling me he would steal mine little treasure, if I failed to give it to him?"

"Oh, Da!" Elfgifu embraced her father and the tears flowed.

Hywel stroked her golden hair and kissed the top of her head. "This Wulf of yours, Cariad. He may not be what you think he is."

"I know he loves me. Is that not enough?"

"It may not be later. Love on its own isn't always enough." Hywel kept his daughter tight to him.

"What else do you think of him?"

"Not sure, really. It seems he fought for Harold against the new king. To do that he must be at least your age. When I first saw his face, I thought he was about fourteen or fifteen, with only fluff on his cheeks like. When he had taken off his hood, I saw the silver-streaked hair and I wondered. When I saw him walk, I was sure he was well past his prime. I wasn't certain if thou weren't cradle snatching or getting thyself a quick widowhood. What do I make of this man of thine? This young man—old man. Not sure, really. But ..." and he again kissed his daughters head, "...if thou loven him and he keeps telling me he loven thee, then what can a poor daft old man like me say?" He gave a deep, chesty laugh. "Come, Cariad, he will do thee fine, I'm sure. Just don't expect life to be easy, though."

* * *

Hywel came to the steps of the small chapel of St. Mary

with Elfgifu on his arm and all his wife's relations about him clucking like a flock of hens. Godfrew turned from facing the altar, smiled and held out his hand to his soon to be wife.

* * *

Godfrew enjoyed the gardening, but the work proved difficult with his sore leg. Despite using the healing water from the mountain spring mixed with his willow bark infusions, he still spent most days walking on the toes of his left foot, never able to put his full weight on that leg without the sharp reminder of pain. Elfgat, the landholder, had been introduced and had given Godfrew work taking the pack horses up to Maidstone. Sometimes he carried finished cloth, sometimes fruit from the orchards. Once he was sent with crocks of honey to Canterbury as part of the tithe that Elfgat owed to the Archbishop of Canterbury. The land, once so fair, was now scarred with the Christ Church all burnt down.

But life was still fair for Godfrew with his Elfgifu. She was of Celtic build and Saxon colouring—all golden hair and milky skin, her flesh a soft plumpness that delighted the touch.

Hywel had made room for them by adding a small lean-to on the side of the cottage. He and Godfrew got on very well, often working together in the garden in the evenings. Godfrew sat pulling weeds whilst Hywel dug.

But Elfgifu's mother was another matter. Things remained cold between her and her new son-in-law. None of that mattered today, as the sun shone with the start of summer.

"Well, boy, warm it must be for you to leave that old cloak of thine off." Hywel and Godfrew walked with the other freemen of the hamlet toward the mount. The Hundred Moot had been called and all had to attend. A gathering was due, but the notice had come suddenly and none knew why.

"It's still in my pack, father-in-law, just in case it gets cold later." Godfrew swung forward the staff that he was using to help him walk.

"I don't know what thou'll do when older, boy." Hywel saw a neighbour and waved to him. "Tovi, what is the reason for the Moot, mon?"

"If thou knowen, then let me know, Taffy Hugh. With so

The Cray

many changes, who knows? I just trusten our landholder is keeping in the Normans good books. We don't wanten a change there." The man had a broad-rimmed hat and the rim bobbed up and down in rhythm with his steps. "Him and old Godwine were lucky to be too scared to fight any more, or they would have been at the battle near Hastings and lost the lot. Even Godwine losing his son at the Stamford Bridge wasn't the tragic loss we first thought. They aren't taking land from those who fought the Norwegians— yet!"

"Well, one landholder is as good as another. We're all freemen."

"So thou sayen, Taffy—but as I hear, Normans don't like freemen. They wanten all to have a master!"

"Well, we're here now, so soon find out."

Hywel and Godfrew stood at the edge of the gathering. On the mound were some that Godfrew recognised—Elfgat, Godwine and their reeves. Others, obviously English from their clothes and long moustaches, were talking to them. Gathered around the group were various clerics, mostly monks, but some dressed as of higher rank. A trumpet sounded and those on the mound sat on the benches set along the top.

The freemen sat on the grass below the mound. Coming from the back and onto the crest, a troop of Norman soldiers emerged with some additional clerics. As they came to the top, the sergeant of the troop removed his helmet and pulled back his mail hood. Godfrew removed his cloak from the bag and pulled it on.

"Freemen of the Bromley Hundred," announced a monk thrice—once east, once west, and once north. By his side stood the sergeant. Despite the loud voice of the cleric, all eyes were on the sergeant —for his face was horrible to behold. The man had a scar that ran from his forehead to his chin. His nose was reduced to a squat pig's snout. His left eye had been put out in such a way as to leave the socket a mass of scars. For a right hand he had but a stub and a thumb. As he breathed, a strange wheezing snuffle came from his nose and water ran from it continuously.

The monk continued. "You are gathered here to hear of news most important. First, let it be known that Stigand who styles himself Archbishop of Canterbury has been taken into the care of our most beloved Lord, King William. His Grace, after seeking and beseeching the Lord for guidance, has decided that Bishop Odo, his beloved brother and recently made Earl of Kent, will take care of the See till he, our Lord King, resolves what is to happen." The freemen murmured whilst the landholders on the mount looked grim. "Now, also hear this," continued the monk, reading from his scroll. "Haimo, now appointed Shire Reeve of the County of Kent, wants it known that the following have been declared outlawed and named Wolfshead: Rudgang Warband of Walton, Hogin Limpleg of Bromley and Godfrew Longshanks of Garrat." Godfrew pulled the hood of his cloak further over his head.

The sergeant spoke to the monk. "Describe the last one to the peasants. I have a personal interest in him." He pulled out a dirty rag and wiped the watery snot from his chin and snout.

"The last of these, Godfrew of Garrat," the monk looked to the sergeant for confirmation, "is particularly wanted. His features are these." He looked again to the sergeant.

The sergeant strode forward and spoke in a loud voice. "The Wolfshead Godfrew is taller than most. He has golden hair. He speaks the accent of north Surrey. He walks stiffly and his left eye is marked with a white caste, such that he cannot see from it. The bastard owes me and I will pay him back."

"The Wolfshead Godfrew is taller than most. He has golden hair. He speaks the accent of north Surrey. He walks stiffly and his left eye is marked with a white caste, such that he cannot see from it." translated the monk.

"The sergeant says you owe him, son-in-law," Hywel said to Godfrew. Godfrew looked sharply at his father-in-law. "Breton and Welsh ... we are both of the Cymry. The language is not that much changed since his relations fled the Saxons for France, leaving my relations behind to be slaughtered by your relations. Thou knowen him?"

Godfrew leaned near Hywel and whispered in his ear: "He owed me for a friend. Now I owe him for his pretty looks. I shall have to leave, I think."

"I told thee of my brother Dai in the shire of Hereford. His son, Llewelyn, is with my other brother Caradog. The lad returns home soon. It will pay thee to be with him. Dai will look after you for my sake." Hywel suddenly stood up and called out: "Shall we raise the hue and cry? Shall we get this rebel, noble sergeant?" He turned to the freemen: "Who will join me in this most valiant of tasks then?" The freemen, many of whom knew and liked Godfrew, took the cue and stood with Hywel, shouting and cheering. The Moot started to dissolve into confusion. The Normans became worried and, led by the Breton sergeant, moved down the mount toward the crowd, spears crossed, shields locked. The sergeant called back to the monk who had read the scroll: "Get them to sit down. What are they playing at—unless they think him here?" He frowned. "That dark one at the back said something to the one wearing the white-hooded cloak. He said something in English. What did he say?" he yelled in his distinctive snuffle. "He told the other to pay more attention to what you were saying sergeant ... that there could be a reward in it," assured the monk. He then called over the top of the soldiers to the assembly using his loudest voice: "Pray, all of you be seated, for there is time to search for the Wolfshead later and there is more news to impart." Clouds gathered and masked the sun. In the distance, a grey wolf limped into the nearby orchard.

Woden's Wolf

The West March

The travellers stood by their ponies and looked across the land of Somerset from their vantage point on the Mendip hills. Below, green islands stood out in the grey sea of mist. It had been worth the early morning start just to see what the land looked like in winter. The mist would be replaced by surface water and the green hills that they could see would be islands indeed.

"They say that this is the land of Arthur and that far hill over there is the Isle of Avalon where he is buried." Llewelyn spoke to all, yet to no one. Despite his Welsh father, his voice was all English, though his looks showed some of his Celtic ancestry: square and solid. His wife, Rhiannon, also seemed to be of mixed race with her black hair and dark features, but whilst Llewelyn spoke constantly and freely of his family, Rhiannon said nothing of hers. "Glastonbury. Tor, they call it now, of course ... and it's only an island in the winter these days ... but it must have been magic then. You can almost imagine Arthur and his men coming out of the mists to harry the Saxons and then disappear back into their fastness, ready to strike again."

"Arthur? Wasn't he the wog that stopped us from taking all the land till we bribed his nephew to help us?" Godfrew's tone was that of fun rather than argument.

"Oh, stop it, you two! Don't rise to the bait, cousin. Let us just enjoy the magic of this moment, for soon the sun will gather its heat and the mist will be burnt off." Elfgifu stood an arm's length from her small pony. She trusted it only as much as she had to and rode it for transport, not pleasure.

"How far, Llew? Shall we reach there tonight?" asked Godfrew.

"Glastonbury? All being well, Wulf, we shall. Just remember, though, that you have to pay for the lodging. I am quite happy to take this little diversion to the summer land, as long as it does not cost me anything." Llewelyn's pony was like its owner, stocky and of unpredictable temper. It stomped its annoyance at having to stand still. "Easy girl." Llewelyn pulled the bridle down and turned to look the animal in the face, eyeball to eyeball. The pony blinked and Llew loosened his grip on the bridle. "You have to let them know who's the boss, eh, Rhiannon." His wife pulled her cloak closer to her thin body. "So, Wulf, you reckon that the waters from the holy spring at Glastonbury will cure your leg?"

"So your cousin Elfgifu tells me. I am just doing as I am told," Godfrew replied with mock seriousness.

"If you do not believe it will help, Wulf, then let us finish this now and turn around. The spring where Joseph of Aramathea hid the chalice of Christ is the most holy in England. If you are to be cured, it is there—walking on the very ground that we are told Jesus himself walked on as a boy. But the waters will only work if you believe. You have to have faith! Without faith, you will never walk right again." The anger in Elfgifu's voice upset her pony, which started fretting and dancing.

Godfrew left his dark pony and went to calm his wife. "I was only joking, my beloved. Honestly, no one wants to be cured more than me ... and I was pleased that you said we should come this way."

"Then don't joke about it."

Godfrew brought Elfgifu's pony with him to the path's edge where Llew stood, still looking over the summer land. "The next hill to Glastonbury is Althany. That still is an island, when the tide is in. That is where Alfred the Great hid from the Danes when the first great Danish army ravaged the land. He's another hero for me. Can you see my advantage, Wulf? You only have Alfred. Me ... being half-Cymry and half-Saxon ... I have both Alfred and Arthur. Come, let's move, for the women are getting as restless as the ponies."

* * *

The small hamlet of Glastonbury lay huddled around the small abbey that was said to have been erected on the site of an earlier chapel built by Joseph of Arimathea. Marshy land surrounded the isle. All the buildings but the abbey proper were built of wattle and daub. Bringing the stones to build the abbey's chapel must have been a difficult and expensive task. Godfrew speculated on the problems of how it could have been done, as the land was soft—even in summer—and cut off by the flooded plain in winter. The monastery was

The West March

rich, over-running with gifts from the many pilgrims. Even the depredations of the Danes during the years of troubles had not stopped its acquisition of wealth. With money, all things could be achieved.

Glastonbury not only boasted the Healing Well that had attracted Godfrew and his companions, but it was believed by all to be Christendom's birth place in the Isles of Britain. Joseph of Arimathea's crude chapel of worship may have gone—covered over by a much grander building, more fitting to such a holy place—but the holy thorn bush that had grown from the staff he planted in the ground at Weary-All Hill still flourished.

Much of the wealth came from pilgrims who braved the dangers of winter travel to see the miracle of the bush blooming—against all the rules of nature—at Christmas tide. Many of the Cymry came not just for these reasons, but also to visit the grave of their hero, Arthur, who lay buried in the abbey graveyard. Marked with an inscribed cross of lead, it was longer than most and reminded Godfrew of the grave promised by King Harold to the tall King Harald the Hardrada of Norway before the battle at Stamford Bridge. Now that both lay dead, all of England seemed filled with dead heroes.

Godfrew shook himself to break his sombre mood. "If we are to visit the well and get some of the water, we had best move or we will be in a queue all day. I just trust that this is worth the effort. What goes on here seems more like horse trading at Mitcham fair than seeking God's blessing and healing."

"God is never tied to man's ways, Wulf. Just forget the ways of the monks and the people. Have faith in God's healing power." Elfgifu rolled up the wolf-skin cloak that had covered them during the night and tied it to the top of the saddle bags. She then looked across at Godfrew as he struggled to lift his saddle whilst keeping his weight on one leg only. "You are not taking that with you. Everywhere we go you either have the pony or your saddle. Leave it here! No one will take it. It's not as though it is very expensive." An edge of exasperation entered her voice. "If you are that worried about it, put it in the corner and cover it with the hay we slept on."

Godfrew reluctantly complied with his wife's request. "A small, scrubby barn for a room and hay for a bed. At the price I paid, we should have been in the abbot's feather bed with a servant waiting on us hand and foot."

"At least cousin Llew and Rhiannon don't snore ..." Elfgifu carried the saddlebags to the hay and covered them up, "... even if their ponies do!"

"Rhiannon doesn't do much at all—except sniffle and pick at the edge of her sleeves. She is a strange one."

"Makes me seem a better bargain, does it?"

Godfrew sneaked up behind Elfgifu and grabbed her. "I stole you. You are my gift from the elves." He nibbled her ear, then proceeded to lick her cheeks.

"Get off." Elfgifu struggled. She turned her head and licked Godfrew's nose in retaliation. "Bully." She broke free and grabbed a handful of hay before Godfrew caught up with her. She was about to stuff the hay down his undershirt when her cousin came in.

"Play time, is it?" Llew gave a half-smile. Rhiannon stood in the doorway and sniffed, her eyes downcast.

Elfgifu gave Godfrew a quick peck on the cheek and dropped the hay onto the floor. "Time to go, I think. Are you all ready, cousin?"

With his toe, Llew lifted the edge of his saddle—which was lying on the floor—and moved it to one side by a fraction. "Now, I have tidied up ... yes. Don't worry about the security of the bags. I have got a local boy to sit outside the door whilst we are away. I have told him that if nothing is missing when we get back, you will pay him four styca,[13] Wulf. I have also told him that if anything is missing, I will castrate him." Llew gave a twisted smile. Rhiannon looked away and pulled at a loose thread on her mantle. "And he knows the truth of that."

"Then let's away." Godfrew held his hand out to Elfgifu. She took it and they passed Llew to go out into the summer sun. Llew snapped his finger, then turned and followed with Rhiannon walking at his heel.

The day was already warm and the two couples could feel the moisture rising from the ground and adding to the humidity. Groups of people were milling about, gathering into larger groups before setting out to the various sights. Mixing in the crowd were hawkers who sold flasks of water from the

---

[13] Styca: a small copper coin of low value.

holy well, arrowheads—said to be from the battle site of Camlann where Arthur was killed fighting Mordred—and pieces from the holy thorn bush. Elfgifu looked to make sure that Wulf was not watching, then beckoned a hawker over and bought a small cutting of the thorn for a copper styca.

"Elfgifu! What are you up to?" Godfrew had heard the muttered conversation his wife had just conducted.

"Just a small remembrance, my love. I shall keep it fresh and plant it in our garden, when we get one." Elfgifu disarmed him gracefully.

"Then perhaps I should buy a flask of the water from a hawker and save us the effort of queuing up at the well."

"Wulf! It would not be the same ... and you know it." Elfgifu was quite indignant. "The water may not have even come from the well."

"And, my clever one, your twig may not have come from the holy thorn bush!" Godfrew countered.

"I will know if it flowers at Christmas instead of spring," she answered, her tone allowing no argument. "See, we are at the well."

"At the end of the queue," Llew corrected her. "I'll get us something to eat. Some bread and jugged hare should go down well, or maybe some smoked fish. Do you two want some? Rhiannon will keep my place."

"Ah, anything but the smoked fish, thank you, cousin. Wulf, the money." Elfgifu nudged her husband.

"Oh, aye, money." He passed over four copper styca. Llew kept his hand out. "All right, I take the hint, I needed to come here, therefore I should pay."

Llew whispered into his cousin's ear: "Bright this husband of yours. Tight fisted, but bright. I'll be back shortly, cousin." He moved away and Rhiannon shuffled into his place behind Elfgifu.

"It's all right, Rhiannon," assured Elfgifu. "I'll keep his place. Go after him, if you wish."

Rhiannon lifted her eyes to Elfgifu and murmured quietly. "I'll stay. It is what he wants." She then lowered her eyes again and went back to fretting about a loose strand in her mantle.

It took hours to get to the well. By the time they did, the sun was at midday and the need for more food was becoming pressing. Whilst the others took a mere sip from the proffered chalice filled with well water, Godfrew asked for a flask to be filled. The monk with the offering box shook it to emphasise the additional love gift expected. Godfrew held the flask and watched it fill. The chalice was then lowered on its chain into the well to be refilled. This time, Godfrew took the vessel and took a sip. It tasted bitter. He thought that he recognised the taste of iron in it.

"The taste, my son? It comes from the holy grail the sainted Joseph hid there. Not only was it the very vessel used at the last supper, it contained drops of our Lord Jesus' own precious, redeeming blood. Look at the chain! You can see the blood stains on it."

"Yes, Father." Godfrew agreed, but his thought was that the discolouration was more that of rust than of blood. Despite the drink of holy water, the all night prayer session in the abbey he had attended and paying for a mass to be said, he felt no different. After all that everyone had been saying and all the monks had promised, he had expected a miracle—maybe not a major one, but at least something. Indignant, he stomped off, dropping the minimum into the offering box. Elfgifu and the others remained at the mouth of the well where they watched the other pilgrims taking the water. Many praised God and claimed to be cured of their various ills. Godfrew, still in a bad temper, strode back and grabbed his wife's arm. "Come, let's go. There is nothing here." His face was red. The pupil of his good eye was a pinpoint and his breath came in short, noisy pants.

"No." Elfgifu was not looking at Godfrew, so was not fully aware of his mood. "No, not yet, Wulf." Godfrew went to grab her arm, but slipped on the mud. As he hit the soft ground, he heard a sharp click. Knowing what the sound had always meant before, he froze. Elfgifu turned and saw the look of horror on his face. "Wulf! Oh, Wulf, has your leg gone again? Please, dear Lord Jesus, who once walked on this very ground. Please, don't let it be so." She knelt down beside her stricken man "Oh, God, not again." Tears came to her eyes and flowed down her cheeks. Pilgrims who had taken the water at the well pushed past, annoyed at the blockage in the path. "Llew, please help me, I need to try and get him up. If it is like last time, we will need help."

The West March

Llewelyn pushed a slow pilgrim out of the way and bestrode Godfrew. "Out of the way, cousin. I need no help to lift this scarecrow of a man of yours." Bending his back, Llew put his arms under Godfrew's and clasped his hands together "One, two, three." He thrust himself upright taking Godfrew with him.

"It's all right, Llew." Godfrew took the weight on his good leg and gingerly touched the ground with the toes of his left "It's all right. I haven't done any damage, thank God." He turned to Elfgifu. "I'm sorry, it's my own fault. My temper causes me too many problems." His look was sheepish now. "Forgive me?"

"Yes, Wulf. Just don't frighten me like that. The prospect of us having to stay in this place for three months as we did at Croydon is not worth thinking about. You wouldn't like the costs for a start!"

Pilgrims were again getting annoyed at the bottleneck, so the four companions moved off. Godfrew found that his leg was no worse than before. He managed to keep up with the others as they went to see Arthur's grave—at Llew's insistence—for the fourth time since arriving. In fact, it felt good enough later that afternoon for him to join the others when they climbed Weary-All Hill to see the holy thorn bush. It was a nice thorn bush, as thorn bushes go, but nothing special despite Elfgifu's enthusiasm for it. Godfrew was more interested in assessing both the hill and the nearby tor as defensible camps.

"It would be a good stronghold, Wulf?" Llew joined him. Rhiannon, for once, stayed with Elfgifu as she examined the thorn bush in the company of about twenty others—under the stern eyes of a couple of monks. "It has been done before, of course, by the Cymry. This hill and the adjoining tor was fortified and held by Melwas. Before you—in your Saxon ignorance—say 'who the hell is he', I will remind you. He was the king who was strong enough to kidnap Arthur's own wife, Guinevere. Mind you, there is another tale that says that she wasn't kidnapped at all, but ran away with King Melwas. But then, with women," he looked at Wulf closely, "who can tell?"

"Who indeed," rejoined Godfrew, though Llew was unable to tell from either Godfrew's face or his voice, just what he meant by his reply. "Once the women have finished their thing here, I would like to get back to the barn. Despite your assurance about the boy guarding our gear, it is still risky being away too long."

"Right," said Llew. "Rhiannon?" His wife left the others and came to stand by his side, head bowed. Elfgifu turned and, finding her companion gone, walked over to Godfrew.

"Let us move back to the barn." Godfrew set off down the hill. Despite the slope, he found it reasonably easy. He also found that he was able to put more weight on his left leg than he had been able to do for some time.

* * *

"One thing," said Llew as he and Godfrew walked the ponies toward the ramshackle barn at the side of the hostelry. "Now that we are in Herefordshire, don't call the Cymry 'Welsh', or even worse ... 'wogs'. I know 'wogs' is the usual English term for them, but don't use it here."

"Getting touchy about your ancestry, Llew?" Godfrew held only the reins of Elfgifu's pony. His own animal needed no guidance and was happy to just follow her master.

"It's up to you if you want to heed my advice or not. About a quarter of this town are Cymry. Keep calling them wogs and you are likely to end up with a knife in your ribs." Llew gave his ponies a hard yank on the reins to speed them up.

"Hard men, eh!" Having reached the barn, Godfrew brought his ponies inside and took them into a stall. The floor was covered in stale straw and dung. The whole barn reeked of horse piss.

"The women are worse. No, the only Cymry you have met till now have been strangers in your country—always cautious, unwilling to offend, standing out. This is Marcher country where ownership of the land changes from Saxon to Cymry and back again. Even Offa's Dyke [14] is unclear in this county. No, if you want to insult anyone, make it the Normans." Llew dragged his reluctant ponies into the stall and closed the wicker gate. Trapping one of the animals against the wall, he proceeded to take off its saddle.

---

[14] Offa's Dyke: erected by Offa, King of Mercia as a seemingly negotiated boundary between Mercia and Wales.

The West March

"The Normans are here in strength?" Godfrew removed the saddle from the dark pony. The creature turned its head and snuffled in his ear with warm moist breath.

"Have been since our blessed King Edward gave land to the half-breed Earl Ralf the Timid. He may have been timid, but his descendants are not." Llew hung the first saddle over the low wicker wall that separated his pony's stall from Godfrew's and started to unencumber the other pony. "The Cymry say the Normans are worse than the Saxons and the English say they are worse than the wogs. Still," he removed the second saddle and put it over the wall, "at least they give the people something in common, even if it is only shared hatred." Llew yanked the bit out of the pony's mouth. "Mind, with everyone against them, it's little wonder that the Normans get a bit nasty. I don't think they will ever forgive the locals for leaving them to get slaughtered by Earl Elfgar—he and his mixed bunch of pirates and reevers [15]—some ten or more years ago." He dipped the bit in a bucket of dirty water and sloshed it about. "Man, this place stinks."

Godfrew put Elfgifu's saddle on the wall, but carried his own and placed it outside the stall. He then took an old rag and started to rub the dark pony down. "Knowing the Normans, they would have made the folk suffer for that."

"I'm sure," said Llew. He pulled a small sliver of willow twig from the wicker wall. "They would have liked to have burned the town down for revenge—except Elfgar and his Cymry mate, Griffith, had already done it. Shame about the minster that old Bishop Æthelstan had built. It was quite beautiful, if you like that sort of thing." He picked his teeth with the twig, seeming to gain great satisfaction from his excavations.

"I thought Hereford looked a bit rough. I had expected something a bit grander for a borough." Having seen to his own animal, Godfrew moved to Elfgifu's and started to rub it down as well.

"We do have the nice new ditch dug by King Harold, or the Earl of Wessex, as he was known then." Llew spat out some of the bits he had dug from a blackening tooth with a wince. "Well, he ordered and we dug. Even me—a youngster—had to dig. It will be interesting to see if it actually stops anyone." He

---

[15] Reever: raider, or pirate.

sucked on the tooth and his eyes tightened as the air jangled the nerve.

"How long will we stay here before moving on to your hamlet?" Godfrew checked the pony's hoofs.

"Just long enough to sell one of the nags. Can't let my old man see just how much money I'm worth. Besides, it will pay to find out who owns what at present. Once over the river Wye, it gets tricky. Today's Englishman is tomorrow's Cymry. Get it wrong and you are dead." Llew slapped Elfgifu's pony on its rump and headed outside.

Godfrew calmed the beast before joining him. "So, cousin Llewelyn, you are telling me that it is not worth trying to buy land. Just join the right side and I can steal it." Godfrew hurried up to Llew, who had made his way toward the stalls in front of the wooden tower on the earthen mound that served for a castle. Since Glastonbury, his leg has been much better, though whether due to the water or the fall, he wasn't sure.

"Neither. The local lord owns the land and leases it out to a tenant. They have the land for as long as the lord can protect it. If he can't, then the tenant has to pay again to the lord who can, provided they are still alive to pay, that is." He turned to Godfrew "Wulf, this is a dangerous place to live. I don't know why on earth you left London. You were a freeman of the city, I think? Yes? Doesn't matter. Land here is bought by the point of a sword ... and life is cheap—very cheap if you are a tenant."

Godfrew looked at his feet, then up at Llew. "You aren't daft. You know what happened at Senlac hill near Hastings. You know what happened to those who fought against the Normans there. You know I can't stay in or around London. So, what am I to do?" He cocked his head at an angle.

Llew had got used to the fact that having sight in only one eye made Godfrew look at people strangely, so he was not put off as some folk were. He looked him straight in the good eye: "Give up the idea of farming or grazing. Uncle Hywel thought you may have been a warrior of sorts before meeting his daughter and what you have said confirms it. Around here, soldiers are always in demand. Just remember that you are for hire. We don't hold to the Saxon custom of ring giving and dying to the last man for your lord. As long as you get paid, you fight for whoever pays you. If the pay stops, you negotiate with someone else for pay, even if it is the person you have just been fighting against. Choose who you fight for if you wish, but be prepared to change masters if you have to." Llew's eyes were deadly serious.

"That has never been my way. I have always fought for what I thought right and for a lord I trusted."

"Those ways have never worked on the border. Keep to them if you wish, but you will be dead in a month, at most."

"I take it that the casualty rate amongst such reevers is high?" Godfrew's eyebrow was now cocked.

"Yes, but a lot lower than that amongst the tenants on all sides. Take your choice. We all have to die some day."

Godfrew smiled as he gave the traditional warriors reply: "So why not today!"

Llew smirked. "But I prefer to delay it for a while."

"If... and I do say if ... if I follow your advice, I don't think my wife will be too happy."

"Llew shrugged, "When are wives ever happy. The only time mine has ever been happy was before we were wed. From the second the priest told us we were man and wife, she has been unhappy."

"She never talks of her family." Godfrew picked up an axe handle and judged its balance.

"Tenants in the Archenfield region. Caradoc and his men killed them all a couple of years back. That's one of the reasons I married her. Her family and my father's are connected by blood. Marrying her to me was a cheaper option than putting her into a convent. Not that the nuns would have wanted her. I mean how could she have become a virgin bride of Christ when at least twenty men had been through her at one session." Llew looked at Godfrew examining the axe handles. "I didn't know you were a woodsman?"

"God may have made the apostles 'fishers of men'. Me ... me, he made a 'hewer of men.'" Godfrew gave an unholy chuckle. "I—and again I say 'if—if I follow your advice, I will need a new shaft for my axe." He took to checking the grain of the handle he was holding.

"Pick the right master and you will get your gear supplied. There are not too many axemen in these parts. The Cymry tend to be very lightly armed. Many are archers—good ones, too. The Saxons tend to be the same, but wear mail more often. Our late King Harold and his brother Tostig worked out that the only way to beat the Cymry was to fight the same way as they do. The Normans are the odd ones out. They still think they are on the battlefields of France. What good are mounted lancers in the mountains or the forests?"

"You are right." Godfrew passed a few coppers over to the stall holder in exchange for the axe handle. "I had better keep away from the Normans, if I want to live." He gave a slight grin to his cousin-in-law. "And they had better keep away from me, if they want to live!"

* * *

"They are dead." Llewelyn had come back from talking to his brother and sisters. "Not reevers this time, though. Plague. It seems half the village died." Although his voice was gruff, Llew showed no emotion. As soon as he stopped speaking, he took to chewing a thumb nail. That was the only thing that gave any clue to his internal confusion. "That leaves me as family provider." He spat out a sliver of nail.

Rhiannon moved closer to Llew, but did not say anything, merely snuffling and sniffing more than usual. Elfgifu handed the reins of her pony to Godfrew and embraced Llew. "Cuz, oh cuz." Still, Llew did nothing but chew his thumb while Elfgifu wept for the uncle she had never met.

"Shall we move on or what, Llew?" Godfrew had walked the ponies over. Elfgifu shot him a withering look for being so insensitive. Godfrew looked at his wife and shrugged. "Death happens, my love, but we still live. Mourning is for those who have nothing to live for. Llew? What is to happen?"

Llew shook himself out of his thumb chewing meditation. "Stay here to start." He gave a humourless laugh. "There sure is plenty of room here now!" He extracted himself from his cousin Elfgifu's comforting embrace and nodded to Rhiannon. She followed him into the crude cottage that had been the family home. Inside, it was dark, but what could be seen of the interior was tidy. The place smelled of crushed herbs— mainly mint.

Llew walked to the sleeping area and made a mental note of who was sleeping where. His younger brother, Puta, ginger-haired like the rest of the brood, was standing behind him. Puta came forward and stood at Llew's elbow.

"I will take the sleeping place of our mother and father, so you can get your fat hide out of there and take over my place. The brats," Llew motioned to the three girls hiding behind Puta's bulk, "can stay where they are in that rat's nest in the corner." Llew chewed another piece of nail from his thumb and spat it out. "Joanna!" he called. An elven ginger brat popped her head out from behind Puta. "Talk to the village reeve about our cousin taking over one of the empty cottages and tell him that we want one that has been purged. We don't want to be plague struck!"

The girl turned to nod her head in acknowledgment and almost fell over. Recovering, she took off again at full speed. "Should have been a boy that one," he confided to Godfrew. "Oakleaf," Llew called to a plumper ginger brat, "see what stabling can be found for our cousin's ponies." Oakleaf took off more sedately. "And make sure there is somewhere for my pony, too." His sister dipped her head serenely and glided out of the cottage. "Mouse," a tiny brat, hanging onto Puta's considerable leg, swung into view: "some food." Mouse squealed and darted away to do her task. "Right, that has got things organised." Llew, with Rhiannon trailing behind, went over to the wooden table set before the hearth in the centre of the cottage. He ran loving hands over its surface, his fingers caressing the cuts and grooves. "My father made this." He looked at Elfgifu. "My father was a tenant farmer, but he loved the carpenter's trade. Perhaps he should have been one and lived in Hereford, instead of risking his life on the borderlands trying to raise cattle and horses." He gave another humourless laugh, "But then, it wasn't reevers who killed him and my mother was it? It was the plague." He took to chewing the other thumb nail, the original now being bitten down to the quick.

Mouse put platters of food on the table. As she set down the ewer of milk, some spilt. Puta caught her by her hair. "Rag mop, you little brat. Clean it up." He turned to the visitors. "I like everything to be clean and tidy. Would you care for some of my eel and green bean potage? It is fresh today." Puta assumed their agreement and spooned the steaming mess onto bread trenchers. The smell set everyone's mouth to watering. "I'm very proud of this recipe. I put a more balanced mix of herbs in than mother used to. She was far too heavy handed."

Everyone picked up a wooden spoon and started to eat. Despite holding a spoon in her right hand, Mouse ate with the fingers of her left hand. The food tasted as good as it smelled. Whatever else he was, Puta was an excellent cook. After they had eaten the potage and wiped the table with their trenchers, Puta got Mouse to produce a shared bowl of milk curds and honey. Again, the food was gently flavoured with herbs. As they ended the meal, Oakleaf and Joanna came back in.

"Report," said Llew, the meal obviously not being sufficient, as he had returned to nibbling his thumb nail.

"The reeve says to go see him, brother dear," replied Oakleaf with a saucy grin. "He said it was to discuss terms."

"And there's room in the far paddock for the ponies, though it will cost five styca a month per pony in summer and ten a month in winter," Joanna said. She looked up to the left, stared at the thatched ceiling and struggled to remember the rest of the message. "If you have no money, it will be half a day's work a pony in summer and a day in winter, unless it be foul, and then you make it up again in spring," she chanted. Having completed the tale, she looked back at her elder brother and smiled, pleased at having got everything right.

"Hmm, for the moment, I'll pay with labour." Llew flicked his head toward the table. "Now you can eat. Puta, more food." He turned to Godfrew "Well, Wulf, cash or work? This time of year, the work is easy, just sorting stock and watching them graze."

Godfrew ran his hand over his chin, pulling on his almost invisible facial hair. "Let's see the reeve first, then I will decide. Cariad?"

Elfgifu turned sharply at hearing Godfrew using her father's term of endearment. Godfrew did not seem to be aware that he had used it, so she smiled in amusement and replied to his inquiry. "You handle the matter. I will take care of the purse once we have a home. Until then, it is up to you what is done with the money."

"Right! Llew, let's find the reeve and see what he wants of us."

The West March

Llew stopped chewing his thumb and made for the door. As he got to it, he turned and called into the darkness: "Puta, make sure they clean up."

"Don't I always," muttered his pudgy brother. "It's you, brother Llewelyn, who leaves the mess. It's you, brother Llewelyn, who goes to the other end of England delivering horses and leaving me behind with the brats. It's you, brother Llewelyn, who eats the food I prepare without saying thanks. But it is me, brother Llewelyn, who always cleans up afterwards." Puta lightly clipped Mouse's ear. "Rag mop, little one. Get the rag mop. Don't leave me to do everything. I am not your mother." Mouse burst into tears, remembering her lost mother. Her sisters joined her. "Dear Lord Jesus," Puta cast his eyes heavenward, "why did you leave me in a house full of wailing women? Why did you not give me a house full of strong men?" He brought his eyes down again, "But not ones like my lazy, overpowering brother." He gave a deep, meaningful sigh.

"I'll get the mop, cousin. Just tell me where it is." Elfgifu looked around the cottage, but its darkness hid the mop's hiding place. Rhiannon tapped her elbow and proffered the mop. "Thank you, Rhiannon." Rhiannon dropped her eyes to the floor and retreated to the corner again.

"No, cousin Elf... Elfwelda?" not remembering her name.

"Elfgifu, cousin Puta."

Puta took the mop and stuck it on Mouse's head. "No, the brats will do it. They have to learn." He bent his knees and lowered himself to eye level with Mouse and Joanna. "Clean up and don't use the rag mop to wipe your runny eyes and snotty noses. As for you, Lady Oakleaf," he stood up again, "when you have finished putting your snout into my delicious food, you can remake the mess you and your sisters sleep on and then move my gear to where our beloved brother used to be." He started to move away, but then turned back. "But don't think that you can take over my old place. The bitch is about to whelp and will need somewhere clean to nest." He strode outside and headed toward a neat vegetable garden, the rows all symmetrical and weed free.

Godfrew squinted his good eye in the strong sunlight, his blind eye being already closed. The village reeve stood with his back to a wicker fence surrounding a kitchen garden. His feet were spread and he had his arms folded across his chest. "So, Dai's nephew-in-law," his voice carried the same Welsh twang as Elfgifu's father. "It's a cottage you are after then?"

"To start with, Master Reeve, I will need to talk to the landholder about leasing pasture and what stock I can run on it." Godfrew was sure the man could see he was discomforted by the sun and was enjoying holding him at a disadvantage.

"Well, there's complex for you." The reeve picked his nose with great relish and without embarrassment. "The cottage, I can rent. The land can only be rented out by the manor reeve." He flicked the produce of his excavations over his shoulder. "Got money, boy? Or is this another labour only job?" He went back to his nose, delving deeper this time, the action distorting his voice. "I prefer money, see. Less risky, less chasing, less overseeing."

"And less for the landholder?" contributed Llew. His lank, brown hair covered his eyes.

"Now watch it, you." The reeve poked his encrusted finger in Llew's direction. "That sort of talk will get you into trouble. You may be head of household now your Da is dead, but you can't throw your weight around and insult people here, you know. I won't have it, see."

"You forgot the 'you are only saying that because I'm Welsh' bit."

The reeve waved his hands about in the air. "Why I should bother to talk to you, let alone help your family, is more than I know. Trouble—that's what you are. No wonder your poor old Da kept sending you into the Saxon country. Delivering horses? Gaining some peace in his own house, more like."

"Talking of gaining peace, my bogey-fingered friend ..." For the first time, the reeve seemed to be aware of what he had been doing and wiped the snot smeared digit on his tunic. "... you had better get the idea of getting a piece of my sister out of your senile, lecherous mind. Touch her and you won't have any hand left, let alone fingers to probe that pox eaten snout of yours."

"Me? After your ginger cat, Oakleaf? Credit me with some sense, boy. I'd rather catch a cold than catch her, or whatever it is she would give me! She is too bold, that one." The reeve's now cleaned finger was thrust at Llew's face, its cleanliness making it stand out from its grimy companions.

"Who said it was Oakleaf? Ginger cat? She's too young for such!" Llew spat the words out and closed the distance between himself and the reeve to a swinging arm's length.

"Too young? Shows how long you've been away!"

"So you have been perving her, you grimy wog toad! I'd heard that you'd been seen hovering in the bushes when she had gone for a bath in the mere. If it wasn't for the fact that you are too decrepit to get it up, I would be really worried."

"Up, is it? UP! I'll give you up." The reeve reached for the short sword at his waist. "I'll stick YOU up, you half-Saxon whelp."

Godfrew stepped between the two protagonists, placed a hand on the chest of each and forced them apart. Both must have been relived that the fight was being stopped without either loosing face, as neither tried to push him away. "Llew, your sister would best be advised to go with the other maidens when she needs to bathe ... and as her brother, you can ensure she does." He turned to face the other way, " Master Reeve, you can but understand my cousin-in-law's being upset at coming home and finding himself in charge of the family, including careless sisters. Now, please ... ease off."

"Tell the weasel that if he looks at my sister in any way other than charity, I'll castrate him—if I haven't killed him first." Despite the aggression, Llew did not try to get closer to the reeve.

"And you can tell that know nothing that if he can't control his saucy sister from flaunting her body, I will not be responsible if she gets raped, or worse, by anyone foolish enough to risk poxing himself." The reeve eased back from Godfrew's restraining hand.

"Right. Well, that's settled, then." Godfrew eased his outstretched arms inwards, keeping them tensed and ready to distance the men again.

"Right." Llew gave a quick nod.

"Right." The reeve's finger started back toward his nose, but catching Godfrew's eye, he withdrew it and hooked his hand on his belt to keep it under control.

Godfrew sensed that he now had things under control and pressed the advantage home. "Master Reeve, you said you could let me rent a cottage."

Woden's Wolf

"Three styca a week without chattels, six with. Payment four weeks in advance."

"Plague cleansed, I assume?"

The reeve's voice resumed its normal tone and volume. "Naturally."

"Not naturally at all!" Llew interrupted.

Godfrew threw Llew a threatening glance. "Naturally, Master Reeve." Godfrew's voice was consolatory. "So shall we say thirty a month? Thirty-five with stabling for two ponies?"

The reeve stroked his stubbled chin and allowed his finger to grace the inside edge of his nose. "Thirty-seven. Three weeks in advance."

"Thirty-six, two weeks in advance?"

The reeve's finger could take the temptation no longer and delved inside his nose for a quick scrimmage while he considered the offer. "Thirty-six, three weeks in advance, paid now." He examined his finger and cleaned the nail with the with the index finger of his other hand.

"It includes feed for the ponies, of course," insisted Godfrew.

"Well," the reeve drew the word out long, as only a man of his race could. As encouragement, Godfrew rattled the copper coins in his purse. "I suppose so. I'll need to talk with you again if the winter is hard and long, mind."

"Right." Godfrew removed some coins from the purse and counted them into the reeve's hand, being careful to always keep the silver pennies out of sight. As each weeks rent was counted out, the reeve took the coins, formed them into a roll and covered them with a dock leaf plucked from the ground in front of the wicker fence. "Now, when can I see the manor reeve to talk about the grazing land I want to lease?"

"You are fortunate. I'm going to the manor first thing tomorrow. Be here at first light with your pony." The reeve strode off, his purse laded.

"That's a weight off my mind and my purse." Godfrew leaned against a fence watching the man's retreating back.

"Thirty-six styca a month, Wulf. I doubt if the manor reeve will see more than thirty." Llew spat a piece of finger nail out onto the ground.

"And if the landholder sees more than twenty-five he will be lucky. But that," Godfrew turned to Llew and gave a lopsided grin, "is his problem not mine. Three weeks in advance is a bit long, but I can live with it." His look became serious: "Your bad temper, cousin Llewelyn, cost me at least a week's money in advance and five styca a week more than I intended to pay. Worse, that temper could cost you your life, if you don't learn to control it."

Llew looked surprised. "I'll get him yet and maybe your money back, too. These are wild times and this is a wild place. I'll get him."

"If he doesn't get you first."

* * *

"Got a sword then, have you, boy?" the reeve tapped his own short sword hanging in a tatty scabbard at his side.

"No, but I do have this." Godfrew put his hand around his back and pulled out his saxe, the sun glinting on its one sharp edge.

"Now that is a big knife, if I say so myself. Ever had to use it other than to kill game?" The reeve's question seemed genuine.

"Isn't all killing a game?" Godfrew put the weapon away and settled the off-white cloak over his back again, hiding the saxe.

"Depends on how you look on life. Me now, I've seen too much of it—killing, that is—and life too, I suppose. Nasty old business at times—life." Without Llew's threatening menace, the reeve seemed more relaxed—even friendly. Godfrew, however, did not relax. Llew had told him something of the man's background—how he had been the village reeve as long as anyone could remember, reeve to the Welsh, then to the Saxons, then to the Welsh again and yet once more to the Saxons. Each time the land ownership changed, Evan the Reeve remained in charge of the village. Loyalty meant nothing and survival everything. Evan had seen herds taken, people taken, crops taken or burnt. He had seen folk killed, yet always, he remained. Evan and the village were always there—always waiting for the next tenants to arrive, always waiting for the survivors to drift back, always waiting for the newcomers to take up and pay their rent for the empty cottages. Evan always was there to take his cut. He seemed to always know who was going to raid next and when. Evan always knew when to leave the village and when it was safe to return.

Evan the Reeve was a man not to be trusted.

The ponies jogged across the plain and started up the gentle hills on the other side of the River Arrow. Grassland gave way first to scrub, then to woodland. The shade of the trees provided a relief from the heat of the day. Godfrew had first rolled his cloak up and slung it across the front of his saddle, then had done the same with his over shirt. Now, with the cool of the forest, he put his shirt back on again. The plain had been dotted with small hamlets, many burnt and deserted, evidence of the cross-border raiding that had only stopped when King Harold, still only the Earl of East Anglia, had struck the Welsh a blow from which they had only recently started to recover. Harold had brought about the death of Prince Griffith, shattering the Welsh princedom back into its usual squabbling fragments. Now, Harold himself was dead and no one knew what that meant to the borderlands. As Godfrew and Evan had ridden by, field workers had grasped their implements and held them as weapons. In those hamlets still occupied, women had gathered children as a hen would its chicks. Everywhere, there was fear. As they progressed into the upland, the devastation became even more evident. What had been clearings were now young woods. What had been hamlets were now scrub land. Deer had replaced cattle and wild boar had supplanted the domestic swine.

Cresting a rise, the horsemen stopped. Through a gap in the oak trees, they could see a holding in a cleared valley below. A small area was in crop, but most of the land was in grazing. Godfrew noted the fact that the cattle herders were mounted and appeared to be lightly armed. The holding itself was surrounded by a moat and a fence of sharpened stakes. The buildings inside the defenses were quite substantial. A large, long house sat in the centre, smoke curling lazily from a hole in the thatch. The long house appeared to have carved eaves, though it was difficult to see clearly at that distance. Godfrew held a hand in front of his good eye and peered through his fingers, using a gap to sharpen his focus. Even so, he could not make out if they were carvings or not.

The West March

Evan leaned across and pointed with his favourite finger. "Lydbury North. Earl Edric's manor. He also had Lydbury South, but Griffith the Magnificent burnt it to the ground. Powerful man is our Lord Edric. Holds land in both this shire and in Shropshire." Evan moved his pony closer to Godfrew: "I doubt we will see his Lordship, but if we do, don't upset him."

The dark pony sidled, uncomfortable at the closeness of Evan's mount. Godfrew settled her by stroking her neck. "My wife's family refer to him as Edric the Wild."

"Wild all right! Wild as in 'savage'!" Evan reflectively picked his nose. After examining the contents of his finger nail, he continued. "Scourge of the Cymry—enemy of the Normans, prickly neighbour of the other Saxons. Edric the Wild is downright bloody nasty, if you ask me. Not," he turned to face Godfrew, "that I would ever dare tell him to his face. Oh, he would laugh all right—think it very funny—but he would also carry on laughing as his pack of wolves flayed the skin off of my poor old body. Oh, yes, Edric the Wild, or Master as I calls him, whenever I have the misfortune to meet him." He went back to his fingernail. "And don't think telling him about our conversation will gain you credit either, boy. After he'd seen to me, he'd do you too, just to show he doesn't like tale bearers. I've seen it done. Vicious Saxon bastard." Evan gave his nag a nudge and they continued on the path down the slope toward the holding.

The trees did not give way gently to scrub and then grass, but stopped suddenly just below the ridge. There, the tree line zigzagged to the crest of the ridge and back again in a pattern designed to prevent either horsemen or footmen from forming up in large numbers without being seen by those in the valley below. As the two riders came into the open, a cattle herder saw them and called to his companion, who rode at speed toward the palisade. Soon there was a body of twenty or so riders jogging toward the visitors. The band was lightly armoured and carried throwing spears.

As they came within casting distance, they halted. The lead rider came forward at a slow walk until he was about five horse lengths away. "Evan, you thieving old wog. I thought it was you. I could smell down wind." The man wore a helmet with a scared nasal guard and dented crown. He had a deep scar across his cheek and the usual broken nose. He smiled to reveal a missing front tooth and his tongue played with the gap. "Got a new friend, eh? I thought it was young wenches you fancied, not young boys!" The war-band leader gave Godfrew the once over and took in the silver-streaked hair. "Perhaps not so young." He turned his attention back to Evan. "Well, toe-rag, what is it now?"

"I have brought this young man to see the manor reeve about leasing some grazing land outside the hamlet of Martinsfield." Godfrew was again scrutinised. "He is related by marriage to some of the folk there: Dai ap Llewelyn, who married Egath, Sif's daughter." The emphasis Evan placed on the sentence showed how important it was to establish Godfrew's credibility.

The war-band leader shifted in the saddle, then having made a mental decision, relaxed and cradled his spear. "Seeing as it is money for our master you are talking about, we had better get you going. Dagobert is sitting at the hearth today, so you are fortunate." He moved his horse to one side to let the others past.

As Godfrew and Evan rode on, the other riders joined them at a distance. The two were surrounded, but the riders stayed two sword's lengths away. As they jogged down the increasingly gentle slope toward the holding, Evan leaned toward Godfrew and whispered out of the side of his mouth: "That bastard Torquil knew I was coming today. He loves to put on a show, just to remind me who is in charge." Godfrew nodded his head in acknowledgment, but kept looking forward to avoid betraying the conversation. Torquil did not look like the sort of man who would appreciate being whispered about.

As they crossed the moat and came within the palisade, Godfrew saw that the eave boards of the long house were not carved at all. Rather, the decoration was made up of dried heads on angled stakes. Some were very old with withered, leather skin and wisps of straggled hair. Some were so fresh that the skin was puffed up and maggots wriggled in the cut flesh where the birds had pecked away the skin and eaten their fill. The eave boards themselves were stained black and white from dried blood and bird's droppings, both forming coloured stalactites that hung from the bottom edge. The

The West March

doors to the long house were solid oak reinforced with iron straps. In front of them stood two men wearing ring mail coats and armed with spears and shields. The spears were of the heavy boar-hunting type with heavy and unornamented stop bars.

As the riders approached, boys ran out from nowhere to catch the horse's bridles. As soon as the riders had dismounted, the boys led the mounts away. When the last animal was around the side of the long house, there were whoops of joy and the jingle of bits and harness hinted that horses and ponies would be ridden to the paddock rather than walked. Godfrew caught one of the younger members in the escort grinning, obviously recalling his own stolen rides not so long ago.

Torquil led the way into the hall as Evan and Godfrew followed. Behind them came six of the escort. The others headed to the wall of the long house and squatted facing the sun. At the oak door, Evan handed his sword to one of the armed guards. Godfrew watched, then followed suit with his saxe. Inside, the hall was surprisingly light. Godfrew could easily see to the end where, on a raised dais, a man sat behind a long table counting coins into piles and marking the totals on a tally stick. Behind the man stood a striking woman, tall with smooth features and a full body. Her curly golden hair showed beneath a severe white cap. As they approached, Evan removed his broad-rimmed hat and lowered his head. At the foot of the dais, he knelt in the strewn herbs and straw that covered the earthen floor. Godfrew noticed Evan was nervously playing with the rim of his hat, thumbing the edge and moving it around in his hand.

"My Lady Gondul." When he had finished addressing her, Evan raised his eyes to the lady, then lowered them quickly when she made eye contact. The lady then looked at Godfrew imperiously, so he also knelt.

"Evan of Martinsfield. I trust that this time you have brought the correct rents with you?" the lady's voice was high and ringing, like a priest's silver mass bell.

"My Lady. But ..." Evan's voice was low and almost inaudible.

"No buts, Evan," the voice was even and emotionless.

"The plague, my Lady ..."

Woden's Wolf

"Is your problem, not mine. There is a set rent for Martinsfield. You pay the set rent. Getting the rent is your problem, not mine."

"But my Lady ..."

"So, Evan, you would that I told Earl Edric?" there was still no emotion in the voice.

"No my Lady. But ..."

"It is settled then." The lady gently ran her finger around the neck of the man seated at the table in front of her. "Evan wants to pay his rent, Dagobert. Just make sure it all goes in the manor's coffers this time." The voice now had a playful, almost seductive edge to it.

"My Lady." Dagobert, the manor reeve, slowly turned his head and looked into Lady Gondul's light blue eyes. As he did so, he widened his own eyes playfully. "What else would I do?"

Gondul gently laughed and the sound was again that of a tinkling bell. She looked down at Evan. "And who is this with you, pray?" the voice was again emotionless.

"A relation of some Martinsfield folk who wishes to lease grazing. I have brought him with me to discuss terms with Dagobert the Reeve." Yet again, Evan looked up till he met Gondul's gaze, then quickly caste his eyes down to the floor, all the time playing with his hat.

"It is about time you found other tenants." The Lady Gondul ran a speculative eye over Godfrew. "You also seem to have found one of our folk, from his colouring." Gondul ran a finger around the back of Dagobert's neck. When she spoke again, her voice had acquired a hard edge. "I have been concerned recently with those that you have brought into Martinsfield. There are too many of your relation, Evan. I would hate to think that Earl Edric could not rely on the loyalty of Martinsfield, should the Welsh come raiding again!" Evan performed another bob of the eye and his hat fondling became more physical, the rim of the hat getting all scrunched up. "You wouldn't want another heart-to-heart talk with Earl Edric now, would you?" Again she played with Dagobert's neck, only this time the lady finished at the manor reeve's ear. Catching the lob between the nails of her index finger and thumb she squeezed until blood showed. Dagobert closed his eyes in seeming ecstasy, his mouth slightly open, his breath coming in short pants. When she spoke again, her voice had resumed its original emotionless tone. "You did seem to be a trifle distressed the last time he summoned you for a personal interview. It was following that 'incident' last Michaelmas, wasn't it?"

"My Lady." The rim of Evan's hat tore and he dropped the object on the floor.

"Yes. You were even more distressed after the interview if I remember rightly." The lady put her finger and thumb to her mouth and licked off the small amount of blood that had started to congeal on the nails. When she had finished, she held her hand at a distance to examine it, turning it first this way, then that. Satisfied with the cleanliness and undoubted beauty of her nails, she turned her attention back to Evan. "Your fingernails grew again, I trust?"

"My lady." Evan swallowed audibly.

"Loosing them must have made it difficult to count the coins you had stolen from the Earl Edric."

"But my Lady ..."

"But? Evan, but? No buts." Gondul went back to stroking Dagobert's neck. "I wonder," the voice now sounded speculative, "I wonder how well a man can walk after his toenails have been removed?" The question must have been for Dagobert for she took a handful of his thick chestnut hair and pulled his head back to compel him to look at her. "Does it cause much of a problem?" She twisted the manor reeve's hair back and forth so that he seemed to shake his head in disagreement. "No? Does one then have to cut his little pinkies off at the joint to impress on a man one's displeasure, then?" this time she compelled the manor reeve to nod his assent. "But one shouldn't cripple him if he is to continue work, should one." Again there was the forced disagreement. "But do we want him to continue him working for us?" Dagobert smiled and the lady tweaked his nose with her free hand. "Naughty Dagobert. Only the Earl Edric can decide a matter such as this." Gondul let go of his hair and the man's head fell back onto the slight rise of her belly, while she blew on his forehead, causing his hair to dance. "Enough." She moved away, leaving Dagobert to flounder for balance. "See to our beloved and trusted reeve of Martinsfield, Master Dagobert." With a toss of her head the lady

Woden's Wolf

turned and disappeared behind the curtain at the rear of the dais. When he had regained his posture Dagobert still had a silly smile on his face, but when he spoke to Evan it was the voice of a serpent.

"You have been over grazing the pastures, you wog ox. Remember, a hand that takes what does not belong to it is a hand that does nothing. How, my crooked friend, will you ever pick your nose again when your hand is sitting in your pocket—doing nothing, because it has been cut off?" Evan did another eye bob. "And this is another poor sheep you had hoped to fleece?" The manor reeve turned his gaze to Godfrew.

"A good man, related to folk already at Martinsfield. I did not try and take money from him, Master Dagobert. I brought him straight here so that he could deal direct with you." Evan gave a quick eye bob, then retrieved his torn hat.

"So, you have learnt that much." Dagobert addressed Godfrew this time. "There was a small misunderstanding between us over the division of responsibilities. Nothing to do with my Lady's reference to Michaelmas. That was an error of judgment that called Evan's loyalty into question and was dealt with by Earl Edric in person. No, the misunderstanding I am referring to was much smaller, between Evan and myself. It was a matter easily resolved, as indeed are all things between old friends." The unblinking eyes remained on Godfrew. "Right, Evan?"

"Right. Master Reeve." Evan worried at the torn hat.

"Now ...?"

"Wulf, Master Reeve. His family call him Wulf." With Dagobert's attention on Godfrew, Evan risked a proper look at the manor reeve.

"Now, Wulf. You want to lease grazing?" Still his eyes did not blink. "The cost is one hundred shillings a year: cash, no goods in lieu."

Godfrew returned the stare as best he could. "For land that is only yours sometimes, one hundred shillings is a lot of money."

"Is it now?" Dagobert snapped his fingers and a boy came forward with a drinking horn of foaming ale. The reeve downed it in one gulp. A rim of foam clung to the beard around his mouth. "Wulf, let me remind you that few people

The West March

live in the Marchlands because they like it. Either they are born here and, for some reason, can't get away, or they like fighting and haven't been killed yet. Or perhaps they want to hide from someone powerful for a while. You are not local, so that takes out the first reason. If you had enjoyed fighting you would have been after joining the war band instead of grazing, so that takes out the second reason. Which only leaves the third reason—so look upon the leasing fee as containing an element of protection money. When you look at it that way, one hundred shillings a year is not much. Remember, stock here is very cheap, even free sometimes. You have cash?"

"I can get it."

"I'm sure you can. Coins preferably. If you only have broken jewellery, try and melt it down. We don't see much of the King's Justice around here, but someone might recognise it and cause a problem. A deal?"

"Do I have a choice?"

"None." Dagobert gave another silly smile. "Except to lease the land with your money or go back to Martinsfield and wait for us to come and steal it from you." The village reeve spat on his hand and held it out to Godfrew. Godfrew got up off of his knees and went up to shake the man's hand.

"A deal. You will collect the money when?"

"I am a reasonable person, despite what some would say." He glanced at Evan, who quickly took to looking at the floor again. "In view of the problems of continual ownership, I will collect the rent every quarter. The first payment will be when I do my rounds later in the month. I am a trusting man, just have things ready for me. Don't, however, disappoint me. I do not like being disappointed, do I Evan!"

"No, Master Reeve."

"Now leave us, Wulf. Evan and I have other things to discuss."

* * *

"Praise God and Blessed Dewi we are out of that hell hole." After leading the way back to Martinsfield at a trot, Evan finally slowed his mount down when they broke through the tree line on the reverse side of the hills.

"It seems your masters are not to be disobeyed."

"My masters? Yours too now, boy. That lot back at the hamlet know little of what goes on outside, let alone what their masters are like." Evan allowed himself a celebratory nose pick. "Easy now." The pony had jolted, causing the village reeve to scratch the inside of his nose.

"The Lady Gondul. Is that Earl Edric's wife?"

"Yes. Not that he spends much time with her. Mind she finds other ways to amuse herself." Evan pinched the bridge of his nose to stop the bleeding.

"With Dagobert Reeve?" Godfrew got the dark pony to match its pace with Evan's mount.

"Who knows. Lady Gondul's amusements are not those of other folk's." Evan's voice was distorted by the nose pinching. A trickle of blood ran from the side, into his mouth, and he wiped it with his free hand. "You heard that she watched as they pulled all my fingernails out? That was light entertainment for her. Before King Harold plotted and got Griffith the Magnificent assassinated, these lands were Cymry again for a while. Edric still held out at Lydbury North, of course. It would take a miracle to winkle him from out of there. Well, he took some prisoners, see. One of them was a young boy, Nye, a son of my mother's cousin's father-in-law. Don't ask how, but Edric kidnapped me and had me taken back to his manor. Said he wanted me to act as translator while he 'interviewed' Nye. He speaks Cymry fluently, so the last thing he needed was a translator. They started with pliers and ended up with hot irons and a flaying knife. By the time Edric had got all the information he wanted, I'd been sick, Nye was dead, and the high Lady Gondul had pissed herself with pleasure. Nine months later she gave birth to another Saxon whelp, assumably to Edric. Oh, her pleasures are strange to consider. Never cross that one, boy, never."

"Dagobert seemed to imply that Edric and his men control most of the land around here and from what you have said that is even when they don't 'own' the land." Godfrew let go of the pony's reins and rummaged in the cloth bag hanging from the front of his saddle. On finding a flat loaf of coarse bread, he pulled it out, tore it and offered Evan half. "Well, do they?"

Evan leaned across and took the bread, his nose bleed

The West March

having stopped. "Yes. Even when they aren't here in person, the fear of their name is sufficient." Evan bit a piece of bread and let it soak in his mouth before chewing it. When he had finished, he continued speaking. "Edric's reputation is known and feared on both sides of the border. Saxon earls court him, princes of the Cymry make treaties with him, the church forgoes its tithes in order to have an understanding with him. Very powerful is our Lord Edric." Evan took another bite of the bread and slowly chewed it as he thought. "This trouble the Saxons have with the Normans has helped him in a way. There have been many young warriors who have lost their own lord, looking for employment and a hearth to sit around. Edric has attracted many, all keen to show him what they can do, God help us." He pulled a flask from his own saddle bag and took a swig of the small ale it contained. "As I understand it, the Normans are taking land from the Saxons on any excuse, so I don't think it will be long before Edric's new men are fully employed." He took another swig before offering the flask to Godfrew. "And when they are employed, those of us on the land will be lucky to survive." He turned to his companion and took back the flask. "You did not pick a good time to settle in this shire, young Wulf. Not a good time at all." Evan put the flask back in the bag and returned to eating the bread. "Mind, it never has been a good time to settle in this area."

"Yet you stay."

"Oh, yes, I stay. My family has been here since the Romans, see. Can't leave it now just 'cos the Saxons rule it, at present that is." Having finished his bread, Evan wiped his mouth with the back of his hand. The skin rasped audibly on the hoary whiskers. "I was born here and, no doubt, I will die here, too. Trouble is, I've no sons to follow me."

"You have no wife?"

Evan's voice went very quiet. "Not now, boy. I had four in my time and buried them all. The little ones they bore me are all gone." He wandered off into a world of his own and it was sometime before he spoke again. "It's a hard place, this—especially for women and children. When the raiders come, it's always the women and children. Always." Again he shook his head and wandered off into the depths of his mind. Eventually, he returned to the present. "Been married long then?"

"Not long."

"If you want my advice, boy, don't get too attached to her—not if you are going to stay here." Evan watched Godfrew and saw the anger in his face. "Oh, so you love her, then? Now, there's a pity. There's not much use for love in this place. Can't say I ever loved any of my wives. Lusted after them, but never loved them. The only one I ever loved was my eldest daughter, a lovely girl. Her Saxon mother gave her a skin of milk and bright ginger hair. When she shook her head, it was like spun gold." He looked at Godfrew, a wistful look on his face. "Not unlike that cousin Oakleaf of yours. She often reminds me of my daughter, does Oakleaf."

"Your daughter was killed by reevers in a raid?"

"No," the word was drawn out, "she is buried only in my heart, boy. She was taken by my own people. That type of colouring increases a girl's value on the slave market—particularly amongst the Moors—where most of them end up. Why rape and kill them when you can sell them, eh?" He took a deep breath and held it for some seconds before letting it out. "I often wonder where she is now. The hours I've spent in prayer over that one." Evan went silent again and Godfrew dropped back to leave the reeve of Martinsfield to his thoughts and memories.

As they rode back across the plain, Evan remained silent and wrapped in his self-imposed isolation. Godfrew used the time to observe the land. Much appeared to be good soil, but instead of being under the plough, it was left for grazing and there were many herds of cattle and horses. When ever they came toward one of the herds, armed riders came between them and the stock, guiding them away from the animals. Occasionally, the herd was made up of only five or six animals and the herder but a boy, but even he was armed with a sling and made no attempt to hide the weapon. Often the boys would make a show of the fact that he was both armed and willing to use his weapon to defend the stock. Being challenged by a boy of no more than ten summers, amused Godfrew, but Evan showed no emotion.

As they came near Martinsfield in the failing light of the summer evening, Evan had still not spoken again. It was not until they neared the village well and Oakleaf waved to them that he seemed to shake himself out of his stupor. "I wish

The West March

you well, boy. Just make sure you have the money ready on time for the manor reeve and myself. Oh, and keep that half-breed Llewelyn away from me. I'll kill him if I have to, but I'd rather not."

"Wulf!" Elfgifu ran toward Godfrew. Now that she was married and no longer a maid, she wore a white linen cap on her head, but her fine golden hair escaped at the bottom and it trailed behind her as she ran. Godfrew slipped out of the saddle and managed to turn slightly before his wife arrived and embraced him. "Thank God you are back. I hate it when you are not here with me." Godfrew kissed her lips, but she would allow no more than a peck. "Come, leave the boys to take care of the pony. Let me show you what I have been doing to the cottage whilst you have been away." She took Godfrew's arm and put it around her waist before leading him toward their new home.

Godfrew turned and called to the boys gathered around the dark pony: "Leave her in the paddock. Don't take her saddle off and don't go riding her. She has had a hard day. If you behave, I'll take you hare hunting tomorrow and you can take turns to ride her then." He squeezed Elfgifu and snuffled her neck. "So, my elven one, what have you been up to in my absence? Mischief?"

"Work, my beloved. See." The ground in front of the cottage had been cleared and made tidy. The wicker fence around the kitchen garden had been repaired and the earth dug over. In front of the cottage, a small thorn bush had been planted. After she had seen that Godfrew had taken in the outside scene, Elfgifu pulled him into the cottage. The floor was strewn with fresh herbs and hay. The small hearth was tidy and cut wood lay at its side waiting to be used, an iron pot suspended on a rail hung over the hearth, its outside burnished. In a corner stood two leather topped stools and in front of them was a wooden table. On the top of the table, a drinking horn with freshly picked flowers lay perfectly centred. "Do you like it?" Elfgifu's eyes were on Godfrew's, seeking approval.

"I like it, but not as much as I like you, Cariad." Godfrew turned his wife toward him and started to undo her clothing. As the garments fell to the floor, she shivered.

"Wulf, others will see."

"Let them." But despite his words, Godfrew went to the cottage entrance and pulled the heavy leather curtain across the doorway. When he returned, Elfgifu was naked, waiting for him by the pile of hay they kept for bedding, her golden pubic hair standing out like whirls of clarified honey on a bowl of milk. Godfrew pulled off his cloak and lay it on the hay. He then kissed his wife. This time, the kiss was returned and he melted into the warmth of her sweet tasting mouth.

"Dear God, I need you." He put his leg behind her knee, took her off balance and they fell onto the cloak covered bed. Godfrew ran his hands over her warm, soft body, loving the feel of her yielding flesh. Again he used his leg, this time to lever her knees apart. Elfgifu undid Godfrew's belt and pulled down his breeches. Grasping his firm buttocks, she pulled him toward her. "Be gentle with me, husband dear, for I am with child!"

The Gates of Hell

Llew pulled back into the bushes that surrounded the mere. Below him, Oakleaf along with two other maids bathed and played in the cold water, squealing with mock horror as they splashed each other, oblivious of the rest of the world. Despite the lure of the chance to see the girl's naked bodies, Llew was watching for something else. Now, he saw his target.

Evan the Reeve moved silently along the path through the trees until he came near the mere, then he went into the bushes just below Llew. As he neared the shore, Evan found a rounded rock and sat on it, his back to the maids, eyes closed, listening and dreaming.

"You weird bastard." Llew chewed another sliver of nail from his finger and spat it out. Time passed and still Evan did not stir. Llew allowed himself to watch the maids below for a while, enjoying their young bodies. He realised that his young sister Oakleaf had become a woman, as Evan had said. The maids dried themselves and headed back to the hamlet. Still, Evan did not move. Llew stayed too, watching, wondering. As the day drew nearer to noon and the warmth made him drowsy, Llew settled back into the bush and closed his eyes. He listened quietly to the bird song and the drone of bees seeking the bright flowers of summer. With his eyes closed, the moving branches of the bush made dark patterns on the red of his eyelids. Thoughts danced in and out of his mind and sleep beckoned.

Just as the surrounding sounds started to dim and blackness began to enfold him, Llew was brought back to full alertness by the sound of horses. There in front of him, two armed Normans reigned in their mounts and waited. Evan the Reeve slid out of the bushes and joined them. Their voices were low and hard to hear. Llew could make out what appeared to be heavily accented Welsh. Like most marcher folk, Llew understood some of the language. His father spoke it often when dealing with Evan, but Llew was not fluent in it and he was too far from the others to catch what was being said. At one stage, Evan became quite vocal and started pulling his hair. Llew caught the words 'ginger', 'gold' and 'save', but as the volume of Evan's voice dropped, he could catch no more. The Normans finished talking to Evan and headed back the way that they had come. Evan returned to his rock and closed his eyes again.

* * *

Godfrew hung over the wicker fence and admired his ponies. They were solid and deep-chested creatures, ideal for carrying packs or armoured men. Already he had made one trip to Bristol and made good money by selling ten ponies brought to him by one of Edric's men. He had bought them cheap. The man wanted a quick sale and the animals looked scruffy. When he sold them, the ponies were in prime condition and the price was high.

Elfgifu, too, was filling out and—apart from morning sickness—was carrying well. Life was sweet.

"Quick, sound the alarm, reevers! REEVERS!" Llew ran into the hamlet, sending geese and hens scattering. The few men not out with the herds picked up their working tools or headed for their cottages to find their weapons. Women caught what children they could, calling out in shrill voices for those not at hand. Some boys scurried into the paddock and started to mount Godfrew's ponies.

"Hey, what ..."

"We need them, Master Wulf, to tell the others with the herds."

"If they stay here the reevers will get them." A boy with torn breeches and lank hair pulled the gate open.

"But ...."

"We'll be back." The boy with torn breeches grabbed a handful of mane and swung up on a pony's back.

"With the men!" added another boy as he rode past at the rear of the small herd of excited ponies.

"Don't worry about them, Wulf." Llew pushed Godfrew in front of him. "If you lose them, you lose them. If those boys don't get them clear of the Normans, you will loose them anyway."

"Normans?" Godfrew asked stupidly.

"Normans. I saw Evan talking to two of them. They were mail coated and armed. In these parts when you see men like that, you know that there will be trouble. Now get to your cottage and grab whatever weapons you have. Don't try and be a hero fighting them in the open. Keep close to the cottages and try and fight one-to-one. HURRY."

Llew ran past Godfrew and dived into the family cottage.

"Elfgifu?" Godfrew was starting to panic now. "Elfgifu?"

"Here." Elfgifu came from the rear of their cottage, wiping her hands on her apron, the soap suds clinging to the cloth.

"Normans. Quick in the house, now." Godfrew caught hold of her arm and propelled her inside.

"Normans? So what is the problem?" Despite the questioning, Elfgifu moved inside.

"Trouble! Normans are trouble and Llew says so, too." Godfrew moved her toward the far wall. "Take this." He rummaged in the thatch, pulled out his saxe and removed it from the scabbard. "Take this and use it if you have to." Elfgifu reluctantly took the weapon and looked at Godfrew, an unasked question on her face. "If one comes in here, make toward the bed as if you are not going to resist him." Godfrew kicked the scabbard under the table and then took the saxe back again. "Get him onto the bed, if you can ..." He slid the saxe under the cloak that covered the hay bedding. "... then stick him." He looked hard into her face. "Don't tell me you can't, because if you don't, he will rape you and then kill you. This is the way Normans behave. I know! I have seen it." Elfgifu nodded dumbly, her eyes darting. Godfrew took both her hands in his: "Look at me, Cariad. Look square at me." Reluctantly, she did as she was told. "There is no other way. Just pray that there is only one of them." Elfgifu nodded, her assent tears forming in her eyes.

"But you will be here to save me." She sniffed and blinked away a tear.

"No. If I stay here, then you will die. They will be looking for the men so that they can kill them first. They will not worry about the women until after they hold the hamlet safe. I will make it hard for them outside and try and stop that from happening. If I stay in here with you they will come looking for me like terriers and then we shall both die like rats in a trap." Godfrew went to the other side of the cottage and picked up Neckbiter. The axe's new handle was plain, without the carvings that had graced its previous shaft, but it was solid with a straight grain.

Elfgifu sat down on the bed and plucked the edge of her apron. "How do you know that is what the Normans will do if they come here?"

"Because that is what I would do if I was raiding this place." Godfrew shouldered Neckbiter and went out.

In the hamlet, there was chaos. Some of the women had gathered their flocks of offspring and were herding them toward the scrub land that lay two hundred paces away. Others, unwilling to risk being caught in the open, were pushing their protesting brats into the cottages. A group of men were gathered around Llew near the well.

"Yes, it was Evan telling them where to find us. This time I saw him and if, God willing, we survive this raid, I'll see he gets his just deserts for the betrayal." Llew's weapon was a bill hook. The shaft was of ash, the head of rough, sand-cast iron. Its sharpened edge gleamed and winked in the sun.

A young man with the same ginger hair as Llew's siblings spoke from the back of the group. "Do you know how many there are, cousin?"

"No, I only saw the two of them."

"But you are sure they are from a raiding party?" Llew's cousin had started to remove his over shirt, exposing brawny arms covered in brown freckles that matched those on his broad face.

"Armed men always mean trouble. If I am wrong, then I am wrong." Llew moved through the group to face his cousin. "Don't tell me that you want to take the risk?"

"Just asking." The cousin picked up his bill hook, a match for Llew's.

"We've all been here before, so we know the score. Stall the raiders as long as we can. If the other men come back in time—good. If they don't get back in time, we die. Until the Normans get here, try praying that there aren't many of them." The group started to break up, each heading for a favoured spot near the buildings. "Wulf." Llew summoned Godfrew over. "You are new to this game. Raiders come in different shapes and need to be handled in different ways. The Cymry use a mix of horsemen and footmen. They tend to start at one end and work their way to the other—footmen driving people to the other end of the hamlet where the horsemen are gathered. They like to take prisoners for selling on the slave market. If you fancy a life of slavery, then you can live. The Saxons and Vikings arrive on horseback and then dismount. They tend to surround the hamlet and work from the outside in. Men are all killed, women raped and then taken off. Only the children are left. We have only had a couple of raids by the Normans, but they seem to be the easiest to beat. They are horsemen and are loath to get off their horses, probably frightened that we are going to steal them! They tend to charge from one end of the village to the other and back again, trying to catch their victims out in the open. Now one thing a horseman should never do is take on footmen in anything other than an open area. Start to try and fight amongst houses or trees and the horseman is in trouble. The worry today is how many of them are there? If the raiding party is small, we stand a good chance. Keep them around the houses and wait for the others to get back. If the raiding party is large, we shall all die. The others won't join the fight if it looks lost. If the Normans kill the men, then you can forget the women. They aren't interested in prisoners. They have no need of them. They took one of the places over the black mountain last year ... not English, but Cymry. My Da took me there looking for unclaimed ponies and cattle. The Normans had killed everyone and everything ... people, cattle, horses, sheep, fowl. What they couldn't take, they burnt, even the common woods." Llew gave Godfrew a sharp look. "So fight hard, cousin. Fight hard!" He strode off to his family's cottage, bill hook over his shoulder. Godfrew held Neckbiter on the ground and rested his chin on his hands, watching the track leading to the village.

Godfrew felt the arrival of the horsemen before he saw them. The ground vibrated to pounding hooves. The numbers were hard to guess, but the raiding party was not that small. Straightening up, he put Neckbiter over his shoulder and went back to his cottage. Picking his ground carefully, he stood with the end wall to his left. The sound of horses came to his ears and he tried a few warm up swings of the axe. The sound grew louder, so he took a peek around the wall. The Normans were at the end of the village and fanning out down the rows of cottages. The leader had pulled over at the paddock. He seemed put out that they were expected and was calling out something to his men, but the riders seemed oblivious to all but the game.

Godfrew pulled back in and waited, estimating the speed of the first rider by sound and feel. At what he thought was the right time, he stepped out into the street. The Norman was almost along side. Godfrew swung Neckbiter and took the rider's leg off, Neckbiter carried on and stuck itself into the wooden frame of the cottage. Godfrew wriggled it free. Rather than risk striking from the same place twice, he moved down the back of the next cottage and waited for another target. It was not long before another Norman came through. This time Godfrew's timing was not so accurate and he found himself facing the oncoming rider. The Norman was holding a boar spear. He couched it as he saw Godfrew. Godfrew stood his ground, then moved to his right and swung his axe upwards, striking the horse in the neck. The creature buckled at the knees and slid to a halt in the blood sodden dirt. Godfrew rushed over and took the Norman's head off before the man could free himself. He could hear another horseman behind him, but Godfrew could not get out of the way. A burning pain shot up his leg as a spear caught him in the knee. Only the fact that the fallen horse had ruined the Norman's aim saved the blow from being true. Godfrew rolled out of the way and back to the protection of the cottage wall. In the alley opposite, a Norman was trying to stick a villager to the wall, but the man kept dodging. Meanwhile, a companion ducked under the Norman's horse and hamstrung it. As the horse collapsed, screaming down on its haunches, the man jumped up behind the horseman and cut his throat with a butcher's knife.

The would-be victim grabbed a rope tied to a wall post and ran toward Godfrew. "Wait till I say and then pull." It was Llew's freckled cousin. "Now!" they both pulled hard and felt the impact as two horsemen collided with the taunt rope. Godfrew went sprawling in the dirt, but the cousin was already running out to dispatch his victims. Picking himself up, Godfrew went to help, but one of the fallen Normans was already on his feet struggling with Llew's cousin whilst another Norman was stabbing him with his sword. Godfrew sunk Neckbiter into the first, taking him at the bottom of the neck and making his head fly. The other Norman let go of the cousin and reached for his sword, but Neckbiter took his arm off, then his head. Godfrew glanced at the cousin, but he was gone, bubbling his life out in frothy blood. Another Norman was charging down the street, but rather than face him, Godfrew stood in the cottage doorway. The rider yanked his horse to a halt and trotted back. He stabbed at Godfrew with his spear, but could not get near enough. Godfrew did not have enough room to swing his axe to get at him either. Once, twice, thrice, the Norman lunged, only to find himself thrusting into thin air. Then a stone from a sling hit the horse's rump, causing it to rear. Godfrew stepped forward, took off the Norman's left leg and left a gapping wound in the horse's side. Pain crazed, the animal took off. The rider fell from the saddle and was dragged along the street, his remaining foot caught in the stirrup.

A loud desperate cry came from the other end of the village. "They've fired the houses!" Godfrew slung himself against the cottage wall before allowing himself a stolen glance. Toward him came a mass of women and children running and screaming. By the far cottages, he could just make out some Normans, fire brand in one hand, horses reins in the other, lighting the thatch. With the panicking crowd running down the street, the Norman horsemen charged again, trampling all in front of them. The Normans sought out the men as they came out of their hiding places, trying to get their folk out of the horsemen's way. Godfrew forced himself forward against the flow of people. Coming to the first burning house, he moved around to the rear. The armoured back of a Norman greeted him, but Neckbiter relieved the man of his head. As Godfrew approached the front of the burning house, he saw another Norman standing there, holding the reins of two horses.

"Hurry up and get back here, Alan. Fancy wanting to piss in the middle of a fight." He turned his head. As he realised his mistake, Neckbiter opened him up from collarbone to navel, finally burying its head in the dirt. Godfrew took a step foreword and freed the axe.

The house was well ablaze. Hurrying back to where he had come from, he returned to the end wall and smashed a hole in it with Neckbiter. It was only when Oakleaf, Joanna, and

Mouse popped out of the hole that he realised that it was Llew's place that was on fire.

"Get out and stay off the street. Keep to the back alley." The girls took no notice, rather heaving and pulling something through the broken wall. "Leave it and get going, the Normans will be here." Still they tugged. "Get out of the way." Godfrew unceremoniously pushed them away, grabbed hold of the bundle of clothing they were pulling and dragged it through. It was Rhiannon. She was dead. "Get going, you cannot help her. Get going, or it will be you next. Go, you little brats. GO!" A horseman came from the back alley into the gap between Llew's place and the next cottage. The girls screamed and ran. Godfrew showed him the axe and the man pulled his horse back. Realising that the alley was too narrow to turn in and that he could only go forward, the Norman screwed up his courage, lowered his spear and spurred his horse.

As he came near, Godfrew threw himself to his right and flattened himself against the wall. When the horse passed, Godfrew came back into the alley and sunk his axe into the creature's rump. The horse took off screaming. Neckbiter would not free itself and Godfrew would not let go of the axe, so the strange combination crashed through the alley into a milling group of Normans on the other side. The impact of the collision freed Neckbiter. He now had a usable weapon, but Godfrew also faced six very angry Normans. Not giving them time to think, Godfrew went berserk striking out blindly, hitting men and horses at random. He could hear a terrifying scream, but did not realise that it was his own voice that was making it. Suddenly, Godfrew slipped in a pile of spilt, steaming entrails and ended up in a heap. He pushed himself upright to see a dismounted Norman standing above him, two hands clasped on a sword held above his head, about to strike.

"Into thy hands, sweet Jesus, I ..." the prayer was cut short when a bill hook sliced the Norman's hands off and showered Godfrew in blood. The Norman collapsed moaning, shoving the severed stumps into his mail shirt to try and stop the bleeding.

Llew kicked him in the back and looked at Godfrew. "Get up! It's not over, yet."

The Gates of Hell

At the other end of the street, a handful of Normans gathered and yelled at each other. Suddenly they charged, buffeting and trampling the women and children running away from them. The men offered no fight, but moved to one side to let the folk through.

"Don't run, you silly cows. Get into the cottages not on fire. Get out of the road so that we can fight." Some heard Llew and obeyed. Others kept on running. So did the Normans... straight out of the village.

Godfrew looked around him and saw Elfgifu. She was standing with her ginger cousins. At her feet were trampled fowls, piglets, and a crushed Mouse. Godfrew did not join her, but leaned on his axe, catching his breath, coughing phlegm, his wrists aching from the jarring of blade on bone. His arm muscles felt like lead from swinging the axe. Some of the men had got buckets and were throwing water on the burning cottages. Others had started pulling the thatch off, trying to stop the fire from spreading.

In the alley at the back of Llew's place, a Norman prisoner was being questioned. The man had a smashed leg and kept sliding down onto the ground. His questioners kept pulling him up again. Llew sat, Rhiannon's burnt head in his lap, watching the interrogation dispassionately. Godfrew went over.

Llew looked up. "They were from Hereford. It seems that William Fitz Osbern, who styles himself Earl of all Hereford now, has decided to remove Earl Edric. William, with his mate, Roger of Scrobe, have destroyed other holdings of Edric's this week. We were next on their list." Llew stroked the frazzled, matted hair of Rhiannon. "We were fortunate. They broke into several raiding parties. If they had stayed together, it would have been all over for us."

Godfrew knelt alongside him. "They may be back."

"Yes," Llew pulled a handful of fallen thatching toward him and pushed it under his wife's head, "but not today, I think. Not according to our song-bird."

"He speaks English?"

"No. He is a Breton. His native tongue is near enough to Cymry for some here to understand. Bretons ... Cymry ... they are all wogs."

Woden's Wolf

The Norman had slid to the ground again and lay there moaning, clasping his smashed leg. A bright white bone protruded through his torn leather hose. Llew got up and selected a broken wooden post from the ruined wall of his cottage. Standing behind the Norman, he hit him hard across the neck. As the man fell, Llew moved him over with his foot and then hit him full in the face with the end of the post. When he pulled the post out of the Norman's pulped face, there were bone fragments and teeth embedded in the wood, but the Norman did not move anymore.

* * *

They had laid Martinsfield's dead out in a row, ready for burial. Some, mainly men, showed the injuries expected from combat, sword slashes, spear holes, smashed or severed limbs. Most, however, had been trampled and crushed. Women and children were scored with hoof marks. Elfgifu had gone with the surviving women to lay out the corpses and try to give their remains some semblance of dignity. Godfrew had not been able to bring himself to join her, seeking to avoid looking at the children, particularly Mouse. Instead, he had gone to where the boys and the men who had missed the fight had gathered. These folk had been out with the herds during the fight. Now, they had taken to stripping the dead Normans of their clothes and armour. The bodies had stiffened. When items could not be pulled off easily, the limbs had been broken or cut off to aid in the removal.

Then came the cry: "Horsemen!"

The whole story started over again: the scramble of women gathering children and heading for the security of the scrub land—for none would stay in the village this time. Men got their weapons ready and sought the protection of the buildings. All were ready to fight to protect what was theirs.

Godfrew rested his back against the cottage wall and ran a whetstone over Neckbiter's edge, trying to give the blade some semblance of sharpness. His knee had stiffened like the corpses opposite. The spearhead itself had missed, but the bar at the base of the head had hit his knee joint at a strange angle. After the fight, Elfgifu had insisted on looking

The Gates of Hell

at the wound, but there was little blood. There was much bruising. Already, it had started to turn black. Godfrew did not fancy his chances of putting up much of a fight this time, particularly if the Normans had brought footmen with them. He ran the whetstone over the blade of the axe again, spitting on it first. The blade had several dents in it where it had bitten through chain mail. Fortunately, most of the Normans had been wearing inferior ring mail coats. Ring mail was good for blocking crossbow bolts at a distance, deflecting spears and absorbing slashing sword blows, but it gave little protection against a bearded Danish long axe, especially one in the hands of a trained warrior. Godfrew gave Neckbiter's edge another stroke of the whet stone.

This time, Elfgifu had gone to the scrub lands to comfort her bereaved cousins. Godfrew had insisted that she keep the saxe with her. He had acquired a double edged knife for himself from a dead Norman. He had also found a helmet and a chain mail coat to replace his own that now lay at his father's feet in Tooting. He wore the helmet, but not the coat, as it was torn and needed the attention of a good armourer. It would be more hindrance than help.

Godfrew stopped his sharpening when he suddenly caught the sound of horses. The horses were being ridden at a walk, so Godfrew completed the stroke. The sound of the horses was now joined by voices—some joking, some laughing. The Martinsfield men moved from the cover of their cottages and came to stand in the main street.

Toward them came a colourful party. The outriders were armed with spears. Chain-mail twinkled under their over shirts, but their helmets were hung over their saddles and the spears were resting on the horse's necks. As they came to the paddock, the outriders fanned out to expose the centre party. In the front rode the obvious leader. He was tall and blond, mounted on a pure white horse with a golden mane. The rider had a short, golden beard and long moustaches that reached his chest, their ends waxed to long points. His chain mail coat shone and he wore a long Frankish cloak in bright blue. The horse, too, was well dressed. Its saddle and harness glinted with silver adornments. Behind the rider came three women, dressed for the hunt, falcons on their wrists, and behind them were more armed men. At one side

Woden's Wolf

of the rider walked Llew. On the other side was Evan the Reeve.

Evan's hands were tied behind his back. A wooden stake had been thrust under his arms. The stake had a rope attached to either end and the rider held one rope whilst one of his outriders held the other. They came to a halt. Evan, his eyes standing out on stalks, collapsed to his knees.

"Earl Edric! Earl Edric!" The men rushed to greet their master. The women must have heard the cry, for they too took to calling out his name and came running, children in tow, toward the village.

"Well, good people of Martinsfield. It looks as if you do not need the protection of me and my men." Edric cast his eye over the gathering assembly. He gave a cracked laugh and the village folk joined him. "Mighty warriors, eh?"

"None like you, Lord Edric," someone called out.

"Who said flattery is unimportant?" Edric called over his shoulder.

A small brown-skinned woman moved her pony forward and came alongside the Earl. "Never you, my Lord. Without flattery, life would be very dull." Her eyes were black and Godfrew could not distinguish her pupils. The woman's skin was a dark brown—not the olive colour, common to the Welsh, that turned brown from exposure to the sun. This was a dark skin, almost velvet brown, the like of which he had never seen before.

The man next to Godfrew saw his fascination and whispered in his ear: "Goda, one of Edric's slave women. She was given to him by a Welsh prince, Bleddyn, to buy his help in one of their incessant fights over inheritance. He never goes anywhere without her."

Edric was laughing again "But, my little wog, I need to know what is flattery and what is lying, surely?"

"Wog, indeed!" Goda's accent was strong and strange. Godfrew had never hear one like it. "My Lord, only this morning you said that I was your precious jewel. Now was that flattery, or lying?"

Edric laughed so much that tears ran down his cheek. "What ever would I do without you?" He wiped his eyes with his hands. The hand holding Evan's rope caught his cheek. Edric looked at it as if he had never seen it before. He pulled

The Gates of Hell

on it and, finding resistance, he looked down the rope an arm's length at a time until he saw the unhappy Evan. "Oh, yes, I had almost forgotten you." Evan stood up and faced the Earl. Godfrew could see Evan's face. It held a look of sheer terror. "You have been a naughty boy just once too often to be left in charge of the village, Master Reeve." Edric gave the rope a playful tug, causing Evan to stumble. "But what shall I do with you?" Godfrew expected the villagers to call out for Evan's banishment or death, but they remained silent. "Evan, oh, Evan. It is not the first time is it? Do you remember my having to speak to you last Michael Mass?" He made another tug on the rope. "Evan?"

"Lord Edric." Evan's voice was so quiet it could almost not be heard.

"You promised to behave. Remember?"

"Lord Edric."

"Precious." Edric turned to Goda, who was stroking the feathers of her hooded hawk and clicking her tongue gently as she did so. "What shall I do with Evan?"

Goda continued stroking her bird. "Offer him a different job, my Lord. Something at Lydbury perhaps."

Edric made much of considering the proposal. "I wonder what job I can offer him there?" He leaned over and touched Goda's hand, flustering the hawk. Goda playfully tapped the Earl's hand and wagged her finger at him. Edric pulled back and waited for Goda's reply.

After a long pause, Goda's face lit up. In a bright voice, she announced: "Why not ask your wife? She always seems to have such interesting ideas."

Evan sagged and Edric yanked him upright again. "An excellent idea." Edric threw his rope to an outrider. "Take him back, you two." The riders set off at a trot through the village toward the road across the plain. Evan looked back at the villagers, his eyes wild and full of panic. "And don't wear him out. He will be no good to my wife in a damaged condition." Edric's cracked laugh was short this time. "Now, my good folk, find us food and drink, for we shall stay the night with you. Brother Goshawk, you won't get fed until the dead are buried."

Woden's Wolf

"My Lord," a plump priest rode up on a donkey, his feet almost touching the ground. On seeing the laid out dead bodies, he rode toward them.

"Llewelyn." Edric nudged Llew with his horse "You are the village reeve now. Arrange things." The voice grew louder now. "Boys," Edric waved to the boy with torn breeches and his mates, "take the horses and put them in the paddock." At this, Edric dismounted. So did the rest of the party.

The folk drifted away to prepare for the stay of their master. Godfrew limped back to his cottage, using Neckbiter as a crutch, unsure of what was expected of him. He was worried about Elfgifu and the child she was carrying, hoping the shock of the day's events would not cause her to miscarry.

A hand tapped him on the shoulder. "Oi, the boss wants words with you."

Godfrew turned to find himself facing a short dark youth, fine featured, but with a face marred by a livid scar across his right cheek and a muzzle full of red pimples. The youth nodded toward Edric and started to walk back to the Earl. Edric and the ladies had seated themselves on stools brought for them by the folk. The war-band squatted in a semi-circle behind them. Standing at the far end was Torquil. As Godfrew and his escort neared the group, a rider rode in and spoke to Torquil. Whatever he said was important enough for the leader of the house carls to disturb Edric as he talked and laughed with his ladies. The Earl became serious and questioned Torquil. The answers seemed satisfactory, for Edric nodded agreement to Torquil's whispered suggestion and the leader of the war-band rushed to instruct the rider, who then spurred his horse and disappeared back down the track he had come from.

Godfrew stood in front of Earl Edric, leaning on his long axe for support. His escort had slipped away and joined his squatting companions behind the Earl. Edric seemed not to notice the arrival and continued to exchange flirtatious banter with his ladies. Godfrew shifted the weight on his feet and waited. Eventually, as he turned to answer a comment from the lady on his right, Edric noticed Godfrew standing in front of him. He gave a second take. "Oh, my dear man, have you been waiting long? I am so remiss. These dear ladies are so charming that everything else passes me by. A stool!" He

The Gates of Hell

called out to Torquil. "A stool for this poor man. He has an injured leg. You can't leave him standing there, get him a stool." Torquil sent a young warrior to get one. "Wulf, isn't it? Your cousin Llewelyn was telling me what a splendid fight you put up against those thieving Normans. Very well done. And so they should be well done as well." Edric threw back his head and a cracked laugh echoed out.

"Now, I believe that you are leasing grazing from me. At an excellent price too, from what Dagobert the Reeve tells me. Now, young man," Edric leaned forward and fondled his pointed beard, "I would like to make you an alternative offer." The small sapphire-blue eyes were hard and bright. "Life is going to be, shall we say ... exciting ... in these parts for a while. Rather than stay here and watch the ebb and flow of the action sweep over the plains, I would like you to join my house carls. You have experience, I think?"

"Yes, Earl Edric, but I also have experience in horse grazing and trading." Godfrew gratefully accepted the stool a young warrior offered him.

"No doubt. At the right time, that is both an honourable and profitable trade." The eyes had locked into Godfrew's and never left them. "At the right time. At this time, I do not need lease holders, nor do I need to buy horses when I am in a position to relieve others of them for nothing." The voice still had an edge of humour to it. "At the moment, I need men: men who know how to bear arms, men with battle experience, men who are not afraid." A pause invited Godfrew to reply.

"And you believe I fill the part, Earl Edric." Godfrew kept his stiff knee out straight.

"From what I have heard, I do. Just what particular role you will fill, I am not sure. Time will tell. You will ..." Edric's eyes opened "... and please note I said 'you will'... return to Lydbury with some of my men tomorrow. I, alas," the Earl turned to his ladies who nodded back to him in acknowledgment, "must continue the hunt." He returned to look at Godfrew again. "The prey is elusive, but my scouts are out seeking it at this very moment. Indeed, I am led to understand that they will bring the prey to bay at first light tomorrow." Again, he looked at his ladies. "Now won't that be good!"

"Such fun, my Lord." Goda replied for them.

"Indeed. Splendid fun. Now, I see drinks have arrived. Well done, good people of Martinsfield. Wulf, go with Torquil and make arrangements to leave here. Your wife and others from the family are most welcome to join us at the manor should you wish." Edric took the proffered pewter pot of boiling water and placed it on the ground in front of him. Goda knelt and poured some clarified honey into it, then added a measured amount of dried herbs. Before she had a chance to offer it to the Earl, he got up and moved quickly to grab hold of the youngster who had fetched Godfrew. The youth was bringing foaming pots of full strength ale to the other warriors. From his walk, he had been sampling some of it already. "You drunken little shit-faced ferret." Edric's voice was filled with anger. "There is work to be done and you are pissed out of your tiny brain already." He cuffed the youth's head with the back of his hand, the jolt of which sent the youngster sprawling. He lay there in the ale-soaked dirt, afraid to get up. Earl Edric put his foot on the young warrior's neck. When he spoke, his voice trembled with rage. "Once more, boy, and I will turn you into a bloody eagle. Do you know what that is, boy? Ask the older warriors, the ones who fought the Norwegians with me. It is a very unpleasant Norwegian practice. They cut your ribs up the front and then rip them back to expose your lungs and heart. I have seen it done and noted it. I am just waiting for the chance to try it out myself." He increased the pressure of his foot, causing the youth to gag. "You want to get pissed? Wait until the hunting is done, then you can get as legless as you like. The rest of you," he faced his men "add water to the ale these good folk have provided; half and half. Make it last." He returned to his stool and settled himself, taking the drink proffered by Goda. Godfrew was getting up. Edric smiled at him and spoke in his usual relaxed voice. "The youth of today! What are they coming to?"

"Indeed, Earl Edric." Godfrew inclined his head and hobbled off to join Torquil, who waited for him.

"It was as well you agreed to comply with the master, young Wulf." Torquil walked slowly alongside Godfrew as he sought out Elfgifu and her young cousins. "He hates to be thwarted. It makes him angry. He hates to be angry, because it makes

The Gates of Hell

him vicious." They neared the women who sat by the corpses of the dead folk, waving away the persistent flies, waiting for Edric's chaplain to finish his mutter over the bodies before they could be buried. " I suspect, though, he sometimes likes to be vicious." Torquil's laugh was not a pleasant one.

* * *

Godfrew and his wife stood facing the raised dais in the long house of Lydbury. Behind them stood Oakleaf and Joanna. Llew had felt uncomfortable about them remaining at Lydbury and had persuaded Godfrew to take up the Earl's offer to let other family members come with him. There had been no spare pony for them to ride, as Edric had taken Godfrew's stock, leaving him with only the dark pony and Elfgifu's mount. At the start of their journey, Godfrew had sat Oakleaf in front of himself, leaving the tiny Joanna to share Elfgifu's mount. Oakleaf seemed unused to horse riding, for she insisted that Godfrew hold her close to stop her falling. After the first day, Elfgifu insisted that they swap riding partners, even though there was less room for Oakleaf on her mount, owing to her own extended belly. Elfgifu had been very insistent about the swap, but Godfrew soon guessed why. Despite himself, he had found Oakleaf's body stimulating as it moved against his own. He wished to think Oakleaf innocent of what was happening, but he had caught a sly look in her face after one particularly uneven ride that had forced their bodies into very close bouncing contact.

Now they stood in the great hall, tired from their trek, covered in sweat and dust, awaiting the pleasure of the Lady Gondul who was seated on a high-backed leather chair in front of them. The lady was smiling, but her look was vacant. Her mind was obviously elsewhere. They had been waiting for her attention for a long time. Still, she made no move to recognise their presence. A bird flew in through the open doors and landed on a ceiling beam between Godfrew's family and the lady. Godfrew noticed that it was a raven. The bird wiped its beak on the edge of the beam and winked at Godfrew just as Lady Gondul took a deep breath and came out of her trance. She looked at Godfrew, then followed his gaze.

Woden's Wolf

"You like my pet?" Her voice was still the emotionless bell sound that Godfrew remembered. "He talks, you know. Some wonder why he does not fly away," now she looked back at Godfrew, "but we keep him so well fed." Gondul stood up and moved to the edge of the dais. Godfrew stared at the chair in which she had been sitting. The leather was white with black hair attached to the centre and the top of the seat area. In the fold of the seat was an unusual protuberance. Gondul caught Godfrew's stare. "You are admiring my chair? Beautiful, isn't it." She returned to the chair, took a handful of the black hair and gave it a playful tug. "I thought you might recognise it. The last time you were here, you stood at the side of its previous owner."

"Evan, the village reeve of Martinsfield, my Lady."

"Yes, Evan." She gave the hair another little tug. "Poor Evan, he just didn't want to part with it. It seems he was very attached to it. But it is mine now." Gondul let her hand fall to the seat, she gave the protrusion a flick and it moved to one side, she flicked it back again into the middle. "There, that's where I like it to be." The lady smiled and glided down the steps of the dais to the group.

Godfrew dropped to his knees and the others followed suit. When Lady Gondul proffered her ring hand, Godfrew kissed it.

Coming to Elfgifu, Gondul placed a hand under her elbow and raised her. "Your wife, Master Wulf?"

"Yes, Lady Gondul." Godfrew went to stand, but the lady's look froze him in place.

"Does your wife have skills, Master Wulf?" Gondul's hand still held Elfgifu's elbow.

"Yes, Lady Gondul. She is a skilled seamstress."

"My husband has sent me some beautiful material recently that needs to be made up into gowns for myself and my ladies. A seamstress is always welcome. Let me greet your wife with a kiss." The Lady Gondul took Elfgifu's chin in her other hand and tilted her head. The kiss was full and open mouthed. As Elfgifu's head went back, Gondul's hand left her chin and cushioned her neck instead. The movements of his wife's cheek told Godfrew that the lady was not holding the kiss back. Her tongue was exploring Elfgifu's warm, sweet mouth. Godfrew fought his emotions. He sank his fingernails

The Gates of Hell

into his hands so deep that blood trickled down the palms. Slowly, the lady pulled her mouth away and a wistful smile graced her face. Bringing her hand away from Elfgifu's neck, she stroked her extended belly. "Your wife is with child!" Although she spoke to Godfrew, it was Elfgifu she was looking at. Gondul's hand now cupped Elfgifu's breast. "She has but small breasts to feed a baby with." Her thumb stroked the front of the breast. "But her nipples are proud, so she should be fine." Elfgifu hung her reddening face down as the Lady Gondul moved to the cousins. Joanna she patted on the head, but Oakleaf she kissed as she had kissed Elfgifu. The girl stiffened, but Gondul moved to the girl's side and used her superior height to lean the girl backwards. A hand came to the maid's small, budding breasts and fingers pinched the nipples. The kiss deepened, but as Gondul's tongue entered Oakleaf's mouth, the lady gave a yell of annoyance. "Garlic! GARLIC." She slapped Oakleaf's face and the sound of the slap echoed around the hall. A red hand mark gleamed on Oakleaf's milk-white face. The lady stormed back to the dais, sat down in her leather chair and she went back into her trance. As the day lengthened, Godfrew's knees set and the women folk shuffled, trying to ease their stiffening legs. Again, it was the raven who brought Gondul back to the hall, this time by flying away.

The blue eyes were on Godfrew again. "Wulf, see Dagobert. He will arrange for you and yours to have a sleeping hut. Your wife will attend me here tomorrow and I will talk to her about the gowns. Your elder cousin ..." she glanced at Oakleaf, smiling briefly when she saw the red hand mark. "Your elder cousin, I was going to appoint to my wardrobe staff, where she would have had many privileges, but as she so likes garlic, she can work in the kitchens instead. She can take the brat with her." Lady Gondul wriggled in her seat and closed her eyes. "You may go."

Relieved that the interview was over, Godfrew stiffly got to his feet. His damaged knee throbbed as he led his family out into the welcoming sunshine in the yard.

"All finished then?" Dagobert joined Godfrew, who was examining the damaged palms of his hands. Dagobert nodded toward Elfgifu, who was comforting the distressed Oakleaf. Joanna was shying lumps of dirt at the dried heads on the eaves. "I take it your women folk did not appreciate the Lady Gondul's greeting kiss."

Godfrew looked at the women and then back at the manor reeve. "No, Master Dagobert, they did not. Fortunately I had warned them not to upset the lady, so they did not resist, but they didn't like it."

"Some do, you know. It would surprise you." He nudged Godfrew in the ribs. "Don't worry, she wont pester them again. It's in the first kiss see, if they respond appropriately then ..." he left the words hanging, but seeing that Godfrew had caught his drift, he continued: "Lady Gondul is only interested in willing playmates ... unless it is one of the very special presents sent to her by Earl Edric ... then she appreciates the challenge! Now," he caught Elfgifu's eye and beckoned her over, "we shall arrange for a sleeping hut. Follow me."

"One thing." Godfrew struggled to keep up with the reeve. "That leather chair. Was it Evan?"

"Of course. If you had looked around the back of the chair, you would have seen him smiling at you. I even got the upholsterer to stitch a finger up his nose. Not the correct finger unfortunately, as that one got damaged. In fact, if you examined the leather closely, you would have noticed quite a few places where it was damaged. It's not easy, you know, getting the skin off like that, nothing like removing the pelt off a dead carcass." Dagobert snorted. "It's funny, really, you know. Whenever he came up here to lie to me about the rents or offer excuses about late payments, he was always trying to get the young girls to come and sit on his lap, offering them sweetmeats and the like. I bet he never thought that he would end up having the Lady Gondul sitting on his lap all the time!" They paused in front of a low hut sunk into the ground. It looked like little more than a turfed roof. "This will be your sleeping place. I did have another one over there free, but now that the maid will be sleeping with you, rather than the Lady Gondul, you will need the bigger hut.

Godfrew moved the leather curtain aside and peered in. "There is not much room, is there. You can sleep in it, but not much else."

Dagobert started to clean his fingernails with his eating knife. "Ah, well, you would be used to the new habits. Up here we tend to be more traditional, Earl Edric being more traditional than most. You sleep here and you eat in the great hall. The women work in the side hall." He indicated an extension at right angles to the long house. "There are looms in there and things like that. On the other side is another small hall where the food is prepared."

"And everything else is done in the hall?" asked Godfrew in disbelief.

"Naturally." Having finished one nail, Dagobert moved onto the next. "Oh, don't think that today is like any other. Normally, the hall is a hive of activity. You were arriving today, so our Lady wanted it kept free for the greeting. You are a bit different from our normal recruit, Wulf." Now he pared the nail. "I'm not sure what the Earl has in mind. Maybe he doesn't know himself, but he does not regard you as just another house carl. You must mean something to him. He told me to give back to you the money you had paid for the grazing. Of course," Dagobert gave Godfrew a harsh glance, "my own commission is non-refundable."

"I'm sure that it would have been foolish of me to think otherwise."

Dagobert smiled. "I'm glad to see that we will be able to work together. You asked for your saddles to be brought to you, so I have had them put in the hut already. If you would get your women folk to come and start getting your things sorted out in the hut, you and I should have a little talk." The reeve waved the women into the hut. "All your things have been put inside. I have arranged for sheep skins and bits to be brought over. If you want more, just ask whoever brings them. Now, Master Wulf, let us walk."

Godfrew and Dagobert went out of the staggered gateway and walked around the outer defences. During the tour, the reeve explained the lie of the country and the direction from which an attack was likely to come. They then returned inside the palisade where Godfrew was shown the smithy, butchery, tannery and other important buildings. Godfrew noticed the large holding paddocks and Dagobert explained the need for always bringing stock in at night. He explained how the newly acquired animals were handled and re-branded. From what was said and from the lack of grass in the paddocks, Godfrew gained the impression that the traffic in animals was very high. Despite all that seemed to be done in the holding, there were few people about. In the end, Godfrew broached the matter.

"Where is everyone?"

Dagobert was genuinely surprised. "Almost all the men are with Earl Edric on his 'hunt'. The women are mainly here, weaving, cooking, doing the many things that they do. If you want to know what they do, then ask my wife. I've little idea." He caught the look in Godfrew's eye. "No, not that. My wife failed the welcoming kiss too!" Dagobert's laugh was light and pleasant. "Look, I'm the manor reeve. I keep tabs on the money and goods the manor produces. I mind whatever the Earl finds when he is out hunting. The spinning and weaving that the women do is overseen by the Lady Gondul. The same with the stocking and cooking of the food. I do have one other job ... seeing to the defence of the holding whilst the war band is away ... not that I could do much with the handful of men left to me. Come sit down." Dagobert squatted and Godfrew sat, their backs to the front wall of the great hall, facing the sun. "Now, Earl Edric has many men, but they play different roles. Forget the bondsmen, serfs, and slaves. I mean real men—warriors. The very young and the very old are either here at the holding or close by in other nearby parts of the manor. They are the home-guard, if you like. They only get to fight as a last resort. I'm their leader. The Earl also has thanes holding land from him, or on their own land, further out. They gather when he calls them to join him. Then he has his house carls. Many have been with him for years, fought with him against Welsh, Norwegians, Danes, uppity Normans from Hereford, other English who got too cheeky, even the Scots on one occasion. Others, mainly the youngsters, come and go. Earl Edric has a fearsome name and it increases a man's worth to say that he had once served as a house carl of Edric the Wild. The best men belong to his hearth troop. They never leave his side." He looked closely at Godfrew and gave a smirk "Oh, yes, it's true. Even when he joins the Lady Gondul to celebrate his marriage dues, there are at least two of the hearth troop in the room. I know, for I used to be one of them." Dagobert threw his chestnut maned head back and laughed until the tears ran down his cheeks. "Oh, dear," he wiped the tears away and slowly brought himself back under control. "The things I have seen. You wonder why the Lady takes such liberties with me at times? I'm sure it's because she knows I have seen all. I'm almost part of the furniture—like Evan!" Again, the reeve went into convulsive laughter, holding his ribs and banging his head against the wall. "Poor Evan, the look of confusion at his last 'interview', when Lady Gondul told him that she had always wanted to feel his naked flesh against hers. Then ..." the laughter this time was so uncontrollable that Dagobert rolled onto the ground and kicked his legs "... then, oh God, then ..." still he rolled about "... when he saw the flaying knife and realised what she had in mind. His face... his face ..." It was a long time before the reeve regained his composure. Several times, he seemed to be under control, then he would mutter, "... his face ..." and he would be off again.

When Dagobert sat still at last and began using the bottom of his overshirt to wipe the tears from his eyes, Godfrew brought the conversation back to the original matter. "You were telling me about the hearth troops."

"Eh? Oh, yes, the hearth troops. Well, I've told you about them, but there are other men as well. Sometimes, when things get particularly difficult, Earl Edric has small bands of men led by a house carl stirring up trouble in lands held by those giving him grief. They pay him his seventh of their plunder and keep the rest ... very informal. There is one other group, a group you should give care to when you deal with them. Lady Gondul has her own hearth troops ... a round dozen. Special men, her hearth troops. It was they who were guarding her this afternoon when she was greeting you. You didn't see them, did you?" Godfrew shook his head "No, you wouldn't. Few do. In fact, you won't see much of them ... ever. No one knows much about what they get up to and no one dares ask." For the first time that afternoon, Dagobert looked serious. "Not even me." He picked up a small clod of earth and took to breaking it up, then cleaned his hands on the damp edge of his shirt. "But Evan's face!" Godfrew left the manor reeve as he walked around the ground laughing.

* * *

"That kiss?" Godfrew and Elfgifu were snuggled up at the end of the sleeping hut, the two cousins asleep at their feet.

"Yes?"

"That kiss?" Godfrew levered himself up on his elbow and leaned across to try and see his wife's face in the dark.

"That kiss? Did I enjoy it?" Elfgifu pushed her buttocks into Godfrew's belly and wriggled.

"Did you?"

"No," the wriggling stopped.

"To be kissed like that by another woman." Godfrew dropped back down and encompassed his wife with his arm.

"So, what's the matter with it being another woman? That was not the problem. It was the fact that I only like being kissed like that by you. It has nothing to do with it being a woman. Now, go to sleep."

"But she fondled your breast?"

"Hands are the same, man or woman. In the dark of this hut, you think I would know whose hands played with me?"

"Mine." Godfrew pushed his hand through Elfgifu's defending arms and squeezed her breast.

"Leave me alone and go to sleep." Elfgifu wriggled her buttocks into Godfrew's belly again.

"Later." Godfrew started to kiss his wife's neck and slowly began to make love to her. At his feet, Oakleaf watched.

* * *

Dagobert had not really known what to do with Godfrew, so he had let him fill his time as he wanted. The first job was to get an awl and thread and check his saddle for wear. Then there had been the visit to the blacksmith. The chain-mail shirt had been about the right size and did not need much altering, but the axe damage was worse than Godfrew had first thought. A week later, he still had not got it back. In order to get something done for him, the blacksmith had altered the helmet Godfrew had taken from the dead Norman at Martinsfield. Godfrew had cheek and eye-guards added to the existing nasal. He had asked for the eye holes to be narrow; trading off the restricted view for sharpened vision at a distance. The blacksmith had taken Godfrew for a traditionalist and had found for him a small brass boar which he had

The Gates of Hell

soldered to the front of the crest. The trouble was, the helmet was pointed and the boar looked as if it was sliding downhill, but the man had meant well. Godfrew had toyed with the idea of only having an eye hole for his good eye, but Elfgifu, on hearing of the idea, told him it was foolish and would make him look daft, so it never happened.

From the very beginning, the women had been fully occupied—even little Joanna. Elfgifu had been cutting and sowing gowns. Lady Gondul had been pleased with the results. Oakleaf and Joanna had worked long hours in the kitchens. Despite there being few folk around, there was much salting of meat and rendering of fat going on. Most evenings, it was dark before the girls got back to the sleeping hut. Usually, Oakleaf had a sleeping Joanna in her arms.

Godfrew had taken to riding out on the dark pony. Sometimes he would just ride, but often he would help the youngsters in charge of the diminishing herds of cattle and sheep. Today, he had kept to the holding. At first light, two riders had come in and announced that Earl Edric had finished his hunting and was coming home.

That news had set the cat amongst the pigeons. Now there was activity everywhere. Dagobert had sent Godfrew off with some helpers to double check the security of the palisade's stake wall and to ensure that the moat was free of debris. Elfgifu had been told to go to the kitchen and help prepare for the night's feast. The girls were relieved of their job of salting the meat. They sat with other young women and children outside the kitchen, cutting and peeling turnips and parsnips in great quantities. Godfrew had been puzzled by the root crops, as he knew there was no plough land at the holding and precious little elsewhere in Earl Edric's lands. Dagobert dismissed the question, saying something about a donation from a local Norman.

Godfrew and his men had just come back inside from checking the moat when a guard in the watch tower called out that a rider had broken cover on the hill.

Dagobert grabbed his helmet and ran toward the paddock holding the horses "Get the mounts out boys, get them out." He turned his head and yelled over his shoulder: "House carls, man the walls. Albricht, Clunn, Turvey, Wulf: grab your gear and get mounted. We go to meet the Earl." The men did as they were told. Dagobert must have spoken to the stable boys earlier, as they had saddled up only those horses needed. As they rode out of the staggered gate, Dagobert looked across at Godfrew. "Wulf, where is your mail coat? I can't see it under your shirt."

Godfrew quickened the dark pony's gait to get alongside. "It is still with the blacksmith. He had promised to have it ready by now, but it is still not finished."

"He will be. He knows armour comes first. I will remind him of what can be done with those tongs of his. Your coat will be with you by tomorrow, I can promise. Still, it is too late for today. I just hope Earl Edric doesn't notice. He expects everything to be done right. Now," he looked at the other riders, "remember to let me get ahead. Keep ten horse lengths behind. After Earl Edric and the ladies have joined me, fall in behind as we all ride past. Got it?" He looked to them for confirmation. "And Turvey, try not to let your horse fart this time as the Earl rides past." Turvey went red and the others all laughed.

Ahead, on the ridge of the hill, riders were emerging and lining up just short of the tree line. Already there were far more than Godfrew had seen at Martinsfield ... and still they came. Dagobert had spurred ahead. The others from the holding fell in behind, each rider carrying a spear. Godfrew felt uncomfortable with his spear, as he rarely used the weapon and never from horseback. As they reached a spear's throw from the ranked horsemen, Dagobert stopped. The horsemen had finished disgorging from the trees. All waited. The horses stomped and chewed their bits. Eventually, laughter could be heard—women's laughter, with the occasional cracked addition of Earl Edric's. Still they waited. Then the Earl rode out with a lady riding on either side and another one to the rear. Dagobert nudged his mount and rode slowly toward the Earl. A sword's length apart, they all halted.

"Ah, Dagobert, what a delight to be home again. The perfect end to a perfect hunt. Would you not agree, ladies?"

"Indeed, my Lord, but the day is not ended, so perhaps we may find more perfection yet." Goda answered for them all.

"You always are full of promises, my precious jewel. Come, Dagobert, let us go and greet my wife. I am sure she will be delighted to see me." Dagobert turned his horse and led the party toward the holding. Before he fell into place in the escort, Godfrew noticed that wagons were now emerging on the road through the trees—heavy ox-carts, laded with goods. As each wagon started down the slope, horsemen fell in alongside it.

Dagobert paced his horse to that of the ox wagons, so the procession proceeded at a very leisurely pace. Once they came through the staggered gateway and into the holding, things moved very quickly. Edric and the ladies went to the front of the long house where Lady Gondul was waiting, but everyone else dismounted and passed on their mounts to the young boys waiting nearby. As the wagons came in, they were assigned to a storehouse. The men started to unload them and stack the booty away. Godfrew ended up with a party unloading barrels of ale and cider. After four wagon loads, Godfrew gave up trying to keep track of how much drink they had handled. It seemed to be enough for a small town rather than a manor. By the end of the day, the storehouse was full and Godfrew's back was breaking. Having a stiff knee had got him out of the task of rolling the tun and half-tun barrels down the cart tail and into the storehouse. It was a task fraught with danger that had seen two men slightly injured. Godfrew had been given the job of lifting the quarter-tun barrels from off the top of the larger barrels and 'walking' them to the sides where others were waiting to carry them on their shoulders. Once his job was finished, Godfrew wandered over to the gate.

When he had come to Lydbury, Godfrew had wondered why it encompassed so much land when it seemed to have such a small number of folk living there. Now the place was full. As he stood by the gate, he could see large herds of cattle, sheep, goats and horses filling the valley. The animals were being looked after by the boys of the holding. Obviously, all the men had been drafted into the heavier task of unloading the wagons. A glint caught Godfrew's eye near the tree line. He realised that some of the men were still armed and watching the roads and the passes into the valley. Nothing was being left to chance.

"Slacking, Master Wulf? That is not like you."

Godfrew turned and found Dagobert by his shoulder, sweat tricking down his face and dripping from his chin. "From the fact that all knew what to do, I assume that this is not a rare occurrence, Master Reeve." Godfrew put his hands to his back and eased the tight muscles, silently praying that he would have no reoccurrence of his earlier problems.

"Often enough, though, with all the goings on elsewhere. Last year was pretty quiet. Mind, with things shaping up as they are at present, we are going to need this lot." Dagobert caught Godfrew's raised eyebrow. "Not for a siege. Oh, no. Most of this will be to restock and replenish hamlets and smaller holdings that the Earl's enemies have devastated." He slapped Godfrew's back and propelled him back into the holding. "If only it was as easy to store and then restock the places with folk!" Dagobert guided Godfrew to one of the holding paddocks. "Now this one is an easy one. Just wait until those fellows there call, then join in and drive the cattle to the chute. There is to be a big feast tonight. If we are to have properly cooked meat—and God help us if the Earl thinks it isn't—we have to complete the butchering shortly." Dagobert left Godfrew with some other men, including the short, dark youth who had taken him to Edric back in Martinsfield.

"Wulf, isn't it?" the youth hung over the wicker fence, leaning on his hands with a straw bobbing in his mouth.

"That's right. You are?"

"Nathan."

"Nathan?"

"My father was a priest, my mother a nun, so a scriptural name was natural, I suppose." Nathan spat a chewed piece of straw into the dust. "Know how to work cattle?"

"A bit. I know more about horses." Godfrew joined Nathan and the others leaning on the fence.

"I wouldn't have guessed that from the look of your scrawny nag." Nathan smirked. So did his companions. Godfrew noticed that they did not have a full set of teeth amongst them.

"Looks aren't everything, as I am sure your mother kept reassuring you."

Nathan sharpened his look at Godfrew, but once he saw that Godfrew had meant it as a jest, he roared out laughing,

The Gates of Hell

disturbing the nearby cattle. On seeing Nathan laugh, the others joined in. "I can see, Wulf, that you have a sharp wit. But be careful! Many here have sharp swords. Often they strike first, then see the joke afterwards."

"Or your guts," a big blond bear pushed past and went to a fence post where he proceeded to urinate, spraying the post up and down, marking the spot much as a dog would.

"You would never get the joke anyway, Gavin the Slow-Witted."

Gavin did his breeches up and walked back to Nathan. Grabbing him by the shoulders he started to shake him like a terrier with a rat. Nathan reached behind his back and started to pull out a double-edged dagger. Before he could use it, voices called out asking for more cattle to be driven in for killing. Gavin kissed Nathan on the forehead and put him down. "Till next time, little one."

"I look forward to it, bear's breath." To Godfrew's surprise, everyone laughed, then vaulted over the fence and started to drive the cattle. Being stiff from the earlier work, Godfrew climbed the fence and joined them.

The cattle could smell the blood and did not want to enter the chute. The men smote the animals on their rumps with the flats of their swords and yelled out loudly. Godfrew did not carry a sword and his saxe was too short to use, so he contended himself with yelling and waving his arms. Fortunately, the butchers only wanted five animals, as it was very hard to get any into the chute. When the last steer went into the race, Gavin and another man pulled a gate closed behind it and stopped it from trying to back out of its date with death.

The stench of killing hung over the area. As an animal was dispatched and dragged away to be cut up, the wicker barrier behind it was pulled out of the way by unseen hands. The next animal was forced forward and the barrier was slid back into place. As each animal went into the killing yard, the one behind became more and more reluctant to go forward. No amount of blows could force the last steer forward. In the end, a heated rod was brought and used on the creatures rear to get it to move. As it was dispatched by the blacksmith by hitting it with a pole-axe, Godfrew went into the yard. He was used to animal slaughtering, both at his home holding

157

and in the local villages, but it did not prepare him for what he saw here. How many animals had been killed was hard to say, but there had been many. Steaming skins hung over the fencing. Buckets of thickening blood were continually taken away and new ones brought in by men in dirty, blood-splattered clothing. Full-gutted carcasses hung on pole spits. Joints of meat—still dripping blood—hung by hooks from racks tended by small boys whose job was to shoo away the ever present flies. Buckets overflowed with offal. Guts hung over parts of the fence nearest the kitchen where maids took them, squeezed them empty, then washed them clean in baths of blood-clotted water. Barrows were filled with stomach contents and wheeled away to the midden heap. Everywhere, there was blood. The ground turned to mud with it. No battleground was ever as bad as this.

Overseeing the carnage was a big, brawny man who stood a good two hands taller than everyone else. First, he was slitting the throat of a bull that had not been killed by the blow from the blacksmith's pole-axe, then he was helping to dismember a carcass. Next, he was chasing up the men with the barrows to get the chewed and partly digested grass out of the way. Then, he was seen chastising a youth for nicking a pelt he was skinning. Godfrew wanted to continue watching, fascinated by the organised chaos, but the smell was getting to him, so he went off in search of his wife. He found her slicing and washing beans.

"I will see you later, Wulf. I have too much to do here and I will be in trouble if I don't get this lot done." Reaching up, she kissed him on the cheek. "Not that I will see much of you tonight. Whilst you are eating and drinking, I will be still preparing the food."

"The wait will make the meeting so much sweeter."

"Not tonight, it won't. Sleep will be all that I will be thinking of."

Godfrew left Elfgifu to her work and went to prepare himself for the feast.

* * *

The heat in the hall was stifling. All the windows had been unshuttered to get the air flowing, but it was still unbearably

The Gates of Hell

hot. Godfrew sat at the end of the hall, as befitted a new member of the earl's host. Although the feast was but a couple of hours old, most of the men were already drunk. Ale, cider and mead flowed like water. Godfrew's head swam, but more from the heat than the drink. After a hard days work, he was hungry and wanted to keep his food, not spew it up like the fool opposite who had had his head rubbed into his own vomit by those on either side of him. Whilst there was noise and drunken banter in the hall, all was serene at the top table on the dais. There, Earl Edric sat in state with his wife, the Lady Gondul, at his side. Their golden head bands glittered in the torch light. Gondul occasionally sipped wine and water from a heavily decorated gold cup, but Edric drank only the herbal drink prepared for him by the dark Goda. Neither the Earl or his Lady ate anything. Godfrew was very aware of the contrast between the tranquillity of the top table and the noisy mayhem at the tables below. He also noticed that it was only on the top table that there were any women. Even the serving at the other tables was being done by men. These well-scrubbed, tidy serfs were being very careful not to upset or spill anything on their betters. Once the meat and vegetable dishes were finished, sweetmeats were brought in. Still, the top table did not eat. After the sweetmeats, fresh fruit was served, but the Earl and his company still abstained while the host in the hall sat back, stomachs full, drinking horns and mugs overflowing. The men belched and picked their teeth with the points of their eating knives. When a drum started beating, Godfrew stopped what he was doing and looked toward the entrance door to the great hall from whence the sound came. Gradually, the hall fell silent and the sound of the drum got louder. A procession entered the hall. At its head was a drummer. Behind the drummer was a roasted goat on a spit. The spit was borne on the shoulders of two warriors in full armour. The goat's carcass still had its head and the head had not been skinned. Behind the goat came a procession of prisoners chained together, escorted by more warriors in armour. The last warrior was very tall and broad. Godfrew recognised him as the butcher who directed the slaughter yard.

The procession halted in front of the dais. Earl Edric beckoned the goat bearers up and they placed the roast carcass

Woden's Wolf

on the table in front of him and his wife. At another signal, the prisoners were lined up facing the Earl. Behind them, others had entered the hall carrying a wooden frame, which they set up in front of the hearth. Although the prisoners could hear the frame being brought in and erected, they dared not look to see what was happening, as any movement brought them a swift smack from one of the escort. Godfrew's table companion belched contentedly and then leaned over to whisper in Godfrew's ear: "The Lady Gondul's hearth troops." He gave another belch, smelling of mead and roast mutton. "Now the entertainment starts."

Earl Edric watched the erection of the frame. Once he was sure that it was finished, he addressed the prisoners in Welsh. "Now who else, other than the Troop Captain, speaks Breton? None? Then you may all sit down." Only one man, a thick set, dark-haired man in dusty torn under clothing sat. Although Godfrew recognised the language as Welsh, it sounded flat—like English— lacking the musical intonation normal with the Welsh tongue. It marked the Earl as a fluent, but not a native speaker.

"Goshawk." Edric snapped his fingers and his chaplain came forward. "Tell them to sit down. Then tell the captain to stand up again."

"The Earl says for you to squat in the dirt like the pigs that you are, except you, sir Captain. God help you, he wants to have words with you." Goshawk translated in his best French.

Edric turned his head slightly and looked full in the Captain's face "So, my friend, only you speak the Cymry tongue," he said in flat Welsh.

"I can follow you, Lord Earl, if you speak slowly. Breton and Cymry are very alike, but not quite the same." The Captain was standing, but had to stoop as the chain connecting him to his fellow prisoners did not have much slack in it.

"I will try. I do so hate to be rude. Please forgive me if I talk too fast." Goda ran a knife along the back of the roast goat and peeled the crisp skin back. "Now that I have established that your friends only speak French, I can speak more freely with you. I wish to know about the defenses at Hereford and Shrewsbury ... not the general things ... I know that already from my own visits... but the more intimate details and little local wrinkles. I am sure you know the sort of thing I am after."

"I know little and what I do know, I won't tell," the Captain stared hard into Edric's eyes, trying to read his thoughts.

"Now there's a pity, or maybe not." Goda cut a thin sliver of meat from the back of the goat, rolled it with her knife, then speared it. "The problem with hearing the tale from only one source is that you often don't get all the details." Goda held the meat in front of Edric's mouth. He extended his tongue and pulled it in. Edric chewed the flesh slowly and thought. Having resolved what he was going to do, he smiled. "You are a brave man, perhaps braver than you realise. I am a connoisseur of brave men, you understand. I think you are right: you won't tell me what I want to know. So I won't waste time asking you. My wife gets bored if things become repetitive. I have decided to leave the questioning to the others here, your French friends. I will use you as an example to encourage them to open their hearts to me." Goda started to cut another thin slice of meat from the goat. This time, she offered it to the Lady Gondul, who closed her eyes and opened her mouth, allowing Goda to put her knife inside and deposit the flesh. Edric watched his wife with amusement before continuing. "Now, dear Captain, I really should introduce you to Wendlewulf. You have a lot in common, as he is the Captain of my wife's very own hearth troops. You have heard of those famous lovers who can make just one act of passion last all night? Rumour has it that you French often claim such prowess. Well our Wendlewulf is just like that, a lover of the flesh. Only he is much more physical, as you will see, or should I say feel. But why should I ruin your surprise. You have understood what I have said? I didn't speak too fast? Good. Now, to prevent you from lapsing into French, a most barbarous tongue, if I might say so, I will have to ask you to wear a little mask. Bear with me, please."

Before the Breton Captain could say a word, two of Gondul's hearth troop kicked away his knees, sending him sprawling. Another warrior jammed a metal mask over the man's face, pulled the sides together and dropped a pin in the clasp at the back. When the Captain tried to yell out in protest, all that could be heard was a muffled roar. That seemed appropriate to the assembly, as the mask was designed to look like a bear's head. The man next to Godfrew nudged him in the ribs: "Bear mask. Very droll, don't you think? Isn't it? Oh, you don't speak Welsh? I only know a little myself." With that, the man closed his eyes and slid under the trestle. At the head table, Lady Gondul had opened her eyes and was chewing the goat flesh with relish.

Without looking away from the masked man, Earl Edric called his chaplain forward again. "Goshawk, ask our guests if they would be so kind as to turn around and face the frame. I want them to see something they may find interesting. I would prefer that they remain seated."

Goshawk went to the edge of the dais. In the meanwhile, Gondul's hearth troops had unshackled the Breton and were dragging the struggling man toward the frame. "All right, you pox ridden flea bags. The Earl wants you to turn around and watch what is going to happen to your Captain. Lift one buttock off the ground and he will castrate you and make you swallow your own balls."

The assembly roared with laughter at the antics of the Frenchmen as, still chained together, they tried to turn around without getting off the ground. Meanwhile, Edric raised a finger and beckoned Goshawk over. When the priest stood at the earl's side, Edric indicated that he should kneel. Once Goshawk had complied, Edric spoke to him in a low voice so that only he could hear: "Now, correct me if I am wrong. I get the suspicion that you are not translating directly what I am saying. I know I don't speak French, so I may be completely wrong in this, but it seems to me that for every one word I say, you say two. This, together with the antics of our French guests, indicates that you are playing games with me. My beloved confessor, you above all others, know what I am like. If you are playing me false, you know what to expect. For this offence, should it continue ... and here I do allow you to repent and make amends as should all Christian men ... I would expect to change you from a chicken to a capon. And Goshawk..."

"Lord Earl."

"... I would ask my wife to oversee the matter."

Goshawk swallowed hard. "Lord Earl."

The Breton was tied and spread-eagled across the vertical frame. Additional ties ran from the base of the bear mask to

The Gates of Hell

the top of the frame to prevent him from moving his head. The butcher walked around, checking that his men had secured the prisoner correctly. Satisfied, he stood back and looked to the head table for instruction.

Edric took his time to consider what he wanted to do. The noise level rose until the Earl beckoned Goshawk over and gave him instructions, then all fell silent again. Goshawk went to the edge of the dais and called out in a loud voice: "Captain of the French troops, my Lord Earl Edric wishes to know what you can tell him of Hereford and Shrewsbury. Hearth troop leader, give the Earl his reply." The masked man made growling noises that could have been anything.

The butcher stood at his side and made a show of listening. "Nothing that we don't know already, my Lord."

"Nothing that we don't know already my Lord," translated Goshawk for the benefit of the prisoners.

Earl Edric took another proffered thin slice of meat from Goda and slowly chewed it. Goda then did the same for Gondul. When he had finished the meat, Edric ran his tongue over his teeth. "That is bad news, Captain. What shall we do now, I wonder. Shall I show you my etchings, beloved wife?"

The Lady Gondul sank back into her chair and wriggled a trifle on the seat before chewing enthusiastically on her mouthful of goat meat. Despite the fact that he had not looked her way, nor had Edric ever taken his eyes off of the trussed Captain, the Earl assumed his wife's agreement. "I think it would be polite that we make the dear Captain more comfortable. It is so hot in here. Perhaps it would be best if our guest was allowed to strip off." The hearth troopers on either side of the frame cut the Breton's clothes off, leaving his hairy body exposed and naked. At the top table, Lady Gondul chewed even quicker. "Wendlewulf, my wife would like to see the etchings, if you would be so kind." The Lady opened her mouth and waited for more meat to be inserted in it by Goda.

The butcher inclined his head to the Earl, then looked to one of the hearth troop, who went outside. The trooper reappeared shortly bearing a stone bottle that must have held about a gill. The butcher took the bottle carefully and removed the cork stopper. Smoke drifted out. Walking behind the Breton, the butcher then tipped the contents of the bottle over the man's shoulder. The liquid ran down his chest

Woden's Wolf

and into his groin. The flowing liquid smoked as it coursed over the flesh, causing it to blister and pop. The man gave a muffled roar and strained against his restraints, struggling as much as his bonds would allow him. As the fluid reached his genitals, he gave several spasmodic jerks and then sagged.

Earl Edric considered what had happened. Refusing more meat, he took a sip of the herbal drink from the cup that Goda held to his lips. When he had finished, the small, dark lady dabbed his lips with a napkin. Once she had completed the task, the Earl came to a decision. "Enough of the acid etching. Neutralise it and then revive him. Goshawk, when he comes around, ask the same question as before."

Wendlewulf the butcher threw water over the Breton. All around the hall, the man's laboured breathing could be heard. When he came to, the muffled sounds he was making got louder. Goshawk coughed, then made his pronouncement. "Captain of the French troops, my Lord Earl Edric wishes to know what you can tell him about Hereford and Shrewsbury. Hearth troop leader, give the Earl his reply."

Again Wendlewulf stood at his victim's side, pretending to listen. "Nothing we don't already know, my Lord."

"Oh, dear, that is most unfortunate. Maybe something more drastic is called for, much as I regret it. Goshawk translate and remember my promise to you."

"Oh, dear, that is most unfortunate. Much as the Earl regrets it, something more drastic is called for." Goshawk turned to the Earl. "It is what you said, my Lord. I only changed it from the first to the second person."

Edric waived the priest silent. "Wendlewulf, your specialty, I think."

Wendlewulf checked the tightness of the bonds. Satisfied, he pulled out a small saxe. Skillfully, he cut the skin and muscle around the shoulder joint. With a quick wrench, he dislocated the joint and pulled the arm off. Taking a fire brand held by an assistant, he cauterised the wound. The Breton passed out again. The man's weight was now being held partly by the neck straps of the mask. Wendlewulf indicated to his assistant to revive the victim and then looked to the top table for instructions.

The Gates of Hell

"My wife did not see all of that, I'm afraid. Perhaps you would be so kind as to repeat it, but first, Goshawk, the usual, if you please."

"Captain of the French troops, my Lord Earl Edric wishes to know what you can tell him about Hereford and Shrewsbury. Hearth troop leader, give the Earl his reply."

Again Wendlewulf stood at his victim's side, pretending to listen. "Nothing we don't already know my Lord."

"Then continue."

"The Earl says to continue."

Wendlewulf removed the Breton's other arm. Lady Gondul wriggled in her chair and breathed heavily. When Wendlewulf's assistant revived the Breton this time, the noises issuing from the mask were broken and had no flow to them. "Wendlewulf, I don't think the Breton captain is as brave or as strong as he led us to believe. It may be time to put him out of his misery. I am perturbed though, as I heard he was a virgin. Now as you know, Wendlewulf, it is against the law of the realm to execute a virgin. I wonder what we should do. Well, looking at him at present, he does seem to be excited at the thought of loosing his virginity. Shall we oblige him, dear wife?" Gondul gave a short gasp and started panting. "Quite. Unfortunately, Wendlewulf, the poor man looks as though he needs a hand in this matter. I shall send my wife's maid to assist." Edric tapped on the arms of his chair and a dull-eyed young maid with no breasts shuffled forward. "Get my Lady's toy, the one she sometimes lets you share. Quickly now, child, or I shall be cross." The girl shuffled out of sight behind the rear curtain and returned with a polished cow horn, the end of which had been cut off. "Good girl, take it to the nice man down there, the handsome Wendlewulf. Quickly now, child. Goshawk!"

"Captain of the French troops, my Lord Earl Edric wishes to know what you can tell him about Hereford and Shrewsbury. Hearth troop leader, give the Earl his reply."

Again Wendlewulf stood at his victim's side, pretending to listen. "Nothing we don't already know my Lord."

"Then proceed."

"The Earl says to proceed."

As the maid came down the hall, Godfrew saw Wendlewulf's assistant heating an iron bar in the hearth fire.

Woden's Wolf

He guessed at what was to happen. Feeling sick, he made for the door.

A warrior blocked the way. "Not leaving are you? I'm not sure the Lord Edric would appreciate that."

Godfrew started gagging. "Drink, too much to ..." he started heaving and the warrior quickly made way for him. As soon as the cold air hit Godfrew, he spewed up all that he had eaten. His stomach gave such strong spasms that he had to grab a wooden buttress for support. Tears were running down his face. No sooner had one spasm finished than another started—and each time the muffled bellows of the Breton commenced. It took a long time for the bellows from the hall to cease—by which time Godfrew's stomach felt as if it had been kicked in. Taking a deep breath, he looked around. Propped up against the outside wall of the hall were a few drunks, but otherwise he was alone. Remembering Earl Edric's temper, he made his way back in. The stench of burnt flesh hung in the air and Godfrew's stomach started to heave again. It was with difficulty that he made his way back to his place on the bench.

Wendlewulf's men had cut the remains of the Breton down from the frame and were dragging it outside, followed by a pack of hunting dogs which they were having difficulty in keep off. In front of the frame, the other prisoners sat terrified, unable to move. As Godfrew sat down, he glanced at the dais and saw Edric looking at him.

"Goshawk, advise our treasured guests that they will be taken outside and assigned their own personal confessor. Should I be unhappy with what they say, I shall hold another 'interview' tomorrow night and it will be their turn to be the featured act."

Goshawk glanced at the Earl and decided to take a chance. "Tell him what he wants, or it will be your turn tomorrow." He turned to the Earl. "Anything else, my Lord?"

"Nothing more for now. Thank you, Goshawk." Edric stood up. So did the Lady Gondul. They moved from their seats and headed toward their curtained sleeping area. Goda walked between them and the other ladies who had been with the Earl at Martinsfield. As they neared the doorway, they all held hands and went in together. Two of Edric's hearth troops pulled the heavy curtains over the doorway, then went through as well. As the little slack eyed maid went to follow, she was turned away by another of Edric's hearth troop. Wendlewulf beckoned her to come to him.

The party over, drunken warriors staggered off to find somewhere to sleep for the night or slept where they had fallen. Godfrew left for his sleeping hut and the comforting sanity of his wife's arms.

* * *

The heat from the previous night's feast still filled the long house, even in Earl Edric's bedroom. The room was quite large. Along the walls were windows covered in thin, uncured animal skins, but the windows were wide open and the wall hangings were pulled back. The wall hangings were beautifully embroidered, but unlike those that had graced the walls of his parent's holding at Garrat, the scenes on them were of naked women in unusual poses rather than the martyred saints of England. Despite his best intentions, Godfrew had problems not looking at them. Edric was still in bed, sitting up with his back supported by a heavy bolster. The bed cover was an embroidered sack that was puffed up, obviously filled with down from the eider duck such as the warriors from Iceland always took with them on campaign. From the wall post—above the Earl's head—hung an iron ring. From that hung leather thongs. A similar ring with thongs was set in the floor at the foot of the bed. Edric beckoned Godfrew over. After last night, Godfrew did not know what to expect, especially as the Earl had seen him coming back into the hall after the 'interview' had been completed. That morning, on the way from the sleeping hut to the long house, Godfrew had seen the bodies of the Normans, hanging from the palisade. Some were so freshly hanged that urine was still dripping from them. Godfrew nervously wrung his hands, a habit of his father's that he had sworn never to imitate.

"Cold, Wulf? I find it most bracing, at present." Earl Edric slapped his naked chest. Edric's chest was covered with a mat of light golden hair, except where it was marked by a scar. There were many of those—old scars of bunched white flesh, newer scars of tender pink, and a very recent one that was still purple and still had brown scabs attached to it.

Godfrew was surprised at the variety of colour in the hair of Edric. The hair on his head was a white gold. His body hair was a light, yellow-gold. His moustaches were a bright, yellow-gold, except at the ends, where they were waxed. There, they became a reddish gold, topped with a beard of rich honey gold. The Earl must have realised what Godfrew was thinking, because he laughed and pulled the hair on his chest. "They say, Wulf—those that have seen—that you have almost no hair on your body at all! How can you keep warm without hair? Perhaps that is why you are cold now!" Edric threw back the covers and moved to the edge of the bed. One of the hearth troops put his head outside the curtain and called a name which Godfrew did not catch. Within a minute, Goda and the other two ladies came in. Goda put a mug of steaming herbal drink and a plate of white bread on the side table whilst the other two dressed the Earl. Over his scared chest was pulled a fine undershirt of saffron yellow. Edric lifted his feet off the ground and knee length breeches of the same colour were pulled over his legs. As he stood up, a lady pulled them up and secured them with a soft, light-brown leather belt that was tied rather than buckled. Edric sat down on the bed again and the other lady pulled very fine stockings over his legs and secured them with a garter of the same soft leather.

Godfrew recognised the material that the Earls' clothes were made of ... silk from Damascus. In the year before the invasions, Godfrew had accompanied Harold Godwinson—then Earl of Wessex—to Northampton. There, he had met the earls Edwin and Morcar. Morcar had deposed Harold's brother, Tostig, as Earl of Northumbria. Godfrew had been but a young warrior with no experience. His family was just able to claim thane right. His family owed loyalty to Harold Godwinson through a tangled web of indebtedness to the Danish Royal House of Knute—through the Earl's mother, Knute's step sister—and thus to Harold. But Harold had sought him out and spoken to him with encouragement. Harold had worn Damascus silk.

Earl Edric stood up, took the drink from the table and slurped a mouthful. "Ah, wonderful! Whatever would I do without you, Goda and my other ladies? Thank you. Now, if you would, leave us. I am grateful." The ladies left and Edric

The Gates of Hell

went back to sitting up in his bed. "Well, young Wulf, though with those silver locks ..." He drank some more. "... now where was I? Ah, yes. What are we going to do with you, Wulf? I had thought to have you in my hearth troop, but I don't think our ... shall we say 'ways'... would suit you. I suspect that last night was not to your taste. Was it?"

"No, Lord Edric." Godfrew looked at the floor expecting the worst.

"No? Well, it's not for everyone. Tell me what you can do. You are a thane, yes?"

"Just, my Lord." Godfrew now found the courage to look up. "I am trained as an axeman. I have always worked with a shield bearer. I can use a sword and shield, but the axe suits me better."

"Your eye?" interrupted the Earl.

"My eye. Not having the eye makes me vulnerable on the left, my shield arm. I can use a spear, but, again, it is not my best weapon."

"You carry a saxe. I assume you can use it and don't just carry it for the sake of tradition." Edric downed the contents of the mug and wiped his mouth with the back of his hand.

"I can use it. In fact, I am quite good with it. I am not afraid to get close to an enemy when I have to. I'm not very fast, so I prefer to be crafty."

"Excellent." Edric twirled the ends of his moustaches. "I know just the job for you. Lead one of my wolf packs. Work ahead of me, or where people think I should be. Cause trouble, but avoid pitched battles. Keep moving, but always be ready to come to me when I call. You can read and write?"

"English and a little Latin."

"Excellent. I can't understand those who either cannot or will not learn those skills. As my old father used to say, 'If it was good enough for King Alfred the Great to read and write, it's good enough for you.' But ... and here is the tricky one ... can you read the Runes?"

"Norse ones, yes, but only some South Saxon ones. I was taught by an Icelander."

"Good enough." Edric got off the bed and went to an oil lamp hanging from the sloping wall. He wiped his finger on the wick and came back. Taking a piece of bread from the side plate, he used his oily finger to write on the bread. "See that, Wulf? If you get a letter from me with those Runes at the bottom, then you know the message to be true. If the Runes are not there, kill the messenger and get out fast." Having said that, he took the bread and ate it. When he had finished, he took Godfrew to the door way and showed him out. He spotted Godfrew looking at the red marks on his wrist. "Ah, those? Well that is another game of mine that would not be to your taste. Good hunting with your pack, Wulf." The Earl turned and went back into his room. The hearth trooper outside moved Godfrew on.

Godfrew sat in the trees and watched. Smoke curled from the cottages as wives prepared the evening meal, while the hamlet lazed in the sun—unsuspecting. Children played in the dirt or tried to catch a goat to ride.

"That tall boy. He has some 'go'. He must have run a mile trying to get that Billy goat. Mind, when he does, he won't like it. I can smell that Billy from here, and I ain't got a good nose!" Dunstan, big and solid, spoke with the same flat, clipped, north Surrey accent as Godfrew.

Dunstan spoke often of his time with the Godwinsons: of Swein, Harold, Tostig and Wufnoth. Dunstan was a talker. He spoke of the time in Ireland when Earl Godwin and his sons were exiled, of the trouble between Swein and his cousin Beorn, of the wars against the Welsh when he served with Harold before he became king, and of much more. He talked when others were interested. He talked when they were not. The others joked that he even talked when he was alone. Godfrew had verified this when he heard him talking when no one else was around.

Clunn, almost the exact physical opposite of Dunstan, spat on the ground in front of his feet, then kicked dust to cover the gob. "You haven't got a good nose, our Dunstan. In fact, you haven't got a good anything. Even your willie is shrivelled." Clunn smiled a yellow-toothed smile, his thick beard a blend of black and dark auburn.

"Yes, but even shrivelled, it's more than twice the size of yours, you little black rat."

"That's 'cos I put it to constant use. It's getting worn down." Clunn pulled his threadbare, battered-pointed wool hat down over his eyes and settled down to pass the time away in comfort. "I bet it gets more use than yours does."

"Ah, maybe now, with my current missus. When I was living with my lovely Adia, things were different. She loved me, that one did ... would do anything for me. I just wish I hadn't been so stupid and started chasing my current missus. I still hear from her sometimes, you know ... my first missus, Adia.

I'm sure she would have me back, it's that evil old father of hers that's ..."

"Dunstan," Godfrew stopped Dunstan from telling the story of his life for the umpteenth time since they had started this trip a month ago. "Do me a favour and check young Ragnor and Tosti. Make sure they are watching where the village men are and where the animals are kept. Check to see that they are out of sight."

"Right. Oh, Wulf. One thing."

"What?"

"You know... thing, Stanley."

"What about Stanley?"

"Thing ... you know, is he supposed to be watching as well or, you know ... thing?"

Godfrew had soon learnt that all conversations with Dunstan involved an element of guess work. "He is with Bjorn the Wainwright and Dagobert the Lathe-maker, getting things ready."

"Dagobert? Oh yes, thing, Dragon's-breath." Dunstan gave his slow smile "Fancy having a nick-name of Dragon's-breath. Serves him right for eating onions all the time, but fancy having to live with that name."

"Fancy being called Dunstan," chipped in Clunn. "Dirty stones, maybe, if you washed them now and again you would be called Britstan. Maybe that was why your first wife left you ... because you never washed your stones!" Clunn stayed where he was, but braced himself in case Dunstan made a dive for him.

"Dunstan." Godfrew watched the big Surrey man. "Leave him and see to the others. Go now."

Dunstan moved off with an occasional backward glance. "Dirty little rat, he's only got one stone to wash anyway. If he doesn't watch his tongue, he won't have any stones to wash."

"I wore it out, which is more than can be said for yours!" Clunn called after the Surrey man.

Godfrew watched Dunstan go, then grabbed Clunn's beard, taking a handful of whiskers on either cheek "Clunn, you evil rat, save the fighting for the Normans." Godfrew shook Clunn's face by the whiskers. Clunn smiled and laughed. Godfrew pulled his beard a bit harder: "You really are a rat."

The Wolfpack

"Normans, Saxons, wogs ... who cares who the fight is against. I'm only in it for the fun."

Godfrew noticed that Clunn's teeth were not only yellow, but also pointed like a rat's. "When you are with me, you fight only who I say you fight. Do you understand, rat?"

"Squeak, squeak, Master Wulf."

Godfrew let him go and sat back on his haunches. "Do you only have one stone, or is that just another taunt?"

"Only one. It's all I need. Didn't wear it out, though. Well, only in a way. I was a bit late in leaving when a certain house carl came home to perform his marital duties. He sort of insisted I left him with a keepsake."

"You can joke about it?"

"Well, I left him with another keepsake. That keepsake is five summers old this year. He thinks his wife was delivered three months early! Silly bastard."

"You really are a little rat."

"Into any little hole that presents itself, or any big hole, if it comes to that. I ain't fussy."

"God preserve us. Just behave yourself on this raid. I want confusion and alarm, not terror and men of mine leaving intimate bits and pieces behind."

Clunn picked up his fallen hat and replaced it. After getting his hat settled, Clunn nestled back into his bush. "Yes, Master Wulf. Anything you say, Master Wulf."

"Sweet dreams, Master Rat."

"Dirty dreams, Master Wulf."

Godfrew made his way back through the trees to the small clearing where Bjorn and the others were working on a hay wain. Bjorn looked up from his work. "Are you sure you want to do this, Wulf? There are other places around here we could do easier. It's an awful lot of trouble for such a poor place." Despite his seeming concern about the venture, Bjorn picked up another wooden dowel and hammered it into place with his leather mallet.

"Yes, this is the place. Earl Edric wants certain people harassed and I want to harass Normans. This place fits both bills." Godfrew lowered himself down by bending his knees and keeping his back straight.

"I supposed so." Bjorn hammered in another dowel. "Just seems a lot of work for very little return."

"Can I do that?" Stanley, bright eyed and eager as a puppy, held the final wooden dowel and put his hand out for the mallet.

"Oh, I think I'd better do it. I want it to be a proper job." Bjorn took the dowel and hammered it home "Yes, I suppose that will do." He stood back and ran his eye over the hay wain. "When do you want to go, Wulf?"

Godfrew looked up, shielding his eye against the sun with his hand. "Twilight."

"Seems a bit late to me. Dragon's-breath, what do you think?"

"Whatever the master says. It's his plan." Blond, amiable Dragon's-breath continued sharpening the edge of his sword with a whetstone.

"I think it's a good plan," added the still eager Stanley.

"You haven't been around long in this game. Leave it too late and you might as well not bother. I'm not sure why I am bothering this time. I've been on too many of these outings as it is. I have other things that interest me now. I should have given up raiding years ago." Bjorn started to collect his tools together and put them into his leather carry-all bag.

"The Earl told me that I would need a skilled man like you, Bjorn the wainwright," Godfrew remained squatting. "The next time, we may be all right on our own, but this time I need you."

"I suppose so. What nags have we got to pull this thing, Dragon's-breath?"

"I'd offer my horse, but she's a bit unused to pulling wains." Dunstan reappeared from the bushes where he had gone to relieve himself.

"I don't think that would be any good. Dragon's-breath?"

Bjorn dropped his bag on the ground just in front of Dragon's-breath who seemed to have drifted off into a world of his own. The strokes of the whetstone on his sword became an automatic movement.

"What? Oh, horses. Well, mine is used to pulling and I think Stanley's is too."

"Yes, mine is good with wagons and carts. In fact ..." Stanley started to say, but he was overridden by Bjorn.

"I suppose it will have to be my poor old nag again ... it is well past its time. When it dies, I won't replace it. I'll give up the raiding then." Bjorn wandered off in search of his horse.

Godfrew saw the disappointment in Stanley's young face. "Stanley, you can ride with me. It will be far better than having to hide in the false floor of the hay wain." Stanley rewarded Godfrew with a smile. "Dunstan." Godfrew turned to face the big man. "How goes it with the watchers?"

"Fine ... just fine. Those lazy beggars like sitting on their arses all day watching other people work. No, thing."

"Thing? Where are you going to go? I think you are too big for the false bottom. Can you drive a wain?"

"Yes, I can drive one all right. When I was with Earl Tostig on the last campaign, I drove for days. King Harold—or Earl Harold, as he was then—travelled down the coast by sea whilst his brother, Earl Tostig, came down the mountains. That was a campaign, that was. The wogs didn't know what hit 'em. Travelled light, we did."

"But you drove a wain?" Stanley was the only one of the band that could never get enough of Dunstan's battle stories, though even he shied away from the more convoluted tales of Dunstan's domestic problems.

"Most were on horse ... well, those stunted little ponies the wogs use. But we had to have some transport for the plunder. I must have travelled hundreds of miles. You should have seen the problems we had with those mountains. Why, one occasion ...."

"Dunstan." Godfrew broke the flow of words. "Finish the tale later. Check the lads and send one of them back for something to eat. When he returns, send the other. You can eat when they are both back on watch."

"Yes. Well... me ... I can never eat before a fight. Now Earl Tostig, he could eat a whole cow and never worry. Me ... I wait until it's all over. My guts, they play me up."

"Your guts play you up all right. They overhang your belt so much I wonder they don't trip you up at times." Dragon's-breath added his words of wisdom and then went back into his dream world.

"At least I've got guts, Dragon's-breath. I have yet to see yours." Dunstan went off to double check Ragnor and Tosti.

Dragon's-breath did not hear what had been said, being fully engrossed in sharpening his sword.

"Food. Stanley. Dragon's-breath. Bjorn." Godfrew made to the tail-gate of the hay wain, where a jug of cider, a wheel of cheese and some flat, coarse bread lay.

"Just a little bread." Bjorn tore a hand-sized piece off of the loaf and went off to sit with his back to the wain's wheel, where he commenced to morosely chew it.

"Not for me." Stanley was already pulling on a sheep-skin coat, wool inside. "Later, after it is over." He looked up from tying the coat with a large battered leather belt. "Nerves." He looked apologetic. "Sorry."

"We are all different," Godfrew reassured him. "Dragon's-breath? Food?" There was no reply from the man, so Godfrew left him in peace sharpening his sword.

"Food? Did I smell food?" Clunn forced his way through the bushes and joined Godfrew at the tail-board. "Cut me a bit piece of cheese."

"Rats like eating cheese?" joked Godfrew.

"Almost as much as suckling soft breasts. Now, a hunk of the bread if you please, Master Wulf." He took the proffered food. "Excellent. Cider?" The question was accompanied by a blast of cheese fragments as yellow as Clunn's teeth. "Cleans the pallet to make ready for the next taste." Clunn tipped the jug right back and a trickle of golden fluid escaped, running down his chin and into his beard. "Got any apples? No? Well maybe we'll get some from the hamlet tonight." He took another swig. "And maybe we will get other tasty morsels as well."

"Just remember what I said, Rat," Godfrew took the cider jug back, "and ease off the drink."

"Hardly wet my whistle. Hey, Dragon's-breath." Clunn nudged the man none too gently. "Sharpen my weapon, too?"

"If you wish." Dragon's-breath lay his own sword down and held out his hands for Clunn's. Clunn started to drop his breeches. "Oh, no, not that dirty old thing. If you kept it out of damp places, it wouldn't get so rusty."

"Rust?" Clunn looked into his breeches "Is that all it is? Thank God. I thought I had the French pox!"

The Wolfpack

"French pox will make your willie go green and yellow," informed Bjorn.

"Mine is green and yellow," insisted Clunn "I had it painted those colours so that any innocent maid seeing it lying alongside her would think it an adder."

"That would be an advantage, Rat?" asked Godfrew

"Of course. If she thinks it an adder, she would durst not move for fear of being bitten. Nor would she be surprised if it hid in a dark, damp place." Clunn cut off another piece of cheese and munched it with relish.

"How you can eat with the same hands that have touched that foul thing, I'll never know." Dragon's-breath picked up a piece of oily sheep skin and commenced to wipe his sword blade clean.

Ragnor Redhead slipped up to Godfrew and nodded his head toward the bread. "A little, Master Wulf. Enough to kill the butterflies."

Godfrew cut off a lump of bread and passed it to the lad. "You are all right about tonight?"

"I have been on raids before, but only to hold the horses. Yes, I will be all right. I just wish we could go now and not wait."

"I've already said that," interjected Bjorn who had taken the whetstone from Dragon's-breath and was sharpening his own sword with it.

"Gentlemen, we will go when we are ready ... and that is not now. Ragnor, you will be in the wain floor."

"Wain?"

"Wagon," interpreted Bjorn.

"The wain ... wagon ... has a false floor. You, Bjorn, Dragon's-breath, Clunn and Tosti will hide in there when we go to the hamlet."

"Don't worry, little redhead, I will be next to you, giving you courage," assured Clunn.

"Courage I will take. Any of your filthy tricks, I won't. Keep your hands and that smelly thing of yours away from me."

"Oh, thing?" mimicked Clunn in a poor representation of Dunstan's accent.

"You know what I mean, Rat."

"Oh, I hope to have better drains to scuttle up than yours, copper knob."

"Clunn! Remember what I said!" Godfrew's voice had a hard edge to it.

"Yes, Master Wulf. I remember." Clunn's smirk hinted that he may yet chose to ignore Godfrew, given the chance.

Godfrew got the distinct impression that Clunn was winding him up, so he left the band and sought out Dunstan and Tosti. They were watching the hamlet. The watchers were only a hundred paces away, but the trees and bushes were so dense that all sound of the others was gone. Dunstan sat behind a bush, his back against a tree, asleep. Tosti lay on his stomach at the very edge of the undergrowth.

Godfrew joined him. "How did you know it was me and not a Norman?"

"Because a Norman would be on a horse and he would not make half as much noise as you did, Master Wulf." Tosti, despite his Norse name, was dark with a beard and moustache that consisted of a few thin sprigs of hair kept in place by grease. "Have you been watching the hamlet too, Master Wulf?" Tosti kept his light, grey eyes on the hamlet and its folk.

"A little, Tosti." Godfrew wriggled further forward and squinted, trying to see clearly. Giving up, he took a fallen leaf, made a small hole in it and peered through the hole, using it to sharpen his distant vision. Tosti turned and watched. "A trick, Tosti, for those who lack your long sight."

"Ah, I see."

"Better than me no doubt."

Tosti giggled. "Indeed, Master Wulf. You know, you don't realise what a lot of activity people get up to in a day with so little result. I've been watching them." He indicated the hamlet and its population. "I've been watching them all morning and most of the afternoon. They have hustled and bustled about, but very little has been achieved. A bit of garden has been dug, some wood chopped, animals moved, washing done. But nothing important, nothing meaningful. Is life always like that I wonder?"

Godfrew rolled onto his back and closed his eyes. "You are wasted here. You should have joined a monastery and become a great philosopher priest."

"Ah, no. Ladies. I need ladies."

"In one so young?" Godfrew rolled back onto his stomach and observed the young man beside him. "You could not do without the ladies until you became a Bishop and could afford a mistress?"

"In these parts, Bishops have their mistresses, but priests have wives. Ask Nathan the house carl. Across the border, the Welsh clerics all marry. No, it's not being clergy. It's the spending of time thinking when I want excitement. I crave ladies and fighting—preferably both—one after the other and in no particular order. Hmm. I love the wrench in the guts when you get into a fight. Don't you, Master Wulf?" Tosti still kept his eyes on the hamlet.

"Sometimes, but not often. I always seem to come off worse for wear."

"And you have been chosen by Earl Edric the Wild to lead us?"

"I am still alive. Despite having two shires declare me outlaw, I am still free. I can't be that bad can I?"

"I hope not. Still, as long as it is exciting. We all have to die some day."

"But not today. Not if I can avoid it. My wife is with child. I fully intend to see it born. Go and get some food, Tosti. Stretch your legs. I will stay here with our sleeping friend, Dunstan, and keep watch."

The day slipped into evening. Godfrew watched the boy chase the Billy goat and ride it. He had also seen the boy get a thrashing from the goat herder when he caught him. Apart from that, all had been quite, except for Dunstan talking in his sleep. Now, with the light just fading, it was time to move. Godfrew gently kicked Dunstan, but nothing happened, so he shook him and the big man stirred.

"Adia, darling, I'm sorry." Dunstan reached out and started to embrace Godfrew. "I know the girl is having a baby, but I didn't mean to ..." Dunstan broke out of his dream with a start. "Wulf? Oh, I am sorry. I thought I was back in Mordon with thing."

"Sorry, Dunstan, only me. It's time to move. Come on." Dunstan got up and followed Godfrew back through the bushes to the hay wain. Bjorn had harnessed the horses and put them in the shafts. Dragon's-breath's heavy cart horse towered over Bjorn's. The two made an ill-matched pair.

Woden's Wolf

"Are you sure they will pull together, Bjorn? They look out of balance."

"Too late now. You should have said something earlier." Bjorn stood by the head of his nag. "I said I didn't think it was a good idea. We can still call it off. I know another place just over the way."

"That's one of Earl Edric's holdings," reminded Dunstan.

"Is it? Didn't use to be. Everything keeps changing. I should have given all this up years ago."

"It's Earl Edric's. So?" asked Clunn the Rat. "What's the problem? As long as there is killing to be done and women to be consoled."

"Clunn, my evil smelly rat. If you raided one of Edric the Wild's holdings he would be wild indeed. I believe he would remove not only your last precious gem, but he would cut up your pet adder. The time has come to move. Bjorn, never mind the horses, Dragon's-breath, stop sharpening your sword before you wear it all away. Clunn, slide into your rat hole. You too, Ragnor and Tosti." Godfrew strode to the tail gate and helped them all in. Seeing them settled, he pulled up the tail gate and slid the pins in place. "Dunstan, get this thing on the road. Come on, Stanley. Mount up. Just all look tired and worn out. We must not look a threat to anyone."

The hay wain lurched off. Dunstan had to pull continually to the right in order to hold Dragon's-breath's big mare in check. With the lowering sun shining behind them, they came out of the woods and travelled over half the way to the hamlet before they were seen. The goat herder saw them first and ran off calling out. They were only a few paces from the first of the mean cottages when the mounted men stopped them.

There were three of them. The leader was taller than the others. He was dressed as an Englishman and wore the long moustaches favoured by the English. When he spoke, it was with a heavy and thick French accent. "Say why you here." The leader had a boar spear which he had couched. On his left arm, he carried a light, rounded shield.

"Ah, Master." Godfrew rode slowly forward, stopping only when the spear was raised and aimed at his chest. "We've been sent forth by our master to try and find some feed for

The Wolfpack

his kine." Godfrew was good at accents and his Herefordshire one was faultless despite his short time in the district. "Would you have any you could spare him, Master?"

"I spare no one nothing." The Frenchman leaned forward and moved Godfrew's cloak out of the way with the point of his spear, obviously looking to see if there was a mail coat underneath. "Who your master."

"Thing, Master. My master be Thing."

"Thing? Who this thing?" The Frenchman turned to his companions: "Thing?"

"Could be Thingfirth. He is sometimes called Thing. Not to his face though, Master."

"No matter." The Frenchman faced Godfrew again. "No sale. You go way. Now."

"Water the horses? They're tired. At least, let us water the horses," Godfrew whined. "Please, Master? Water?"

The Frenchman looked at the horses. Bjorn's nag was in a lather. Dragon's-breath's horse was stomping and fidgeting in the shaft. "Water. Only water." He turned again to his companions. "Water only. You stay with them. Watch. Yes?"

"Yes, Master. We'll watch." The Frenchman rode off toward his hall, a building only a little better than the cottages of the hamlet. "All right you. You heard what the Master said. Water only. Follow us." The two remaining riders escorted the hay wain to the well and the stone trough in front of it. Stanley stood with the horses and watered them while Dunstan engaged the escort in conversation, a thing he was very good at. Godfrew walked to the rear of the wain and pulled the pins near the tailgate. The false floor dropped down at an angle and the concealed men slid out. The first thing that the escorts were aware of was falling, as Clunn cut the girth straps on their saddles and gave their feet an upward shove. Both of them fell to the ground. Dunstan and Stanley quickly dispatched them. Stanley grinned from ear to ear at his first kill.

"Dunstan, Bjorn. Get the stock." Godfrew reversed his cloak, pulling the wolf mask down over his face. "The rest of you come on."

"I don't know about leaving my pony. It's been good to me. There are years left in her yet."

"Take the bloody thing and the wain. I'm after cattle. Cattle is thing." Dunstan grabbed an unsaddled horse and, with an agility he shouldn't have had with his bulk, vaulted onto its back.

"Money," clarified Bjorn. "I suppose I could cut the traces. I suppose I had better bring Dragon's-breath's horse too." Bjorn used his knife to free the horses and Dragon's-breath's ran away to find her master, joined by the dark pony. "I'll tie Stanley's horse up, just in case."

"Come on, Bjorn. Thing!"

"Indeed. Thing, Dunstan. Thing."

Clunn and Tosti headed for a small chapel, but the rest stayed with Godfrew as he made for the Frenchman's house. It had a staked fence around it, but many stakes had fallen down. There were burn marks on others. As they entered the yard, a man made as though to challenge them, but Dragon's-breath cut him down with a swinging stroke from his sword. Another also saw them, but dived through a hole in the fence. The door to the house was ajar as the band entered. They spread out through the house, slaying only when they had to. The Frenchman was in the pantry.

"Ah, Master Frog. I remember my Master's name now. It is Edric the Wild."

"Edric? Bastard." The Frenchman lunged at Godfrew, Ragnor stuck him in the chest with his saxe. The blow was well aimed. It took the man in the heart and he died instantly. A woman came in, saw the dead man and screamed. Another joined her.

"Why you, Wolfshead? Why?"

"He is Norman. This is our land."

"He came here at King Edward's invitation. He stayed here at King Harold's invitation. He married a local girl. This is his wife. She was born here. What right have you to do this?" The woman tried to restrain and comfort the Frenchman's distraught wife.

"This is England, not France. Get out of here and take her with you," the wolf replied. "This place will be purged by fire. Tell your neighbours that Edric the Wild has unleashed his wolf pack. Those not the friends of Edric had best move out before we visit them. NOW GO!" Ragnar bustled the women

The Wolfpack

out. "Scavenge, my wolves. Scavenge, then burn. We have but little time."

The house was small and rather poor. Plundering its treasures took little time, burning it even less. No one from the hamlet interfered. They ran. It seemed that the evacuation was well practised.

First the band gathered what horses they could find, then they returned to the well and were joined by Clunn and Tosti.

"Where have you two been. We may have needed you," the wolf growled.

"Is that you under there, Master Wulf? Very appropriate. Where have we been? Look!" Clunn threw an alter cloth on the ground and unwrapped two candlesticks. A chalice and a small gold cross also rolled out. "Who would have thought this place would have such as these, eh? He should have spent more on armed men and less on these baubles."

"Pick it up. Come on, let's get going." Godfrew found the dark pony at his shoulder. "Get a horse. Get mounted. Let's get out of here before they realise there are so few of us. Stanley, fire the hay wain."

They rode out under cover of the burning wain and the fired hay rick nearby. At the clearing, they took stock. Dunstan and Bjorn had brought out some twenty head of cattle. There was the small treasure from the house and, of course, the plunder from the church.

"Well, Master Wulf," Clunn stretched out on the ground by the little pile of treasure. "I think the church provided for us best of all. Materially and spiritually."

"Spiritually, Clunn?"

"Yes. We found a female anchorite in the chapel. She provided spiritual comfort for both myself and young Tosti here."

"Clunn!" Godfrew stood over the small man. "I said no rape."

"Oh, it wasn't rape. She quite enjoyed it. Seems she used to be the local Abbot's bit of stuff till he found a new novice to play with. Put her away so to speak. Seems she missed the comfort of a man's company. You should have seen the smile on her face when we left!" Clunn put his hands behind his head and smiled up at Godfrew.

"You went with a woman after the rat had had her?" an incredulous Stanley asked Tosti.

"Before. Following him is the last thing any sane man would do. But he is right. She did have a big smile on her face!"

* * *

The heat was making things very unpleasant. Buried in the middle of the hay rick, Godfrew and Ragnor were near to passing out. This was the third day of watching the manor of Newton near Leominster. Dragon's-breath was supposed to be with Ragnor, but the dust from the hay had affected both his eyes and his nose. As a result, he could neither see nor stop sneezing. Neither was desirable in someone who was supposed to be secretly spying out the land. Godfrew had found the noisy, boisterous behaviour of the others tiring, so he had left Dunstan in charge and taken Dragon's-breath's place today. Newton was to be their fifth raid in five weeks. The other raids had produced some booty, but not a great deal. Bjorn had taken one herd of cattle back to Lydbury, but had returned that morning, bemoaning the fact that he had not stayed at the manor. The last raid had produced only a few scraggy sheep. These were used to fill the band's pot, rather than increase the flocks and wealth of Earl Edric. The other raids had been easy and the targets relatively soft, but Newton was different. This was a fortified manor. When the herds of cattle and horses went out, they had armed men to guard them. The main manor was within a stake fenced palisade with only a few other buildings outside the fence. Inside the palisade could be seen a watch tower that was always manned.

"This is not an easy one, Master Wulf. Shouldn't we go elsewhere?" Sweat tricked down Ragnor's freckled forehead and dripped off the end of his nose. Godfrew was aware of Ragnor's strong body smell. He was certain that he smelled as bad himself.

"Our beloved Earl gave me quite a free reign, but this was one place that he specifically mentioned we should visit." Godfrew wiped his own forehead with his sleeve and looked at the resulting damp patch on the material. "It is a hard nut

The Wolfpack

to crack, though. We may have to limit ourselves to just being a nuisance."

"A nuisance?" Ragnor irritably struck out at a persistent fly that was feeding on his sweaty face. " How pray?"

"Horses. They are keeping a herd of horses corralled in that paddock outside the palisade each night. Yes?"

"Yes, Master Wulf. They bring them in at sunset. But there are always armed men with them. Even at night we would have trouble getting near the paddock without being seen. Two men sneaking into a hay rick five hundred paces away is one thing. Seven men—with swords drawn—going right up to the paddock to steal horses ... that is another thing." Ragnor was shaping up well as a warrior. He was a thinker, rather than a berserker.

"With swords drawn? Surely, not till the last moment? But I know what you mean, Ragnor rust head." Godfrew took a piece of hay stalk and started to pick his teeth. He worked hard at a piece of mutton flesh caught between two back teeth. Having got it loose, he spat it out. That task done, he turned his attention back to Ragnor. "Your mare is in heat, isn't she?"

"Yes."

"Well, so is mine."

"It's lucky all our mounts are female, Master Wulf, else we would have our hands full."

"What has luck got to do with it?" Godfrew went back to picking his teeth. This time, he attacked the lower front ones, using a split stalk and working the sliver backwards and forwards.

"So the choice was deliberate?"

Godfrew threw away the stalk he had been using and selected a replacement. "Ah, you are learning young man. You may make a warrior yet!"

Whilst Ragnor continued watching the manor, Godfrew closed his eyes and started planning the raid of Newton, but thoughts about Elfgifu and their soon to be born son—for Godfrew was sure it would be a son—intruded. Eventually, the thoughts became dreams.

Godfrew and his nine sons had just rounded the horses up on the Wandle water meads before Garrat when the woe waters broke. The flood swept the horses and Godfrew's sons away. Frantically, he forced his dark pony against the flow and managed to rescue three of his boys before blackness descended. Suddenly, he could hear Elfgifu calling him.

"Wulf, Master Wulf." Ragnor gave Godfrew another shake. "It is fully dark. We should be going now. Otherwise, the others will have eaten all the meat."

"Hmm." Godfrew struggled to open his eyes. Seeing Ragnor, not Elfgifu, he shut them again.

"Master Wulf!" Ragnor was getting desperate now.

"All right, my red-headed friend. All right."

"You seemed disturbed and in anguish, but I did not know if it was safe to wake you."

"Waking people from a dream is not fatal, Ragnor ... and that is all it was ... just a dream." Godfrew forced himself awake and eased himself up to look out of the observation hole in the hay rick. "So the horses are in the paddock with their armed friends. The procedure was the same?"

"Yes, Master Wulf. The same."

"Good. Now, let's get back and fill our stomachs with that burnt offering Clunn claims is roast mutton." The men crawled out of the small chamber that had been hollowed out of the hay rick and covered over the entrance. Keeping low to the ground, they made their way to the scrub land that covered the crest of the low hills to the west. Once in the bushes, they followed the smell of cooked flesh. Before they came into the clearing, Dragon's-breath had emerged from nowhere and walked back with them.

"How was the hay rick? Nice and dusty?" The blond man's eyes were still red and hot, but his smile was warm.

"No, never was. You just couldn't hack the pace. You always were a poor, wee thing," said Ragnor, who was half Dragon's-breath's size.

"Watch it, runt. My eyes are still the colour of your hair." Dragon's-breath broke through the bushes into the clearing. "Hey boys, the dust mites have returned for food."

"And drink. Most definitely, the drink." Godfrew picked up a crock of cider and took a mouthful. He swilled it around his mouth, then spat out a thick, dirty phlegm. "That's better. Now for a drink." He took a long swig before giving the crock to Ragnor. "Hello, who's this?"

The Wolfpack

Standing in front of the fire, leaning on a boar spear, was a medium-sized man with curly, fair hair. He was watching Godfrew with interest. Bjorn cocked his head toward the man. "Godwine. He used to come raiding with us years ago. You gave it up what ... three, four years ago?" Godwine nodded his agreement. "He was wise. I should have given it up then, too. I'm getting too old for raiding. This is my last trip, believe me."

"So what are you doing here, Godwine?" Godfrew took the crock of cider back and drank some more, feeling it fire his belly and lighten his head. A taste of yeast hung on his pallet.

Godwine fluffed up his moustaches with his free hand and moved his weight from one foot to the other. "Well, Master Wulf. Earl Eric himself asked me to go back on the prowl."

"He must be getting bloody desperate," chimed in Dunstan. He held a blackened and burnt leg of mutton in his hands.

Godwine gave a silent laugh. "He's up to something bigger than the usual raid, I think. Anyway, I thought I would see how you were getting on and make sure that we don't get in each others way."

"What worries me is not us getting in each others way, but rather how you managed to find us." Godfrew poked around the bits of mouldy cheese until he found a suitably runny piece, which he then ate.

"I just followed the smell of Clunn's burnt meat."

"Poxed meat, don't you mean?" Tosti asked.

"Maybe," conceded Godwine. "No, Bjorn told me where I would find you when he was dropping off the cattle. I just hoped that you hadn't moved on. We used this place in the old days. Remember, Bjorn."

"Only too well." Bjorn carefully sliced off a sliver of half-raw flesh from the roast sheep's side. "Clunn, you little rat. Can't you cook the flesh properly instead of burning it on the outside and leaving it red on the inside?" Despite his complaint, Bjorn ate the meat. Clunn, his small eyes burning, sat in a bush and gnawed on a shoulder bone, occasionally spitting out a piece of gristle.

"How many in your band?" Godfrew was still sorting through the cheese for smelly bits.

"Six. Ulf the Swede, Paul the Monk, Alarac, Krak the Small ..."

"And Kevin the Tall!" added Dunstan, to the amusement of the others.

"Yes, Kevin the Tall'."

"Kevin? Isn't that Irish?" asked Godfrew who, having selected a good apple, was polishing it on his shirt.

"On his mother's side." Godwine moved his weight again and resettled his position. "Norwegian on his father's, or so his mother says. I've also managed to get Jan-Jan's son to come along."

"A good boy is Jan," contributed Tosti. "I wish I was as good with a sword as he is."

"A bit reckless, though. I remember when he and I were raiding thing last year. Slashing about everywhere but thing."

"Thing, Dunstan?" Godfrew admired his shinny apple.

"Yes, thing. Got himself cut up bad. Some wogs caught him from behind." Dunstan turned to Godwine. "He's all right now, is he?"

"I hope so. He's the best I've got. The rest are either young or out of practice. Ah, here comes the wife." A blonde woman, twice Godwine's size and dressed like a man, came into the clearing holding two naked children, both dripping with water.

"It's a long way to the pond, Godwine. I could have done with your help." The woman dumped the soggy children in front of the fire. Clunn threw them the mutton bone that he had been gnawing on and laughed as they fought over it. "Stop that now." The Valkarie smacked both of her offspring on the back of their heads and they began to cry. "Here, share this." Godwine's wife hacked two strips of flesh off of the roast sheep's flaps. "As for you, Clunn the Rat," she walked over and smacked Clunn's head. Clunn laughed.

"I see you have everything in hand, my beloved." Godwine seemed completely unphased by what was happening.

"No thanks to you, Godwine Good-husband. Cider?" Clunn brought her a crock of cider and then tried to grope her backside. Godwine's wife rewarded him with another smack around the head. Again, Clunn thought it funny.

The Wolfpack

"My evil wolf pack. Gather round." Godfrew ate his apple, core and all, whilst the others drew near. "Where's Stanley? Oh, there you are." The youngster emerged from behind a bush with grass on his back and in his hair. "We will strike tonight. Once Stanley has wakened properly, I will tell you how we shall do it."

* * *

Clunn rode his horse, keeping as close to the saddle as possible. Behind him, on tethers, were Ragnor's mare and Godfrew's dark pony. Clunn brought them as close as he dared to the paddock, ensuring he was down wind. As the stallions in the paddock caught the scent, they became agitated and started running the fence line, ears pricked, calling out to the in-heat mares. At first, the guards took no notice, preferring to continue to doze in the saddle and hope that their charges would settle, but soon the stallions started to jostle and bite each other. That stirred up the rest of the herd. It was the guards riding into the paddock to stop the fighting that caused the herd to stampede and break down the paddock fence. Clunn, still leading the in-heat mares, rode for his life, pursued by a herd of forty or so horses. Behind them came the guards, quickly followed by others emerging from behind the palisade. Meantime, a wolf and two men entered the small buildings without the fence, checking the contents and removing those deemed edible.

* * *

"What do you mean: 'Earl Edric wants Newton discomforted'. Isn't that what we did earlier in the week?" Godfrew stared at Etheljarl, the anger clearly showing on his face.

"Master Wulf. I am but a bearer of the Earl's desires. He is pleased with your actions so far. He is grateful for the twenty fine horses you took from Newton and sent to him. He wants you to stay here and wait for Godwine and his band to join you. He wants you to 'discomfort' Newton. He wants the manor itself attacked. He wants you to either take it or besiege it, until told otherwise. He wants the attack to be on the first night with no moon. He told me to give you this."

Etheljarl proffered a tatty piece of parchment. On the back were some prayers in Latin. Godfrew took it and opened it. Inside, written in Norse Runes, were the same statements the messenger had brought. At the bottom was the Rune signature Edric had shown Godfrew back at Lydbury, the signature only he and Godfrew knew.

"All right, Etheljarl. It is just the prospect of tackling Newton with such a small force. You will be able to join us?"

"I'm a bit out of practice, but yes, I look forward to it. So, do you have a plan?"

Godfrew pulled his top lip, still only covered with fluff, rather than whiskers. "Not yet. I will have to give this a lot of thought."

* * *

As the black velvet of night embraced the land, a grey wolf moved from the cover of the hay rick and very slowly, stopping often, moved toward the buildings outside the fenced palisade of Newton. Each time he stopped, the wolf looked to the palisade and watched, noting where the watchmen were stationed, seeing which one moved and which one did not. In no hurry, the wolf closed the gap between rick and fence. As he got closer, he determined which of the watchmen were awake and which dozed at their post. The wolf changed his direction and came near the buildings under the closed eyes of a sleeping guard. There were four buildings. The wolf made for the furthest and entered.

Godfrew could not understand why the master of the manor had left the buildings standing when the staked fence had been built. A stream had been diverted to create a moat two man-lengths wide that encircled the palisade for all its circumference, except the gateway. The buildings were on a slight downward slope. That would explain why the buildings had not been enclosed by the moat and the fence. Even so, they should not have been left standing to give cover and material to an attacker. Godfrew put down the short plank of wood he had brought with him and the leather bag containing some of Bjorn Wainwright's tools. On the earlier raid against Newton, he had explored the out buildings. One served as a butchery. Another contained a rendering vat and workings. The third held raw, uncured hides. It was this building that interested him most, for it contained barrels of oil and lard. Against the wattle and daub wall were two long planks of wood, obviously used to roll the barrels on and off wagons. Godfrew took the planks. Using Bjorn's auger bit, he drilled holes in them, four apiece. Having done that, he put the short plank underneath, matching the holes in it with those of the long planks. The wooden dowels had been precut. All he had to do, once he had hammered them into place with the leather mallet, was saw the heads flush. Godfrew now had a plank long enough to span the moat.

The nearest watchman was at least fifty paces away and still asleep. Godfrew pulled his long plank to the edge of the moat and pushed it across to the other side. The weight was more than he expected. The end of the plank took several dips in the water before Godfrew got the end to touch the far bank, but he could not lift it over the lip. Cursing, Godfrew went back to the building and retrieved several small barrels. Using one as a fulcrum, he was able to lever the plank up over the lip. The watchman still slept. Godfrew used the first barrel to test the strength of the joined plank. Slipping into the moat, he waded through the water and rolled the barrel along the wood. Fortunately, he had thought to test the depth of the water on his previous visit, so he was not surprised that the water came only to his waist, but the coldness of the water was a shock. It took his breath away. The plank held, so Godfrew returned to bring more barrels across.

Once he had four barrels on the other side, Godfrew pulled himself out of the moat and onto the narrow ledge betwixt the fence and the moat. Using the pommel of his saxe, Godfrew stoved in a barrel's bung, splashed the oil over the fence and poured it through the arrow slits. Satisfied with the results, Godfrew emptied the other barrels and went back for more. The work was hard and tiring. By the time he had reached the fence in front of the sleeping watchman, Godfrew's arms ached and his joints creaked.

Here, there were no arrow slits. Godfrew assumed that the watchman's stand was built of earth from the excavated moat. It would also explain why, during the day, he had seen the odd watchman disappear from one stand and reappear at another. Instead of being able to walk along a catwalk, they obviously had to climb up and down artificial mounds. Godfrew chuckled at the poor design of the defences which, at a distance, had seemed so impressive.

The chuckle must have disturbed the watchman, for he stirred. The wolf flattened himself against the fence and watched. The watchman stood up, using his spear as a prop, and massaged his face with his hand, picking sleep out of his eyes. The wolf pressed its face against the fence, feeling the rough surface, smelling the resin from the wood, appreciating its dryness. The guard hung over the fence, but his eyes were on the plain and he never looked straight down. Cramp started to set into the wolf's legs. He moved them up and down—slowly—to try and gain relief, while never taking his eyes off the watchman. The cramp got worse and the wolf's leg muscles started to lock, but just as he was about to howl, the watchman sat down again and settled himself for another sleep.

Godfrew knuckled his calf muscles and slowly managed to restore movement to his legs, but he was cold and his clothing still wet. Feeling very uncomfortable, he went back to the plank, crossed the moat and returned to the building, taking his plank with him. The clouded sky was still black. It would be a while before the others arrived. Godfrew wanted to sleep, but knew he dared not. Instead, he thought of Elfgifu and what name to give to his son. As the first streak of dawn started to lighten the clouds, the sound of horsemen could be heard. Godfrew left the building and crossed the moat. Striking his flint and steel, he set fire to the oil. Soon, a large section of the fence was ablaze. The watchman called to others inside and rushed to the fire. Godfrew moved around the moat's edge to the side of the palisade opposite the fire.

Godwine led the band. They had twice as many horses as men and they made enough noise for four times their number. They used the smoke and confusion to make the occupants of Newton believe that they were under attack from a vast army. Some defenders were trying to put the fire out with water, but the oil floated in it and spread the flames. Others beat it with hides and blankets, but Ragnor and Stanley found them easy targets for their sling-shots. Some men ran from the gateway, around the ledge toward the fire,

The Wolfpack

but Clunn and Bjorn's arrows from their Welsh long bows[16] reached them before they reached the fire.

On the other side of the palisade, Godfrew threw a platted walrus-skin rope at the fence. The noose fell over the point of one of the stakes. Pulling himself up, he used his saxe to cut through the rope that held the fence stake to its partner, planning to open a hole in the stake wall. Having done this, he lowered himself down and cut the matching rope at the bottom. He crossed the moat, taking the trailing end of the walrus rope with him, and waited. Soon he was joined by some of Godwine's band: Jan-Jan's son, Ulf the Swede, Krak the Small, and Kevin the Tall.

Godwine's wife and children rode up with horses in hand. The horses were joined together with a crude rope harness. Godfrew threw the end of the walrus rope to Godwine's wife, who attached it to the harness. With much whipping and yelling, Godwine's wife and children drove the horses forward. Nothing happened. They tried again. Still, nothing. The third time, Godwine's wife grabbed the bridle of the horse nearest her and charged. With a groan and a crack, the fence gave way. As Godwine's wife swerved the horses to run parallel to the gap in the fence, a whole string of posts pulled out. Before the walrus rope broke, there was a hole in the fence wide enough for twenty men to enter shoulder to shoulder.

A soldier ran up to see what was happening, but when he saw the wolf walk through the torn fence, he screamed and ran back the way he had come. He managed five paces before Krak's arrow took him through the back and sent him spiralling along the dusty street. To Godfrew's surprise, the area inside the fence was jammed with small cottages and animal pens. The fence on the other side could not be seen, except at the end of the narrow streets that transversed the grounds. Apart from the one soldier, there was no one in sight. Noises from the cottages told of people hiding and waiting, but no one showed to challenge the small band. The

---

[16] Long bow: the long bow is generally accepted as being of Welsh origin, though bow staves of similar length have been excavated in Denmark. Use of the weapon is known to have spread to the Welsh Marcher counties quite early on via Welsh mercenaries. Eventually, the weapon became England's own.

guard in the watch tower had seen the fence go down. He was calling for help, but no one came.

"Keep away from the cottages. Leave the folk. Follow me." Godfrew ran down the street toward the fence at the end, slowing only when he was ten paces from it. The others bunched up behind him.

In front, the defenders were frantically fighting the fire, oblivious to the watchman's warning cry. Smoke billowed up and the heat could be felt by Godfrew and his men. Some of the men were armed and mail coated, but most were in their night clothes. They were shovelling earth at the wooden stakes. Where the heat was less intense, they beat the flames with horse blankets or whatever else they could find at hand.

"Like a scene from hell, Master Wulf. Shall I?" Krak notched an arrow. His bow was far longer than any Godfrew had seen before, about two of his own arm's lengths. It dwarfed its holder.

"Just wait a moment, then you and Kevin can shoot as you will. Count to fifty so that we can work along the back of this cottage and take them in the flank whilst you shoot at those in the middle."

Krak looked worried. "Count to fifty? I can't."

"How many can you count to, Krak?" Godfrew watched out the corner of his eye as the rest of the band started to sneak around the cottage to the staging point.

"Ten, Master Wulf."

"Kevin, can you count?"

Kevin gave a beautiful smile, showing wonderfully white teeth. He was the only member of either band, except for Wulf, with a full set, "Of course I can. To ten."

Godfrew took a deep breath, which he let out slowly. "Krak, you count to ten. Kevin, you count how many times he has counted to ten. When you get to five, then you can shoot."

"That sounds easy enough. Off you go, Krak."

"One, two, three, four ...."

Godfrew ran to join the other two. He had just come around the corner when the first of the arrows started to cut the defenders down. Jan gave a blood curdling scream and ran forward, slashing out wildly with his sword, the others followed.

"Out, out, out, out ..." Ulf rammed the boss of his round shield into the back of an unsuspecting victim and smashed his sword into the man's unprotected ribs as he fell. Godfrew pulled another's neck back and severed his throat, the blood hissing as it sprayed onto the burning fence in front. "Out, out, out ..." Ulf took out his next victim, but Jan had already dispatched three and was striking another two. His voice was stuck in a quavering scream. His movements were crazed, as he wound himself up into a berserker's frenzy.

Krak and Kevin kept a rain of arrows coming from the street. The defenders started to panic, never stopping to count their attackers, never thinking to fight back. Flight was their only clear thought. Easy victory seemed at hand—until the reinforcements from the area of the watch tower arrived. They caught Jan Jan's son trying to free his sword from his tenth enemy. A thrusting spear crunched through his back and out through his guts. Jan kept on trying to free his sword, but his movements became slower and slower, until they finally stopped. Krak sought revenge by coming out of the cover of the cottage to gain a better aim. A throwing spear lodged in his spine between his shoulders. A soldier rushed over to finish the job, but as he lifted his sword, an arrow from Kevin's bow struck him in his unprotected armpit, the head appearing at the base of the man's neck. Instead of slaughtering the defenders, the remaining attackers were themselves about to be slaughtered. Ulf took a blow that shattered his shield and forced him to the ground. Three soldiers closed in for the kill.

It was then that the fire burned through the first posts and the fence fell. Through the gap, firing arrows at the soldiers, came Clunn and Tosti. The rest followed, yelling, brandishing their swords and calling out their war cries. The reinforcements faltered, gathered their remaining comrades, and made toward the area of the watch tower.

"Close, Godwine. Almost too close." Godfrew knelt by the side of the fallen Krak the small.

"But did it look good?" Godwine sheathed his sword and joined Godfrew at Krak's side.

"It looked good, but may God help us when they realise we are so few." Godfrew lifted Krak's head "Krak how do you feel?"

"I don't. I feel nothing from the neck down. From the neck up it hurts." Krak moved his eyes, searching. "Kevin, where's Kevin." Krak's face and lank, curly hair were covered in dust. As Godfrew watched, several fleas abandoned him.

"Here, cousin." Kevin was beautifully made—clear skin with straight, honey-coloured hair. He had bright, blue eyes, long moustaches and was very well-muscled. Everything about him was in proportion, but—like his cousin lying before him—he was small. "What's to do?"

"You can't leave me like this, cousin."

Kevin took Krak's head from Godfrew and wiped a stray hair from Krak's eye. "You are sure?"

Krak blinked his eyes and nodded.

"Come on, Master Wulf. We had better catch up with the others." Godwine took Godfrew's elbow and propelled him along toward the watch tower.

Kevin stood well back, blinked a tear from his eye, took aim and sent an arrow through the heart of his cousin, Krak the Small. "Farewell." He then stooped and grabbed all the arrows in Krak's quiver before running off to join the others.

"Bleeding hell, Wulf. You see it? You seen the thing? It's a bleeding tiny castle that." Dunstan's face was smeared with soot. Only his teeth and eyes stood out. "That moat goes under the wall and runs through in here. The wall thing, you know."

"Dunstan!" Godfrew pulled Dunstan around to face him fully. "Dunstan. Start again. What moat ... what wall ... do you mean the fence?"

"Fence, wall ... it's all the bleeding same."

"The fence is wood. We can burn wood. Walls are dirt or stone. Which do you mean?"

"Fence." Dunstan started to pull away.

"Dunstan. The fence! What about the fence? Forget the others for a moment. What about the fence?" Godfrew's patience was wearing thin and his voice was getting shrill and loud.

"Thing, you know, thing," Dunstan insisted.

Godfrew took a deep breath, counted to ten, then spoke slowly and calmly. "Dunstan, you followed the defenders. You got to where the watch tower is. What did you see there?"

The Wolfpack

"The fence, it comes inside the outside fence. It separates the watch tower and bits from the rest of the holding. We are in one bit of the holding. There's another bit behind yet another fence. It has even got another moat. We ain't gained nothing."

"All right, Dunstan. Take me there, slowly. Just take me there."

"Right." The big man ambled off with Godfrew following him. They passed four streets of cottages before they reached the fence that had upset Dunstan so much.

"Hell!" Godfrew squatted down. An arrow buried itself at his feet, so he quickly got up again and moved to the side of a cottage for cover. As Dunstan had reported, there was yet another wall and moat. The wolf pack had only succeeded in breaching the outer defences. Godwine joined Godfrew. Somehow he had found himself a strong thrusting spear. He leaned on it in his customary manner.

"An interesting situation, Master Wulf."

"Interesting? I've just realised ... here we are inside the walls of the outer defences with hostile soldiers in front and the manor folk behind. We are going to get cracked like a cob nut between the rock and the stone."

"Oh, no. Don't worry about the folk." Godwine brushed his moustaches up and then smoothed them down. "Only worry about the soldiers."

"Look, when we were attacked at Martinsfield, we fought and we fought hard. We drove the raiders off. Don't tell me the folk are nothing to worry about." Godfrew pulled back in as an arrow flew between him and Godwine. Godwine remained unmoved.

"Ah, but you were tenants, owning your own stock, minding your own land, taking care of yourselves. These folk are all serfs of the lowest order. Some may even be slaves. They own nothing and they care for nothing except their lives. They will fight to save their lives, but not their current owner's property. Leave them alone and they will leave you alone."

"Clunn!" A look of panic struck Godfrew's face as he remembered Clunn's bad habits. In the present circumstances, Clunn's actions could prove fatal. "CLUNN!"

"He's over there trading arrows with the defenders. No, I've seen this sort of place before. It's the Norman way of running things. This lot has been here for years, since early in Edward's time. I believe that he thought these French would keep the wogs in order, but they didn't. We did. Some got thrown out by Earl Godwine and his brood, but many stayed. These Normans are not very popular with their folk. Now, they are running the whole country. It does not sound very good, Master Wulf." More arrows skimmed past Godwine, who continued to ignore them.

Godfrew caught hold of Godwine's elbow and pulled him behind the cottage. "For God's sake, man, do you want to get killed?"

"If they kill me, they will have my wife to answer to. They won't like that! No?" Godwine returned to where he had been standing "There are at least ten archers firing at us, some with those complicated crossbows, too. I saw at least twenty men running as we came through the burnt out fence. They would not have left the inner defences unmanned while they made that sally." Godwine at last returned to the safety of the cottage wall, "I think, Master Wulf, that they have about thirty or forty to our ...what ... nine or ten?"

"Nine or ten?"

"Krak, Jan, and Etheljarl are dead."

"Etheljarl?"

"Arrow. Ulf isn't too healthy, and Bjorn's got a broken leg."

"How?"

"He fell off his horse as soon as we arrived. Silly bugger. He won't live that one down. It will cost him a few drinks at the tavern, that one will. So, at best ten, maybe not even nine."

"I was taught all I know about fighting by an old Icelander called Snorrie who had served with Sven Forkbeard and Knute the Mighty all over the north. He always told me that when you attacked a walled borough or castle, you had to have at least four men to every defender." Godfrew slumped down the wall to sit on his bum.

"So, we really are in the middle of the midden heap!" Godwine brushed up his moustaches, but this time left them up. "But we will look good. Even if we die, we will look good."

"Die! My wife is carrying our son and you talk of us dying. The last thing that I intend to do is die, looking good or otherwise." Godfrew pulled a bruised apple out from inside his shirt and started to eat it.

"We'll die. We will—unless we have great luck. Even our daft friends behind the fence will soon realise that there aren't many of us. And daft they must be to have let us get this far. Be honest. Even if they just twig that we are attacking them only on one front. No, we will have to be very lucky this time not to die."

"Are you lucky, Godwine? Have you been lucky?"'

"Not yet, but there is always a first time," Again, Godwine brushed his moustaches up.

"Oi." Dunstan lay against the wall of the cottage on the other side of the narrow street "Oi, catch this lot." He rolled a barrel over. "And this!" He threw two short bows across. The end one landed short and Godwine had his shirt nailed to the dirt by an incoming arrow as he tried to retrieve it. Godwine gave a tug and tore himself free, bringing the bow with him.

"That has torn it." Godwine examined the tattered shirt sleeve. His mail coat gleamed underneath. "My wife will not be happy about that." He fingered the rent. "She made it herself, see. She told me to put on an old one in case it got damaged or blood stained, but I couldn't. We have to look good, don't we, Master Wulf?" He looked at Godfrew for confirmation. "Of course, we do! I just hope there is enough plunder to take her mind off the shirt."

"If we live to take the plunder." Godfrew watched as Dunstan shot off some badly aimed arrows at the soldiers in the watch tower. "Tell me, Godwine. Your wife. What is her name?"

"Brunhilda." Godwine pried the lid off of the barrel and pulled out some of the arrows it contained.

"Somehow, I'm not surprised." Godfrew leaned around Godwine and called across the street to Dunstan, "Oi, Dunstan. Where are these from?"

"What, thing? Oh, they came from our friends over there. They left them behind near the arrow slits in the wall ... sorry ... fence. Thoughtful, eh!" Again, Dunstan unleashed some badly aimed shots. "I think I'm getting the hang of this, you know. If I keep practising, I could get quite good at it." The next shot didn't even make it the twenty paces to the fence before buried itself in the dirt. Dunstan laughed. "Well, I did say that I needed practice!"

"How goes it with the others, Dunstan?" Godfrew ran into the street and made two quick shots before ducking back behind cover.

"You know, Etheljarl is dead? Silly sod! He had been away too long and got slow. Bjorn broke his leg, so we had to stick him in one of the buildings, knock a hole in the wall and make him shoot arrows. He was pissed, especially when the roof caught fire." Another loose shot buried itself in the planks of the gate. "His hair got burnt off! Moan, moan, moan. He is now ... well, very pissed. We didn't have any water, so that was what we used to put his burning hair out. You wouldn't think that a little bloke like Clunn would have such a big bladder ..."

"Dunstan, I know about Bjorn. I know about Krak, Jan, and Ulf. What of the others?" Godfrew took a quick shot, then moved out of the way for Godwine, who calmly stood in the street and fired three well-aimed shots before strolling back behind the cottage wall. "Well, Dunstan?"

"Oh, thing. Dragon's-breath, caught an arrow in his thing."

"In his thing?" Godwine had pulled the rest of the arrows out of the barrel and was holding them up so that he could check their straightness. He put the best to one side. "Do you really mean in his thing, Dunstan?"

"Yes, in his thing ... his leg. He is still able to use a bow ... well, one of these short ones, anyway. The rest are all right, except for cuts and bruises." Dunstan's next arrow appeared to clip the helmet of one of the soldiers in the watch tower. "Oh, nice one. Did you see that? I'm getting good at this. I might even become an archer, if I find the time."

"Dunstan, are there many more barrels of arrows?" Godfrew was getting very dry and the effort of shouting across to his sergeant was not helping his voice.

"No, not many. There might be some more down near the main gate, but I can't get there. The cottages are catching fire and the manor folk are leaving with all their bits and bobs. It's very crowded at present." Dunstan took another shot, but the arrow slipped its notch and the bowstring caught his fingers. "Oh, shit." Dunstan sucked his stinging fingers.

"Oh, shit, indeed." Godfrew looked at Godwine.

"Don't look at me, Master Wulf." Godwine collected the best arrows and started to stick them in the ground against the cottage wall. "I'm the one ready to die. As long as I look good."

"No thing," Dunstan called across before starting to examine his reddening fingers. "There should be just enough to last."

"Dunstan, you said that there were not many barrels of arrows left. How can there be just enough when we haven't got many?" Godfrew kept his voice level, but the volume and tone was high.

"Well, they only have to last till Earl Edric and the others get here." Dunstan took to shaking his sore fingers.

"And how many days is that, pray?" Godfrew's voice started to crack.

"Days?" replied Dunstan puzzled. "No, thing."

"Thing, Dunstan?" Godfrew knocked the back of his head against the cottage wall.

"Yes, thing. You can already see them coming across the plain. They will be here in an hour or so."

Godwine stepped into the street and fired an arrow. It went through an arrow slit in the palisade and they all heard a high, gurgling scream. "Now, was that luck, or was it skill?"

* * *

Godfrew walked over toward Earl Edric's tent. The chill of the early morning cut his face and tingled his ears, so he kept his cloak tight about his body. The temperature had dropped low during the night and the resulting heavy dew was soaking his shoes and leg wrappings. As he came near the tent, the flap was thrown back and Edric appeared. Behind him came Goda and the two other ladies. One lady opened a folding stool and put it behind the Earl. The other lady placed a small table beside the stool on the Earl's right side, then Goda put a steaming pewter pot on the stool. Without checking that it was in the right place, Edric sat down on the stool and observed the scene in front of him. The fires had been put out. Already, men were pulling the remaining outer defenses down. Only the watch tower and its surrounding fence remained. Its defenders were still defiant. Most of Edric's troops were destroying the cottages. The folk no longer needed them, so they gathered their few goods and made ready to leave for their new home—wherever Earl Edric would send them. Edric sipped his hot drink and smacked his lips with pleasure.

Godfrew stood near the Earl, but Edric seemed not to see him. With much noise, three wagons pulled up between the Earl and that part of the fenced area held by the defenders. Those manning the wagons were all dressed alike—short, boiled-leather jerkins over light, blue shirts with purple breeches and bright, yellow leg bindings. On their heads were small, boiled-leather caps trailing sparse, yellow feathers. When they spoke, it was in Norse. Systematically, the men pulled an assortment of wooden beams and heavy ropes from the wagons and laid them out on the grass, being very careful about the order the pieces were laid out in. Once the wagons were empty, they were driven off and the men commenced to assemble the pieces in front of them.

"I love to watch them work. I am always interested in watching skillful men ... people who know how to extract the maximum result from the minimum effort. Have you ever seen them before, Wulf?" Edric keep his gaze on the men assembling the siege engines.

"Never, my Lord Earl. I have only heard about such things."

"They are very clever. They all served together with the Eastern Emperor, except those youngsters at the end ... sons, I believe, brought in to replace casualties. Since they returned to the north, they have been in great demand." Edric took a sip of his drink. "Even this campaign had to be timed to fit in with them. I had to delay two months whilst they completed a contract in Ireland, though goodness knows what dirty dung hill in Ireland needs these fine experts to make it fall. I'll never know. Two months ... still, they are worth it. Two months that enabled me to employ the wolf packs to soften things up a bit, so it was not wasted." For the first time, Earl Edric the Wild broke his gaze away from the scene in front of him and stared at Godfrew with his cold blue eyes "You have done well." Edric snapped his fingers and Goda came forward and handed him something wrapped in fine silk. "For you," Edric passed the object over.

The Wolfpack

Godfrew unwrapped the gift. It was a gold arm band of ancient design, embossed with biting dragons, each with a garnet eye, a diamond tooth and claws. "It is a royal gift, my Lord Earl."

"It was a royal service you did, particularly with the poor material that I gave you. But your task is not yet finished. This ring is payment for both that already done and that which is to come. Now let us watch." Edric stopped looking at Godfrew and returned to observing the men with the siege machines. The men had divided into three teams, one per machine. Working in a well-rehearsed routine, they had soon put all the parts in front of them together, making three huge catapults. Two of the catapults had been got ready to fire. The third was being readied. Four men— two on either side— cranked the wheels. As they did, so the arm of their catapult was pulled down. Each crank of the wheel brought a click from the ratchet. The arm almost touched the end of the catapult's frame before the captain called for a halt and a wooden frame was brought up to trap the spindle on the end of the arm. Into the cup on the end of the arm of each catapult, a barrel of oil was placed. The bung on the first barrel was knocked in and an oil soaked wick inserted. The captain walked to the first machine and spent much time looking at the watch tower, then at the machine. Eventually, he called for wedges to be brought which were inserted under the front on the machine. Again, the captain did some visual measuring before taking a long-handled mallet and lightly tapping the wedges. Satisfied, he gave a nod and one of the men lit the fuse. As soon as it was well ablaze, another swung a mallet and knocked the frame away from the spindle. The long arm of the catapult shot up until it was arrested by the cross bar with a deep thwong. The burning barrel arched overhead and hit the side of the watch tower, splitting and throwing burning oil everywhere. The captain adjusted the wedges with another couple of light taps and then went on to set the other catapults whilst the team for the first one started to crank the arm down again.

"Oil is best for this type of defence, of course." Earl Edric finished his drink and held the empty pot out for Goda to take and refill. "Very spectacular. I love it when they use boulders against stone walls. It is often very hard to get the range right, with the boulders varying so much in weight. That is where the skill comes in. But when the boulders hit the wall, showers of sharp shards of rock fly everywhere. That is indeed an inspiring sight. Talking of sights Wulf, what is that poking out of your cloak?" Although the Earl had been facing away from Godfrew as he spoke, he must have caught the movement in Godfrew's cloak out of the corner of his eye. Godfrew looked down and a long, pointed black nose had indeed poked out of the top of his cloak just below his chin.

"That, my Lord?" He looked at the protruding muzzle.

"Yes, that." Edric turned to face him "Is it a rat? or have you taken to consorting with demons? If you have, I'm sure my chaplain Goshawk would love to interview you!"

"Ah, neither, my Lord Earl. It is a lurch."

"A lurch, eh? What is a lurch?"

"A dog, Lord Earl." Godfrew loosened his cloak and the creature struggled to get its head and front paws out. It stared unblinkingly at Edric. "A small greyhound. The locals use them for hunting hares."

"Plunder, Wulf? You know I get first claim on plunder!" Edric narrowed his eyes.

"A gift, my Lord. One of the folk gave it to me. He seemed pleased we did not rape and pillage when we took the place."

"They have nothing to pillage anyway! Nor, from what I have seen, anyone worth raping. I have seen some poor places in my time, but this is the poorest. I just hope that they have all the wealth in that small castle of theirs ... provided my siege engineers don't burn it, of course."

"Would you like Shock ... ah, the dog, my Lord?"

"Oh, no. What would I do with a scrawny, wee thing like that—except perhaps feed it to my hounds. You keep it. The man who gave it to you won't need it either. There aren't many hares in the wooded place I am sending him and his folk to. It has been in waste for ten years or more since Griffith destroyed it in a fit of temper."

"Will it be safe now, my Lord?"

"The Welsh are my friends now ... at least for the present." Edric reached over and pulled Godfrew close to him. Godfrew bent his head to listen to what the Earl wanted to say. Shock took the opportunity to lick Godfrew's neck and face.

"And you, too, are my friend ... yes? I need friends at present. I need them in the town of Hereford."

* * *

Godfrew, Shock and cousin Llew sat on the bench outside the tavern near the main gate of the borough of Hereford. The town was crowded. News that Edric the Wild, accompanied by the Welsh princes, had come reeving had sent many hastening to him with gifts to buy peace. Those who hated him—or against whom he bore a grudge—went scuttling for the security of Hereford's ditch and palisaded earth banks.

Normally, secreting a band of armed men into a town where they were strangers would have been difficult, but the tide of humanity sweeping into Hereford from the southern half of the shire had made it easy for both Godfrew and Godwine to bring the remains of their bands inside the town. Even as they sat watching, another group of refugees came in.

Leading the group was a man dressed as a Norman mounted on a war horse. He was without his helmet and mail coat, but carried a spear and kite shield. Behind him was an ox-wagon carrying a well-dressed woman surrounded by maids and young children. Other wagons and carts laden with goods followed. One cart—with crates of chickens and other fowl—screeched, squawked and honked with each turn of the uneven wheels. Walking in the dust behind the carts came a huddle of manor folk, uneasy at leaving their homes. Their uncertain eyes flicked up at the unfamiliar surroundings, then flicked back down again to their tired feet. The folk were surrounded by the Normans' armed and mounted men. The Normans were shepherding the folk like sheep. Heels of the sluggards were soon nipped by the spear points of their guards.

Attached to the tail of the group were many others: beggars, wanderers, waifs and strays. Among them were Ragnor and his new hand-fast wife, Kriemhild. Kriemhild, Ragnor's personal plunder from Newton, was slender, but with a delicate softness to her flesh. Her softly waved chestnut hair flowed free to her waist. Kriemhild had quickly made herself indispensable to the band with her cooking skills. It was Kriemhild whom all desired, but Kriemhild had eyes—and shameless hands—for only Ragnor. Kriemhild had won Clunn's undying respect by kneeing him in the testicle for putting his hand where it was not welcome, then pouring cold water on the bruised organ to ease the pain. The recollection of the latter made Godfrew smile.

"Something tickle your fancy, cousin Wulf?" Llew worried a sore, loose molar.

"No, I was just remembering someone else's fancy getting more than tickled. Godfrew put down his tankard of ale. Shock leaned forward and drank the remains. When Godfrew spoke again it was loud enough for only his wife's cousin to hear. "No, cousin Llew, that passage sees the last of my band in. Now that they are all here, I shall have to find out what to do with them!"

"May we join you ?" Godwine, Brunhilda and their two brats approached the bench.

"Certainly, friend." Godfrew indicated the space next to himself. "The town is getting very crowded. I wonder where all these new comers will stay?"

"My wife and I ..." Godwine indicated Brunhilda, who was dressed in woman's clothes for the first time since Godfrew had met her. She went coy and blushed as a chaste wife should. Godwine continued: "My wife and I are most blessed to have rented a corner in the priory tithe barn."

Godfrew pulled Shock away from Godwine's boy child, whose face he was licking. "More fortunate than us. My cousin and I have nowhere to stay. We have been spending the nights sleeping under the eves of any convenient cottage." Shock looked at his master. Seeing his attention was diverted, the dog returned to cleaning the remains of that morning's breakfast from the boy's chops.

"It is not right that you should be so discomforted, friend. Perhaps you would care to share our humble abode with us for the night." Godwine had left his usual spear behind. Instead, he held a quarter-staff in his left hand. He used it for support as he swivelled around to look Godfrew full in the face: "It would be an honour, sir." He winked.

"Perhaps you should first ask your good lady wife? She may find it embarrassing to have two rough fellows such as us for company." Godfrew again pulled Shock away from the boy.

The Wolfpack

Again, as soon as his masters attention moved from him, the dog returned to washing the child's face.

"My dear." Using the quarter-staff as a pivot, Godwine swung around to face his wife. "I'm sure, in the name of charity, you would not object to these poor fellow travellers joining us, would you?" Brunhilda pulled the edge of her head covering across the lower half of her face, fluttered her eyes and simpered. Only Godwine saw her tongue poke out. "See?" Godwine swung back to Godfrew. "All is arranged. So let me buy you an ale to seal the bargain."

Godfrew caught the eye of a serving wench and beckoned her over. "One for your wife?"

"No, my wife would never drink ale. She is too delicate!" Godwine winced as Brunhilda kicked him in the ankle. "Perhaps a fruit or herbal cordial?" Brunhilda gave him another kick and Godwine had problems keeping a straight face.

"Maybe she would make an exception, as a token of friendship." The bar maid stood behind Godfrew and leaned over his shoulder, brushing her breasts against his arm as she did so. "One tankard of small ale ... and one of your strongest, please." He put the required coins into her outstretched, well-scrubbed hand.

"Will that be all, sir?" The wench moved herself on Godfrew's shoulder and he could smell the chamomile she had washed her hair with.

"Ah, nothing this time." He gave her an additional copper coin. "Have a drink yourself."

"If you change your mind, just call." The bar maid moved to the back, then moved away to get the drinks. Godfrew watched her swaying hips and thought of Elfgifu, still at Lydbury. As he turned back, he noticed Llew watching him.

"Oh, no. Just looking. So what's this about you marrying again?"

"It is hard for a man to live alone, particularly around here." Llew reached for the piece of coarse bread that he had half eaten, but it was gone. Shock licked his lips.

"I must admit, I was surprised, so soon after Rhiannon." There was no condemnation in Godfrew's voice, just curiosity.

"She is the widow of my cousin. You met him at Martinsfield."

"Big, ginger hair, freckles?"

"Like most of my relatives, except on your wife's side. He died in the raid by the Normans ... the same raid as Rhiannon."

"I remember."

"The family thought it best for us to wed, what with the four kids." Llew shrugged his shoulders. "What can you do? She's a good enough woman, but she and my brother Puta don't get on ... always arguing about cooking and tidiness." He finished his ale and put the tankard on the ground. Shock got down and examined it to ensure it was empty. Finding it was, the dog contented itself with licking the dried foam on the tankard's outside with slow and deliberate strokes. "The thought of getting away from the noise made me keen to join you."

"And I thought it was out of friendship! Such is life." The bar maid came with the tankards of ale. Brunhilda leaned across and took the one containing the strong ale, leaving a bemused Godwine to take the small ale.

* * *

One by one, the members of the two bands made contact with their leaders and moved to the priory tithe barn. Soon, all were safely gathered in. Llew and Dunstan were the only ones really familiar with the town. They took turns showing the others about. The fact that the place was crowded with strangers helped. No one challenged them. At first, it all seemed like a big party with plenty of food and drink. Following Earl Edric's generous pay-out at Newton, there was plenty of money. Godfrew had sent most of his plunder back to Elfgifu at Lydbury with the injured Dragon's-breath and Bjorn, but even he had enough to keep himself well fed and watered. Four weeks after Ragnor's arrival, Earl Edric and his allies—Prince Bleddyn and Prince Rhiwallon—camped in front of the borough and the gates were closed. The second the gates slammed shut, the price of food doubled and that of ale tripled. Rumour had it that the price of a whore had quadrupled, but Clunn always did exaggerate.

The Wolfpack

For two weeks, the siege engines fired boulders and casks of oil at the town's defences. One catapult was stationed permanently at the rear of the town. It fired its large boulders at the castle's stone tower. The two other machines fired burning oil barrels at the stake fence atop the earthen ramparts. Each day followed a routine. From first light to noon, the catapults would fire their missiles. From noon until dusk, all was quiet. From dusk until full dark, the catapults fired again. Each night, the catapults firing the oil were moved to a new location. Each attack followed a routine. A bursting barrel of oil would strike the fence and start burning. The defenders would tip containers of sand and dirt over the wall to put the fires out. The Welsh archers would try and shoot any defender who kept his head above the fence top for more than a second or two. Then the next barrel would strike and the routine would continue. Godfrew wondered where Edric was getting all the barrels of oil, as there must have been hundreds used over the fourteen days.

On the evening of that fourteenth night, a dark pigeon with distinctive red and blue markings on its wings landed at the priory dove cote. Clunn brought it to Godfrew, who called Godwine over before examining it.

"This should be it, Master Wulf. I thought it would have been here before now." Godwine brushed his moustaches up and then smoothed them down again. A restless girl child hung around his leg, occasionally putting out a hand to pull at Godwine's quarter-staff.

"Our beloved Earl has a timing all of his own. Now, if you want to tell him he has got it wrong ..." Godfrew crooked his eyebrow.

"I would live to regret it. No one looks good when Earl Edric has finished with them. I have sufficient humility to recognise that even I would not look good should the Earl think I was being too bold in questioning his judgment." Again, Godwine brushed his moustache. "Read on, friend." The thin piece of silk attached to the bird's leg was covered in runes, the last being Edric's own. Godfrew read and then reread the message before sitting down and indicating for Godwine to join him. Normally, the barn was full of people and noise, but this evening a barrel of flaming oil had over-shot the fence and set fire to the tavern by the main gate. People had crowded from all over the town to the fire. Some helped put it out. Others, such as Clunn and Tosti, helped by moving the stock to a safer place.

Godwine settled himself down on the hay. His daughter sat between his knees, teasing Shock, who was playing tug with the girl's leg wrappings.

"Well?"

"Well?" Godfrew replied mockingly.

"Cut the crap. What does it say?" Godwine pushed Shock away and wagged his finger at the dog, who wagged its tail back at him. "Come on, what does it say?" Shock went back to playing with the girl's wrappings.

"Very little, actually. Your boys have brought their mail coats and helmets with them, I trust?"

"As the Earl instructed. I've told you that already. I don't defy the Earl!"

Godwine leaned forward and grabbed hold of Shock's jet black muzzle and pried his jaws open to remove the now sodden and ragged leg wrapping from the hound's mouth. The little girl grabbed hold of the black lurch and flipped him on his back, cuddling him like a mother would its baby. Shock licked her face and snuggled into her arms.

"Tomorrow night. The Earl thinks it may be getting a trifle cold and suggests that it might be advisable if the boys lit themselves a fire . . . several in fact."

* * *

At dusk, the curfew bell tolled. Clunn and Tosti slipped out of the barn toward the animal pens to cut the hinges on the gates. Whilst the other occupants of the barn indulged in the beer that was liberated from the burning tavern the previous night, the members of the band gathered at the door. One by one, they disappeared into the moonless night, leaving the others at the ends of the streets. Godfrew—with Ragnor and Kevin—made toward the main gate. There they hid ... waiting.

The evening barrage from the catapults was coming to its usual conclusion. The last volley of burning barrels flew over the wooden fence and landed in the street of bakers, setting the area alight. The last shot of the night was at the castle's stone tower. Instead of it being a boulder, it was a barrel of oil and it burst into spectacular flames as it struck. Seeing this signal, the band started to set fire to the cottages at the opposite end of the town to the already burning bakeries. Godfrew and his companions waited, watching.

As the fires spread, so did the panic and confusion. Terrified people left their burning dwellings—some to fight the fire, others to run. Frightened animals milled around their pens until they pushed the weakened gates over and joined the confused people in the crowded streets. Those trying to escape the fires got in the way of those fighting them. The guards on the wall and by the gate shuffled about. They were annoyed at the lack of order and precision amongst the fire fighters, angry at the aimless wanderings of the others, frustrated at having to man their posts. Eventually, the Captain of the gate guard made up his mind. "Alan, Jean, Henri, Rollo, stay here. Don't let anyone out, and keep an eye on the plain. This could be a ruse, so be aware. Alan, you're in charge. The rest of you, follow me. If we can pull down some cottages ahead of the fire. It will stop it from spreading. Now hurry!" The captain and his men set off at the trot, shields slung over their backs, swords swinging at their hips, throwing spears held at quarter arms.

Alan barked out his orders, obviously pleased to have been left in charge. "Jean, up here with me. You two watch the gate and don't sleep!" As soon as the other man joined him, Alan peered into the darkness of the plain. He watched for movement, trying to separate the usual noise from that of the besieging army.

The wolf kept to the shadows of the embankment until he was directly behind the Norman called Rollo. He watched the shadows opposite until he discerned a slight movement, then he slipped the walrus rope over the man's head and tightened, crossing the rope over and locking his wrists. As the man began to silently choke and scrabble with his fingers at the garrote, the wolf knocked his knees away. With the man now kneeling in front of him, the wolf put his own knee into the Norman's back and sped his death. The man's flailing arms made contact with nothing but air.

Ragnor did not have the experience with the rope he had claimed. He had allowed his victim to get all his fingers under the rope. Ragnor's bungled attempt at garroting had silenced his victim, but had not strangled him. Ragnor and Henri danced together, the Norman fighting for breath, trying to get Ragnor off balance, Ragnor trying to match the Norman's movements and, at the same time, to tighten the rope around the man's neck. The scuffle was starting to make a noise, so Godfrew threw back the hood of his cloak and kicked Ragnor's knees. They, in turn, knocked away Henri's knees. The two sprawled on the ground. Godfrew started to pull out his saxe, but then realised that he could not kill the Norman without endangering Ragnor. Instead, he pulled out his small double-edged eating knife. Godfrew tried to get at the man's throat or eyes with the knife, but got badly kicked for his troubles. At the next attempt to kick him, Godfrew sat on the man's leg. When the other leg came across to kick him, he grabbed it and splayed the legs. It took three stabs with the knife, but eventually Godfrew managed to sever the main artery that ran through the inner thigh. Ragnor kept the rope tight. Slowly, the Norman's fingers slackened their grip, but he eventually bled to death, rather than succumb to the choke hold, so the ending was slow.

Godfrew left them and cautiously looked up at the ramparts. Alan and Jean were still there, standing at attention, skewered to the wooden fence by Kevin's arrows. Godfrew saw Kevin making toward the ramparts. Kevin gave him a beautiful smile: "Just going to try and get my arrows back. No point in wasting them, even if the feathered flights will be bloody from being pushed through."

"Don't be too long. I will need a hand to open the gate." Godfrew stepped over Ragnor and the almost dead Norman. "Leave him. He's not going anywhere. Help me lift the bar on the gate. Ragnor reluctantly loosened the rope and stood up. The lower half of the youth's body was soaked in blood as dark and red as his thick hair. "Come on Ragnor. Over here. Get your shoulder under the beam."

Kevin joined them. Three men were about to do a task that normally took six. "Only managed to get one free." Kevin pointed to his arrows. "The others broke. Caught in bone, I think."

"Spare me the details and get under this. We need to hurry before the garrison realise what has happened." Godfrew watched as Kevin joined them with his shoulder under the oak beam. "One, two, three. Lift!" Despite the padding of his cloak, Godfrew felt the heavy wood dig into his shoulder, causing the chain mail of his shirt to cut into his flesh. "A bit higher," he commanded. As the pain increased and sweat started to drip off of Godfrew's brow, his back creaked. "Just a bit more. That's it. Now to your right. THE OTHER WAY KEVIN!"

"Sorry." Another beautiful smile.

"Keep it up. A bit longer."

"You sound like my Kriemhild."

"Shut up, Ragnor. Up, up, AWAY." Godfrew and his companions moved away as the oak beam bit the dust at their feet. "Come on, use it as a lever to open the gate." The men pushed the beam away from them, but the end was digging into the ground, making the task hard. "We will have to get under the beam again and drop it completely clear. Don't look at me like that, Ragnor. I don't fancy it any more than you do. My back is killing me."

"Then let someone else do it for you, Master Wulf." Godwine brushed his moustaches up.

"Godwine, don't sneak up on people like that. You will give me a heart attack," Godfrew's legs started shaking.

"Heart attacks are for the old and lazy. You are more likely to die from the swords and arrows of outraged Normans if we don't get these gates open." Godwine turned and called into the darkness, "Hurry up, the lot of you. Stop watching the pretty fires. We have work to do." Members of the band came to help lift the beam and push the gates open. In the distance, from the plain, came the sound of galloping horses. "Right, boys. We won't be the only ones hearing the horses. Wulf's band take the right, my band the left. Get up on those ramparts and keep the Normans away from the gates." Godwine looked to Godfrew for confirmation. "Right. Don't be silly enough to go too far toward them. Make them come to you. Now hurry."

Godwine turned to Godfrew. "Are you all right? You look puffed."

"Only my back. I hope I haven't put anything out." Godfrew put his hands to his back and massaged the aching muscles.

"You volunteered for the job." Godwine kicked the dead Norman, called Henri, who was lying in a pool of his own thickening blood. "Trouble?"

"It was my specialty, but not ... it seems ... Ragnor's. I shall have to train him better, I think."

"You won't be training anyone." Godwine took Godfrew's arm and led him out of the gateway. "Not if you stand here for much longer."

They had just got clear when the first of the horsemen charged through.

They were small, squat men with boiled-leather caps on their shaggy heads and dyed horse tails dancing on the tops of the caps. Their chests were protected by banded-steel breastplates strapped over sheep skins—fleece side in. Their legs were naked and hairy—black hair, like a bear's. One hand held a throwing spear, the other the reins. They carried two spare spears and a small target shield on their arm. Hanging on to the stirrups were runners, one to each side, using the horses momentum to increase their own running speed. The runners wore no armour. In fact, they wore very little, only a thin shirt that came to just below their crotch, their privates covered by a cloth clout. The legs, arms and faces of some of the runners were covered in patterns made out in blue paint. As they entered the town, the horsemen ran at a gallop up the streets in front of them. The runners detached themselves from the horsemen and ran along the bottom of the earthen ramparts— splitting to either side as they headed toward the flames of the burning houses. No one seemed to be in charge, yet all knew where they were headed.

"The Hounds of Hell." Godwine spat and wiped his mouth with the back of his hand. "God and all his angels sleep when that lot are on the loose."

"You sound very bitter." Godfrew watched Godwine's face, trying to determine the man's mood.

"I have spent half my life fighting against them and half fighting with them. I still do not know which is the worst. I just hope our beloved Earl knows what he is up to in getting involved with them again."

"Are you going to ask him, friend Godwine?"

The Wolfpack

"Me? I'd rather keep company with the Hounds of Hell than risk upsetting Edric the Wild!" Godwine went silent for a moment, then laughed. His mood suddenly changed. "Come on, let's see what the boys are up to." The boys had a fight on their hands. On the left, Godwine's band had built a low barricade of dirt-filled barrels. Dark-haired Alarak—eyes flashing—was hacking at any Norman foolish enough to try and get near. At his left shoulder stood his best friend, Paul the Monk. His tonsure had long grown over, but he still was wearing his dishevelled habit. Paul's slow and deliberate blows contrasted and complemented Alarak's frenzied slashes.

Behind them, the rest of the band shouted encouragement to their mates and insults to their foes. When the opportunity presented itself, Kevin shot an arrow from his Welsh long bow. The fight on the right side was not going so well. Despite Godwine's instructions, Stanley, Ragnor, and Tosti had run too far ahead in their youthful exuberance. Passing through one of the raised watch towers, they now found themselves cut off from their companions by the tower's occupants. Whilst they fought with more desperation than skill, Dunstan, Llew and Clunn were forcing their way toward them. The big Surrey man filled the whole width of the path atop the rampart. His blows were few, but telling. His borrowed kite shield soaked up the blows without splintering. Clunn and Llew stood back and shot arrows over Dunstan's shoulder when the chance arose.

Godfrew could do nothing but watch. The youngsters were fighting desperately. As soon as it became apparent that the Normans from the tower were more concerned about being cut off from the castle than with killing the youths, Ragnor went down to a blow and stayed down. Tosti took a knock to the head, but kept fighting—though his sword was staring to droop in his hand. Stanley revelled in his situation and made a big slaughter. Finally, Stanley made a mistake and a Norman flattened him against the wooden fence with his shield. The youngster gasped as his breath was forced from his chest, but the Norman did not strike at him. For some reason, he held him there until the rest of the tower guard had run past. Seeing Dunstan ambling toward him, the Norman dropped his shield and jumped off the rampart. The man's fall was broken by the thatched roof of the cottage below, so he slid down and ran off. Stanley had got his breath back and was joined by Llew, Clunn and Tosti. Tosti's left ear was hanging by a thread, flopping about as he moved. He set off in pursuit of the retreating Normans as Dunstan ambled after him.

Godfrew examined Ragnor. The boy was badly cut, but would live. He tore a strip from Ragnor's shirt and bound the lad's wounds. Just as he finished, Godfrew was struck across the head and shoulder. He fell into the footpath. As he rolled over, he could see a Norman, who was bleeding profusely from a neck wound, holding a piece of wood and looking to see where to strike next. Godfrew tried to move, but the pain from his shoulder was excruciating. It was such a bad pain that he wished the man would hurry up and finish him off so that the pain would go away, but it did not come to that. Godwine hit the man behind the back of the neck with his quarter-staff and sent him toppling over the rampart to crunch on the hard ground below.

"Dear Master Wulf, where would you be without me?"

"In less pain than I am now, friend Godwine." Godfrew dragged himself upright, his right arm useless.

"What a funny grey colour you have gone. Do you want a hand to help you get up?" Godwine lowered himself down to squat in front of Godfrew, his hands still clasping the quarter-staff.

"No, I will do it myself. Where are the boys?"

"Gone off like the mad march hares they are. They might all be killed by now, I shouldn't wonder. Still: 'Who ...'"

"... wants to live forever?' I know, I've heard it before, many times. Sweet Jesus, give me relief ... the pain ... I think I am going to die." Godfrew pulled his cloak under his damaged arm and made a crude sling out of it. One of his fingers was mashed and dangled by a sinew. "Godwine ... friend ... tie this off, please ... or something."

Godwine did the best he could, but stood back, as requested, when Godfrew struggled to stand up. In the distance, a trumpet brayed. All along the rampart wall, Normans—whether engaged with members of the wolf packs or the Hounds of Hell—left off the fighting and made for the protection of the castle and it's stone walls. Covering flights of arrows came from the castle, discouraging pursuit.

How long Godfrew stood there with his back to the fence, he did not know, but the temperature seemed to have dropped dramatically by the time the bands had reassembled by his side. Stanley had lost more teeth and his ring-mail coat had arrows hanging from it, both back and front. Tosti had another cut on his face. Dunstan had arrow grazes on his bare forearms and a trickle of dried blood near his ear. Clunn showed no signs of having been in battle. Godwine's band had lost Ulf the Unlucky. Otherwise, they were unscratched.

"Time to go. We must get back to the barn before the Hounds of Hell find it." Godfrew moved slowly back along the rampart toward the gateway. Every step sent a jolting pain through his body and he shivered uncontrollably. As he neared the steps by the gateway, he turned and seemed panic struck. "Ragnor?"

"He is being carried, Master Wulf. Trust me." Godwine leaned on his quarter-staff. "Are you sure that you don't want a hand?"

"NO. Thank you." Slowly and painfully, Godfrew made it down—one step at a time.

Standing by the gate, holding a horse, was Torquil, the leader of Earl Edric's house carls. "Been in the wars, have we?" He held out a folded cloth. "Earl Edric said to take this and hang it over the door of your lodgings." Godwine took it and opened it up. It was a banner with a raven embroidered on it—in the old style. "Hopefully, our allies will recognise it and keep away. No promises, mind you. You are at the priory tithe barn, yes? As instructed, yes? Return there by way of the monier's street. We hold that—as we know what it is worth. I doubt our allies would know what they were getting their hands on, seeing as they hardly use money for trade." Torquil waved them out of the way as a group of mounted house carls rode out through the gates driving a flock of confused sheep before them. "I would not hang around. Things are wild now, but they will get wilder before this night is out."

Godwine led the way back to the barn. Although the soldiers had all retreated to the castle, the screams and sounds of fighting and slaughter did not cease. The Hounds of Hell were butchering unarmed civilians—men, women and children. Their desperate cries and appeals went unheard. The Hounds of Hell were dragging women out their hiding places and raping them in the streets ... woman after woman. The next victim, seeing what was being done to the present one, screamed and struggled unsuccessfully to be free. Drunken Welsh warriors rolled around the streets, some literally swimming in a vat of ale standing in the burnt ruins of a brew house. Order was only found where Edric's house carls held the land, but they kept to their allotted place. What went on elsewhere, they treated with indifference.

The barn was guarded by Brunhilda. Her long bow was drawn, her arrow notched. Her two brats had their slingshots ready. "Only us, my love," Godwine called out as they came near. "Look what I have brought. A pretty flag to hang over the door!"

As the wolf packs slowly filed into the barn, Godfrew hung back to be last in. His final view of the mayhem outside was of Clunn about to mount a nun old enough to be his mother. The poor woman was stretched out on a tomb, her arms and legs held by Hounds of Hell, no doubt awaiting their turn.

Godfrew vomited.

* * *

"Strong wine, Wulf!" Brunhilda proffered Godfrew a clay cup filled with a dark red fluid. All around was the sound of drunken snoring, the smells of drink and vomit from the barn's inhabitants, saved from the hell of Hereford by Clunn's free booze and Brunhilda's courage.

"No. Thank you. I couldn't. The smell. I feel sick." Godfrew swooned in and out with the pain in his head and shoulder.

"Wulf, that is not an invitation. It is an order! I am going to have to set your shoulder and cut off your finger. You want to be conscious while I do it? Don't be stupid. Drink the strong wine. Drink as much of it as you can, as quickly as you can. Then, I can get on with my work." Brunhilda thrust the cup and a full jug at Godfrew, then went over to where Kriemhild was stitching up Ragnor's torn arm and side. Ragnor's gasps and squeals were matched by that of the serving maid from the tavern by the gate. She had been "rescued" by Clunn and Tosti yesterday with the barrels of ale and wine. She now lay naked on the straw as the members of the bands took their pleasure of her. She made no objection to their actions until it was Dunstan's turn. A big man in all ways, she made a painful gasp as he entered her and was silenced only when he settled down and put his full weight on her small, but well-shaped body.

Godfrew drank the wine and felt its affect—waiting for blackness, comforted only by the warmth of Shock's body and the thought of Elfgifu, safe at Lydbury.

* * *

The fine rain had put the fires out. The resultant damp, burnt smell reminded Godfrew of the woods above Garrat. He felt sick. In front stood the tent of Earl Edric. Two of the Earl's hearth troop guarded the entrance. Inside, voices could be heard—at times low, at other times loud and angry. Godfrew stood and waited. Finally, the flap was thrown back and the hearth troopers tied it up. Earl Edric strode out, dressed in light blue silk, the colour matching his eyes. He was followed by two short, stocky men. One was dark of skin and hair—almost dark enough to almost be a Moor. Godfrew had once seen a Moor in London when he was but a child. The other was fair enough to be a Saxon—white skin, blue eyes, with wavy golden hair hanging in twisted ringlets down his back. The man's beard and moustaches were white gold.

"Look, Edric, just make sure we get our fair share." The golden one had his arms crossed over his barrel chest.

"I will, Bleddyn. I said that I would, so trust me." Earl Edric's voice was even, but there was a slight edge to it. Again, Godfrew noticed that although the Earl spoke the Welsh tongue, he spoke it as an Englishman. It lacked the music that the language needed to make it come alive.

"Trust you? Now there's a worry! Only as far as I can throw you, Saxon!" The dark one spat, legs apart, his finger wagging at the Earl.

"Look, Rhiwallon, you dirty little wog. You were the one who broke the truce, not me. You got what you asked for."

Woden's Wolf

Edric's tone made his hearth troopers cringe and take a step back.

"Dirty wog, am I, you vile snake's spawn!" Rhiwallon took a step forward to wag his finger closer to the Earl's nose. Edric brushed the man's arm aside and grabbed him by the neck of his grubby shirt, lifting him off the ground.

"Now, now," Bleddyn ducked under Edric's arms and stepped between the protagonists. "We are all in this together. Edric has said that he will share things evenly between us." He turned his head to face his countryman. "Rhiwallon?"

"Not just the plunder. He must also share the fighting. It was us who rode into Hereford. We took the town. Where were his men? Eh? Taking the silver, that's what!" Being held off the ground was making the dark man's face go a strange reddish-brown colour.

"Who let your filthy dogs in? Eh?" Edric tightened his grip on Rhiwallon's shirt.

"Quite so, Edric. We all played our part. No doubt we shall all get our share of the profit." Bleddyn spoke slowly and calmly. "Now, Edric, put Rhiwallon down. Please, Edric."

Edric put the now spluttering Rhiwallon down.

"Thank you, Edric. Don't worry about Rhiwallon. He and I will take a walk and I will explain things to him." Bleddyn guided a still protesting Rhiwallon away. As the two princes walked off, the dark-skinned Goda came from inside the tent, followed by the two other ladies. Edric's stool, table and drink were laid before him. He sat down. It was not until he had drunk two pots of his herbal drink that he acknowledged Godfrew's presence.

"A seat, Woden's Wolf?" Edric stood up and indicated his own stool. Godfrew dared not decline and sat on the stool. "Who would deal with the wogs, eh? I don't know how long I can keep this lot together. I may have to cut my expenses and call things off." Edric cupped his chin and paced the grass in front of the tent, oblivious to the rain. After a while, he came to a decision. "Wulf, you and Godwine, with your bands, shall return to Lydbury. You will join the escort in taking home my share of the plunder from Hereford. Wait for me there at Lydbury. I shall keep things stirring here until I can see ahead more clearly. Our new king is an unknown to me. Will he allow the Welsh to invade his lands? Will he allow his earls to have their own private spats? Will he have the time to sort things out himself? Until I have a better idea of things, I will stay here ... at least, until I have stripped Hereford bare. I doubt that I will be able to take the castle ... not unless this William, the would-be King of England, is very lazy and willing to let me besiege the place for a year or so. Somehow, I don't think he will." Edric made for the stool. Godfrew painfully got up and moved aside to let the Earl resume his seat. "Till then, Wulf."

Woden's Wolf

The Calm

At first, Godfrew had ridden his dark pony, but the animal's gait had sent biting pains through his shattered shoulder and out through his amputated finger. Godfrew was reminded of the toothache he had suffered the previous spring, an ache that never left and gave constant sharp spikes of pain. The tooth problem had been solved by the village blacksmith at the cost of a copper styca at Mitcham Fair, but arms—unlike teeth—could not be pulled. The next day Godfrew had the dark pony tied to the tail gate of the wagon carrying Ragnor and Krimhild and joined the couple atop bolts of cloth. The swaying made him feel sick. When the wagon's wheels fell into ruts, the jolts made him cry out in pain, leaving his teeth chattering and his brow pouring sweat. Twice, he was thrown loose from his seat and struck the stump of his finger. Each time, he was sick and passed out. The third day saw Godfrew back on the pony, but he needed to constantly stop and rest. The escort soon became tired of stopping the convoy. As soon as they spied a small abbey ahead, they sent riders to ask sanctuary for Godfrew and Ragnor, whose wounds were starting to fester and throw him into delirium.

They transferred Ragnor and Godfrew to a small cart, normally used for carrying food to the advance guard. The dark pony followed, not needing to be tethered. Awaiting them at the gate were three nuns. Two were quite young, slim of build—their habits hanging from them, then expanding as the wind caught them and made them look like ravens with feathers puffing up and down during a dust bath. The middle one was a mature woman, full of figure and good food. As the cart halted, the nuns came to the tail gate.

"What have we here?" The plump nun cocked her head and removed her arms from her voluminous sleeves. She lifted the covering over Ragnor and looked at the wounds on his arm and body, now almost as red as his hair. Kriemhild watched protectively, ready to spring if Ragnor looked in danger of being hurt. "Your stitching?" the nun looked at Kriemhild inquisitively.

"Yes." The girl's reply sounded defensive. She tensed like a dog waiting to be struck for stealing a bone.

"The stitching is well done, but you should have cleansed the wound better." The nun's face softened and so did her voice. "But battle wounds are hard to keep clean. Who knows where the sword that cut your man had been before. Come child, help the sisters to get your man down and into the abbey." The nun turned her attention to Godfrew: "You don't need a hand, you can get yourself down. Just follow me."

"Oi, lady!" Dunstan stood up on the cart's seat. "What about his horse?"

"His horse will have to wait. If it is still there, later on someone will bring it in." The nun turned, followed by Godfrew and the dark pony. She entered the gate without looking back.

"Oi, Wulf. Thing."

"Thing, Dunstan?"

"Be lucky!" Dunstan sat down on the seat and flicked the reins. As the cart moved off, Godfrew started to raise his good arm in acknowledgment, but couldn't get it above waist height before it started to pull on the bad one. He hoped Dunstan had seen the movement. He did not want the big man to think he was being snubbed.

The plump nun set a cracking pace. Soon Godfrew was left behind in her wake. She did not take long to catch up with the other women. Despite their slim build, the two young nuns seemed to have little difficulty carrying Ragnor. They formed a bandy chair with their arms. Kriemhild trailed behind them, waiting to catch Ragnor should he fall.

"Get him into one of the empty cells. I'll look at him there, rather than in the infirmary." The plump nun went ahead and opened a door set within a pointed arch. By the time Godfrew had made it through the arch, the two young nuns were laying Ragnor down on a bed. The plump nun stood by the open door of another cell. "Come on, young man. You are not dead. You can walk faster than that. In here."

Godfrew entered the cell. It was unlike any other he had seen. The bed was soft and pumped up. There was much furniture—all richly carved. The floor was strewn with fresh, sweet-smelling herbs and the walls were adorned with woven wool hangings showing scenes from saint's lives. "It is not what I expected." He shuffled over and sank, exhausted, into a padded chair.

"What did you want? If you are after bare walls and a draft, you can sleep in the stables with that over bold horse of yours!" The nun arched her brows and stuffed her hands back into her sleeves.

"Only a fool would want that. It is just that I have never seen such comfort in a guest's cell before." Godfrew let his head fall back onto the head rest and allowed the nag from his arm to wash over him.

"This is not a guest's cell. It belongs to one of the sisters. At present we have several spare cells. When the Normans from Hereford went on the rampage and Earl Edric loosened his wolf packs, some of the sisters thought it best to move back to the mother church. You have been brought here because it was less of a distance to carry the boy. Normally, you would have been lodged in one of the guest's cells." The nun removed her right hand from its hiding place in the sleeve and gestured, encompassing the room. "Enjoy this, for the guest's cells are not so well disposed." Godfrew looked at her hard, an unasked question on his face. "Guests are only here for a night or two. We have to feed them for no charge. It would not pay for them to feel too much at home. We would never be able to move them on!" The nun walked over to an exquisitely carved table that showed etched scenes from the Exodus and poured a goblet of wine from a silver ewer. She gave the wine to Godfrew.

"But I have been a guest at convents, abbeys and monasteries many times. I have seen the cells the nuns and monks have. None are like this." Godfrew took a sip of the smooth, sweet wine. As he swallowed the first mouthful, he could feel it warming his gullet, then slip snugly to his stomach.

The nun set the ewer down and walked to the foot of the bed. She pulled back the wall hanging to reveal a high window. The light threw a mixed pattern on the bed—various browns from the small sections of thin horn set in the window. "What would you rather have? Keep us all living in damp, mouldy caves so that we are crippled with rheumatism and can't bend our knees to bow before the Host on the altar? Sleeping on stone floors so that we are too stiff to kneel in prayer? Wearing hair shirts so that we spend most of our time being distracted by the desire to scratch, rather than devoting our minds to thoughts of the Lord Jesus Christ and what he has done for us by his blessed passion? Well? Well?"

Godfrew took some more wine and thought before he answered. "No. I was merely comparing you to others. Who is to say who is right. It is not for me to comment. At this moment I am all too grateful for the warmth and comfort." Godfrew finished the wine, closed his eyes and soon fell into a deep and dreamless sleep. When he awoke, the light had almost gone. He found himself looking at the plump nun and three others. He took the proffered goblet of wine. This time, the wine was bitter. Before he could comment, the blackness enfolded him.

* * *

Godfrew came into the cell. Kriemhild, sitting at Ragnor's side, had fallen asleep with her head on his fevered chest. Godfrew was moving easier now. His shoulder and arm had been reset and the new bindings were more comfortable than those hastily put in place by Brunhilda after the taking of Hereford. Using his left hand, he clumsily moved the girl's hair from her face. Her skin was soft and unmarked. The only blemishes were two small, flat moles on her cheek bone. In the flickering light of the oil lamp, her complexion took on a golden hue. Godfrew thought that she looked like an angel. He was unable to resist stroking her cheek, but his movements were clumsy and the girl woke with a start.

"Master Wulf!" Kriemhild blinked her eyes and sat up. The cheek that had lain on Ragnor's chest was creased and flushed pink. The girl opened her eyes wide, then half closed them. She seemed confused, as if trying to separate dream from reality. "I ... I must have fallen asleep. Ragnor ... is he all right?"

"No worse than before." Godfrew caught himself studying the girl's neck and soft rounded shoulders. He gave his head a shake. "You must be tired. You should be in bed." Godfrew's voice sounded thick, his breath shallow. His body

The Calm

stirred as he caught the girl's scent, and he watched her through narrowing eyes. "Yes, bed. You need to be in bed ... tucked up."

"But not in this one, young woman!" The plump nun strode in and brushed Godfrew aside. Fortunately, she touched on his good side. "Well?"

"Perhaps I could be near his side. In case he needs me?" Kriemhild pleaded.

"To your room, child." The nun's voice was brisk and brooked no answer. "Do you ever pray the 'Our Father'?"

"Yes, Sister, sometimes," confessed Kriemhild.

"Then when you next get to the bit that goes: 'And lead us not into temptation', say it twice!" The nun closed the door behind Kriemhild. "The same goes for you too, young man. Wulf?"

"Some call me that. But why should I say that line twice, Sister?"

"Wulf, the eyes are the mirror of the soul. Now ..." The nun stripped the covers off of Ragnor's bed. They were soaked in sweat. "... give me a hand. I will roll him, you pull the under sheet away." Godfrew hesitated. "Go on. You only need one hand. You are not a cripple, even if you like to think so. Pull the sheet away, now!" Godfrew obeyed. "Pick up the clean one from the floor near the door." Godfrew did as he was told. "Put it on the bed. Tidy now, no rucks." The nun rolled Ragnor the other way and pulled the sheet tight on her side, then bustled Godfrew out of the way to tighten his side. "Easy, wasn't it!" She then opened the door and brought in a basin and ewer, together with some cloths. When she poured the water from the ewer into the basin, Godfrew caught a strong familiar smell—not unpleasant, but strong. "Balm of Gilead," informed the nun. "Keep your dog away from the lad. I don't want the infection to get even worse. Now, take that cloth and wipe his body. Keep away from the wounds. I will do them. Oh, and you had better do his private parts."

"Lead us not into temptation? Is that it?" Godfrew took the cloth. He found it very hard trying to wring the excess water out, but eventually succeeded by combining his good hand and his teeth.

"The temptations I suffer from—and the sins I fall into as a result—are between me and God. Would you be my Confessor, Wulf?"

"No. Sister ... Sister?"

"Clotild."

"No, Sister Clotild."

"Good, for I am sure you would be horrified at what you learned of me!" Sister Clotild examined the inflamed wounds. "Under the bottom of the basin ... the thin yellow cloth ... bring it here, but be careful not to let it undo." Godfrew retrieved the cloth and found that it contained finely chopped herbs. "Mainly comfrey," Clotild told Godfrew.

"That is a new one on me. My mother used many herbs, but I have never heard of that one." Godfrew leaned over and sniffed the poultice, but all he could smell was the putrefaction of Ragnor's wounds. Shock sniffed the wounds and gave a cautious lick, but even he found the smell and taste too strong.

"The Norwegians use it. They brought me a cutting. Their cousins, the Rus, use it a lot, apparently. It is good, but, like the Vikings who gave it to me, it needs to be contained or it takes over everything!" Clotild placed the cloth around Ragnor's body, mounding the herbs over the wounds. Once satisfied, she lightly bound the herbal poultice in place. "Tomorrow you will meet the Abbess, The Lady Ethelburger. Be sure you are clean and presentable and watch your manners." Sister Clotild looked flustered. "Oh, dear. Where on earth is the other poultice I made for his arm?"

Godfrew had a question of his own: "Why does the redheaded Ragnor have freckles on his private parts when they are so rarely exposed to the sun?"

* * *

The Lady Ethelburger, Abbess of Sedgebarrow, sat at the end of the hall, enthroned on a high-backed chair complete with a wooden awning. Around her sat young novice nuns, sewing and chattering. Godfrew found the scene more like that of an earl's court than of a convent—even to the armed men standing at either side of the Lady Ethelburger's chair. As Godfrew drew nearer, he noticed that the Lady's habit was

The Calm

made of fine wool and her head covering of purest silk. Her crucifix was gold with inlaid silver nails and thorns, whilst Christ's wounds wept rubies for blood. An arm's length away, Godfrew knelt as gracefully as he could. Shock imitated his master.

"My Lady Ethelburger. Greetings. May Christ's peace be on you and your house." Godfrew saw the lady's slippers. They were the softest of doe skin, stitched with gold thread.

"Greetings to you, Wulf the stranger, in Jesus name. Though it is a bit late to wish peace on my house I fear!" Lady Ethelburger's voice was deep and sultry, like her dark brown eyes.

"Indeed, my Lady. On the way over, I noticed some of your outbuildings were burnt. Was it by natural causes?" Godfrew shuffled his knees, wishing the flagged stone floor was rush strewn rather than carpet strewn.

"Yes. The Norman, Sir Richard of Scrope, sent his men visiting. Show a Norman a priory or an abbey—or indeed any building that isn't his—and he naturally wants to burn it down." The young nuns laughed at their Abbess' joke, their voices sounding like the bells hung in fruit trees to scare away the birds at harvest time. The Lady locked her eyes onto Godfrew's and half closed them, breathing out slowly through her nostrils.

Godfrew acknowledged the jest by smiling. "I have observed the same habit, Lady. However, I must comment that you were lucky to lose so few buildings. I am surprised to find no scorch marks on any of the main ones." Godfrew found himself unable to break eye contact. The whole world was shrinking to Lady Ethelburger's eyes alone.

"There is no such thing as luck, Wulf." The lady's eyes widened and Godfrew sank even deeper into them.

"Indeed not, Lady." Godfrew started to get short of breath. "I am sure you will remind me that all is in God's hands."

"No," the Abbess laughed a deep, deep laugh. At last she released Godfrew's eyes. "It was not luck, or even God who saved the abbey and we poor, defenceless women. It was Edmund and the rest of my hearth troop who saved us." The tall warrior at the lady's right hand side cracked a smile and shook out his mane of bright, gold hair. "Clever Edmund. He knew he didn't have enough men to beat the naughty Normans outside, so he let them into the abbey yard. He then closed the gate and they remain with us still. Every Sunday my chaplain says a mass for their souls—all thirty of them."

"One, my Lady," whispered Edmund, the leader of the hearth troops.

"Of course, one." She looked across at Edmund. Her eyebrows arched. Her tongue explored her upper lip, teasing him. "Plus thirty!" Again, the laugh. "Wulf." Their eyes locked. "I am from the royal family of Mercia. My ancestor, Wulfhere, King of the Mercians, gave the land that this abbey stands on to his cousin, our forefather, Berhtferth, in 674 Ana Domino. My family has always provided the Abbess. It also continues to provide well-trained hearth troops, thank God. No rat-faced, snivelling, half-Viking Norman is going to take it away from either me or my family." Godfrew could see only her eyes and hear only her voice. "So, that is that." Ethelburger's voice deepened. "Tell me about yourself. You are Earl Edric's man?"

"Yes, Lady. I am Earl Edric's man." Godfrew knew giving the Abbess that information could be dangerous, but he felt unable to resist.

"You were hurt in the fight for Hereford?" the voice asked.

"Yes Lady. I and my men took the gate. We were inside the town. I was struck down after the gates were opened." Godfrew wondered why he had said so much.

"Earl Edric is coming this way?" the voice was silky smooth and alluring.

"Yes, Lady. Back to Lydbury."

"When?" enquired the honey voice.

"I do not know, Lady. If I knew I would tell you."

"I know. Now about yourself. Are you married?"

"Yes, Lady. My wife is expecting our first child soon."

"You have not seen her for a long time, having been about the Earl's business?"

"Not for a long time, Lady." Godfrew found he wanted to tell all—everything—even to bare his soul to the voice.

"And you want to be with her?"

"Yes, Lady, I do."

"And you crave for the touch of her body?"

"I ache, Lady."

The Calm

"And you have not sought to ease this ache?" The voice allowed a hint of amusement to creep into its tone.

"No, Lady. I see others, but I think only of my wife." The only thing Godfrew felt able to withhold was Elfgifu's name. That alone was his and not to be shared.

"What a wonderful man! Your wife should be proud of you. Sin, repentance, confession, absolution and then free to sin again. It is such a natural circle. Learn to enjoy it." The Lady Ethelburger clapped her hands and Godfrew was released from the spell of her eyes. No one said anything when he looked around, but the young nuns were smiling secret smiles at him. Godfrew could not remember what had happened, but he was sure it was something he would regret. The Lady indicated that he should rise, then she beckoned him over. Shock followed. "Well, Wulf, what are we going to do with you? Your friend will not be capable of travelling for a while yet, provided he recovers at all. I suspect Sister Clotild will leave him a weakling, unable to fight again. She thinks it is a waste of time repairing warriors who will only go out and get chopped up all over again."

"My Lady!" protested the plump Clotild from the doorway where she stood.

"Oh, fie, Clotild. I only jest. I am sure he will soon be up and about, chasing all my young ladies around the abbey." The tinkle of laughter from the novice nuns echoed around the hall. "Wulf."

Godfrew tried not to look at the Lady Ethelburger's eyes, but fight as he would, he could not resist. Once his eyes met hers, they locked. "Lady."

"What am I to do with you? Your comrade in arms, provided he lives, can work in the grounds to pay his keep. His young woman can work in the kitchens ... but you ... what am I going to do with you?" The abbess played with the crucifix around her neck.

"I can read and write English. I can read some Latin. But I need to get home to my wife Lady."

"It would be tempting to find some personal work for you, Wulf. I would find that interesting, I think." Ethelburger looked at the crucifix and thought before speaking again. "But I feel moved to employ you in reading to my young novices ... maybe help those whose reading is slow. When you are healed, you may return to your wife. Now ..." Lady Ethelburger held the crucifix in front of Godfrew's face and moved it till it caught the sunlight. "... look at the image of our Lord ... look ... look at our Lord."

The cross seemed to come alive, writhing and flexing in the sunlight. Jesus moved his arms off of the cross and held them out to Godfrew.

"Look at our Lord ... feel his healing enter your shoulder ... your arm ... your head ... your hand ... feel him push the pain away ... rest in his power ... trust in his healing." The Abbess left Godfrew looking at the crucifix for sometime before she clapped her hands. Again, Godfrew came out of the spell ... again, the secret smiles ... again, he could remember nothing.

"My Lady?"

"You are to read to me and my young Sisters every morning at this time."

* * *

Godfrew stood in the hall, surprised to find it empty. For the past month he had come every morning at this hour, excepting Sundays, to read and to teach reading to the young novice nuns. His shoulder was much better and no longer needed to be so heavily strapped. His amputated finger was a bigger problem. The stump poked out and was always getting knocked as a result.

He had come from talking with Ragnor, who was convalescing with light duties in the kitchen, aided and encouraged by Kriemhild. Now, Godfrew found himself alone in the hall. Unsure what to do, he sat at the foot of the Lady Ethelburger's chair and started to flick his way through the volume he had brought from the library. Shock sat at his side and nestled his head in Godfrew's lap. The book was in Latin. Godfrew found it hard work, though a lot easier than he had done when he had started the lessons a month ago. The big problem was that although he could read it well enough, he didn't understand a lot of it. Most of the books in the library were in Latin. Surprisingly, many were not on religion. Many were poetry—some even full of love poems, particularly those written by a man named Ovid. In view of his position as a married man amongst a veritable flock of unmarried and, mainly, young women, Godfrew left the love poems behind. Instead, he used the lives of saints or history books for his readings and lessons. Today, it was an historical text by Livy. Godfrew had just found a piece that seemed both interesting and not too hard to understand when he heard the nuns coming in. He put the book down and stood up.

The nuns were not in their usual black habits with white head coverings. Rather, their heads were uncovered and they wore only their white under garment. Each nun carried a lit taper. Except the Abbess, they all had their heads bowed. It was the silken-voiced Lady Abbess who led the procession into the hall. Her chestnut hair with its golden highlights was tied, knotted and lay in the nape of her neck. As the last nun came in, Lady Ethelburger's hearth troops followed. There were twelve warriors and Edmund, the leader of the hearth troops.

Three other entrances led to the hall, in addition to the main one. Two hearth troopers opened each door and went out. Their footsteps indicated that they stood just the other side, guarding the entrance. Another hearth trooper stood with his back to the door, guarding it from the inside. Edmund walked to a small door that Godfrew knew led to a small side room and stood guard there. Once all were in place, the nuns turned to face the main entrance of the hall and sat on the floor. The door opened and a wooden frame was brought in by two warriors and a priest. The frame had restraining ropes at each corner. Godfrew remembered the Breton Captain at Lydbury and he felt sick.

"Wulf, come sit by me," the Abbess commanded. Godfrew did not move, frozen to the spot by anticipated terror. Lady Ethelburger turned her head and looked at Godfrew, seeking his eyes. "Wulf, come and sit by me." Godfrew left his place and joined the Abbess, where he sat on the floor at her feet. "It is time for our monthly confession and penance. The nuns will be heard in order of their time here. I will go last. It is not appropriate that your penance be meted out in the hall. Yours will be in private, but you will help me with my penance."

"Yes, Lady."

The priest went to the door that was guarded by Edmund and entered the room. After a minute of contemplation, he opened the door again and called in a high, clear voice: "Who has sinned and wishes to be confessed and absolved?"

A small, very young nun got up and entered the room. The priest closed the door behind her. The nun must have been fairly sinless, as she was not in the room long before she re-emerged. The youngster walked to the small statue of the virgin and child set into the far wall and set her burning taper on the flag stone floor in front of it. She then proceeded to the frame. The member of the hearth troop guarding the main door came over to her and undid the ties at the back of her undergarment. The wool chemise dropped to the floor, leaving her naked. The nun stepped over her fallen clothing, walked to the frame and stretched out her arms. The warrior tied her wrists and ankles to the frame, then returned to his place in front of the door. The nun next in seniority to the youngster got up off of the floor and walked to the warrior. He untied a knotted leather thong from his waist and gave it to the nun, who then proffered it to the novice. The novice kissed the tool of punishment. When Shock saw the knotted thong, he slinked away to hide behind Lady Ethelburger's high chair. The young nun commenced to say a prayer in Latin. As she said the amen, the other nun struck her back with the thong. Red weals appeared on her white flesh and the youngster gave a cry of pain, but she immediately started to say another prayer. Five prayers were said. Five strokes were administered. When the penance had been completed, the more senior nun walked to the front of the youngster and presented her with the thong. The youngster kissed it, then kissed the cheeks of the other nun. Once that was complete, the warrior came and unbound the young novice, who put her chemise on again and sat down.

The nun who had done the flogging returned to collect her taper, then entered the room where the priest was awaiting her confession. This nun took longer, but she too came out, was stripped naked, trussed to the frame, said her prayers and was flogged by the nun next in seniority to her. Her punishment was ten prayers and ten strokes of the thong. The nun administering the punishment had a strong arm. By the time the penance had been made, the penitent's

The Calm

back was bleeding. Godfrew was surprised to see that, once released, the nun looked serene, rather than hurt by the experience. One by one, the nuns went to confession, put their taper in front of the shrine, were stripped, flogged and released. Some cried out in pain. Some groaned. Some moaned—almost with pleasure.

What struck Godfrew most was the variety of shapes and sizes the female form came in. Some had unblemished skin, others had spots and moles. Some had big breasts, while others were small and dainty. Some had round buttocks while others hung and sagged. Some were skinny and others had rolls of fat. Some had protruding bellies while others had hard, muscular ones. Some had hair that laid like a mat on their bellies. Others had almost none at all. Sister Clotild had spotty skin, big breasts, hanging buttocks—complete with dimples—rolls of fat, a protruding belly and far more hair on her body than Godfrew had on his. The Lady Ethelburger laid into her with the thong as hard as she could, cutting Clotild's back and buttocks badly. The older Sister had to be helped back to her place once her ordeal was complete.

The Lady Ethelburger returned to pick up her lighted taper: "Wulf, you are to help me with my penance, wait for me by the frame of repentance and forgiveness." The Abbess looked deep into Godfrew's eyes: "Go now, Wulf, and wait for me." The Lady Abbess went into the confessional room and was there a long, long, time.

Godfrew waited by the frame. When the Abbess came from the room and stood by the frame, he knew what he had to do. The warrior undid the ties and Ethelburger's silk chemise slid to the floor with a light rustle. The lady was not young, but had born no children. Her body was firm and taunt. By the time Ethelburger had stepped to the frame and been secured by her own hearth trooper, Godfrew had enough time to register that her skin was not white, but pink, as if it had been exposed to the sun. Godfrew proffered the thong to Ethelburger to kiss.

"Do not hold back, Wulf. I have been very sinful and deserve punishment." Her eyes locked onto Godfrew's: "Remember, Wulf—fifteen stokes, never the same place—and do it with feeling." She then kissed the thong.

Ethelburger's back and buttocks were criss-crossed with little scars from previous administrations of the thong. Some marks were still purple. Godfrew listened to the chant of her prayer. When the "amen" came, he smote her buttocks with the thong far harder than he thought he ever could hit a woman. Ethelburger gasped and let out a long sigh. Another prayer. This time Godfrew smote her shoulders and Ethelburger strained against her bonds. After ten prayers and strokes Godfrew was sweating and so was the Abbess. Sweat ran down Ethelburger's back, down the crack between her cheeks and dripped onto the floor. The whole of her body glistened. By the fifteenth stroke, Godfrew's arm was hanging off and he wished his other arm was fully mended so that it could have shared the burden. As the Lady drew her undergarment back on, she shivered as the silk caressed her bruised skin.

"Come, Wulf, follow me. It is time you were confessed and served whatever penance you are given." Ethelburger's eyes and voice were deep and turgid.

"Yes, Lady." Godfrew followed the Abbess into the confessional. It was not long before the priest led the nuns out of the hall in procession. Edmund, with Shock at his side, remained on guard outside the small room, but the other hearth troopers followed the nuns out.

"I don't know about you," a tall trooper confided to his only slightly shorter comrade. "I'm going to look up my wife. I don't care what tasks she has been given in the kitchen today, I have an even bigger one for her."

When Godfrew left the hall, he found it strange that nuns and members of the hearth troop alike looked at him differently and smiled at him a lot. Why, he could not imagine. All he could remember doing since he had arrived at the abbey was read ... and what was there to smile about in that?

* * *

One of Earl Edric's convoys passed through the area the week after the general confession and Godfrew had joined it with the Lady Ethelburger's blessing. In fact, the blessing had been most full and had made Godfrew feel somewhat special. Ragnor and Kriemhild had stayed behind. Ragnor was much better, but still not fully healed. Kriemhild fitted in well with the abbey lay workers and Ragnor appreciated the fine food everyone was served. By now, they had married and moved out of the spare nun's cell and into a small hut. It was bigger and warmer than anything at Lydbury. Godfrew suspected that it would be a while before the pair made an appearance at Earl Edric's main manor.

It was early autumn. As the convoy broke out of the forest on the ridge above Lydbury, they plunged into a clinging fog. Soon moisture was dripping off of the dark pony's reins and from Godfrew's hooded cloak. The fog was so thick that they had almost reached the gate before the watch guards saw them and raised the alarm. The convoy halted whilst they identified themselves, then slowly wound through the staggered entrance and into the holding proper. Godfrew let the wagons and other riders carry on to the storehouses, as his shoulder would still not let him do much physical work. He knew that Dagobert, the manor reeve, would not let those bringing in plunder count up their own goods. Godfrew looked for Elfgifu, but could not see her amongst the many wives and girl friends who had rushed into the yard looking for their loved ones. He was still looking when Oakleaf tugged at his cloak.

"Cousin Wulf. You are back. We heard you were hurt. We received your letter from Sedgebarrow Abbey. It is good to have you home again." The mist had already started to soak into the girl's hair, making it seem more ginger than usual. By her side, her little sister Joanna nodded her agreement.

"Elfgifu? Where is my wife? Is she all right?" Godfrew slipped slowly out of the saddle and handed the reins of the dark pony to the boy waiting to take her.

"Elfgifu is fine." Oakleaf played in the mud with her big toe. "She is in the sleeping hut. She spends most of her time in the hut." Oakleaf held out her hand. "Come, cousin Wulf, let me take you there!" Hand in hand, the pair ran toward the sleeping hut, Shock at their heels. As they neared, the leather curtain across the entrance was pulled back and a bloated Elfgifu heaved herself out. Godfrew let go of Oakleaf's hand, though the girl seemed reluctant to do the same.

"Elfgifu, Cariad. All is well? I feared that I would not get home in time!" Godfrew went to embrace his wife, but she took his hand instead and waddled him inside the hut.

Woden's Wolf

"It's is nice to have you back again, Wulf. I have not had an easy time." Elfgifu moved along the hut, using the wooden sides of the sleeping pallets for support. "I could have done with you here. Oakleaf is lazy. She always seems to vanish when I need her. Joanna is always either getting under my feet or elsewhere. She never comes when I call her. Wulf, I needed you at home."

"Elfgifu, I am home now. Come and let me hold you." Godfrew at last embraced his wife, but was greeted by the sound of liquid hitting the floor. He held Elfgifu at arm's length, looked down and saw that water was dripping off the edge of his wife's skirt. "Elfgifu?"

"My waters have broken." Elfgifu looked stunned and just stared at the dripping fluid. Godfrew grabbed the night bucket and put it between his wife's feet.

"Stay there." Godfrew ran to the entrance "Oakleaf! OAKLEAF!"

"You will be lucky to find the wench. She is never around when I want her." Elfgifu wandered to the entrance. Godfrew ducked back inside and retrieved the bucket, which he again placed between her feet.

"You wanted me, cousin?" Oakleaf smiled her sly smile.

"Elfgifu's waters have broken. I think that means that the baby is coming." Godfrew looked to Elfgifu for confirmation. His wife vaguely waved her hand. "Yes, the baby is coming. I will get her back inside. You go get the midwife. Now, please, Oakleaf ... now!"

Oakleaf walked to the great hall, swaying her hips as she had seen Earl Edric's ladies do. Once inside the hall, Oakleaf made for the side hall, then the kitchen. She looked around, seeking the withered old crone of a midwife who doubled as the chief herb selector for the manor's food. The old woman was sprinkling dried leaves onto some goose carcasses. "Mother Chickweed. My cousin Elfgifu is about to deliver her child."

"Eh? What?" the midwife cocked her head and offered her best ear to Oakleaf, gesturing that she should repeat what she had said.

"My cousin, Elfgifu, is about to deliver her child," Oakleaf repeated, her voice now so loud that all in the kitchen stopped work to listen.

The Calm

"Oh, why didn't you say so. Daughter!" Mother Chickweed called across the unfortunate geese to a slightly younger version of herself. "Get the birthing stool. That woman of young Woden's is about to whelp. Hurry now, I hate having to clean mud and dirt off of babies that can't wait and drop on the floor!"

Oakleaf moved out of the way, knowing that she was no longer wanted. As she turned to go she bumped into the Lady Gondul.

"Oh, my Lady. I am sorry. I didn't see you there." Oakleaf went red, as only one with ginger hair could.

"It's the little garlic girl." Lady Gondul looked at Oakleaf with her sharp blue eyes.

"Oh, madam. After what you said last time, I have stopped eating garlic. See." Oakleaf came close to Gondul and parted her lips, keeping her mouth just from the Lady's. Gondul moved her face closer. Oakleaf closed her eyes and kissed the lady of the manor, accepting Gondul's warm, clove-tasting tongue—sucking it gently, as she had seen Elfgifu do once when Godfrew had kissed her.

It was the lady Gondul who broke the kiss. "Definitely, no garlic. So, you have learned a good habit from me." Gondul undid the ties on the small leather purse at her waist and took out a silver penny which she put in the palm of Oakleaf's hand. "A small reward. Perhaps later I shall be able to get you to change some of your other habits."

* * *

Mother Chickweed need not have hurried, as it was a full ten hours before Elfgifu gave birth to her first son, Jaul. The child was small and weak. It was thought that he might not live, particularly with the cold season starting. Jaul proved them wrong. By Yuletide, he was as healthy as—if somewhat smaller than—any other child of his age. Elfgifu was exhausted by the experience and did not thrive as well as her son.

Godfrew celebrated Yuletide in the hall with the Earl and his full host, but Elfgifu and the baby remained in the sleeping hut.

Godfrew sat at the top table with Dagobert, checking the books and accounting for the plunder that Earl Edric had amassed from the summer's raiding. With his arm still not strong, Godfrew found himself becoming more and more of a clerk and administrator as time went by. The role suited him, as it kept him at the holding and Elfgifu had become very dependent on him. She seemed to need his help with all of the tasks involving the baby, with the exception of breast feeding. Even here, his wife was having problems, but Elfgifu refused to let a wet-nurse suckle her son. She preferred to introduce the boy to solids earlier than most mothers would.

Many of the tasks were ones better suited to Oakleaf, but Elfgifu seemed to have developed a strong dislike for her young cousin and rarely asked her to do anything. Even more rarely, would she accept Oakleaf's offers of help. Sometimes, when given a task to do that seemed to be more of a woman's job, Godfrew passed it on to Oakleaf without his wife knowing. Oakleaf seemed to enjoy the deception. Godfrew felt that the young maid was not the problem that Elfgifu sometimes made her out to be, but Elfgifu was right about Oakleaf's tendency to disappear and not be around when she was needed. Even today, Godfrew had been looking in the kitchen for the girl. He needed some finely chopped greens for Jaul, but it seemed that she had taken some hot soup to Lady Gondul an hour ago and had not returned. Godfrew had started to chop the greens himself, but was so clumsy that one of the kitchen women took pity on him and chopped them up instead. On his way back to the hall from delivering the greens to Elfgifu, he had looked in at the kitchen again, but Oakleaf had still not returned.

"Don't look so worried, young Wulf." Dagobert put down the ale horn and wiped his mouth with the back of his hand. "If you worry any more, the rest of your hair will go white. Not that there is much of it that isn't white now. It's a shame about the bald patch of yours, too."

"Bald patch?" Godfrew put his left hand to his pate and felt. "What bald patch? I am not going bald!"

"Of course not." Dagobert tipped the dregs of his ale onto the stale bread in front of him. As soon as it looked as if the

The Calm

bread had softened, he ventured to eat it, being careful to keep it away from the two back teeth that had become very sore recently. "You only wear a hat, or that hooded cloak of yours to keep the sun out of your eyes. It has nothing to do with your hair falling out on top."

"Yes, I do ... and no, it is not!" The indignant Godfrew again felt his pate. It seemed sufficiently hairy to him. "Besides, I have always had very fine hair."

"Yeah, so fine it looks as if you are going bald." Dagobert winced as he accidentally bit on a cracked barley grain. "I will have to see the blacksmith soon. I can't keep this up forever." Dagobert leaned over, picked up Godfrew's ale horn and tipped a small amount of the drink on the rest of his bread.

"I am NOT going bald!" Godfrew was still running his hand over his head. Satisfied that Dagobert must have been teasing, he used his right hand to recover his ale. As long as he was careful, Godfrew was starting to regain the use of his favoured side. "Thinking of going to the blacksmith, eh?" Godfrew went on the offensive. "You were saying that when I first came back. Then it was 'After Yuletide'. Don't tell me the famous house carl, the great Dagobert Fearnaught, reputed dragon slayer, is frightened of having his teeth pulled?" Having worked closely with the manor reeve since his return, Godfrew was on very friendly terms with Dagobert, terms almost as friendly as that between the reeve and his ex-comrades in the Earl's hearth troop.

"I never said I was a dragon slayer. I said I was a Dago slayer. Things were quiet here one year. Earl Edric hired me and some of the boys out to the Dublin Norse for raids against the Moors in southern Spain. Few came back, but those that did were very rich." Dagobert picked up the sloppy bread and sucked it into his mouth. A few crumbs dropped to the floor and Shock slipped from under the table to retrieve them.

"Which is why you are here with me counting someone else's profits." Godfrew finished his ale and put the horn down. It was a beautifully made piece with the lip and point overlaid in chased gold—old-fashioned, but beautiful.

"The Earl took his cut—as was his right—but I do have some stashed away somewhere in case I need it. The truth is, I like it here. I have spent most of my life either in the Earl's service, or that of his father. Now I am a bit too old to fight. Don't let the hair fool you. My wife washes it in a special herbal brew that allows it to keep its colour. No, I am too old to fight. It is good to be given a job that gives me some power without too much physical exercise." Dagobert decided to resume work and pulled his book toward him, together with some tally sticks from the wool cloth store.

"And keeps you near your Lady Gondul?" Godfrew probed.

Dagobert became very serious. "Never joke about that one, Wulf. Not even when you think you are alone." He drew very close and whispered in Godfrew's ear: "The little games between the Lady and I are but small things. I durst not touch her, nor dare any other man here. The Earl allows her to have her amusements and her maids, but never think of going near her yourself. Any man who touches the Lady would provide an awful amusement for Earl Edric the Savage." Dagobert looked around the hall to ensure there was no one else near. "A man once accidentally brushed against her—not a slave or a serf—but a messenger from one of the Welsh princes. It took five days for him to die!"

"I think, Master Reeve, I had better keep my mind on my job." Godfrew pulled his book toward himself and checked the balance.

"It would be wise." Having completed the conversation, Dagobert visibly relaxed and even started to whistle as he worked.

"Working hard, Dagobert?" Lady Gondul's bell-like voice tinkled in the men's ears.

"Oh, indeed, my Lady." Dagobert directed a beaming smile at his mistress.

Gondul stood behind him, looking over his shoulder at the book with her eyes running up and down the columns. Once she had completed her scrutiny, she ran her fingers through the reeve's hair, then started to slowly part the flowing chestnut mane. "Dagobert."

"My lady?" Dagobert tried to look up at Gondul, but she was too far back.

"Your roots are showing. Tell your wife to wash your hair again."

"My Lady."

The Calm

"You will need to look your best, Dagobert, my trusted reeve, when we visit the cattle being held near Clunn. Clunn? Don't we have a house carl called Clunn?"

"A wee black rat, Lady, who likes his cheese too much." Dagobert closed his eyes and enjoyed the hair massage he was getting as the Lady Gondul sought out more grey roots in his thatch.

"Ah, yes. I can place him now. When you see him next, tell him if I catch him sniffing around my favourite cheeses again, it won't be just his nose that will be cut off. Master Wulf," Gondul acknowledged Godfrew for the first time, "where was I?" The massage was getting more powerful and Dagobert's head was rocking backwards and forwards.

"You are taking Dagobert to visit the cattle at Clunn, my Lady."

"Oh, yes, so I was." Gondul suddenly let go of Dagobert's locks and he almost fell face first onto the table. "Dagobert, I am concerned at the possibility of the new stock breeding before I have had a chance to vet them. I have no intention of letting inferior bulls loose to mate with anything and everything." Gondul picked up Dagobert's eating knife from the table. "Those not suitable will have to be disabled." The knife slashed down onto an apple, cutting it cleanly in half. "If you see what I mean." Gondul stood at Godfrew's side and put forward her cool hand with its long delicate fingers. She touched, then stroked, the stump of Godfrew's severed finger. "It is interesting, Wulf, the way they have folded the skin over the stump. It is so neat and tidy." She stroked some more. "Normally, when I see severed fingers, they are rough and jagged. I do believe that this is the first time I have seen, let alone touched, one that had been cleaned up." She then turned and smiled sweetly at Godfrew. "See that Dagobert is clean, tidy and ready at cock-crow tomorrow morning." The Lady Gondul went as silently as she had arrived.

"You heard, Master Reeve." Godfrew himself looked at his stumpy finger. Often it felt as though the bone was trying to push its way through the pad of flesh that had been formed at the end, especially when it was cold, like today. "Where was I? Oh, yes, be ready, Master Reeve, for I am under instructions from the Lady Gondul herself to ensure that you are ready on time. If need be, I shall have to winkle you out of your sleeping hut, even if I have to pry you off of your beloved lady wife!"

"It isn't me that will need chasing to be ready on time. It will be that hoary old hearth troop leader of hers, Wendlewulf." Dagobert counted the notches in the first tally stick and noted it in his book.

"And who will I have to pry him off of? The Lady Gondul's little maid with no tits?" Godfrew's tone was only half joking.

"Only if the Lady is with the Earl and his ladies tonight." Dagobert started counting the next stick.

"He is a big man for such a little wench. I'm surprised he doesn't break her back when he mounts her." Godfrew had still not re-started work and watched Dagobert's face, seeking to watch his expression.

Dagobert lost count. When he spoke again, his voice was a trifle agitated. "He doesn't mount her. He can't mount her any more than he could mount the other flat-chested young maids that ..." Dagobert dropped his stick and moved closer to Godfrew: "... any of the other flat-chested young maids that have kept the good Lady Gondul warm at night when the Earl did not need her."

"Can't?" Godfrew's voice matched the deep whisper of Dagobert's.

"Look, many years ago, when he was one of Earl Edric's house carls, we were raiding deep into the Welsh princedom of Powys. We had taken a small town ... I forget the name ... the wogs counter attacked. Well, we all got out fast, except Wendlewulf. He was caught coupling with the local gentry's eldest daughter against her wishes. If it had been us and we had caught one of them doing the same, we would have killed him, slowly of course. They didn't." Dagobert took a glance around to make sure that there was no one else within earshot.

"They castrated him?" suggested Godfrew.

"No, more than that. Let's just say that next time he gets a skin full of beer and needs to let it out, follow him out to the bushes. Whilst you will be letting it all hang out, he will squat!" Dagobert picked up his fallen stick.

"If he can't mount the maids, then what does he do with them?"

The Calm

Dagobert put the stick down again. "I don't know. Something no doubt, but not much." Again the furtive glance. "He can't be doing much, the Lady Gondul wouldn't allow it. She only sleeps with young maids with no breasts. As soon as they get past buds, she marries them off to a house carl, but no man dare mount one till then." Dagobert fingered the notches in the stick and looked sideways at Godfrew, waiting to see if he could resume counting or if he was going to get interrupted again.

"I remember the welcoming kiss. I got the impression she sleeps with grown women, too." Godfrew dug, as the question of Lady Gondul's kiss had continued to tease him like a sore tooth. He found that he could not leave it alone—even a year later.

"She 'plays' with grown women, yes ... but does not 'sleep with them' ... as you so delicately put it. But those grown women are always other men's wives or mistresses. And don't ask why!" Dagobert cautioned. "She is not as other women. She has her reasons and she wants them kept secret. I wish to live." Dagobert faced the front and started counting the notches on his stick, indicating that the conversation was over.

"Which you may not do if you are not ready to accompany her at cockcrow tomorrow morning!"

Dagobert sighed, put his finger at the beginning of the stick and began to start recounting yet again. "It won't be me that is late. Go and make sure that Wendlewulf is awake, if you have the balls."

"Which is more than he has?"

"Do you want to remind him of that?" Dagobert waved his stick under Godfrew's nose.

"Not if I want to live." Godfrew picked up his tally stick and started counting.

* * *

Spring turned to summer and summer to autumn. Dagobert rode often with the Lady Gondul, inspecting the plundered herds, arranging breeding programmes and culling the unwanted, or undesirable. More and more of the regular reeve's work fell on Godfrew. He did not object. The job was easy and it kept him near Elfgifu and his young son Jaul. Elfgifu still spent most of her time in the sleeping hut. She always seemed to be unhappy and despondent. At first, Godfrew had tried to get her to join the other ladies in the hall, or at least to eat there, but eventually gave up. He even did most of his own eating in the sleeping hut, although he knew the Earl did not like it.

It was only months after the birth of their first born that Elfgifu found herself pregnant again. Unlike before, Godfrew did not look forward to the birth. The smell of soiled napkins and baby vomit in the hut was already overpowering at times. The prospect of it being doubled was not enticing. Whether it was the smell, or what, Godfrew did not know, but Oakleaf frequently excused herself and spent the night elsewhere. Even little Joanna was often 'elsewhere'. Occasionally, such as today, Godfrew left Lydbury and travelled abroad in his role of manor under-reeve. Although he hated to admit it, he was glad to be free of family involvement for a while.

The family still figured in his thoughts, however. Even on this journey, he was travelling to Martinsfield to see Elfgifu's cousin—Llewelyn the village reeve—about the rental for pasture and of the Lady Gondul's need to find additional grazing for her cattle. One of the things Godfrew had learned during the time at Lydbury was that the Lady Gondul effectively ran the manor. Dagobert was the reeve. He kept the books and looked after the books for all Earl Edric's other holdings—large and small—but it was Lady Gondul who ran Lydbury. It was she who saw to the ploughing, the crops, the pastures, the herds, the breeding and oversaw the stocking of Lydbury's larder and armoury. Although he was never quite certain where he stood with the Lady, nor was he comfortable with the Lady's amusements, Godfrew had only admiration for her skills as farmer and quartermaster. Godfrew frequently pondered on Dagobert's words that "Lady Gondul is not as other women." He agreed with him whole-heartedly.

The land showed more signs of devastation than when Godfrew had travelled through last—almost a year before. More villages and hamlets were abandoned. Those that were still occupied seemed to have smaller herds that were kept close to home. It was not until they neared Martinsfield that

The Calm

things became more productive. The herds were bigger—signs of Earl Edric's protective power. For reasons of discretion, Godfrew, Clunn and Tosti kept well clear of the armed men tending the herds. They were replacements for the young boys who would have had the task in more peaceful times. In the wood before Martinsfield, they stopped and put on their mail. Godfrew's gift from a dead Norman was a good mail shirt of fine hammered links. It was reasonably light. He put it on over his under shirt and beneath his over shirt. The other two had ring mail coats, large rings of steel sewn to boiled-leather coats. To avoid overheating, Clunn and Tosti took their over shirts off and stuffed them in their leather saddle bags. As they cleared the small wood before Martinsfield, they saw a herd of horses with five men guarding it. On seeing the three riders, the herders drove the horses off, leaving one herdsman to gallop to the village to raise the alarm.

Godfrew looked at his companions. Clunn seemed even more dirty and dishevelled than ever—eating with both hands, steering the horse with his knees, crumbs of runny yellow cheese adorning his beard. Tosti, with his mixed parentage showing in his black hair and grey eyes, was quietly chanting to himself. Tosti's skin was pure white, like the marble images in church, but he was no saint, as the chant was a vulgar one learned from the Norse skald that Earl Edric had entertained the week before. Its words would have made a whore blush, though obviously not Tosti. They were now but a hundred and twenty paces from Martinsfield. A man stood at the edge of the village. He was holding a Welsh longbow. At one hundred paces, he notched an arrow. The riders dismounted and stood. The archer fired and the arrow arched through the air, burying itself two paces from Godfrew's feet. Clunn walked forward and pulled the arrow free, then all three walked toward the archer, their horses and Shock following behind.

As they closed the gap, Godfrew recognised the archer. "Cousin Llew, so it was you. I am glad that we are on the same side. I wouldn't have liked that arrow fired at my chest rather than my feet!"

"Which is why you took the precaution of wearing mail!" Llew leaned on his longbow, two hands taller than himself.

"How come he didn't know it was Llewelyn?" Tosti asked Clunn. "I saw it was him even before he shot the arrow."

Clunn picked a piece of sticky cheese from his beard and popped it into his mouth. "Maybe he is loosing his eyesight as well as his hair."

Godfrew turned to face Clunn. "Look, Rat. I am not loosing my hair." Going forward, he then embraced his wife's cousin.

"I am not loosing my hair," Clunn quietly mimicked, getting Godfrew's voice and accent almost perfect. "And I am giving up women."

"You are?" asked an incredulous Tosti.

"Only if he is not going bald." Clunn wiped his beard with the back of his hand, then stooped and wiped his hand on his leg wrappings. "Women, food and fighting. What else is there in life? Now let's get into the village proper and find a large buxom woman to help me get this stinking mail coat off, amongst other things." He flashed Tosti a yellow-toothed grin and ran his tongue across the jagged edges of his pointed teeth.

As they came down the main street of the village with Llew, the men folk stepped out from the alleys between the cottages, weapons in hand. Cottage doors were opened, as women and children poked their heads out—blinking in the sun—all curious to see who it was. Many of the folk recognised Godfrew from his short stay with them and called out to him, but there were also many new faces, folk brought in by the Earl to make up for those killed in the earlier fighting. Llew took Godfrew into his new cottage, leaving Tosti and Clunn to their own devices, which pleased the men. The cottage traditionally belonged to the village reeve and was twice as large as the one that Llew had previously. The floor was flagged with flat stones and the walls were lined with wooden lathes. There were even some wool wall hangings.

"You are doing well, cousin Llew." Godfrew gratefully accepted the offer of a stool and sat down. "May I?" He indicated his mail shirt, showing at the cuffs of his over shirt. Llew nodded and Godfrew stripped it off. He had just removed the mail coat when a rather fat woman with ginger hair and many freckles came in.

"Cousin Wulf, this is my wife, Agnes."

The Calm

Godfrew struggled to his feet. The mail shirt hung from the end of his arms like quicksilver. Agnes skipped over, her body all aquiver beneath her loose gown.

"Ooh, cousin Wulf, the hero of Martinsfield!" She gave him a hug that almost cut his breath off and planted a wet, warm kiss on his mouth. "Welcome. Has my handsome new husband been looking after you?" she asked.

"I have just arrived. Look ..." Godfrew managed to pull the mail shirt off and let it fall to the ground, where Shock promptly sat on it. "I am sorry to be undressed."

"Oh, don't worry, my lovely. I likes my men undressed, now don't I, sweetheart?" Agnes put her hand across and pinched Llew's buttocks. "Now you just make yourself comfortable while I go and get you something to eat and drink." As Agnes headed for the kitchen, four ginger heads popped around the door. Each head had a hand and each hand had a crust of bread dripping with honey. Shock licked his lips. Agnes came back and set down ale, cider, bread, butter, honey and blackberries before the men. She saw the inquisitive heads at the door. "Out you go, my little puppies," she shooed them away with her hands. "Out, now, or I'll have to tan your bums." She picked up a birch broom and skipped, all a-jiggle toward them. The children laughed, squealed, and squeaked—knowing it was a game—and ran away, pursued by a giggling Agnes and a salivating Shock.

"Your Agnes is nothing like your Rhiannon, Llew, either in looks or temperament!" Godfrew helped himself to the cider, washing away the dust of the road.

"Thank God." Llew poured some ale from the jug. "She may not be the tidiest of build, but she is one good woman, in all ways."

Godfrew crushed the last mouthful of cider against his pallet, savouring its rich, yeast free flavour. "In all ways, cousin?"

"It is no accident that she bore my late cousin Hwel four kids in four years, nor that she is already bearing one of mine. Yes, I am well pleased. If only she could get on better with my brother Puta." Llew took his knife and spread a thick layer of butter onto his bread. "Two good housewives in one household causes problems." He added thick honey to the bread, taking pleasure in watching it flow.

"Puta. What can be done there, I wonder. I would take him back with me, but Elfgifu would be unhappy with yet another to share the sleeping hut. You know we still have to use sleeping huts at Lydbury? Yes, I'm sure you do. I shall see if anyone else needs a hand. I don't suppose you could marry him off?"

"Puta? Marry him off?"

"Sorry. No, leave it with me." Godfrew took his turn with the butter and honey. All went quiet while they ate. Sitting in the warm cottage with a full stomach, it would have been easy to drift off, but there was business to do. Godfrew, at last, reluctantly broke the peace. "You know why I am here, I trust?"

"Big bad rent man, I assume." Llew poured the last of the ale into his mug.

"Good news and bad news." Shock had reappeared and snuffled around the table looking for scraps.

"Unlike some, I will take the good news first please, Wulf."

"Well, Lady Gondul needs pasture for her prize cattle. She wants to graze them here on the lakeside pasture and is willing to forgo a year's rent of the top pasture in exchange for the grazing and guarding of the herd." Godfrew watched Llew's face.

"Reasonable, I suppose. At present, the lake pasture is being grazed by another, but I am sure he would be willing to give precedent to the Lady Gondul and be in her favour—especially as I can offer him good terms now that the top pasture will be rent free for a year." Llew gestured. "Go on."

"In view of the current uncertain times and the possibility of raids by Richard of Scrope, Earl Edric is reducing the overall rendering for Martinsfield by a tenth."

"All good news! The Earl must have made a killing in the raid on Hereford to be so generous with the rents. He's never been so before, even when we were getting hit month after month. What's the catch, Wulf? There has to be one." Llew used his foot to dislodge Shock from his ale mug, the dog having got it stuck on his pointed muzzle.

"Ah, you always were shrewd, cousin. Yes, there is a catch. There has to be." Godfrew smiled apologetically and spread his hands in emphasis. "Earl Edric has been looking at the way the Normans run things. He has talked to prisoners—not the standard 'interview', you understand. He believes that there is some merit in their methods."

"Get on with it. Don't try your London soft sell methods with me. What is our glorious and clever Lord up to now?" Despite the words, Llew's tone was humorous.

"He wants to put a thane here, with four or five house carls; permanently."

"I see. And how will they be paid, pray?"

"Earl Edric calculates that it will cost about one tenth of Martinsfield's annual render. Plus houses will have to be built ... a one-time cost."

"Did I say clever? Did I say clever?"

Godfrew got up, went to the doorway and looked out. Llew joined him. "The thing is, Llew ... from a defensive point of view, it makes sense. In many places thanes have, for years, held land and dues from villages. In times of trouble, they have provided protection in exchange. This is just a variation. The Earl retains ownership of the land and the thane holds it at his pleasure. If the thane does not perform, or upsets the Earl ..."

"He gets his bollocks cut off?" suggested Llew.

"No, he gets the land taken from him and the Earl gives it to someone else. Think about it. Wouldn't it be nice—the next time there is a raid—to have trained, armed men here to help protect the village and its folk?"

"Do we have a choice?" Llew took to chewing his thumb nail, though Godfrew could see little nail there for him to chew. "Well, do we?"

"No. Earl Edric has already decided."

"And you are the thane?"

"Again, no. It will be someone of higher standing than I. You and me cousin, we are but reeves." Godfrew put his arm on Llew's shoulder. "And things may get tougher yet. The Norman king is still smarting over Hereford, I think."

"From what I hear, he has enough problems at present with the troubles in Northumberland and York. I hear only rumours, but you would know more than I."

"Troubles yes, but disorganised from what I can gather. If it had been more than just troubles, Earl Edric would have been out in the field exploiting it to the full, instead of only conducting nuisance raids against Scrope and the new Earl of Hereford, William Fitz something."

"Osborne," correcterd Llew. "William Fitz-Osborne."

"Quite. No, you were right earlier. Our Earl is clever. He won't take the field unless he is certain he can win and his allies are trustworthy and steadfast."

The cousins stepped out and walked to the well where Clunn, Tosti and Puta were talking together.

"Unlike his Cymry friends?" Llew suggested. "If they would only stop fighting us and each other, they would be all right. It wasn't them that caused Earl Edric to give up his siege of Hereford. But you are right, they can be a bit dodgey."

As they reached the others, Puta came to his brother, looking all excited. "Llew, I am leaving Martinsfield. I am going back to Lydbury with Clunn."

"Clunn?" Godfrew questioned.

"I have to take him, Master Wulf. I have just sampled his apple dumplings and I can't live without them!"

The Storm

In the autumn,

Elfgifu gave birth to her second son, Moithar. Her love for the boy showed in the great care she lavished on him, but it was at the expense of others, including herself. The child was kept clean and groomed, but Elfgifu gave up washing her body and combing her hair. Moithar was well fed, but Jaul was forgotten. Godfrew spoke hard and long to Oakleaf. She and Joanna took care of his eldest son. They brought him back only at night to sleep in the fetid atmosphere of the sleeping hut, whilst they removed themselves off to the kitchens to keep warm sleeping by the hearth. As the year aged, Dagobert returned to Lydbury, allowing Godfrew to spend more time with Elfgifu, but he found it hard to break through to his wife. She withdrew more and more within herself. Despite his love for her, Godfrew was becoming unhappy. He now looked forward to the times he was asked to go abroad on the Earl's business.

With the new year there was much coming and going and often Godfrew found himself riding over the snow-covered hills to hand over written messages to other lone riders. Something was afoot—and it was big. Winter became spring. Despite Elfgifu's self absorption, she and Godfrew had spent enough time together for her to conceive another child. The result was that Elfgifu became even less caring of herself and often sat for hours in the corner of the sleeping hut holding Moithar, rocking herself and the baby, saying nothing. As Godfrew's family life became more tense, so did the atmosphere at Lydbury. In was on mid-summers eve that Godfrew was sent with Clunn and Tosti to meet a rider and bring him back to see Earl Edric.

"There are two of them." Tosti, as always, liked to show off his long-sight.

Godfrew screwed up his eyes and squinted at the distant blob waiting at the ford over the river Lug, "You are sure?"

"Believe me, Master Wulf: two of them. You can see them can't you, Clunn?"

"Ah, yes. I can see two ... definitely two of them." Clunn scratched his crotch, deriving much pleasure from the action. "Two riders. You weren't expecting two were you, Master Wulf?"

"No, only one. Stay in the woods and watch. If I need help, come quick. Otherwise, wait and make sure they are not being followed." Godfrew nudged his dark pony forward, still squinting to make out the two riders more clearly. As he got nearer the ford, the two riders separated themselves from the one blob. On seeing Godfrew approach, they dismounted and walked their horses toward the river. "I am a stranger here friend, but it looks as if this river would be good for fishing." The two riders were of the same height and skin colouring, but the speaker had golden, brown hair and the other wore a broad-rimmed hat. The hat covered his head, but long white hair hung beneath it. It was the white of a young child rather than that of an old man.

"Trout, yes, but we also have many eels." Godfrew called across.

"On my manor we have many eels, too," golden hair replied.

Godfrew was satisfied that the password had been given and dismounted himself. "Why don't you cross and we can talk some more."

The two men remounted and splashed their mounts through the cold water of the river. Once at Godfrew's side, they dismounted. "This place was not easy to find. Even so, we have been here most of the day waiting for you to arrive. My companion ..." golden hair indicated the other man, "... had just persuaded me to return to the hamlet yonder for refreshment when we saw you coming."

"I have been here a while. I am just cautious." Godfrew noticed the accent of the other man and tried to place it.

"In these times, it pays to be cautious, friend." Golden hair nodded his head toward the other man. "I hope you don't mind me having company, but my master thought it best to bring him with me."

"I don't mind, but the final decision will lie with my master. He told me to only expect one." Godfrew looked at the white-haired man.

"Bjarki. This river is good for trout. Never mind the pass words. I wouldn't mind living here. I appreciate good fishing."

The Storm

The man had teeth so white they seemed almost invisible against his white beard.

"Your name is Bjarki? You speak Norse? You are Norwegian? You want to live here? You like the fishing?" queried Godfrew.

"Yes, I am Bjarki, but I am Danish. This is the first time I have been in your country, but I like it. Is it time to go yet? I am getting very hungry." the Dane slapped his stomach to emphasise his hunger.

"You want to go? You are hungry?" Bjarki nodded agreement. "Right, let's go then." They mounted and headed up the slope of the river valley and into the woods.

"Nice trees ...plenty of oak ... very good for raising pigs and building houses," Bjarki commented pleasantly. Godfrew dropped back a trifle and tugged at the sleeves of the golden-haired man.

"If it was not for my concern about the Normans, I would be worried about the Vikings. This man is really sizing the countryside up for settlement."

Golden hair smiled. "Which is what my grandfather and his crew did when they arrived with Svein Forkbeard," he laughed. "My mother may be English, but I am all Dane on my father's side, as are most of my neighbours in the fens."

"I was trying to place the accent. What is your name?" Godfrew maintained his position at the fenman's stirrup, leaving Bjarki to ride ahead and admire the land.

"Bjorn. Bjorn the Canny: I can fight with my left as well as my right. Your name is?"

"Some call me, Wulf."

"And the rest call you?"

"You wouldn't want to know." Bjorn the Canny laughed and his laughter bounced off the trees, causing all the birds in the area to take flight.

At the wood's edge, Clunn and Tosti sat on their horses and watched the ford for new arrivals. Tosti ate a juicy apple. Clunn contentedly scratched himself.

* * *

The great hall of Lydbury was crowded. The day was bone-chilling cold and the huge fire in the hall was the only warmth that could keep teeth from chattering. Those near the fire felt sick from the heat, while those near the wall froze. There was a constant movement of people to and from the fire. Sick with heat or half-frozen, they all coughed from the smoke.

Outside, the rain fell. The mush brought into the hall increased the general misery, but it was better to be in the hall than in the sleeping huts, where pools of condensation made the floors treacherous.

Jaul hung to his father's leg and picked at the sheep skin Godfrew had used for his leg wrappings. Godfrew dangled his right hand, using his fingers to keep in touch with his eldest son's white-haired head, as he was very aware of Jaul's tendency to totter off at every opportunity. Looking up, he saw Dagobert standing on the dais searching the crowd. As their eyes met, Dagobert beckoned him. Godfrew scooped his son up and forced his way through the press of people to the dais, then mounted it to stand beside the manor reeve.

"You want me, Master Reeve?" Jaul fidgeted to get down, but Godfrew held him tight.

"Not I, the Lord Earl. You are to go to him in his private room." Dagobert looked at Jaul's struggles and pulled a face at the boy, making him laugh. "Where is your wife?"

"In the sleeping hut, as usual. I had to be in here to stop the lad from freezing to death. The baby is fine, wrapped in his mother's shawl, but you can never keep this one still long enough to cuddle him." Jaul hung down to annoy Shock, who stood at his master's heel, shivering.

"You had better not take your dog—or worse your son—in with you to see Earl Edric. Even his own sons and daughters only go into his private room by appointment. Where is that buxom cousin of yours ... Acorn, or something?"

"Oakleaf? She is working in the kitchens and won't have the boy in there. He is into everything. She is frightened that he will get himself burnt or—worse—upset Old Mother Chickweed." Godfrew searched the crowd in the hall looking for Joanna, but failed to see her. "Look, can you hang onto him? If you see my wife's other young cousin, Joanna ... about nine ... ginger hair ... acts like a boy ... she will look after him. Please?"

The Storm

Dagobert held out his arms. "I suppose so. I've done it before often enough with my own." Godfrew passed Jaul over. Jaul greeted Dagobert by grabbing a handful of beard and twisting the whiskers. "I can see that this is going to be an interesting time, Wulf." Dagobert undid Jaul's fingers and released his beard from the boys grip. "If you could only grow your own beard, perhaps the lad wouldn't be so fascinated with other people's!"

"Sorry, I've tried, still can't. But thanks. I had better go. I would hate to keep Earl Edric waiting." Godfrew went to the door of the Earl's private room and spoke to the hearth troopers guarding it.

Dagobert threw Jaul up in the air, much to the boy's delight. "I can see that you will be a right terror when you get older. A reever, rather than a reeve. Come on, let's find your ginger cousin Jo ... whatever."

Godfrew entered the room. There was little smoke, but the fumes from the charcoal burner in the centre of the room bit the eye. Earl Edric—encased in a huge, black, sheep-skin cloak—sat on his bed, his golden hair for once hidden under an embroidered wool cap. In front of the Earl, on stools, sat Bjorn the Cunning and Bjarki the Dane. Edric motioned Godfrew over, nearer the burner.

"Warm yourself, my Wolfshead. We have been talking about you and your talents. I have need of those talents again ... and I am not referring to your administration skills." Edric took a sip from his cup of steaming herbal drink.

"I am your man, Earl Edric. Command me and I will do it."

Edric looked over the rim of his cup, blinking in the steam. "Rubbish, Wulf. There is no need to impress my visitors. You know as well as I that if I commanded you to help me 'interview' someone who had upset me, you would be as sick as a dog and about as useful as a mule in a breeding programme." Edric saw the worry in Godfrew's face and chuckled at the discomfiture he had caused. "But you do have other talents. That's why I have kept you on, despite your failings." He put the empty cup on a side table. "Send word to your other wolves to gather. You and Godwine shall 'sniff out' the shire of Shropshire for me. I have many holdings there, so it won't be a hard task. Oh, and forget about asking Stanley to join you, I have other plans for that promising young man, I am sorry to say." Earl Edric did not look at all sorry. "There is a vacancy in my hearth troop. He should fill it nicely, judging by his performance at Hereford."

"When would we be moving, Lord Earl?"

"As soon as possible. Time is not on our side I am afraid, Wulf. These gentlemen," he gestured toward Bjorn and Bjarki, "have brought me some unfortunate news. The sons of our late beloved King Harold have returned to their homeland. Again they have brought their Dublin Vikings and their mad Irish friends with them." Edric started to wind up, his voice getting louder and more angry. "Last year they made a mess of things. They forget that when an Earl ravages his own earldom as punishment, the people may bitch—as they did when Harold returned from Ireland during the dispute between the Godwine family and that facile religious idiot, King Edward—but they will accept it. But when others try the same—others who have no claim on the land—they fight back. They may have been forced out last year, but did you know they killed my friend, Eadoth the Staller? Eadoth ... there was a good man ... bought all the horses I could get my hands on for the king's house carls. He never once questioned where they came from—not like that jumped up Norman twit, Ralf, who did the staller's job for Edward. 'Where's this one from? Where's that one from? Why has the brand been over written?' Bastard!" Foam flecked at the corners of Edric's mouth and the pupils of his eyes became pin pricks. "What was I saying? Oh, yes ... Harold's boys ... they have come back ... up to their old games. We knew they would. We told them they could, but they still got it wrong and struck too soon." Edric got off the bed and went to the charcoal burner to warm his hands. "God preserve me from fools and the English summer."

"Too soon, my Lord?" asked Godfrew quietly.

Edric smiled. When he spoke, his voice was its normal self. "Best to forget what I have said, Wulf. All will become clear later." Edric sat down on the bed again. "You have sons, don't you, Wulf?"

"My Lord."

"So have I. So had our late, lamented King Harold. Don't expect your sons to have the same abilities as you have, nor think that they will follow you in all your ways. They never do. To think that shrewd Harold, the master general, the great planner, the wonderful strategist, could have such incompetent sons as his. They can't even get the dates right." Edric shook his head in disbelief. "Go now, Wulf. Tell Godwine of my instructions and gather your wolf packs."

"My Lord," Godfrew made for the door.

"Your English summer. I like it. I could live in a climate like this." Bjarki commented as Godfrew closed the door behind him.

* * *

The ox cart driven by Brunhilda trundled down the gentle slope of the road toward the green plain ahead. Godfrew and Godwine rode their ponies side by side, slightly ahead of the cart, so as to avoid the dust.

"Flat land. I haven't seen much of that since we left Hereford last year. It almost reminds me of home." Godfrew eased himself in the saddle and let the air move over his bare legs, evaporating the sweat.

"Flat, eh? I've never lived near flat land, except for the valley floor that is." Godwine slapped and squashed a fly as it settled on his neck. He looked dispassionately at it before letting it fall to the ground. "My place is very hilly, only enough flat land to build the holding."

"Much land?"

"Three hides. My grandfather was granted ten when it was taken from the Welsh. He had two sons; so five each. My father had two sons as well. I got three and my brother got the other two. His are more productive than mine."

"A thane, eh!" Godfrew took off his broad-brimmed hat and wiped the sweat off of the inner band before putting it back on.

"A thane, yes. Although we have less than the five hides, both my brother and I have the thane-right. I am the one who serves in the Fyrd, though. Our Earl Edric has made me an interesting offer. He wants me to take over a place called Martinsfield for him. He will continue owning it, but I get perpetual lease. I still have to perform the Fyrd duty, the road repair duty and pay the Danegeld, of course, plus his lordship's cut. It's 10 hides of good land, so it could be worthwhile." Godwine brushed his moustache up and wriggled his upper lip before brushing the moustache down again.

"I know the place. It could well be worthwhile. You have always been the Earl's man?"

"I and my brother, as my father was his father's man and my grandfather was his grandfather's man. I can take my land with me to any lord, but Edric's my Master." Godwine nodded his head, more to himself than to Godfrew. "They are a good family to have as lords. Earl Edric always looks after his own. Any trouble from the Welsh ... he will get word to you before they strike. Twice, since I have held the land that I have, I have had to get out of my holding with all my folk. The first time was a false alarm, but the second time was when that snake Griffith came over the border. We spent almost six months living at Lydbury till Harold Godwinson cleared him and his hell hounds out. You should have seen the damage they did. I practically had to rebuild the whole place. Welsh, I'll give them bloody Welsh."

In the back of the cart, Godwine's brats pushed each other and squabbled. It got to be too much for Brunhilda, so she flicked the whip backwards toward her children, rather than over the backs of the ponderous oxen pulling the cart. The boy brat yelped and started crying. Godwine looked over his shoulder.

"Problems, my love?" Godwine had his boar spear across his saddle. As he turned, the spear arced, forcing Godfrew to move slightly away to avoid being hit by the shaft.

"No problems, my love." Brunhilda smiled at her husband.

"What a wife." Godwine turned back and spoke to Godfrew "Indeed, Wulf, what a wife."

"Your wife has many admirable talents, Godwine." Godfrew kept an eye on the shaft of Godwine's errant spear.

"Indeed! So she has. I see that the stump of your finger has healed nicely."

"Yes," Godfrew examined his shortened finger, "thanks to your wife and her talents."

"She was always good at stitching ... skin, leather, wool, linen ... even silk, if I can get my hands on it. Yes, she is very good at stitching ... amongst other things, of course."

"Of course." Sensing that Godwine had settled, Godfrew moved the dark pony closer. Ahead, Shock searched for

The Storm

hares, sniffing in clumps of grass and cocking his leg over them when they failed to have any interesting scent.

"Mind ... she will find it hard when we reach Earl Edric's manor of Minsterly ... what with us supposedly going there at the Earl's behest to check the running of the place, she will have to assume the role of the good and gentle wife. That will grate ... so will having to wear women's clothing again." Godwine turned his shoulder to catch his wife's eye and smile at her. Godfrew watched the spear's shaft, ready to take evasive action. "Your wife has never thought of joining you on your journeys, Wulf?"

"No, I am afraid not. She is very much a 'home' person. Myself, I think it would do her good ... at least on less warlike trips such as this one. Unfortunately, Elfgifu does not agree. I do miss her." Godfrew started to drift off into a world of his own, but Godwine dragged him back.

"Well, this one should be harmless enough. Send the boys out in pairs ... let them gather information about the Normans ... the feelings of the folk ... the lie of the land ... all that sort of thing. Meantime, we sit back at one of the Earl's manors—me at Minsterly and you at Westbury—and live like lords. What could go wrong?"

* * *

The hare started and ran a zigzag course across the meadow. Two hounds streaked after it—one long and rangy with a white and brown brindle, the other small and jet black. The hare straightened its course, then looped back the way it had come. Shock turned tightly and almost stuck his nose up the creature's bum before it changed tack again, leaving the lurch aiming off in the wrong direction. The bigger hound tried to take the hare head on, only to have the animal turn at the last moment, leaving the dog with no target in sight. The hounds met each other and started sniffing the hare out. In the meantime, the hare sat bolted upright on its hind legs, watching them, but never moving.

"Shock, you stupid thing. Look in front of you. It's staring you in the face! SHOCK." Godfrew gesticulated in the direction of the hare, but to no avail, Shock's eyes lifted no higher than his nose, which was just above ground level. "SHOCK!"

"Give it up, Master Wulf. Your hound is as stupid and useless as mine. At least, being smaller, it won't eat so much." The reeve of Westbury had a nature as sunny as his yellow hair.

"Don't believe it. My father had huge hounds—deer hounds that stood as high as my elbow. That little runt eats as much as the two of them together." Godfrew looked around for a stone to throw.

"Would you take a wager on which hound catches the hare? Just to make it interesting, of course." The reeve kicked a stone loose and picked it up.

"Gambling, Siward? What would the Earl think?" Godfrew's voice mocked.

"The Earl would only be thinking of what odds to offer me! Mind, if my hound won, he would want to buy it and would make me an offer that I couldn't refuse." Siward tossed the stone up and caught it.

"Have you been to the Earl's main holding at Lydbury North?"

"Once. That was enough. I saw plenty to convince me that I should never refuse Earl Edric anything he requested." Siward gave Godfrew an amused smile. "Yes?" He showed the stone.

"Why not?" Godfrew grinned. "An ale to the winner and another for the winner's owner,"

"I can almost taste it now." Siward threw the stone. It landed just in front of the hare and the hare took off. The hounds saw the movement and gave chase. Again, the creature ran an erratic course, allowing the smaller Shock to get close more often than his larger opponent. Shock turned tighter on the turns, but the chase went on too long. As Shock tired and slowly dropped behind, the big greyhound came alongside the hare, grabbed it by the neck and threw it into the air. The hare landed back on the ground with a thud, it's neck broken.

"Leave it, leave it." Siward with Godfrew in his wake ran across, trying to beat the hounds to the hare. "GET OFF IT, LEAVE, Sleipnir, LEAVE." By the time the men reached the hare, only the rear legs were salvageable. Godfrew pulled the body away from the hounds and cut the rear half away with

The Storm

his saxe. As the battered remains of the shredded carcass hit the ground Shock and Sleipnir, red muzzled, fought over it.

"Oh, well, Siward, at least we got the best part." Godfrew stuffed the legs into the coarse sack hanging from his waist.

"The best part will come, Master Wulf, when I and my hound down that ale you owe." Siward tried to get the bits of dead hare away from Sleipnir, but each time he got close the greyhound ran to a safe distance and continued chomping. "Stupid hound." Siward looked back to Godfrew and shrugged his shoulders "Well, that's it for today ... with a full belly he won't be doing any chasing. Perhaps we should head back to the manor."

"Huh, giving up before I can get the chance to gain revenge. Your hound may be full, but mine still has an empty gut." Shock stood at Godfrew's heel, licking the blood dripping from the bottom of the sack.

"Would I dare try and cheat you, Master Wulf? Not if I want to keep in the good Lord Edric's favour." At last, Sleipnir, having bolted the remains of the hare, came over to his master and stretched, putting a paw on each of Siward's shoulders and licking his face with gusto. "Yes, yes ... I know. Good boy. Now, get down. No, not my mouth, you filthy animal ... you stink." Siward lifted the hound off of his shoulders and made it stand at his side. "Honestly, Master Wulf. His breath is worse than a house carl's after a Yuletide's drinking bout."

"No, you wouldn't cheat and you haven't cheated. I've studied the books, so I know." Godfrew laughed and Siward, the manor reeve, joined him.

"Well, Master Wulf, that is good news. Are the other holdings as honest? I know that several of your men have already reported back."

"So far, so good." Godfrew nudged Shock away from the sack. The hound waited until Godfrew bent down to wipe the blade of his saxe clean on the grass before licking the bloodied sack bottom again.

"The Earl must be concerned about something ... what with you here and the other house carl over at Minsterley. Mind, he would have an easier time ... with that being book land. The monks would ensure that they got their full tithe."

"Maybe the Earl is concerned that they might be getting more than their tenth part."

"Maybe the Earl has other things on his mind than the honesty of his reeves."

Godfrew looked seriously at Siward. "The last man I met who thought he knew the Earl's mind ended up with out one."

"Ah, no offence meant. I did not mean to pry. Of course, the Earl needs to ensure that his holdings are being run properly and efficiently." Siward's voice had gone very quiet.

Godfrew broke the silence. "Now, Master Siward ... that ale. My throat feels it has been cut, if you will excuse the expression."

"Indeed, Master Wulf." Siward cheered up, but as they walked back across the meadows toward the manor, he pondered on Godfrew's words and decided that he had better be more careful with what he said in the future.

The pair walked in silence to the old Roman road that headed in the direction of Shrewsbury, but they turned the other way toward Westbury, nestled under its wooded hill. As the manor came in sight, so did a boy running toward them.

"HO, MASTER SIWARD, HO." The boy was all arms and legs, trying to run and catch the reeve's eye at the same time. Siward looked across at Godfrew, who looked back.

"I wonder what this is all about, Master Wulf?" Siward called out to the boy: "Slow down, wait till you get here, slow down." Siward then stepped out to close the distance between himself and the runner. As they got nearer, he called out again: "Aldrich, what is it you want?"

"Trouble Master, trouble. We're calling the 'Hue and Cry'." The boy bent, holding his knees and drawing lungs full of air. "Gesta, the goose-girl ..." again the lungs full of air "... someone tried to rape her ..." the boy now stood up, his breath still coming unevenly, "... a short, dark, smelly man. He headed for the hill."

"Clunn," muttered Godfrew.

"What was that, Master Wulf?" enquired Siward.

"I said, 'Hmm'. I hadn't expected you to have that sort of problem here ... not unless there was raiding going on."

"Nor did I. But we must get back. As the reeve, they will be waiting for me to get things organised." Siward patted the boy on the shoulder: "Aldrich, get your breath back and fol-

The Storm

low us as best you can." Siward inclined his head toward Godfrew. "Shall we run, Master Wulf?"

"If you insist, Siward, but I regret I am not as fast my hound." Godfrew set off with Siward at a steady jog, the two hounds playing and bouncing around at their heels, finding the whole process fun.

The manor was in an uproar. Women with their children stood in huddles, talking and looking worried. Men gathered together in knots, waving their farm implements and shouting. Gesta was nowhere to be seen, but her geese waddled and hissed in front of the priest's small cottage. Siward rushed over to the well and called his men together. Godfrew hung by the gap in the hedge, unsure what his role should be.

"Master Wulf," the voice came from behind Godfrew's left side.

"Tosti. What in the name of all the saints possessed that little black rat to rape the goose-girl of the very manor he was supposed to meet me at?" Godfrew hissed, anger showing in his voice.

"It's not quite as it seems, Master Wulf," Tosti continued in Godfrew's ear. "He didn't rape her." Godfrew started to turn around. "No, wait. We were on the way back from Shrewsbury. We saw this comely wench on the road ahead of us ... and you know Clunn."

"Don't waste my time, Tosti. I know Clunn very well ... and his disgusting habits. Get on with the story." Shock joined Godfrew and amused himself by sticking his nose into Tosti's crotch and sniffing. Tosti pushed the dog out of the way.

"She looked very comely and Clunn only wanted to chat her up ... get himself into her good book and set himself up for tonight, as it were," Tosti wheedled.

"And? And?" Shock reattached himself to Tosti's crotch. This time Tosti gave up trying to dissuade the animal and took to playing with Shock's ears.

"She was comely from the back, but not from the front. Goose-girl? Thirty years ago perhaps. More moles on her face than in a meadow ... wrinkled like a ploughed field ... hair like straw and little more than two peas rattling around inside her head. She is a girl only in her mind."

Woden's Wolf

"And? And?" Godfrew watched as the men finally got themselves sorted out and headed toward the hedge, the hounds at their heels.

"She had heard what he was saying as he caught up with her and liked what he suggested in her ear. She didn't like it when he changed his mind, after seeing her face. There was no rape. Perhaps that is what she is complaining about. Fortunately, she didn't see me. Perhaps she only had eyes for the handsome Clunn." Tosti started to laugh. Shock sat on his haunches and stared up at the young warrior.

"I don't find it funny. Where is Clunn now?"

"Headed back to Shrewsbury. He said he would see you there later."

"If he beats the hounds." Godfrew patted his thigh. Shock left Tosti and sat by his master.

"He should. He covered himself in horse shit to cover his scent."

"That would be an improvement." Godfrew's tone lightened. "I only hope he has enough of a head start. I need him to get away, just so I can get my hands on him."

"I think he will make it. He is still as cunning as a rat."

"Hmm. I hope the information you have gathered is well worth all this aggravation, Tosti."

"Oh, it is, Master Wulf. It is pure gold."

"So is horse shit." Godfrew and Tosti joined the Hue and Cry as it set off for the hill at the back of Westbury.

* * *

"So what is this event that will help us take Shewsbury?" Torquil, the marshal of Earl Edric's house carls, put his aching foot on the table. They had gathered in the room that Godfrew had rented at the inn. Removing his soft leather shoes, he massaged the sole and arches. "Dear God, I was made for riding horses, not walking. Come on, Wulf, cough."

"A hanging."

"A pleasant entertainment—particularly if the hangman has used only a short drop—but how will it help us?" Torquil took out his eating knife and started to clean black crud out from under his toe nails, wiping the residue on his bare legs.

The Storm

"The man is English, the hangman Norman. The townsfolk don't like the idea." Godfrew put his hand to his face and discretely blocked his nose with his thumb and finger stump, keeping the acrid smell of Torquil's feet at bay.

"Ah, innocent, is he?" Torquil examined his handiwork. Being satisfied, he proceeded to par his toe nails.

"Of what? He killed a man in a drunken brawl. The other man was a young Frenchman, popular even with the English, by all accounts."

"So ... why the resentment?" Torquil gave a short gasp as he cut a little too deep and nicked his big toe.

"The Normans were offered Wergild,[17] but wouldn't accept it. The killing wasn't deliberate, so Wergild is appropriate."

"Wergild is not always acceptable to the victim's family." Torquil put his bleeding big toe in his mouth and sucked. Godfrew winced.

"Only family can opt not to take the Wergild. The Frenchman has no family here. His lord says he is the one who has suffered the loss and he wants blood, not money."

Torquil stopped sucking his toe, held it a distance from his face and tried pinching it to stop the blood. "So, it is not justice that is the problem ... it is the Normans riding rough shod over the law of the land, despite what their king has proclaimed in all the cities." The bleeding would not ease, so Torquil got up and searched for a cobweb, dripping blood on the floor as he went.

"Does it matter? The event will suit our purpose." Godfrew went to his bedside table, picked up the water ewer, slopped water on the spots of blood and spread the watery mix across the wooden boards with his foot. "Are all your men in the city, Torquil?"

"I think so ..." Torquil found some cobwebs and settled himself back at the table to wrap them around his big toe. "... I hope so. I also hope they can keep out of trouble long enough. If this goes wrong, Earl Edric will be very wild, in-

---

[17] Wergild: a man's monetary value. Instituted to prevent blood feuds, each man had a value according to his rank. These values varied from time to time and kingdom to kingdom. One example is Thane = 1,200 shillings, Fyrd serving ceorl = 600 shillings, ceorl (carl or freeman) = 200 shillings. Other, lower ranks, had, at various times, lower values down to: slave = 20 shillings. Interestingly, Welshmen were all at half price! The money was payable to the family of the victim. In some legal codes, an additional amount, or part of the Wergild itself, could be payable to the man (or woman's) lord, especially in the case of the non-free.

deed. He has sent all his men here, retaining only his own hearth troop to guard him against the Welsh."

Godfrew stayed at the other end of the room, away from the smell of foot rot. "Aren't they supposed to be his allies?"

"What did that ever mean to the Welsh?" At last Torquil's toe stopped bleeding. Much to Godfrew's relief, the marshal put his shoes back on again. "No, this had better go well." Torquil poked his tongue through the gap in his front teeth. "This is the biggest thing we have ever tried. It had better go well, or we are all in trouble."

"It will," assured Godfrew. "I think," he added under his breath.

* * *

It was a good day for a hanging. The sun was covered by light cloud. Although its warmth could be felt, its light did not get in the eyes of the spectators—and there were plenty of them. Despite the warmth of the day, several of the men in the crowd wore old, thin cloaks, held close to their bodies—cloaks that held within other things than body heat within them. From the mix of the crowd, it was as though it were a holy saint's day. Thanes rubbed shoulders with serfs ... serfs with merchants ... merchants with ceorls ... ceorls with Welshmen. Only the slaves seemed to have been left at home. Yet, the crowd was unbalanced. The women and children were missing.

Godfrew was pleased by this. The dissension he and his men had sought to sow in the town and the surrounding districts had found fertile ground. A crowd's temper was always tense at a hanging, but the tenseness today was that of anticipated violence, rather than expected entertainment. The men stood in small groups, talking low—constantly glancing at the other groups around them—as though frightened that they might be overheard. Moving through the crowd were the usual hawkers, but they found few buyers for their food. There were no buyers for the mannequins of hanged men, popular items with the children in previous hangings.

The gallows looked new. The timber was still bark covered with the ends cut raw and white. The cross beam had five

The Storm

ropes dangling from it. That reinforced the impression with the folk that that the recently installed Norman garrison expected there to be more hangings in the future. In the past , the lowest limb of the oak tree by the green had been sufficient for the task.

Above the murmur of the crowd, Godfrew managed to catch the sound of a muffled drum and the squeak of an ill-oiled wagon wheel. Despite being taller than most, he still found it necessary to stand on his tip toes to see the execution party heading toward them. Norman foot soldiers in full battle gear marched ahead and alongside the ox cart containing the condemned man and his priest. The hangman was suitably dressed and hooded in black. As the procession wended its way to the gallows, the soldiers used their spears to force the crowd back. At each push of the soldiers, a growl went up as the men in the crowd bumped into each other. The soldiers seemed unaware of what was being said to them, but they could not help but catch the threatening tone. They constantly looked back at their sergeant for reassurance.

Once at the gallows, the soldiers formed a circle around the structure and kept the crowd back ten paces. They doubled the ten paces in the front to ensure that the wagon could trundle forward and leave the condemned man dancing from the rope's end. The Norman sergeant paced behind his men, encouraging and steadying them. In the wagon, the occupants had been joined by the Captain of the Guard and two soldiers who were helping the hangman get the reluctant victim to his feet. As the condemned man wriggled and struggled to free himself from his tormentor's grasp, he knocked the kneeling priest over, but the man kept praying aloud whilst moving himself to the side of the wagon out of the way.

The hangman placed the rope around the man's neck and tightened it—checking the angle, the amount of slack and pulling once again to ensure that it was well secured to the cross beam. The drum stopped its slow beat. The Captain unrolled a scroll of vellum that had been tucked into his sword belt. Before commencing to read it, he looked up toward the wooden fence of the castle's outer bailey. A figure waved back and the Captain turned to the crowd.

"Be it known to all that Leofwine of Raebrookham has been charged and condemned for the slaying, without legal right, of Yves from Le Man. For this heinous act, he is to forfeit his life by hanging. May God forgive him." The Captain obviously could not read, as he did not once look at the scroll. He coughed before repeating the message in heavily accented English. "Know ye all that Leofwine of Raebrookham was charged and condemned for killing, without legal right, Yves the Frenchman. For this heinous act, he is to hang. May God forgive him." The Captain nodded to the hangman who went to the front of the wagon and picked up a whip, making ready to stir the ox into movement. Two soldiers stood on either side of the condemned man, restraining him, as he continued to struggle. Godfrew stood on an upturned bucket at the back of the crowd to watch what was happening

Godfrew whistled between his teeth and Clunn pulled the stave of his bow from the pile of hay at his side. After stringing the bow, he replaced Godfrew on the upturned bucket. As the hangman raised his whip, Clunn took aim. Before the whip could descend, an arrow took the man full in the chest. Only the feathers of the flight showed at his front as the arrow destroyed his heart. The hangman toppled forward, vaguely gesticulating as he fell to embrace the rear end of the ox. The Captain was stunned at the sight and looked to see where the missile had come from. Confusion was on his face and his words were locked in his throat. Shortly, one of Clunn's arrows was also locked in his throat. The two Norman soldiers, who were keeping the crowd back from the front of the wagon, heard the flight of the arrows. They turned their heads to watch where they were landing. This distraction was enough for some of Earl Edric's house carls. Their fine chain mail glinted beneath their over shirts as they forced their way through the ring of soldiers and start to attack their enemies from the rear.

Stanley slipped his hand beneath his thin cloak and released the leather thong holding the long-axe on his back. The weapon glided into his hands as he stepped forward to face the ox. The dumb creature had felt the hangman embrace its rump, but was unsure what to do. Seeing Stanley come toward it the ox started to walk forward to meet him. Stanley set his feet firm, adopted the stance Godfrew had taught him and swung the axe in a great arc. When the blade struck, it split the animal's head in twain, dashing

The Storm

brains and blood onto the earth. The two soldiers hanging onto Leofwine—the condemned man at the rear of the wagon—felt the forward movement. When the wagon stopped, they realised that the condemned man still had his feet on the edge of the deck. Using the hafts of their spears, they pushed the victim off the tailgate—only to have Leofwine swing back at them, his feet kicking and dancing. They fended him off and again Leofwine danced in the air, only to return and collide with one of them again. Before they could repeat the performance, one of Clunn's arrows took a soldier in the back. The arrow did not kill him, but it did cause him to topple from the cart. A house carl took out the other with a throwing axe that struck the man on the helmet and stunned him long enough for others to drag him through the slatted side of the wagon and finish him off. The priest cowered in the corner, ignored.

By now, the crowd had joined the house carls in the melee. The Norman soldiers had disappeared in a tumult of yelling struggling men. Godfrew looked to his band.

"The castle, now." Godfrew caught Neckbiter as Stanley threw it to him and started to run. On his left, Godwine and his band also started to run forward—all intending to catch the watchmen off guard.

"Close that gate! Hurry, HURRY." The Frenchman's cry was cut short as Kevin let a yard arrow loose that caught the man in the face, sending him spiralling off the palisade wall.

The bands crashed into the soldiers belatedly coming down from the palisade walls to try and close the gate. The fight was uneven, as the Norman's were fully armed and armoured whilst Godfrew and Godwine's men were armed only with saxe, sword and bow. Only the two leaders were wearing mail under their shirts. The first to fall was a young man who had joined the band only two days before and whose name Godfrew had not had time to memorise. With no shield to protect him, he had taken a sword blow to the body and just crumpled. Dunstan stood over the boy's body, protecting it—hoping that the blow had not been fatal.

"God I wish I had a thing." Dunstan struck out at a Norman, but the soldier took the weapon on his kite-shaped shield and twisted it sideways, almost wrenching the sword from Dunstan's hand. Dunstan managed to wrench the sword free, but was off balance and was unable to avoid the Norman's counter stroke. The big man's left arm was opened up from shoulder to elbow. "Oh, Lord, a thing. Why haven't I got a thing?" Dunstan slashed at the Norman's legs without success. Another Norman caught him on his sword hand, taking off the top joint of two fingers. "THING, shit and THING." Dunstan's backhand swipe clipped the second Norman's helmet, throwing the man to the floor. "What I want is a thing!"

"I always thought those rumours about you were true, Dunstan." Clunn, bow across his shoulder, ran to the Surrey man's side and passed him a blood-stained shield. "No thing, eh?"

"You know what I wanted." Dunstan grabbed the proffered shield, but his lack of attention caused him to be felled by a sword blow that missed him, but allowed the sword's pommel to hit him behind the ear. Clunn stuck his short sword into the unprotected area under the offender's arm, but had to let go of the weapon in the process. It was bending down to grab Dunstan's sword that saved his life, as a spear whistled over his head. Diminutive new comer, Edgar from Weobley was not so lucky, as the errant spear smashed into his shield and sent him spinning. More Normans were joining the fight by the gate and the bands were falling back.

Bjorn the Wainwright, slowed by his badly-healed leg, had his hand severed. He staggered away from the fight—shoving the stump into his shirt—trying to stop the pumping blood. "Oh, er, no. Not this. Not now. Oh, dear, I really am getting too old for this game. This is definitely the last time I go raiding." A crossbow bolt struck him down and left him slumped against the wall.

Local recruit, Magnus, was leading the wolf pack's defence—flailing about with a bill hook, keeping all around him at bay, but without landing a single blow. At his side, another new man—the dark, curly-haired Swein—protected his comrade's back each time he moved forward, blocking blow after blow with shield and sword. At Swein's feet, Dragon's-breath coughed blood onto the ground. His golden ringlets were covered in red slime, dirt and pieces of dried grass. At the very gate itself, Godwine just managed to hold on with the remnants of his band. Kevin lay in front of him, his once

The Storm

handsome face no longer able to smile, since it had been stoved in by a mace. Young Alarac screamed and created mayhem amongst the Normans facing him, trying to avenge the death of his friend and constant comrade, Paul the monk, who was transfixed to the gate by a spear, blood still pumping out through a ragged hole in his torn, bloodstained habit.

Godfrew, swinging Neckbiter at every opportunity, joined Tosti and Clunn over the fallen Dunstan's body. "Be ready to turn and run."

"Run? You, Master Wulf, run?" asked Clunn as he smashed the boss of his shield into the unguarded face of a young Norman with bad acne. "I thought only us rats ran." He took another blow on the edge of his fast splitting shield. "Wolves that run. That's a new one."

"Then stay and die, Rat."

The fight closed in and the time for words was lost. Godfrew stole a glance over his shoulder to see if he would still be able to get back out through the gateway when he saw the house carls headed by the small, dark Nathan Priestson and his shield companion Gavin the Slow-Witted, charging toward the gate: "Out, out, out ..."

Godfrew did not linger on the scene, but returned to the ring of Norman shields that faced him. He feinted twice. Each time, the shields turned to meet the undelivered blow. The third time, the Normans ignored the movement, waiting to catch the axeman off balance, but the blow was sent home and two men went down, one with no head and the other with a shattered collar bone. Godfrew did not get in another blow before the tide of house carls washed over him and swept the Normans away. Behind the house carls came a hoard of local men who were armed with whatever came to hand. Several stopped to kick over dead Normans and take their fallen weapons. They joined the house carls as they charged across the clear ground of the courtyard and headed toward the inner defensive wall in front of the keep.

Godfrew shook Clunn's neck, getting him and Tosti to leave the rest. The three men climbed the now deserted palisade wall and headed to the watch tower over the gate. Finding lamps, they spread the oil over the wooden structure and then set it alight as a beacon to Earl Edric and his allies, telling them that the town was now open.

Along the wall, the remains of the Normans retreated toward the gate of the inner bailey wall. The last man turned to look hard and long at Godfrew before joining his comrades. The man had the face of a pig. Where his nose should have been was a sheen of silver snot.

As the stragglers reached the inner bailey, they crashed into the house carls fighting to keep the gate open. Some of the Normans made it through the lines to join their comrades and help force the English out. Suddenly, the gates closed and all the house carls could do was vent their frustration on those Normans caught on the outside.

Godfrew climbed down the ladder and went toward Godwine by the outer gate. Godwine was looking down at his foot. It was skewered to the ground by a spear. He rocked the broken shaft of the spear. Although the spearhead freed itself from the dirt, it remained embedded in Godwine's foot. Sweat pouring down his face, Godwine sat down on the trampled dried grass. He pulled his saxe from the scabbard hanging at his waist. Slowly, Godwine cut away his leather shoe. The spear head was barbed. Godwine shook his head in disappointment, knowing that he would never be able to extract the weapon from his foot by pulling straight out. Taking a deep breath and chewing on the ends of his moustache, he made a deep and deliberate cut between his big and adjacent toe until he hit the iron spear head. Having cleft his foot, he pulled the spear head out through the new wound. When he finished, he crumpled and vomited.

"All well, Godwine, my battle friend?" Godfrew knelt beside his companion, undid the top of his cider flask, and poured the fluid over the damaged foot.

"No, good friend Wulf, but I will live, God willing." Godwine winced at each flow of the cider over his foot. Digging into his bag, Godfrew pulled out some honey smeared bread and applied it to Godwine's foot as a poultice before binding it with strips of cloth cut from a dead Norman's cloak. Godfrew helped the other band leader up onto his feet, allowing him to lean on his shoulder. Before going out of the gate and back into the town, they turned and looked toward the other gate—that of the inner bailey. As they slowly made their way

The Storm

back toward Godfrew's lodgings, Godwine started to laugh. "My beloved and talented wife will not be happy with this days work, I am afraid, friend Wulf."

Godfrew stole another glance toward the unconquered inner defences. "Nor, I regret to say, will our master, Earl Edric."

* * *

"You are wrong ... you are wrong ... you are wrong. Haven't you and your lot ever learned anything? After all these years, you must have learned something—surely to God and all his saints." Earl Edric looked at Prince Rhiwallon, his bloodshot blue eyes standing out on stalks. "Look, you! I learned all I know about fighting in this part of the world from my father ... and he learned it from his father ... and he learned it from the Cymry ... ambush ... raid ... cut off ... assassinate ... befriend the locals and intimidate those you can't befriend. Never, never, never fight a pitched battle unless you have to. Fight only when you are either cornered, you have overwhelming numbers, or you have surprise on your side."

Rhiwallon ignored Earl Edric, poured himself wine and drank some before pouring the rest out onto the carpeted floor of the Earl's tent. "Small minds have small ambitions." He picked up a sweetmeat and nibbled it, dropping sticky crumbs. Shock stuck his nose under the greyling of the tent and smelled the air. Crawling on his belly, he made his way to the crumbs and cleaned up. He had just started to lap up the spilt wine when the Earl's harsh voice made him run and duck back out of the tent.

"So, at last, the truth. The reconquest of England. Never mind the past six hundred years ... give the whole place back to the Cymry ... and using English men to help you. You filthy little wog." Earl Edric made toward the Welshman, the veins on his neck standing out in knots.

"Is that any different from you wanting to get rid of the Normans by using Cymry troops?" Rhiwallon selected another sweetmeat to eat.

Earl Edric had his hands out in front of him and had almost reached the dark Welshman when the tent flaps were opened by a member of the hearth troop and Prince Bleddyn of Gwyneth came in. He quickly sized up what was happening and stepped between the two men. Rhiwallon, meantime, had acted either unaware of or indifferent to Edric's malicious intent.

"Edric. What is it this time? Nothing we can't sort out, I'm sure." Bleddyn gave a disarming smile. He took the Earl's arm and led him to the other end of the tent. "Just what is it that my cousin of Powys has been saying to upset you so?" he continued, the light glinting off his white teeth.

Despite his anger, Edric allowed himself to be led away. His anger showed only in the constant clenching and unclenching of his fists. "You intend to head for Stafford to take the town and shire. This—despite the fact that Shrewsbury castle is still holding out and despite the news we have received. Not only are the Normans headed this way from the south east—where they crushed those young fools of King Harold's—but the Norman King William himself may be headed this way. The time to fight a pitched battle has gone, Bleddyn ... gone ... at least for now." Edric allowed the Welsh Prince to keep him away from his countryman, but the Earl's eyes were all the time on Rhiwallon.

"The time may yet be right yet, Edric. William's appearance is only rumour. There are still big troubles to the north and east. Count Brian? Well, we are not a band of mercenary pirates held together only by lust for plunder. We cannot spend all our lives waiting in the hills for the right time." Bleddyn smiled reassuringly at Edric. "Sometimes we have to not take, but make the opportunity ..." he gave a little chuckle, "... like King Arthur."

"Don't forget it was us that set up and armed his half-son, Mordred. And it was in a pitched battle that he died." At last Earl Edric stopped staring after Rhiwallon and looked at the man in front of him. His voice was quieter now, edged with a need to convince. "Bleddyn, it will not work. Trust me, it will not work. Some of my men have fought the Normans in pitched battles. Things have changed ... things are changing. We will not win a pitched battle, believe me."

Bleddyn sighed and let go of Edric's arm. "Edric, this is not easy for any of us. You know how difficult it is to get any Cymry to act in unison. I have managed to get the most difficult of all, Rhiwallon. The men of Staffordshire have risen to back us .. the men of Cheshire have flocked to the banner.

The Storm

You command many of the men of Herefordshire and Shropshire. Never have we had so many men under the one banner. The time is right and it is now. We must take the opportunity." He gave a short smile. "Please, Edric. One battle and it will be over ... the west will be ours. We must fight."

"Then you will do it without me. I am not afraid to die. I just refuse to throw my life away on something that will not ... cannot ... succeed." Edric lowered his head and looked at his feet. "Go now and take that thing with you."

"So be it. But remember, Edric. When we rule the west, you had better look to your defences. When we win the west, it will be back to the good old days between us and ours." Bleddyn collected Rhiwallon, pushing him out of the tent. "Time to go. Time to get the men ready, cousin. Time to gather the Cymry and cleanse this land." Rhiwallon grunted and snatched a last sweetmeat before leaving.

Earl Edric sat down on a leather folding stool and waited while dark Goda and her ladies brought in his hot herbal drink.

Godfrew leaned across to young Nathan priest's son. "Bad news?"

Nathan trimmed the nail of his bandaged little finger with his teeth. "From what I understood, yes."

Shock stuck his inquisitive nose under the greyling again and sniffed. Thinking all was well, he crept inside and returned to cleaning up the wine that was now staining the carpet.

"Wulf, a word." Earl Edric held his hot drink in front of him and bent down to inhale the steamy fumes. Godfrew got up off the floor and stood in front of his Lord. Shock left his cleaning up and went to sit at his own master's heels. When the Earl spoke, it was almost a whisper, a voice meant for only Godfrew to hear: "It is all turning to a crock of shit." Edric returned to sniffing the drink.

"My Lord. The inner gate, I am sorry we did not manage to take it. I know that—with the lack of the siege engineers—all depended on it being taken. The timing was slightly off and the resistance stronger than we thought." Godfrew noticed that the Earl's mind seemed elsewhere. "I am sorry, my Lord."

"Hmm?" Edric snapped back to the present. "Oh, yes. You are sorry. So am I. But things are changing, Woden's Wulf.

Woden's Wolf

We should have learned that at Hereford. Twice now, we have carried the town and the outer castle defences, but did not manage to get through the inner ones." Edric pulled his bottom lip and drifted off again. When Shock started scratching, the noise broke the Earl from his musing. "Castles are not boroughs. They are like onions. No sooner than you get through one layer than you strike another. No, the Normans have brought new arts with them. Castles and men who fight well on horseback. We will have to change, Wulf. We will have to change." The Earl took some drink and drifted off yet again. Godfrew stood and felt his back start to stiffen. At his feet, Shock lay down and closed his eyes. Godfrew had just reached that point of discomfort where he had decided to risk his master's ire and sit down when the Earl stirred himself and spoke again: "You did your best, Wulf. We all have ... and it is not enough. I am not a religious man, but it is as if God is punishing us. No matter what we do or how we plan, things go awry." The Earl held out his now empty cup for Goda to take and refill. "You did your best. Now do so again—for me. Take those of your men fit to travel and head eastward toward the Isle of Ely. First find the Earl Waltheof—whom you know—and then find an old acquaintance of mine called Hereward."

"The Wake, my Lord?" asked Godfrew.

"You have heard of him? Good. Yes, Hereward the Wake. Tell both of them what has happened here. Tell them I am going back to my hills with my men. Make your journey near Stafford where the Welsh and the rest are headed. Keep tabs on them. Don't get involved in any of their troubles. They will lose, Woden's Wulf. I wish I were wrong, but they will lose. Take the news of their fate to Waltheof and Hereward, but I fear it will be only bad news you will bring them."

The Eastings

The wolf pack rode eastward in silence. They had been that way since the combined Welsh and English army, led by Blenddyn and Rhiwallon, had been shattered outside Stafford by King William and his men. Following the battle, William the Bastard had sent out war bands to harrow the land. The bands had taken all livestock, burned the holdings and the villages, and killed all they came in contact with. They punished the guilty and innocent alike for the uprising.

Godfrew remembered the instructions of Earl Edric and obeyed them. He did not seek out the Normans. Twice, Godfrew came across parties of Norman raiders about their gruesome work. The wolf pack slaughtered them—hanging the bodies from nearby trees, pierced with their own spears.[18] Food for the ravens.

Despite being late summer, Godfrew continually felt chilled and took to always wearing his wolf-skin cloak, fur side out. The wolf pack felt the anger and sadness of the land. The sky wept gentle tears, hiding the shame of the country's rape. Godfrew recalled the words of the prophet Jeremiah, read from a book whilst languishing with the monks at Croydon a lifetime ago:

> The earth has no form,
> The heavens no light.
> The mountains all reel.
> Askip are the hills.
> Seen nowhere is man.
> Missing are all birds.
> Farmland now wilderness,
> Razed are the towns
> By the hand of a foreigner,
> Strong tool of the Lord.
> The whole land stands desolate,
> A small remnant surviving
> The earth in deep mourning.

---

[18] All hanged men were considered a sacrifice to Woden, those stabbed with a spear whilst being hanged especially so.

> 𝕳eavens have turned black.
> God shows us his purpose.
> No change, no relenting.

The devastation did not stop until the wilderness of the Pennine hills—where the desolation was the creation of nature, not of man. Once they made it to the other side, the rain stopped and the land greeted them with freshness and bounty. It seemed almost another country.

The wolf pack kept from the sight of man. They obtained their food from hunting and gathering and drank only Adam's ale. They were headed for Godmanchester, in the shire of Huntingdon—Waltheof's earldom. Godfrew had an aunt there—Mildred, his mother's sister. It had been many years since he had seen her and her then new husband. Mildred and Godfrew were of a similar age—they had grown up almost as brother and sister. Once, they had been so close, but Godfrew did not know how he would be greeted now—a Wolfshead and in arms against the new king.

The journey had, of necessity, been slow and winding. Once, near where the Fossway approached the town of Nottingham, they had seen bands of mounted Normans and their foot mercenaries heading north in a sombre mood. The wolf pack waited two whole days before feeling safe enough to cross the old road and cut across country to the inviting depths of the nearby oak forest. When there were no trees to hide them, they split into pairs and kept half a day between each other. Godfrew rode alone—at first leading them, then letting them all pass. Later, he would overtake his men—making certain they stayed on the right roads and ensuring that they kept away from the temptations of women and ale. A day's ride from where he believed the village to lay, Godfrew sent Magnus and Swein ahead to find out if his aunt was still living there. He left Clunn, Tosti and Puta partnered with the reprieved Leofwine to follow on later.

Godfrew rode along the overgrown Roman road that ran atop the high ground above the Greater Ouse River. The sun finally broke through the black, threatening clouds and bathed the village of Godmanchester in a golden light. He squinted and made out the stone bridge that crossed the river. His eye followed the road as it ran along the opposite

The Eastings

bank, parallel to the river, until it met the small town of Huntingdon where Earl Waltheof had his holding.

He rode on. The blur of the village clarified into houses. He saw two men sitting by the bridge, their horses grazing the grass. As he rode nearer, Godfrew was relieved to see that the men were Magnus and Swein. He rode up to them and dismounted, leaving the dark pony to join their grazing mounts. A hopeful Shuck ran over to see if the men would share their bread with him.

"Greetings, friends. Are you bound for Huntingdon?"

Magnus ran a hand over his cropped golden hair, then pulled up his hood to keep out the cold wind that was blowing off the Pidley Fen. He looked at Magnus, then looked back at Godfrew. He nodded: "Yes, Master."

Godfrew smiled. "I intend to go there soon, to speak with the Earl Waltheof—if he is there. He held land near me in Surrey before the troubles. Meantime, I hope to stay with my Aunt Mildred."

"Oh, I understand that there is a lady of that name here, Master," Swein added, joining in the game. "We will be returning this way in a day or two. Would you like us to bring you news of the Earl on our return?"

"That would be kind." Godfrew reached into his purse and pulled out a silver penny. Shock ran to his master—hoping he had taken out some food. Seeing only a coin, the hound went off to make his mark on a nearby shrub. Godfrew gave the coin to Swein. "Thank you for your trouble." He retrieved the dark pony, removed his cloak from the front of the saddle and put it on—wool side out. "I will see you on your return. You say my aunt is in the village. Do you know where? It has been many years since I was here. I seem to remember her cottage was further up from this bridge."

Magnus pulled up a stem of grass and put it in his mouth. "Nay, Master. She lives in the small cottage right at the beginning of the village. You must have ridden right past it. It has a small apple tree in front of it."

"Again, thanks." Godfrew mounted and rode back to the beginning of the houses. As he reached the cottage with the apple tree, he dismounted and walked around the back of the cottage. There, working in the garden, was a childlike figure. "Mildred? Is that you, Mildred?"

The figure straightened and turned. "I'm Mildred. Who are you?" The woman's face was as childlike as her height. Only the odd silver strand amongst her chestnut hair poking out under her head covering told the truth of her age.

"Have I changed that much? You do not recognise your little nephew?"

"Frew? Is that really you? Surely not!"

"It is me, big Aunty." Godfrew at last allowed himself a grin.

"Big Aunty! Little nephew, indeed. It is many years now since I was taller than you." Mildred put down her hoe and came to embrace her nephew.

Godfrew was not prepared for the strength of the hug and gasped for air. Mildred loosened her grip and Godfrew bent and kissed her covered head. "Didn't recognise me, eh? Have I changed that much?"

"No, not now I look properly." She pulled herself away to arm's length. "But your hair."

"Has turned white, like when I was a young boy."

"More than that it ..."

"Is much longer than I usually wear it. I have been on the road for a long time and have not had the time to care for it properly."

"No, I was going to say it is ..."

"Oh, you can wash and cut it for me before I go." Godfrew pulled his aunt close again and swung her around. "Mildred, Mildred. So many years." He put her down. "You heard the bad news about my parents?"

"Yes ... from your father's brother. He sent word. He also said that you ran off with his serving maid and married her."

"And am now a father. Two sons with another due soon." Godfrew became serious. "Did he say more? Did he say what I am now doing?"

"No. It was but a short message. There may have been more, but the carter who brought it could not read and he brought the message in his head. Knowing the amount of ale he drinks, I am lucky he remembered that much. I cried when I learned what happened to my sister." Mildred started to weep. Godfrew comforted her and for a long time they hung onto each other, sharing their sorrow. At last Mildred let go of her nephew She took hold of his hand and walked him toward the cottage. "Enough of tears. You married, eh. And

The Eastings

sons. We must forget the sadness of the past and think of the future, Frew. Sons."

"You and your Toki. You have children?" Godfrew looked around the garden looking for signs of toys and the usual muddle of children, but there was none.

"Alas, no. Not for want of trying on my husband's part, mind." Mildred allowed herself a chuckle. "But we are happy," she assured Godfrew.

Mildred pulled the leather curtain aside and went into the cottage. Godfrew followed her. The end of the cottage they entered was cluttered with furniture and bits of building timber. The other end resembled a building site. Half-finished dividing walls with half-woven wattle filled the spaces. Mildred caught Godfrew's eye. "Toki is making a separate sleeping area and some storage space for me. I'm afraid it is taking longer than expected. It should have been ready before the haymaking."

"Toki always was building and altering things, as I remember. I know it is a long time since I visited you here, but I seemed to remember you living nearer the bridge. How time warps the memory." Godfrew picked up a wood shaving and started to split it with his thumb nail.

"We did." Mildred proffered Godfrew a pottery mug of ale. The mug was in the shape of a mouse and the tail curved around to make the handle. "We had to sell it. Toki got carried away and bought more timber for its re-building than we could pay. The price for the house was the same as the price of the timber. Silly Toki ... he will never change." A weak smile crossed her face. "But a house is a house and Toki will always reshape any place we live in, just for me. We have plenty of timber to do it!"

"Is he still carpentering for the Earl?" Godfrew's voice had an edge of concern in it. Shock caught the tone and nestled against Godfrew's leg, looking up at his master to reassure him that with his love, all would be well.

"It was the Earl who eventually made us sell the house. He waited over a year for the money, so I can't blame him. Unfortunately, Toki had also overspent on a building he was putting up for the Earl at the same time, so that did not help. Still, Lord Waltheof did find him another job ... this time as a swineherd."

Woden's Wolf

Mildred went to fetch some bread so Godfrew could not see her face. "And money? How are you managing for money?" Godfrew caught her by her elbow and looked over her shoulder. "Money, big Aunty?"

"Oh, we are doing all right. We went on pilgrimage to St. Albans at Easter. Such a nice place." Mildred's eyes brightened at the memory.

"So you have money to spare, even though Toki is now only a swineherd. The truth Mildred."

"I told you, we are all right, provided the Jew at Nottingham does not call his debt in or increase the interest again." Mildred gave a giggle and gave Godfrew the 'little girl' look he always remembered her for.

"You haven't changed, Mildred. No sense with money."

"And never worried about it, nephew!"

"Mildred!"

"Frew!" After putting the bread down on the crowded table, Mildred placed her hands on her hips while she wagged her head at her nephew. "If I never worry about my debts and how I am going to pay them, why should you? Now listen to your big Aunty. Sit down and eat."

The afternoon slipped away in talk of yesterday and family, though Godfrew managed to avoid the detail of his recent activities, only mentioning that he acted as an under-reeve for a landholder in Herefordshire. As the shadows lengthened and the chill of the fens started to creep along the ground, Mildred became anxious. She constantly looked out of a crack in the now shuttered window that faced the cottage path. It was almost dark before she saw what she wanted, came back to the table and gave an audible sigh. Godfrew was about to ask the question when the door curtain parted and in came a short, round figure with a belly as big as its nose. The light from the rush lamp shone on its bald pate.

Toki sniffed and grunted. "Come on, woman. Where's me food? It should be on the table. Don't make we wait." It was then that he realised that there was another figure in the room. Toki screwed his eyes up and peered at Godfrew. Again he sniffed. The sniff was as inquisitive as any Shock made. "Who's this then, Mildred? Entertaining visitors, are we?" He spoke further, but it came out as an unintelligible mutter that Godfrew could not catch, but the tone was unpleasant.

The Eastings

"It is my nephew Frew, my sister's boy. He came to stay when we were first wed. Remember?" Mildred hastily intruded.

"Frew? Ah!" The tone changed. "After all these years. Frew, eh. We ... I ..." the rest became a happy mutter, "so I ... yes, I do." Toki beamed a gap-toothed smile at his visitor.

Godfrew looked puzzled. "Sorry, Toki."

"How long will you be here, Frew. That's what he wants to know," interpreted Mildred.

"Oh, yes. Sorry! Toki. I don't know. Most likely a few days. A week at best, I think. I hope to see the Earl before heading off."

"The Earl ... well, he ... I shouldn't think ... but I could be wrong." Toki took two lumps of bread from the table and dunked them into the steaming bowl of pottage Mildred had hurriedly placed in front of him. "York, now that is a long ..." the sodden bread with pieces of herbs and fatty meat attached to it disappeared into Toki's gaping maw. After a quick, open-mouthed chew, the mess was swallowed and more bread grabbed. "So he ..." Toki laughed at a private joke, then stuffed the dipped bread into his mouth. With barely a pause, he continued. "But I am only a humble swineherd so what ... but then I often ... so take it for what it's worth." As he was now looking directly at him and smiling, Godfrew assumed the flow of information was completed.

"Thank you, Toki. I shall bear it in mind. Now, my horse. I need to stable her."

"No problems. I know ... a very reasonable price, don't you ... so if you will take her ... I'm sure she will be all right till morning." Again, the gap-toothed smile with a nod of the bald head for confirmation.

"Yes, I'm sure you are right, Toki. Thank you again." Godfrew spooned some pottage into his mouth, then watched in amazement as Toki matched him four spoonfuls to one.

* * *

"The lads are keen to be moving on, Master Wulf." Swein shuffled on the upturned bucket he was sitting on, jammed against the unfinished wall in Mildred's cottage. "Clunn reckons that if he stays on that water-logged island in the Pidley Fen much longer, he will develop webbed feet."

"To go with his forked tongue and pointed tail?" Magnus lolled on the pile of wood shavings that served for Godfrew's bed. "Doesn't your aunt's husband ever finish a job or clear up?"

"Not that I know of." Godfrew kicked at a half-cut piece of wood propped up against the wall.

"Didn't think so." Swein pulled Shock up by his ears and stared him out, wet nose to wet nose, unblinking eyeball to unblinking eyeball.. "I was talking to the priest in Huntingdon. As a penance for eating meat during Lent ... eating meat ... by all accounts it was a whole hog that had drowned in the mere ... Tosti was told to make a new rood screen for the Earl's chapel. That was last year and it is still only half done." Shock sneezed and a wet-faced Swein quickly let go of the dog's ears. "Master Wulf. Please, when shall I tell the lads that we are moving on. It is getting very hard to persuade Leofwine to keep off the booze and Clunn the women. He is already stalking the milkmaids."

"Tell them patience. They will all have to learn patience."

"Even poor Puta, whose nice clothes are getting dirty?" Swein pushed away the inquisitive nose of Shock as he sought out the smelliest part of the young man's crotch.

"All of them. First, I need the news of Earl Waltheof. Then I will decide what we are to do." Godfrew rested his head on his folded hands and screwed his eyes up to keep out the light shafting in through the unshuttered window.

"Well, the news we bring is that the Earl is not at his holding. Nor, in fact, are very many folk at all. The only man of standing was an under-reeve of some sort. I told him you could read, so he got a cleric to write this down for me. I didn't know if you could understand the Roman tongue so I told him to put it in English—though with the strange version they speak here about, maybe Latin would have been better." Swein passed over a soft, well-worn piece of vellum.

"I think you are right. Latin would have been easier." Godfrew read and reread the scrawled message, often stopping and frowning before carrying on. "Hmm. It looks as if Clunn will get his webbed feet after all." He got up and walked toward the hearth, rubbing his tired eyes as he went. "The Earl

The Eastings

is in York, or thereabouts. You, Magnus and Swein, must take a reply back to his man to be forwarded on. When you return, we head deeper into the fens and seek out Hereward the Wake. Not that our news will be of much cheer to him." Godfrew picked up a burnt twig and started writing on the reverse side of the velum. "Be careful not to scuff the message. It is only in charcoal and will easily rub off. Take this now and join me with the others first thing tomorrow morning." He passed the script over. "There is no longer any need for subterfuge. The Earl is in arms against the Norman King. He has joined the Danes and the men of Northumbria to take the city of York."

* * *

"I will get your ... I hope she hasn't ... cabbages for years ..." Toki wandered off to the back of the cottage to retrieve Godfrew's dark pony. Shock followed, always hopeful that some of the food that always seemed to be in Toki's hand would fall his way.

Godfrew looked down at his tiny aunt. "Mildred, Toki has been told to take us into the fenland to find a friend."

"Yes, I know."

"If you think that the life of a widow would suit you, tell me now."

"You always were one for a jest," Mildred chirped, but her eyes told that she was unsure if Godfrew's offer was indeed a jest or a serious offer. "We are happy. I told you so."

"Indeed, so you did, big Aunty." Godfrew took his aunt's hand and squeezed it. As he walked away, she found ten silver pennies in her palm.

"What's that?" Toki held the dark pony back, squinted at his wife's hand and sniffed.

"Money. No doubt intended to clear our debt with the Jew of Nottingham." Mildred watched Godfrew as he threw his cloak on, wolf-skin side out.

"It would buy some nice fancy cedar panels for the bedroom and ... maybe a bit left over for a couple of legs of prime beef which we ..." Toki grunted in delight at the thought of spending the coins.

"Myself, I was thinking that next year we could go on pilgrimage to Canterbury. Of course, I would need some new clothes for the trip." Mildred's eyes glazed over as she started to think of what she would need for her wardrobe.

"Just wait till I get back from taking this lot on their voyage through the wetlands, woman." Toki's voice became low and menacing. "Don't get tempted to spend it before I return."

"If you return, Toki. The Vikings are at large in the fens as well as Englishmen." Mildred gave her girlish smile. "If you die, I shall just have to spend the money on widow's needs."

"Just remember what I said and heed it!" Toki stomped off, yanking the pony away from the soft grass she was munching.

"I always remember what you say, my love," Mildred called after her husband. She turned and walked to the cottage, jingling the coins in her hand as she went. "But I take no notice of it," she added under her breath.

* * *

The dark pony's hoof would not pull free from the mire. She struggled to make any movement. Eventually, it pulled out of the cloying mud with a slurping plop and the pony lurched drunkenly forward again. Godfrew wiped a mud-encrusted hand across his forehead, trying to clear the mix of sweat and drizzle that threatened to run into his eyes. He looked back at his men. They and their filth-covered mounts were also struggling to make headway on what was supposed to be a causeway through the fen. Ahead was Toki, holding a gnawed meat bone in his right hand and fending off a besmirched Shock with the left. The fat man was skipping from one small mound of damp earth to another with an agility that denied his considerable weight.

Toki stopped and turned. "Yes, well, it's ... yesterday's rain has ..." He smiled and shrugged his shoulders. Shock leapt at the lowered bone, but missed. "So, I'm sorry, but it will ..."

"Toki, we will have to go back. The horses can't cope with this. If the causeway is this bad, God help us if we wander from it."

"Ah, well, I did warn ... but he ..." Toki shrugged again, but this time he remembered to keep the bone shoulder height. "So back to my beloved swine. I ..."

Godfrew fixed Toki with his eye. "No. With or without the horses, we must reach Hereward." Water ran into his good eye and Godfrew blinked rapidly. "If we are going to get wet, dear uncle Toki, so are you." The dark pony shuddered and started to loose her balance. At the last moment, she managed to pull a hoof free and regain her equilibrium. Godfrew leaned across her neck and settled her down.

Toki had a dark look on his shining face. Water ran down the crown of his hood, trickled onto the bridge of his nose and dripped off the tip. After glowering at Godfrew for a couple of minutes, he suddenly regained his composure and assumed his gap-toothed smile. "Well, I know a ... he would not charge much and, eh ..."

Godfrew cut short Toki's mumbling "No. We return to Huntingdon and leave the horses with Earl Waltheof's men. I need to know where they are. With all the going's on around here I want the horses with people I know and trust." Godfrew nudged the dark pony's flanks and persuaded her to start the difficult manoeuvre of turning around on the narrow strip of the causeway. "Don't just stand there muttering, Toki," he called over his shoulder. "My mind is made up. We move." He shifted his weight in the saddle to help the pony gain traction. "And we move NOW!" Godfrew whistled out to his men and gestured for them to turn around and head back.

Toki gave Godfrew's back a black look and spat a piece of gristle into a puddle. As Shock walked past, trying to catch up with his master, Toki put his foot under the hound's belly and flipped him into the puddle. Shock staggered to his feet and shook—almost falling over in the process. On seeing the gristle floating on the muddy surface, he bent down and ate it.

* * *

The minute the wolf pack had climbed on board the punt at Huntingdon to head back into the fens, the rain stopped and the sun came out. They soon left the river and started mov-

Woden's Wolf

ing through extensive reed beds, following small slow-moving streams and waterways. Occasionally, they passed small islands with stunted trees and rich green pastures. Mist rose from the islands, matching the steam that rose from the sodden clothes of the men in the punt.

Godfrew had removed his cloak and spread it in front of him. The rain had soaked through the cloak unevenly and his shirt showed patches of varying dampness. Godfrew sat on the crude plank seat at the punt's blunt nose and kept his legs splayed to try and dry the inside of his trousers, his long legs filling the full width of the craft.

Each time he needed to move forward to manoeuvre the punt with his pole, the puntsman had to step over Godfrew's legs. The first time he had to do so, the taciturn fenman had turned to speak sharply with Godfrew, but on seeing the young man's white, thinning hair and one eye, he thought better of it. Thence forth, he took great care to ensure that he did not physically touch the Wolfshead.

The other passengers in the punt were not so lucky. They were regularly cursed at, jostled, and subjected to a wetting from the fenman's punt pole. Toki sat at the end of the craft and watched it all in seeming amusement. Drink and food were never far from his hands. Shock sat under Godfrew's seat shivering and watching Toki's food. Toki took pleasure in watching the hound, teasing him by eating the food with slow and exaggerated gestures.

The further into the fens they went, the quieter it became and the scarcer the islands. Of the few islands they did see, none was inhabited. The autumn rains had already caused the water level to rise and turn them into waterlogged bogs.

So quiet had it become that when the occasional water fowl took fright at their coming and took off with a flap and a squawk, every man took fear and drew his weapon, staying tense until the bird's noise had faded into the silence.

As darkness fell, the puntsman headed his vessel into the rushes and grounded it on a low mound of mud. "Out here then, Toki Outlander." The fenman stepped over Godfrew and leapt onto the mound, landing with a resounding squelch. "Come you all. The night is to be spent here." He gesticulated to his reluctant passengers. "Toki, move they, this is it."

"Oh, right ..." Toki stood up, upsetting the balance of the punt and almost causing it to tip over. Ignoring the insults of the wolf pack, he waddled forward. "Come on, this is the night's resting place. Don't forget the supplies. I'm sure we will be ..."

His mutter was lost as he got off and splashed after the fast disappearing fenman, leaving the others to follow.

"You heard him." Godfrew slowly stood up and gingerly disembarked. "I don't know where we are going, but it must be better than sleeping on the punt."

"Any women around, Master Wulf?" asked an optimistic Clunn.

"Only mermaids, Rat," commented Tosti, as he accepted Godfrew's proffered hand to ease himself onto the soggy soil, "or maybe female water rats would do, knowing your lack of discernment, 'cos I think that is all you will find around here."

Clunn gave only an evil look in reply and trudged off into the growing darkness, a sackcloth bag bouncing over his shoulder. Godfrew helped Leofwine and Puta ashore before striding past the others and catching up with Toki and the puntsman.

They walked for what seemed hours, at times up to their knees in water, until at last, hidden in the reeds, invisible to anyone but those ten arm's lengths away, stood a thatched hut standing above the surrounding water on stout poles.

"Here she be." The puntsman had a look of immense pride on his face. He fondly patted the willow poles which held the rope bridge that led to the hut. "No fires, mind, Toki Outlander. Warn they that." He glared at the dishevelled members of the wolf pack. "I'm off to make sure we are expected tomorrow at Ely. I'd die for Earl Waltheof if need be, but not from an English arrow."

After avoiding contact with Godfrew, he pushed his way through the others and headed back to the punt. Once out of sight, he turned and made a sign to ward off the evil eye and said a silent prayer to St. Michael to protect him from evil spirits, Woden in particular!

The wolf pack watched the fenman go, half glad to be rid of him for a while, half wanting him back to help them cope with the strange world of the fens. Whilst they dithered in front of the hut, Shock cautiously stepped onto the rope bridge. Finding that he did not like the swinging motion, he turned back, but the bridge swung even more. He ran forward and scampered onto the board veranda. The men heard the sound of his claws on wood. They knew that the dog was already at the hut and decided to follow.

Clunn and Tosti set off together. The short bridge swung in frightening rhythm to their steps. The others followed, one at a time, their hands gripping the damp rope handrail, their knuckles white from the tightness of their grip.

Watching the men crossing to the hut, realising that he would not be alone, Shock nosed open the wooden-framed thatched door and entered the dark hut to explore its interior.

In the first corner, by the door, eels had been hung up to dry on frames, rows of them. Some were like hard uncured leather. Others were still moist and supple, their black skins glinting in the small amount of light getting in from the doorway. Over on the other side, Shock snuffled and, to his delight, found slivers of fish stuck to the floor together with pools of dried fish blood to lick. A mound of tacky innards lay under a crude bench where fish had been gutted and dressed. Shock took great pleasure in rolling on them, sniffing his shoulders and back after each roll to ensure he had gained an even spread of scent. Next he wandered over to the far corner where a cage had been erected. The outside was covered in coarsely woven sackcloth.

Shock stood by the wood frame and sniffed the game birds that had been hung up inside to ripen. Along the wall, piled in the last corner, were mattresses filled with feathers. They had come from the water fowl now hanging in the cage— these and many others. The last mattress was only half-full and the top was unstitched. Shock stuck in his weasel-shaped nose to snuffle and snort around. When he pulled his head out, he looked prematurely aged. His muzzle was covered with fine white duck down. He was just about to see if he could find a way into the bird cage for a quick snack when the sound of the men's laughter disturbed him. He quickly ran out to see what was happening.

"Come on, Puta, my pretty. Just hang on to the rope and you won't fall in." Clunn called out in encouragement to his

The Eastings

petrified companion. "Come on now." With an evil glint in his eye and a yellow-toothed smile, Clunn gave the handrail a quick shake.

"Clunn, I saw that." Puta's voice went up in pitch. "In the name of all the saints, don't do it!" Puta grabbed the oscillating left-hand rope rail with both hands. The now off-balanced bridge swung alarmingly, threatening to dump plump Puta into the stagnant water beneath. Leofwine and Toki were weeping tears of laughter. Swein and Magnus sniggered whilst Godfrew looked on amused.

Tosti became serious. He held out his hand to the now panicking Puta. "Forget the others! Trust me." He shook his hand encouragingly, "Come on, Puta. Be brave! Let go of the rope and take my hand." Puta let go with one hand and reached forward, but Tosti's helping hand was just out of reach. "Come on, let go, my ginger-headed friend. Trust me."

Puta plucked up his courage, let go of the rope and lunged for Tosti's hand. Tosti withdrew it at the last moment. The unfortunate Puta fell forward and ended up prone, his head through the laced rope side of the bridge, his face just inches from the water.

Tosti and Clunn stepped forward and started bouncing the rope bridge, thereby dunking poor Puta's face.

"You are always telling me we need to wash regularly, my lovely. And you've told me more than once that mud cleans the complexion." Clunn cackled and bounced up and down with even more enthusiasm.

At first Godfrew had let the boys have their fun as Puta's simpering ways had often got on his nerves, but once he realised that his plump cousin was getting hysterical, he called a halt to the torment and helped Puta get off the bridge and onto the veranda. It was not an easy task, as his fingers seemed to be welded to the rope. Even when the motion of the bridge ceased, Puta would not stand up, preferring to cautiously crawl along the rope way, not relaxing until his hands touched the wooden decking.

Godfrew left him to join the others at the entrance to the hut. Shock sat at Puta's side and licked the tears from his face.

"Go on then, Toki, you are the local man. In you go." Clunn pushed him toward the door. "In you go! See if there are any trolls in there. Go on!"

"Oh, well ... strange things in the fens, sometimes lights that just ... not that they would ..."

"Get on with it." Tosti opened the door and pushed the reluctant Toki inside.

As the fat man fell on the floor, Tosti quickly pulled the door closed.

"Let me out, there's ..." Toki started coughing and reaching. "In God's name let me ..."

"What's up? Trolls?" Tosti drew his short sword and held the door closely shut.

"No. No trolls, just ..." Toki took to pulling the thatched reeds off of the door in order to try and get out.

"Let him out, Tosti," Godfrew commanded. Tosti obliged and Toki fell out of the doorway, floundering on the veranda deck. Once Toki made his appearance, Tosti jammed the door shut again and stood with his back to it. "Well Toki?" Godfrew asked. "What is in there? Are there trolls?"

"No, just stench." Toki crawled to the edge of the decking and vomited into the water. "It smells like ..." the rest of his sentence was lost as he emptied the remaining contents of his expansive stomach.

"Well, if that's all," the now emboldened Leofwine moved Tosti out of the way, pulled open the door and strode into the hut. He did not stay in there long. "The Devil's breath could not be worse." He went and stood at the water's edge and took several deep breaths before continuing. "Toki, what do they do in that place?"

"Well, I, never ... I know of them. Each family has one somewhere in the ... fishing all year, eeling, catching water fowl in season, and cutting reeds for ... but I've never actually been in one." Toki scooped up a handful of water and dumped it onto the top of his bald head, rubbing it over his face as it ran down.

"Right! I notice that there are windows, each covered by a drop-down shutter. They must be designed to stay open." Godfrew walked up to the nearest one and lifted it up. As he caught a whiff of the stench within, he dropped it closed again. "Right! Then each of us takes it in turn to go inside and prop one of the shutters up. With all of them open, the smell must clear." Godfrew looked over his men. "Tosti, you are first, then Clunn. Go in and open the one opposite the door. We will help from this side."

"Thank you for the honour, Master Wulf. I don't suppose you would like to take my place?" Godfrew closed his blind eye and stared hard at Tosti with his good one, biting on his back teeth and making his jaw harden. "Well, I only thought it would increase your standing." Tosti looked again at Godfrew, but there was no humour in his leader's face. "No? Well, I was only jesting." Tosti glanced at Clunn. "Ready to open the gateway to hell, Master Rat?"

Clunn nodded.

"Let's go then," Tosti ordered. As the reluctant Tosti ran into the hut, Shock joined him, glad to be back in the treasure hoard of smells.

Whilst Tosti struggled to find a prop to use, Godfrew and Leofwine opened the shutter from the outside. They gratefully stood well back until Tosti finally got the prop in place.

Once he got outside, it was noticeable that his pale complexion was even whiter than usual.

"All right, Clunn, you're next, and I think we will leave the door open to encourage more draft." Godfrew went over to his cousin to see if he was able to help yet, but Puta was still sobbing into the hem of his overshirt, so he went to his aunt's husband instead. "Toki," Godfrew prodded the ample body of the bald man, "a hand, if you will. We need to open the shutters and get fresh air into the place if we are to sleep there tonight. Toki?" Toki looked up at Godfrew, then reluctantly got up and joined him.

Clunn opened the window by the bird cage, Leofwine the one opposite, and Magnus the one nearest the door. Swein was nowhere to be seen.

By the time they had finished, it was fully dark. The darker it became, the noisier the fen. Frogs competed with the wind through the rush beds, water fowl competed with who knew what, as one weird sound competed with another. Above all was the humming of winged insects.

Leofwine and Tosti claimed that they could hear high-pitched squeaks and squeals, as if someone or something was being tortured, but the others could hear nothing.

Occasionally, they heard the flap of a flitter mouse as it sped past the hut on leather wings. If they had been allowed to light a fire, they would have taken off their wet shoes and leg-wrappings and dried them, but without a fire the exercise was pointless.

Now their wet feet added to their discomfort. The feather mattresses eased the hardness of the uneven planked floor. Slowly, the men stopped talking and drifted off into sleep.

Shock spent most of his time learning the past history of the hut with his nose, but eventually even he tired of it and crept under the wolf-skin cloak to join his master. Godfrew felt the warmth of the hound's body and pulled him close, dreaming of Elfgifu.

Only Clunn remained fully alert as he comforted the drowsy Puta.

As light started to filter through the reed thatching and into the eastward-facing windows, the men stirred. All felt as if they had not slept at all.

Godfrew was the first to move, his full bladder compelling him to go out and relieve himself. As he walked onto the veranda he was shocked to see the fenman and a companion asleep outside, each man under a fine meshed net hung from the eves of the hut.

Godfrew scratched the angry red insect bites on the back of his hands and neck and made his way over the rope bridge to find a convenient place to piddle. On his return, he found the others were up, talking and scratching. The two fenmen, legs and feet bare, stood apart talking with each other.

The newcomer was dressed the same as the man who had brought them by punt thus far, but was much taller and his hair fairer. From his belt hung a saxe and a hand axe held by a leather wrist strap. Against the thatched wall stood his battered, round linden-wood shield with more scars than paint, its device long since chipped and peeled into no more than an occasional splotch of faded colour.

Godfrew strained his ears to catch what they were saying, but the dialect contained much old Norse and he had difficulty in following what was being said. It was obvious that the puntsman had greatly modified his speech when talking with them yesterday.

Godfrew went over to the fenmen and spoke with them. "Will we reach the Isle of Ely today?" Godfrew scratched his wrist again and then stopped when he saw the fenmen watching his actions with amusement.

"Yes," said the puntsman.

"Yes," echoed the other fenman.

"And Hereward is there?" Godfrew went to scratch the irritation on his wrist, but fought the compulsion.

"Yes," said the puntsman.

"Yes," echoed the other fenman.

"Do we have time to eat?" Rather than scratch, Godfrew took to rubbing his wrist against his leg, but his actions did not fool the fenmen. They watched with a half-smile on their faces. "Can we eat?" Godfrew repeated.

"Yes," said the puntsman.

"Yes," echoed the other fenman.

"Thank you." Godfrew walked over to the others, glad to be able to scratch his bites to his heart's desire.

"Off soon are we then, Master Wulf?" Magnus sipped cider from a flask before passing it to Swein.

"As soon as we have broken our fast." Godfrew accepted a hunk of acorn bread Clunn proffered to him, but he only played with it before giving it to Shock who took it into the hut to eat in peace. "I don't know about you, but that smell still lingers. It has ruined my appetite."

Godfrew looked at his men and found that they too were not eating much, except Toki who had acquired a dried eel from the hut and was tucking into it with relish.

Shock reappeared and sat behind Toki, just out of his sight. Whilst Toki used his fingernails to strip pieces of dried eel flesh from the leathery skin, Shock gnawed at the tail.

The taller fenman walked over and addressed Godfrew. "Close the hut up. We're off now." He and the puntsman then crossed the rope bridge and headed off.

Godfrew and his men hurriedly shut up the thatched hut and scampered off after their hosts. Puta closed his eyes and held out his hands to be led over the bridge by Tosti at the front and Clunn at the rear. Being full daylight, it was easier to see where they were going and they did not get so wet on the journey this time. As they embarked on the punt, the new fenman remained in the bow. His shield was slung over his back and his hand shielded his eyes as he scanned the banks and rush beds.

The longer they travelled, the more little green islands of wet bog appeared. Finally, they entered the clear waterway of Soham Mere. The punt was kept close to the shore until they turned off again into the fens. Yet more small islands of green had appeared amongst the reeds.

Then they saw the Isle of Ely. Anywhere else, it would have been regarded as but a low hill, but in this flat land, its appearance was dramatic. Soon they could see the tower of Ely Abbey above the reeds and the stunted trees of the Isle's shore.

A duck quacked.

The fenman in the bow replied.

A warbler called. Again the fenman replied.

Soon they came to a small jetty where the punt headed in, bumping alongside it. The man in the bow got out. He took a rope with him and tied the punt up. The wolf pack unsteadily disembarked and stood about, unsure of what to do. Godfrew heard a whooping swan pass overhead, but when he looked up, he saw nothing.

The sound came again, this time a duck gave an alarm signal in reply. Godfrew looked for the duck, but found it was the taller fenman.

Before he could say anything, men with short bows came out from a clump of reeds and stood an arrow's shot away. The two fenmen grabbed Toki by the elbow and quickly marched him toward the awaiting party.

The wolf pack watched as the two groups talked and gesticulated. Eventually, Toki and the fenmen came back.

The fenmen got back into the punt and got ready to leave.

"So this is it, Toki?" asked Godfrew. "The famed Isle of Ely?"

"Oh, ere, yes, the ..." Toki seemed unduly agitated.

"Off back to Godmanchester. In some ways, I envy you." Godfrew gave his neck a discrete scratch.

"Err, no. That's the problem. I ... err ... owe someone some money for supplying me with ..." The rest of Toki's words were lost as he turned to look at the men by the reeds who still held their arrows notched. "Look, Frew, nephew," Toki's voice started to whine. "When the chance comes, put in a word for me to get home." He gave a lopsided smile. "I mean the Earl's

The Eastings

reeve will be after me for not looking after the swine and your poor aunt will be worried silly." He shrugged and tried hard to keep Godfrew's eye contact, his feet jiggling and dancing.

"Just what do you owe?"

"Oh, err, you sound just like my wife, she's always ..." again the glance back. "I thought he would be more ..."

"Toki. How much?" Godfrew gave Toki the eye contact he had sought, but Toki did not like it when he got it and tried to look away. Godfrew grabbed him by the shirt. Twisting it in his fist, he jammed the resultant lump under Toki's several chins and forced the fat man to look at him. "How much?"

"Twenty silver pennies," Toki gasped. "Please, Frew, let," he struggled for air, "let go, please!"

Godfrew let Toki go. "For once you will not be bailed out. I haven't got that much, not now, not here." He pushed his aunt's husband around and prodded him toward the waiting archers. "If you need that sort of money you had better stay with us and hope for some good raids and plenty of plunder, or you may have to spend the rest of your life enslaved here."

Toki went to turn around to plead again, but Godfrew gave him a hard shove that sent him stumbling forward. The rest of the wolf pack followed, hands on weapons, just in case. Two sword's lengths away from the archers, Godfrew stopped. "Greetings, I come from Earl Edric called 'The Wild', in search of Hereward called 'The Wake'. Men call me 'Wulf'."

The leader of the archers unnotched his arrow and came to stand in front of Godfrew. "I am Brynoth. I trust you are more trustworthy than the thief you came with." Brynoth turned his head and spat at Toki's feet. "We have heard of your Earl and his hobbies." The man had a wry smile on his pockmarked face. "If only half of them are true, he is a very distinct person. To be his trusted messenger must be a great honour. Come." Brynoth turned and strode off, his men parting to let Godfrew and the wolf pack through. As Toki passed, they gently restrained him and led him off in another direction, laughing as they went.

The main camp was some way from the landing place. A haze of wood smoke betrayed its presence long before it could be seen. It lay in a slight hollow before the abbey.

The streets were laid out all higgledy-piggledy. The camp had obviously grown haphazardly with the increased number of outlaws seeking refuge there. Women and children strolled about and sat in front of the thatched reed huts, completing their outside tasks while the weather held.

At the far end of the camp, cattle were corralled and men could be seen undertaking the autumn slaughter. As Brynoth led the wolf pack in, the younger children ran indoors while the elder gathered at the ends of the alleys between the rows of huts and watched curiously. Brynoth caught Clunn and Tosti eyeing the women. "Tell your men to keep hands and other things to themselves. These women are all spoken for. If they are after loose women, they will have to talk to the Danes. They are always bringing in spares." Godfrew raised an eyebrow. "They have their own camp over the hill," Brynoth explained. "Just tell your men to be careful."

"Any reason?" Godfrew went to scratch his itching wrist, but saw that it was already a bleeding mess and fought the temptation.

"Just be careful. At present they are our allies against the Normans, but things are not as we had hoped." Brynoth rubbed his chin with his free hand.

"What had you hoped for?"

"Well, as you know, many of us in these parts are half-Dane. With King Harold dead and Harald the Hard-ruler dead, Swein the king of the Danes, has next call on the throne, unless you count Edgar the Aetheling—and he is no warrior, so who would want him." They reached a large hut and Brynoth stopped. "We thought Swein would come with men to reclaim the kingdom his kinsman Knute ruled so well, but he sent his brother Earl Osbjorn instead. The Earl seems more intent on plunder than conquest." The warrior looked at the hill where the Danish camp lay and slowly shook his head. "Who knows where they stand in this matter. The Lord Hereward still hopes, but does not know for sure. And if he's not sure, what hope have I, a humble soldier."

Brynoth's thought went elsewhere, but Godfrew and his men were tired and wanted to rest, so Godfrew did not allow him the luxury of private thoughts.

"We are staying here?" Godfrew indicated the hut.

"Oh, yes, sorry," Brynoth apologised. "Please make yourselves at home, I will send food and drink for you. Whatever you do, do not drink the water, not if you want to live."

"You said 'us' earlier, but by your accent you are not a fenman. Middlesex or Essex perhaps?" Godfrew probed.

"Essex. My father was English, but my mother Danish. She came from these parts. When things went wrong, after the King was killed, I came back to stay with her family." Brynoth unstrung his bow and wrapped the string around the stave. "I will go and find where Lord Hereward is. I believe he is gone from the camp today, but he should be back by nightfall. Rest." He glanced at Godfrew's bloody wrist. "In addition to the food, I will get my woman to bring herbs for your bites and nets for you to sleep under."

"Thank you, we will be very grateful. It is good of you to think of us."

Brynoth laughed: "I'm not thinking of you, I'm afraid. I'm thinking of us. The more trained warriors we have, the better. Unless I keep you fit, you will be no good to anyone!"

* * *

It was late afternoon before anyone came near the hut occupied by the wolf pack. The men had dozed and lazed about, making up for their disturbed sleep the night before. They had just started to question Godfrew about when they were going to get something to eat when a short, dumpy woman came in.

"I'm Brynoth's woman, Edith. You are Edric the Wild's men. The wolves? We've heard something about you." She glared at Clunn, "So keep yourselves to yourselves, then we will get on fine." As she returned to face Godfrew, Clunn blew her a kiss behind her back. "I've brought you all some oatmeal poultice steeped in local herbs for they bites. Use it sparingly! Happens oats don't grow here about, so them are expensive." A pot of steaming water with a cloth pack in it was set down on the ground. The reclining Clunn took the opportunity of the woman's bending to glance up under her kirtle. He rolled back shaking his head and kissing his fingers. "Now I supposes you and they others want food as well."

"Please," said Godfrew politely.

Woden's Wolf

"Come on in, you," commanded Brynoth's woman to an unseen figure outside. "Get that food in here." With a toss of her head she faced Godfrew again. "I hope you like fish pie. It's all we've got at the moment, till the beasts are all slaughtered."

"Fish pie," Godfrew smiled pleasantly. "Why I was almost raised on it."

"Good, you won't be disappointed then." Again she turned to the doorway, "I said come on in you."

As no one came in, Edith went out. She returned leading a fat figure by the ear. It was Toki carrying a basket containing several cold fish pies. He was wearing a muzzle. "Now set that food down and then get some small beer for these men," Edith gave Toki's ear a tweak, "but be quick. I have plenty for you to do in the kitchens tonight. If you try and sneak off ..." She left the threat unsaid and breezed out of the hut.

"Oh, Uncle Toki, what have they done to you?" Godfrew went over and examined the muzzle on Toki's face. It was well made and tight fitting. Only the smallest pieces of food could be slid into the man's mouth. Toki gave a wild-eyed look and started to cry. "They won't ... until ..." His mutterings turned into sobs.

"Oi," interjected Magnus "don't drop those pies, fat man. I'm looking forward to them. They smell delicious."

"Oh, yes, and hurry up with the ale. I need a drink. Just remember, if it is only small ale, I will need twice as much of it to make me mellow," added Leofwine as he helped himself to a pie.

"Uncle Toki, it does look as if they mean to get payment, doesn't it." Godfrew embraced the man to comfort him, but the wolf pack saw Godfrew's amused smile. "We will think of something, but not today I fear. I will speak to Brynoth when I see him."

Toki shook his head sadly and went out the door.

No sooner had he gone than everyone fell about laughing.

They were still laughing when Brynoth entered. "Good joke, is it?"

"Toki!" exclaimed Swein and laughed again.

"Yes, I thought you would appreciate that." Brynoth seated himself on one of the straw mattresses.

The Eastings

"How long will you keep it on him Brynoth? Seriously," asked Godfrew.

"Seriously? Till he pays up." He saw the question in Godfrew's face. "No, honestly, that man has caused me and mine some considerable grief. I'll not starve him to death, but he will get a lot slimmer."

"It is your right, I suppose, but he is my kin by my aunt's marriage," explained Godfrew as he gently dabbed the slime from the poultice onto the bites on his wrist.

"Your kin? I am sorry, but it won't change things." Brynoth poured himself a cup of ale and sipped it. "I'll tell you what: if you pay it, I won't charge the interest I would have charged him. Fair enough?"

"Fair enough." Godfrew started applying the poultice to his neck. "Was there anything else you wanted to say to us, Brynoth."

"Oh, yes. Lord Hereward is back. He wants you to dine with him at the Dane's camp tonight." The men started to get up, but Brynoth gestured to them to sit down again. "No, just Wulf." He picked up a bit of pie crust and threw it to Shock. "Oh, and I would leave your hound behind as well as your wolves. The Danes may eat it. They seem to devour everything else they see."

* * *

Whereas the English camp was sprawling, the Danes' camp was a proper military one. As they mounted the hill, Godfrew saw the earthen ramparts surrounded by a deep ditch. The lack of trees had prevented its constructors from building a stockade on the top, but they had found sufficient wood to construct a watchtower on each of the four corners. Brynoth took him around the outside of the whole camp so that Godfrew could see its full size. There was a gate in each of the four sides. On all but the west side, the gates were protected by an embankment before and aft of the gate. On the west gate were woven wooden hurdles ready to be pulled across the entrance. There was an embankment inside the walls to stop a concerted rush. The earth of the embankments was too new to have grass growing. The recent rains had cut grooves in them, leaving pools of soft slurry at the foot. In front of the west gate, people were queuing up to go in.

As the people went up, two fully mailed and helmeted guards searched them and took away their weapons, giving them a wooden token in exchange. Brynoth knew the score. When it was their turn, he handed over his hand axe and sword. The guards were laughing amongst themselves as they approached Godfrew. As the first guard came, he looked at Godfrew with the setting sun behind his back and stopped. He carefully took in Godfrew's wolf-skin cloak, the old man's hair, the boy's face and the blind eye. He stopped laughing and grabbed his comrade by the elbow. Two ravens, hoping no doubt to scavenge food, landed at Godfrew's feet, walked toward the guards, and passed into the camp. The first guard muttered in his mate's ear. He, too, stopped laughing. They waited in silence as Godfrew approached them, handed over his saxe, took the token from the first guard's slack hand and went in. The first guard fingered the small silver hammer of Thor that hung from the thong on his neck whilst the other crossed himself.

"Your looks have a strange effect on people, even if they don't know that men call you Woden's Wulf," Brynoth chuckled.

"My looks may not appeal to women, but they do have advantages," agreed Godfrew.

Before them stood the long house. On either side ran rows of huts neatly set out in a grid-iron pattern.

As they came up to the armed men at the door, the men recognised Brynoth and let them pass. As Godfrew passed, there was again the touching of talismans and crossing of the body.

Inside, there was much noise, smoke, and confusion. Three rows of tables ran the length of the hall to a head table. At the table sat two men, deep in conversation, with a third tall man occasionally being brought into the talk. The big, golden-haired man was obviously Hereward the Wake. The one beside him was in Danish dress and of slender build. Behind the men stood a row of very tall warriors. Every other warrior faced the wall whilst the man next to him faced the other way.

The Eastings

"Lord Hereward's Frisians," enlightened Brynoth. "After Lord Hereward was outlawed by the old king, Edward the-would-be-priest, he went to Ireland. He left there after some trouble and went to live with the Frisians. Pirates to a man, but very loyal. He goes nowhere without them. He trusts them implicitly." They made their way along the wall of the hall to the top table. As they neared, it started to get crowded with drunken Danes and serving women carrying food and drink.

Brynoth carved his way through. There was a gap a sword's length wide between the crowd and the tall Frisians. Brynoth stopped short and called out: "Stig Gullwing, it's me! Brynoth."

A Frisian, tall enough to be seen as tall even in the company of tall men, turned and stepped up to Brynoth. "What?"

"We have come to speak with Lord Hereward," Brynoth replied.

"So?"

"So, we wish to talk with him."

Stig Gullwing turned and resumed his place.

"Come on." Brynoth guided Godfrew away. "We might as well get some food and drink while we wait." They found a space on the right-hand table and sat down. "Men of few words, the Frisians. When they talk slowly you can understand them easily enough. When they talk quickly you just get out of the way. It always means trouble."

A serving woman passed by. Brynoth beckoned her over and took some meat for him and Godfrew. "Any chance of some bread and some ale?"

The woman went off. Later, the rest of the meal arrived. Godfrew chewed on the meat. It tasted like the horse flesh so beloved by the Icelanders—a taste he had been introduced to so long ago in Wandsworth by old Snorrie. Brynoth took a mouthful of ale and puckered up his face, "Weasel's piss. Now, when are these fen dwellers ever going to learn to brew some decent ale?" He smiled a toothless smile. Godfrew stared at him. "Oh, the teeth? Lost them in the great battle against the Bastard. Were you there?"

"No. I arrived only in time to take part in the fight at the fosse. I had been injured at Stamford Bridge."

"You were at Stamford Bridge? So was I. I was in the rear so didn't get to take part in the fighting. Plenty of plunder, though. I even managed to put mine in a safe place before going to the Hoar Apple Tree fight. I say 'safe', but I haven't been back to dig it up, so I am only assuming it's safe, I mean." Brynoth broke up the horse flesh and started to cut it into small pieces with the blunt knife the serving woman had provided for him and Godfrew to share. "What's the point of having gold around in these times when some other bugger is likely to steal it from you." He put the small pieces of flesh into his mouth and washed them down with ale from his earthen-ware cup. "The fosse, you said? I missed that. By the time that one started I was out of it all. I got hit in the face with a mace when in the shield wall. Lost all me teeth, had me nose spread over me face and had me eyes closed up on me. I was lucky not to get killed. Someone, I don't know who, got me away and left me with a hermit. He looked after me till I was able to travel. He did a good job of straightening me nose. Look!" Brynoth held his pocked face up for examination. "Not bad, eh?" He diced some more horse flesh and washed it down. "I went back to my place in Westminster, but it had been burnt down. I don't know what happened to the wife. I found my kids hiding in the nearby marshes. Even they don't know what happened to her."

"You lost your wife, did you say? Then who is that back at the camp? A new woman?" Godfrew looked puzzled.

"No, that is my first wife. It was my second wife who went missing." Brynoth started breaking up the bread into small pieces. "I married one of the daughters of my mother's cousins. You remember that she was from the fens?"

"Yes." Godfrew's mind turned to his own burnt out home at Garrat. He stopped eating his meal and settled for drinking ale instead.

"Well it was silly, really. We had an argument. I went off to London on business. A piece of young skirt caught my eye and I didn't come back. At least, not till a long time later. The wife, this one, not the other one, gives me lip about the time I spent in the south, but she loves those kids as well as her own."

"You left your first wife and your children? Why?" Godfrew held up his cup for a refill.

"I told you. It was silly ... but then we all get tempted by a bit of young and willing female flesh, don't we?"

The Eastings

"No, I ..." Godfrew never finished as a drunken Dane opposite caught part of the conversation and butted in.

"Female flesh? Do you want some female flesh? I have some to sell or hire."

He pushed off the comrade who was leaning on him and started to fill the cup he was holding with thick mead. "Now I am in the position to hire you a very desirable woman. In the very prime of life she is—soft, warm flesh. Long brown hair. Wavy. Not one of your camp whores either. A widow, in fact. She accompanied her husband from Orkney when he joined the Norwegian king's fleet. Unfortunately, he didn't return from the fight at Stamford Bridge. Few did. I caught her when we sacked York last year."

"No thank ..."

Now, I will admit," the Dane stopped long enough for a gulp of mead, "she may not know all the tricks that a camp whore does, but she is very gentle and loving."

"No, I ..."

"Loki," the Dane shook his comrade. Loki just stared ahead blankly, his head wobbling slightly. "Loki, that woman of mine, lovely isn't she, very gentle." Loki slowly leaned forward and rested his head on the table, his cheek lying in a pool of spilt ale and meat gravy. "Yes," continued the Dane, "very gentle. Would suit a man like you missing his wife." Ignoring the cup in his right hand, the Dane swigged mead from the flask he held in his left.

"No, honestly, I don't want to hire your woman," insisted Godfrew.

"Very wise too," agreed the Dane after he had taken another swig from the flask. He proceeded to pour some mead into Brynoth's cup, despite the fact that it was still half-full of ale. When it came to Godfrew's cup, the flask was empty, but the Dane held it over the cup none-the-less. "You want to buy a woman. Excellent decision. When you take her home just tell your wife that you have got her a handmaiden." He laughed, spittle catching on the untidy whiskers of his beard. "A handmaiden, very handy for you, too, I think—especially if she uses more than her hands!" The Dane laughed so hard at his own joke that tears ran down his cheek.

"No, I don't want to buy a woman from you!" Godfrew moderated his exasperation, not being willing to cause trouble in the Danes' own camp.

"You are right," agreed the Dane. He went to take another swing from the flask. Finding it empty, he threw it against the wall. The movement dislodged the sleeping Loki, who slid to the floor, curled into a ball and started snoring. "No, the women I have for sale at the moment are all rubbish. Now men, not that I think you are like that, of course. Men, I have. Frenchmen, unfortunately. Tradesmen, I believe. We kill all the warriors, but tradesmen are different. They have a decent market value. We will have to find someone who speaks their barbarous tongue and see what their trades are. If they have no trade, it reduces their value, but they can still be sold as farm labourers." He suddenly found that he was still holding a half-full cup of mead in his right hand, so downed it with lip-smacking relish. "So, do you want to buy a Frenchman?"

"No, I ..."

"Selling our Frenchmen already, Tor?" another Dane tripped over the sleeping Loki and crashed onto the bench by Tor's side. "We've only brought them in from York this afternoon and you are trying to sell them already." He tried to prop his head up with his hands, but his elbows slid on the spilt ale. He contented himself with looking up at Tor from the table. "Just ..." he wagged a stump of a finger at the other Dane "... just make sure you get Irish prices, not Iceland ones."

The stumpy finger wagged in a circle before the effort became too much and the man's hand flopped onto the table top in front of his face.

"Yes, yes, Lief." Tor leaned over and patted Lief's back with his right hand whilst his left removed a mead flask from the slack hand of the next Dane along the bench. "Only Irish prices."

"Irish prices?" asked Godfrew.

"Always pay a good price, the Irish. Always wanting more good-looking women and skilled tradesmen. Pay well, not like the Icelanders. Very bad at the moment, Iceland prices." Tor picked up his fallen cup, couldn't make his mind what to do with it, so put it down again. "Iceland prices?" Godfrew was only managing to pick up part of the conversation now as

Tor's speech was becoming more slurred and getting beyond Godfrew's understanding of Norse.

"Iceland prices. Damned Kjell ruined the Iceland prices. Damn Kjell." Tor shook Lief, "Damn Kjell."

Lief opened his eyes with difficulty, "Dam Kjell," he murmured before he went back to sleep. His breath stirred ripples on the pool of ale on the table.

"Flooded the market," Tor took another swig. "I said Kjell ruined the market, Olaf," Tor turned and prodded a man sitting at the table behind. The man turned around. Next to him was Bjarki Whitehair. He smiled at Godfrew and raised his cup in salute.

"Kjell? Oh, yes, he ruined the Icelandic market ... flooded it with cheap slaves. Wendles weren't they?" Olaf extracted himself from the bench with great difficulty and came over. Seeing Lief asleep, he pulled him off the bench and dropped him alongside Loki on the floor.

"Yes, Wendles."

"Wendles indeed. They are cheap for a good reason, them Wendles. Skinny, that's what they are." Tor passed his flask to Olaf for a swing. "They will be back, those Icelanders. Skinny Wendles are all right in the summer. You loose a few in the heat, but still cheaper than a normal slave, mind, you just wait till winter."

"Drop like flies, that's what they will do. You get what you pay for."

Tor rolled the recumbent Lief over with his foot inquisitively. "Then they will be back, but they won't get any quality slaves from me at anything under premium prices, I can assure you. Mind, I only sell quality. No skinny Wends."

"Skinny Wends," agreed Olaf. "Even their women are skinny."

"Skinny, yes skinny. No tits on them."

"No tits?" yet another Dane from the far bench turned and joined in. "Are you sure? No tits?"

"Just puffed up nipples," Olaf assured the newcomer.

"Nipples," agreed Tor. "Now if you want big tits, you need a decent Slav."

"Yes, but the trouble with Slavs," Olaf rested his feet on Lief's belly, "is that it's not just their tits that are big. They are big all over!"

Tor joined Olaf in his laughter until they both cried. "Now the biggest woman I ever saw was that Slav woman Rus had when we were in Kiev with the Swedes. Rus, hey, Rus!"

Tor leaned across and plucked at the belt of a short red-headed man on the other bench. "Rus."

"What?" Rus turned and tried to focus his bleary eyes. "Oh, Tor. What do you want, you old bear."

"That woman in Kiev. The big Slav. She was big, wasn't she?"

"Big? Oh, yes, she was big, all right," Rus snickered.

"So big," Tor held his arms out wide to illustrate the woman's size and almost knocked Olaf off the bench, "so big that when you mounted her that first night you fell in and it took a search party two days to find you."

"Don't lie!" Rus looked stern, and the others listening in went silent, waiting to see if there would be a fight. "It took them three days to find me and, boy, did I have a smile on my face when they did!" The bench erupted into laughter.

Godfrew accepted that he and Brynoth were no longer part of the conversation and went back to drinking his ale.

Brynoth took advantage of the Danes' preoccupation to help himself to a cup of their mead. He offered to refill Godfrew's cup, but Godfrew didn't like the sweet, sticky fluid. "This mead, Wulf. These Danes drink it like water." Brynoth sipped his cup. "I don't know where they get it all from. Do you know how much honey it takes to make just one flask of this stuff?"

Before Godfrew got a chance to answer, Stig Gullwing came and tapped Brynoth on the shoulder.

"Now."

As Brynoth and Godfrew followed Stig to the top table, they saw the straw and rushes being cleared from the floor at the far end of the hall. A large, blue cloak was being spread out and two young men, stripped to the waist, staggered onto it.

"Knuckle fist fighting. Very bloody." Brynoth shook his head "Can't understand them doing it, getting hurt for no reason."

Godfrew squinted and noticed bets being taken while the two youngsters were being held back from getting at each other. Bjarki caught his eye and waived. Godfrew waved back and then jogged to catch up with the others. As they came to the row of tall Frisians, Stig signalled them to wait while he went and spoke to Hereward.

After a few words, he returned. "Hereward will talk now." The Frisian's did not move to let Brynoth and Godfrew through. They had to squeeze through the gap left by the absent Stig. As soon as they passed inside the wall of men, Stig resumed his place.

Godfrew was disappointed in Hereward the Wake. The man's fame had him as being big, and he was, but he was stocky rather than muscular. Already there were signs of fat on his waistline and the golden hair looked as if it had been died with saffron to cover streaks of grey that even now showed at the roots. There was a man on either side of Hereward. One was the tall man who had been occasionally called in when Hereward had been speaking with the richly-dressed Dane. The other was quite short with brown hair that hung across his forehead in a fringe. His moustaches were cut short and he had the most piercing blue eyes that Godfrew had ever seen.

On the table, before them all, lay the sword, Brainbiter, naked in all her glory, red rubies glinting from her gold-gilded hilt and pommel. Hereward motioned them to sit. The short man sat with pursed lips, his hands held as if in prayer under his chin. His blue eyes looked at and through Godfrew. The tall man paid them no attention, seemingly more interested in the fist fight at the end of the hall. Hereward swilled the ale in his cup, ignoring everyone.

Eventually, he downed the drink and turned to Godfrew. "Well, my man, you bring word from Edric the Wild, I hear. Not such good news, either."

"It is old news now, my Lord." Godfrew was shocked to see the plumpness of the face and the puffed baggy eyes. He had expected more of a hero. "In the West Country, the sons of our late king arrived too early, attacked the wrong places and failed. The revolt in Mercia failed when Earl Edric's Welsh allies would not listen to his advice. Earl Morcar made the mistake of joining them and also came unstuck. All the land of those who supported them had been ravaged and much lies waste. You are right, my Lord. Not good news." Godfrew turned his head to find himself still under scrutiny from the man with blue eyes.

"So it would seem. Just as well things are going better at this end, what!"

"My Lord?" Godfrew broke away from the eyes and looked at Hereward again.

"York. We have it."

"We have it, my Lord?' Godfrew couldn't resist the temptation to see if blue eyes was still looking at him. He was.

"Hogni, stop it!" Hereward shouted at blue eyes.

"No harm meant, Hereward, my Lord."

"Nothing you ever do is harmless, you odious toe rag. Leave him alone and help Martin Lightfoot here keep track on that fight. I have a gold ring on the Goth with the red sash against Earl Osbjorn's man with the blue one. Don't fail me." He turned his attention back to Godfrew. "Now, York. Yes, we have it. That was the news I got this morning. The men of Northumbria, with help from our Danish friends, took it. Such tales I have heard of Waltheof felling men at the gate with his long axe as if he was chopping down saplings ... of the Normans burning down the Minster of ... of ... well all sorts. So, things are moving. You will be able to tell your master. All we have to do now is agree who will be king, once we have either killed the Bastard or sent him packing."

"Who will be king, my Lord?" enquired Godfrew.

"Yes. The Mercians are for Edgar the Aetheling. The men of the Northumbria and the Fens are for Swein of Denmark. Apart from that small problem, all is going very well."

Hereward refilled his ale cup and concentrated on watching the fight. Godfrew and Brynoth knew the interview was over and left.

Outside the long house, the air was chill. "Apart from that small problem, all is going very well. Dear God and all his saints, have mercy on us poor English." Godfrew shook his head and accompanied Brynoth back to the English camp.

* * *

They had prepared to leave the following day. Godfrew had taken two flat pieces of smooth wood and carved runes on them telling Earl Edric the news. One piece of wood he gave to Swein and Magnus, telling them how to conceal the wood in a horse saddle before sending them north. The other he

The Eastings

gave to Puta to keep safe, in case he himself did not make it back to Lydbury. But Godfrew's party never left the Isle of Ely.

The night they were due to leave, Godfrew and Clunn developed a high fever and the shakes. Despite all that Puta could do, their temperatures soared and they started hallucinating. Godfrew was again plagued by the nightmare of Elfgifu with his nine sons and the river Wandle's woe waters washing away his wife and all but three of the boys while he watched. As the image played in his mind, he called out and yelled, but those standing by him could make nothing of the babble that came from his mouth.

Clunn's mind was also on a woman, but this one was a whore. Every time he got near enough to grab her, she changed—the first time into an armed warrior, the next time into a dragon, then into a witch. Finally, he grabbed the whore and she turned into Earl Edric, who then called in his hearth troop and started to prepare Clunn for the type of interview only Edric the Wild could conduct.

Nearby, those tending to the sweating man's body wondered why he stopped yelling in anger and started to whimper in terror instead.

Puta sent for Brynoth. When the Essex man heard what was happening, he sent his wife to the wolf pack's hut. Once inside, she clucked in dismay and sent for some other women folk to join her.

While she waited, she lit smoking tapers soaked in sharp-smelling herbs and mutton fat. Whilst the men coughed, she stripped Godfrew and Clunn naked. Godfrew muttered Elfgifu's name, his first coherent words since the fever had struck. When it was his turn, Clunn screamed and fought. Tosti found this hysterical, as he had never seen Clunn fight to prevent a woman stripping him before. After the other women arrived, they helped Brynoth's wife, Edith, wash the sick men down.

Clunn struggled so much they had to tie him to the frame of his cot. Though the water used was cold, both men cried out as if it were boiling hot.

"You! What's your name?" Edith called to Puta.

"Puta," he lisped.

"Right then, boy. Keep they warm." She pointed at the tossing men. "Don't let them throw off them covers."

"But," protested Puta, "they are hot."

"Don't argue with me, boy! Just do as I say. Keep they covered." Edith nodded thanks to the other women as they left to go back to their own huts. Puta went to touch the red-faced Clunn, but Edith caught his arm. "They may be hot, but keep they warm. Every hour now," she pulled Puta to face her, "every hour, mind, wash they down with cold water, and make sure them get plenty to drink. They won't want to drink, so force it down them if you must."

"Where do we draw the water?" Puta started to cast his eyes around for an empty flask.

"To wash?" again Edith pulled Puta around to face her.

"And drink," Puta tried to pull away.

"Don't ever do that, boy." The woman was far too strong, even for a big boy like Puta. When she pulled him back to face her he almost fell over. "Wash them in the water in that there bucket. Never, ever, let them drink the water. I will send over some small ale with one of my kids."

"Clunn being forced to drink ale. That's a new one!" Tosti started to give a braying laugh, but Brynoth's wife slapped him on the face.

"Don't you laugh, boy. Them there have the fen ague. Look after them or they will die." She grabbed Tosti's wrist and examined it. "You've got the red bites too. It will be your turn next."

While Tosti studied the marks on his wrist, the woman left, leaving behind dust motes from the decaying floor rushes to join the odorous smoke from the tapers in seeking to escape through the smoke hole in the roof.

"I don't know about letting a woman slap me in the face." Leofwine, already half-drunk, flopped his arm over Tosti's shoulder.

"That?" Tosti felt his glowing cheek. "That's nothing! My mother does it to me all the time. I'm more worried about the fact that if I get this ague I won't be able to stop her from stripping me stark naked and running her coarse red hands all over my body."

* * *

The Eastings

By the time Godfrew and Clunn had recovered, the others had gone down with the ague. Godfrew wondered how the departed Swein and Magnus were faring.

Weeks became months as Clunn and Tosti suffered another bout of fever. Then all in the camp went down with the bloody flux and the wolf pack knew that it would be some time before they would escape the damp fens.

As early autumn became winter, the landscape changed: meadow became water meads, water meads became bogs, bogs became meres, and meres became rivers. Meanwhile, the rivers changed their pace from sluggish to swift. Very early on, the few causeways into the fens became impassable, leaving the water as the only means of transport. With the increase in water level, the Vikings sailed their longships up to the Isle and many of the crews joined their rowdy brethren at the hill camp. Then, just as the flux struck, most of the Vikings left.

Soon word came back that Earl Osbjorn of Denmark and his men had not sailed to escape the sickness, but had accepted a bribe from King William the Norman and had sailed away with the silver of a huge Danegeld safe in the holds of their ships.

The coming of the snow and the freezing of the water on the meres was a relief. Those who were fit enough used the opportunity to walk on the ice and seek out those water fowl foolish enough to have remained when their wiser comrades had taken wing for warmer climes. The bird's flesh was a welcome change from the dried eels, fish, and heavily-salted horse and cattle flesh they had been eating.

On one occasion, Godfrew and the others had joined Brynoth and his men. They travelled over the ice pulling a sledge to fill with dried willow and alder branches that had been stored as cattle fodder in a barn on a nearby island.

The wolves had been amused when, for the first time in months, they saw Toki. The muzzle and a bout of the flux had halved the man's bulk.

The weight of winter pressed even heavier when refugees from Northumbria started to arrive. William had retaken York and punished the earldom for rising against him by harrowing the land.

From the river Humber to the river Tees, the Frenchmen had killed all the men and boys they could get at. All the stock they could drive off, they did. The rest, they killed. All buildings and crops they found were burnt. All who escaped the sword and the fire were left to starve or die from the cold. Many of those reaching Ely's camp of refuge were so weak that they died soon after getting there.

As the days grew darker, so did men's spirits. Even the chants of the monks at the abbey had started to sound like funeral dirges. The extra folk meant shorter rations. Soon all came to look as skinny as poor Toki. When the days started to lengthen, the migrating birds slowly returned and the eels began their trek back from the sea.

The advent of spring meant the chance of fresh food, but spring was more welcome than usual that year for it brought good news: Earl Osbjorn the Dane and his fleet may have been bought off, but his brother King Swein had raised another, much larger force, and was on his way to join forces with Hereward in the fens and claim the English kingdom that was his by right.

King William the Norman must also have heard that Swein of Denmark was on his way to Ely, for soon an army of Normans appeared in the fenland set to destroy Hereward's wasp nest before Swein could join him.

* * *

The wolves watched the lumbering ox wagons heading along the sodden causeway toward the island and its scraggly trees. The drivers had to get off and lead the animals through the boggiest part of the path. Godfrew pulled the hood of his cloak over his face, squinting through the eye holes of the wolf's mask. "How many are there, Tosti?"

"Four wagons, Master Wulf. Each has a driver and a guard. Hey, look, that front one has got stuck again!" The other members of the pack came and stood at his side, holding their hands to their eyes to see better. "Look at them! Even the guards are helping them try and get it moving."

"Normans working? I don't believe it." Clunn ran his thumb over the edge of his bill hook. Seeing a thin trace of blood, he

The Eastings

seemed satisfied. "Can't be Normans! Must be hired Flems or Burgandians."

"Flems, Burgandians or even Black-a-Moors. If they work for the Normans, they are our enemies." Leofwine took a sly swig from the flask of ale that was always present.

Godfrew saw the ale flask and took it away. "Drink later. All of you get to work cutting brush for our beloved Norman masters to make the new causeway with."

"Why a new causeway, Master Wulf?" enquired Puta. He cleared some twigs from the grass, then sat down and picked up a bill hook to sharpen with his whetstone.

"How else? The Bastard has little choice. The only other way is by water. Would you like to try and force the passage? He could try and block us by sea, but the Danes are already off the coast and any mercenaries he hired would be no match for them when it came to water craft. No, the only way to take the Isle is by land—or what passes for land in this place." Godfrew stared down at his feet. He moved a foot on the soft ground and water came to the surface. "Now look busy, Puta. And Leofwine."

"Master Wulf?"

"Put the flask down and get on with it!"

"Master Wulf." Leofwine took a last sip and carefully placed the flask by the pile of brushwood he had cut.

The Frenchmen finally got the ox wagon moving again. With much swearing and shouting, they drove it and the others off the causeway and onto the island. As they made their way up the slight slope toward the woodcutters, the wheels of the wagons cut the green turf and exposed the rich black soil beneath.

Reaching the first pile of cuttings, the wagons stopped. The guard on the first one leapt down and walked forward. "Better come and give us a hand to load this lot, Jean," he called back to the next wagon in the French of Picardy. "You can help too, friend," he said to Clunn who stood in front of him. His Flemish was perfect, but spoken with a strong French accent. The man grabbed the first bundle of brushwood and found, to his surprise, that there was a detached head beneath. One of its eyes was closed in a lurid wink. He looked questioningly at Clunn.

Woden's Wolf

Clunn moved back as the wolf closed in. The only reply the Frenchman got was a swish as Neckbiter came to take off his head. The Norman party stood stunned. By the time what had happened sunk in, the wolf pack was on them. Only one escaped and Godfrew pursued him toward the causeway.

As the man passed through the first clump of reeds, an axe whirled through the air and split him in twain, top from bottom. The man fell in two twitching heaps, joined only by steaming entrails.

"Almost let that one get away, Woden's Wulf." The owner of the axe stepped clear of the reeds and was followed by others, including Hogni blue eyes.

"But he was not as fast as a heron?" Godfrew asked.

"Ah, so you have heard of me name sake." The tall, raw-boned axeman bent to wipe the weapon's blade clean on the dead man's torn cloak. Never once did his eye's leave Godfrew's face.

"Wulfric Heron. Your deeds are famous." Godfrew couldn't help but let his eyes wander and compare the plain blade of the Heron's axe with Neckbiter's engraved one.

"And yours are infamous, son of Woden. Or maybe he is Woden himself, Hogni?" Wulfric asked his companion.

Godfrew went red, muttered, and went back to his men. Hogni stared after him and chanted a war prayer from the old times.

The wolves removed the wheels of the wagons and rolled them into the fen. The shafts were smashed and thrown into the wagons. After heaving the dead bodies onboard, the wagons were filled with the brushwood intended for the causeway, then they were fired.

Puta and Clunn walked the docile oxen across the small island toward the inlet where the punts were hidden. As the creatures walked, their heads moved from side to side in rhythm with their steps with their tails swinging the opposite way.

The spring day was mild and the midges were out in force. To keep the insects at bay, Clunn and Puta found themselves swinging their heads in the same manner as their charges. A midge got into Clunn's mouth and he came to a coughing halt.

The Eastings

After much hawking, Clunn managed to clear the nuisance from his throat. The anxious Puta watched and clucked sympathetically. Clunn caught him watching. "Puta, my pretty, how about you serving some nice roast ox heart to your pet mouse tonight?" he said, his eyes watering from the coughing.

Puta gave a gentle, shy smile. "For you I will find some bread and just the right herbs to go with it, for I know how much you love stuffing."

It did not take the Normans long to stop the raids on their work parties by Hereward's men. Soon the armed guards were increased to the point where only a full out attack could succeed in tackling them. Hereward was not prepared to risk his men in a set battle, so he waited, mounting only the odd nuisance raid to remind the invaders that they were in his territory.

The causeway grew. As damp spring turned to dry summer, the land firmed enough for the Normans' work to speed ahead. Their sappers now worked in clear view of the Isle of Ely, cutting away the dry rushes, preparing the ground for an army to be deployed.

It was a fine sunny morning when Martin Lightfoot was seen talking with Hereward outside his hut. Hereward sent the word to all the English and the few Danes still in their hill camp that the Normans were gathered for the final attack and to be ready to meet them.

Godfrew hovered near Hereward and his chief men as they stood talking. None seemed worried. In fact, Hereward spent most of his time laughing and slapping his men on the back. Hogni blue eyes came over to Godfrew and stared at him.

"Woden Wulf! Get they men of yours and join the shield wall by the crossing the other side of the Isle. Hereward commands it." The short man flicked the long fringe of hair out of his eyes without blinking or breaking contact with Godfrew's eye.

"We have no shields, Hogni. You know that. Indeed, we have no armour to fight in the front line." Godfrew looked across to where his men lounged about outside the crumbling wall of their thatched hut. When he looked back, Hogni was still staring at him.

Woden's Wolf

"You need no shields, blessed Woden. There are plenty of warriors with shields. You and your men will stand in the gaps." The wind blew and moved Hogni's fringe again, allowing the hair to lay in his left eye, but again he did not blink. "Some of your men are archers, are they not?"

"Yes, but they have not brought their bows with them."

"I know that, old man, young man. They have been practising with Brynoth's men, and teasing them that their bows are too short. They have taught them to make longer bows, have they not?" The wind now blew the hair out of Hogni's blue eye.

"Yes." Godfrew shuffled his feet, uncomfortable in the presence of Hereward's man.

"Then let them use the bows they have made for Brynoth's men. Hereward will tell them to give the bows up. They will do what Hereward says, feeder of ravens." Only Hogni's lips moved. The rest of his body remained as a statue.

"Then the archers will be there. But again I say that the others should not be in the shield wall. We have no mail coats. When it comes to the fight, we will be cut down easily." Godfrew blew gently on Hogni's face, trying to get a reaction. Hogni remained as a statue, the only change was to his eyes as his pupils became needle points.

"There will be no fight, rider of Sleipnir. I sacrificed nine Frenchmen to you this morning. They hang now in the alders facing the southeast crossing whence their comrades must come. You will honour the gift: there will be no fight."

At last Hogni turned and walked away.

Godfrew looked at his hands. They were shaking and his palms were sweating.

Godfrew called his men over and together they wended their way toward the southeast crossing, away from the camp and over the hill that dominated the isle.

The wolf pack breasted the low hill and walked down toward the broken crossing facing Stutney Isle. In front of them were armed warriors laughing and jostling each other for a place in the shield wall. Between them and the narrow river was a breast-high wall of woven wickerwork. Godfrew and his men stood in a huddle behind some warriors in the middle of the line. They were still unsure what to do when a shrill trumpet sounded across the river. Everyone strained

The Eastings

their eyes to see the glimmer of light shining off the helmets and mail coats of their Norman attackers.

The rebuilt causeway ended a hundred paces from the river, just out of arrow shot for the short bows used by the fenmen. The ground at the end of the causeway, running parallel to the river, had been made hard by the sappers to a width of four men, but from there to the river bank, the ground was soft and swampy, unlike the firm land on the Isle of Ely side of the river.

As the first Normans came off the causeway and started to deploy along the hard ground, Hereward appeared on the crest of the hill and called in a loud voice that could be heard by all. "Form the shield wall. Spear and swords men to the front. Axemen ... two paces back. Archers ... in between the axemen. Slingers and others ... to the rear ready to fill any gaps. Archers ... shoot only on command. Hogni will give each archer a blessed talisman to wear. When I call red, those with a red talisman will shoot. When I call blue, the same ... then, also for yellow. Any archer who disobeys will be used as target practice for the others next Sunday afternoon!" Hereward laughed and the archers all joined him. "So be brave, men of Ely! Hold firm, men of Ely! Be victorious, men of Ely!" Hereward lifted high his sword, Brainbiter, and waved it.

The men cheered three times.

"To the wall!" Again the men cheered and then took their posts.

Godfrew looked along the line and saw how pitiful it was. Of all the men gathered there, only half had mail coats. Most of them were only ring mail. There were several well-armed Danes, but they were the older men who had been left behind to keep the camp ready should their King Swein have need of it. Of the English, fully half of them were new arrivals from Northumbria. They were half-starved, many still showing signs of injuries received in the harrowing of their beloved north.

The man to Godfrew's left saw him looking and read his thoughts.

"Aye, that's right, lad, a poor bunch, a forlorn hope. But then, do you want to live forever?" A livid scar ran from the crown of the Tyke's head to his chin. Crude stitch marks broke the red line in a random pattern.

"It's a good enough day to die! Why not today?" replied Tosti as he stuck a collection of arrows into the ground by his side. Tosti saw Godfrew turn suddenly to face him. "They say Saint Guthlac himself appeared last night to Hogni, walking across the fens from where his bones rest at Croyland," the youth hastily explained, going red at his leader's obvious annoyance. "Apparently, he promised us victory. If Saint Guthlac appeared, why should we worry?"

"I have seen more of Hogni than you have. I have spoken to Hogni more than you have." Godfrew's voice had a resigned hardness to it. "If anyone ever appears to Hogni it will be Satan claiming his own!"

"In that case, maybe we will die." Tosti went on with his task, somewhat quieted.

"Did someone say St. Olaf had appeared?" asked a rather corpulent Dane on Godfrew's other side, his breath tainted by last night's mead.

"Saint Guthlac of Croyland," said Godfrew, trying to keep downwind of the man's breath.

"Saint who?" asked the Dane, cupping his ear.

"GUTHLAC," shouted Godfrew.

"Guthlac, did you say?" the Dane looked to Godfrew and waited for his confirming nod. "Guthlac? Never heard of him. One of yours?" Again he waited for the nod. "I trust he is good. No point in him appearing if he isn't any good. Waste of good prayers and candles, saints are, if they are no good." Another trumpet call sounded and the Dane broke away to look to his front.

There, coming along their causeway and headed by sappers carrying thick wicker mats wide enough to protect five men, came the Normans' foot soldiers, ten abreast in a long silver snake that stretched way back. They halted on the hard ground facing the river whilst more sappers moved through the ranks bringing more of the large mats of woven wattle with them and dumping them in front of the host.

The English fell silent and took the opportunity to settle themselves, each man making sure that he could wield his weapon without interfering with those next to him.

The Eastings

Although the Normans were out of reach of the fenmen's short bows, they were easy targets for the longbows used by the wolf pack.

Both Clunn and Tosti tried to interest Brynoth into letting them shoot, but after glancing at the imposing figure of Lord Hereward, all they got was a shake of his head.

Leofwine sat down and took a swig of his ale as soon as the archer's captain had passed.

Brynoth moved along the shield wall, continuing to stop and talk quietly with each of the archers, advising them on wind strength and direction, indicating suitable targets.

He paused by Godfrew. "Tosti told me you were worried about how few men we had." Brynoth showed none of his usual humour, his voice being very gentle and thoughtful.

"It is not the strongest army I've seen in the field." Godfrew snuck another look along the ranks.

"No, but only about half our strength is here. The others must be elsewhere."

"Elsewhere?" Godfrew closed his blind eye and gave a puzzled look.

"Lord Hereward was about very early. Long before he roused the camp." Brynoth gave a sad smile. "It's me bladder, if I get up once in the night to piddle, I get up four or five times. It's getting worse as I get older," he shrugged. "Age, comes to us all." He ran a hand over his pocked face and played with the ends of his moustache before continuing: "Him and Wulfric Heron were organising the local men into groups and sending them off. Even before that, just before daylight, I saw his Frisians getting into punts and his top man, Winter, instructing the puntsman before each craft set off into the reeds. Something is up, Master Wulf."

"What, Master Brynoth?" Godfrew's single-eyed stare grew harder.

"You tell me! I'm only the captain of the archers. No one tells me nothing. All I do know is that Lord Hereward is very shrewd and he is very devious. He has something planned. Something neither I, you, or the Normans are expecting."

Suddenly a wild-eyed woman pushed her way through the Normans who waited behind the sweating sappers labouring to pile up their mats. The woman started dancing and singing French words in a strange high-pitched voice:

Woden's Wolf

"The English are food to the fishes.
The Danes all be meat to the eels
Oh such tasty fine dishes
Sweet and crusty as their blood congeals."

"What's she saying? That woman, what's she saying?" asked the foul-breathed Dane.

"No idea." Godfrew shook his head, as much to get away from the Dane's smell as to show that he did not know the answer.

"What did that Dane say?" asked Brynoth as he came alongside Tosti.

"Something about wanting to know what that women said," Tosti informed him, stealing a glance at the seemingly possessed woman who still sang and pranced in the no-man's land between the English and Norman warriors.

"What did you want to know, old man?" The Dane had not heard Brynoth call to him, so Brynoth pulled at the man's sleeve.

"What? What do you want?" asked the startled Dane.

Brynoth gave the Dane a gummy smile and replied in corrupt Norse. "You want to know something about what the old hag is saying. I picked up some French when I lived in London." Brynoth had stood directly in front of the man and moved his mobile lips slowly and deliberately.

"The old hag? Oh, the old woman. Yes, what is she saying?" the Dane seemed genuinely happy to be talking to someone he could understand.

"Something about feeding the English and Danes to the fishes. I couldn't catch it all. Her French is not that spoken by the Normans." Brynoth watched the Dane's eyes to see if he had understood.

"Not Norman? But she is being nasty to us, I think. Yes?" The Dane kept his mouth slightly open. A small steam of saliva ran down the deep creases either side of his mouth and into his silver beard.

"Very nasty. Shall we get the boys to give her a reply?"

"Oh, I think so, yes. Just make sure it isn't the chant used by your lot at Maldon. I know we won, but it might stir up

The Eastings

the old feelings, eh!" The Dane gave a foul laugh, Brynoth caught his breath full in the face and started coughing.

Brynoth wiped his eyes, "I'll get our Hogni to start something, something we all know." Before he left, Brynoth stopped by Tosti's side and spoke quietly to him, making sure that no one else heard.

Still the Frenchwoman skipped and capered, all the time singing out her curse.

Suddenly, from the side, Hogni ran and jumped the wicker fence, turning a somersault in the air before landing on his feet and facing the English shield wall. He wore no mail, but held in his hand a long sword and a battered linden-wood shield with a raven device on it. Once he was certain he had the men's attention he started to bang the sword's pommel against the shield in rhythm. Those with shields followed his lead. When the beat steadied, he started to call out the war chant of King Harold's house carls. All in the line joined him:

> "We are warriors
> Holders of sharp sword
> We are ring men
> Wielders of bright axe
> Give us ground
> We take your heads
> Give us battle
> We feed the wolves
> We are dragon men
> Reevers of your land
> We are ship men
> Carriers of plunder
> Give us treasure
> We take all gold
> Give us women
> We steal our own
> We are avengers
> Slayer of foemen
> We are taking you
> Out, Out, Out Out, Out."

The beating of shields and the battle cry of "OUT, OUT, OUT ..." reached a crescendo when Hogni stopped pummeling his shield and held his sword above his head. The men stopped. He then cried out in a voice that sent shivers down Godfrew's spine: "For our foes are all going to DIEEE."

It was then that Tosti shot his arrow on a high arc. The sun caught the arrow head as it reached the top, before plummeting down and transfixing the mad Frenchwoman to the soggy ground.

It was some minutes before what had happened sank in, then the Normans gave a roar and surged out along the front of the causeway. Two footmen carried one of the large, woven-wicker mats between them. In pairs, they advanced toward the river bank until the ground became very soft, then they threw the wicker work onto the soggy ground. They let the pair following do the same, thus they progressed toward the river bank. Hereward let them gain thirty paces before he acted: "Red archers! Fire at will." The archers bearing a red talisman started a desultory fire at the advancing foe. If anyone used his arrows at too fast a rate Brynoth went and spoke to him and told him to slow down.

Some Normans fell, but most carried on with the job of getting across the marshy ground, arrows sticking from their mail coats like quills on a hedgehog.

"Why doesn't he let all the archers fire, Brynoth?" Godfrew asked as the Essex man went past on his way to slow down another over-keen archer. "At least let them that are firing do so quickly."

"Don't ask me, Master Wulf, but Lord Hereward will have his reasons. It looks to me as if he wants to draw them on. Look ..." Brynoth glanced at Hereward and saw his leader waving him impatiently on to get to the fast-firing archer, "... I must go. No doubt I will catch up with you later, God and his saints willing, of course." Brynoth scuttled off.

The Normans had now made forty paces toward the river and Tosti could see some sappers coming off the causeway with prefabricated bridges that they started to assemble before moving them forward.

"Master Wulf, they have brought bridges to get across the river."

"Where?" asked Godfrew, the Norman sappers being just part of a blur to him.

The Eastings

"There, near the causeway. And they are bringing yet more pieces of wickerwork to throw on the marsh." Tosti pointed in the general direction with his bow. "Oh, why won't he let us shoot!"

"Blue archers, fire!" commanded Hereward. The increased density of fire slowed the Normans somewhat, but still they advanced. Godfrew turned and watched Hereward. The Wake was talking to his confidants and pointing to the rear of the Normans. Martin Lightfoot, who seemed to be a man of clear sight, was giving a running commentary of what was happening at the back of the Norman advance, off in the reeds along the causeway. None of the commanders seemed interested in those Normans trying to cross to the river bank. It was Brynoth who went over to inform Hereward that there was now only twenty paces between the leading Normans and the bank and that the crossbow men had started scuttling to the front. Hereward then gave the command for the yellow archers to join in. Even then, the order was given in an off-handed manner, his attention still being the Norman rear. Just as the first man reached the bank and the sappers rushed forward to bridge the river, Martin Lightfoot said something to Hereward, who responded by giving a whoop of joy and slapped Martin happily on the back. Hereward then yelled for Brynoth to come to him.

After getting hurried instructions, Brynoth ran to the shield wall, grabbed Tosti and took him back to Hereward.

Godfrew heard a cheer rise up from the Normans and turned back to see the first part of a bridge going across the river.

It was then that a flaming arrow from Tosti's bow streaked across the English lines and fell into the reeds to the Normans' west flank. Instantly, flames engulfed the reed beds, enclosing the Normans on the west and north sides.

The English fell silent, watching the burning reeds slowly getting nearer the Normans. As they realised what was happening, the Normans still on the causeway started to push forward, trampling those before them. A temporary change in wind direction brought the faint sound of a clash of arms to the Norman rear.

"Must be Stig Gullwing and his Frisians putting the stop in the bottle." Brynoth stood behind Godfrew directing a work group of women and non-combatant men who were delivering baskets of arrows to the archers.

"Why has the fire only been set on two sides, Brynoth?" Godfrew yelled behind him. He was unwilling to break away from watching the Normans panic as they spilled off the causeway and crashed into those on the hard ground at its mouth, thereby forcing everyone forward until the men at the front were forced off of their wicker mats and into the soft-sucking marsh.

"No point firing those to the south. That's Wicken Fen. No matter how dry the summer, that place is always treacherous. Often the ground looks firm, but put a foot on it and you find yourself under water. If they want to ..." Brynoth broke away and grabbed the now skinny Toki, "You get moving, these are to be taken to members of Wulf's pack, special yard long arrows for their long bows." Toki scuttled off, dragging his basket. "And tell fat Puta to stop mooning around Clunn and get back for another load." Brynoth yelled after him. "Where was I? Ah, yes. If the Normans want to try their luck in Wicken Fen, then good luck to them. Even the locals keep away from it."

"Archers," Hereward called at the top of his voice, "fire as you will, but make sure you are aiming at a target. Fire the feathers of the grey goose, my bringer's of death!" The men around Hereward burst out laughing. At first Hereward did not join them, but as the volume of fire increased and fell into the now packed ranks of Normans scrabbling over each other to get away from the burning reeds, he laughed too.

Godfrew felt something cold touch his leg and looked down to find Shock smelling his leg. Godfrew bent down and fondled the hound, whispering a gentle rebuke in his ear. "How did you escape from the hut, you little rogue. You were left there to keep you from harm. If you are going to stay here, behave yourself!" Shock licked Godfrew's face in reply. The deaf Dane watched and wiped the edges of his mouth with the back of his hand.

"Some are across!" exclaimed Tosti as he changed his aim to pick off the leading Norman. Shock caught the excitement and barked. As he barked, he hopped forward toward the Norman line. Stiff-legged and ears erect, he barked again and gave another hop.

The Eastings

"That hound, it is calling your name!" an aging Dane shouted across to the deaf one. He did not hear what had been said, so Brynoth went and nudged him and pointed to the other Dane.

"What?"

"I said," explained the other in a loud exaggerated voice, "that hound is calling your name, Hroff."

Hroff bent down near Shock, who obliged with a bark and a hop. "Yes, he is calling me." Hroff looked up at Godfrew, who despite the warmth was still wearing his wolf cloak. He then turned to the other Dane: "Woden spoke to his hound, and now it calls my name and points me to the foe. I have no choice. My doom is cast! I must go, so who will join me?" Hroff left his place and walked along the back of the shield wall behind the archers. "I am called by Woden to join him this day in his mead hall of Valhalla. Who is with me?" Soon Hroff found himself joined by a group of equally ancient Danes, all with silver beards and stiff joints. He raised his sword above his head and cried out in a deep voice: "To Valhalla!"

"To Valhalla!" echoed the other Danes as they elbowed through the shield wall, pushed the wicker breastwork over and formed up.

"St. Olaf!" cried Hroff and lumbered forward toward the Normans who had made it across the river.

Shock ran alongside them, much to their obvious delight. Despite their age, the Danes made short work of the mud-caked Normans, exhausted by their efforts to extract themselves from the swamp and in crossing the river. Hroff slew five of them before he too went down, hit by a stray English arrow.

The killing went on as the Normans trampled each other down into the mire, were laid low by arrows, or fled into the fastness of Wicken Fen to sink, or drown in its black waters. As the ring of fire closed in on them, so their desperate attempts to escape increased, but death was inescapable. Only the choice of how to die was left to them. As the day waned, so did the supply of arrows. Those left were used only when it looked as if a Norman was going to extract himself and escape. By late afternoon the shield wall was no more. The men sat and ate as they watched the final death throes of the enemy army.

The fire had swept across the fens as far as the eye could see and the blue sky was obscured by a dense haze of smoke. The men who had been responsible for the torching started to arrive back, walking the marshes with their wide, wicker swamp shoes, leaping the river with their long poles.

By night there was only the glow from the embers of the burnt reeds, the smell of burnt flesh, and the occasional cry from a drowning Norman to remind the English of what had happened.

With the moon starting to rise, the Frisians came up the river in their punts and disembarked to join the others. Hereward, thoughtful as ever, supplied ale and mead in plenty. Soon the men forgot everything else as they celebrated their victory.

* * *

Edgar of Weobley sat by the hearth. He was cracking cob nuts with his teeth. As he shelled the kernel of one, he looked over at Godfrew. "We all thought you were dead, Master Wulf."

Godfrew picked up a nut and put it on the hearth stone before tapping it with a large pebble. Shock sat at his elbow, salivating. "Not yet, though when I caught that fen ague, I wished I was. Tell me: my wife, what did she have?" He shared the nut with Shock who swallowed his share without tasting it.

"Another boy: Njarl. Both are well. Though ..." Edgar looked across to his own wife who sat in the corner of the hut breast feeding her first-born son. Her three young step daughters were hovering around trying to help. Edgar's wife was as small and delicate as her husband, but as dark as he was fair. Her face was covered in freckles. She shook her head from side to side.

"Though what?" asked Godfrew, reaching for another nut.

"Nothing. He is a fine child, your new son. Strong and healthy and very long. He will be taller than you when he is grown!"

The Eastings

"Another long shanks." The nut shell cracked and Godfrew broke it open.

"You hesitated! My son has not got an elf- smitten eye like me, has he?"

"No." Edgar looked again at his wife for reassurance before proceeding. "Your wife had a hard time giving him birth, but she is fine now. That was all. It was not helped by the fact that she thought you were dead. Young Swein and Magnus arrived back, but they had no news of you and you sent no word. The youngsters said that they thought you were going to come back through the north country. When we heard what the Norman king did to that land after he retook York, we were certain you were dead."

"I never intended to stay." Another nut cracked, but the shell broke badly and pulped the kernel. Godfrew threw it away in disgust and picked up another. Shock salvaged the damaged fruit. "One thing and another. Now, I am staying in the hope of some plunder. Hereward keeps promising those scavenging Danes on the hill that he will find them some. If he doesn't, King Swein may have a mutiny on his hand!"

"Plunder, Master Wulf? That's not like you. I know you take it if it comes your way, but I've never known you to seek it out." One of Edgar's daughters came and sat on her father's lap. She played with his moustache, twisting the ends and making them stand out.

"Never had to, until now. My aunt's husband is the problem. I brought him here and he is now enslaved." Godfrew grabbed Shock, turned him on his back, jammed him between his legs and started examining the hound for fleas. "He owed money, unfortunately, and came face to face with his creditor. It's only twenty silver pennies, mind. When we first got here I could have bought his freedom. I had ten with me. All I needed was my aunt to send up the ten I had left behind with her, but she never sent the money. Now I only have three left. I don't suppose you have any cash you can lend me till we get back?" Godfrew held a captured flea between the nails of his thumb and middle finger and cracked it.

"Master Wulf, you forget my position. Seven silver pennies," he turned to his wife, "we would like seven pennies, wouldn't we, my love!" He turned back. "Sorry! Earl Edric gave me four when I left, but that was to get us here and back. We only have one and a half left as it is."

"And Earl Edric forbade you to go scavenging for more, didn't he, Edgar!" interjected his wife as she pulled the now sleeping baby away from her breast with an audible plop. She wiped the child's mouth with a rag.

"Yes, no opportunity for scavenging now that he has come to an agreement with the Norman King and made his peace." Edgar sounded disappointed.

"So, that's why you are here. Not seeking me out after all. You have come as Earl Edric's messenger to Hereward the Wake." Godfrew caught another flea and executed it.

"Peace, yes, and who knows what that will bring."

"There is some sort of peace around here as well. Earl Waltheof has settled his differences with the Normans too." Godfrew let his hound go and Shock ran off, only to return again as soon as Godfrew picked up another cob nut to crack. "That's making life very difficult for us." The shell cracked and a piece of the kernel flew up in the air. Shock leapt and caught it. "Now that Earl Edric has made his peace, I should return to Lydbury with the men, but I must buy my aunt's husband's freedom first."

Godfrew lay the nut's kernel to one side and picked up another. He took the flat pebble and hefted it in his hand before striking the nut lying on the hearth stone. The shell cracked and the sound disturbed the baby, who gave a little cry before settling down again. "I brought Toki here. I must take him back again. I'm afraid plunder is the only thing that will let me do that now, peace or no peace."

* * *

"Why do we always get the good jobs, Master Wulf?" asked Leofwine, his bloodshot eyes trying to make out his leader's shape in the pitch black.

"Shut up moaning, Leofwine," muttered Edgar, as he swatted an insect against his neck.

"Yes, shut up moaning, Leofwine," Tosti called from the punt he was sitting in. "We will still get a share of the plunder, even if we are just looking after the punts."

The Eastings

"I must admit," added Clunn from the next punt, "I wouldn't have minded taking part in the attack on Peterborough. A bit of excitement to brighten my weary life." He dangled his hand in the brackish water of the river. "A bit of rape and pillage would have gone down well."

"Especially the rape," lisped Puta, sitting at Clunn's feet. "You think too much about women." He glanced up at the dark figure above him, "Women are smelly creatures. I don't know what you see in them."

Clunn bent down and whispered in Puta's plump ear, "I don't."

"Oh, you don't?" Puta's voice had an air of excitement to it.

"No." Clunn put a grubby hand to the youth's cheek and stroked it, "Because I always close my eyes when I do it with them, my petal."

Puta struck Clunn's hand away, "You are a rotten tease, Clunn," he cried.

"Will you all keep quiet!" hissed Godfrew. He pulled the wolf's mask lower over his face to help him see into the darkness by using the edge of the eye hole to sharpen his vision.

"Will you all keep quiet," mimicked Clunn in a voice so quiet that only Puta, who was resting his head on Clunn's lap, could hear. Puta giggled.

"Look!" Godfrew turned around. For a second, the moon came from behind a cloud and its beam caught the white of the cataract on his blind eye. "I told you all to be quiet!"

"What was that, Master Wulf?" asked Tosti.

"I said ..."

"I know what you said. I meant what was that? That sound? Could it be the attack has started?" Tosti got unsteadily to his feet, feeling the flat-bottomed punt move under him.

He cupped his hands to his ears: "Yes, I am sure I can hear shouting and swords clashing."

"Rubbish!" Leofwine got up and sat down again quickly. The punt moved under him and water started to slop over the sides. "Are you certain, Tosti? Master Wulf, can you hear anything?"

Godfrew strained his ears, but picked up nothing. "Sorry, no. After that whack in Hereford, my ears are often full of hissing. Tonight, that is all I can hear."

Woden's Wolf

"Were you at Hereford then, Master Wulf?" Leofwine made another attempt at standing. This time he made it. He stood with his arms stretched wide to keep his balance, like the mountebanks that walked on the high ropes at the fair.

"Shut up, Leofwine!" chipped in Edgar in a weary voice.

"Yes, shut up, Leofwine," mimicked Clunn. Puta started to giggle. Clunn bent over and tried to cluck him quiet, but it caused Puta to giggle even more.

"And shut up Clunn!" Edgar sounded angry this time. The tone caused Puta to cease giggling and Clunn to mutter quietly to himself. "Yes." Edgar listened again "Yes. You are right, Tosti. The attack has started."

"Oh, yes, very exciting for us brave punt warriors!" Clunn pushed Puta's head off of his lap and sulked.

Puta eased himself onto the narrow seat next to Clunn. Suddenly he stood up and almost caused Clunn to fall over the side as the punt rocked: "What was that?"

"What was what, you ginger-headed weaponed wifstra? [1] I'll give you 'What was that!' I almost got a soaking!" Clunn looked about for the punt's pole to whack his young companion with.

"No, look!" Puta grabbed hold of Clunn's shoulder and shook it. "Look!" When Clunn turned and looked, he saw the rest of the wolf pack watching a flaming arrow arcing into the air.

"Oh-oh!" Clunn began searching even more frantically for the punt pole. "There go the reeds again. Where is that damned pole? We may have to get out of here in a hurry."

"Don't be stupid, you little rat," snapped Edgar, "You don't know how to pole a punt. Anyway, the arrow is going to hit the town. It's the signal for the Danes to start the attack proper from the northern side."

"All right, smart arse. How did they get the other side of Peterborough ."

Edgar tapped the side of his nose. "They came up the river Welland from the Wash, and then along the old Roman canal. The Goths were to be left to hold the island of Spalding,

---

[19] Weaponed wifstra: literally *armed wife* . The term could be used for an effeminate man, a transvestite, or even an hermaphrodite. Then, as now, men often referred to their sexual organ as their weapon.

not that there would be much left to hold after those savages had been through it."

"Ooh! Privy to Hereward the Wake and King Swein's council, are we? I'm sure they tell every punt guard they see what they intend to do." Clunn at last found the pole and almost knocked Puta over with it as he put it over the side into the water.

"I heard that captain of Hereward's, Winter, telling one of their jarls."

"Oh, yes," spat out Clunn. "He got where he is because he often makes a habit of talking about the war plans in front of strangers. And you are pretty strange, Edgar, if I say so myself."

"Look, Rat." Edgar got out of his punt and started to walk along the river bank toward Clunn's punt.

Clunn pulled the pole out of the water again and held it ready to strike at Edgar. Edgar looked around the scrubby trees lining the river bank. Seeing a handy piece of broken branch, hg picked it up and continued his approach. "That Dane was thick, or couldn't understand English, or something. But I don't have to put up with this crap from a smelly rodent like you!" he yelled at the defiant Clunn.

Edgar had just started to try and board Clunn's punt when Godfrew put his arm around the small man's neck, lifted him up off the ground, turned him around, and dropped him down again on the bank.

"Save your fighting for the Normans, Edgar. And as for you, Clunn, Edgar is right. You are a smelly little rodent. Shut your mouth!"

Clunn started to carefully move across the punt as if he was going to try and take Godfrew on.

Suddenly, Tosti called out again: "Listen!"

"What now?" asked Leofwine, disappointed that the impending showdown between Godfrew and Clunn had been halted.

"Listen!" insisted Tosti. "The Danes must be having a hard time getting into the town." All stood still, turned toward Peterborough and tried to hear what Tosti could hear.

Puta closed his eyes to help him concentrate. For a long time no one other than Tosti could hear anything other than the murmur of the frogs, the whirl of flying insects and the occasional cry of a water fowl. Then, above the sounds of nature, came a ragged cheer.

"They must be through." Tosti turned and smiled, "I told you."

"I told you." There was a bite of sarcasm in Clunn's voice. When no one laughed at his joke, Clunn put the punt pole into the water and played with it, digging out water weed and flicking it into midstream.

Godfrew and Tosti continued to stare in the direction of the town, trying to interpret the sounds that drifted their way.

Edgar and Leofwine went back to dozing in the bottom of their punts. As the night lengthened, the clouds grew thinner and the moon broke through more often, throwing the branches of the scraggy willow trees into relief.

The sound of battle increased, then almost as suddenly as it started, it stopped.

"Look lively, lads." Godfrew moved along the bank from one punt to the next, making sure that everyone was awake. "This could be it. Winter said that Hereward and some others would be along to take the punts as soon as the fighting was over." As he reached Clunn's punt, he stopped.

Clunn was standing on the seat, his hands clasped over the end of the long pole, his chin resting on his hands, his eyes half-closed. At Clunn's feet lay Puta, who had his arms around Clunn's legs and his head resting against the man's calf. "Clunn, look lively and wake your Puta."

"Oarlocks!" exclaimed Clunn.

"What did you say to me?" Godfrew brought his right hand up to the leather thong that held his axe, Neckbiter, across his back.

"Oarlocks! I can hear oarlocks." Clunn continued to look across the river, past where it joined its larger sister, the Nene. "Someone is rowing—and rowing hard—on the main river. Tosti, listen this way."

Tosti turned and cocked his head in the indicated direction. "True, more than one boat. Could be two or three. At least ten oars aside." He broke away from listening and looked at his leader: "Is the river here deep enough for large boats, or is it too shallow?"

"A longship could make it. It is too shallow for a merchant cob, though."

The Eastings

Godfrew came aboard and stood by the younger man. "Winter told me that there were few soldiers in the town and no ships. They must be ours."

"We are safe then, Master Wulf?" Tosti's question was low, but urgent.

"Would you trust the Danes?"

"The Norman king did when he paid them off last winter."

"And they came back in the spring." Godfrew patted Tosti on the shoulder before making his way back to Clunn in the punt furthest downstream.

"What are we doing now? Do we get ready to fight?" Clunn had not moved, but his eyes were now wide open.

"Tosti says three boats, twenty oars apiece. I make that one hundred and eighty men." Godfrew pinched an insect against his earlobe just as it started to bite. He looked at his thumb and finger. It was covered in bright, red blood. "No, we do not fight. We have instructions to guard the punts and wait for Hereward and others to come." Godfrew looked up the line of five large punts bobbing on the black water. "If—and I do say say 'if'—if the longships come down here, we will move the punts downstream. We will also have to cross the river to keep out of sight of the village of Fletton."

Godfrew turned and glanced toward where the village lay. He tried to make it out, then turned back to the men. "On the way up here I noticed a stream—down where the reed beds take over again. We can hide the punts there."

"All is well for you to say that, but we don't know how to punt like the fenmen." Still, Clunn did not face Godfrew, preferring to address his reply to the opposite river bank.

"Then, my smelly water rat, you will have to learn very quickly!" Godfrew moved on to tell the others.

"You will have to learn very quickly," repeated Clunn in his imitation of Godfrew's north Surrey accent.

"You will have to learn very quickly," copied Puta in a poorer version.

"Don't be cheeky." Clunn bent down and clipped Puta's ginger head. "Now stop your crying! Undo the rope that ties this thing to that tree and then get into your own punt."

The sound of the longships increased and the grunts of the crews as they bent their backs to the oars could be heard.

Woden's Wolf

The wolf pack slipped their moorings and inexpertly punted their way downstream, keeping close into the east bank.

The first dragon-prowed vessel nosed around the river bend and came into sight. The crew hung over their oars, allowing the craft to glide through the water. The skipper called something to the man at the steering board and the longship changed direction slightly.

"What did he say?" Godfrew asked the sharp-eared Tosti as he walked past, holding the dripping pole in his hand.

"No idea. It wasn't English. It wasn't even Norse." Tosti slid the pole into the water and pushed on the pole. "They must be some of those Letts or Estonians that King Swein brought with him." Another longship poked its dragon snout around the bend and followed its sister downstream.

"I suspect they are headed for Fletton. That's about all there is down here. Besides, after Fletton, the river would be getting too shallow, even for a longship."

The third longship rounded the bend. The others had now stopped moving and lay dead in the water.

To stop the current from taking them back, the front oarsmen occasionally dipped their blades into the water. The movement was quiet and easy, never causing a ripple. As they came alongside each other, the skippers called across in low voices. A cloud covered the moon and made it hard to see anything.

Godfrew caught Tosti's arm as he walked past on his way to give the punt another push. "Steady, no noise. We don't want to attract the attention of the Vikings."

"Couldn't we tell them who we are, Master Wulf?"

Godfrew caught the scent of a woman on the youth and wondered when he had had the time to go chasing one. "Sorry, Tosti. Even the Danes have problems talking to their pagan allies, let alone controlling them. Just take it gently, no splashing of the water."

Gradually, the punts edged past the unsuspecting village of Fletton. After rounding the next bend, they crossed back over and searched through the reed beds for the small tributary stream. Tosti saw it first and headed his punt into it. A few boat's lengths downstream, on the right hand side, the reeds gave way to pussy willow.

The Eastings

Just as the last punt, unsteadily poled by Clunn, made its way into the mouth of the stream, three drums started beating together. They were immediately joined by the sound of oars striking the water in unison. When the sound of the oars ceased, it was replaced by savage war cries, then shouting, yelling and eventually screaming.

When the noises finished, the flames started. The village was put to the torch.

"What about Lord Hereward, Master Wulf?" Edgar had taken off his shirt and had commenced to wring out the sodden sleeves.

"Yes, Hereward." Godfrew closed his eyes, lifted up the wolf mask, dropped the hood back, and massaged his face.

"And our share of the plunder?" added Clunn, water dripping from his elbow onto the floor of the punt. "If we don't pick up Hereward, we won't get our share of the plunder. I don't know about you lot, but I am quite looking forward to spending my share of the plunder."

"Yes, yes." Godfrew's voice sounded weary and he continued to massage his face, washing it with dry hands.

"I asked about the plunder," insisted Clunn.

"Shut up, Clunn," said Leofwine.

"Yes, shut up, Clunn," repeated Edgar, his voice muffled as he pulled his shirt back on again.

Godfrew stood with his back to the others and covered his eyes with his hand as he thought. At last, he came to a decision. "We will continue down this stream. It will get closer to the island further down. Then we will have to get back to the meeting place across land."

Tosti started to pole the punt along, "I knew you would have a plan, Master Wulf. You always have. Just as well that you know where this stream goes." He pulled the pole out and walked back to the front to start again.

Edgar of Weobley moved his punt alongside. When he came level with Godfrew, he whispered, "You don't, do you, Master Wulf." Godfrew just looked at him. "Didn't think so. Just as well that I trust you then."

"What was that, Edgar?" asked Tosti as he walked back to the rear of the punt, his hands firmly grasping the end of the pole embedded in the stream bed.

"I was just assuring Master Wulf how much we trusted his judgment, young Tosti the Far-sighted," said Edgar, amiably. "Good leaders are hard to find."

"So is good plunder," muttered Clunn as he reached the bow of his punt and stuck his pole into the water.

"And so is good ..." Puta stopped short as he caught the evil look on Clunn's face. Puta went bright red, pulled his pole out and walked carefully down to the front of his punt, leaving the glowering Clunn to propel his craft at the rear of the slow-moving convoy.

The stream grew narrower and narrower until soon it was only just wide enough for the punts to pass through.

Godfrew grew anxious and quietly whistled through his teeth. A turn in the stream and then, on the right, firm land appeared. Godfrew tapped Tosti's shoulder as he passed by and pointed.

Tosti nodded and stopped poling. Once all five punts were around the bend, Tosti stuck his pole into the soft muddy bed of the stream and stopped his punt's forward movement. The others gently bumped into it.

"What the ..." Clunn stopped yelling when he saw Godfrew's outstretched hand. "This is it?"

Godfrew grabbed hold of a weeping willow sapling and tied both his and Tosti's punt to the branch. He got out and looked around.

The ground was springy, but firm enough. It slopped gently upwards. "Tie up! Bring your weapons." Godfrew pulled his hood on again. As he adjusted the wolf's mask, he caressed the fur around the nose. For once, like the others, he carried a shield on his back. For some reason, Winter had insisted that all the men taking part in the attack on Peterborough had shields. Godfrew's was an old one with big bites out of its edge, the leather hand grip replaced with fraying rope.

As Godfrew walked, the shield banged annoyingly on Neckbiter, hidden from view under the wolf-skin cloak. Godfrew stopped to adjust the thong holding the shield on. Hearing the others catching up, he called back quietly: "We shall see if we can get back to the meeting place this way," before resuming his walk.

The Eastings

Clunn looped his rope around a willow stump and pulled on it to test it. "See if we can get back. It's so dark, we can't see anything."

"Shhh!" Puta held his finger to his lips and glanced to see if Godfrew had heard Clunn's comment, but Godfrew had set off up the slight slope with the others following him.

The rise was very gentle. Even when they reached the top, they were scarcely above the height of the reeds below. The ground had become quite firm and the walking was easy.

Soon the coppiced willows gave way to grass. The wolf pack walked on, hidden only by the darkness of the night.

Godfrew strode ahead as if knowing where he was going. After some time, he held up his hand for the band to halt. "Tosti."

The youth moved to his leader's side. "Master Wulf?" Earlier, Tosti had to give his longbow back to the fenman that he was ordered to make it for. He was now armed only with his saxe and a bill hook. The bill hook was old. Its handle was smooth with use. Pig fat had been wiped on the blade to stop it from gleaming in the dark.

"Can you see or hear anything?" Godfrew stared into the black night, unable to pick anything out.

"I'll go forward, away from Clunn and Puta's chatter." Tosti went twenty paces ahead and stopped, his body tense with concentration. He stood alone, turning this way and that. Eventually, he came back to Godfrew's side. "What are you looking for, Master Wulf?"

"The river. Can you see or hear the river?"

Tosti looked at Godfrew to try and read his leader's face. All he could see was the wolf's mask. "The river? No, we are far from the river. There is no moon to see, but I am sure we have come far to the west. The nearest river would be the Nene, not the smaller one we were waiting in."

"The Nene. Are we near it?" A slight breeze stirred the fur on the cloak, giving it a life of its own.

"The Nene? No, I can neither see, hear, or smell it. But there is a small holding ahead, so we must be somewhere near water." Tosti put the handle of the bill hook on the ground and rested the blade under his arm pit. The grease stained his already dirty shirt.

"A holding? Where?" asked the wolf.

"Ahead. I can hear it. It will be just over that small ridge ahead."

"A ridge ahead?"

"Yes. Can't you see it?"

"Would I ask if I could?"

"Sorry, Master Wulf. So would you like me to take the lead and get us there?" Tosti moved his bill hook to snuggle it under his arm better.

"Yes. You have the far sight, you lead. But," the wolf waived his shortened finger under Tosti's nose, "but when we get twenty paces away, you stop. I will then decide what we are to do."

They did not reach the small holding, because just before it stood a small stone chapel of ease. Someone was in the chapel and candlelight showed through the partially open door.

The wolf pack closed in. Satisfied that all were in place, Godfrew slipped inside, followed by Edgar, the others being left to keep watch outside.

"Good evening," said the wolf.

The priest turned around and gave a startled cry. He stuffed his fist into his mouth and the sound became a muffled whimper. Edgar came forward and turned the priest around before putting his foot into the back of the man's knees, making him keel before his own altar.

Godfrew came and sat on the edge of the altar. He stroked the man's cheek with his saxe. "Where are we, priest?"

"The Chapel of Our Lady Before Orton." The priest tried to glance over his shoulder, but Godfrew's saxe stopped him. "The wolf, tell me, where is the wolf?" the man was twitching and sweat formed beads on his brow.

"I am the wolf!" Godfrew leaned forward and came face-to-face with the white-faced priest. "Tell me what I want to know or I shall change back again."

"Ahhhh!" the priest gave a gurgling choking sound before continuing. "Ah, I will do as you say ... just please ... please, don't take me back with you to hell. I know I have often done wrong, but ..."

"I know all about you. What about your vow of celibacy?" Godfrew let his saxe run under the man's chin, leaving a thin cut that weeped blood onto the priest's vestments.

"I ... she ... it was ..." The priest crossed himself. "Dear, sweet Jesus, save me."

"You should have thought of him when the temptation came. Now you are mine to do with as I please." Godfrew tilted the sweating priest's chin upward with the point of his saxe. "This Orton of yours, it is a way from the Nene is it not?"

The priest gulped and tears started to run down his fat cheeks, "I ... she ... we only ..." The saxe started to bite and remind him of the question he had been asked. "Yes, the Nene, away a bit."

"And Fletton?"

"Fletton, yes, Fletton. Twice as far, that way." The priest pointed behind him. "Fifteen minutes—twenty at the most. Look, that woman ..."

"Cut your babbling. Gather candles, lots of them. You are coming with us." Godfrew put his foot on the priest's back and pushed him over.

As the priest scuttled around gathering candles, Edgar came and stood by Godfrew's side. He whispered into his ear: "How did you know he had been lifting some woman's skirt?"

"Show me a priest that hasn't." Godfrew allowed himself a chuckle." Have you got them all?" he yelled at the fat priest.

"Yes, yes."

"Then get that white vestment of yours off. Show me your hair shirt."

"Hair shirt? I haven't ..."

"But you should have! Your Bishop told you to wear one didn't he?"

"Yes, but I, I, I ..."

"Shut up!" Godfrew looked at the collection of candles. "Stick them in a sack. Look at your undershirt. It is filthy! A whitewashed grave, indeed. Still, it will be less easy to be seen in the dark. Come on, you are coming with us."

"To hell?"

"Who knows!" Godfrew nodded to Edgar and they pushed the priest outside.

As he bumped into the evil-looking Clunn, the priest gave another cry of fear and started weeping again. "Shut your noise, or you will get to hell even quicker! Now move! Take us to Fletton." Godfrew pulled his hood on again.

Woden's Wolf

The priest knew the way well. He took them along paths and through areas of dense scrub until they finally saw the village of Fletton beneath them.

Drawn up in front were the dragon ships. The wolf pack could see Vikings loading plunder and slaves aboard the crafts. Most of the buildings had burnt out, but some were still on fire. The flames reflected on the surface of the mere that lay behind the village. When he saw what was going on, the priest crossed himself and started to tell his beads.

Godfrew did not leave him to his devotions long before forcing him to lead them back to the meeting place north of Fletton. When they arrived, Godfrew was relieved to find that Hereward had still not arrived.

"You, priest," the wolf grabbed hold of the man, bunched his fist into his grubby undershirt and jammed it under his throat, causing him to choke. "There is a stream, back toward the island."

"The Mogg stream. It is called Mogg stream." The priest started to gag.

"Vomit on me priest and I will open you from nose to navel." The wolf relaxed his grip. "Take these men with you to the Mogg. Avoid being seen from Fletton, unless you fancy a trip to Iceland." The wolf snatched the sack of candles, selected the biggest candle, then gave the sack back. "My wolf cubs will all take a candle each. the rest, you will place between here and the Mogg—one for each of your unconfessed mortal sins. Pray for forgiveness as you go. When the sin is forgiven, the candle will be lit."

The priest looked into the sack and started to hand out the candles to the wolf pack. When he had finished, he stole another glance into the sack. It was still almost full.

"I, I ..." he looked at the wolf with the blind white eye. "I haven't committed this many mortal sins, have I?"

"You have!" replied the wolf. "Think on them. If you can't recall them, they will not be forgiven. Then I will come after you again and take you straight to hell!"

The priest and his escort set off, leaving Godfrew and Edgar. "Edgar, catch them up. Make sure the candles are screened from the riverside. I don't want the Letts, or whoever they are, seeing them. The men should have theirs behind their shields. Have young Tosti the Long-Sighted at the rear, say a hundred paces behind. Tosti can light the candles. Don't worry about him getting lost. He has the sight of a cat. He will see the candles, even if they are unlit. I will see you back at the punts, my friend." Godfrew patted Edgar's shoulder. "I just hope Hereward hurries up and gets here before the candles have all burned out!"

Edgar clasped Godfrew's arm and smiled. "Until then, Woden's Wulf." Edgar then let go and trotted after the others.

Godfrew had to wait sometime before the expected party arrived. By then, the sky had turned red as Peterborough caught fire. From his place amongst the pussy willows, Godfrew watched as a group of warriors and black clad monks wound their way along the narrow river bank.

He knew it was Hereward's party, for there at the front strode Stig Gullwing and some of his tall Frisians, mail coats rustling and the flames reflecting off of the low iron caps on their heads.

"Stig Gullwing," said the wolf as he stepped into the path of the Frisians.

"Quick!" Stig signalled his men and they formed an outward-facing circle around Hereward and his captains. Behind the circle of swords, the monks crossed themselves, then knelt in prayer.

"Stig Gullwing, where is your leader, Hereward the Wake?" asked the wolf in a commanding voice.

"Strike the demon!" yelled out a priest at the back. "Iron, they are vulnerable to iron."

"Silver," corrected one of his brethren. "Silver, through the heart."

"This wolf likes silver all right, but in his hand rather than through his heart." Hereward tapped Stig on the shoulder and the tall Frisian stepped forward to let the Wake through.

Hereward stood like a hero of old. His silver mail coat had a double row of yellow gold at the ends of the cuffs and the hem. The mail was of fine links and looked elven-made. On his head was a low cap of the Frisian type, but it had a gold band from back to front and another from side to side. In each of the quarters were pictures of animals set in bright enamel. Hereward's eyes were protected by raised eyebrows of red gold on either side of a silver-gilt nasal piece. Gold edged, silver-gilt cheek guards came out of the helmet and joined at the point of his chin. As Hereward walked toward Godfrew, Frisians left the circle to walk either side of him. "Where are the punts, Wulf, Edric the Wild's man?"

"Hidden, Lord Hereward. We have had some company. Three longships have come and taken Fletton."

"Fletton? Bugger. I should have known the Danes would not be able to keep their heathen hordes in hand." Hereward gnawed at his knuckle. "Too late now."

"Perhaps we should scatter a few Norman bodies around Fletton tomorrow morning, Hereward." Hogni stepped from behind a Frisian and stared at Godfrew with his sharp blue eyes.

"Yes, talk to Wulfric Heron when we get back to Peterborough. See that it is done." Hereward indicated to Godfrew with his thumb. "Come, we should talk to the priests."

The Frisians allowed Godfrew to join Hereward before escorting them both to where the monks knelt in prayer. Godfrew threw back his hood, grateful to let some cool air get to his head. Hereward came to a halt in front of a thin monk. "Finished praying yet, Yswre? I can't spend all night here. I have a battle to finish."

"Battle, Hereward? Sacrilege, more like!" the thin monk got to his feet and wiped the dirt from his knees. "You have done wrong bringing those thieving Vikings here."

"Ever grateful, aren't you, Yswre the Sacrist. You haven't changed since we were boys swimming together in the meres. You were a poor swimmer and I was always saving your bacon. Even then, you never thanked me. No, times don't change, nor do you," Hereward sneered.

"You were a bully then and you are one now. No, you are right. Times don't change," rejoined the monk.

"I didn't have to let you and the English brethren escape with your baubles, now did I?" Hereward crossed his arms across his broad chest. "Peterborough was my father's bequest. He gave it to an English church. I am his heir. If I want to take it back to stop it from falling into foreign hands, then I shall."

"And give it to the Danes?" Yswre thrust his hands into the ends of his sleeves, as if to restrain them.

"You would rather I left it for that thieving Frenchman, Torauld?" Hereward's voice was getting angry.

The Eastings

"Torauld is the church's choice as the replacement abbot for the holy Abbot Brand, God rest his soul. It is not for you to dispute it!" Yswre's anger started to match Hereward's.

"Church's choice? My arse! William the Bastard's choice. Every Englishman who dies, be he noble or churchman, is replaced by one of his foreign creatures. Well, Torauld shall not have Peterborough."

Hereward's voice was now getting so loud that Godfrew feared that the Letts across the river would hear him.

"You saw to that, Hereward. By now it will be burnt to the ground!" Yswre spat out.

"Good!" Hereward stepped forward, stuck the pommel of his sword, Brainbiter, under Yswre's chin, and forced the monk to stand on tip toe. "For old times sake and in memory of old Brand, you have your life. You also have some of your treasures. Think yourself lucky."

"I think he dislikes losing the beautiful trappings he and his like have garnered from their impoverished flock over the years." Hogni stood at Hereward's elbow and fixed Yswre with his blue eyes. "Strange habits for followers of a man who only owned the clothes he stood up in."

Yswre pulled his hands from his sleeves and eased his fingers between the sword's pommel and his chin. "Hereward, perhaps I have been too hasty. You spared our lives." Hereward lowered the sword a little, allowing the monk to regain his footing. "I thank you for your mercy."

"Good." Hereward sheathed Brainbiter. "Go with the wolf. He will take you to the punts. From there you will be taken by Pig Water and the Whittlesey Mere to Ripton. You will have to get yourself from Ripton to Huntingdon. I am sure Earl Waltheof and his Norman friends will be only too pleased to listen to your whimpering." Hereward turned and walked away.

---

[20] Woden (Odin to the Norse) was the supreme Germanic god. Usually regarded as the god of war, he was also regarded as being a somewhat benign god, despite the fact that the slain of battle were his and human sacrifices were sometimes offered to him. His wisdom came when he drank from the magic cauldron, Odhrerir, in exchange for one of his eyes. To learn the runes, as a young man he hung for nine days on a gallows tree pierced through with a spear which he had dedicated to himself. Always associated with wolves, he was also connected with ravens, two of whom—Huginn, thought and Munnin, memory—came to him each night and told him all the news they had gathered from flying over the earth all day. Woden often travelled the earth disguised as an old man. The number nine is significant to Woden and his worship.

"Woden." [20] Hogni sidled up to Godfrew. "Martin Lightfoot and some local men will go with you as guides. Make the monks pole the punts. They are skilled at it, unlike your men." Godfrew nodded his head and went off to find Martin. Hereward had, in the meantime, signalled to Stig that he was leaving. The tall Frisians formed up around him and Hogni. They then headed back toward Peterborough. At their approach, the monks scrambled to their feet and moved out of the way, dragging their precious belongings with them.

"Follow me, but if you want to live, keep quiet." Godfrew pulled down his hood. Taking a steel and flint, he struck a light, got the candle burning and held it behind his shield. He took care to mask the light by keeping the shield facing Fletton as he led the party of monks off.

As they went up the hill, another candle glowed at them from a bush of willow, then further on another. Godfrew trudged on toward the lights that led to the hidden punts. The monks and Hereward's men followed the wolf into the dark night.

The Return West

"Look, Toki, I risked my life and the lives of my men to get the silver to buy your freedom. The least you can do is help us get our horses back."

The wolf pack lay in the bushes overlooking Earl Waltheof's hall at Huntingdon. Toki, a quarter of the size he had been when he left on the venture to the fenlands, lay on his back munching a leg of roast swan. The swan was only partly cooked and the half-eaten flesh showed pink in the moonlight.

Toki rolled over and edged on his belly until he was alongside Godfrew. "Look, nephew-in-law. If I thought I ... but as it is I could only ... the staller is a decent enough ... but we all have to ..." Toki continued in his usual incoherent mutter.

Godfrew waited until he thought his aunt's husband had finished, wiped some bits of half-roasted swan from his eye and sighed. "Toki, do I understand you right. You are willing to talk to the staller to see if he has our horses. If hc has them, you will try and get them back for us, but you think it will take a bribe to get anything. Right?"

"Right." Toki gave one of his silly gap-toothed smiles and continued chewing the swan meat. Little crumbs of it escaped the edge of his mouth and slid down his chin.

"The bribe is for who, Toki? You or him?" Godfrew held back Shock, who was licking his lips and trying to get at Toki's face.

"Well ... of course, but then ..."

"Will a silver penny do?" Godfrew slipped his hand down to the small leather purse tucked inside his britches. While he tried to get the coin out, Shock gave him the slip.

Toki held Shock at arms length and smirked, eating with the other hand. Satisfied that he could glean no more meat from the leg, he threw the bone over his shoulder. Shock tried to chase after it, but Toki managed to hold him in place by pushing on his chest with his free hand. Eventually, Shock managed to slip sideways and escape Toki as he clutched at his legs. "Your hound is ... would taste nice with a bit of ..." Toki gave a funny chuckle. "Now, the money. You have found a ... amongst the other ... have you?"

Godfrew held out a coin between his thumb and middle finger. The stump of his index finger pointing accusingly at Toki. "If I thought that this was going to you, Toki, after all I have done for you." He dropped the silver into Toki's open palm and the fingers snapped closed on it, like a rat trap.

"Oh, er, by the ... before I, er ..." Toki mumbled and mumbled as he rummaged in the small sack that he had tied to his now slim waist. The first items he brought out were all edible, including a piece of honey comb that was covered in fur from the dead hare it shared its space with. "I thought I had ... must be near the ... ah, here it is." Toki produced a small leather-bound book. He licked a piece of honey from the cover, then held it out to Godfrew. "For your new son, a gift."

"It is beautiful." Godfrew took the book and opened the clasp. Inside, the colour from the illuminations jumped out at him from the page. "This is magnificent. Where did it come from, Toki?"

Toki just smiled. "I looked at the ... Noah's ... lots of animals in ... would suit a child!"

"Thank you, Toki. I am touched." Godfrew looked for somewhere to put the book.

"Master Wulf," Tosti edged forward. "Can I look after it? I am learning to read." Tosti gave an embarrassed smile: "Never too old, eh. Puta started to teach me when we were in the fens. May I?"

Godfrew passed the book over. "Keep it safe for me till we get back home."

Tosti took the book, reverently opened it, and looked inside.

"Puta taught me." Clunn's yellow teeth glowed in the dark. "You are all turning into monks. No fight in any of you."

"Clunn," Godfrew's voice came in an urgent hiss: "Clunn, shut up."

"Yes, Clunn. Shut up!" echoed Edgar and Leofwine together.

"All right, Toki. You have the money. Now go and find out about our horses." Godfrew gave Toki a prod in the ribs. "Go on!"

"All right, all right," moaned Toki. He eased himself to his feet, made his way out of the shrubbery, and edged toward the holding. There was a guard at the gate. Toki slowly walked over to him. For a moment, Toki and the guard spoke quietly, then the guard gave out a loud laugh.

"You, Toki?" There was more laughter. "Stand here in the light. It is you! Isn't it?" The guard called back into the yard: "Hey, Stan, come over here. Come on. Leave that for a moment. I have something funny to show you."

"What's want now?" a powerful figure wearing an apron joined Toki and the guard.

"Guess who this skeleton is?" asked the guard of the newcomer.

"I don't know."

"Toki! Fat Toki the Swineherd!"

"Never!" the big man replied. "Let me see better." He yanked Toki under the light of a burning torch in the gateway. "Well, I'll be buggered." He slapped Toki on the back "What on earth happened to you, man?" Toki and Stan went into the yard and Toki's reply was lost to the wolf pack.

"What will we do if the horses are there, Master Wulf?" enquired Leofwine, still half-drowsy from the ale that he drank with the earlier meal.

"Edgar and his brood have their mounts already. If we find we can get the rest of the horses, they can wait for us at the lake—in the woods at Grafham—on the old Roman road, heading east. We will join them there. If we can't get the horses? Who knows? There's no use in planning too much ahead when we do not know what the story is. We must just be patient." With that, Godfrew rested his head on his hands and went to sleep ...

... Godfrew drove the dark pony against the force of the Wandle's woe waters to try and save his other six sons. The three boys he had rescued hung on to him as he encouraged the dark pony forward with his knees. He forced the reluctant animal to move against the current, but it stumbled. As Godfrew looked down he saw blood surging around the ponies legs and swirling past. The pony started to stumble even more, then stagger. Godfrew noticed that as the pony bled, it changed from dark brown to white. As the pony started to buckle, a bloodied hand grasped his shoulder. Godfrew looked up. "You fiend! What have you done to my pony?" he screamed ...

"What?" asked a very shocked Tosti, as he rolled back onto his heels. Godfrew sat up and blinked his eyes. He looked closely at Tosti, then looked around for the pony and the water, but they were not there. Instead of water, there were trees silhouetted against the moonlit sky. Tosti moved across and held Godfrew's arm. Godfrew slowly looked, then he smelled the fruit and realised that the youth's hands were stained with the juice of early blackberries, not blood. "Are you all right, Master Wulf?"

"A dream, Tosti. Just a dream. And not a pleasant one." Godfrew eased the cloak's hood off his head and ran a hand over his face. "What's happening then?"

"Toki, he's on his way back."

Godfrew turned and looked in the direction of the holding at Huntingdon. There, slowly heading toward the woods where they lay, was Toki. In one hand, the now skinny man held a large slice of black bread thick with honey that dripped off as he walked. In the other was an uncorked ale flask. Toki stopped to take a long swing of ale. He belched, then entered the trees twenty paces from the wolf pack. Even before Toki came in sight. Godfrew could hear his unfathomable mumbling.

"... so it should be ... to think that they ..." Toki laughed at his own joke. "All right, nephew-in-law ... the plan for you to ... and then I can go ..." Toki cocked his head to one side questioningly.

"Toki," Godfrew pulled clear of the bushes and stood up. "Start again from the beginning. Can we get the horses?"

"Yes." Toki took another bite from the honey bread, leaving a smear of golden stick across his face.

"How, Toki? How do we get the horses?" Godfrew put his hands into his back and eased the ache that had set in. "Slowly, Toki ... and with your mouth empty."

Toki took a final swig from the flask, draining the ale. He tipped the empty vessel upside down. When nothing came out, he tossed the flask into the nearest bush. "Easy. It seems Earl Waltheof is expecting a party from the Earl of Kent, so when they ..." Toki's mumble ended in a belch. Toki smiled, then farted. "Who ... was that ... I suppose it ..." Toki then noticed Godfrew's hard stare. "Oh, yes, well ... when the Normans have arrived, you all ... and you shouldn't be noticed in all the ..." Toki shrugged his shoulders. "Just see the ... Gyrth. Easy, eh!"

"Earl of Kent?" asked Leofwine of no one in particular. "We haven't got an Earl of Kent. Kent is part of Wessex, surely?" He then moved to the bush where Toki had thrown the flask, hoping to find some dregs in it.

"We haven't, but the Normans have." Edgar started to gather his gear together, ready to head for Grafham Woods to join his wife and children. "I heard Earl Edric talking before I left. The Norman king has made his fat brother, Odo the-Nun-Chaser, Earl of Kent." He looked around. "Has anyone seen that hunk of bread I was eating?" Puta pointed to Shock who was hunched over his prize. Edgar bent to pull the bread away from the hound, but Shock growled and bared his teeth, so Edgar changed his mind.

"He's a priest or abbot ... or something like that in the church, isn't he?" Tosti rolled his cloak up and started to tie it. "They aren't supposed to be earls, are they?" He attached the rolled cloak to the top of his haversack.

"Hey, get into the real world," Edgar called over his shoulder as he departed. "They are Normans. They do as they please." Toki shot a glance at Godfrew. He, too, was busy getting ready to leave, so Toki tagged on behind Edgar, walking away with never a glance behind him.

The wolf pack did not have to wait too long for the Earl of Kent's party to arrive. In pairs, the wolves came out of the woods, each man with a bundle of small branches over his shoulder, thus disguising his haversack with the animal fodder. Tosti, Leofwine and Clunn had tied the staves of their newly made long bows to hastily cut quarter-staffs. The tall poles still had the odd leaf attached. They pushed their way into the yard, side-stepping nervous horses and arguing retainers from both the Kentish party and Earl Waltheof's. Odo's party was a mix of all races. The wolves were hit with a babble of different tongues. Despite Odo's reputation, there were no women to be seen amongst the visitors. Most of those in the yard were servants and horse handlers, but there were some men-at-arms present. The wolves kept well clear of them. Godfrew jammed himself into a corner by the main horse stable. By observation, he worked out who Earl Waltheof's staller was, but waited for the press of people to thin before making an approach to the man. Leofwine had purloined an ale flask, which he reluctantly shared with the others. His eyes carefully measured the volume of each man's swig.

At last, the yard emptied—though the odd rider still came in and out, gaining little attention. Godfrew stood near the staller and whistled quietly between his teeth until the man cocked his ear. "Toki has spoken to you? All we are after is getting our horses back. We left them here last autumn."

"And very handy they've been too. I hate having to give them back." The staller loosened the girth strap of the roan pony in front of him. "In fact, one of them is out at the moment. I trust you will be happy with a replacement." He pulled the saddle off and swung around to take it into the stable, almost knocking Godfrew over in the process. "Sorry, I thought you would have seen me."

"Not that side friend." Godfrew gave a lopsided smile. The man then saw the dead, white eye and blanched. "The pony that is out," continued Godfrew. "What colour is it? Not the dark pony, I hope."

"Oh, no, Master." The staller found it hard to look at Godfrew in the face. Instead, he wiped his sweaty palms on his leather apron. "Lord Waltheof's nephew rides that one. It is gentle and well behaved—ideal for a young boy. That pony only goes out on short rides. She is in the next stall. In fact, you can hear her whinnying now. Perhaps she can hear her master's voice."

Godfrew listened. "You are right. She is calling me." He smiled with pleasure at the thought of riding his beloved pony once more. "Is there any problem with us taking our mounts?"

"Yes, there will be, but nothing that a little silver won't cure. Even the disappearance of your dark pony can be managed with the aid of silver." The staller stole a glance at Godfrew, then looked the other way—casting his eye over the other members of the wolf pack who were standing in a half circle in front of him. Clunn pulled out his eating knife and pared his finger nails, eating the parings in the process. The staller watched him—horrified. Godfrew took a deep breath and let the air out loudly down his nose. "Oh, sorry Master. Yes, a little silver will grease the wheels. It need not be too much."

"More than the silver penny I told Toki to give you?" Godfrew felt a numbness in the stump of his severed finger and massaged it between his middle finger and thumb. "Well?"

"Silver penny, Master? What silver penny?" the staller persisted with his habit of talking to Godfrew without looking at him.

"No matter." Godfrew stopped working the stump and used his other hand to remove a gold ring from the middle finger of his right hand. In the centre of the ring was an image of Jesus on the holy rood, carved from walrus ivory. Before passing it to the staller, Godfrew took a final look and rubbed the image with his thumb. "If a little silver brings your grudging co-operation, then this should bring it in full measure."

The staller took the ring and examined it. As he saw the carving, he gasped. "This ring ... this ring ..." he gulped. "... I have seen it before. I kissed it once when it was on the hand of Abbot Brand at Peterborough!"

"Brand is dead, so he no longer has need of it. Take it, it is valuable. You can be a rich man. Or, if you prefer, you can buy the new Norman Abbot's favour by returning it to the abbey. Myself, I think it is too beautiful for some crude, half-educated Norman to wear." Godfrew looked toward the stall where he knew the dark pony to be. "The horses ... we will need them saddled and ready as soon as possible. My men will leave first." Godfrew pulled out his saxe, held both his arms out wide and circled them before re-sheathing the weapon. The staller's eyes followed the movement of the saxe, relaxing only when it was put away again. "As I said," continued Godfrew. "My men will go first. I will stay here until I am happy with all the arrangements you have made. Now ..." he held out his left hand, his right still on the handle of the saxe. "...the ring. You will get it when I go and not before."

The staller reluctantly passed the gold ring back, his finger tips caressing it as it passed through them. "Of course,

Master." He reluctantly started to move away, then stopped. " Master?" his voice was quiet and he averted Godfrew's eyes as he spoke. "Toki said that he had been captured by pirates who beat him daily and tried to starve him to death, but that you came back and rescued him. He said that you led Yswre the Sacrist and the other English monks out when the Danes sacked and burnt Peterborough. He also said that you can ..." the man hesitated, "... that you can change into..." again he hesitated, "... change into a wolf. Is it true?"

Godfrew smiled and pulled his hood over his head, "Gyrth the staller, look at me."

Gyrth did as commanded and saw the wolf. "You know my name? God help me!" He crossed himself and hurried away to ensure that Godfrew and his men were out of Huntingdon as soon as possible. While the others loitered, Godfrew went in to see the dark pony. The pony was restlessly pacing until she saw her master, then she came straight over and nuzzled him. Godfrew closed his eyes and put his arms around the animal's neck, letting her sniff and blow hot air around his neck and hair. For a long time, they hung together, soaking in each other's scent.

"Master Wulf." Tosti stood at the door of the stall, almost afraid to interrupt. "Master Wulf, Gyrth has the horses ready. Leofwine wants to go first. Is that all right?"

"It is fine." Godfrew undraped himself from the dark pony's neck. "Let Leofwine go first, before he gets too drunk to ride." He put his nose to the pony's. It wrinkled its top lip and mouthed his chin. "I will come and watch, to make sure all goes well." The dark pony started to get agitated as Godfrew went to leave: "Easy, easy. The nice man will saddle you up and then we will leave here for good. You and I, together." The pony quieted at Godfrew's voice, but still stood with her head over the wicker hurdle, waiting to be gone.

Leofwine mounted his pony—with the help of Gyrth and Tosti—and slowly walked the beast out of the yard. The others watched, but no one took any notice. Satisfied that all was going well, Godfrew jerked his thumb at Puta. The ginger-headed boy went into the main stable. When he emerged again, it was on a sturdy piebald that was capable of taking his considerable weight. Clunn got his mount without waiting for Godfrew to tell him. As he trotted the pony out of the yard, he could not resist letting the animal step on the toes of one of the Norman man-at-arms lingering by the gate. Tosti and Godfrew waited for some time before getting the next horse out. They thought there could be trouble from Clunn's provocation, but it never came.

Tosti's mount was a dark grey, taller than the others. Because of its size, it carried some of the excess baggage hanging over its sides in pannier bags. As Tosti rode toward the gate, the Norman with the sore foot looked up and scrutinised his face, but did nothing to stop him leaving. Now it was Godfrew's turn.

The dark pony stamped her feet as she stood outside her stall, keen to be gone. Godfrew double checked, adjusted her straps and bridle, then gave her bit more freedom than the staller had allowed. Slipping the staller the promised ring, he edged the dark pony into the yard and looked toward the gate. The Norman men-at-arms were still there. There was another man, a stocky man in a mail coat, but no helmet, walking toward them. Godfrew decided not to wait any longer and mounted. As he headed to the gate, the bareheaded man turned and looked at him. Fear struck Godfrew's stomach as he realised the man had only twisted scar tissue for a left eye and a pig's snout for a nose. He dug his heels into the dark pony's flanks and increased her pace to a trot. The pig-faced man stared at him. As he came alongside, the moonlight caught Godfrew's face and the man gasped, waiving the remains of his right hand at him.

"You—you bastard Saxon! I thought I could smell you!" He turned to the men at the gate: "Hey, you useless piles of shit. Those men who left—they are the Wake's men. Rebels! And you've let them go!" Godfrew kicked the dark pony and she broke into a gallop. A man grasped at the pony's bridle as she ran past, but Godfrew had seen him coming and drawn his saxe. As the man buffeted alongside, Godfrew struck him a backhanded blow. The man gave a burbling scream as he let go and fell under the pony's back hooves. Pig-face started running after Godfrew: "Stop him. He is the leader ... a Saxon Wolfshead. STOP HIM!" He screamed from the top of his lungs. As the gate came nearer, Godfrew leaned forward and clung to the dark pony's neck. He did not see the ox cart that the Normans pushed into their path until it was too late.

The dark pony tried to jump over the cart, but instead crashed into the wooden side and stopped dead. Godfrew sailed over her head and smashed into the cobblestones the other side. As he was dragged unsteadily to his feet, he could hear the pony screaming and screaming. Her noise did not cease until the staller cut her throat and put her out of her misery.

It was then that Godfrew fainted.

* * *

The Norman men-at-arms dragged Godfrew into Earl Waltheof's hall and walked toward the head table. The Breton Captain strode behind, his arms swinging. The torch light reflected off his mail coat and caught the thicker rings where it had been repaired inexpertly. As they progressed up the hall, heads turned and the assembly watched with a mixture of amusement and horror. As Godfrew's body slid and bumped along over the dirty rushes on the floor, his wolf-skin cloak seemed to develop a life of its own. With its wearer's head hung low, the cloak's hood swayed from side to side and the wolf's mask grinned as it swayed, as if seeing if it knew any of the hall's occupants. The party stopped in front of the Earl of Kent, Bishop Odo—the Norman king's brother—and dropped Godfrew in front of him. The Breton Captain put his foot on Godfrew's back. After searching unsuccessfully for any hair on his scalp to grab, he put his mutilated right hand under Godfrew's chin and jerked his head backwards for his master to see.

"My Lord, Earl. We caught this Saxon Wolfshead stealing one of your host's horses. I know him of old. He is wanted in three counties for murder." The Captain dropped Godfrew's head back down on the rush-covered floor.

Bishop Odo studied the prostrate figure before him with hooded eyes. He held his fat, ringed fingers in an attitude of prayer, the tips touching and parting rhythmically. The hall mimicked his silence. Even the hounds ceased their usual rummaging amongst the rushes for scraps. Finally, the fingers stopped tapping and the hands clasped. Odo turned to

The Return West

his host and—in a quiet, but very audible voice—asked, "Waltheof, what company have you been keeping in my brother's absence?"

Earl Waltheof's chaplain moved forward and interpreted in the earl's ear. Waltheof nodded to show that he understood, then turned to face Odo. "Surely, Abbot Odo, you do not think that I have been harbouring the King's enemies?" His French was slow and halting, marked by a strong Mercian accent. "Even the best households suffer from mice in the stables."

Bishop Odo's eyes closed even further. His voice became as an adder's hiss: "Old habits can take a long time to ..." Odo paused for effect, "... die."

Again Earl Waltheof listened for the translation before replying. "Or, in this man's case," he pointed to Godfrew, who was starting to stir the rushes with his right hand, "you might find it more appropriate to say: 'You can't teach an old dog new tricks.'" Waltheof waited for a reaction from Odo to his deliberate deflection of the question. When the Abbot allowed his eyes to widen slightly, Waltheof continued: "Or should I have said: 'an old wolf'." The Earl threw his head back and laughed until the tears ran down his cheeks and into his thick brown beard. The English in the hall joined him in laughter, though few understood what he had said.

Odo closed his eyes and ignored the merriment. He seemed asleep, but the knuckles on his clasped hands showed white. When Waltheof ceased laughing and wiped the tears from his eyes, the English stopped too. They whispered loudly to one to another—seeking to find out what they had been laughing at—knowing only that the great earl had cracked a joke at fat Odo the-Nun-Chaser's expense. At last, the noise in the hall died. Earl Waltheof took his mead horn and raised it to fat Odo. "Do the French never laugh, Lord Abbot?" he asked in all innocence.

Odo slowly opened his snake like eyes. "When there is something to laugh at, Waltheof of Huntingdon." He cast his watery, hooded eyes at the Breton Captain: "You are sure that this horse thief is an outlaw, Captain?"

The Breton nodded his affirmation. Watery snot ran from the mangled remains of his nose and shook off the end of his chin with the movement of his head. Odo waived his hand at him and screwed his face up in disgust. The Captain pulled a stiff piece of rag from his sword belt and wiped his face. "Yes, my Lord. I know him well. He has been declared outlaw and Wolfshead in Surrey and Hereford—even in Kent." He wiped his face again before giving Godfrew a sharp kick in the ribs. Godfrew commenced a low moan.

"Kent? My own County?" Odo looked across at Waltheof. "As he is wanted in my own County, Earl of Huntingdon, I claim the right to hold him and take him back with me." He gave a slit-mouthed smile that contained no warmth. "I assume you have no objections?"

After the chaplain translated, the Earl replied: "How could I object, Lord Abbot? Surely, you must take him with you if he is wanted in Kent." Waltheof swirled the mead in his horn before downing it in one gulp. "As I said earlier: 'Even the best households suffer from mice.' I just wish you could learn to keep the Kentish mice in your own pantry instead of letting them run abroad in mine." He glanced in the direction of the Breton Captain. "Mind, I am sure they all run away when they see the face of your chief cat!" This time, the chaplain joined his master in laughing and, again, the English copied the great earl. Waltheof laughed and laughed, setting the table rocking. Odo audibly hissed. The Breton took the opportunity to kick Godfrew again. Mopping his eyes with his table napkin, Waltheof stood up. "My, Odo, you are such fun company." Laughter again shook his bear-like body. It was some time before he could control himself. "Oh, dear," Waltheof wiped his eyes again and sighed. "Yes .. well ... take your prisoner to my stone storehouse and keep him there till you leave. Being stone, there shouldn't be any mouse holes for him to escape through." Waltheof threw his head back and roared, then left the hall, taking with him his chaplain and the leader of his hearth troop. The earl's laughter hung behind him like the incense in a church after mass.

Bishop Odo stood up at the table and flicked his dimpled hands at the Breton Captain. "Take him away and keep him safe. I can see from the evil glint in that eye of yours that you wish to be alone with him for some intimate conversations." The Captain snuffled his agreement. "Just keep the noise down, Captain. Some of us want to sleep."

The Return West

Odo moved his chair and pulled his considerable weight around it. "Sleep! With that Saxon dog Waltheof guarding his maidens like an old bantam hen that's ALL I will get in this place!" he commented to his mass priest as he waddled down the steps of the dais.

* * *

"Who's that? Open the door. Come in, so that I can see you." The Norman soldier tightened his grip on his sword and held his left hand out for better balance. He listened hard. The faint scuffling noise outside the door continued. Cautiously, he edged toward the closed door. "Cover me, Yves," he called to his companion. "Put those dammed dice away and get here, now." The other man-at-arms reluctantly stuffed the dice into a small velvet bag hanging from his belt and came over, unsheathing his sword as he walked. The first Norman nodded to Yves and threw the door open. Shock walked in, went straight over to Godfrew and started to lick his face. The two Norman men-at-arms on duty outside the stone storehouse burst out laughing.

"Very funny. Ha, ha!" The soldier slammed the door shut. "Pillocks, what are they trying to do? Give us heart attacks?" he asked Yves.

"You are getting jumpy, Ralf. I really think that you believe the story that this wretch," Yves stuck his foot under Godfrew's ribs and flicked him over onto his back, "does turn into a wolf at midnight." Yves kicked Shock out of the way, but the hound returned to his ministrations as soon as the Norman wandered back to the barrel he had been using as a seat.

Ralf joined Yves and was laying his weapon across a third barrel that they were using as a dice table when a voice asked: "Do you want some food?" Ralf dropped his sword with a clatter. Quickly scrabbling to grab the hilt, he turned and saw a tall figure standing in the doorway. "Do you want this food or not?" The man walked into room and at last Yves could see him properly. It was Red, the leader of Waltheof's hearth troop. The lamplight reflected dully on his bald head and gold wire bound the remains of his ginger hair into pigtails. "Well?" Red proffered one of the plates of food he held.

"What did he say?" Yves half stood, his hands on the edge of the temporary dice table.

"I don't know, but I think he is offering us some food." Ralf put down his sword and held out his hand. "Thank you, yes." He took the pewter plate Red offered him and put it on the barrel in front of him, pushing the dice to one side first. "Yves? Do you want some?"

"Don't ask stupid questions." Yves stood properly and held out his hand for a plate. "Do you have any women you could bring us as well?" he casually asked Red. Red stared back blankly. "No? I suppose if there were some, our lord and master would have grabbed them." Yves held the plate to his nose and appreciated the smell of the stew it contained. "They say the English can't cook, but this lot smells beautiful." He looked at Red. "Thank you. You go, now," he said in his best Flemish.

"First, I feed the wolf." Red knelt down and rested Godfrew's head on his thigh. Godfrew opened his eyes and looked at Red uncomprehendingly. "Do you want anything to eat, little wolf cub?" Red fiddled around at his back and produced a small wooden spoon. Godfrew tried to pull himself up, but failed and flopped down, whimpering. Shock made the most of Red's distraction and licked the edge of the plate.

While Red tried to spoon some stew into Godfrew's mouth, Ralf left his meal and came over. "You no feed. Him sick." he explained to Red.

"Sick?" asked Red, puzzlement crossing his scared face. "Hurt, yes. Not sick."

"Sick," insisted Ralf. He stomped on the stomach of the recumbent Godfrew, who rolled over and vomited over Red's leg wrappings. "Yes, sick. See?" Red pulled himself from under the retching Godfrew and walked to the door, shaking the contents of Godfrew's last meal from his leg and emptying the plate of stew on the ground as he went. Before he left, Red took a final look at the injured man's face and grunted.

"He's a strange man." Yves pointed his piece of black bread at the closed door. "If that had been me, I would have killed either you or that puking wolf on the floor. Yet, he took it ... despite the fact that to look at him you would think he ate babies boiled in their mother's milk for breakfast. He's a strange one, no?"

The Return West

"Perhaps we have finally knocked the fight out of these Saxons." Ralf blew away the steam from the stew on his plate and cautiously edged some into his mouth with the piece of bread Red had left on the edge of the plate. "Oh, very nice. A bit hot," he sucked some air into his mouth to cool the food, "but very nice."

The door opened yet again. Ralf was about to yell abuse at the outside sentries when the Breton Captain came in and walked across to where he sat. The Captain smacked Ralf across the back of the head: "Guarding my wolf well, are we?" He took the plate from Ralf and, using a wedge of black bread, shovelled the remaining stew into his mouth. Yves stopped eating in sympathy with his mate. The Captain saw this and ate his portion too. "The trouble with being a Captain is always having to stand guard around the master. One never seems to get the time to eat," he snuffled. "I see he has been sick. He must have eaten too much rich food stolen from his better's table, no doubt." He stopped and peered with his good eye. "What's that thing? A giant rat?" Shock was cleaning up the stew that Red had thrown away, but looked up at the Captain's voice. "Get away." The captain stepped forward and aimed a kick at the hound, but Shock was too quick and scampered to safety behind some bales of wool. "Never mind the rat, let's have a look at our wolf." The Captain sidestepped the pool of vomit, went over to Godfrew and pushed him into it. Godfrew snorted and coughed before bringing up what little else his stomach still contained. "Messy dog, is he not?" The Breton studied his victim in detail, then stood back. "All right, get him up."

The two soldiers grabbed Godfrew's arms. "Just keep his filth away from me." The men put their arms under Godfrew's and lifted—trying, without success, to get him to stand.

Godfrew lifted his head as best he could. "My leg," he gurgled. His stomach went into a spasm and he tried to double up. "My leg. I can't stand."

The soldiers were having trouble holding Godfrew as he started dry retching. "Captain, there is something wrong with his left leg." Yves slipped in the vomit and had trouble regaining his feet. "Captain, we can't hold him up much longer."

"Then let him go." The men obeyed and dropped Godfrew into a crumpled, moaning heap. "Give the leg a pull." Yves did as he was told, but the moaning did not increase. "Move it." Yves followed instructions and again the moaning remained low. "Nothing broken, eh. Now, there's a pity. We could have had a lot of fun with a broken leg. I wonder ..." the Captain snuffled as he kicked Godfrew's bad leg. "... I wonder just what is wrong with the leg. Ah, I know. Twist it." Yves twisted the leg. Once it got past a certain point, Godfrew screamed and tried to reach out with his right hand, but seemed unable to support himself with his left arm. "Got you!" The Captain seemed delighted. "Torn muscles. I should have been a physician." He paced around his victim, hand on chin, thinking. "Well, if he can't stand on his own, then we will have to help him." The Captain looked around the store. "Yes, that's it." He went over near the door and glanced upwards "The pulley. They must use it to lift the bails of wool. What's good enough for sheep shearings is good enough for a wolf's screaming. Bring him over here."

To avoid the pool of sick, the soldiers grabbed Godfrew's feet and dragged him under the pulley. While they waited for instructions, Yves took the opportunity to discreetly pick his nose. The Breton Captain investigated the pulley before speaking again. "Shame, him not having the broken leg, but torn muscles may prove interesting enough. Tie his hands behind his back. Come on, look around for some rope. Otherwise, use your belt." Ralf found some coarse flax rope. When he pulled Godfrew's arms back to tie them he was rewarded with a scream. "Excellent, Ralf, excellent. We shall have our entertainment yet. Now, undo the rope on the pulley and stick the hook under his bindings." Ralf obeyed. "Now, the two of you pull him up—just far enough to make him stand on tip-toe." As the full weight of his body went onto his damaged shoulder, Godfrew's screaming became louder. "Excellent," commented the Captain. "Lower him and take the weight off of his arms. Now, twist his legs—one at a time." Ralf twisted Godfrew's right leg, but all he got in response was a moan. Then he twisted his left leg and got deafened as Godfrew gave a roar that increased in pitch as the angle of the leg increased. "Now, at least we know where to start." The Captain brought one of the barrels over and sat on it facing the dangling man. "My fine wolf, let's hear you howl. At first for pleasure, then for revenge." He took out his rag and wiped his snout. Seeing Yves picking his complete nose, the Captain glared at him. Yves embarrassedly stopped and wiped his tacky finger on his ring-mail coat. The Captain then continued: "Finally, for information. I am sure you know many things about that adder's nest infesting Ely."

"If we can get good information on that outlaw Hereward, there could be a decent reward in it for us, eh, Captain." Yves let the rope go slack and Ralf found himself struggling to keep Godfrew hanging at the right angle.

"Us? Us?" yelled the Captain. "What is this 'us'? If you let that creature fall to the ground, your only reward will be to take his place!" Yves quickly grabbed the rope and pulled hard on it. Godfrew screamed. "That's a good idea, jiggle him up and down a bit. Not too hard, mind. I don't want his shoulder dislocated. That can wait until last." With each jiggle, the pitch of Godfrew's scream changed. The higher he went, the higher the pitch. The Breton Captain gave a snuffling, snorting giggle and wiped his eye with the rag.

Suddenly the door swung open and one of the sentries popped his head in. "Captain, you must have disturbed his Lordship. He is hanging out of the window and looking this way."

"And his mass priest has just come out of the door and is headed toward us," added the other sentry, who was hidden from view.

The Captain got up and stuffed his snot rag into Godfrew's mouth. "Shit." He chucked Godfrew under the chin. "You will keep until morning. All right, you two," he said, "take him up on tip-toe and leave him there for the night."

* * *

Red went through the open door of the stone storehouse holding the plates of food in his hands. As he entered, the stench hit him. It was the smell of a human confined in his own filth. He stopped breathing through his scared and broken nose and held the plates nearer his face to let the odour of the food cover the stink within. "Food. Goose in blackberry sauce together with peas and fresh beans." He went to where the soldiers were playing dice to while away the evening. As he passed the suspended Godfrew, he gave him a casual glance. "He's still alive after four days in your hands?"

"What? Goose and berries with beans? I right?" enquired Ralf in halting English. "You come here four days? Yes, four days." He turned to Yves, "I suppose I will get the hang of their language in time. At least, I try, even if you don't."

"Flemish is near enough. Let them make the effort." Yves looked at Red questioningly, "Where is the wine? You've brought us wine for the last two nights." He screwed up his face and mimicked drinking."Wine."

"Ah," said a repentant Red, "I forgot your wine."

"Yes, that's it: W-I-N-E." Yves smiled encouragement to Red. "W-I-N-E."

"Wine," Red agreed. "I'll get it." He turned and headed for the door.

"Where's he going. I asked him for the wine." Yves used his eating knife to prod the goose flesh and see if it was cooked. The flesh fell from the bone.

"I think he said he was going to get it." Ralf turned from Yves and called out to the retreating back of the hearth troop leader: "Don't close the door, we need some fresh air. You no close door." The door slammed shut as Red went out. "Never mind." Ralf picked up the leg of goose and licked off some of the tart blackberry sauce. "You can open the door again, Yves, after we've polished off this lot."

It was quite some time before Red returned with a flagon of wine. Accompanying him was a monk, hands in his sleeves, his hood over his head. The sentries crossed their spears as he approached the door. "You, yes. Who him?" the senior sentry asked in a passable accent.

Red surreptitiously passed the sentry a silver penny. "The wolf: dying. Father get confession."

"Yes, well ..." the man discretely examined the coin. "... if it was left to me, he could spend the rest of eternity in Hell." He glanced at his fellow sentry who was watching and flashed him the coin. The other man raised his eyebrows in agreement. "I suppose so. A man's got to live and fat Odo's wages are poor. Yes, you go. Quick. No take long."

Red opened the door for himself and the monk and went inside, gently closing the door after them. He crept over to

Ralf and Yves. They were sleeping quietly with their heads on the barrel top they used for their table. Red tickled Ralf's nasal hairs, but got no response. He turned to the monk with a smile that showed he had his two front teeth missing. "Like babies. The bag?" The monk pulled out a leather bag from his voluminous sleeves and threw it over. Red opened the bag and took out two cooked geese legs, which he used to replace those on the sleeping soldier's plates, first taking a bite from each. Then he pulled a small flask from the bag and doused the legs with blackberry sauce. After second thoughts, he removed one of the legs and put it by the blackberry stained muzzle of the sleeping Shock. "Whoever wakes first gets the goose!" He went and stood by the monk's side. "Shall I lower him down? I know he can't stand." The monk nodded his assent. Red untied the rope and eased it through the pulley until Godfrew was laying face down on the floor. The monk threw back his hood and eased Godfrew onto his side. Taking the flask of wine that Red had brought in, he trickled some into Godfrew's mouth. After coughing and spluttering a little, Godfrew drank. Slowly, he gathered his strength until he felt able to open his eyes. When he did, he looked confused, for there in front of him was Waltheof, the Earl of Huntingdon.

"So, it is you, young thane of Garrat," Waltheof said, as he proffered some more of the watered wine. He looked up at the leader of his hearth troops. "You were right, Red."

"I know. I told you so, Waltheof. I may be getting old, but I am not getting daft. At least, not yet." Red sat on the floor beside Godfrew. "Careful with the wine, Waltheof. Don't give him too much."

Godfrew sipped the wine while he could, never taking his eye off of the earl. "Yes, young thane, I wondered if it was you when they brought you in the other night, but you have changed somewhat. Your hair? Where has it gone? That's why I got Red to come and take a look at your eye. That eye of yours certainly marks you." He chuckled "No, you are not dreaming, young man, nor is your nightmare over." Waltheof put the now empty wine flask down. "You have caused me some embarrassment. I wish you had come for your horses before the odious Odo arrived. I had told my staller to help you and the others when you came back and asked for them, so there should not have been any trouble. I may have been forced to make my peace with the Normans, but it doesn't mean I like them any the more. Bad timing though, young thane ... bad timing." He tapped Red on the knee. "Shall I risk feeding him, Red?"

The hearth troop leader thought for a while before shaking his head. "Too risky. If he vomits, those Breton buggers will add two and two together and know that it wasn't just tiredness that made them sleep. Just get some fluid into him and hopefully he will last a while."

"You don't know Red, do you, young thane?" Waltheof asked Godfrew, not expecting an answer. "When I was eight summer's old, my father took me away from my nurses and the priests and gave me to a young house carl to foster." He turned his attention to Red. "You were a lot better looking in those days, Fostri ... and you had more hair."

"I lost them both looking after you, you young bugger." Red fingered the remaining top half of his left ear lobe. "That escapade of yours at Stamford Bridge almost finished me off for good."

"Do you like his new beauty mark, young thane?" Waltheof asked Godfrew. "Show him, Red." The old hearth trooper smirked and tipped his bald pate down for Godfrew to see. There was a red scar that ran around the back of his skull from ear to ear and ended at the jagged end of the reduced left ear lobe. "Some Viking with an axe decided to have a look and see if old Red had any brains!"

"He didn't find many, Waltheof," Red chuckled.

"What to do with you, young thane. What to do. I don't think you should be left to the Norman's tender mercy, but I can't set you free either. Red and I will ponder the problem. Meantime, I'm afraid you will have to stand up with help from the pulley, though I'm sure Red will let you keep both feet on the ground." Earl Waltheof got up and wandered over to where the soldiers lay sleeping. Casting around the back, he found the wolf-skin cloak and Godfrew's axe and saxe. He rolled the saxe in the cloak, undid the rope belt at his waist and shoved it up his habit. The axe, he threw to Red—who had re-hoisted Godfrew. Red slipped the weapon under his cloak and tied it across his back by its leather thong.

The Return West

"If we meet again, young thane, I trust it will be in happier circumstances." Waltheof pulled the hood over his head and waited at the door for Red to open it. "Benedicti," he said, before going back outside.

Ralf opened an eye and looked at the snoring Yves opposite him. Relieved that he had not been caught out sleeping on duty, Ralf stretched and then resumed eating his meal.

* * *

"Saxons pigs." The Breton Captain rode at the head of his mounted party as it passed along the well-travelled Ermine Street and through the Chipping Woods.

The plump, freckle-faced soldier holding the reins to the pack horse that was burdened with Godfrew called across to the dark, squat soldier riding the other side: "What's up with old pig-face?"

"Shhh." The dark soldier looked intensely at the Captain's back, but there was no sign that their leader had heard what had been said. "Honestly, Rainald, you will get us flogged with that mouth of yours."

"Saxons pigs," repeated the Breton Captain, as he took off his conical helmet. "Goddamn those Saxons." He pulled down the mail hood of his hauberk and wiped the top of his balding head with his snot rag before muttering again, "Saxons pigs."

"Robert, what did old ... you know who ... say? Something is eating him." Rainald gave the pack horse a yank to make it quicken its pace and ease the strain on his arm.

"Keep your voice down!" Robert hissed. "Look, do I now speak Breton? Well, do I?" The squat man-at-arms nudged his horse forward until it was near the rump of the horse in front. "Yves. Yves."

Yves allowed his horse to drop back a little. "What's up, little frog? Need another wee-wee stop?"

"Stop pissing around." Robert paused to see if the Captain had noticed the change in the position of the riders, but the Captain seemed engrossed in getting his mail hood back on again. "Pig-face is in a mood. What's he saying? You're a Breton. What's he moaning about?"

"He is complaining about the poor quality of his men and saying how he is going to have them all beaten and branded when he gets them back to Rochester." Yves looked sideways and watched to see how the other man had taken the information. Robert went red, then white. "No, only joking. I think he is bitching about us having to leave Huntingdon and take the prisoner back to base to finish off the interrogation."

"You're an evil bastard, Yves. No wonder you get on so well with ..." Robert stopped himself from using the nickname for the Breton Captain. "... with the Captain." The horses bumped and Robert's mount skittered before allowing itself to be manoeuvred back alongside the other horse again. "I don't know why he is unhappy about leaving. It was getting nasty there. Arrogant Saxons! It was bad enough when we first got there, but at least it was a cold hostility. The last couple of days they started deliberately bumping into you in the hall or the yard—spilling their drink down you, spitting at your feet, flicking their nose pickings in your direction. Oh, yes, it was all right for you in the store ... with only a trussed up Saxon to deal with ... do you know that when I was on sentry duty, yesterday morning, there was a group of them with their hunting hounds ... and they were getting their goddamned dogs to come over and piddle on our legs! Arrogant Saxons."

"I thought you smelled nice," Yves smirked. "I think it was the noise that did it. The old Lord and Master Odo stopped any work on the Captain's toy at night. From what I can gather, the noise of your friend ..." Yves nodded his head back toward the pack horse where Godfrew was draped across the animal's back, his wrists tied to his ankles. "... got on our Saxon host's nerves. They didn't seem to appreciate our way of asking their fellow countryman questions." Yves rested his lance in the crook of his left arm and tilted his helmet back by the nasal guard to try and get some cool air around his face. "It is sticky. I thought it would get cooler once we got in among the trees." He half-removed the helmet and was tempted to hang it on his saddle, but a look at his Captain's back made him change his mind. "A bit squeamish ... the Saxons... surprising, really ... especially as most of the ones I've met seem to be half-Viking ... from what you hear told about these Vikings, one would have thought they would have enjoyed a 'vigorous' questioning. No, I think we had to leave after that Earl ... Wal ... whatever ... complained to the old Lord and Master. The mass priest thought that Wal ... what is his name, anyway ...the priest said something about not being able to 'guarantee our safety' .. and 'In view of our Lord King's wish to reconcile the peoples, it is not really appropriate' ... these things and the like."

"Yes, I'm pleased to be on the way back home. I've a little Saxon of my own I want to be vigorous with ... though hopefully we won't have to bother with talking!" Robert let his horse slow until he was back on station with Rainald. "It's all right, young Rainald. The Captain is just not pleased with having to go back home with that thing." He jerked his thumb at the pack horse and the trussed up Godfrew. "I take it that he is still alive?"

"He grunted a bit when I prodded him a while ago." Rainald twisted in the saddle and glanced at the pack horse. The movement caused a trickle of sweat to run down his nose and drip onto his chin. "He is still breathing ... though I'm about to croak myself with the heat. I thought it wasn't supposed to get hot over here?"

"Keep quiet." Robert inclined his head toward the Captain, "I believe 'It' is getting ready to say something."

The Captain held up his left hand. After allowing a few seconds for the party to halt, he turned his mount around and faced his men. "You ignorant lot have no doubt failed to notice that we are now well into the woods." The horses all fidgeted. Their tails swished and their flanks twitched, as gnats and flies settled in to irritate them. The Captain pulled on his reins and steadied his animal. "There is a slight bend ahead. The locals seemed to have failed to keep the trees cut back from the roadside. If there is going to be trouble, it will be along this stretch. I want you all to be on the alert. Keep your eyes peeled ... keep close together... and ensure that you hold your lances ready for action." He gave his head a quick shake to dislodge a fly that had crept under his helmet, attracted by the salt from his sweat. "There will be no dosing. It does not pay, does it Jean? Is your back still sore from the flogging you got last time? Yes? Good! Let's get moving again ... just be ready." A quick kick in the mount's ribs... a pull on the reins ... and the Captain was off again ... but at a slower pace. As they neared the curve in the road, the trees closed in and formed an arch over their heads. The density of the trees muffled all sound.

Even the birds fell silent.

Just as he reached the apex of the curve—just where he expected it—a man came out of the bushes, stood in front of the Breton Captain and held up his hand for him to stop. The man was not tall—but looked taller than he was—for he stood on his toes with his right leg and he leaned on a quarter-staff for support. The Captain looked him over. The man was dressed in badly-cured leather garments. On his head was a peculiar hat made from a badger skin that looked as if the animal was still alive and sitting on the man's head.

"Get out of my way filth!" yelled the Captain. The man stood his ground. "Ralf!" called the Captain. "Ralf, get over here. You speak some English. Tell this filth to get out of the way or I will have him run down."

Ralf obediently rode to the Captain's side: "You, man. You go. You go quick. You go or die. Big chief say you go fast." He shook his lance at the man.

"Piss off," replied the badger-hatted man. "This is common land. I have the right to be here. Have you, Frenchman?"

Ralf looked at the Captain. "He said he won't move, Captain."

"Run him down. I don't like the idea of hanging around in one place for too long." The Captain turned and called to the others in his snuffling voice. "Keep your eyes peeled and be ready to move fast." He turned back to Ralf: "Go on then, run him down. Just make sure that you kill him. I don't want to have to stop to finish him off."

Ralf couched his lance and charged at the man. Badger hat just stood and smiled. At the last possible moment, he moved to Ralf's left—thus avoiding the lance head—and struck the rider across the stomach with his staff. Ralf crashed to the ground with a resounding thump. Before he had a chance to get up, the badger man struck him under the chin with the end of his staff and Ralf's head went back with a loud 'snap'.

"Charge!" yelled the Captain at the top of his voice. "Charge and keep going. It's a trap!" The other Frenchmen were only too happy to obey and spurred their mounts forward. The badger man, despite his physical infirmity, leaped out of the way and back into the bushes.

"You're keen!" quipped Rainald, as one of the two back riders overtook him. "Oh, shit." The rider had an arrow that came out through his chest. The shaft had passed right through his ring-coat and had sunk into his horse's neck. The maddened animal charged on, overtaking all the others. Rainald looked over his shoulder. The other back marker was lying on the ground, an arrow protruding through his neck whilst another transfixed his leg, slowing him down as he tried to scrabble toward his horse that had now stopped to graze the roadside grass."Shit, shit, shit." Rainald tugged on the pack horse's reins and dug his spurs into his own mount. It was then that he was hit in the back by three arrows, the top and bottom one coming through his chest, the middle one only showing as a bump under the front of his coat. He fell from the saddle and his horse ran on after the Captain and the others. As the pack horse slowed, the badger man came out of the bushes and grabbed its bridle. He held the horse still and waited for the others in the ambush party to join him.

"Did you see that, Leofwine? I always said you were a big girl. Tosti and me sent our arrows right through the bugger. You only just managed to get yours to stick in." Clunn kicked Rainald back over on his face. "Hey, Gareth," he called to the badger man. "Have the rest gone, or are they on the way back?"

"On the way back." Gareth led the pack horse back down the road past the wolf pack, as they lined up across the track. Tosti, Clunn, Leofwine and Edgar pulled their bowstrings back to their ears and let their arrows fly at the approaching French. Yves took two arrows in the chest and Robert one in the leg. The fourth arrow hung from the chest of the Captain's horse. The two remaining Frenchmen reined their horses to a halt.

"You silly sod, Leofwine," chided Clunn, "You were supposed to get the big one with the ugly face. I had already marked that one at the front. What's the point of putting two arrows in one man when one arrow will do."

The Breton Captain shook his mangled fist at the wolves. "Saxons pigs. I will be back for that wolf later!"

"What did he say?" Tosti asked Gareth, as the badger man and Puta started to untie Godfrew and lower him to the ground.

"Who knows." Gareth stood up. Using his quarter-staff, he swung up the road to face the Breton who still sat watching. "Piss off!" The Captain saw Edgar notching another arrow and decided to follow Gareth's advice. He turned and rode away, taking the wounded Robert with him.

"My, Master Wulf," chirped Puta as he cut through the leather thongs binding Godfrew's wrists. "You do smell, somewhat."

"You get used to it, Puta." Godfrew gladly took a proffered flask of ale and sipped it slowly. "You hold your water for the first day, then you have to let it go. You think you can hold your bowels. How long did they have me?"

"Nine days, Master Wulf ... and another one and a half on the road." Edgar sat behind Godfrew and let his leader lean back to rest his head on his chest.

"That long? I lost track," Godfrew croaked. "But, Puta, your bowels ... you cannot hold them forever, no matter how you try." He took his left hand in his right, pulled it from the dirt of the road and laid it across his lap. "Man, I stink. I didn't notice till now. Having my nose under a horse's crotch, I thought it was him!"

"There will be no horses near your nose for a while. From here we walk, though just what we are to do with you wolf man, I don't know." Gareth leaned forward on his staff and observed Godfrew.

"And you are?" Godfrew asked.

"Gareth," the badger man replied. "Gareth the Forester."

"Welsh, then are you?" Godfrew allowed Puta to undo his belt and start cutting down his soiled and stinking britches. Shock edged forward on his belly and commenced to gently lick his master's dirty face, nibbling at a stubborn piece of regurgitated food stuck to his cheek.

"My father was. So my mother tells me. I am from near Chester. At times, the Welsh raid that far from Offa's dyke. She says she gave me a Welsh name to remind her of where I came from." Gareth showed no emotion as he told his tale. "Earl Waltheof sends his regards and says that he is sorry he had to wait so long before helping you. He said it was due to 'necessary politics'." Gareth went back into the bushes and came out with Godfrew's wolf-skin cloak, the saxe and Neckbiter. "He told me to give you these."

"Where do we go from here, Gareth of Chester?" Puta had removed the fouled britches and had started to clean Godfrew up with a wet rag, being very careful around Godfrew's damaged left leg.

"I'm on my way to visit my family in Chester. I always go there to celebrate Michael Mass with them. Each year, the Earl lets me go. I'll take you part of the way back. I know the hidden routes."

"Thank you, Gareth." Puta helped Godfrew roll on his side and then started to clean Godfrew's buttocks.

"Hey, look at this!" Clunn beamed a yellow-toothed smile, "Look!" His right hand held a long sausage and his left an opened cloth wrap containing thick, ham flavoured pea pudding. "Gifts from the Normans. I think that this is going to be a rewarding return home."

* * *

The wolf pack spent the rest of the summer and early autumn limping its way back to Lydbury. At first, Godfrew's injuries prevented him from either walking or riding. The wolves moved slowly from place to place—keeping to the woods, always seeking a safe haven to leave their pack leader and the extra burden of Edgar's family. They sought out small priories with only English inhabitants, or sole hermits. Once satisfied that Godfrew and the others were safe, the pack would disperse and scavenge. Where the woods were thin, they raided farms and holdings held by the Normans or their Frenchmen. Where the woods were thick, they plundered any travellers who spoke the wrong tongue. Only when the pickings became thin—or the outrage too great—did they move on.

On one occasion, Godfrew had the amusement of listening to an outraged French prior complaining in heavily-accented Latin that he and his party had been robbed by a "yellow-toothed rat and other obnoxious vermin" who had not only taken their asses with all their food and clothing, but also the sandals from their feet because: "Jesus walked bare foot with his cross to Calvary and you are supposed to be walking in his footsteps."

By the time the wolves had reached the expanse of Sherwood, Godfrew was able to walk slowly by tying a rope to the end of his left foot and lifting it like a puppet master. From then on, he no longer needed to be carried by the men or transported in a stolen cart. After crossing the Pennine hills, Gareth left to go to his home at Chester—well past his usual date of Michael Mass. By now, Godfrew's leg muscles had mended sufficiently to allow him to walk unaided, but he now walked with a distinctive rolling gate. It took a conscious effort to get the leg to make its first move.

The leg may have improved, but the shoulder had not. The movement had never come back. He could no longer raise his arm above his shoulder. During the day, the nagging pain merged into the background, as other matters filled his mind—but at night, pain was all there was. No matter how much love Shock showed him—or what herbal infusion the monks or nuns gave him—Godfrew rarely slept. Unable to earn his keep with physical work, Godfrew wrote and translated for his hosts. At night, when the pain became unbearable, he got up and worked by flickering candlelight in hope of losing himself in a drowsy dozing the next day. As the tiredness increased, his judgments became less reliable. The wolf pack consulted him less and less.

Slowly, Clunn had assumed the leadership of the wolves. After Gareth left, he took total control. As a result, the actions of the wolves became less predictable. They were less selective in their targets. Soon, any English working for Frenchmen began to contribute to the pack's survival. The need to move on became more frequent. By the time they reached Earl Edric's land, they were being hunted by every man wanting to claim the five silver pennies for a Wolfshead. Long gone were the times when they could count on the English to give them shelter from the Normans. Even religious houses bolted their doors when they saw them coming. Gone, too, were the stolen horses that had made them too easy to track. As they stood at the tree line on Lynchgate Hill, overlooking the holding of Lydbury, they were foot sore, hungry and filthy.

The Return West

A party of horsemen left the holding and headed toward them. As they neared, Tosti studied them, fingering the thick white scar that ran along the ear that had almost been severed at Shrewsbury. "Here comes Nathan Priestson, Gavin Gormless, Magnus Wild Swipe ... and guess who's in the lead? None other than Stanley Sharpsword. He's come up in the world." A wry grin crossed his face. "I wonder how the others have taken that! I bet Nathan is well pissed-off. He always thought he should be top dog."

"Come on." Clunn started forward. "Let's show them that the mighty warriors have returned home for their rapturous welcome."

The others moved forward with him. "Come, Master Wulf." Puta put his hand under Godfrew's elbow and helped him get going. "I'm sure you will be glad to see your wife and the children. You've a new son you that you haven't met yet." Godfrew walked at the rear of the wolf pack, his thin matted hair flopping as he carefully moved down the slope. The incline did not suit his rolling gate. At his heel walked Shock. His black coat was covered with dried mud.

At ten paces, the horsemen spread out in a line and halted. Stanley rode up to the men. "So, it is you, then. We thought as much." He turned his horse—the other riders did the same—and they all slowly rode back to the holding, leaving the wolves to follow.

"Not very friendly," Clunn said to no one in particular. "They could at least have given us a ride down." He led the others to Lydbury, using his bow stave as a walking stick, no longer worrying about keeping it ready to use as a weapon.

They straggled in through the gate and looked for familiar faces, but the yard seemed empty. The few people around were too busy with their tasks to notice them. Leaning against the wall of the hall was Dagobert the Reeve. "Before you do anything else, you lot, go and get yourselves cleaned up." The wolves started to head off. "Master Wulf, a word first."

Godfrew slowly made his way over. "My wife?" Godfrew's voice still had the harsh tone it had acquired from his days in the stone storehouse at Huntingdon. "Have you seen my wife?"

"At prayers in St. Michael's chapel, no doubt. It is where she spends most of her time these days." Dagobert ran his eyes over the dishevelled figure in front of him, visibly shocked at Godfrew's appearance. "I did not call you over to tell you of your wife's new obsession, Wulf." His voice and eyes became serious. "Earl Edric wants to have words with you as soon as you have tidied yourself up."

"From your voice, it is not to congratulate me on an errand well run, Master Reeve." Godfrew propped himself awkwardly against the wall, using his right hand to position his left arm more comfortably.

"Not for me to say, old friend." Dagobert allowed sadness to tinge his voice. "But do try and look smart. The Earl always goes a lot on looks. Look smart, for your own sake."

"Does my wife still sleep in the same hut?" Godfrew let his eye wander to the familiar turf roofed sleeping place with its unflowering thorn bush.

"Yes, when she does go to bed. Now go and get ready to see the Earl. Don't keep him waiting too long." As Godfrew slowly walked to the hut, Dagobert shook his head sadly before going past the guards into the hall.

Godfrew was amazed at the change to the hut. Instead of confusion and smelly baby clothes, all was clean and tidy. He slowly removed his filthy garments and washed his body in herb scented water from the bowl by the bed. Inside a new plain wooden box, he found some of his clothes—all washed and darned. He put them on and then made his way to the bed. He slid a panel of the wooden ceiling to one side, put in his hand and retrieved the gold dragon arm band that Earl Edric had given him, put it on, then slid the panel back in place. He went out again into the yard and looked around, trying to guess what was going on in what had now become unfamiliar surroundings. When he looked toward the chapel, he saw figures heading toward him. He squinted to try and make them out.

"I thought you were dead." Elfgifu had changed as much as the sleeping hut. Gone was the unkempt hair and the unwashed body. Gone were the baggy, food-stained clothes. Before him, Godfrew saw what looked like a novice nun in a clean white habit and shorn hair.

The Return West

"Elfgifu?" His wife seemed taken aback when she heard Godfrew's changed voice. "Beloved, is that you?" After a false start when his left leg refused to move, Godfrew rolled forward to embrace his wife. Instead of throwing her arms open wide, she held out her hands to take his and kept him at arm's length.

"Things have changed since you left." Elfgifu's face was serene and peaceful.

"Yes, I saw the hut." Godfrew tried move in closer, but stopped when he felt his wife resist.

"I thought you were dead. There was no word. I thought you were dead."

"I nearly was. Now, gift of the elves, give me a kiss. I have waited so long." Godfrew turned Elfgifu's left hand around so that her arm was locked against the joint and levered it out of the way. "Just a kiss, for now." He moved to a hand's breadth from her face: "Elfgifu? A kiss?"

"A kiss," she agreed, "but a kiss of peace only. When I thought you were dead, I thought that I would die also. My heart and mind were in turmoil. I found peace with God." Godfrew gave her a puzzled look. She continued: "Jesus healed my broken heart. After Njal's birth I took a vow of chastity."

Godfrew laughed and pulled back to study her face, "Elfgifu, you jest? I am back now. The vow can be broken." He closed in again, put his lips to his wife's and kissed her, but she did not respond. "Elfgifu?" Godfrew's hoarse voice had an air of desperation to it. "Elfgifu?"

"I love you, Wulf. I always will, but from now it will be a chaste love." Elfgifu studied Godfrew's face, her eyes darting: "You do understand?"

"No, my love, I do not understand." Godfrew pulled away. "I must go now to Earl Edric and hear my doom. Return to your God and pray for me."

"I will pray for you. I will pray that you understand. I will also pray for your protection and that you will be able to change your way of life." Elfgifu let go of her husband's hands and started to return to the chapel. It was then that Godfrew remembered the others standing with Elfgifu.

"Welcome home, cousin Wulf," Oakleaf smiled. In her arms was Godfrew's latest son Njal and hanging on to her skirts were his elder boys, Jaul and Moithar, kicking dust at each other. "It is good to have you back. I will find some better clothes for you tonight."

"Thank you cousin, yes ..." Godfrew couldn't help noticing that Oakleaf was very much a woman now, broad of hip and full in breast, "... yes, I would appreciate that."

"Till later, then." Oakleaf smiled again and, gathering her brood, went with a hip-swinging sway toward the hut. Shock trailed behind her, keeping just out of reach of the grasping Jaul.

Godfrew watched her until she entered the sleeping quarters, then he went past the guards into the hall. Inside, Dagobert sat at a side table sharpening quills with his eating knife. "Ah, there you are, Wulf. You have seen your wife?" Godfrew nodded. "She did think you were dead. We all did. Still ..." he broke off to muse for a moment, "you'd better come and see Earl Edric."

The two men crossed the hall, mounted the dais, and stood before the door to the Earl's private chambers. Torquil stood guard, but he showed no sign of recognising Godfrew. Torquil knocked on the door and went in. A few seconds later, the hearth troop leader came out again and indicated to Dagobert and Godfrew to go in. Seated on the bed, dressed in a loose flowing red silk gown, sat Earl Edric. He watched Godfrew's rolling gate and noticed the slumped left shoulder.

"Things have not been kind to you, Woden's Wulf." The Earl pointed to a stool in front of the bed. "Pray, be seated. You have seen your wife?"

"My Lord." Godfrew gratefully sat down and used his right hand to pull his left into his lap.

"She thought you were dead. We all thought you were dead. In view of what has been happening recently, it might have been better if you had been dead." Edric's watery blue eyes ran over Godfrew. "Clunn seems over bold these days."

"My Lord."

"Come on, man, explain." Edric's voice rose a little, "Tell me of Clunn the Rat."

"I am not fit to lead the men at the moment. I don't sleep much. I, I ..." Godfrew's voice started to crack. Edric looked at Dagobert and indicated that he should pour Godfrew a drink. Godfrew sipped the thin ale before continuing. "I don't seem to think so clear at the moment, my Lord."

"That is apparent ... that rat Clunn runs feral ... if not kept under a barrel." Edric went silent for some time. Eventually, he spoke again: "I like you, Wulf. You have always done your best for me. Even when things did not go right, I always knew it was not for want of either planning or trying." The Earl closed his eyes, then slowly opened them again. "What am I going to do with you? You know that I have had to make my peace with the Norman king? That has restricted my actions, both with you and for myself. What am I going to do with you?" Again, Edric fell into silent, deep thoughts.

The ale—thin though it was—started to affect Godfrew and he started to doze. Earl Edric's voice brought him back: "... so as part of my 'bond of good behaviour' I have had to agree to betroth my eldest daughter to that upstart Mortimer's son, young Ralf. I suppose it is not a bad marriage—a reasonable alliance that will help me if I get any more trouble from the Welsh. Well, anyway, they are due here next week. Guess what he wants for a betrothal gift? The heads of certain wolves that have ravaged his lands of late." Edric shook his head sadly. "If only I didn't like you, Wulf, my life would be so much easier."

"My Lord." Godfrew's mouth went dry again and he finished sipping the ale.

Edric got off the bed and slowly paced the floor in front of Godfrew. Suddenly he stopped, "Got it!" he exclaimed. "Right, young Wulf. You spent time working with Dagobert, yes? So you know book-keeping and records. You can read and write Latin as well as English, yes? You have a band of men who need a new home and a fresh start. Yes, it is all falling into place." Edric sat down again, his face alight, well pleased with himself. "When I was at court, eating humble pie, I became friendly with young Ralf of East Anglia." He looked at Godfrew and laughed. "No, he is not a Norman. His father was brought up there with old King Edward the sword shy, but he was English. Mind, Ralf's mother is a Breton. Still, I am sure that you can put up with that. After all, I understand that your wife is half-Cymry. Anyway, Ralf was telling me that he is having problems getting anyone to properly assess some new holdings for him. Everyone is on the make, particularly now that there is so much confusion. I shall send word to him that I have found the very man to do the job." Edric clapped his hands together with glee. "You will have a new job and I won't have to hand you and the others over to the mercy of that evil old thief, Mortimer. Excellent. I do surprise myself at times."

"Where did you say I was to go, my Lord?" Godfrew screwed up his eye and tried to see the Earl better.

"Suffolk. You'll like it. I went hunting there once ... it was very nice." Edric played with the ends of his moustache. "Wulf," he became serious again, "you have served me well and I hope that I have been a good Lord to you."

"The best, my Lord. I don't really want to ..."

"But you have to," interrupted the Earl. "Things have changed ... perhaps forever. I cannot keep you here. I even had to move that old friend of yours, Godwine, away from his new holding at Martinsfield and back into the hills to keep him safe. The Normans' have long memories and they hate wolves ... particularly successful ones! You have to go. This way, you can go with honour." Edric pulled a small ring from the little finger of his right hand. It was in the shape of a sword curled around on itself—the blade silver, the hilt gold, the pommel a bright ruby. "Take this and remember me." Godfrew got up and tried to kneel. Edric caught his elbows and stood him back on his feet. "Wulf ... we are friends ... remember that. I will send your wolves with you."

"The Earl of Kent ..."

"Fat Odo the obnoxious? You don't want to work for him, surely?" Edric returned to his place on the bed, flicking the edges of his silk gown clear so that he did not sit on them.

"He has a dislike for me, my Lord."

"Fortunately for you, Ralf of East Anglia has a dislike for him, too. I doubt he will come visiting." Edric smiled pleasantly. "It really does seem as if this job is made for you."

"Clunn ..."

"Forget Clunn. He will be a kitten rather than a rat when he leaves with you. I shall speak with him."

As Godfrew opened the door to go out, Edric's wife, the Lady Gondul, came in holding hands with Joanna, Elfgifu's cousin. "Ah, Edric, my beloved, I believe we are to be entertained this afternoon by one of your errant wolves?" She plunked herself on the bed beside her husband. Joanna sat at her feet and the Lady stroked the maid's straight ginger hair. "What fun."

Outside, Clunn stood between two of the Lady Gondul's hearth troopers and behind him stood the bulk of Wendlewulf.

* * *

When Elfgifu came into the sleeping hut, she found Godfrew sitting on the floor digging a hole in the earth floor where the bed normally sat. Jaul and Moithar played in the dirt whilst Oakleaf nursed the baby on the displaced bed. Elfgifu went to where her husband sat. As she neared, Godfrew pulled a thin gold bar from the hole and passed it to Oakleaf who put it alongside the other two lying on the bed covers. "Elfgifu, my love," Godfrew went back to digging and his voice became muffled by his body as he worked, "your prayers have been answered. I am to have a new life style. Just keep praying about me gaining understanding for our new relationship."

Woden's Wolf

The Peace

"**D**o you really have to go, Wulf?" asked Elfgifu, as they stood outside their small house in Ipswich.

Godfrew stroked his left arm to ease the numbness that constantly plagued it. "It is my job. I have to go." He reached and stroked her cheek affectionately. "I have spent all winter with you whilst I went over the books and studied the details of Earl Ralf's holdings. Now that it is spring, I must actually go and look at them." He studied his wife's face. "You do understand, don't you?"

"You are always leaving me, Wulf. Always." Elfgifu started to cry. Pulling a small rag from her sleeve, she turned and went back into the house. Oakleaf followed her. Njal hung over her right shoulder, a struggling Moithar was tucked under her left arm and Jaul was hanging to her skirt, pulling faces at his younger brothers. As she was about to go through the door, Oakleaf turned and gave Godfrew a smile before disappearing into the darkness within.

Godfrew sighed and stared after the women. He stood there for some time before finding the strength to break away and head toward his men waiting with the horses. "Ready to go, are we?" he asked them, not expecting an answer. Tosti and Clunn the Earless were already mounted on their small mounts. The animals hung their heads and occasionally sniffed. "Ready, Puta?" Puta cupped his hands and bent his knees, waiting to boost Godfrew into his saddle. Godfrew put his leg into Puta's waiting hands, grabbed hold of the pommel on the saddle with his right hand, then nodded to Puta, who heaved him up. Godfrew then sat in the saddle—his head bowed like the horses—and waited for the pain in his hip and left shoulder to pass. The men waited patiently. Eventually, Godfrew looked up. "Let's go. We have much ground to cover," he croaked.

Puta quickly mounted his stocky pony and rode alongside Godfrew. "Do you like your rouncy, Master Wulf?" The question was tinged with humour.

"Rouncy, Puta?" Godfrew turned slowly in the saddle to face the ginger-headed youth alongside him. "What on earth is a 'rouncy'?"

"You are riding one, Master Wulf. It is what the locals call a hack pony." Puta giggled at his own jest.

"Rouncy. It is a new one on me. You learn a new thing every day." Godfrew nudged his pony to quicken its pace. "I am sure that we will have a lot to learn in these parts." The party rode off toward the town gate. Godfrew led the way—followed by Puta, Tosti and the earless Clunn riding side by side at the rear—with the pack ponies trailing behind.

After leaving the town, they rode to the north and the low-lying wooded hills. Near noon, the road crossed with another. Around the crossroads was a larger party of well-dressed men sprawled on the grass verges, eating and drinking. Closing ranks, Godfrew and his party tightened their reins, ready to run. They were almost past the picnickers when a short, well-dressed balding man gave instructions to a youth who then ran across.

As he came up to Godfrew, the youth grabbed his horse's bridle and pulled it to a stop. Godfrew nervously fingered the hilt of his saxe. "My master would know who you are." Despite being almost as tall as Godfrew, the boy's voice had not yet broken. He sounded like a girl.

When he replied, Godfrew's hoarse voice grated. "I am an under-reeve for Ralf, Earl of East Anglia. I am to conduct a survey for him of his new lands in this county of Suffolk."

"Greetings, Master Reeve." The high pitch of the boy's voice unsettled Godfrew's rouncy. "Perhaps you would meet with my master and tell him of your business?"

Godfrew looked slowly about. The other party consisted of about twenty. Although they were only equipped for hawking, they looked too formidable to upset or run away from. "Your master. May I ask who he is?" The road dust made Godfrew sound even more gravel-voiced than usual.

"William Mallet," the youth squeaked. "I trust you have heard of him?"

"He lost York to Earl Waltheof, I believe." Godfrew watched the boy's face. The boy squirmed. "Don't mention it, Master Reeve. My master lost many friends in that escapade." He looked across to where the Mallet lay sprawled on his side

The Peace

watching them. "My master was a councillor to King Edward the Confessor."

"And to William the Bastard."

The youth went red. "Come, Master Reeve. Come and greet my master."

Godfrew dismounted with difficulty and the others followed suit. The tall boy was soon joined by some others who ran up to hold the horses. Godfrew looked at his men. Puta preened himself, spitting on his hands and smoothing his hair down. Tosti stood stiff legged and stared at the Normans. Clunn fingered the torn remains of ears, his lips curled over his yellow teeth. All were dressed in dusty, patched clothing and looked quite dishevelled. "Steady lads," Godfrew muttered. "Steady. We are on legal business. We are in the right. Steady."

As they came near William Mallet and his inner group, they caught parts of the conversation. They were surprised to find it a mix of both English and Norman French, sometimes both tongues being used in one sentence. As they stood before the great man, he signalled his companions to cease their banter.

"Greetings. May I ask who you are and where you are going?" Mallet's English was perfect and unaccented.

"My Lord, I am Geri Wendlewulf, an under-reeve to Earl Ralf of East Anglia. I am undertaking a survey of his new holdings in the county of Suffolk. We are travelling to his holding of Combs. These are my men." Godfrew eased his weight onto his good leg and stood askew.

William studied Godfrew and the others. "A drink, Master Geri? I insist." He turned and beckoned the squeaky-voiced boy over. "Walter, get some ale for our guests." Mallet then rolled back to face Godfrew's party. "I am sorry to have detained you, but these are troubled times. Please accept refreshment as recompense."

Godfrew looked at his men to see if they liked the idea. Puta was busy eyeing the muscular body of the recumbent man at Mallet's side, but both Tosti and Clunn were rubbing their hands together and licking their dirt-encrusted lips. "Thank you, my Lord. Your generous reputation is well founded." The boy waved them over to a shady oak tree where other youths were getting food and drink ready for them. Shock sat expectantly at the heel of Walter, his tail wagging and tongue drooling.

As they walked away, William Mallet smiled at his nearest companion. "My, my, Frank. Young Ralf must be getting desperate—or they are liars."

"Then why let them go, my Lord?" Despite speaking French, Frank—like his master—wore his hair long and bore dangling moustaches in the English fashion.

"The story is too fabulous to be false." William gave a chuckle, "I doubt young Ralf knows just what he has taken on with that crew ... Geri ... the wolf-skin cloak ... the others ... all ruffians to a man. Wendlewulf! Wolfshead, more like." He picked up his cup of wine and carefully picked out a drowning ant with his well-manicured index finger. "Frank?"

"My Lord."

"Just make sure that our boys check the stock if those wolves pass by any Mallet holdings."

* * *

It was late evening when they arrived at the holding of Combs. The moon was full in a cloudless sky. As the sun had set, the temperature had quickly dropped. The men had wrapped themselves in their cloaks, closing up to try and retain the heat from their horses. Despite the fact that Godfrew had not sent word of his arrival, it was obvious that they were expected. As they rode in, men stood in knots near the horse paddock. Women hung by the doors of their cottages— supposedly watching their children play in the road—acting as if it were normal for their young ones to still be awake after dark. Godfrew led his men toward the paddock and the waiting locals. One of them had two big wolf hounds by his side straining at their leashes, sniffing the air and grumbling in their throats. Shock dropped back behind the pack horses to cover his scent.

Godfrew stopped in front of the man with the hounds. "Are you Ulf, the head man?" Godfrew's voice cracked. He tried to summon enough spit to hawk out the afternoon's road dust, but failed. "Well?"

The man with the hounds shook his head. A man further back moved through the others and stood by Godfrew's bridle. "I'm Ulf. Why do you want to know?"

"You are a Dane?" Godfrew let go of his reins and used his right hand to pull his left down by his side. "I asked if you are a Dane. Well, are you?"

"I am English. So are we all here." The man's belligerence showed in his voice. "What is it to you?"

Godfrew ignored the question. "If you are English, why speak Norse?"

"I speak as my father spoke and his father before him. What is it to you? Are the Normans going to try and make us all speak French? Is that why you are here?" Ulf deliberately trod on the paw of one of the wolf hounds, starting it barking.

"I am not from these parts, but I like the Normans no more than you do. If you insist on speaking Norse, then at least slow your speech down so that I can understand you." Godfrew tilted his wide-brimmed leather slouch hat back from his face. "Now, Ulf, you ask why we are here." Godfrew removed his hat, put it in his left hand and looked down at the man. The moonlight illuminating his face clearly, showed in his blind white eye. "I am Geri Wendlewulf. I have been sent by your master, Earl Ralf of East Anglia, to value his holding here."

Ulf tapped the hound to stop its barking before replying, "We are freemen here ... sokemen. We have no Lord." Ulf stared at Godfrew's face and his voice faltered. "We are sokemen," he reiterated. The statement sounded lame and Ulf knew it.

Godfrew looked at the hounds. They had stopped their straining. As he continued to stare at them, they sat down—first on their haunches, then on their bellies, their heads resting on their paws—watching him. Once happy that the hounds had settled, Godfrew eased himself out of the saddle. He left his horse and stepped around to where Ulf stood. A gentle breeze stirred the wolf-skin cloak. The moonlight reflected off the strands of silver fur at its edges. "I do not argue with you being sokemen." He looked at the faces of each of the local men. "But as each longship has its captain, so each holding has its lord." The men muttered to each other and Godfrew waited for them to cease before continuing: "You are

Woden's Wolf

fortunate. Although your Lord Gyrth, Earl of East Anglia, brother of our beloved King Harold, died in the fight at the Hoar Apple Tree—no doubt with your own sword thane by his side—you have not had a Norman put over you."

"Ralf is Norman," one of the men interjected.

"Earl Ralf is English born of an English father," Godfrew again looked at each man's face, "and he is your Lord—Earl of East Anglia. Consider yourselves lucky. If he had been a Norman, do you think he would have sent us to visit you?" He turned and indicated his sorry and dusty companions. "Well? Do you?" The men again muttered amongst themselves. Godfrew cut through their mumblings, his voice rasping: "No, a Norman would have sent an armed band ... and seeing your insolence they would have burned this place down and killed you one and all ... men, women and children." Godfrew looked at Puta, Tosti and Clunn and gesticulated with his head that they should dismount. "We come from your Lord ... Lord Ralf. Sokemen or not sokemen, he is your master. Now get someone to take care of our animals and find us a place to sleep." Godfrew started to untie his bundle from behind his saddle.

Clunn nudged Tosti in the ribs and raised his eyebrows. Tosti took the hint. "Master Wulf? Food and drink?"

Godfrew turned back to Ulf, "And some food and drink," he added before heading off to relieve himself behind a bush, his distinctive rolling gate made more pronounced by his stiffness from the day's ride.

* * *

The door of the hay barn squeaked open and a shaft of early sunlight edged its way into the darkness. Godfrew stirred from his mead-induced sleep and squinted at the doorway. A young boy peered in at the strangers. Godfrew could see the lad's lips moving as he counted the heads, his breath hanging in the chill air. Shock had heard the noise, too. He struggled free from Godfrew's arms and poked his head out from the wolf-skin cloak.

"Ah!" squealed the boy. "You've got two heads." He turned to run "The wolf man has two heads!"

"No, I haven't. Look!" the boy swivelled his head to look and Godfrew let Shock go. The hound ran over, leaped up on the

The Peace

lad and licked the child's breakfast from his cheeks. "It is only my hound." Godfrew rolled himself onto his good side and slowly got to his feet "Who are you, boy?"

"Robin. Everybody knows that." Robin sat down on the floor, put his arms around Shock and pulled him over for a cuddle. Godfrew opened the barn door more fully and looked out at the houses of the holding, noting that they were in better order than most he had seen in such a holding as this. He turned back to look at Robin. The curly-headed child was wrestling with Shock, blowing in his ears and trying to avoid the hound's responding licks.

Godfrew stiffly went to each of the men and stirred them with his foot, massaging away the numbness in his bad arm as he went. The task complete, he propped himself in the doorway again and watched the hamlet come to life. For the number of houses, there were few people. The number of animals seemed small for the number of stalls, byres and sties. Godfrew sniffed the sharp air and detected wood smoke, so someone was cooking food. He called to the boy. "Robin, can you go ask Ulf where our breakfast is?"

"You want me to see Ulf about breakfast?" the boy asked.

Godfrew nodded his response.

"I don't run errands!" Robin replied indignantly. "Why do you speak so funny?" he asked, changing the subject.

"If you can go and ask Ulf about the food, I will tell you ... and maybe teach you to talk the same way. I'll even let you play with my hound if you like."

"If I want to play with your hound, I shall. I do what ever I want! Everybody lets me. I'm Robin." The child played with Shock's ears, swaying the hound's head from side to side, "But I am very hungry again. I will make Ulf give me some food ... and maybe I will get some for you, too." Robin let go of Shock and stood up. "Come, dog. Follow me." Shock looked at his master. Godfrew pointed to the disappearing back of Robin and Shock scampered after the boy.

"Obnoxious little brat," complained Puta as he pulled his darned wool shirt over his soft white flesh. Beside him, Clunn mumbled and stirred as the shaft of sunlight sought him out. Puta bent down and pulled at the drowsy man's dark beard, "Come, Clunn, my sweet. 'Tis time to rise and eat."

"Eat?" Clunn whispered, his eyes still closed. "Did you say eat?" He rubbed his eyes with his horny hands. "Are you cooking it, my precious?" Clunn propped himself upon his elbows, eyes bleary, pieces of hay poking out of his unkempt hair.

"No, my little Rat. I am not a slave. That nasty Ulf is going to provide it for us." Puta sat behind Clunn and set about removing the hay from Clunn's brown hair prior to combing it. The engraved bone comb lay ready on his plump thigh.

"You are not cooking it?" Clunn opened a blood-shot eye and tried to turn his head to look at Puta, but the youth would not let him interrupt his work on the little man's hair. "Then I don't want it." Clunn tried to slip down into the hay to resume his sleep, but Puta tightened his thighs under Clunn's armpits and clamped his victim in place so that he could finish the grooming.

"Shut up, Clunn ..." Tosti gave Clunn a good-natured smile as he emerged from his bed of hay and stretched luxuriously, "... food ... any food ... sounds good." He strolled over to the door, leaned against the post and looked out onto the green, scratching his crotch contentedly. "A lovely place ... even if it all is a bit flat for me." Tosti's attention was caught by some activity at the end house. "Ah, here comes head man Ulf and that bossy little Robin."

"Have they got food?" asked Clunn, his body still clamped between Puta's thighs, half his hair neat and the rest remaining ragged.

"Well," commented Tosti, "Ulf is carrying pails that steam ... so they either contain hot food, or shit." He glanced across at the restricted man. "Which would you prefer?"

"Food of course!" Puta answered for Clunn. "He hates shit. Don't you, sweetness. Can't even stand the smell of it ... so delicate and precious he is." Clunn struggled, but without success, as Puta ignored him and fluffed up Clunn's hair with his hands, "Don't you look nice? Tosti?" he called across: "Clunn ... doesn't he look nice with his hair combed like this?"

Tosti took a quick look before going back to watch the holding come to life, "Clunn ... look nice ... he would only look good if you combed his hair over his face!" Tosti stretched his neck toward the approaching Ulf: "No, it is food, I can smell it. Eggs mixed in milk and oatmeal porridge. Smells good."

"Any food smells good to you, Tosti the empty-bellied." Puta relaxed his grip on Clunn and shuffled back to drop the man's head into his lap. Satisfied that he had Clunn's head in the right place, he tightened his grip to stop the rat from squirming and commenced to comb his beard, stopping occasionally to hand pick or fret out pieces of dried food. Clunn lay back and enjoyed the attention, getting anxious only when the youth came near the ragged ends of his torn ears. Puta was most careful, so Clunn soon relaxed again.

As Ulf came up to the barn door, Tosti moved inside and followed him. Robin and Shock capered and scampered together—getting under everyone's feet—as they came over to where the head man had put the food down.

"Thank you, Ulf." Godfrew used his good arm to keep his balance on the wall, whilst he carefully slid himself down onto the floor. "Your food is most welcome."

"Robin told me to get it for you, so I had to hurry. My wife was still in bed, so I had to cook it myself." Ulf put his hand around his back and pulled out a bag. From it, he produced wooden platters and horn spoons, which he handed to the men.

"You always do what the child Robin tells you?" asked Godfrew his voice still thick from last night's mead.

"Do I always do what Robin wants?" Ulf waited for Godfrew to confirm that he had understood him correctly. "Of course. We all have to make sure that our Robin is happy and has what ever he wants. It wouldn't be right otherwise."

"I'm Robin," the child called out from a pile of hay where he and Shock were playing hide and seek. "Everyone loves me, don't they, Ulf."

"Of course, Robin. We all love you." Ulf straightened his back and turned to go.

Godfrew tapped his spoon on the side of his platter and the head man turned at the sound. "Ulf, today, before I look around, I would speak to the Manor Moot. At say, midday. Perhaps it would be best if you and I spoke before hand."

"If you wish," Ulf replied indifferently.

"Oh, I do ... in fact, I insist." Godfrew's voice had an edge on it. Ulf caught the changed tone and sharpened his eyes before looking carefully at Godfrew, ready to give a tart reply. It was then he that he noticed Clunn watching him whilst carefully picking his teeth with the point of his saxe.

"As you say ... before the meeting of the Moot." Ulf left, stopping at the door for another appraisal of the strangers before going back to his own house.

As the sun warmed the houses, so the folk emerged—like chicks from their eggs—and went about their business. Godfrew's men wandered about, checking their horses and gossiping with any of the locals who cared to stop. Godfrew stayed in the barn and tried to doze, making up for another night of broken sleep. Although he found that strong mead helped, his night's sleep was always shallow, disturbed by the pains in his shoulder and arm. The sun was not far from its zenith when Ulf came in, accompanied by young Robin—still with Shock in tow. Godfrew half opened his good eye and watched the approaching man from under the wide brim of his hat. Ulf was of medium height and slightly plump. His hair was light brown, receding from his temples, with wisps of silver that showed in his short beard. A white scar on his left cheek spoke of a time when he might have been a warrior—long before his pot belly had appeared. Underneath Ulf's bold exterior, a nervousness was displayed with his constant need to run his fingers under the soft leather belt with bright embroidery that encompassed his girth. Godfrew waited until Ulf was almost upon him before speaking: "At last, Ulf. I had started to wonder if you were going to come. I would have hated having to send for you."

Ulf jumped. "I thought you were asleep." He ran a hand over his hair.

"I never sleep, Ulf." Godfrew pressed his back against the wall—half-rolled against it, then pushed himself up. Despite his care, Godfrew knocked his arm and he stood with his face to the wall until the waves of pain had washed over him and faded. His face still lined with pain, he turned and faced the village head man. "You do not seem keen to speak to me, Ulf. You wouldn't have a bad conscience, would you?"

"Did you say a 'bad conscience'?" Ulf went red. "To have a 'bad conscience', I would have had to have done wrong!"

The Peace

"And have you?" Godfrew pulled the straw stopper out of an ale flask and spat it on the ground before taking a swig in an attempt to unclog his throat and voice.

"I don't have to take this. I am going." Ulf turned and went to leave. Tosti and Clunn stepped into the barn. Both had their saxes in their hands.

"Are you, Ulf?" Godfrew took another swig whilst the head man backed into the hay barn, warily watching Tosti and Clunn as they followed him. "Perhaps you are right. You are going ... but where, I wonder? Earl Ralf's dungeon?"

Ulf stood in front of Godfrew: "You wanted to talk, Master Geri. I am here."

"Good, good." Godfrew looked over Ulf's shoulder. "Tosti, Clunn. Would you be so kind as to roll a couple of barrels this way for us to sit on ... and another for a table." Godfrew changed his focus. "I find all this standing hard, Ulf. Old age I suppose."

"Old age, Master Geri? Your face says that you are but a young man." Ulf studied the under-reeve's boyish face.

Godfrew pulled off his hat, revealing his balding pate and tossed it onto the top of the barrel Tosti had placed there for use as a table. "Looks can be deceptive, Ulf." Godfrew sat down and indicated that Ulf should do likewise. "Now let us talk about Combs and what has happened here since your Lord Gyrth died."

"Lord Gyrth ... now he was a good Lord ... he spoke the same tongue as us." Ulf sat, but sat on the barrel's edge. The iron rim cut into his legs and caused the flesh to hang either side.

"Lord Gyrth was half-Danish, like his brother, our late King Harold. That is why he spoke your tongue as well as mine. I once met his mother—a very powerful lady with a strong mind, most definitely the Danish princess." Godfrew emptied the flask and put it on the floor.

"You met the Lady Gutha?" Ulf seemed surprised.

"I meet all that family. I fought with King Harold's house carls, though I owed no man lordship, except by choice." Godfrew's voice at last started to free itself.

"The King's house carls all died at the battle on the hill ... so did his brothers!"

"So they did ... so they did." Godfrew pulled out a small book from inside his shirt and laid it upon the table. "And yet, here I am! It is a strange and complex world, Ulf." He opened the book: "Ah, here we are. Combs: 12 sokemen all owing rent and no service, except you. You pay no rent, but render service by keeping the hall ready for the Earl and arranging for his demesne to be worked until he puts in a reeve. In exchange for this, you get the fourth penny. A good arrangement is it not, provided you do the job!"

"I do my job." Ulf fidgeted on the barrel's edge, his hands holding the iron rim either side of his thighs. "You can't say that I don't do my job."

"You do your job?" Godfrew was now having less problems understanding the Danish Norse the locals spoke, but he still found it hard at times to pick out the words when Ulf spoke, as the man's tones were seemingly affected by his damaged cheek. "Let us see how well you do your job." Godfrew opened the book and turned to the appropriate page. He studied the writing—one side in an old crabbed hand, the words fading, the other ornately written in bright red ink. "It would seemed that since the survey conducted by Earl Gyrth—when he took over from the late king as Earl of East Anglia—and the survey conducted by Earl Ralf's man last spring, the amount of stock held by you on behalf of the Earl had decreased by two thirds." He looked up and cocked his head. "Doing your job, Ulf?"

"The thane who held the holding for our beloved Earl Gyrth was a better farmer than I." Ulf slid himself back on the barrel top to relieve the discomfort caused by the iron cutting into his legs. "Then we had the cattle murane for the two springs before Ralf's man came. Also," continued Ulf, warming to his story, "the Vikings raided last year and carried off most of the swine. Things have been bad here since Hakon the thane died at Earl Gyrth's side."

"Oh, I am sad to hear of such misfortune, Ulf." Sarcasm dripped from Godfrew's tongue. "The crop returns are lower too. More misfortune?"

"Bad harvests," agreed Ulf, "and a lot less land under the plough."

"So more pasture then?" Godfrew asked pleasantly. He placed his elbows on the open book, fingers steepled.

The Peace

"More pasture, yes. But not the animals to graze it." Ulf smiled ingratiatingly.

Godfrew closed his good right eye and left Ulf to stare at the blind whiteness of his left while he contemplated what had been said. "I find your information most distressing, Ulf," he eventually said. His eye was still closed and his voice dreamy. "I see things differently: I see most of Earl Ralf's cattle being looked after by the men of Stow. I see his herd of swine hidden in Barking's Wood and cared for by the men of Battisford. All this in exchange for doing the same for them when Earl Ralf's county reeves come calling." Godfrew slowly opened his eye and looked at the stunned Ulf. "I may have only one eye, but it is far-sighted, Ulf the thief."

Ulf half got up off the barrel as if to reach out for Godfrew, but Clunn and Tosti came and stood by their leaders side, saxes drawn. Clunn put one hand on the barrel top, pushed his face within a hand's breadth of Ulf's, and breathed his foul breath on him. Ulf sat down suddenly, buried his head in his hands and burst out crying. In the end the sobs ceased and he looked at Godfrew, red-eyed and snotty nosed, "My wife ..." he started.

"Liar."

"I didn't mean to ..."

"Liar." Godfrew folded his arms and watched the pathetic man in front of him. "Ulf, I know all. I always have known all."

Ulf looked at Godfrew with new eyes, "All Father," he said, using the familiar term for Woden. "What is to become of me?"

"That depends. Certainly you will never become the reeve. Whether I pass on news of the theft to Earl Ralf depends on many things, including restitution."

"Yes, yes, I will give it all back."

"And more besides, for I also know that you have silver hidden from the time you sailed with Earl Gyrth to Ireland and back and raided with him against King Edward, the would-be-monk." Godfrew pushed himself upright, slowly walked to the door and opened it. "Call the Moot together now, Ulf. You can tell them of our conversation—or not tell them, as you wish. Just remember that they will need to tell me the truth, for I know all." Ulf scuttled out of the barn. In the distance, the boy Robin, Puta and Shock played a game of 'he'.

* * *

"We should have killed him." Clunn pulled his wool cap over the ragged edges of his ears to keep the morning chill out.

"Or taken him prisoner, Master Wulf? Why did you let him off?" Tosti asked. A small dew drop formed on the end of his nose.

Godfrew pulled his cloak closer and hunched himself to ease his cramped arm. "If we had killed him, we would have been killed. All the sokemen are in on the fiddle. If we had tried to take him prisoner, we also may have been killed—or, at best, stuck with the worry of taking him with us on the rest of our journey ...watching him ... feeding him ... giving us yet another horse to look after ... and all the rest." Godfrew let go of the reins and used his right hand to work at the pain in his left shoulder. "Even if we had lived, neither killing Ulf or taking him prisoner would have got Earl Ralf his money, nor would it have made the others willing to set things right for the future. Tosti," Godfrew carefully turned to look at the young man riding slightly to his rear, "can you see if there is anyone ahead of us?"

Tosti stood in his stirrups and used his right hand to shield his eyes against the rising sun. "I can't see anyone, but there is some dust being raised a way ahead. Someone could be riding hard."

"A sokeman from Combs going to Stonham, no doubt." Godfrew slowed his pony enough to allow both Tosti and Clunn to come alongside before addressing them. He was trying to save his hoarse voice. "I am sure that the thane and good folk of Stonham will be all the more honest as a result."

* * *

"Come in, come in." Stigand, the thane of Stonham, hustled Godfrew into his house. The inside was bright with embroidered wool hangings on the wood-panelled walls and light streaming in through the open window shutters. "I had heard that you were in the district and wondered if you would be visiting us." The thane pulled up a stool for Godfrew in front of an adze-hewn table of solid oak. "Something to eat? Some ale perhaps?"

"Thank you. Some ale." Godfrew gratefully eased himself down onto the sheep-skin covered stool and removed his wide-brimmed hat. Dust covered his face, but stopped in a clean circle where his hat had been, leaving his bald head shining white. Godfrew wiped the side of his nose with the back of his hand and noticed the dirt. "I wonder if you would be so kind as to arrange for me to have a bowl of water to wash my face in?"

"Of course, of course." Stigand finished pouring the large mug of ale from the small wooden barrel on his sideboard and passed it to Godfrew before disappearing into a side room. Whilst he was gone, Godfrew looked around at the wealth of the room—the enamelled plates displayed above the doors, the gold gilding on the holy statue in the shrine nook complete with its silver water bowl and candle sticks. Stigand came back in: "My maid will bring it in shortly. She is boiling water for you now."

"Cold water would have sufficed, Master Stigand ... but thank you." Godfrew rolled some of the ale around his parched mouth and wished he was in an old cottage or barn so that he could spit the contaminated fluid out. Politely, he swallowed the thick ale and took another mouthful, this time enjoying the taste of the rich, malty brew.

"It is no trouble, Master ..."

"Geri."

"Yes, Master Geri. Some more ale?" Stigand held out his hand for the now empty pewter mug.

"Thank you, yes. It is an excellent ale. You brew it yourself?" Godfrew asked appreciably.

"Yes ... well, my wife and the maids brew it ... but you are right. It is excellent. We grow the barley here, of course."

"But not as much as you grew before—in Earl Gyrth's time." Godfrew took the mug from the now unsteady hand of Stigand the thane.

"These have been troubled times, as you know, Master Geri ... and as we explained to the last man Earl Ralf sent around. The Danes came visiting on their way to York."

"So I heard." Godfrew pulled out the land book and Stigand fingered his top lip nervously. "Between Earl Gyrth and Earl Ralf you seemed to have dropped your revenue by over a half."

"Yes, but things have improved miraculously this last year. We are now only a fourth part lower," the thane offered optimistically.

"That's funny, I thought that you had done so well that you were now up a fourth—even on the days of Earl Gyrth. I also seem to get the idea that your ale is so desirable that you have been selling surplus barrels off at Stow market."

"There is nothing illegal in that," Stigand blustered.

"No, but you keep forgetting to pay the Earl his fourth penny on the returns." Godfrew put the mug down on the bee's-wax polished table. "Now about the difference in what you claim to have and what you really have. Tell me the truth before I let that ragged-eared rat of mine and his none-too-delicate friend take over the questioning. I know the surplus swine have been driven into the Middlewood and that Odd of Thorpe, your brother-in-law, has the set of true account books that the village priest carried to him last Monday—so why bother lying?"

Stigand picked up Godfrew's mug, filled it to the brim and downed it in one gulp. He looked long and hard at Godfrew. "And what is this correction to my audit going to cost me, Master Geri?" he finally asked in a subdued voice.

"No more than you owe our master, the Earl. I am not an unreasonable man." A noise behind him made Godfrew turn as quickly as he could, drawing his saxe as he went, but it was only the maid with the hot water. At the girl's side, a year old boy child hung on her skirt. Stigand went over and picked him up, allowing the child to tug his moustaches without complaint. "Your son?" asked Godfrew politely.

"No, this is not my son, handsome though he is. This is our Robin."

* * *

From Stonham to Debenham, to Rishangles to ... at each stop, the deceptions became smaller, so that at each stop it became easier to assess the Earl's rights and dues. By late

The Peace

summer, the circuit was almost complete. Ahead lay the village of Bradley. The Earl owned the manor, but the Church of St. Edmund, King and Martyr, had been granted the rights of soke and sac in exchange for prayers for Earl Ralf's father, Ralf of Norfolk.

As the party came to the brow of the hill, they met a bullock cart carrying a few sacks of salt. A man sat on the front board holding a long whip whilst his wife and children sat on the almost empty tray. The man called to his three beasts and they stopped. He waited for Godfrew to reach the head of the lead ox before he spoke to him: "Greetings, Master. A fine day to travel."

"Indeed a fine day, Master Salt. You have travelled far?" Godfrew cleared his throat and spat into the dust on the road. Puta took the opportunity to slide off of his mount and head into a nearby bush to relieve himself.

"We are just up from Bradley, bound for Dallingho before returning to Ipswich." A toddler crawled up, grabbed hold of the driver's shirt and pulled himself onto the man's lap, where he sat and played with the drawstrings on his father's shirt.

"Dallingho! That's interesting. We are due there, too." Godfrew touched the brim of his hat as a nun and a priest walked by, headed to the village. "Bradley is a good place?"

"Very nice, Master. I wonder if you could be of service to us?" the man turned to his wife, encompassing his son whilst he did so to prevent him from falling. "The letter, my love." The small, brown-skinned and heavily freckled woman passed him a folded letter. He carefully turned back to Godfrew, still guarding his small son. "We were supposed to deliver this, but forgot. Master?"

"Geri, the under-reeve of the county for Earl Ralf." Godfrew took off his hat bowed his bald head to the woman and the three young maids hanging onto her.

"Thank you, Master Geri. Well ..." the carter passed his son back to his wife, "... we must be off if we are to make Dallingho before dark." He leaned forward, called to his lead ox and the cart slowly moved on.

The youngest of the small maids hung over the cart tail watching Godfrew and his party disappear into the whirl of dust thrown up by the cart. Satisfied that the men could no longer be seen, she walked back to the front of the pan—being careful not to step on Leofwine, who was lying in a drunken stupor. She sat down in her step-mother's lap. "Mum, why did he say his name was Geri? I thought he was called Wulf?"

The woman stroked the girl's hair and kissed her head. "Edgar? Would you tell your daughter the answer to that one?"

"Certainly, Buttercup." Edgar checked the road ahead, but it was clear and he could see no bad pot holes, so he left his beasts to walk on and turned to sit and face his brood. "Well, my little one, everyone of any worth has more than one name."

"We call father 'Dad', but others call him Edgar," the eldest girl informed her little sister.

"And ... and," the little one added, "we call Buttercup 'mum' and daddy calls her 'squeezy bum'!"

Puta turned at the sound of laughter, but could see nothing of the cart through the cloud of dust. "Women are such frivolous creatures," he said to no one in particular.

Clunn looked at him, his reddened eyes running, the tears washing off the road dust around them. "But useful." Clunn rocked to the slow rhythm of his plodding pony.

"What uses have they got that I can't better?" asked the indignant youth.

Godfrew ignored the banter of his men and opened the letter Edgar had given him. The words were written in Runic with a fine straight hand. Godfrew smiled. Despite many hours, Edgar was still unable to write anything other than his own name—and even that badly—but Buttercup had proved a different matter. In a very short time, she had mastered both the Latin and Runic alphabets and had proved a more adept pupil than even the enthusiastic Tosti. Godfrew ran his eyes down the letter, checking the contents and memorising the details of the manor of Bradley and of the attempts to deceive its master—Earl Ralf—of his rightful dues. It was a ritual he had practiced before visiting each of the previous holdings and villages on his circuit. Edgar had always been there ahead of him, selling his salt and gathering information and gossip. Once happy that he knew enough, Godfrew put the letter inside his shirt and looked ahead

The Peace

along the road toward Bradley. Though small, the village and manor looked prosperous enough. They were expected, for there—standing in the middle of the road—was the current thane of the holding, Roger the Norman.

Godfrew rode ahead of his men and reined up in front of Roger. "Master Roger, Thane of Bradley, I presume?"

"I Roger. Who you?" Roger had wisps of hay attached to his fine, but patched garments. He had obviously been working in the fields. He carried his sword in a baldric strung across his shoulder.

"I am Geri Wendlewulf. I am Earl Ralf's under-reeve. I am sure you have heard of me." Godfrew removed his hat and tapped it against his knee, dislodging the accumulated dust around its brim.

"You Geri Reeve? I expect you." Roger looked at the others who had now arrived and formed a semicircle around Godfrew. "You want check books. Yes?"

"Yes, Master Roger." Godfrew put his hat back on. He coughed and spat on the opposite side to the thane.

"Yes ... speak French?" asked Roger hopefully.

"No. English only." Godfrew smiled.

"Damn. No person speak French. Make hard for me." Roger felt uncomfortable being on foot in the company of horsemen, so he stepped back to save craning his neck, "You go village ... speak Bundo. Later I send chaplain. Him have book."

"Bundo? Thank you, Master Roger. I hope to meet you again later." Godfrew nudged his pony forward allowing the creature to brush against Roger the Norman, enjoying the idea of having an invader under his authority. Roger watched them go before returning to his house, dusting off the hay and muttering in French as he went. Godfrew and his men did not have to travel far into the village before they found Bundo.

Standing in front of his well-kept house—complete with its own hay loft—Bundo beckoned the party over and pointed toward the jugs of ale and loaves of bread awaiting them on a rough cut table set up in his front garden amongst the crab apple trees. Thoughtfully, he had arranged for two buckets of water to be there, also—though a sheep was drinking from one of them. Godfrew and his men walked over from their tired ponies. "Greetings, Master Geri. I have been expecting you." The language was English, but the accent Danish. "We have heard of your work in the other holdings and villages of Earl Ralf's."

"Then you will know what to expect, Bundo." Godfrew took off his hat, then rolled up his sleeves and scooped up handfuls of water from the bucket to wash his face. Puta stood behind awaiting his turn, leaving the less fussy Clunn and Tosti to use the bucket of water the sheep had drunk from. Clunn gave his face but a cursory dab. Tosti stripped to the waist, making ready to wash himself fully. Godfrew accepted the rag Bundo offered him and commenced to rub his face and hands dry: "I assume that you are the head man for the village?"

"I am the senior freeman. There are seven others—Leuric, Lewin and Ulwin hold their own land, the others rent." Bundo gave a pleasant smile. "You will, of course, have met our new thane, Roger the Norman."

"Yes. He spoke English with a Danish accent!" Godfrew sounded surprised.

Bundo laughed, "Well, so do we. You know, when he first came here—this spring—he only spoke French. He has done well to learn what little he has in such a short time."

"You sound fond of the man." Godfrew made his way to the table and started to pour out a drink. Puta followed suit and began pouring ale for the others.

"He means well, this Norman. A good farmer, I think. Our previous thane was Olf, but he got killed at Ely when it fell."

"Ely has fallen?" Godfrew gasped spilling his drink.

"Around Easter. But I can tell you more of that later, perhaps this evening." Bundo inclined his head toward a priest scuttling toward them with a ledger book in his hands. "That sort of matter is not for idle ears to hear." When the priest arrived, Bundo took the book graciously and flicked his hands at the man to go away. "Daft Matthew," he offered Godfrew, by way of explanation, "does not speak French, English, Danish or anything we can recognise. But who knows what he understands." He watched the retreating priest's back, "Olf bought him at a slave market from the Danes at Ely and sent him here, knowing we had no priest. I suppose he felt a Christian duty to save him from being sold to the heathens

The Peace

or Moslems. It is a shame he did not try and speak to him first. He knows how to keep books, but only in Latin. I suppose you ..."

"Yes." Godfrew wiped his mouth with the back of his left hand and poured another drink. As his hand fell back to his side, Shock took the opportunity to lick it clean.

"Of course, you do. Earl Ralf would not use a reeve who could not read and write Latin as well as English. Our Norman speaks a little Latin. That is how he talks to Daft Matthew, I do not believe that he can read it, though." Bundo looked around until he saw a buxom woman heading toward them. He gave a broad smile and waved her over. "Master Geri, I have an apology to make." Godfrew looked at him, uncertain what to expect. "You see, Father John and Sister Edda have come to join us for our harvest celebrations. Norman is a bit of a stickler for the new way of things and will not let them sleep under the same roof, let alone together in the same bed as they are used to doing!" Bundo laughed pleasantly. "These new ways of Norman and his friends." He signalled for the woman to hurry. "Anyway, Norman will look after Father John, but I am afraid I will have to care for Sister Edda. Talking of caring for people, I want to introduce you to someone." The woman Godfrew had seen Bundo beckoning over came and held Bundo's hand. "This, Master Geri, is my sister-in-law, Freja. She is a widow and has spare room. I would be grateful—even honoured—if you would stay with her. Your men will be made comfortable by other villagers who will be only too pleased to look after them."

"I am not sure ..." Godfrew looked at the woman. She was in her early thirties. Thick chestnut hair spilled from under her head scarf and flowed down her chest and back. Her body was full and strained at the seams of her clothes. Godfrew took a deep breath and smelled the musk of her body mingled with the smell of crushed herbs. "I am a married man and I am not sure if it is ...."

"Of course you are married, Master Geri," smiled Bundo. "All good men should be." Again the smile. "Freja is a widow. She understands the ways of married men ... that is why it is appropriate. Please, it would be an honour."

Freja smiled secretly at Godfrew and slowly walked off, casting her head back to ensure that he was following her.

Godfrew shrugged his shoulders stiffly, went to his mount, undid his travelling gear and followed Freja to her house.

* * *

It was late when Godfrew returned to Freja's house, slightly befuddled by the malty ale he had been drinking whilst Bundo told the sad tale of the final siege and fall of the Isle of Ely—the sack of the Camp of Refuge, the punishment meted out to the defendants, the mutilations, the bold escape of Hereward the Wake with his followers and their continuing harassment of their Norman foes. The ale and the food had been excellent. Bundo's company was refreshing, despite his seeming surprised that Godfrew had been unaware of Ely's fall, but Sister Edda's high-pitched voice had irritated Godfrew. When she retired early for the night, her constant snoring had become too much, hence Godfrew left, despite the fact that he wanted to find out more about Ely and the fate of individual defenders. Bundo had known several of the Ely men that Godfrew had met, as several of the local men had fought there and had been fortunate enough to make their escape before the Normans had the chance to capture them. Now Godfrew stood at Freja's house door and wondered what awaited him within. The prospect half excited and half frightened him.

He was still thinking about going in when the door opened. Freja stood in the doorway, framed by the light of the oil lamps inside. Her voluptuous body was covered by a fine linen underdress. Where it touched her body, it clung—displaying the soft mounds and ripples of her flesh. "Master Geri, at last. I had wondered if you had resumed your travels. Please, come inside." Freja moved to allow Godfrew's entry, but she had not left a generous gap. He had to turn sideways and rub against her curvaceous body to get in. Much to Godfrew's surprise, there was a handsome young man sitting in a chair with his feet on the table, a clay cup in one hand and a half-eaten leg of chicken in the other. The youth looked at Godfrew with little interest and resumed eating the chicken. "Have you finished yet, Robin?" Freja asked the young man.

The Peace

"Trying to make me leave, Widow Freja?" Robin drank some of the ale, then belched loudly. "Why should I go? I am quite comfortable here."

"I have a guest." Freja lightly touched Godfrew's arm. "I should like to talk with him and offer him some refreshment and entertainment. I am sure that a young man like you would not want to stay around and listen to us 'old' folk gossip."

"You, 'old', Widow Freja?" Robin half-closed his eyes and stared at the woman, his cheeks glowing red. "Let me stay the night with you and see if indeed you are 'old'."

"R-o-b-i-n." Freja dragged the name out. "You know that you are not to indulge in that sort of behaviour. What would Father Matthew or Father John say if they could hear you?"

"Father Matthew wouldn't say anything. If he did, we wouldn't understand him. We don't even know if he even speaks Latin properly." Robin swung his feet off the table and stood up "Freja, why can't I go with a woman? All the other boys do. Some are even married with children." He sounded like a petulant child. His bottom lip protruded. He looked at the half-eaten chicken leg and threw it on the floor. Shock scampered out from behind Godfrew's legs, snatched it up and disappeared under the table to eat it.

"Oh, Robin ... honestly. Boys boast about what they would like to be doing, not what they really are doing." Freja's grip on Godfrew's arm tightened slightly and her fingers casually started to stroke him. "As for marriage, you are too good for the local girls, Robin. But you will be twenty-one next week and all the girls will gather here for the harvest celebrations. There could be a special girl amongst them. What do you think, Robin? Will you join us for the dawn gathering?"

"I always go to the service at the Chapel, but I've never been to the dawn gathering. I thought only the women folk went to that." Robin came over and, ignoring Godfrew, stood in front of Freja, looking hungrily at her body. "Lots of girls there, did you say?"

"Lots, Robin ... and they will all be looking at you. I can promise that. Now please, leave me with my guest. Please, Robin?" Freja touched a finger to her lips and blew a kiss at the youth.

"All right, just this once." He brushed past Freja, forcing his body against hers and knocking into Godfrew's bad arm. "There had better be lots of girls at this gathering, Widow Freja, because if there isn't ..." his voice faded as he closed the door and walked away.

Freja turned to Godfrew who was standing with his eyes closed as the waves of pain from his arm washed over him. "Oh, Master Geri, you are hurt?" She ran her hands over the arm and shoulder. Godfrew gave a muted groan. "Yes, you are." She took the hand of Godfrew's good arm, led him to the table and made him sit on it.

"I, I ..." Godfrew took a deep breath before continuing: "I don't sleep much. Not without the help of strong drink." Godfrew opened his eyes. The white of the cataract on his blind eye gleamed in the light of the nearby oil lamp.

Freja put her hands on both his shoulders and looked hard at him—the way he sat with his damaged shoulder drooping and his weight off of his bad leg. "Well, I was thinking of a more pleasurable form of entertainment tonight, but it looks as if my time is to be spent straightening your body out."

"Widow Freja ..." Godfrew looked her in the face. Freja smiled and shook her head. "Sorry, Freja. I am a married man. It is not my way to sport with women other than my wife."

Freja started to strip off Godfrew's shirt. She tried to pull it over his head, but he was unable to lift his arms, so she rolled it off over his shoulders and neck. "I understand, Geri the wandering wolf, the traveller, the old man, the young man." She looked at his scared body and then ran the back of her right hand inquisitively over his hairless chest. Godfrew shuddered. "Battle scars?"

"Some." Godfrew looked first at his right shoulder with its criss-crossed white tracings and then his left, which although unmarked was swollen and lumpy. "Others from when I hung."

"For nine days, to learn the Runes. I know." As Freja put her hands to Godfrew's waist, he fluttered his hands, unsure of how to protect his modesty. Ignoring him, she undid the belt of his britches, eased them off of his hips, wriggled them down his legs, pulled them off of his bare feet and cast them to the floor.

The Peace

"Don't believe all you are told. I knew the Runes long before then. All I learned from that experience was pain and how to try and deal with it." Godfrew looked at his nakedness and wondered what to do about it.

Freja slowly walked past Godfrew. "Pain ... pleasure ... where does one end and the other begin?" Coming behind him, she put her arms under his armpits and pulled him along the table. Godfrew, his mind still clouded by alcohol, did not resist. He sat there at the middle of the table, his head drooped, his chin on his chest. Freja rested her head on his good shoulder and whispered in his ear. "I understand about not sporting with all the women who would have you to their beds. Only the royal ones get to couple with the All Father. But then, I carry your wife's name, so am I not also her?"

"My wife?" Godfrew allowed Freja to lower him down onto the table. Kicking off her soft felt slippers Freja mounted the table, flounced her underdress over the prostrate Godfrew and sat astride him. Godfrew could feel her naked thighs and buttocks resting on his stomach. "But ...."

"But, my Master, you need caring for." Freja leaned forward and sunk both her hands into the torn, knotted muscles of Godfrew's damaged shoulder and started to work them. Godfrew gave a sharp cry and then began moaning as Freja's probing fingers sunk ever deeper into the damaged flesh.

"Did you hear that?" Clunn and Tosti stopped outside the Widow Freja's house on their way from the ale house to their lodgings. Clunn cupped his hands over the ragged edges of what had once been his ears. "I said did you hear that?" he hissed.

"Hear what?" Tosti's normally sharp hearing was deadened by the whirling sound in his head and the flashing lights that had plagued him since his tenth mug of strong ale.

"Over here," insisted the equally inebriated Clunn. "Look!" Through the uncured skin of the window, the men could make out the silhouette of Freja astride Godfrew on the table, her body moving rhythmically as she worked on his body. Clunn pushed Tosti away and stuck his naked ear against the window and listened to Godfrew's moaning and sighing. "Well if the old wolf can find time to howl, so can his cubs. Come on, let's go find some willing maids."

***

Godfrew woke to find that the sun had already risen and that Freja had a fine smelling pot of porridge on the hob. He looked around, but could not see her. The sunlight coming in through the uncured skin windows filled the room with a warm orange light. He was tempted to drift back to sleep. Out of habit, he stroked his sore arm, then realised that it no longer felt numb—nor was there a sharp pain as he sat himself up in the bed. He pulled back the bed covering and put his feet on the floor. Again, although his movement was still poor, he felt no pain in his either his hip or his shoulder. Godfrew stood up, closed his eyes and stretched. His right hand touched the low ceiling. Although he could not get his left arm above his shoulder, he did feel good.

The door opened and Freja came in. She looked at him as he stood at the bedside stretching his naked body. "It is good to see you up so early, Master."

Godfrew opened his eyes and saw Freja. He went red, grabbed his britches and hurriedly put them on. "I ... I ... I thought you were out," he mumbled.

"So I was ... and now I am back. You slept well?" Freja took a wooden platter and spooned some of the porridge out of the pot. "You should have after that work out last night. You almost wore me out!" She put the platter on the table and found a spoon to go with it. "I have been to find you some mead, for I know that it is all that is drunk in Valhalla."

"I don't live in Valhalla." Godfrew watched the dimples in Freja's elbows as she poured the mead into a drinking horn for him.

"Silly me. Of course, you don't live in Valhalla." Freja passed the horn to Godfrew and got some porridge for herself. "You live in your own hall. Valhalla is only where you feast the heroes after their daily battle." She came back and sat opposite Godfrew, after kicking her slippers off, she caressed his feet with hers. "How is your shoulder and your leg? Better, I trust." One foot got under the hem of Godfrew's britches and commenced to massage his calf muscle.

"Much better. I actually slept." Godfrew put down his spoon and considered what he had said. "Yes, I actually slept." He

The Peace

took Freja's plump and dimpled hand and kissed the back of it. "Thank you, Freja."

"'Tis not all over yet, my Master. I will have to work on you again tonight and every night till you leave."

* * *

The bees hummed around the flowers in front of Bundo's house and occasionally around the flask of ale in front of the two men sitting around a table under the trees.

"Well, Bundo, I see from the books that in Earl Gyrth's time, Olf the thane had three plough teams, one rouncy, twelve cattle, sixty swine, twenty sheep, seven goats and one hive of bees, whilst you and the other freemen paid twenty-two shillings and six pence." Godfrew moved his finger across the page and started to go down the figures in red ink. "Now, when Earl Ralf sent his man around last year, there were only two plough teams, one rouncy, six cattle, twenty swine, five sheep, two goats and one hive of bees—with you and the other freemen paying ten shillings and two pence." Godfrew raised his eyebrows "And now?"

Bundo smiled, poured a mug of ale for Godfrew and himself and passed over the manor books prepared by Father Matthew. "See for yourself, Master Geri."

Godfrew looked at the figures and compared them. "I don't believe this." He looked up at the still smiling Bundo. "The number of animals and dues paid are even higher than in Earl Gyrth's time and almost triple that of last year!" Bundo raised his mug in a heil wassail. "Bundo, now I know that animals can be made to breed well, but this tripling of stock is physically impossible."

Bundo finished his drink and put the mug down on the small round table beside the books. "We have been well blessed."

"And Roger the Norman is a good farmer."

"And Norman is a good farmer," agreed Bundo. "So, yes, we have been blessed."

"Blessed, my arse." Godfrew put his hand over the top of his mug to prevent from Bundo refilling it. "Don't lie to me, Bundo. The last survey did not have the correct figures. Would you like to tell me why?"

Bundo took a thin wafer and carefully spread some clotted cream on it with his little finger. Satisfied that the spread was even, he cleaned the finger by sucking it. Watching Godfrew's face, he ate the wafer before replying. "The under-reeve who came here last year was a Breton. Perhaps we could not understand him properly."

Godfrew also took a wafer and spread cream on it. He brought it to his lips, but asked his question before eating: "He would have spoken his own tongue and, of course, French. Your Roger the Norman speaks French."

"Our Norman was not here then. Olf was still the thane." Bundo gave a bland smile.

"To have been given the job, I would assume that this Breton would have spoken—or at least been able to write—Latin. Your priest would have understood that."

"You have met Father Matthew. None of us can understand him, so how could he translate properly? Besides, perhaps the Breton just asked the wrong questions."

"Or perhaps the animals had been sent out to other holdings to be looked after ... and perhaps poor Father Matthew had been led into the temptation of keeping two sets of books—one for Olf and one for Earl Ralf."

"And where would he hide such a set?" Again Bundo gave a bland smile.

"In the bell tower of the Chapel, jammed between the first rafter on the right at the top of the ladder and the second purlin."

Bundo stopped smiling and put down the second wafer he was about to eat. "You really do see all, don't you." He popped the wafer in his mouth and thoughtfully munched it. "Strange things happened under poor Olf's stewardship. Our Norman would never have anything to do with dishonesty."

"I think you like Roger the Norman, don't you? Is he good ... for a Norman, that is?" Godfrew poured himself a small drink.

"He is not 'Good for a Norman', he is just plain 'good'." Bundo went to pour more ale into Godfrew's cup, but again found it blocked by Godfrew's hand. Seeing Bundo distracted, Shock put his paws on the table and stole a cream-covered wafer. "You don't believe me, Master Geri?" Bundo went to pick up his wafer to eat, but not finding it, he shrugged and prepared another. "Our Olf got himself killed at

The Peace

Ely, as I have already told you. Silly fool, he and some of the others had heard about the earlier defeats that Hereward the Wake and his crew had handed out to the French and thought that this would be the same. You know, lots of honour and glory, but little risk ... with a chance for a bit of plunder on the side. But they got it wrong. Anyway, after he got killed, Earl Ralf sent our Norman to look after the holding. The first thing he did was to propose marriage to Olf's widow so that she and her family wouldn't be thrown out of the manor house. Proposed to Grizelda!" Bundo laughed heartily. When he stopped, he put the wafer down to wipe his eyes. When he lifted the snack to his mouth, he was surprised to find that the cream was somehow missing. Shock sat under the table licking his muzzle. "Well, she refused him, of course. Not only was Grizelda past child bearing, she had had enough of men anyway, after being married to that old ruffian Olf. She only wanted to get out of the place and into cloisters."

Godfrew slipped Shock a wafer under the table in the hopes of halting his thieving. "So the family had to move after all?"

"Bless you no. Norman married the eldest daughter. I think she was only too glad to see her mother become a nun and let them all get on with their lives." Bundo felt a wet nose touch his hand and looked down to see Shock. "A lurch, Master Geri? I'd have thought a wolf more suitable company."

Godfrew picked up his cloak that was lying at his feet and draped it over his shoulders. "I am the wolf, Master Bundo!"

"Indeed you are." Bundo gave Shock the remaining wafers and the scrapings of clotted cream still in the small crock. "You will stay with us for the harvest celebrations on Sunday?"

"Sorry, no. I have to be in Dallingho by Saturday evening. My men and I leave on Saturday afternoon at the latest. As it is, I had intended to go today and take a slow ride, but I think another night in Bradley will be preferable to a night under the trees by the roadside." Godfrew drained his cup, but kept it close to prevent it being refilled.

"You are enjoying your stay with my sister-in-law? She is looking after you well?" Bundo's smile this time was far from bland.

"Yes," agreed Godfrew. "Yes, she is. In fact, she has been just what I needed."

* * *

Godfrew sat on his pony, just ahead of the others, waiting for them to get ready. He stretched his left arm out straight and turned it this way and that, marvelling that he felt no pain. He turned for a moment to check on his men's progress. His face was relaxed and his position in the saddle much easier now that he was sleeping properly. He no longer suffered from jolting pains in his hip each time he moved.

"Master Wulf seems happy with himself." Tosti fiddled with his reins, settling them in his hands, finding the familiar loops and notches in the leather.

"So would I be if I had ridden that plump mare he was stabled with." Clunn pulled his wool cap from his belt and slapped it against his thigh to reshape it. "His being taken up by that comely widow sure upset that brat Robin who was always sniffing around her tail. I reckon that Robin thought she should have been his. Must have been the only time he has ever been refused anything."

"It's funny how all of the villages around here seem to have a spoilt boy or young man called Robin." Puta leaned toward Clunn as he settled himself into the saddle, ready for the afternoon ride to their next destination. He held the pack horse's lead strap in his hand.

"Yes, funny. They all seem so spoilt ... everything they want, they get." Clunn fiddled in his saddlebag and pulled out a bruised apple. He bit the worst part and spat it out for Shock to eat.

"Except the girls." Tosti scratched his head and caught a flea, which he squashed on his leg. "The older Robins always complain that they never get to lay the girls, even the wantons that lay with everyone else."

"That could be a serious drawback," admitted Clunn, spraying bits of apple as he spoke. "No crumpet. If it wasn't for that, I would like to be a Robin."

* * *

The Peace

At daybreak the women of Bradley came for Robin. Laughing and smiling, they took him to the common field. The two prettiest girls held his hands as they skipped along the path. When they arrived at the field, the girls moved to one side and stretched his arms out wide as the Widow Freja approached him. Seizing his head in both her hands, she gave him a full, open mouthed kiss. After she released him, the rest of the women came and did the same, even babes in arms were held up for them to rub their soft wet mouths on his.

Robin relished the moment and wondered what would happen next— all this on his twenty-first harvest celebration! Freja came to him again and ran her hands over his body, appreciating his firm muscles. She then ducked under his outstretched arms and stood behind him. Again she ran her hands all over his body. When she reached his waist, she undid his belt and let his britches fall around his ankles. Robin smiled and his smile grew even wider when she grasped his firm penis and started to fondle it. When she began slowly pulling on it hard, over and over again, he gave a gasp and closed his eyes. He savoured the combination of pain and pleasure as long as he could—then, in front of all the women, Robin spilled his seed onto the ploughed soil.

At the conclusion of the act, Robin opened his eyes again and wondered what other delights awaited him. He did not have to wait long. Freja kicked him in the back of his knees. At the same time, the girls holding his arms quickly moved forward and knelt. The movement forced the surprised Robin face down in the dirt. Freja knelt on his back, grabbed a handful of hair and jerked his head back. Using her eating knife, she severed his jugular vein and let the crimson blood pour out. Robin did not struggle for long. Once he was dead, the women quickly left to get themselves ready for the harvest celebration at the chapel.

Bundo and the rent paying freemen watched from the woods. Once they were satisfied the women had gone, they went to the corpse. Bundo thrust a wooden pole through the sleeves of the dead man's coat whilst the others pulled up his britches and retied them before pushing another pole up the back of his coat. Bundo pulled back the coat's collar and lashed the two poles together. The men then raised the scarecrow.

"He was a big lad. He will guard the crops well for the next twenty-one years. Especially, as he had met the All Father in person." Ulwin the freeman wiped the dirt from his horny hands.

"I wonder when our next Robin will come?" asked cross-eyed Leuric, ramming the dirt at the bottom of the scarecrow's upright with his foot.

The freeman, Lewin, pulled the scarecrow's hood over its face. "Well, Edith, Alf's wife, she is due in the next month ... and so is Albricht's missus. I am sure that they both got pregnant at the right time in order to have the honour of bearing the next Robin."

* * *

Godfrew and his men encouraged their mounts into a jog, keen to reach Ipswich before dark. They were curious to find out why there were so many ships in the estuaries of the Stour and Orwell. The lowering autumn sun reflected off of the wavelets in the river Deben as it made its way to the sea. Even here, there were ships tied up in big numbers. As they continued along the higher land to the north of the village of Woodbridge, Tosti the Far-Sighted kept up a commentary on the ships that he could see along the rivers and the men working on them. He tried to guess what they were doing, whether they were English, Danish or Norman. Concern for the safety of his family caused Godfrew to force the pace, so the ponies were nudged into a trot. As they came down onto the level ground before Ipswich, the view of the ships was reduced to that of masts.

"A good sign, Master Wulf. Look!" Tosti rode alongside his leader and pointed at the ships masts. "Most of the ships have taken their masts down ... and there goes another."

Godfrew screwed up his eye and squinted in the direction Tosti had indicated. "You are sure?" he asked, for all he could see was a blur and the only mast he could make out with any certainty seemingly had two others alongside it.

"Yes." Tosti turned in the saddle and called back to his crop-eared friend, "Clunn? You can see that, can't you?"

The Peace

"See what?" Clunn caught the line of Tosti's gesticulating. "Oh, the ships? Yes, very nice. I hope they aren't Norman ones." Clunn peered at the horizon, lowering his head to cut the glare from the setting sun. "Look, some of them are unstepping their masts. They must be expecting to stay awhile. Could be a good sign."

"Is there any smoke, Tosti? I can't see any smoke, but can you?" Puta rode at the back of the group with the pack pony in tow. He was struggling with its lead strap, trying to prevent the animal from overtaking his own mount.

"No smoke," Tosti confirmed.

"A good sign. The houses looked all right as we came along the ridge, didn't they, Tosti? I thought they did." Clunn had got his pony alongside Godfrew on the opposite side to Tosti and was shouting across at him.

"They looked all right to me," Tosti shouted back. Godfrew gave a cold look, first to Tosti and then Clunn. They both let their mounts drop back.

"As long as the ale houses are still there." Clunn flashed a yellow-toothed smile.

"And the pie shop." Tosti licked his lips.

"And the brothel!" Clunn gave an evil snigger.

"Clunn! You promised me," Puta yelled from the back.

"Sorry, precious, but I have to ... just this once. I have a little mouse that is looking for a nice warm nest to rest in." Clunn scratched his groin with his free hand. "Oh, my, yes."

Puta pursed his lips and snorted down his nose. "Men!"

With their ponies in a lather, they made the town gate before sunset and clattered into the town. There were people everywhere. On what had been spare grassy lots when they left last spring, new houses had either been built or were being built. Godfrew peered at the timber as he walked his pony by. The timber was freshly cut and green, oozing sap. Godfrew shook his head in disgust, knowing that the new dwellings would not last long. He wondered why they were being thrown up so fast. Passing the market, they had to slow to an interrupted walk, forcing their way through the throng of people. Godfrew's mount shouldered into a scraggy man, his wispy hair poking out at odd angles from beneath his pointed leather cap.

"Oi, watch it mate," he yelled out angrily, bad temper written all over his lined and scared face.

"Brynoth!" Godfrew tried to quieten his pony. "Brynoth, you old bugger. It is you! What on earth are you doing here? Were you still at Ely when it fell?"

"Master Wulf!" The angry look left and the old archer's face wreathed in smiles. "What am I doing here? I should ask the same of you. Ho!" He caught sight of the others. "Tosti, Clunn, and, and ..." he scratched his forehead, tilting the cap to show his receding hair line. "... thingee."

"Puta. The name is Puta," the youth said seriously, a trifle annoyed at being forgotten.

"Yes, that's it. Putty." Brynoth shook his head. "I'm sorry, Putty. You spent more time in my house than all the others, but you spent most of that time in the kitchen helping and advising my good wife on her cooking, rather than with me and the lads supping ale."

"Your wife?" asked Godfrew. "She is with you?"

"Yes ... and the little ones. I got them all out before the camp fell. They lived with her relatives while I stayed on to fight." Brynoth grabbed hold of the bridle of Godfrew's mount to steady it. "Bad move."

"A hard fight, Master Brynoth?" Tosti leaned over the neck of his pony trying to get nearer to Brynoth and make himself heard over the babble of the crowd.

"No. We got bottled up, but could still have held out with most of the women and kids gone. Someone betrayed us and showed the Norman bastards one of our secret paths." Brynoth spat, being careful to avoid his own foot. "Bastards. If I ever find out who, they will smile from a second mouth."

"Brynoth," Godfrew interrupted, "it is too crowed here. Do you know The Swan ale house?"

"You know me, Master Wulf. It's my second home." Brynoth gave his toothless smile.

"Then we will see you there later tonight. For now, we must go." Godfrew looked at his companions. "Well, I must go. I must see my wife. I have been away for almost half a year. I seem to make a habit of it, so I must go."

"Oh, not seen the wife for that long, eh?" the archer chuckled. "Then you must hurry home. I'm sure she will have something waiting for you."

The Peace

"If only," Godfrew muttered. He took a deep breath before facing Brynoth again. "Till then, friend. The Swan, right?"

"Indeed ... at The Swan." Brynoth released the bridle. The pony snatched its head up and crashed into the back of a man in front of it before resuming its push through the crowd. As they approached Godfrew's house, they could see two of his boys playing in the dusty street. They were building houses and ships out of horse dung, a matter that amused Clunn and Tosti, annoyed Puta, but did not surprise Godfrew, as he had played the same game in the paddock outside his own home at Garrat when he was a child. Godfrew caught a sight of a woman's long hair and saw his youngest son, Njal, being carted indoors.

"Puta," he looked at the ginger-haired young man as he got out of the saddle, "take my horse and put it in the house paddock. I will see to it later, after I have seen my wife."

"See to it later," Puta said to himself, "and pigs might fly." He came alongside Godfrew and took the pony's reins. "Don't worry, Master Wulf. I will see to it all. You see your wife. I'll get the saddle off, give the nasty beast a rub down and get it stabled," his voice dropped low, "as usual."

"Thank you, Puta." Godfrew stopped at the porch of his house, "I appreciate the help you are to me ... and to all of us." He turned and went in.

"Crawler," snipped Clunn, as he too dismounted and commenced to walk his horse around the back to the yard.

In the house, Godfrew stopped and listened. All was quiet. Then he caught the sound of Njal protesting as he was being washed. He followed the noise into the scullery and saw his son floundering in a wooden bucket being held in place by the plump shape of his wife, her long hair cascading down her back. He slipped his hands around her waist and cupped her breasts. "It is good to be back." He snuffled her scented hair and stroked her breasts with his thumbs, feeling the nipples tighten. "Oh, how I have missed you."

"Have you?" The tenor of the voice seemed too high and the accent wrong. Godfrew then realised that the breasts he was holding seemed bigger than he remembered.

"Wulf! What on earth are you doing?" demanded Elfgifu from the doorway.

"Elfgifu?" Godfrew let go of the soft and pliant bosom he was holding and turned around. He squinted and tried to make out his wife's face in the gloomy room. "Is that you? Then who is ..."

"Welcome home, cousin Wulf." Oakleaf turned her head from her struggling charge and smiled at Godfrew. "It is nice to have you home."

"But ... but ..." Godfrew took steps toward his wife. It was not until he was less than five paces away that he clearly saw her. Then he remembered her cropped hair. "Oh, dear." He went red. "Elfgifu, I am sorry. I thought that was you. The hair .. you see, I forgot ..."

Elfgifu did not let him finish. "You are so seldom here, I am not surprised that you forget what I look like. Did you say 'hello' to your other sons? They are outside, you know. You must have walked right past them."

"Well, I wanted to see you first." Godfrew kissed his wife's proffered cheek. "You see, I saw the hair and I thought it was you. That's why I came straight in."

"I'm sure." Elfgifu turned to leave. "You had better come into the main room. You have guests. They have been here for over a week now, eating us out of house and home."

"Guests, my love?"

"Dunstan Thing and those two young boys who went with you to the fens, but came back early." Elfgifu's eyes moistened.

"Magnus and Swein. Look don't worry about the cost. Earl Ralf said that I should have the tenth penny on any improvement in the books. We have done well, so don't worry about the cost."

"It isn't the costs I worry about, Wulf, it is you." Elfgifu embraced her husband, "I worry about you getting killed ... or worse, especially after Huntingdon."

"Well, my elven gift, I am back and in one piece." Godfrew tried to hold the embrace, but his wife pushed away.

"I must see to your guests." Elfgifu allowed her hand to stray to Godfrew's for a moment before pulling it away. "But I am glad you are back."

Godfrew watched her go, screwing up his eyes to try and keep her in focus.

The Peace

"And I am glad you are back, too." Oakleaf brushed past Godfrew to go in search of her next victim for the bath, the twin mounds of her buttocks momentarily caressing his stomach.

"Look, Oakleaf," Godfrew called after her. "I'm sorry about ... you know. I really thought it was Elfgifu. I am sorry."

"I'm not," Oakleaf said under her breath as she went out into the gathering gloom to find Jaul and Moithar."

* * *

Godfrew accepted a cup of ale from Brynoth. "When did you join the gang?" he asked as his stump of a finger met the short stumps of Brynoth's index and middle fingers.

Brynoth laughed. "Ely, mate. Dammed stupid." He sat down on the crude wooden seat opposite. "I was still there when the Normans took over the camp."

"I hear that the Wake is still loose. I thought you would have been with him." Godfrew took a sip of his drink and licked the foam from his lips.

"Well, I should have been." Brynoth settled himself down on his seat. "As soon as they knew we couldn't hold out with our main exit route gone, the so called 'leaders' decided that we would have to talk terms. Hereward wasn't having any of that. He knew Norman mercy and wasn't willing to be subject to it ... after all he had done to them. So, the Wake and his crew slipped out whilst the others were arguing about what to do and what terms to accept. My boys went with him." He took some drink and smacked his lips in appreciation. "Not bad for an Anglian brew, this!" he paused before continuing: "No, the boys left and I was with the others when I did something very silly. I remembered that I had left some silver in my old hut." He pushed back his leather cap and gave a resigned smile. "Too greedy ... too greedy by far ... always have been. You know what silver I am talking about, of course?"

"The money I gave you to redeem Toki." Godfrew rested his elbows on the table, being careful to avoid the pools of spilt ale. "But your fingers. You are supposed to be telling me about your fingers," He gave Brynoth an encouraging raise of his eyebrows.

Woden's Wolf

"Well," Brynoth sighed. "I got the silver, but didn't get out fast enough before they put the stop in the bottle. Lovely people, the Normans." He sipped his ale "Yes, a good brew, no? Well, the leaders may have struck a reasonable deal for themselves, but the lower orders copped it. Some had hands chopped off, a few were even blinded. Us archers were luckier, they only chopped off our arrow fingers." He held his mutilated right hand out at arm's length and admired it. "I can't complain though. They might have asked which hand I favoured."

"And you are left-handed?" Godfrew took another sip, all the time watching his friend's face.

"Yep. Silly buggers! I can still shoot a better arrow than most, especially with one of them Welsh long bows your boys introduced me to." Brynoth laughed and laughed. "Silly buggers."

Godfrew waited for Brynoth to cease laughing. "So, after that you came here."

"A lot of us did. You see, the only good condition that the twots in charge at Ely did manage to wring from the Norman bastards is that any English that want to leave the country for good, can. Some are going back to Norway and Denmark where their folk are from. But others like me ... well, we haven't got anywhere as easy as that to go to. So we are going reeving ... and if we survive, we'll see if the Greeks want us. They always seem short of good warriors." Brynoth drained his ale and turned to find a serving wench to buy another.

"My round, Brynoth." Godfrew called a girl over and gave her some copper coins to buy a jug of ale. " That is a similar tale to what I've already heard from my boys."

"Where are they? I've been looking for them." Brynoth turned and scrutinised the room.

"They have met up with some of my other lads from Lydbury and headed for what passes for a brothel in this town. The others came down here as an escort for a local landowner. He has sold out and brought his family here to join the group going to Greeceland. Just how effective he thought my little wolf cubs would be against an armed Norman force, I don't know ... particularly young Magnus ... all enthusiasm and little skill. From what they have been saying, I don't think things are too exciting back home. I might have to find

The Peace

useful employment for them here, unless they intend to go with you."

"I must admit, I am surprised that the bastards are letting us go. I keep expecting to see them let us gather together and then come in and wipe us all out." Brynoth scratched his head whilst still leaving his cap in place. "But I suppose, mate, letting all the trouble makers leave the country for good without having to fight them isn't too stupid when you think about it."

Godfrew topped up his cup and did the same for Brynoth. "But what if—having all gathered together—the trouble makers decide to form an army and take the Normans on again?" He pushed Brynoth's cup toward him. "Now, if I can think of that, I am sure the Norman King and his Witan could have done so as well."

"That must be why there is a Norman army camped at Colchester."

"And, Master Brynoth, what is to stop that Norman army from squashing the English flea before it sails away for foreign climes?"

"Nothing. That is why we have a war band watching Colchester."

"Oh, how we have all come to trust each other in the short time we have been together." Godfrew held up his cup and Brynoth chinked his against it: "Heil, Wassail!"

* * *

That winter was wild and stormy, but still people continued to arrive in Ipswich. They filled the houses, both old and new. The lesser folk camped on the common fields and paddocks, turning all to churned mud. With such demand, the merchants increased their prices. Some of the folk wondered if they would have the money left to buy passage in the fleet that the great Lord Siward Barne had assembled. Having extra mouths to feed, now that Godfrew's men had gathered, caused Elfgifu great worry, despite her husband having silver and gold to spare. In mid-winter, Edgar and his family left and settled in Catawade with its salt pans. Edgar had developed a liking for salt trading during his travels around the county. Godfrew encouraged Edgar, for he felt it wise to ensure that he had continued access to good information. Once the spring storms had passed, Siward Barne ordered the fleet readied for sailing.

Godfrew sat outside his house on a rickety bench that he had made during the long winter. The bench had been made with more enthusiasm than skill, for it rocked on its slightly uneven legs. Godfrew changed his position, easing his arms. He was getting cramped from holding the sleeping Moithar. His eldest son, Jaul, ran up and down the street dragging a piece of sheep skin attached to a rope as Shock chased after him. Having caught the wool scrap, the hound shook it to death before letting it go again. No matter how many times Shock caught his toy, Jaul continued to play. Both boy and hound seemingly had an inexhaustible supply of energy.

Elfgifu joined Godfrew. The bench gave a protesting groan as she sat down. "You are deep in thought, Wulf. You have been quiet ever since you came back from the wharf this morning." She moved a strand of Godfrew's few remaining white hairs from the corner of his eye and tucked it behind his ear. "Does the idea of sailing away with Lord Siward interest you that much?" Her voice was gentle with no condemnation in it.

"Ah, Elfgifu, my gift from the elves, I have no secrets from you." Moithar stirred and Godfrew took the opportunity to ease his back before the child returned to his sleep. "I have thought about it. Sorry, I am thinking about it."

"And my love? Are we to leave all behind and sail away to Greeceland, or beyond?" Elfgifu took a staple of wool from the bag at her side and threaded it onto her spinning whorl.

"And if I said 'yes', would you come with me?" Moithar gave a cry in his sleep and struck out with his arms. Godfrew kissed his white-haired head and clucked him quiet.

Elfgifu slipped into her native Kentish dialect for the first time in years. "Thou knowen that I wouldst ... to the ends of the earth. I loven no other but thee, Wulf. Never hast I loven another so." Elfgifu stood up, settled her distaff in the crook of her left arm and set the spindle spinning with her right hand.

"You love another more than I, Elfgifu, as you well know."

"Never ask me choose between you and God." Elfgifu did not let her talking upset the rhythm of her spinning. "You know

The Peace

what I mean, Wulf. The choice as to whether we go or not is yours. You are the head of the household."

"Thank you, my love. I just love it when you say that." Godfrew risked disturbing his sleeping son by turning his head toward his wife. "To go or not to go? Now, that is the question." He took a deep breath. The silence was broken only by the whirl of the spindle as Godfrew ran the problem through his mind. It was some time before he spoke again. By this time, Moithar had awakened and got off of his lap in search of Oakleaf and a drink. "I would like to go," Elfgifu stopped spinning and waited, "but it is not practical." Elfgifu gave the spindle a twist and started spinning once more. "The boys would find it hard if we went. You would find the sea journey hard to deal with ... and we don't know if Oakleaf would be with us to help with the boys, but we would manage." Godfrew stretched his arms, his left still unable to reach higher than his chin.

"So why dost thou not rushen down to book us passage my husband, for I would follow thee," Elfgifu dropped again into her own Kentish dialect.

"Because it is not practical, Cariad." Godfrew gave a wry smile, "I am no longer a warrior and I would have to be a warrior to go with them."

"You are still a warrior, Wulf. Your men still talk of you and your skills." Elfgifu dipped her head in acknowledgement to Oakleaf, who had brought out some small ale for them both.

Godfrew waited for the girl to go back indoors before continuing. He failed to see Oakleaf hover just inside the doorway, listening. "I am skilled only in craftiness these days. With my shoulder as it is, I could never swing a battle axe again. And my leg would prevent me from doing the battle dance that keeps you alive when the weapons sing."

"A sword?" suggested Elfgifu, putting her spinning down on the bench to sip her drink.

"Ah, the voice of a woman!" teased Godfrew. "To use a sword and shield well enough to live long, my love, you have to start learning when you are seven, as I did with the axe. I am too old now to start again."

"Why did you use an axe rather than a sword, Wulf? I have often wondered."

"See this?" Godfrew pointed to his left eye with its blinding cataract. "That is why. My father knew that I would have to be the sword thane for our holding. I know that I have told you he was daft, but he was not that stupid. He knew that with a blind eye I would always be one step behind others when it came to sword play. With an axe, now that's a different story. I would have a shield bearer to cover my blind side. Being the left eye, I swing with the right rather than the left, as others do. That alone gives me the advantage of surprise." He took a drink and went quiet. When he next spoke, his voice was subdued. "You never met my shield bearer, Godwine."

"I met Godwine. He had a wife that used to dress up as a man at every opportunity." Elfgifu put down her empty cup and made ready to resume her spinning.

"No, not that Godwine. My Godwine died in the fight at the English camp after the King was killed." Godfrew's voice went even quieter. In order to ensure that she could hear him, Elfgifu refrained from spinning. "He was the son of my father's reeve—five years older than me. Master's son, reeve's son. We were more like brothers. He was always there, keeping me from trouble and getting me out of it when I did manage to get into it. Even before I started battle training, he always protected my back." Godfrew swallowed the lump in his throat before continuing: "I often wonder whether the revenge I wrought was for the deaths of my mother and father or for my beloved shield bearer." He shook himself before getting up and standing in front of Elfgifu. "I am past being a warrior now. I am a book thane, not a sword thane."

"Oh, Wulf." Elfgifu put her spinning down, embraced her husband and kissed his cheek. The nearness of her body stirred him. Elfgifu felt the movement in his groin. "Is that all you ever think of?"

"I'm sorry my love." Godfrew left and went indoors, almost bumping into Oakleaf as he went.

* * *

A month after the great fleet of Siward Barne and the English sailed, taking Brynoth and his family with it, Godfrew received a summons from Earl Ralf to attend him at his castle in Norwich. He demanded that Godfrew bring his family and his men with him. Light showers accompanied them all the way. As they travelled along the paved road through the densely populated, but wooded countryside, they made good time. Dunstan and Godfrew drove the horse carts loaded with family and furniture. The other men rode as escort. Only Edgar of Weobly remained in Suffolk.

As they moved through the land, Godfrew was surprised and pleased that for once there was no sign of war or devastation. The well-worn Roman road brought them to the top of the gentle rise. They saw the town of Norwich before them—embraced by those gently-wooded hills, its feet washed by the twin rivers. Godfrew called a halt and arranged for Magnus and Swein to stay back and enter the town just before nightfall. They were to stay at an inn, just in case he needed some assistance, should his interview with the Earl of East Anglia not be as friendly as he anticipated.

At the town gate lounged four guards. Three of them looked the same—both in dress, hair colouring and face—except one wore a boiled-leather cap, with its pointed top hanging over one ear. Another wore a wool cap of the same design. The third wore no cap at all. The fourth man had white, straw-like hair and strangely-shaped eyes that never blinked. Saliva ran out of his slack mouth and down his naked chin. Unlike the others, he had no English-style moustache. As Godfrew's party came to the gate, Clunn and Tosti fell back to join Puta at the rear of Dunstan's cart.

Godfrew acknowledged the guards with his whip, "Greetings, I am Geri Wendlewulf. Earl Ralf has summoned me to Norwich with my family and men."

"Has he now!" said leather cap.

"I wonder why?" said wool cap.

"Not in trouble, are we?" added bare head.

"I think not," Godfrew assured them. "If I had been in trouble, I think he would have sent you brave sword dancers and shield cutters to fetch me!" He raised an eyebrow. The three guards looked hard at him to see if he was being sarcastic or not. Godfrew gave a slight smile, and they all laughed.

"Very funny," said leather cap.

"Very droll," said wool cap.

"Very amusing," agreed bare head.

Woden's Wolf

"I think we have seen you before."

"I think we have."

"Were you at Stamford Bridge in the fight with the Vikings?"

"Yes, I was," agreed Godfrew. "So, you were there as well then?"

"I remember your white eye."

"You fell at the bridge."

"They dragged you off so the army could get across. You looked dead."

"But I am here now ..." Godfrew stood and gesticulated to the wagons and the outriders, "... with my family and my men ... to see Earl Ralf."

"Take your wagons inside."

"Into the bailey."

"We'll find out where you are to go."

"I'll get hold of his nibs' steward, Conlan," said leather cap.

"Colin!" insisted wool cap.

"Colon?" asked bare head.

"Gogmagog."

"Come here."

"Hurry."

The white-haired man with the funny eyes came over and stood before the three brothers, his shoulders hunched, his neck bowed. "Huh?"

"Fetch Conlan."

"Tell Colin that Geri Wendlewulf is here."

"Earl Ralf sent for him. Fetch Colon now."

"Cohlam, come. Geriwulf here. Earl want. Yes?" Gogmagog's blue eyes fixed on Godfrew and he weaved his head from side to side. Although his head moved, his eyes remained fixed on Godfrew's eyes.

"Good boy," affirmed leather cap.

"Hurry now," encouraged wool cap.

"Go get him," reminded bare head.

The strange man shuffled off with an unusual gate in the direction of the partly completed castle with its ant-like workers.

"Take no notice of Gogmagog."

"He's harmless, except in a fight."

"Then he is a berserker and unstoppable."

The Peace

Godfrew touched the back of his lead horse with the long whip and the wagon jolted forward to be guided through the gate. Once inside, Godfrew stopped his wagon and dismounted. His men followed his example. Elfgifu and Oakleaf got out of the front wagon and took the children into some nearby bushes to relieve themselves after the long day's journey. Puta watched them, waiting for their return, so that the men could follow suit.

Godfrew walked back to the gate and the brothers. "You say you were at Stamford Bridge. Were you with Earl Gyrth?"

"House carls," confirmed leather cap.

"Been with him for years," informed wool cap.

"Even went into Irish exile with him," added bare head.

Godfrew propped his back against the wooden town gate, "I heard that all of Earl Gyrth's house carls died with him at the king's side."

"So they did," said a saddened leather cap as he entwined his right leg around the shaft of his spear and hung his head.

"To a man, around their lord," agreed wool cap with a catch in his voice as he hooked his right leg around his spear.

"Oh, that we could have been with him that day," asserted bare head, as he rested his left foot against his spear shaft.

"A Lordless man is a sad creature."

"A lost soul seeking a new master."

"Blessed are we who found one."

"But you were at Stamford Bridge with Earl Gyrth. Why weren't you with him at the Hoar Apple Tree on Senlac's ridge?" asked Godfrew as he bent and scratched a gnat's bite on his bare knee.

"Diarrhea," said leather cap.

"The shits," expanded wool cap.

"Terrible squirts," clarified bare head.

"Probably the mussels."

"Or the pork."

"Maybe the eggs."

"Eggs?" queried leather cap.

"I don't think so!" insisted wool cap.

"It smelled like it," assured bare head.

"Ah, here comes Conlan the Steward."

"Colin the Breton wog."

"Colon who speaks some English. So beware!" A barrel-shaped man with short-cut hair and clean-shaven face strode purposely toward them, the gangling and shuffling Gogmagog in his wake. The man's self importance surged before him like the bow wave of an overloaded ship.

The Earl's steward stopped and put his hands on his indefinable hips. "Who this 'Geri-ulf'?"

"I am Geri Wendlewulf." Godfrew removed his broad-rimmed leather hat and inclined his bald head toward the pompous man. "I have served Earl Ralf as an under-reeve in his county of Suffolk. He has summoned me here."

"We no know 'Geri-ulf'." The Breton gave Godfrew an imperious stare "We only expect a 'Wulf.'" The stare continued.

"You have never heard of Geri Greedyguts?" Clunn moved forward, taking his wool cap off and wiping his sweaty brow. "Geri, my friend, is the wolf!"

"What you say?" asked the steward, struggling with Clunn's Herefordshire accent, "Geri is Wulf?"

"You stupid wog. The wolves have eaten such as you for breakfast and then vomited them up for their pups. You are nothing more than a fat capon waiting to be plucked and stuffed and I have the steel to do it." Clunn's hand reached behind him for his saxe.

Godfrew caught the movement: "Clunn. Heel."

Clunn fingered the ragged edges of his torn ears and gave the steward one more evil look before spitting some dust-laded gob at his feet.

"Geri-ulf, what man say?" demanded the steward, his face going red with anger.

"He is my jester. He is concerned that you are unaware of my fame. He was about to tumble for you before I stopped him. Would you like to see him tumble?" Godfrew kept his face straight, testing the man's command of the English language.

"I think not." The steward looked at Clunn and studied the short, dishevelled and grubby man who glared at him. "He jester?" The Breton changed his look back to Godfrew. "I think not. Him troll!" He strolled to the wagons and looked in. On seeing the women and children in the lead one, he called back to Godfrew: "Wife and mistress? You greedy."

The Peace

"Another comment like that, wog, and I will let my pet rat tumble you," Godfrew muttered under his breath. "Wife and cousin," he loudly called out to the steward.

"Wagons and wife go in bailey. Find Brian of Cherbourg," the steward gestured in the general direction of the castle. "You," he pointed at Godfrew, almost poking his chest, "come to me. I take to Count Ralf." Turning around, he strode off without checking to see if Godfrew was following.

Godfrew called his men over. "Puta, you do the talking when you find this 'Brian'. Clunn?" The scruffy man put away the crust of bread that he was nibbling back into the open neck of his shirt. "You, my little Rat, keep your tongue between your teeth. I don't want to hear that you have caused any trouble." Taking just long enough to ensure that all had understood him, Godfrew went after the steward—as fast as his rolling gate would let him go along the cobbled street. Whilst the others organised themselves to head toward the castle, Clunn just glared after Godfrew's back, fingering the tatty red rumps of his savaged ears.

The steward had almost reached the wooden bridge over the river Wensum before Godfrew managed to catch up with him. By then, his hip joint was aching badly. Godfrew fell in beside the pretentious Breton and matched his pace, his chest heaving after the exertion of doing the nearest to running he could manage. They headed for a wooden hut beside a building site. The door was open. Inside, two men sat with a large book between them on a wooden travelling table. The taller of the two had his dark-brown hair cut somewhere between the long locks of an Englishman and the shaven-necked crop of a Norman. His moustache was cut short at the edges of his mouth. The other, shorter man, had his head between his hands and kept shaking it from side to side in apparent disbelief. As Godfrew and the steward came to the doorway, the taller man stared hard at them. His eyes were such a dark brown that, even close up where he could focus properly, Godfrew could not tell where the pupils of the man's eyes began and finished.

"Lord, this is the Saxon dog we have been waiting for from Ipswich ... the one you sent for," the steward explained in Breton. He indicated Godfrew's presence with an out-turned hand. Without bothering to look at him, Earl Ralf stared at the steward. "Count Ralf, this is the one you called 'Wulf' and others apparently call Geri." Earl Ralf continued to give the steward an unblinking stare with his unreadable eyes. "Wulf, my Lord. The no-good Saxon soldiers at the gate seemed to know him from somewhere. Perhaps he worked here before." Still no reaction from the Earl. "Before he served that Saxon rebel Edric the Wild, that is."

At last Earl Ralf spoke. When he did, it was in an even voice with a slight edge to it: "One day, Connan, you will remember that my father was a Saxon too ... or rather, English. So this is the one my friend Edric sent me." He changed his stare to Godfrew. "A good reputation for shrewdness and maybe a reputation for fighting. Edric only hinted at that part of his past." He pulled at his moustache, "Connan, talk to the house carl brothers at the gate and see what they know of his reputation as a fighter." Connan went to leave, but the Earl put out a restraining hand whilst still staring at Godfrew. "On second thought, get one of the others to do it. You seem to get the backs up with our English troops and workers."

Ralf let his steward go. "So, Geri the wolf, you have arrived." His English was flawless.

"My Lord." Godfrew breathed deep to try and still his heaving chest.

"You did a good job for me in Suffolk," Earl Ralf said in his even voice. The other man also turned to look at Godfrew. His face was heavily lined and he had a tired look to him. Ralf flicked his eyes to the other man, who looked guilty and returned to scrutinising the open book.

"Thank you, my Lord."

"Yes, Edric was right about you. You do have a way of getting things done." Ralf caught a nasal hair between his thumb nail and that of his index finger and pulled it out, dropping the hair onto the wooden floor of the hut. "There was quite a discrepancy between the information Connan brought back from the shire and what you brought back. Would you say that there had been a degree of dishonesty?"

"My Lord?" Godfrew was unused to such a degree of openness and was not sure how to reply.

"Do you think that my steward is stealing from me? Or my thanes and tenants?" Another nasal hair came out.

The Peace

"My Lord, I got honest answers because I knew what questions to ask and how to ask them." Godfrew fought the redness he felt creeping into his face.

"I bet you did, Wulf. I bet you did." At last the Earl allowed himself a small smile. "No, don't bother telling me how you did it. I am only interested in results." Ralf turned back to the other man: "Well?"

"No, Count Ralf. I can't sort it out. I am sorry!" explained the sad-faced Frenchman. The stress caused a small tick in the corner of his left eye to start.

Earl Ralf turned his expressionless eyes back on Godfrew: "So, Master Geri Wulf, I trust that you have the procedures and processes in place to ensure that this honesty my people are now displaying in Suffolk will continue?"

"My Lord." Godfrew's leg ached. He would have loved to sit down, but his new master showed no sign of offering him the courtesy.

"Good. You can do Norfolk next." Without pausing, Ralf changed the subject. "You are loyal, I understand?"

"I have always served my lord well and to the best of my ability." Godfrew slipped a hand into the small of his back and knuckled an ache that had commenced in his spine.

"Which lords have you served, other than Edric?"

"King Harold was my father's lord, even before he was elected king by the Witan." Godfrew tried to see if there was any reaction in the Earl's eyes, but if there was he could not detect it.

"You fought with Harold at Senlac, beneath the apple tree?"

"No, my Lord. I was hurt in the Stamford fight."

"Just as well. I would have had problems explaining my employing you to our beloved king, should he have found out." Ralf broke his eyes away from Godfrew for a moment and examined his hands, pulling at a loose piece of skin on a callous. "I was there."

"My Lord?"

"But I was on King William's side." Ralf looked up at Godfrew again, "My father's holdings in England were poor. My mother's, in Brittany, were rich. So that is where my loyalty has lain till now. Some men call me Ralf the Gael, after my mother's land. I don't like shifting loyalties, Master Wulf. Where are yours?"

433

"My loyalty is with my lord. King Harold died, so I was released from my family's oath. Lord Edric sent me here to serve you. I am a freeman. I have the right to give fealty to which ever lord I wish. Earl Edric told me to give it to you, therefore it is yours—till either of us die, or you release me."

"Quite a speech." Ralf turned back to the table, picked up a chased-silver wine ewer and poured wine into two thin stemmed goblets. He gave one to Godfrew and retained the other. "I demand total loyalty. In exchange, I give total loyalty." He held up his goblet in a toast and took a sip of the rich red wine within. Godfrew did the same, but found the taste too much like red ink for his palate. "I had a sergeant serving me when I came here. He came from my estates at Gael. He fought for me at Senlac. He got himself in a fight around the baggage train later, though I don't know what on earth he was doing there." Ralf looked hard at Godfrew, "He got his face all smashed, his nose cut off and an eye put out. He was always on about a white-eyed Englishman with a stiff walk that he was after for doing it." Godfrew swallowed hard. "I had him looked after. I paid for him to be nursed and cared for. Once he had recovered, he left me and went to serve Odo, the King's brother, now Earl of Kent." Godfrew found it hard to stop from breaking out in a sweat. "That was disloyal. I have never spoken to either of them since." Godfrew let out his breath and momentarily closed his eyes in relief. "I know it is the English custom for a lord to give his man an armband or a ring," Ralf continued. "I have neither, but pray, keep the bauble in your hand as a symbol of our bond."

"My Lord, thank you." Godfrew screwed up his face and downed the goblet's contents.

"So ... Norfolk. You will review it the same way as Suffolk, starting ..." Ralf suddenly stopped talking and swung around to look at the Frenchman hunched over the book. "Hmm." He swung back and looked at Godfrew. "Do you know how to build a church?"

"I have never done it before, my Lord."

"But you can do it?" Ralf's brow furrowed slightly.

"Well, my Lord, I suppose I ..."

"Good. You start tomorrow. There is a problem with the books. I am not sure if there is a thief or just a

The Peace

'misunderstanding'. Also, it is behind time. I have to attend the king shortly. He is taking an expedition to Scotland to dissuade Malcolm from raiding into England in support of Edgar the Aetheling. He has called out the Norman equivalent of the 'Fyrd'. Your men can stay here and help you sort things out. I understand from Earl Edric that this is the way you operate. Yes?"

"Tomorrow, my Lord. I shall be here." Godfrew inclined his head and stiffly walked away, examining the wine goblet as he went, admiring the semi-precious stones set in it.

"Well, Louis, you are lucky." Ralf poured himself another wine—which he sipped and savoured, rolling the fluid around his mouth and over the back of his tongue before swallowing it. "The English side of my folk will come to the rescue of the French side." Louis the Frenchman looked up from the book and gave a sigh of relief before closing it with a resounding bang.

* * *

The rain thundered on the wooden shingles of the hut and poured off the eaves. Godfrew screwed his face up in concentration and tried to ignore the sound. Despite the increasing length of the days, it was dark in the hut. The only light came from a sputtering oil lamp. Godfrew paused for a moment and watched the pages of the book dance as the draft from the closed window shutters caught them. Through the cacophony of sound and the ever present hissing in his ears, he detected the squelching sound of someone approaching the hut.

The door swung open to admit Tosti and Clunn. Godfrew slammed his hand down hard on the book to stop it closing. He ignored the men as they closed the door behind themselves and looked for somewhere to sit in the crowded quarters. Eventually, Clunn just jammed himself in the corner opposite the door and arranged his heavy, stained-wool cloak out around himself, letting it stick to the plank floor. Dye-tainted water ran down from Clunn's sodden-wool cap. It coursed across his inclined face and into his beard before appearing again—clean and filtered—at the point of his beard and plopping onto the out-laid cloak. Tosti found himself an empty nail barrel and rolled it in front of Godfrew's table. Like Clunn, he arranged his wet cloak to minimise its contact with his body. He removed his tattered, wide-brimmed straw hat and held it in his hands, watching Godfrew.

Godfrew marked a place on the page with the index finger of his left hand, then picking up a quill pen he dipped it in red ink and made a short comment alongside the contentious entry. As he wrote, the stub of his right index finger poked out at right angles to his hand. He read what he had written and grunted before looking up at his damp companions. "So, how are the new recruits on the building site getting on?"

Tosti rolled his hat around in his hand before answering. A bead of water ran around the rim, falling to the ground only when the movement finally stopped. "Swein and Magnus have asked me to ... to ..." he hesitated, "... to mention..."

"To protest, don't you mean?" interrupted Godfrew. As he spoke, Godfrew moved forward a trifle. Shock took the opportunity to slide from his master's lap and stick his pointed nose behind Godfrew's back. He fidged, causing Godfrew to move forward a little more. It was enough for Shock to push his way in behind Godfrew's back and snuggle down in the increased warmth.

"Protest, Master Wulf? A bit strong, wouldn't you say, Clunn?" Clunn said nothing, offering but a baleful glare to his friend. "Not so much a protest as a comment," continued Tosti. "They are not used to this type of work and they find the task of unloading the hewn stones from the wagons, difficult."

"They said 'shifting them bleeding heavy rocks in this pissing rain was sodding dangerous,' and 'only a piss-head or a madman' would have them doing it," Clunn explained gleefully.

"An interesting and perhaps valid comment," conceded Godfrew, fighting Shock for chair space, "but seeing as they are always boasting that they enjoy the dangers of life and are always talking of the risky situations that they have been in—and, so they claim, overcome—I thought they would be happy."

"You can't win them all, Master Wulf."

The Peace

"Indeed not, Tosti." Godfrew checked the ink. It was still not dry, so he sprinkled a little fine sand on it. "Anything else?"

"Yes. Despite their short time on the site, they think that you are right. The head of the free masons is not being completely honest in the returns he is making for materials and labour."

"Information so soon, Tosti? I am impressed." The ink now dry, Godfrew shut the book and slipped the gilt clasp to keep it closed. "You are sure that they haven't just 'created' this information to cut short their endeavours on the building?"

"Just good luck. The head mason—a big, bearded man with a beer belly that hangs over a funny little leather belt ..."

"Bernard of Bec," proffered Godfrew.

"A big man with a pot belly and a breath stinking of garlic?" Tosti asked. Godfrew nodded his head. "Well, Bernard Bec, the mason, was talking to some of the contractors—including the man who was delivering the stone from Normandy—and some of what he was saying didn't sound right."

"Bernard makes a habit of betraying himself in front of day labourers, does he?" Godfrew's voice had a tinge of sarcasm. Shock poked his head around the front and rested it on Godfrew's lap, his eyes flicking from Tosti to Clunn.

"Bernard was speaking in French. I'm sure he didn't know that Magnus was a sailor and understands a bit of the language. Besides, he didn't totally betray himself. It was just that it seemed wrong ... the totals and all that. Magnus reckons that he carried the stones, so he knew how many there were and it was less than Bernard said he was going to put down in his return for the day. That's all." Tosti took another look at the damp and despondent Clunn, sitting there and surrounded by an ever-increasing puddle. Clunn ignored him.

"Interesting ... enough to wet my curiosity, but not enough to prove anything." Godfrew tapped the hard cover of the book. "It does seem to tie up with what I suspect. However, with such flimsy hearsay, only a confession would be sufficient to convict him." Godfrew put his hands together and pursed his lips, thinking. Finally he came to a decision and called to Clunn in a loud voice: "Clunn, my pet rat. It seems to me that you are getting bored and that you need some stimulating company ... perhaps some sparkling conversation." Clunn looked at Godfrew through slitted eyes and glowered. "I know just the thing. Why not go out tonight with Tosti here and visit my chief of the free masons, Master Bernard. I am sure he will prove to be amusing company!"

Clunn smiled and his yellow fangs glinted in the flickering oil light.

* * *

Puta placed the thick log of oak on the block and stood back. Godfrew shifted his shoulder to free his arm from the encumbering wolf-skin cloak and swung his axe, Neckbiter. The log split cleanly down the centre, the axe's blade resting on the block, not leaving an indentation. Godfrew stood back whilst Puta cleared the wood away and replaced it with another. Again, Godfrew split the thick log with a single blow. Escorted by Clunn and Tosti, Bernard the mason hobbled toward the wood splinters.

Godfrew locked eyes with Bernard and, without looking, split a third log cleanly. "Greetings, Master Mason. I trust you speak English?" Godfrew split a fourth log before putting Neckbiter in front of him, handle to the ground, axe head under his hands.

"I speak, yes." The Norman mason looked for a seat, but found none.

"You seem uncomfortable, Master Mason. An accident, I assume?" Pockets of mist rose from the wet ground and hung around Godfrew's ankles whilst small wisps of steam issued from Godfrew's body in the sharp early morning air.

"Accident?" Bernard stole a glance at Clunn, who fingered the rough peeling bark of the quarter-staff he was leaning on. "Maybe you say that."

"Pray, have a seat." Godfrew indicated the chopping block and a smiling Puta brushed off the raw splinters of wood from the top of the block.

Bernard sat down. His right leg—with a swollen knee—stuck straight out, while his left foot with the bloody bandages was carefully tucked out of harm's way. "Your men say ... you want talk."

"Ah! So my men have been to see you?" The silver fur in Godfrew's cloak caught the sunlight that was breaking

The Peace

through the clouds and sparkled. "That was social of them, wasn't it, Bernard."

Bernard frowned, then having understood what was said, gave a grunt. "They see ... they tell ... I come."

"It is most fortunate you dropped by. I have been meaning to have a word with you about the book work."

"Book work?" asked Bernard. He closed his eyes as he moved his damaged leg with both his hands. "They say nothing ... 'book work' ... they say only speak."

"Oh, how rude. I had better have words with them later about their manners." Godfrew moved Neckbiter slightly so that the sunlight caught its blade and reflected into Bernard's eyes. "But, yes, the book work. There seems to be a problem with some of the figures ... a problem with translation, or perhaps one of the clerks being careless ... minor, I am sure. I doubt if you would even think of cheating the Earl, now would you?"

Bernard turned his head to avoid the glare from the axe and found himself looking into the leering face of Clunn. His face was made all the more disquieting by the traces of dark-red dye from his wool hat staining the creases in his gargoyle like features. "I cheat Earl? Never!"

"Good. So I assume you will send your clerk around to see me later this morning ... to correct the 'misunderstandings'?" Godfrew readjusted Neckbiter. The reflected glare bore into the side of Bernard's eyes.

"This afternoon ... yes, he come ... I talk him first." Bernard carefully and painfully got up and made to leave.

"Oh, Master Mason," Godfrew called to him.

Bernard turned back and hobbled over "Yes. You want?"

"I must congratulate you on your command of our language. I understand that you have only been here for a year. It is very good for only that short length of time." Godfrew half-closed his good eye, leaving his blind, white one open.

"My woman ... English ... she teach." Bernard snuck a glance at Clunn and Tosti lounging near the chopping block, watching him. He shuffled closer. Nearing Godfrew, he bent forward and spoke in a garlic-laced whisper: "Please, Master, your men. They no come again. They no go near my woman again."

Godfrew turned and whispered back. "And you no steal ... otherwise, you will be used as part of the foundations ... a pillar of the church, perhaps?" Godfrew started chuckling. The chuckle became a laugh. By the time Bernard, the mason from Bec, had stiffly hobbled from the scene, Godfrew was almost bent double with laughter. Clunn and Tosti came over, full of smiles and good humour.

"A good result, Master Wulf?" asked Tosti, his grey eyes sparkling.

Godfrew stopped laughing. When he spoke again, his voice was harsh. "What was that about the woman, the English woman?"

"It seemed a good move at the time." Tosti glanced at Clunn, who stared back.

"Clunn? Was it Clunn?" Godfrew ran a finger down the edge of Neckbiter's blade and let the blood trickle down till it dripped from the axe blade's bottom.

"Well, both of us really," explained Tosti. Again he glanced at his companion for support. Again, Clunn stared back at him. "After we tied big Bernie up, I held her, and he ..."

"He?" prompted Godfrew, his face getting redder.

"He ... did what she wanted him to do, really. I mean it may have looked bad to Bernard the Norman, but Clunn only did what she asked him to do."

Godfrew pushed Tosti to one side. "Clunn?"

Clunn shrugged his shoulders. "She whispered instructions in my ear. I only did what she instructed. Personally, I think she had 'exotic' tastes." He stared hard at Godfrew, "I mean, she groped my crotch not long after we started 'interviewing' the mason. That's why it seemed to be a good idea. That's all."

"Honestly, Master Wulf," insisted Tosti. "She was willing and ..." he gave a smile to Clunn "... I would have called her tastes 'perverted', rather than 'exotic' myself."

"That's because you are still half-virgin and haven't much idea about what a man and a woman can get up to," retorted Clunn.

"I have plenty of experience, you filthy rat. I just wouldn't want to do some of the things you did with that whore the mason keeps."

"All right, all right." Godfrew held out his axe to Puta, who took it and headed to the hut, carefully wiping the blade clean with an oily rag as he went. "Just remember, both of you: I don't like rape. I particularly don't like it in front of a woman's man, even if she is a whore." Godfrew turned and made his way back to the hut, Shock at his heels.

"And a bloody good whore she was, too. She taught me a couple of new tricks." Clunn took hold of Tosti's elbow and guided him toward the town proper. "Now, young Tosti, let us see if the brothel is open yet. I know it is early, but I want to try out some of those tricks I learned last night before I forget how they were done."

Godfrew crashed into the chair and held his damaged shoulder, rocking backwards and forwards with the throbbing pain that using his axe had caused. Puta closed the door and came to stand behind his leader. Removing Godfrew's cloak, Puta started to massage the muscles attached to Godfrew's shoulder blade, trying to work out the knots. Once the initial work had been done Godfrew, let the ginger-headed youth pull off his shirt and start on the joint, but despite Puta's enthusiasm, he lacked the skill and knowledge of Freja from Bradley. Eventually, Godfrew had enough and decided that the residual pain was better than Puta's ministrations. He had half-pulled his shirt back on when the door was thrown open and two monks came in. They took in the scene displayed in front of them.

"I did not know that the English were in the habit of keeping catamites, Brother Philadelphia? I thought that was only a Greek practice." the French monk's habit was mud-splashed and speckled with horse lather. His skin was as soft as his face was hard.

"Roman, surely, Brother Theophilus," corrected the second monk, as he tapped the side of his pointed nose with a tightly-rolled scroll.

"Do you not know about the sins of the Greeks? My, you have led a cloistered life." Both monks laughed at the pun.

"I know something of the wrongs of the Latin church, though, Brother Philadelphia. Our abbot is Italian!"

"Hush, Brother Theophilus, or your abbot may make it your turn in the barrel tonight!"

Woden's Wolf

"Maybe our English friend would like to take my place. What do you think?" the monks looked at Godfrew and sniggered.

Godfrew had seen the looks. Although he did not understand French, he gathered the inference and did not like it. He flicked away Puta's continued attention to his state of undress and struggled to tie his own neck string. "You two have a reason for being here, I trust?"

The two monks stopped their bird like twittering. "What did he say, Brother Philadelphia? I regret I still can't understand the dog bark they call a language."

"Perhaps you should see if someone will sell you one as a slave. Then you may find yourself able to get in the habit of learning what to do with the Saxon tongue!" The monks started twittering again at the wit of Brother Theophilus.

Godfrew gave up with trying to do up his shirt. In three steps, he was on the monks, grabbing them both by the throat and slamming them against the wall of the hut. Fortunately, the shorter Theophilus was on the left, so Godfrew was still able to reach his windpipe, despite his left arm's restricted movement. "If you enter my patch, you speak to me. You do not carry on as if I do not exist." He gave them a shake. Brother Philadelphia, who was being held in Godfrew's stronger right hand, started to turn a strange blue and purple colour. "If you want to speak to me, do so," another shake, "and do so in English. This is England and we speak English. Understand?" Godfrew noticed that Brother Theophilus was making fluttering movements with his hands and uttering funny hissing sounds. "Well, monk? What are you trying to say?" Theophilus fluttered his hands around his grasped throat. "Oh, I see." Godfrew let go of the monks and they slid to the floor. Brother Theophilus sucked in huge amounts of air and kept coughing them back again, but Brother Philadelphia just lay there and gurgled. Puta came over, lifted the monk's head and massaged his windpipe. Godfrew slammed himself down in his chair and poured himself a drink. "Arrogant French bastards. They treat us like shit and think that we are so damned thick that we can't see through their machinations."

"Master Wulf," Puta had managed to get Philadelphia breathing properly again and was struggling to pull the monk

The Peace

up against the wall. "I don't know whether that was really a wise move."

"Getting critical, are we, Puta. You can end up like them if you don't watch your flapping tongue." Godfrew downed his ale and let his head fall back, nursing the pain that had returned to his shoulder now that the adrenaline had started to wear off.

"I speak only as your wife's cousin, Master Wulf. I am sure they meant no insult. Brother Philadelphia here has always shown himself most considerate to me and indeed has taught me many new things."

"Speak French and Latin now, do we, Puta?" Godfrew asked, his teeth gritted against the pain that flowed over him. Flopping forward in his seat, he poured another cup of ale and downed it in one gulp.

"He speaks English .. well, at least he speaks some English ... actually not much English ... but he is good with his hands," Puta explained as he moved over to see how Brother Theophilus was getting on.

"Spare me the messy details, Puta. Just hurry up with those black frogs and get back here. Try and get this shoulder loosened up again." Puta scrambled over and tried to undo Godfrew's shirt, "No you ginger fool, leave the shirt, just get on with the pummelling." Godfrew picked up an apple and bit on it hard, leaving it in his mouth as a gag to block out any sounds or signs of weakness that might escape during Puta's ministrations.

"Dear God," croaked Brother Philadelphia, "I thought he was going to kill us." He tried to make eye contact with Godfrew. "I excommunicate for this. Understand?" His voice broke on the last word, making him sound like an adolescent boy.

"Did you say something about 'excommunication'?" Brother Theophilus whispered hoarsely. "Oh, do shut up, you fool." He washed his face with his dry hands. "Threatening him may start him off again. You may seek martyrdom. I don't!" Theophilus went into a coughing fit.

"Excommunication?" asked Godfrew quietly, taking the apple from his mouth and signalling Puta away. Brother Theophilus groaned. "Excluded from the body of the Church? Typical of you monks and priests. Sitting yourselves between

God and man, making yourselves the intercessors and interpreters, taking your forty pieces of silver for every bit of help and information, keeping the poor very poor and yourselves and your noble masters rich." He had another drink of ale. "I care nothing for your threat." He stood up and Shock came out from his hiding place under the chair—his tail between his legs and his ears down on his head— waiting for his master to explode again in anger. "You speak English, after a fashion, monk. What is it you want."

"Tell him and watch your tongue." Theophilus risked standing up. Seeing as Godfrew made no move toward him, he held out his hand and pulled his fellow monk up onto his feet.

"All right, but I am reporting him to both the Count and to the Bishop when I see them." Brother Philadelphia wiped his running eyes and glared at Godfrew.

"Are you going to tell me, monk, or am I going to have to throw you out?" Godfrew took a step forward.

"Yes, yes, all right," with the back of his hand, Philadelphia caught the stream of water that was issuing from his nose and wiped it on his habit. "I have letter ... it from Earl Ralf. He go Scotland. He call men here. You stay ... you have Connan big boss."

"Give it here." Godfrew held out his right hand for the scroll.

"I tell you message." Philadelphia held the parchment protectively across his chest.

"I said 'give.'" Godfrew clicked his fingers impatiently.

"It written Latin."

"Still insisting on being the only interpreter?" asked Godfrew, his eyes narrowing. "Give it to me or I will squeeze your throat until your eyes pop out."

"For Christ's sake, if not for your own, give him the scroll," pleaded Brother Theophilus. "Brother Philadelphia, please."

Godfrew took the scroll from the hands of the reluctant monk. Holding the bottom carefully in his left hand, he extended it fully with his right. The writing was appalling and obviously scribbled down in haste. "The Earl needs a better scribe," Godfrew commented.

The Peace

"He writes his own letter," informed Philadelphia, glad at last that he was able to be one step ahead of the Englishman.

"Unusual for one so high." Godfrew browsed through the letter till he finished it, then read it fully. "Has Colin Steward seen this?" he asked Brother Philadelphia.

"Colin no here at moment. I look him next."

"Fine." Godfrew handed the scroll back. "When you see him, tell him I want to see him urgently about the gathering of the East Anglian Fyrd."

"Tell? I ask!" insisted the monk.

"As you like, so long as he sees me before they arrive." Godfrew rested his hands on the wolf's mask hood of his cloak that lay across the table. "I hold you personally responsible for making sure that he sees me. If he fails to see me, I shall seek you out and deal with you in my own way!"

Falling over themselves, the two brothers left. Godfrew listened to their footsteps slopping away through the puddles and podgy earth around the building site. He waited until he could hear them no more before turning to Puta, standing quietly in the corner of the hut, fondling Shock's ears. "Sorry, Puta. Showing off to the mason with the axe hurt me more than I thought. I did not mean to shout at you. You know how it is."

"Yes, cousin Wulf, I know how it is." Puta clicked his fingers at Shock and the hound followed him out of the hut. "I know how it is, all right, Woden's wolf. Cousin Elfgifu said 'No' again last night. Oakleaf told me."

* * *

Connan the Steward gathered the men of the counties together the day before the Fyrd was to ride to Nottingham. There, they were to join Ralf, Earl of East Anglia, for the Norman king's invasion of Scotland. Despite their complaints about rising so early, they assembled in the half-completed great hall of Norwich castle an hour before sunrise.

Smoke from the peat in the braziers on either side of the dais made the half-lit hall uncomfortable, as the acrid fumes burnt eye and throat alike. At either side of the raised dais stood Tosti and Clunn. Both were wearing new forest-green cloaks with the hoods drawn over their heads and faces.

Woden's Wolf

They had their long bows strung with arrows notched. Behind them, at the rear of the platform, stood Dunstan, wearing a chain-mail hauberk borrowed from Connan. On his head was Godfrew's boar-crested helmet. He was frightened to move, lest the tight-fitting coat split. Dunstan bore a linden shield with a freshly painted red and black raven on it. In his right hand, he held a naked sword, which he held point down. The smoke thickened. The wolf stood on the dais and surveyed the men gathered in the hall. At first, only one or two saw him. They nudged their neighbours and told them. Soon, the hall fell silent. All looked toward the wolf—and he looked at them.

A draft blew through the shuttered windows. The smoke swirled, stinging eyes and starting coughs. When it finally cleared, the wolf had gone and an old man stood in his place. He was cloaked in white and wearing a broad-rimmed hat with straggling wisps of white hair poking out from the sides.

The old man stiffly walked to the edge of the dais with a rolling gate. "I am the old man," he said. His voice was high and weak. "I travel far ... I travel wide ... I ask... I hear ... I see." The old man removed his hat and dropped it to the ground. Those at the front gasped as they saw the face of the man and realised it was that of a whiskerless boy, soft of skin and free of wrinkles. "I am the young man," said the youth, his voice strong and powerful, full of vigour. The young man put his hand under his cloak and undid the leather thong holding the axe across his back. As the axe slid into his hands, he brought it around, put the shaft firmly on the wooden flooring and rested his hands on the axe head. Its silver inlay picked up the hall's scant light. "I am Wendlewulf ... I am the raven feeder." The young man closed his good right eye and stared at the gathered host with his blind white eye. "I go everywhere ... I know everything ... all things are known to me. The only thing I do not know is a master, for I serve whom I please." The axe was brought to the shoulder and the blade caressed the man's cheek. Blood trickled from the thin cut. Godfrew brought the blade around under his bare chin that the axe might taste the red blood and feed. "Be it known amongst you all, that Earl Ralf—of the East Angles—summoned me here that I

The Peace

might travel his lands and that I might have the amusement of judging his people in the scales of my pleasure. Suffolk I have seen ... Norfolk I will see. Beware of my wrath." The smoke increased. When it cleared, the man and the others on the dais had vanished.

The men of Suffolk knew who he was and they told the men of Norfolk. The priests and monks present crossed themselves and prayed.

Two weeks after the host of East Anglia departed and their supporters returned to their lands, Magnus the Sailor and Swein Four Whiskers rode out from Norwich on their ponies with their pack horses behind, bent upon following their new careers as peddlers of ribbons, buttons and fancy goods with the whole of Norfolk as their market.

* * *

As Godfrew delved deeper into the book concerning the building of Earl Ralf's new church, he came across more discrepancies. However, he was pleasantly surprised to find that, when challenged by him, the miscreants quickly confessed and set things right. But there was more amiss than just plain thieving. The whole building project had been mismanaged. Plaster sat outside in the wet, timber warped in the sun, stone sufficient for two years building was on site, but there was only enough lime to make mortar for a month. There seemed to be only half the Norman masons needed for the job, but there were enough carpenters—English to a man— that had arrived to finish everything in a summer. Yet, the building was not at the stage where they were needed. With nothing to do, the carpenters made it their job to annoy and distract the masons. Within a week of the carpenter's arrival, the building site threatened to become a second Senlac Hill, so Godfrew summoned the master carpenter.

By lunch time he had still failed to appear, despite Godfrew's sending for the carpenter in the early morning. Godfrew had been busy enquiring about where quantities of lime could be bought and writing letters to obtain quotes for supply, so he had not noticed the carpenter's discourtesy. Sitting outside under a shady tree, he brushed away the crumbs of hard, white cheese that had fallen on the parchment he was writing on, then someone coughed.

"Well, do yer want ter speak to us, or don't yer?" The man coughed again and his chest rattled. "I means, I'm 'appy ter stand 'ere all day if yer wants. Don't worry abaht me poor old back."

Godfrew raised his eye from the parchment and observed the stoop-backed, black-bearded man in front of him. "And you are?"

"Athelmere, Master Carpenter, London Guild." The carpenter screwed his eyes up and folded his arms across his chest. "And you?"

"I am called many things, Master Athelmere. To you, I am the clerk of works on this site, but I can be what I need to be, should I so desire." Godfrew pointed his finger at a wiry younger man at Athelmere's side. "And he is?"

"Alderbrook. He represents the men," replied Athelmere. He looked at his companion.

"S'right," confirmed Alderbrook.

"London men. I was told the carpenters were coming from Peterborough." Godfrew pushed his writing away from him and sat back in his chair to better see the Londoners.

"Peterborough was for us to quote on. Vey expected us to start on the re-building of ve abbey, but we told 'em 'pull it dahn, start again, don't mess abaht'. That's what we said."

"Don't mess abaht, that's what we said," confirmed Alderbrook.

"Bloody mess, Peterborough. Vandals, vat's wot vey were; used ter be a beautiful place."

"Beautiful place." Alderbrook shook his head in sorrow at the thought of the destroyed abbey.

"My old man worked on vat place. Bloody vandals."

"So, Master Athelmere, seeing that the Peterborough job could not go ahead at this stage, you came here ahead of schedule." Godfrew watched as the master carpenter eased his weight from one leg to the other, confirming his tale of a bad back.

"No. We could 'ave made good money staying on vere. Despite what uvers may say about vat Norman Ivo Tall Boy, 'e made us a very generous offer ter stay vere and work on some uver projects until the abbey site 'ad been cleared. But we

The Peace

remembered our contractual h'obligations ter comes 'ere. Now, as contracted." Athelmere was getting decidedly uncomfortable and was casting around for a seat or chair to sit on.

"We remembered our 'contractual obligations'. We knew we mustn't break 'em, didn't we, Master Athelmere." Godfrew noticed that Alderbrook had one brown eye and one blue one.

"Yers. Fank you, bruvver Alderbrook." Athelmere put his hands into his stooped back and eased the muscles. "Look, Master? Well, clerk of works ... I don't suppose yer can find me ..."

"Find you some work?" Godfrew smiled. "Yes, of course. Look I'm sorry about the scheduling problems. I have only just taken over and things do seem to be a bit of a mess. Things and people that should be here ... are not ... and things and people that should not be ... are!" He watched amused as the carpenter kept glancing around, looking for something to sit on and get the weight off of his back. "Now, Master Athelmere, I am most concerned about what is happening between your men and the masons. Before we go any further I should like to sort this out."

"Look, wot ever yer name is, can yer ..."

"Tell you what you can do? Certainly, Master Athelmere. Get your men off the Normans' backs and get them working before I have to go against my principles and get my own men to sort them out. Much as I would hate to set English against English in order to help some Normans, if I have to do it, I will."

"A chair, a seat, anyfing. I can't sit on ver wet grahnd. I've got piles of piles! Please?" Athelmere whined.

"Is there anything they can get on with now ... even though the church is not ready for your carpenters to start work yet?" asked Godfrew in a steady even voice.

"Chair, seat, please."

"So, they can start on making chairs, seats and the inside furniture. Good." Godfrew held up his hand and Puta came over. "A stool for Master Athelmere and another for his companion, if you please." Godfrew saw the relief in the master carpenter's eyes. "Oh, and Puta, see if you can find a sheepskin cover for one of them to ease Master Carpenter's piles."

"Wood, timber, 'ave yer got any?" asked Athelmere before turning and watching Puta's back as the youth went off on his mission.

"Yes, but I am not sure how good it is. It may be all right, but it is badly stacked. You may have to build some sheds as a first move," suggested Godfrew.

"We could build some nice ones, ven vey could double as sleeping quarters, Master Athelmere," added Alderbrook.

"Yes, yes. I'm sure vey could. But it would corst extra of course." Athelmere stared desperately around. "Oh, Gawd, w'ere is that boy wiv ver stools?"

"Have you seen the plans for the church yet, Master Carpenter?" Godfrew played with the cheese crumbs, rolling them into a ball and placing it by the edge of the small table so that Shock could try and get at it.

"Ah, vere you are, boy. Give it 'ere." Athelmere took the stool and placed the sheep skin on it before gratefully sitting down. "Me back, I did it in working on the Westminster, you know ... that fancy abbey old King Edward the sainted built on Forney Island, just ahtside London. Fell from the ceilin', I did. Almost killed meself."

"Have you seen the plans yet, Master Athelmere," insisted Godfrew. Shock's head appeared at the table side and his tongue chased the ball of cheese right to the end. He caught it as it fell off the edge.

"The plans? Oh, yers. Rubbish, vat's what vey are. Rubbish."

"Rubbish," confirmed Alderbrook.

"The problem is, yer see," continued Athelmere, "those plans were drawn up by a mason." He looked at Godfrew and waited to see if the clerk of works had grasped the significance of the matter. "A mason!"

"A Norman mason to boot!" clarified Alderbrook.

"And that means, Master Athelmere?" Godfrew spread out his hands and smiled. "I'm afraid I don't see the problem."

"Masons don't know wood. They fink it is either the same as stone, or worse, regard it as somefing you use to prop up a wall wiv whilst yer build rahnd it wiv stone," explained Athelmere, his voice tinged with exasperation.

"Wood is living, stone is dead," added Alderbrook, as he accepted a small cup of strong mead from Puta.

The Peace

"Fine. Everyone designs for their own material. But what is wrong with this plan?" Godfrew unrolled the church drawings and put his empty cup and ale flask on the ends to prevent it from rolling up again.

"The roof would stand all right ... and the bell would hang in its tower. But it is all rubbish, frown togever, no skill, no artistry. We, the English, are the best carpenters in Christendom. Vese plans are an insult to our talents. English talents."

"London talents," clarified Alderbrook.

Godfrew waited for Athelmere to taste his drink before he continued the conversation. "I trust you are not refusing to work on them, especially in view of your 'contractual obligations', Master Athelmere."

"Can't use 'em. Sorry."

"Sorry," confirmed Alderbrook.

"Yer see ver contract states 'as per plans supplied, the said plans being of a good standard', an' these ain't. Yer understand, of course."

"The Guild lawyers would take ver mattah to ver king's own court if you forced ve issue," Alderbrook added.

Godfrew pinched the end of his nose and thought. He looked again at the plans before speaking again. "I have seen the workmanship in the Westminster at Thorney. I was very impressed." He looked from Athelmere to Alderbrook and then back again. "I agree that the English are the best carpenters there are." The two men nodded their agreement. "So, it would be a shame—if not criminal—to try and force such skilled artisans as you and your men to complete a shoddy job."

"Quite right," insisted Athelmere.

"Quite right," echoed Alderbrook.

"So, I have a proposal." Godfrew indicated to Puta to refill his guest's cups and waited for them to drink before continuing. "I will let you draw up your own plans."

"Hammer beam ceiling, four way joints an' all?" asked Athelmere as he and Alderbrook accepted another refill of mead.

"Whatever. You draw up the plans and I will find some extra money to cover the cost of the work. However," both the carpenters paused mid swig, "you and your men will commence straight away to build the sheds." The carpenters smiled and downed their drinks. "Once built, you will start making the church furniture ..." Godfrew paused for the men to accept another drink from the attentive Puta, "... but this part of the work will be at no extra cost to me." The men coughed and spluttered, spraying their mead over each other and their own clothes. "If you don't accept these very generous terms, I will tie you up in court for so long that you will not be able to take on any contracts for a year."

"We've fought longer." Athelmere wiped his beard and flicked the drips of mead onto the floor. As he lowered his hand, Shock came and cleaned it for him.

"Oh, yes, much longer," agreed Alderbrook, licking the sticky mead from his lips and moustache.

"I am sure you have. I have heard of such cases." Godfrew folded his arms. "But whilst you may have the patience, I haven't. I would then have to consider my options. Master Bernard the Mason knows some of the options I may think of employing."

"Oh." Athelmere remembered the mason's limp and his bandaged foot. "I fink we may be able ter agree terms. In fact, I am sure we can."

"We would 'ave ter take it to ver men, of course," insisted Alderbrook.

"But I am certain that such good negotiators as yourselves could persuade them." Godfrew caught sight of the monk, Brother Philadelphia, in his stained and dirty habit. "Well, master monk? What have you got for me now?"

"Geri the Wendlewulf, this from Earl." The grubby monk proffered a tattered and finger-marked scroll.

Godfrew took the parchment. It was written on both sides, but the writing on the outside had been crossed through. After he read the message on the inside, he looked up at the monk "Thank you, Brother Philadelphia. That will be all." He turned to the carpenters: "Shall we talk again this afternoon? Over a jug of mead, perhaps?"

"Yers, vis afternoon," Athelmere stood up carefully, followed by Alderbrook. "Till ven."

Godfrew waited till his visitors left before turning to Puta, "Another summons from our lord, Earl Ralf, cousin Puta. This time we are to go to him in Scotland."

The Peace

"Your wife won't like that, Master Wulf."

Godfrew gave him a wry smile, "No, cousin Puta. I doubt that she will."

* * *

Godfrew stood at the jetty alongside the river Welsum and watched Earl Ralf's goods being loaded aboard the merchant ship. She was of the Norse knorr-type, broader beamed and with a higher freeboard than the longship from which she was derived. Leaves, small branches and other jetsam floated past her—touching and caressing her side before spinning off and continuing downstream. "No!" Godfrew caught his eldest son, Jaul, as he ran toward the edge of the wooden jetty.

"Sorry, cousin Wulf. He slipped past me." Oakleaf came toward him with his other sons. Moithar strained to escape her broad hand and Njal clamped against her large, soft breasts. With her unbound ginger-gold hair streaming behind her in the breeze and her white apron billowing to her broad side, she reminded Godfrew of the very ship he was standing near. He lifted Jaul under his arm and ignored the boy's squirming as he walked toward his wife's cousin.

"Oakleaf. I did not expect to see you here." Godfrew looked toward the ship. Her crew was working hard with the local men to get all the Earl's goods stowed amongst the already loaded shipment of pottery from the local kilns. The kilns were run by the descendants of the Rhinelanders brought there by the Danes in the time of Alfred the Great and Jarl Guthrum. "Not come to find a husband from amongst the sailors, have you?" he teased.

Oakleaf went red, as only a person of her complexion could. "Cousin Wulf, how could you? I don't go chasing men. Besides," she glanced at the noisy and sweating crew beneath, "they couldn't match up to the man I want to marry."

"Confession time, is it, cousin?" Godfrew found the maid's embarrassment amusing and enjoyed teasing her.

"No." Oakleaf finally let Moithar go so that he could stand at the wharf's edge and watch the ship being loaded. "Only a priest is entitled to hear confession. To have a clear conscience, I would have to spend most of my time in the church."

"Like your cousin?" Godfrew bent and let Jaul join his brother.

"Like your wife, cousin Wulf." Oakleaf rested her chin on Njal's head and looked at Godfrew with unwavering blue eyes. "Perhaps I am more like you, cousin Wulf. You never go to church."

"I never go to church," agreed Godfrew, moving slightly behind Oakleaf so that he could watch both her and his sons, "let alone tell my dark secrets to some smelly old man who hasn't the right to know."

"Then," conceded Oakleaf, "perhaps I am a compromise between you both ... for I go to church, like Elfgifu, but I only tell the priest what I think he should hear ... not what I don't want him to hear."

"Hang on, Oakleaf." The maid turned to face Godfrew properly. Her plump, freckled face was all smiles and dimples. "I just remembered. At present, I am going to church every day!"

"From what I have heard, cousin Wulf, it is more to hand out the judgements of God on the dishonest and the lazy, than to worship or confess." She leaned forward and tucked a stray wisp of Godfrew's scant hair behind his ear.

"Who told you that, young Miss?" Godfrew stroked the head of his son Njal, buried in Oakleaf's bosom. The boy moved slightly and Godfrew's hand caught the top of Oakleaf's breast. Godfrew looked at his wife's cousin, but rather than pull away she moved imperceptibly closer. He could smell mint on her breath. The maid's body warmth reached him. He took a deep breath, took in her body musk, and his loins tightened and stirred. Oakleaf moved forward again and Godfrew could feel her yielding body against his.

"Dad, dad." Moithar's shill voice cut through the air. "Jaul's in river. He fall."

* * *

"Where's the boss," asked a slurred voice.

Tosti the Long-Sighted looked up from stowing his gear in the ship's hold. "Hello, Leofwine." Tosti put his foot on the sack with his spare clothing in it and gave it a push. "Master Wulf is busy. He is with the ship's Captain at the moment. What do you want him for?"

The Peace

Leofwine swayed as he rummaged in his shirt. Being unsuccessful, he put his other hand in and the rummaging became even more frantic. Eventually, he gave up. He undid his belt and let a piece of air-cured deer skin fall to the ground. "A letter." Leofwine leaned over to pick the parchment up and fell over. Flailing his hands about, he finally managed to catch the letter just as it was about to be blown into the river. Leofwine smiled at his victory, then tried to work out how he was going to stand up again. "Letter ... from Edgar." He looked at the letter, puzzled. "Letter from Edgar, but Buttercup wrote it." He cast his head about until he managed to see where Tosti was. "The letter ... is it from Buttercup or Edgar?"

"Does it matter, Leofwine?" Tosti put his hands on the jetty and eased himself over the ship's gunwales. He reached Leofwine and helped the inebriated man to his unsteady feet. "Here, let me have the letter." Tosti pulled the parchment from Leofwine's hands, leaving him to blink and wonder where it had gone. Tosti took a quick look around to see if there was any sign of Godfrew, but there was not, so he took a sneak look at the letter. "Bugger."

"What's up, virgin?" called Clunn, only his bum visible above the stacked pine planks of the deck.

"It's written in Runes."

"That will teach you to try and find out things you aren't supposed to know about." Clunn Cropped Ears stood up and looked to the jetty. "Leofwine, you pissed again?"

"Don't ask stupid questions, bilge rat." Tosti grabbed Leofwine's elbow and turned him around to face the town centre. "Leofwine, leave the letter with me. The alehouses are that way." He gave the drunk a shove.

"Wait!" Leofwine stumbled forward and then stopped. "Edgar said to give to Master Wulf and wait." He tapped the side of his nose. "Very important." Suddenly, Leofwine's face went white and then a grey-green colour.

"Get him to the river, Tosti." Clunn struggled to get out of the ship and across to where Leofwine was wobbling around in a circle, his face getting greener by the second. "Tosti, for crying out loud. He is about to chuck." Clunn grabbed the errant Leofwine and none too gently shoved him toward the edge of the jetty. "Do you want to spend the rest of the morning smelling Leofwine's breakfast, dinner and God knows what?"

Tosti joined Clunn. Together, they got Leofwine to the jetty's edge and his head hung over the water. Immediately, the drunk's stomach started to go into spasms.

"Leofwine teaching you all how to pray, is he?"

Tosti looked up. "Master Wulf!" Leofwine started to lift his head. Tosti quickly turned back and helped Clunn force the drunk's head down again, just as the vomit started to pump. "Leofwine has brought a letter for you from Edgar."

"It will be just a report. It can wait until we have sailed." Godfrew started to make his way toward one of the wharfside huts.

"No, Master Wulf." Tosti put his full weight down of Leofwine's back to hold him in place whilst he turned to call after Godfrew. "Master Wulf, he said it was urgent and that Edgar told him to wait until you had read it." Tosti held out the parchment with his left hand, using his right to help Clunn keep Leofwine's head down.

Godfrew took the letter and scanned it. "I told you it was just a routine report—village, population, ploughs, sheep, kine, horses, mills, fisheries ... just the usual stuff. Ah!" Godfrew stopped at the last paragraph and re-read it. "Leofwine!" Clunn and Tosti let go of the man and let him lift his head and turn toward Godfrew. Sick and spittle hung in candles from the corners of his mouth. "Leofwine, you are to come with us to Scotland."

"Master Wulf!" Tosti sounded most indignant.

"Taking him is a bad mistake," added Clunn. He forced Leofwine back over the water as the drunk started spewing again.

"I am afraid we have to." Godfrew tapped the last paragraph. "It seems that when Leofwine gets into the booze, he also wants to get into Edgar's wife." Godfrew rolled the parchment up and continued toward the hut.

"Bloody marvellous." Clunn maliciously dunked Leofwine's head into the water and held it there until the man stopped blowing bubbles. "Here we are ... about to go to sea ... and we get stuck with a man who gets sick just standing on dry land." He held Leofwine's head up by its hair. Water streamed

The Peace

off of it and Leofwine started coughing. "Just wait until we get on the deep and briny. He will be sick all the time."

"And you won't be?" Tosti helped pull Leofwine back onto the jetty proper and prop him onto his side. "I'm not sure about it myself. I've never been to sea before."

"Nor have I," confessed Clunn.

"And you were complaining about Leofwine likely to be sick! I think we all are doomed to it."

* * *

Godfrew looked at his men and wondered. So far, they had enjoyed their voyage. Only Leofwine was sick, but even he gave up once his stomach was empty. However, up until now the journey had only been down the rivers Wensum and Yare. At present, they sat on the mud flats in Breydon Water. Once the tide turned, they would sail from the Great Yarmouth harbour. To the north lay the bright green of the Halvergate Marshes with red-coloured cattle wandering across land that the hot summer had made semi-firm. Attendant boy herders played mock battles with each other, using reeds as spears—careless of their lumbering charges. To the south, on a ridge far from the marshes, another wooden Norman castle rose. The sound of hammering could occasionally be heard as the breeze started and stopped at whim. Godfrew sniffed the air. Its scent was pungent with strange smells of decay overlaid with that of the sea. The ship rocked slightly and Godfrew looked over the side to see that there was now shallow water lapping the tar coated sides of the knorr. Again, Godfrew looked at his men. Leofwine was sleeping off his hangover. Clunn slumped in a corner out of everyone's way. Tosti sprawled along an empty chest, sleeping and letting his white skin turn pink. Puta sat at Clunn's feet, sewing up a tear in his friend's new green cloak. Godfrew couldn't see Dunstan. Dunstan—the Surrey man who had kept out of Godfrew's and everyone else's way since his arrival in Ipswich, Dunstan the formerly talkative, on this journey from Ipswich to Norwich—had hardly said a word.

"Have you ever been to sea, Wulf?"

Godfrew turned toward the speaker. "Ah, there you are, Dunstan." The big man came and stood at Godfrew's side.

Woden's Wolf

"Sea? Me? Never. I've seen it, of course, when I visited my relations in Sussex. But been on it? Never. You?" Godfrew asked.

"Yes." Dunstan stared at the entrance of the haven and watched the incoming water. "I must have told you that I was with King Harold in Ireland when he and his father, Godwine and the rest of the brood, were exiled by King Edward the Norman lover."

"Yes, you did." Godfrew took in another deep breath. This time, the salty smell of the sea was stronger than the rot of the marshes. "Somehow, I never connected that with sailing. Funny, really."

"We sailed to Thing and then sailed back, raiding all the way. The king—Earl of East Anglia, he was then, of course—said it was to punish the people for betraying his father. He was then thing of Wessex. But how can the people be traitors when their own king, Edward Sword Shy, tells them not to help the Godwinsons?" Dunstan slowly shook his head. "It all gets a bit complicated for a simple soul like me. I just do what I am told. Go here, fight there, travel here, sail there ... even though I hate sailing."

"You hate sailing?" interrupted Godfrew, resting his back against the gunwales. "So why did you come?"

"You asked, so I came."

"All right, that I understand. But, Dunstan, why did you come east at all? Why leave the west country and Earl Edric's service?"

"Ah." Dunstan went quiet again.

"Dunstan, tell me why," Godfrew commanded.

"I left my wife. I came to look for my other wife. Not the one in Lydbury, the other one, Adia, the one I left in London."

"And?"

"And? She wasn't there. That's where I went after I helped bring that family to Ipswich. London. Adia had gone. She's gone and now I can't go back to my missus ... my current one .. not the one in London ... or was in London ... 'cos she ain't there now. I didn't know what to do, so I came back to you and the lads."

"And got stuck with a sea trip to Scotland."

"Yes." The ship gave a lurch and then a sucking sound as the keel freed itself from the clinging mud. "And I hate the sea. I always get sick."

The Peace

* * *

As the ship hit the wave, Godfrew felt the decking beneath his feet move and lift as the ship's hull flexed. Godfrew bent his knees and moved with the roll. Salty spray smoked over the curved prow.

"Keep thee clear, land lubbers," yelled the steersman, holding the tiller lightly, letting it move in his hands.

"Dublin Norse," explained Dunstan before hanging his head over the side and dry retching.

"I wondered. The Captain speaks very clear Norse with an Icelandic accent, but the rest are hard to understand. You would know their speech from your time with King Harold Godwinson in Ireland, wouldn't you, Dunstan." Dunstan did not reply, so Godfrew turned from watching the crew getting ready to make the tack to look at Dunstan. "Dunstan?" The big man was beyond listening, as he clung to the gunwales and groaned softly to himself.

"STAND BY TO GO ABOUT!" yelled the Captain. "TACK!"

The crew leapt into action. Men manned the two front and two rear most oars on the steering board side and held the oars out parallel to the water, ready to dig them into the foaming sea. The bow party stood by the sheets, ready to pull the leading edge of the sail around.

"GIVE WAY TOGETHER!"

The crew flung themselves into their work. Ropes flew in the air and slid freely along the deck. The sail fluttered, turned and flapped, before billowing out again over the opposite side. The protruding oars bit the sea as the horny-handed sailors bent their backs and almost came off their sea chests. They straightened their backs and knees together—water running off the oars and down their arms—as they lifted the blades ready for another pull. The ship took the new tack and caught several waves. The hull twisted and flexed. The spruce roots held the ship's strake-planked sides, groaning in ecstasy as she strove on the whale's road. Godfrew's eyes lit up with excitement at the joy, the skill and the danger of the manoeuvre. He looked at Dunstan, but Dunstan was collapsed in the corner, eyes glazed. He looked over to where Clunn and Tosti were, but they were ashen-faced, hanging on to whatever was at hand for balance. Puta alone was not being sea sick. He was bent over Clunn, cleaning vomit out of the man's dark brown beard. As a last hope, Godfrew searched for Leofwine to share his exhilaration, but Leofwine had found some ale and was striving to replace the fluid he kept bringing up.

"Enjoying yourself then?" The heavily-bearded Captain came over to where Godfrew stood, carefully stepping over the prostrate Dunstan. He looked down at Dunstan. "I hope he is not being sick on board. It reduces the value of the goods in the hold to no end and makes the goods owners very unhappy." He shook his head at Dunstan's stupefied face. "Never mind. But you ... you are enjoying yourself, yes?"

"Yes, yes, I am." Godfrew moved inboard to avoid the spray from a buffeting wave, his feet still well spread to maintain his balance.

"Yet when we spoke earlier, you said you are not a sailor." The Captain broke away to check the set of the sail. Happy with the way she was taking the wind, he relaxed and carried on talking with Godfrew. "I think you said you had never sailed on the sea before."

"No, I haven't. This is a new experience for me."

"Now me ... I have spent all my life on boats and ships ... and my father ... and his father before him. Perhaps if I traced my family back far enough, I would find old Noah sitting at the end!" The Captain gave a deep chuckle. He gave another look at the sail and turned his head to feel the wind. "Excuse me." He went over to the steersman.

"STAND BY TO GO ABOUT!" yelled the Captain. "TACK!"

The crew leaped into action, manning oars and waiting by the sheets to pull the sail around.

"GIVE WAY TOGETHER!"

As last time, ropes flew in the air and oars bit the water. The ship shuddered as she changed course and shook herself like a swan that had just landed on a lake. The Captain came back to Godfrew, "Beautiful, isn't it, when everything goes right. Mind, you should see it when it goes wrong. I've been shipwrecked four times so far. The last time, I was the only survivor. Yet, still I come back. The salt water is in my blood." He pulled out a piece of dried meat and offered it to Godfrew. Unsure of what it was, Godfrew refused it. The Cap-

The Peace

tain shrugged and bit the leathery meat, sucking on it with relish. "The sea is like a mistress, capable of giving so much pleasure, but very demanding ... and jealous ... oh, so jealous. When you are riding her ... dare to think of anything else other than mastering her ... and you will find out just how cruel she can be."

"Yet, despite the problems ... you still love her."

"Of course! Can you understand that?" Fragments of dried meat interwove with the Captain's stained, silver-streaked yellow beard.

"I think I can," conceded Godfrew. "Love runs deeper than just ..."

"Watch that bearing, steersman. Take her more into the wind, just a nudge." The Captain beamed at Godfrew. "Always on the alert when dealing with the sea. You have always to be on the alert. So," he took another bite of the dried meat, "you are enjoying the voyage. Good. You nearly didn't make it you know. See that lot?" He indicated the crew with his head. "After seeing you—with your one eye and boy's face on an old man's body—the Christian half didn't want to sail with you on board, as they thought you were in league with the Devil ... mind, the heathen half thought you would be a good luck talisman. Seamen, they are a superstitious lot. The sea makes you like that. She is so fickle."

"Your crew are Dublin Norse, yet you are what? An Icelander?" Godfrew asked.

"They are from Waterford, actually, but Dublin is near enough, I suppose. And me? Icelander, yes. I only sail the Silver Goose on contract. A summer away from my wife is long enough. Not that I don't trust her, but there are plenty of fisherman's sons sniffing around, believe me." He saw Godfrew's bemused look and smiled. "I may be suffering from a few old, rotten planks in my hull and I may be in need of a re-caulk, but my wife is freshly painted and quite recently launched!" He laughed, his eyes twinkling with merriment. "I bought her about four summers ago from some old Danish pirate in Wexford. Two hundred English silver pennies—a bargain price compared to normal—and well worth it, even if it has taken her all that time to learn to speak Norse. Do you know," he nudged Godfrew in the ribs, "I still haven't worked out where she is originally from. She does tell me, but it is as if she is talking with her mouth full. Lovely girl, wonderful cook," his eyes took on a far-away look. The ship bucked and the sail started flapping as the wind backed off. "See what I mean about how jealous the sea is!" The Captain went to the steersman. As they changed the ship's heading, others in the crew adjusted the angle of the sail. Once satisfied that all was back under control, the Captain returned to Godfrew's side. "Here," he proffered a small earthenware jar. Godfrew looked inside it and found that it was full of grease, so he sniffed it.

"Swine grease?"

"For your face," informed the Captain. "Put it on your lips and nose and cheeks, otherwise you will be very salt burnt by tonight when we seek a safe beach to camp on."

"We are not going to make Wells-Next the Sea today, then?" Godfrew dipped his fingers in the pot and started to smear the evil-smelling grease onto his face.

"Sorry, no. The wind is wrong, hence the frantic tacking. But you will be comfortable in one of our nice tents with a belly full of salted mutton." The Captain prodded the comatose figure of Dunstan with his foot. "I don't think your boys will be eating much, so there should be plenty to go around!"

* * *

At Wells-Next the Sea, they had unloaded the Rhenish earthenware. They dumped the breakage into pot holes in the wharf side road. For the first day in harbour, Godfrew's men had remained in the hastily-erected tents and recovered from the sea trip. By the second day, they were out and about, though still not eating. By the afternoon, they had even joined the ship's crew in loading aboard the new cargo of dried eels and barrels of salted beef. Godfrew spent the whole of his time with the Captain, checking the goods in and out. The men's renewed health disappeared the next morning when they sailed on the high tide and hit the sea's big swells. Dunstan was the first to change his complexion to the same green as the sea. The others soon followed suit, even Puta who had kept his stomach on the first leg. The further north they sailed, the more boisterous the sea became. The Silver Goose hissed along the tops of the white-capped

The Peace

waves with her sail half-reefed. The spume flew from stem to stern, leaving mist on the clothes of those in the stem, but soaking those at the stern who stood outside the protection of the sail. Each time they cut through the top of a big wave, the Captain would take off his wool cap and hold his arms out wide to embrace the incoming heavy spray, then laugh as the salt water poured off him, draining out through his beard and running onto the planking of the deck. As the ship took more water, some of the crew went down into the hold and formed a chain to bail out the water from the bilge. As time went by, the sea grew rougher. Even members of the hardened crew started to suffer from sea sickness, much to the Captain's amusement.

Godfrew lost his sense of time and felt that they had been at sea for more than just a day. "Captain. How much further will we sail today?" He saw another wave about to strike, turned his back to it and let the water cascade over his hooded, white wool cloak. "We seem to have been at sea for ages."

"How far?" The captain looked at the sail. "Steersman, two fingers to you, if you please."

"Aye, aye. Two fingers to me it is." The steersman made an imperceptible adjustment to the steering board.

"Now, how far?" the Captain pulled out a notched wheel from underneath his soaking wet shirt and passed it to Godfrew. "Don't drop it, for crying out loud. I'll never be able to get a replacement in the God forsaken hole we are headed for." He pulled a black lodestone out of a pocket. "Give the wheel here." He took the wooden wheel from Godfrew, set the hole in the lodestone onto the spindle of the wheel and held the assembled instrument in his hand. Squinting at the moving stone, he adjusted the wheel until the stone settled. He then cast his eye over the starboard side and glanced back at the wheel. "That, over there, is Saint Abb's Head. So with this wind, we should be at Edinburgh before sunset. We will have to start our turn soon. Mind, if the wind eases too much or changes its quarter, we may have to settle for Dunbar for the night, but Edinburgh should be attainable. Your boys will prefer that, I think. Besides, the instructions you received were to meet your Earl at Edinburgh, were they not?"

"They were, Captain." Godfrew ducked his head as a heavy sea crashed over the Silver Goose's prow. The Captain saw it coming and quickly shoved the lodestone and wheel back into his pocket. "I just hope Earl Ralf is still there. An army on the march is often a hard thing to find."

"So is a raiding longship!" rejoined the Captain, his eyes alight and his teeth flashing a broad smile.

"Not that you would know, of course!"

"It's only what I have heard, of course." The Captain did not loose his broad smile. "An honest seaman such as I, would never know of such things as reeving. Would I, Ulfkettle?" he asked the steersman.

"Never, Captain," replied Ulfkettle with a smile as broad as the Captain's. "Such things are for pirates, not the likes of we."

Godfrew looked puzzled and cocked his head.

"He said 'never'," explained the Captain. "I'm afraid they have spent too long interbreeding with the Irish ... and their Norse is atrocious ... often with Irish words all jumbled in. Mind, many of your people speak a jumble of English and Norse ... not that it is too hard to follow, as long as they speak slowly." The old seafarer stepped away and again stared at the view of Saint Abb's Head. He grunted, then pulled out his wheel and stone. After adjusting it, he made a calculation. He then pulled out a strange grey stone and held it toward the sky. It glistened with sunlight, despite the clouds. The Captain's lips moved as he did some mental sums. He nodded his head, satisfied with his mental workings. "Master Geri, we turn in one hundred counts." He checked the steersman, who was nodding his head as he counted down. "We will then be entering the Firth of Forth, so the seas will ease and your men will start to feel happier. Things are going to be very busy, so I will see you after we tie up in Edinburgh. You can buy me a drink!"

Godfrew leaned over the side and watched the sea, revelling in the smell and movement. Gradually, as the Captain had promised, the seas eased and the heavy swell was replaced by short, chopping waves that slapped the tar-coated hull and tried to force their way in through the sealed holes of the oarlocks. As they progressed deeper into the Firth, the clouds lowered and the sky darkened into a pinkish purple. As the hills closed in, they too appeared the same colour. Godfrew felt as though he were being forced into a purple velvet box. Silver Goose slowed as the tide turned and added its strength to the current of the river Forth on its way to meet the open sea. Then the wind changed and joined the river in its seaward surge. The Captain became worried and made the crew man the oars—two men to an oar, seated on their big sea chests—twelve oars to the side. As the oars went into the water for the first time, the Captain took a wooden club from his own sea chest and started beating out the strokes on the deck planking with the end of the club. He then called out the first line of a chant:

"Sea maidens wait for us in the deep,"

The crew replied with the response: "in the deep." The ship surged forward.

"Sea maidens call out to us from the deep, from the deep.
Sea maidens yearn for us, so they weep, so they weep.
Sea maidens dream of us in their sleep, in their sleep.
Sea maidens will feel for us in their deep, in their deep, in their deep."

Just as the purple became black, Silver Goose kissed the stone jetty with her worn side. Godfrew held onto the taunt mooring rope that ran to the ship and pulled himself ashore, onto Scottish soil, only to find that it moved under his seatrained feet.

* * *

Despite twice washing himself down and letting the still queasy Puta pour buckets of fresh water over him whilst he stood in an empty barrel, Godfrew still felt the stickiness of the salt water on his skin. The sea had also affected Godfrew's clothing, both what he had been wearing and the spares that had been stored in the hold. Fortunately, the Captain had used his contacts and arranged for all the wet gear to be put into the local smoke house to be force dried. Even so, Godfrew found that his clothing was stiff, sticky, and now smelled of kippers. Before going out, he looked at the men. Naked as babes, they lay around the warehouse on bales of unwashed wool. Their dried clothing had been laid in neat piles at their side by the thoughtful Puta.

In the light of day, Godfrew saw that the hills on the Edinburgh side were still distant, but the clouds were sitting low and cutting off their heads. He almost felt that, should he stand on tip toe, he could touch the yellow grey clouds.

"Looking to see if the weather will stay fine whilst we unload, Master Geri?" asked the Captain. He had a half-eaten loaf of flat bread in his hands and a beard full of crumbs.

"I have never seen clouds so low in my life," explained Godfrew, accepting the offered bread from the Captain.

"Many things are different here near the edge of the world. The further north you travel, the closer you are to heaven, or so my cousins in Orkney tell me." The Captain started to walk down toward the ship, so Godfrew accompanied him, finding it hard to match the Icelander's pace. "There has been a change of plans by the way. It seems your Norman King has brought the King of Scots to bay at Abernathy, so my contract compels me to go there." He looked at Godfrew, "It's only a short way from here—just out of the Forth, turn left and into the next firth. Half a days sail—one at most—even with the wind against us, as it is at present."

Godfrew screwed his face up. "Another day at sea? That gives me a problem. I don't think I will be able to get my lads onto a ship again, even for a short run."

"You could press the point." The Captain pulled out some dried meat to complete his breakfast. This time, Godfrew accepted the offer of a stick.

"Press the point, did you say? I suppose I could, but I couldn't guarantee the outcome, so I wouldn't want to risk it."

"The other alternative is to unload and cart it over the hills and hope that the army is still where it is today by the time you arrive. It will piss my boys off though, having to unload part of the cargo." The Captain ran his hands over his beard and grabbed the end before giving it a shake to eject its garbage. "But they will do it. We have to come back here anyway to load up with wool for London, so the whole trip has turned messy."

The Peace

"I would be grateful, Captain." Godfrew put a finger into his mouth and worked at a piece of meat stuck between his teeth.

"I would want to be away as soon as possible. There are some twenty ships due with supplies for the Norman king. I want to get in and unloaded at Abernathy before they arrive and clog up the works ... and drive down the price for getting the wool down south. As it is, we are bound to be delayed while the navy gives us the once over, making sure that we are not on the Scot's side." The Icelander offered Godfrew some more dried meat, but Godfrew showed him that he had eaten only half of the original stick. "Do you think your men are fit enough to help us get off your goods?"

"If it means not having to go back on the sea, I am sure they will have miraculous recoveries Captain."

* * *

"How much?" Godfrew yelled at the carter.

"Suit ye self, see if I care." The man pushed his flat wool cap forward so that the end of it almost touched his nose. "That's the price, take it or leave it. You'll noo get anyone else cheaper, ye know!"

"They told me Scotland was a poor place. At your prices, it won't be for much longer."

"Haimish. You can call me Haimish."

"I can think of many other names I could call you other than Haimish."

"Oh, very dry! Ye're a right wee joker."

"And you, Haimish, are a right wee thief."

Haimish chuckled at Godfrew's passable imitation of his accent. "Aye, 'tis a buyer's market. Me price is no sae bad, considerin' the risks."

"The only risk, at present, is that I will get my lads to drop you in yonder river and drive off with your ox wagon and team." Godfrew leaned on the head of Neckbiter. Its blade was freshly burnished with sand, its edge brightly honed.

"An' ye think ye'll get far?" Haimish looked over Godfrew's motley crew lounging on the barrels they had just unloaded from the now departed Silver Goose. "Aye, they all look as if they be right wee fellahs, especially him wi' noo ears and the rat's teeth. Ye may get oot of the toon, but ye'll never get through yon hills."

"So, I am paying for protection?"

"Aye, so ye are. In a way ... sae ta speak."

"With your King of Scots talking treaty with our Norman king, do you think he will be happy about you letting the outlaws get us?"

"Outlaws did ye say? Ach, no. Help and guidance ... protection from the natural dangers ... that's all I'm charging ye for. Besides, the King's law only runs as far as he can see at any one time." Haimish spat on the palm of his hand and offered it to Godfrew.

Godfrew looked at his men, then at the enclosing hills before looking back at Haimish the carter. "And you reckon that we can cross the river by ferry?"

"Aye, sae ye can. At the Queen's Ferry."

Godfrew took the man's wet hand and shook it to seal the deal. Haimish went off to back his team of shaggy-haired oxen into position for loading the wagon. Godfrew went over to the men: "All right, we are using this man Haimish to get us to where Earl Ralf is." The men stirred. "Just get all the barrels on the wagon as soon as you can. I want to be off." He started to walk away, then on a thought, turned back: "I know I said to hurry, but for God's sake, don't drop them."

"Why, Master Wulf?" asked Tosti. His face had returned to its normal chalk-white, despite being sunburned before the sea trip.

"Because it contains the special sheep's cheeses and the red and white wine that the Earl told me to bring for him."

"Wine?" exclaimed an exasperated Clunn, pulling his partially bleached-wool cap off before wiping his sweating face with it.

"Wine, Clunn. Special wine, according to the Earl." Godfrew turned and left.

"Wine? Bloody wine?" Clunn stomped around to the barrels and gave one a hearty kick, "All this way, putting our stomachs—not to say our lives—at risk, just so his nibs up there can have some of his special wine. Bollocks." He gave the barrel another kick. "Wine, I ask you. Why wine? Why not some decent ale? Wine tastes like sheep's piss."

The Peace

"Sheep's piss, Clunn? You really do exaggerate." Tosti bent his knees, lifted the first barrel up and put it on the bed of the wagon for Leofwine to roll into place. "How can you know what sheep's piss tastes like?"

"Oh, it's not too bad. You can get used to it in time." Dunstan lifted up his barrel and went to get another.

"What was that, Dunstan?" asked Clunn, incredulously.

"Sheep's piss. If there's nothing else. You see when I was fighting in Wales with the King—Harold the Godwinson, that is, not the Norman one ... well, he wasn't king then, of course. He was only thing, you know, Earl of thing ..."

* * *

It was with great relief when, the next afternoon, Godfrew and his band came out of the pass through the hills and saw the spread of the Firth of Tay before them. Leaving Leofwine, Tosti and Clunn to bring the slow-moving ox wagon to the camp of the two kings, Godfrew and Puta rode ahead along the riverside road. In the river was a ship under oar. As Godfrew watched, the oars were shipped and the sail unfurled. He recognised her as the Silver Goose, bound again for Edinburgh and its next cargo. They came to a shamble of huts where men were working furiously at unloading another ship. Goods and barrels were stacked high. A column of carts and wagons formed a ribbon from the waterside back inland to the distant camp. Patient oxen stood and chewed the cud, their heads swaying, whilst inpatient draught horses champed at the bit and stamped their feet, raising dust and leaving piles of horse dung.

The camp was neatly laid out. The Normans and their English followers were on one side of the road. The less numerous Scots—their English allies and refugees—were on the other. Despite the numbers, the men in the camp seemed to be getting on well with little more than occasional insults being thrown across the divide by the different English factions. Much to his delight, Godfrew saw Dagobert—Earl Edric the Wild's reeve.

Reining in his pony, Godfrew called out to him: "Ho, Master Reeve, still fiddling the books?"

Dagobert looked up from the cauldron of stew he was stirring with a wooden spoon, "Who's that?" He peered through the mixture of wood smoke and steam. "Wulf? Is that you, you old crook?"

"Everything I know about dishonesty, I learned from you, Dagobert." Godfrew slipped out of his saddle and embraced his friend. "Man, but it is good to see you."

"How's that arm of yours? Still playing you up?" Dagobert patted Godfrew on the back and then looked hard at Godfrew's face. "You don't age, do you. Everything else about you may be falling apart, but your face never changes."

"But what are you doing here, Master Reeve. Don't tell me that our illustrious Earl now has holdings in Scotland?"

"He wouldn't be the first Englishman to seek lands here." Dagobert scratched his thick beard. The silver was showing, now that it was not being regularly washed with the herbal dye that his wife made him use. "No, I am actually here as leader of Earl Edric's war host."

"Where's Torquil? It's not like him to miss out on the chance of a bit of rape and pillage, let alone the opportunity of a decent fight." Godfrew bent and slackened the girth strap of his pony.

"Dead," explained Dagobert. "Woke up the morning before the troops were due to leave, looked at his wife as she brought him his morning ale and bread, went a funny blue colour and flopped back on the pillow ... dead. I never thought he would go that way." He flicked his head over his shoulder and glanced at the cauldron. "Would you like some stew? It should be ready soon."

"Yes, we can have something to eat while we wait for the others. You do know where Earl Ralf of East Anglia is camped, I assume?" Godfrew gratefully accepted a proffered leather stool and sat down.

"Oh, yes. Earl Edric has been there several times. Your Ralf is very matey with Roger, the heir to Herefordshire. Our Lord Edric is keen to settle his differences with that family, now that his circumstances have changed."

Puta pulled the spoon out of the stew and tasted it, screwing up his face. Seeing a well set up tent that obviously belonged to one of the richer nobles, he headed off to scrounge some herbs from one of the cooks.

The Peace

"Changed circumstances, Dagobert?" Godfrew stretched out his legs and ran his fingers along his tired muscles.

"Well, you know that his daughter was getting married to Mortimer's whipper-snapper. She is his only hope now. The plague carried away two of his sons and the youngest, Alnod, went into the church. Now that ..." he picked up a twig and threw it into the fire beneath the cauldron, "... now that did surprise Edric, after his careful upbringing. Well, that basically leaves his daughter as his heir. So, all his hopes are tied to his girl. You know," he turned to Godfrew with a wry smile on his face, "I often wonder how she and her husband get on ... him only speaking French and her only English with a smattering of Welsh. They must get on ... at least in one aspect of their lives, that is ... as she is carrying his child at present."

"Earl Edric a grandfather?" Godfrew shook his head in amusement. "A strange thought, that. I wonder how the Lady Gondul feels?"

"Lady Gondul? Ah, another of the Earl's worries. You know her liking for the company of young, unbudded maids?" Godfrew nodded and Dagobert continued: "Well, she got the last one pregnant![1]"

"Rubbish!"

"Remember ... I told you that she was not as other women. I know ... I used to be leader of Earl Edric's hearth troops. There is nothing that I did not see—inside the bedchamber and out of it. She was quite capable of getting the maid pregnant, believe me. A genuine weaponed wifstra!"

Godfrew half-laughed and half-spluttered in disbelief, "But ... but ..."

"Yes?"

"But she bore children of her own!"

"The ways of God are mysterious beyond belief." Dagobert the Reeve picked up another twig and drew in the dirt in front of him "Lady Gondul has now been placed away into a convent." He looked up from his scribblings. "You know that he also lost Goda, the dark one?"

"What?"

"Some of her fellow countrymen came to Lydbury. Edric called them wogs and laughed at them ... their outlandish dress and manners. When they went, she went, too."

"Did he know she was going?"

"No." Dagobert threw the twig into the fire. "So with one thing and another, Earl Edric believes himself cursed by God for his past sins. Goshawk the priest is feeding him, of course. He keeps telling him that it is all a sign of the end times, especially Lady Gondul's curse. He keeps quoting the Prophet Jeremiah: 'For the Lord has created a new thing in the earth: a woman turned into a man.'" Puta came back, threw some herbs into the stew and stirred the mess. "Myself, I think that he is after the Earl founding an abbey and putting him in as abbot."

"Hello, cousin." Barjarki White Hair rode past on a piebald pony.

"Cousin?" Godfrew asked Dagobert. "What does he mean by 'cousin', pray?"

"Didn't I tell you?" Dagobert gave a quick smile. "The maid Lady Gondul got pregnant was your wife's young cousin, Joanna."

"Joanna? She was supposed to be going back to the family at Martinsfield when Elfgifu and I left." Godfrew accepted a plate of stew from Puta, who, on hearing his sister's name, stopped to listen.

"Well, she is there now ... and Barjarki, her husband ... well, he is the new thane of Martinsfield!"

* * *

"You no go in." Connan the Steward put his hand on Godfrew's chest. "You wait ... I go." He turned and flicked his fingers at the two soldiers guarding the entrance to the tent. Holding the flaps in his hand, he turned and gave Godfrew a searing look. "You late, should be here two day ago."

"Have you ever travelled by sea, Master Steward?" Godfrew asked evenly.

"Yes. Normandy ... England." Connan flicked his head arrogantly and disappeared inside.

"Makes you feel thing, don't it, Wulf."

"Thing, Dunstan?" Godfrew adjusted the gold clasp to his cloak and turned the wolf skin back under so that only the white wool showed.

The Peace

"Yes, thing ... welcome." Dunstan fidgeted. "Bloody hell, these clothes are stiff. They have never been them same since they got soaked in that God-cursed ship."

"You are not the only one." Clunn wriggled. "My trousers are so stiff they have chaffed the inside of my legs and brought up a rash in my crotch."

Puta lightly touched the short man's elbow. "Don't worry, Clunn. I'll rub some soothing balm on the sores tonight, before you go to sleep." One of the soldiers at the entrance swallowed and his eyes widened. Puta stared hard at him with his unblinking blue eyes.

Connan poked his head through the flap, "You in now."

"And my men?" asked Godfrew.

"Yes. They quiet, you only speak. In now." Connan's head disappeared. Godfrew and his men passed the guards and ducked their heads through the entrance.

The inside was bright with lamplight. At the end of the tent, seated on stools with a folding table in front of them, sat three well-dressed men.

"Earl Ralf, Earl Edric ... and I assume the other one is Roger of Hereford." Tosti informed his short-sighted master.

Around them, sitting on the ground, were Norman knights—men-at-arms, together with English thanes and house carls. All were eating and drinking while a bard plucked at a lyre and sung out verse. Godfrew strained his ears to try and make out what was being sung, but the babble from the half-drunken men drowned all but a few of the singer's notes. Even the language being used was unclear.

"Master Wulf," Tosti Far-Sighted tapped Godfrew's elbow, "Earl Ralf is beckoning you to go to him." Godfrew raised his hand in thanks and made his way carefully over the men lying in front of him, taking great care not to step on anyone. Eventually, he made it to the head table. Edric the Wild saw him and gave a tired smile before lifting his glass cup of water in a salute to his loyal servant.

"Ah, Geri, you are here at last." Earl Ralf stabbed the small circular cheese in front of him with his dagger and held it aloft. "It is good to have some decent food and wine again. My thanks." He held the round of cheese under the nose of the man to his right. "Roger, cheese?" he asked in French.

Woden's Wolf

Roger of Hereford smiled, pulled the cheese off of the dagger and started to eat it with great relish.

"I am sorry for the delay, Lord Ralf." Godfrew spread his hands. "The journey took its toll ... on men, if not cargo."

"You were just in time, Master Geri. King William has just concluded an understanding with Malcolm, King of the Scots. He will be staying a few more days, then will be going back to London, taking his hostage, Malcolm's young son Donald, with him."

"Hush, Ralf. The King has ears everywhere. Donald Malcolmson is not his hostage. He is his guest," insisted Edric.

"Guest, my arse." Earl Ralf turned to Roger. "Hey, Hereford, Edric here says that Scot's ankle biter is William's 'guest' and not a 'hostage'. What do you say?"

"Guest? Good behaviour bond, more like." Roger wiped the soft, golden cheese from his mouth with a piece of white bread, which he then ate.

"So, Geri. While the King takes his leisure, we," Ralf indicated Edric and Roger, "we leave tomorrow morning." He filled his glass cup with white wine and swirled it around whilst he observed it in the light. "Things are well in my Earldom?"

"My information is that Suffolk goes well. Norfolk has a problem or two." Godfrew eased his weight onto his good leg. The tent was warm and sweat was forming on his brow.

"Then solve the problem. That is what I employ you for." Ralf looked and managed to catch Edric's eye. "Geri ... he is good at solving problems, is he not."

At first Earl Edric seemed not to have understood what had been said, then the ever-present Goshawk, hovering at his shoulder, whispered into his ear. "Ah, yes. Geri? Geri the Wendlewulf. Solve problems?" A memory of a twinkle entered the Earl's watery blue eyes. "Oh, he can solve all sorts of problems. Often before they even happen."

Earl Ralf threw back his head and laughed. Roger looked at him puzzled, but Ralf waved him away, unwilling to translate. "So, Geri ... my wonder wolf ... solve my Norfolk problems whilst my friends and I wend our merry way back to Nottingham where we will dismiss our following. You can head straight back to Norwich and start getting things straight." He picked up his glass again and held it to his nose, enjoying

The Peace

the bouquet. "But tonight, you and your men should join us and enjoy some good food and drink."

Godfrew dipped his head to Earl Ralf, then looked at Earl Edric and dipped his head again. Ralf smiled and downed his wine, crushing the last drop against the roof of his mouth and forcing it over his back teeth. He shook his head with pleasure and smacked his lips loudly.

Godfrew gingerly made his way back across the crowded tent to where his men still stood. "All right, lads. Grab some food and drink. Sit down and enjoy yourselves."

Godfrew took off his cloak and rolled it, using it as a prop for his bad arm. He sat on the floor and watched the mixed crowd of men in the tent as they ate, drank, laughed and struggled to converse. Puta came to sit by his side and placed some titbits on a thick slice of trencher bread by his side. "Ale or wine, cousin Wulf? I can get some wine if you prefer. One of the butlers out the back is proving most friendly." The youth's soft hand rested on Godfrew's for a moment. "Master Wulf?"

"Just ale, please, Puta ... but see to yourself first." Godfrew picked at the food by his side, wishing that they had been serving the wholesome and filling stew that he had shared that afternoon with Dagobert the Reeve instead.

"Master Wulf." Tosti slid alongside Godfrew. "Do you see that curly-headed kid over there?"

Godfrew moved his eyes to the youth indicated. "Rennie, or Reggie, isn't it? Stroppy little git ... always up himself. One of Colin's Bretons."

"Clunn says that he is talking about you and not being very nice, either."

"Clunn?" Godfrew creased his brow. "He speaks Breton?"

"Welsh. They are all wogs." Tosti wiped a trickle of sweat off the side of his face just as it was about to go into his eye. "I can only grasp some of it, but Clunn understands most of it."

"So what is he saying, this Reggie the wog." Godfrew kept watching the Breton. Rennie saw him, nudged his drinking companions and muttered something to them that started them all laughing. "Tosti?"

"He is making jokes about you and your family."

"Such as?"

"I'm not sure you want all the details, Master Wulf." Tosti wiped his brow with the back of his hand, then looked at the sweat before wiping it clean on the side of his trousers.

"Give."

Tosti bent back and conferred with Clunn, who was at present stroking the cropped remains of his ears and staring at Earl Edric the Wild, who had locked eyes with him. Without looking away from his old master, Clunn whispered to Tosti. The young man grunted and then leaned forward to talk quietly into Godfrew's ear: "It seems that young Reggie has suggested that, having left your nun of a wife and fat ginger mistress behind, you have now brought your ginger catamite with you. He also seems to think that maybe you will shortly be looking for one of the local ginger cattle or perhaps a ginger goat to sleep with instead, particularly as you haven't brought your regular bed companion with you." Godfrew furrowed his brows. "Shock. You usually have him with you and he sleeps under your cloak to keep you warm on cold nights."

"I see." Godfrew's voice was expressionless. "Thank Clunn for me. Tell him I am sorry his ears are no longer what they were, but tonight they have served me well."

Godfrew drank little and waited until later into the night when young Rennie left the tent to relieve himself. Godfrew followed. As he passed the place where Connan was sitting, he tripped. When he stood up again, Godfrew held Connan's cloak in one hand and the steward's double-edged dagger in the other.

The youngster was standing facing a dense gorse bush when Godfrew joined him. The youngster finished urinating and shook the drips off. After unsteadily tightening his britches, he turned to go back to the tent, but Godfrew blocked his way. "Move out of the way," he spat in Breton. He realised that Godfrew had not understood him, so he tried French. "Out of the way." Godfrew looked blankly at him. The youth swayed and gathered his clouded thoughts before trying English. "Get away, yes?"

"No, bad English. Not get away, but rather 'get this'." Godfrew threw Connan's cloak over Rennie's face, thrust the steward's dagger up into the youth's heart, twisted it and pulled it back before giving it another thrust. Satisfied that the boy was dead, Godfrew let him fall into the bush and walked away. The other side of the bush, hidden from view, Clunn watched. After Godfrew left, he walked to the bush and used a long stick to push Rennie further into the gorse.

* * *

At the rear of Earl Ralf's tent, Dunstan levered the top off of one of the barrels of white wine. He dug a wooden jug into the wine and pulled it out. Yellow fluid ran down the side of his broad hand. He quaffed the lot in one draught. "Sheep's piss," he asserted to Clunn, his fellow conspirator.

Clunn held up another wooden jug and replaced the drunken wine with the yellow fluid it contained. "Sheep's piss," he confirmed.

* * *

Bryan de Morlaix strode into the hall of his manor, glad to at last be home from the tiring campaign in Scotland. He dropped his saddlebags in the corner and headed toward the head table in search of some wine. It was then that he saw the wolf seated in his high-backed chair.

"What the hell do you think you are doing sitting in my chair?" Bryan the Breton gestured with his fingers and his squire came to stand alongside him. He switched his language to French. "I said, what are you doing in my chair?"

Brother Philadelphia moved out of the shadows and stood at Godfrew's elbow. "He ask what you do in his chair?"

"Sitting!" Godfrew could smell the dried horse dung on the monk's habit. It irritated his nose. He fought back the desire to sneeze.

"Good Sir Bryan, Master Geri Wendlewulf says that he is sitting." Philadelphia translated.

"Is he? By God, he will not be for long." The Breton drew his sword from the scabbard that hung from the brightly-coloured baldrick across his shoulder. "Tell him that he does not frighten me like he does the others. I know that he is only an ordinary man."

"He says, Master Geri, that you are only an ordinary man."

Godfrew pulled back the wolf mask hood, grateful to get its tickling fur away from his already irritated nose. Looking at the irate man, he gave a beaming smile, then chuckled. "Oh, Bryan the More Lax, how right you are. Philadelphia, you tell him ... and tell him that they are ordinary, too."

"Sir Bryan, he says you are right, he is only ordinary," explained the monk. The Breton grunted and strode forward with his naked blade in his hand. "But he says that these are only ordinary men, too." Bryan stopped and looked puzzled, until he noticed Tosti standing on one side of him holding a hand axe and Leofwine on the other with his saxe drawn. Bryan's squire went to pull out his dagger, but when he grabbed the hilt, he found a hand already on it. A leering, earless Clunn was smirking at him. Bryan's slit eyes started to calculate his chances of making a fight when the sound of shuffling feet told him that more men had arrived.

"And," said Godfrew pleasantly, "you can tell him that these are only ordinary house carls." The brothers three and Gogmagog came down the side of the hall and stood two to a side by the table. "Oh, I don't know, Master Monk. Why bother! He can see for himself."

Bryan's eyes opened wide and he started to breathe hard, "This is outrageous. I will complain to Count Ralf about this!"

Godfrew grasped what had been said and put a staying hand on the monk. "Tell Ralf, did you say? You will see the Earl only too soon."

Philadelphia looked at Godfrew, who nodded his assent for him to translate. "You will see 'Earl' Ralf too soon."

"You see, Bryan More Lax, you have indeed been lax ... lax in giving the Earl his dues. Your unlicensed market, for example ... and the twenty swine that somehow failed to get on the books before they ended up being salted away in barrels and sold to the Norman king's army agents. Then we shouldn't forget the fact that the Earl is only being sent the fourth penny on the fines levied in the manor court, instead of the third. There is more, but I won't bore you. I gave you and the rest of the landholders the hint before you all went north. You had men coming back to your holding. They understood what had been meant when I spoke to you all. You should have ensured that things were put straight then."

The Peace

"You want me tell him all that?" asked Brother Philadelphia.

"No. But tell him that he is to accompany us back to Norwich to await the Earl's pleasure." Godfrew poured himself a drink from Bryan's ewer into Bryan's chased-gold goblet and took a mouthful. "Wine? Don't you have any decent ale or cider?" He poured the fluid onto the stone floor. "Get on with it, monk. We have a long way to go today."

Brother Philadelphia pushed past the house carls and stood directly in front of Bryan."The sword, Sire, please." Bryan glanced around the room, still thinking of making a fight, but soon accepted that the odds were not good, so he went to sheath his weapon. Leofwine gently took it from him instead, checking the sword's balance and weight as he did so. "Now, Sir Bryan. There are certain matters that Earl Ralf is uncomfortable about, so he has asked Master Geri to come and escort you back to Norwich, so that you and he may clear matters up."

"Norwich ? You will have accommodation ready for me?"

"Yes, Sire. All is arranged. Your squire will accompany you. So will your priest."

"My priest?"

"Yes, he who has offered you advice and comfort for so long."

"Who will look after the manor? I know that the reeve has been taking care of things, but he did have Father Luke to help and advise him."

"That has been taken care of. Claud Bent Leg will serve as landholder for the present and I will remain to look after your folk's spiritual instruction."

"Now, look here monk. This is outrageous. I want a full explanation."

Philadelphia tilted his head to one side and licked his thin top lip. "I am sure that the Earl will tell you everything when he sees you. Now if you could go with these men, they will help you select a fresh horse and get it saddled."

As Bryan and his party left, Brother Philadelphia went back to Godfrew's elbow. Godfrew looked up. "Well, what did you tell him?"

"I tell?" asked the monk. "I say him that he get accommodation and priest come too."

"Ah, Master Monk, did you tell him that the accommodation we have ready for him is the damp dungeon that sits beneath the level of the moat at Norwich castle, or that the priest has already been persuaded to sing his litany and will now be retired to the secluded life of a anchorite?"

"I thought I leave that as nice surprise." The monk had a slit-mouth smile that did not look very pleasant.

* * *

Godfrew stood in the half-completed church and watched the masons at work building the walls with the imported Norman stone. Earl Ralf had given extra funds to employ more stone workers. Now that his holdings were bringing in much better returns, he could afford to indulge himself. Godfrew went to a wall and ran his hand over the cold surface.

"Back from yer country jaunts ven?" Athelmere stroked the stone. "Terrible stuff. As cold as a robber's grave." He stood at Godfrew's shoulder, but his stooped back put his face nearer the wall. "Dunno why yer fashion is ter build in it."

"Perhaps because it lasts longer?" Godfrew gave the carpenter a sideways glance.

"An so deprives good workmen of steady employment," Athelmere sighed. "It's just as well us carpenters is versatile. No matter 'ow much yer likes stone, it still takes wood ter finish it orf. Just imagine what stone seats would do ter yer piles on a winter's night!"

"Versatile?" Godfrew tapped the carpenter's elbow and indicated with his head toward a pile of stacked flat stones. "Seat?"

"Oh, yeh, why not." Athelmere walked to the make-do seat with a gate similar to that of Godfrew and sat down with a relieved sigh. "Versatile did yer say? Wot yer got in mind ven?"

"I have just been informed by our Lord and Master ..."

"Wot 'im," interrupted Athelmere, looking to the clouded sky above them.

"Silly bugger, you know who I mean."

"Only a joke, Master Geri, but seein' as wot we is buildin', I fought you may 'ave 'ad a divine message or somfink."

The Peace

"Earl Ralf, my earthly Lord and Master, has informed me that the Norman king has summoned all his chief men. He says the king has called it a 'Witan', but that he doubts anyone will get a chance to say anything other than the king himself."

"So wot's new?" Athelmere pulled out a small single-sided blade and used the opportunity to polish it on the flat surface of the stone he was sitting on.

"Our lord—Ralf, that is—believes that the summons is to raise an army to help the king crush a revolt by some of his subjects in France."

"I fought 'e bought 'em. Soldiers vat is."

"Perhaps he is running short of money, or maybe no one wants to fight for him anymore, considering he is always late in paying and so many of the soldiers seem to end up dead. Either way, he seems likely to be raising an English army to fight with him."

"Wiv 'im, not against 'im? Vat er'd be a novelty." The carpenter spat on the blade and then continued working it.

"They way he talks, Earl Ralf will try and dodge going, but he will have to send a contingent of men and he told me to look after the supply train."

Athelmere stopped stropping the blade. "'Ere, wot's all vis got ter do wiv carpenters?"

"Wagons. We need some new ones. Now we normally get them from a wagon wright in Hethel. They are a bit crude, but they are quite strong. Now, normally if you take an army to other shores, you have to beg, steal or borrow your transport when you get there. After my experience in Scotland, I am loath to try and do that. If I do go to France ... which I hope that I won't have to do ... but if I do have to go, I intend to take my own wagons and draught horses with me."

"Vey did vat, yer know. Ver Norman brought vere own 'orses."

"Yes, and on some occasions, the Vikings did the same. No, transporting horses isn't the problem. It's the wagons." Godfrew pulled off his broad-rimmed hat and ran his hand over his bald head and around his neck. "That's where you may be able to help."

"Oh, no, Master Geri. Versatile we may be. Wain ... I fink vats wot yer means by wagons ... wain builders, we ain't.

Different trade, see ... 'nover Guild, even." Athelmere bent to pick up a straw from the ground and used the blade to split it. Satisfied with its edge, he put the blade away.

"The man at Hethel can build them. You would 'advise'. For a fee, of course."

"Of course," Athelmere turned and gave Godfrew his full attention for the first time. "Master Geri, you 'ave a very devious mind. But I'm buggered if I can see wot you are drivin' at. Just wot sort've advice would I be givin' 'im?"

"I want wagons that pull apart and can be stored flat in a ship's hold. I know you can do it. I have seen your wonderful joints and skillful cuts."

"It'd need metal dowel pins, Master Athelmere," advised Alderbrook as he came and joined the other two. "An ver joints would 'ave ter 'ave greater tolerance so as vey can be knocked aht. Ven we would have ter get ver dowles drilled so as vey can be pinned. Be a bit tricky, but it can be done."

"For a price," commented Athelmere.

"For a price," agreed Godfrew.

The Revenge

Dunstan looked up from his labours.

"Oi, Wulf, where's all the bleeding cherry trees then?" He picked up his wooden mallet. Using a timber block, he drove home one of the iron dowels that held the wagon side in place. Godfrew waited until the big man had moved down to where Leofwine was holding the side ready for the next dowel to be hammered home.

"What cherry trees?"

"Well," Dunstan lined the dowel up with the hole in the side strut, "this place is called Cherryberg, isn't it? So where are the cherries? I fancy some cherries." He gestured to Leofwine: "Up a bit, just a fraction."

"Hungry? The last time I took you on the sea you spent the whole time puking over the side or vomiting into the scuppers!" Godfrew bent and inspected the wheel assembly, ensuring that the axle had been well greased.

Dunstan checked the alignment of the hole and dowel again before covering the iron pin with his block and whacking it home with strong strokes of the mallet. "Yes, but this time it was like a mill pond. I can cope with that." He nodded to Leofwine: "All right, sunshine. This is the last one to go on this side. Use the crowbar to ease it up—if you have to—but don't damage the sides!"

"You are trusting Leofwine with a crowbar?" Godfrew ran his thumb over the iron dowel to ensure that it was flush. Dunstan ignored the fact that Godfrew was checking his workmanship and moved to where Leofwine was gently levering the side with a long crowbar. At the same time, he checked the corresponding holes in the side panel and the side strut on the chassis. "For once, he is sober. I thought he was going to be sea sick, so I kept him away from the piss. It won't last though. He has already sussed out where the ale houses are." Dunstan checked the hole's alignment: "Spot on me, old mate. Just hold her there." Shock cocked his leg and piddled over the wagon's rear wheel.

Godfrew left them to their work and checked on young Swein and Magnus. They were going over the horses to ensure that they had come to no harm from their sea voyage. "Well, lads, are they all right?"

"Good as gold, Master Wulf." Swein Four Whiskers patted the rump of the big Suffolk dray. "Gentle as babes, these beauties."

"Are you sure that using only one horse per wagon will be enough, Master Wulf?" Magnus Golden Hair looked up from checking the hoof of the golden horse he was inspecting. His cropped hair and beard glinted in the weak sun.

"I think so ... I hope so. At least, we have a known quality ... unlike the others." They all stopped and watched as two young squires rode past trailing a string of manky-looking ponies, all fighting against their tethers. "I think that those who didn't bring their own horses will be regretting it later." Godfrew patted the flanks of Swein's horse. "Oh, well, I suppose I had better see how the others are getting on with assembling the other two wagons. I do hope that that young Puta drives a wagon as well as he cooks."

* * *

The trumpet blew and the drums rolled, attracting the attention of the assembled men. William Mallet waited until he was sure that the men were all watching him before he unrolled the scroll in his hand. "Now, listen here ... now listen here." His strong voice carried well, but Godfrew stood by young Tosti so that he could get a translation should he not catch all of what was being said. William cleared his throat before continuing: "First in French, then in English, I will give you your instructions. I will speak first in French, then I will tell you what to do in English."

"We can relax. He is talking to the Frogs first, Master Wulf." Tosti sat down on the crushed grass and the others all joined him. Clunn pulled his multi-coloured wool cap over his face and settled down for a quick doze. Godfrew sat by Tosti and pulled an early russet apple out from his pouch and started to eat it, despite constant attention from Shock's pointed nose. Dunstan rested his back against the rear wheel of the wagon and closed his eyes to dream of the

The Revenge

missing cherries, whilst Puta joined Edgar in the shade under one of the other wagons. As William Mallet droned on in French, so too did the French flies drone, as they sought out any sweaty brow they could find.

"I know that the Earl trusts you, but he is not going himself, so why must you?" Elfgifu held her husband's hands and gently squeezed them. "Why, Wulf?"

"Mainly because he is not going, I think. I suspect I am being used as his eyes and ears." Godfrew returned his wife's hand squeeze and smiled at her.

"And you so short-sighted and going deaf? Wulf, you must do better than that!"

"A kiss, my love, for I must go." Godfrew moved closer to Elfgifu and she to him. They kissed, but Elfgifu kept her lips closed despite her husband's attempts to make the kiss more than just a chaste peck. "I will be back ... and before you know it."

"Promise me, Wulf, that you will be careful."

"Of course. Am I ever anything else but?" Godfrew let go of Elfgifu's warm hands and went through the door of their house. Outside, Oakleaf and the boys waited. Oakleaf held out a plump hand, which Godfrew took.

"Be careful, cousin Wulf."

"You too? Elfgifu said the same." Godfrew could not resist gently running his thumb over the back of the maid's soft hand "Why do the women in my life all think that I am not careful?"

"Because old fat guts is speaking to us." Oakleaf replied.

"What?" Godfrew opened his eyes to find Tosti poking him.

"Old fat guts, the Mallet ... he is speaking to us English now."

"You listen and then tell me. I can't pick out what he says this far away. I'll go and make sure that the others are listening." Godfrew, still half-asleep, stared in the general direction of William Mallet. Once the sound of the war host leader's voice started to penetrate his mind, he got up and checked that his men were paying attention. Only Clunn was asleep. The others were standing on tip toes, straining their ears to hear what was being said. Godfrew left Clunn snoring and went back to Tosti's side. He waited for Mallet to stop speaking. When he stopped, the assembly began to relax and talk amongst themselves: "Well? What did he say?"

"The king has landed his army in more than one place. The various hosts are to assemble at a place called Cairns, or Cains ... something like that. From there, we will go down the river valley and cross some hills. Once over the hills, we will be running under war conditions. Until then, we must all behave, as we will be going through lands belonging to the king or his men. Those with their own transport are to proceed from first light tomorrow. Those without will have to wait here until more mounts and wagons for sale or hire arrive. They are due tomorrow and the day after ... with a horse fair the day after that. He also reminded us that we are to be well behaved ... no trying to re-fight the Battle of the Hoar Apple Tree on Senlac Ridge." Tosti and Godfrew moved out of the way as a group of English house carls came through the gap between their wagons.

An older man at their head, silver streaked through his moustaches and hair, his pointed leather cap set at a jaunty angle, started to slap his thighs as he walked. The younger men following him joined in. Satisfied that they were all making the same beat, he started his war chant:

> Listen to me men.
> Good advice I will give.
> A hoary old warrior,
> A cunning foe man,
> Long skilled in battle
> Skilled reever of old

His followers lifted their voices and joined him.

> Destroy all your foes.
> Lay waste all their land.
> Bring fire and burning.
> Set all things alight.
> Leave them nothing left,
> Neither wood nor field.
> So come break of morning.
> Nothing they eat.
> Begin thus your war.

The Revenge

Heed well my advice.
Destroy first the land.
Then destroy all your foes.

Godfrew watched them pass. "Well, young Tosti, it sounds like the boys have taken the Normans' instructions seriously."

* * *

Connan thumped on the top of the empty ale cask for attention. Behind him, his Breton bodyguard looked at the assembled English with mistrusting eyes. "Now, quiet. I talk." He folded his arms across his broad chest. "You men all belong Earl Ralf. You bring supply for soldiers. Now we left Normandy and in Maine. Supply finish. You go village and take food. No harm people ... no harm houses ... just take food." He leaned forward and looked hard into the Englishmen's eyes. "No trouble like there was at Caen. I already tell soldiers, now I tell you." Connan clicked his fingers and three of his Bretons came forward "These my men. When go villages, you take soldiers. My men in charge. Understand?"

"Very clearly put, Colin Steward." Godfrew turned and gave a sweep of his arm. "I can assure you that my men know very well how to behave in this, your beloved France."

"No trouble, English. Just remember ... no trouble."

"No trouble at all, Master Steward. Believe me ... it is no trouble at all."

Connan gave Godfrew a final belligerent stare before leaving, taking his Bretons with him.

"I wonder how bossy Colin is keeping warm at nights without his nice thick blue cloak, Master Wulf?" asked Clunn. The other men left to get the horses and wagons ready to leave.

Godfrew went red with shock, then turned to Clunn with a smile. "The same way as he is managing to eat without his nice sharp dagger, Master Rat."

* * *

The army of King William the Norman sat before Fresnay and besieged it. The summer sun baked all under it. The besieger's camp sweltered and smelled. Thousands of men and thousands of horses brought in millions of flies. Soon, it was not just the latrines and piles of horse manure that were covered in the winged plague. As soon as any food appeared, so did the flies. If they found no food, the flies sought out any moisture that sweating bodies produced—human and animal. The horses fought back vainly with their tails, the men with their hands.

Godfrew and his men were glad to be heading out of the stinking camp on a foraging expedition. The three wagons travelled along the dusty road in a staggered formation to keep clear of the road grime. Godfrew drove the lead wagon, Dunstan the second, and Edgar the third. Each wagon had an unwanted Breton soldier as a passenger. Riding ahead of the convoy rode Roger the Norman and his men from Bradley, all mounted on their own Suffolk rouncies. Godfrew's men rode in pairs alongside the wagons. The house carl brothers—with Gogmagog—made up a rear guard. All were dressed for war. Godfrew and the fortunate, or wealthy, were wearing chain-mail. The others wore ring-mail or boiled leather coats. All were uncomfortable in the heat, but all were aware of the need for protection in a hostile countryside.

Cresting a rise, Roger held up his hand for the convoy to halt. He rode back and stopped alongside Godfrew's wagon. "There is a small town ahead. I can't see any defences, but there may be covered ditches set as traps. I propose that I go down with my men and check it out. If it is safe, I will send a messenger back. Haggar here speaks a little French. I can then negotiate with the headman and he, hopefully, will organise the townsfolk to gather supplies for us."

"Look, Roger de Bradley. Connan the High Steward put me in charge, so you will do as I tell you." Godfrew's Breton stood up to make himself taller than the mounted Roger. "What we do is this ... you get hold of those barking Saxon dogs at the rear and rush the place. Make as much noise as you can. Put the fear of God into the locals. We will come down and force the peasants to hand over whatever we want. Do you understand?" Roger nodded, ashen-faced. "Good."

The Revenge

"What's happening?" Godfrew asked the Breton sergeant.

"What?" The sergeant looked at Godfrew puzzled, then sat down on the driver's bench of the wagon. "What?"

"Norman?" Godfrew called across to Roger of Bradley, "What is happening?"

Roger gave a defeated sigh. "We attack town, force folk give what we want."

"Fair enough." Godfrew bent down and fiddled under the bench. At last he found what he was after and pulled out his dented helmet with the boar sliding down it. "Thank you, Norman. See you there, then."

Roger turned his steed and his men with him. They rode to the rear to advise the rear guard of what was happening. Clunn and Tosti came alongside.

"What's up, Master Wulf?" Clunn yelled across the face of the Breton sergeant.

"A town lies over the hill. Norman and the boys will take it and then we plunder it." Godfrew looked over his right shoulder. "Hear that all right, Tosti?"

"I don't need telling twice, Master Wulf. I'll tell the others." Tosti dropped back.

"Master Geri." Roger the Norman came back alongside and replaced Tosti. "Tell men ... remember ... no killing ... only use force in self-defence."

"Self-defence Norman? Right. Only kill Frenchmen if they attack you. Don't worry, that has always been my principle." Despite the heat, Godfrew pulled out his cloak from under the driving bench and stood up to put it on, wolf skin side out. Roger shook his head in disbelief and rode off to lead his enlarged band of horsemen to try and take the town.

Godfrew waited until Roger and his men had ridden around the small town, then—just as they thundered in down the main street—he slapped the draught horse hard on its rump and set off down the gentle hill at a cracking pace, the others following. A few of the townsfolk looked as if they were going to make a stand. On hearing—or rather feeling—the approach of Godfrew and the rest of the party, they fled. As they ran through the side streets, they collected others in a headlong panic, crashing into the fields and trampling down anything in their way.

The houses on the outskirts of the little town were little more than mean huts. It did not take long for the wolves to strip them bare before setting fire to them. The Breton sergeant ran over and grabbed Clunn's arm just as the little man was about to throw another brand into an already burning cottage. "No, leave it alone. No fire. No burning. Just take food and plunder!"

Clunn swung around and caught the Breton under the chin. With help from Leofwine and Tosti, he threw the man into the cottage just as the roof started to collapse. "Master Wulf. MASTER WULF," Clunn cried, "the sergeant has been killed."

Godfrew strode over, Neckbiter in his hands. "The Breton killed did you say?" Clunn and the others all nodded. "A great shame that, something also seems to have happened to the other Bretons, too. This is a treacherous place." He hefted his axe in his hands. "Well, lads, this means we must be prepared to act in self-defence." Godfrew went off to further the town's destruction.

Ahead, the house carl brothers and Gogmagog crashed through a group of citizens. They leaped ahead of their mounts and slaughtered all before them—the brothers with their swords and Gogmagog, now naked, with his huge wooden nail studded club. Screams filled the air and the pace of the destruction speeded up. Roger the Norman sat in the town square looking for his Suffolk men whilst they chased down the side streets hunting the townsfolk as though they were hares. For an hour or more, the slaughter continued. As the flames from the burning poor-quarter spread, the English began their plunder in earnest, dragging spoil from the houses out into the streets. The more thoughtful brought in the livestock. Through a mixture of threats and blows, Godfrew gathered his wolf pack together and led them toward the largest dwelling the town possessed. It was three stories high, the bottom two of stone. The door was of solid oak, so it took several blows from Neckbiter to split it near the hinges. Puta drove up one of the wagons and used the last of Godfrew's walrus hide ropes to attach the door handle to it. After a short pull, the door swung open drunkenly and Godfrew herded his wolves inside. Leaving his men to ensure that the house was safe, Godfrew climbed the stairs.

At the head of the stairs, he found three doors. The first two were closed, so he opened them. They were bedrooms, empty of people, but filled with treasure. Leaving Shock to explore them further, he went to the third door. This one was slightly open and he could hear movement inside. Carefully, he eased the door wide open and looked inside.

On the bed, a woman sat facing him, her back to the wall. Her naked skin was a light gold that contrasted with her dark, prominent nipples. Deep auburn, wavy hair cascaded down her body and flowed over her plump thighs. Her body was not that of a maid, as the fine silver tracery of stretch marks on her belly told, but her body's fullness invited the eye. Godfrew moved his eye, from her body to her face. Again, he was aware of her maturity. Again, he found himself attracted. Her dark eyes were half-open. She smiled at Godfrew becomingly. Her lips parted and a dark, pink tongue touched her upper lip as she lifted her hands from the white bed sheet and cupped her breasts. All the while, her smile became more seductive. Slowly, her hands left her breasts and moved down her body, caressing each curve and fold of flesh as they went. When they reached her bush, the woman parted her legs and exposed her inner parts. Godfrew felt a hot flush as he watched, oblivious to the noise of his men below. Slowly, she let her fingers explore her own body. The woman closed her eyes and sighed.

Godfrew ached for her. Since getting married, he had not known a woman other than his wife. Since the conception of their son, Njal, he had not even lain with Elfgifu. The woman moaned and spread her legs even wider. Godfrew could smell her scent, musk overlaid by caramel. His head swam. The woman slid down to lie fully on the bed. With one hand, she kept herself spread to show the pinkness within. With the other hand, she languidly beckoned Godfrew over. Godfrew felt the tightening of his loins. The bitter taste of adrenaline filled his mouth. All he could see, hear, and smell was this woman—mature, full bodied and all knowing. All his body was filled with desire for the woman who beckoned him to join her.

Shock stuck his nose into the door jam and snuffled. Godfrew, not wanting the erotic spell to be broken, went to kick the hound out of the way when he caught sight of a slight movement behind the door. He pulled his saxe from its scabbard behind his back, kicked the door hard, and was rewarded with a scream as it swung into the wall. Behind the door, a near naked man fell to the floor and clutched his shattered nose. Blood ran through his fingers and a gilt-handled dagger lay at his feet. Godfrew stepped forward, kicked the dagger away, tilted the man's head back and cut his throat.

"Wolves, can you hear me?" Godfrew shouted down the stairs.

"Rats can hear as well as wolves, Master Wulf. Have you found me some cheese?" replied Clunn.

"No, but I have found a meat bone for all you wolves to chew upon." Godfrew strode out, followed by his faithful Shock. The woman pulled the bedclothes up to cover herself, unsure of what had been said, but suspecting that it bode ill for her.

Godfrew pushed his way through the men as they headed up the stairs. He wondered why— when their town was being sacked and put to the sword—a woman and her lover would choose to copulate rather than flee.

* * *

Roger of Bradley sat dejectedly in his saddle, surveying the ten wagons of booty and large herd of livestock making ready to head back to camp. On the outskirts of the town, some of the English were amusing themselves by felling or pulling out any fruit trees or vines they could find. The Norman wiped what could have been a tear from his eye. "Why, Geri. Why?"

"Because we had good teachers and we have learned well, Norman. That is why." Godfrew left Roger the Norman to ride off and organise their return journey. He ducked inside the awning of the wagon and took off his cloak and helmet. There, hanging from the ribs of the awning, was the naked woman he had found in the house. The woman's mouth was gagged with a knotted rag. Bruises were already appearing on her bound wrists and ankles. One of her eyes had been

The Revenge

blackened. Checking her globular breasts for any apparent damage, was Clunn.

"Master Wulf." Clunn acknowledged, lifting the woman's chin and turning her face from side to side, tutting at the fact that her ears had been torn when her earrings had been taken from her.

"What is she doing here, Clunn?"

Clunn gave Godfrew a smile that exposed his uneven, buttercup-yellow teeth, "Why, Master Wulf, even rats like to take their old baggage with them." He picked up a long piece of blue ribbon and tied it around the woman's waist.

* * *

Godfrew watched as the house carl brothers, with the daft Gogmagog trailing behind, came toward the wagon. Shock stopped rolling in the horse urine and watched too.

"Not again. We have cleaned out five villages and towns in the last week. We need a break. Even the horses want a rest." Godfrew pushed away the odorous Shock as the hound came over to nuzzle him.

"No, we haven't come to tell you that," said the brother with the leather cap.

"We haven't even come to ask you to get ready for tomorrow," added the brother with the wool cap.

"We've come to say good-bye," explained the brother without a cap at all. "At least, for the time being."

"Where are you going?" Godfrew stood up slowly, then wiped his hands clean on his britches. Shock wiped his neck on the cross banding of Godfrew's leggings.

"It seems the Norman king is pleased with our activities," answered leather cap.

"He promoted Norman of Bradley and put him in charge of an exploratory party going down the river Sarthe." clarified wool cap.

"He is taking all the men of Suffolk with him," added no hat, with a smile.

"I take it he is not wanting us with him, then?" Godfrew shook his right leg, so Shock went around and rubbed Godfrew's left leg instead.

"Afraid not."

"Wagons would be too slow."

"Need to keep on the move."

"He human, who is Devil." Gogmagog picked up Shock, gave him a big kiss on the nose and rubbed the dog's muzzle and neck all around his smiling face.

"Did he say what I think he said? Our Norman thinks that I am the Devil?"

"Afraid so."

"He's a peaceable man, really, our Norman."

"He dislikes pillaging and sacking."

"So," Godfrew picked up a flask from the shade under the wagon and offered it to the brothers, "am I to be left with Colin and his Bretons for company?"

"I'm afraid not." Leather cap took a deep swig before passing the flask on.

"He says he loses too many men when they go with you." Wool cap drank long and hard from the flask.

"So you are to join the men of Shropshire, seeing as you know them." No cap tipped the flask well back and quenched his thirst.

"Here, here, here." Gogmagog took the flask and drained it. "Hempterty," he said before dropping it to the ground for Shock to investigate.

"Now. Master Geri, the Wolf ... our plunder."

"It will get back all right?"

"It won't 'shrink' will it?"

Godfrew patted the side of the wagon. "It will get back, even if you don't. Don't worry, I know who to give it to if you do die here. You are married to the four sisters who own the Twisted Thorn ale house, right?"

The wagon shook slightly. There was a murmur of voices from the rear.

"What's going on?" asked leather cap.

"Got problems?" inquired wool cap.

"Need any help?" offered no cap.

"The only one who may need help is that earless rat, Clunn. He is using the wagon to hire out his woman. So far, he has made more money out of her than we have ever got from plundering. He may need help carrying away all the gold he has taken."

The Revenge

* * *

With a bright, yellow-silk shirt over his coat of mail, Stanley led Earl Edric's men into the streets of Beaumont. The newly risen sun lighted their way as they moved toward the castle. The castle had its drawbridge up, so Stanley set archers to watch it while he organised his men to ravage the village that had grown up around it. Godfrew stood at Stanley's side and listened. Following orders, the men fanned down the streets and waited at the doors of the more prosperous houses for Stanley's signal.

"You have learned a lot, young Stanley." Godfrew undid the leather thong that held his helmet to his belt. The eye hole in the face protector that matched his blind eye now sported a piece of red glass that had come from a destroyed chapel. A metal smith had skillfully made gold tongues to hold it all in place. "You have certainly come a long way from when I first taught you how to use an axe and it was all that you could do to keep your balance."

"Circumstances have just worked my way, Wulf. All men's fate is already written. We just can't always see the cloth for the threads." Stanley looked at the castle. "I do not think that it is our fate to take that castle. That looks like a full siege job." He looked at Godfrew and gave a lop-sided smile. "I know, Wulf, I am all too familiar with the stories about how you almost took Hereford and Shrewsbury."

"You were there at Shrewsbury, young Stanley." Godfrew put on his helmet and adjusted it so that his good eye was looking under the rim of its eye hole.

"Yes, I was ... and I remember that we failed to take it ... lost a lot of good men in the process." He looked down the main street and saw the last of the men get to their target "Unlike you, Wulf, I am not willing to risk it." Stanley left Godfrew and stood in the middle of the street. He took a very deep breath, then called out at the top of his voice: "WE ARE THE BOYS WHO MAKE NO NOISE!"

"OOH-AAH, OOH-AAH," came the shouted reply. The Shropshire men stove in the doors of their target houses.

Godfrew joined his men in the side street that had been allocated for them. He watched as they crashed through the fragile doors and chased out the occupants, letting them climb out through the windows and back doors in various states of undress. Like most of the other villagers, the majority headed for the village church, rather than the open fields. They could see others from Stanley's band rounding up cattle and sheep.

Godfrew's attention was pulled back to the main street by the sound of clashing swords and shields. "Leave them, wolves. TO ME, TO ME." As he ran down the street, he banged on the broken doors and repeated the cry. In the middle of the main street was a knot of English with their coloured shirts over their mail. They fought with ring-mail coated French, tangled in a heaving, bloody shamble. Godfrew and his men took the French in the flank and shattered them. Despite the ache in his shoulder, Godfrew took down a mail-coated opponent with his axe, splitting the man's head in twain. He freed Neckbiter, saw a Frenchman with his back to him, and cleft him apart from shoulder to waist. From the castle came a sharp trumpet call, but there were no Frenchmen left to answer the signal for retreat.

Godfrew stood over Stanley, his bright, yellow shirt spoiled with blood. Dunstan hobbled over with a broken sword in his hand. "Is he all right? He looks pretty .. you know .. thing." Dunstan moved around to look at the other side of Stanley's shattered face and head.

Godfrew knelt and flicked pieces of broken bone away from what had been the young man's nose and examined the damage. "He may live, but he will never fight again. 'All men's fate is already written'." Godfrew stood up and cried out: "Destroy it all. Take no prisoners. Pull everything down. Leave nothing and no one standing."

The men went and set about their task with a grim will, looting the houses and killing all within. The church, they surrounded and burned. The archers picked off any who tried to escape. All the time, Godfrew stalked the village to ensure that his orders were being carried out. Meanwhile, his wolves went about their own purpose.

* * *

The cottage was dark. The only light came from the smoke hole in the roof. That shaft of pure light struck the naked-

The Revenge

white body of the young girl lying on the rough wooden table. Of no more than ten summers, her bound copper hair contrasted sharply with her alabaster skin. She was held face down by members of the wolf pack, but she made no sound. Clunn the Earless stood at the end of the table furthest from her face, looking over her body—examining it like a master chef before cutting the first slice from a prize joint of meat at a king's banquet.

"Such perfection," Clunn sighed. "It is almost a shame to touch it." He tugged at his black and brown beard and moved his head, checking the girl's body over from all angles. "But then, how can one know if it is perfection or not, unless one samples it?" He flashed a yellow-toothed grin.

"Get on with it, you little rat." Tosti tightened his grip on the girl's wrist. "My britches are bursting."

"I thought I taught you patience, young man. A good meal should be contemplated. It should be mused over ... the flavours should be anticipated ..."

"And it should be thing," intruded Dunstan, holding the girl's other wrist. "You know ... thing ... consummated."

"All right, then." Clunn ran two dirty thumbs down the crack in the girl's buttocks "My, this reminds me of that sweet fruit we sampled in Caen. What was it now? Tosti?"

"A peach. Now hurry up. I want my turn."

"A peach! That was it. You ran your thumb nails down the crease and opened it up, so ..." Clunn peeled the girl's buttocks open and Swein and Magnus, at her ankles, spread the girl's legs. Clunn looked at the girl's anus. "Yes, a peach. It even has a little stone." Clunn blew on it, causing it to tighten. "Now, should one attend to the stone first, or should one enjoy the fruit first?"

"Get on with thinging her, Clunn, before I am past thing." Dunstan fidgeted, his face becoming a reddish colour. "She does remind me of my wife .. not my current missus ... the one I have just left ... Adia my first one ... beautiful white skin and thing ... I remember ..."

"Dear Dunstan! At last the truth. You are past it!" Clunn gently caressed the girl's flesh, refusing to be hurried. "Now look at that, no hair, just soft silky skin."

"No hair, eh? Just like those whores in Caen. They had no hair either," said Magnus.

"The difference, my ignorant young friend, is that they shaved it off so that you could see if they were poxed or not. This one is natural ... surprising for a girl whose breasts are budding up ... be they ever so small." Clunn continued, stroking wistfully.

"Clunn!" Dunstan wriggled a bit. "Hurry up, before I make a mess of myself!"

"Oh the problems us connoisseurs have with the ignorant." Clunn finally parted the girl's labia. The girl at last opened her eyes and stared into the dead face of her father, slumped against the cottage wall. "Now, will someone let my tail out so that this little rat may make his nest in this warm, inviting hole?" A pair of hands came around the front of Clunn's britches and undid the belt. "Ah, thank you, friend. A further favour. I am loath to loose my hands from this delectable fruit. Could you be so kind as to point me in the right direction?" The hands tugged the britches down, pulled Clunn's erect penis out and lined it up with the spread-eagled girl's body. "So kind. A final task: unhood me." A hand pulled Clunn's foreskin back, but the other hand placed a saxe under the scared head of the penis. "Ahhhhh," was all Clunn could say when he felt the cold steel sharply contact his member.

The saxe slowly circumscribed the head of Clunn's penis, leaving a red ring of blood. Clunn looked at the others in the wolf pack for enlightenment, but they had released the girl and were edging toward the door. After once more checking that the head of his penis was still attached, Clunn chanced a look over his shoulder and looked into the face of the wolf.

"Ah, Master Wulf. I take it you are not amused by my private interests?" Clunn kept his breathing slow and gentle, not wanting to risk the saxe cutting any deeper than it already had.

"Keep your perversions to yourself and your activities to whores." Godfrew tightened his grip on the little man's large penis and pulled it down again onto the blade "I've warned you before about upsetting me. Once more, you rat, and you will have no 'tail' to tell!" Godfrew released his grip. Clunn, after a quick visual examination, pulled himself together and redressed.

The Revenge

Godfrew went over to the girl, grabbed her wrist and pulled her up. The child threw herself at him and wrapped herself around his body. Godfrew pulled the wolf-skin cloak over the girl's nakedness and left.

With the girl still entwined around him, it was with great difficulty that Godfrew managed to mount his pony. As he rode toward the wagons, the rain bit into his face, then flowed down and joined the tears of the sobbing child clinging to him.

* * *

As the first light of morning turned the inside of the wagon into amber, Godfrew felt cold. He lay there trying to work out why. Then he saw Shock's head. Instead of being inside his master's cloak, he was being cuddled by the French girl. Godfrew eased himself up and edged over to where she lay. Shock's eyes were open. They followed Godfrew's movements, but he did not stir—in fact, he could not stir because of the child's iron embrace. Godfrew rocked on his heels and looked at the girl. Her bright copper hair clashed with the plundered mustard-yellow blanket that covered her and the hound. Shock looked from his master to the girl's face, then back again—explaining without words that he could not leave her side. There was a hint of a noise— a chain chinking—and Godfrew knew that Clunn had released his woman to help prepare food for the wolf pack. The little man had realised that keeping her tied by ankle and wrist with rope was damaging her and reducing her retail value. He now chained her by her neck—using a strong, but fine, silver chain he had acquired from a church that they had pulled down. He only restrained her at night. Clunn's woman pulled back the flap at the front of the wagon and looked in. Seeing Godfrew and the child, she took in a sharp breath. Godfrew looked at her and pulled the blanket down far enough to show the girl's nakedness.

"You dirty Saxon bastard. I suppose you want me to clean up the mess you have made of the poor child," the woman hissed.

Godfrew gave her a puzzled look, then pulled at his shirt. "Clothes. Can you find some clothes? The poor wee thing has nothing to wear." He gave his shirt another tug and pointed to the sleeping girl.

"What on earth are you trying to tell me, Saxon? Boasting about your perversions?" Clunn's woman snarled, wagging her finger at Godfrew. "Well, I am not going to wait for you to start again. I am going to get the wretched girl something to put on. Perhaps then you will find her less desirable!" She left the wagon, leaving Godfrew unsure as to whether she had understood what he wanted her to do. He sat down by the girl, stroked her hair with one hand and his faithful hound with the other.

Clunn poked his head in: "Sort this silly bitch out for me, Master Wulf." He shoved his woman in none too gently. "No matter what I do, she keeps going back to the spoils and grabbing clothes." He wrenched a dress and apron from the woman and threw it at Godfrew's feet. "I keep telling her to leave the spoil alone. It's not even as if the gear will fit her!"

The little girl woke with all the noise and saw Clunn's face. She screamed, scrambled across to Godfrew and hung onto him. Shock gave a rare bark at Clunn and just managed to dodge the responding blow aimed at him.

"The clothes are for the girl, Clunn. Just get out of here. You are frightening her." Godfrew held the child close and kissed her head. Shock stood at her side and licked away her tears.

"Sorry I spoke. In fact, I'm sure that I am supposed to be sorry that I am even breathing!" Clunn left, then poked his head back in. "And tell that silly slut of mine to hurry up and get back out here. She has to help Puta get the food ready. We've got the whole bloody war-band to feed now."

"All right, Clunn. Just stop upsetting my child." Godfrew picked up the fallen clothing, but as soon as she felt his hold lessening, the girl began to cry again. She tried to bury herself in his chest. "Steady, little one. You must have some clothes on." He looked over at Clunn's woman. She picked up the dress and passed it over to Godfrew. "Come little one, see what a pretty dress we have found you. Please ... for me." Godfrew touched her hand with the dress and she peeked at it. "Come on now, you can't run around naked, can you?" She reluctantly took hold of the dress and held it to her side. "Especially with that smelly rat Clunn and the other randy

The Revenge

wolves around." Godfrew added softly as he slowly peeled the girl from him. "Now, my precious, put it on." Godfrew touched the dress and pointed to the girl's body. As if aware for the first time of her nakedness, the girl frantically scrabbled at the dress until she had got it on. Clunn's woman came over and passed the girl the linen apron. "Thank you." Godfrew smiled at the woman as she left. The silver chain around her neck also entwined around her waist, so she tinkled as she disappeared through the flap. The blue ribbon that hung under her skirt stayed for seconds after the rest of her had gone.

Godfrew stroked the girls' cheek with the back of his hand and wondered what he was going to do with her. "Come on, little one. Let's get some food." He held out his hand and she took it, letting him lead her into the strengthening sunlight.

Outside was noise and the smell of burnt houses. Puta and the woman were tending a fire in the centre of the laargered wagons. At the end was a mixed herd of domestic animals, all keen to get at the green grass ouside of the camp. Godfrew jumped down and held out his arms for the girl. She accepted his help, but instead of letting him put her down on the ground, she insisted on clinging to him. With the extra burden, Godfrew made it only to the outside of the laarger before he had to rest. Dunstan came over, avoiding the girl's eyes.

"Oh, you were right, last night they tried to thing." He sat down beside Godfrew on the wagon's shaft.

"I knew they would. What happened? Was there much of a problem?"

"No." Dunstan scratched his thick head of hair "The boys let about a dozen of them get halfway up the high street and then took them out."

Godfrew looked over the top of the girl's head, twitching his nose as her copper hair tickled him. "Many casualties?"

"Heaps."

Godfrew almost dropped the girl. She responded by sinking her fingers into his back to prevent herself from being dislodged. "What?"

"On their side," Dunstan smirked. "We used the archers to pick them off, though I think one or two may have made it back to the castle, but they wouldn't have lived long." He bent down and picked a dandelion, which he offered to the girl. She took it shyly and twirled it in her fingers, letting it rub against both her own face and Godfrew's. "I think she has forgiven me, or maybe she doesn't remember me."

"She remembers Clunn."

"Don't we all." Dunstan went a gentle shade of pink. "Look, Wulf, I'm sorry about yesterday. Maybe I've been too long without having a woman. I didn't think."

"Too long without a woman? Yes, it can make you do strange things." Godfrew moved the girl around to a more comfortable position, sideways across his lap. "I gave the order for total destruction. You were only obeying my orders. After what happened to Stanley, I just saw red. I only wanted revenge ... like you only wanted a woman."

"Yes, but she is not ... is she?"

"No, she isn't."

The girl rested her cheek against Godfrew's. She held out the flower to him. "Flower."

"What did you say? 'Fleur'? Is that your name? It is as pretty as you, my little miss." Godfrew saw some of the war band come toward him. "Steady, Fleur. These big smelly men won't hurt you. It's me they've come to see." Despite her fears, the gentle tone of Godfrew's voice reassured the girl and she remained seated on his lap.

"Ho, Master Wulf." Ten or more warriors stood in front of Godfrew, all wanting to say something, but none wanting to speak first.

"Gentlemen. What can I do for you?" Godfrew accepted a bowl of porridge from Clunn's woman and promptly started to feed Fleur with it.

The warriors were obviously amused to see the leader of the wolf pack spoon feeding a child, but kept their comments to themselves. Despite murmuring and muttering amongst themselves, no one answered Godfrew until, after a lot of jostling, Bajarki White Hair was pushed to the front.

"Cousin Wulf," the Dane smiled and stared at Godfrew.

"Yes, cousin Bajarki?" Fleur took the spoon from Godfrew's hand and began to feed herself. "You have something to say?"

"Stanley."

"Yes? Stanley?" Godfrew accepted a second bowl from Clunn's woman and pulled his cloak across Fleur's lap before resting the bowl on her legs.

"Stanley is badly injured." Bajarki stated, after looking to the others with him.

"Yes, Stanley is badly injured. He may not live. If he lives, he may never fight again." Godfrew dug his spoon into the porridge, lifted it to his lips and blew on it gently. Shock stood at his side and licked some spillage off the side of the bowl.

"Well, what is going to happen?" The white-haired Dane looked at his fellow warriors. They all nodded encouragement to him. "Well, with Stanley injured, will you lead us?"

Godfrew ate his spoonful of porridge and two more before answering. "No." Fleur almost jumped out of her skin when the assembled men cried out in protest. Godfrew gave the warriors a withering look and they quieted down. Before continuing, he gave the girl a reassuring hug. "I will lead us back to the camp outside Freshly, or whatever it is called. But then another leader will have to be found." Again the men went to protest, but Godfrew held up his hand to silence them, then put his finger to his lips.

"Why not, cousin?" Bajarki persisted.

"I served Earl Edric of my own free will. Nowhere could I have found a better lord. See, I still wear this ..." Godfrew held out his hand and displayed the sword ring on his finger, "... and on high days and holy days I wear his golden arm band. No man could love a lord more than I love Earl Edric."

"Then lead his men!" a voice from the back shouted. Godfrew recognised the blurred face as that of young Ragnor, his hair as bright a copper as that of Fleur's.

"I cannot. No, don't start off again. Let me finish." Fleur fidgeted and Godfrew managed to persuade her to get off of his boney lap and sit in front of him. There, she rested her back against his legs and draped an arm over Shock. "I failed the Earl on my last mission. I lost control of my men." Tosti, who had come over to see what was going on went bright red and walked away again. "I caused the Earl some considerable embarrassment. He could have ... maybe should have ... given me over to the Norman authorities. They would have loved that. As you all know, I am wanted in many shires as an outlaw and Wolfshead. But he didn't. He released me from his service instead. If I were to become your leader, I would be defying and insulting him. My love is too great to do that." He took a handful of Fleur's unbound hair and let it run through his fingers like molten copper. "Yes, I will take us back to Fresney. And there you will call a Thing-Moot. All who would be leader of the war band shall come forward with his swearers and state his case. By show of hands and acclamation, one will be voted leader and all will then swear an oath of allegiance to him should Stanley recover. If you wish, I will be willing to sit in judgment with the unsuccessful candidates to decide whether Stanley resumes the leadership or no."

"But cousin ..."

"Stop trying to wheedle, Bajarki. You of all people! You have never even seen me fight, let alone lead a war band." Godfrew got up. As he stood, he found Fleur's hand in his. "Trust me, for of all people, I know best my own mind."

* * *

The day after the news of the destruction of his holding at Beaumont by the English reached the ears of Hubert of Fresnay, he began to negotiate terms for his surrender. Whilst awaiting orders to move on, Earl Edric's men elected Bajarki as the new leader of their war band, for although only a new man in the Earl's service, he was the most acceptable to all parties. He was blessed with a ready tongue, even if he could only be understood by the others when he spoke slowly. Godfrew spent most of his time trying to teach his little maid English. Whenever he gave her a lesson, Clunn's woman sat nearby and listened until Clunn hired her out.

"Why does he call you 'Fleur'? Your proper name of Giselle is so much nicer." Clunn's woman rolled her sleeves up and plunged her arms into the large bucket of soapy water.

"It is because he is English, silly," replied Fleur, bringing more dirty plates over.

"That is not the answer, Giselle, and you know it." Clunn's woman scrubbed a plate clean and put it on a rickety table to dry with those that had gone before.

"Yes, it is Eleanor. I heard the one with the straggly whiskers on his chin say, 'She is as pretty as a flower'. So ... I am

The Revenge

his flower ... his 'fleur'... he thinks that I am pretty." Fleur put the dirty dishes down for Shock to lick off the scraps of food.

"It is not right for a man his age to keep touching and cuddling you like he does. He will do dirty things to you, Giselle. Believe me, one day he will." Eleanor took the now shiny dishes from Fleur and sunk them in the bucket to wash.

"Like you do with the other men around the back of our wagon?"

"You should not be watching!" The older woman put her suds-covered hands on her hips and gave the young girl a strict look.

"You should not make so much noise!"

"Please, Giselle. Just be careful. Men are not to be trusted." Eleanor went back to the bucket and continued the washing.

"He will never hurt me. He is my Papa."

"Little one, you know what happened to your papa. This English wolf is not your father."

"He is my Papa." Fleur sat down and started crying. Shock came and nuzzled her.

"Oh, poor child." Clunn's woman sat by the girl's side and put an arm around her shoulder.

"He loves me. He is my Papa." Fleur lifted up her tear-stained face with a pleading look in her eyes.

"Yes, he is your papa ... and you are his pretty little flower." Eleanor cradled the girl in her arms and hugged her. Shock forced his needle nose up between Fleur and Eleanor. He winked and then licked the fresh tears running down the older woman's face.

* * *

The army of King William continued down the Sarthe valley. Ahead, on both sides of it, the foraging parties of the English spread like locusts. As all was green when they arrived, so all was black when they left. On hearing that the English wolf packs were coming, the people fled—taking what they could with them. Any joy they found in escaping with their lives was lost when they returned to their homes. No house was left standing ... no animals left grazing... no trees not cut down or ring barked ... no vines not pulled out ... no standing crops unfired. As the Normans had done to them, so the English did to the French. The army rode on to besiege Sille, but the men holding it had heard of the destruction already wrought on the land. They surrendered the castle and town to the Norman king without a fight. Now the host found itself before the walled town of Le Mans, where the revolt had started, and the whetstones were brought out so that an edge could be put back onto the blades of blunted and dented weapons.

Godfrew stood by the head of one of the Suffolk draught horses, keeping it steady whilst a smith reshod it. Acrid smoke from the animal's right rear hoof drifted past him as the shoe was fitted. Godfrew hid his head in his shirt and breathed shallowly whilst his eyes watered.

"Master Wulf!" Swein and Magnus came through the fumes, waving their hands before them to disperse the smoke. Swein was sporting a vivid red scar that ran from his wrist to his elbow. Magnus had shaved his head yet again and cropped his beard to no more than a finger's width.

"Seeing you two, I know that there must be trouble." Godfrew rested his head against the horse. "What's up now? Lost more money playing dice? You know I won't give you your share of the plunder till we get back home, so you will be wasting your time, you know!"

"It's not us." Swein came and patted the horses flanks.

"No, it's Leofwine." Magnus rested his back against the horse's side and stretched his arms out along the creature's back.

"What's he done now? As if I couldn't guess." The farrier came around the other side and gave Godfrew the thumb's up. Godfrew let go of the bridle, beckoned Fleur over and gave her the horse's lead strap so that she could walk it back to the horse lines. "All right, surprise me. What's up with Leofwine."

"He's sick." Magnus had not seen Godfrew hand the horse over to Fleur. As the maid led the big animal away, he fell down on his back. Swein laughed at his friend's discomfort, so Magnus picked up a ball of horse dung and threw it at Swein.

The Revenge

Godfrew stepped in before the game turned into a fight. "Tell me about Leofwine." He grabbed Magnus' wrist and made him drop his next missile. "Magnus!" he warned.

"Leofwine?" Magnus wiped his hands on Shock as the hound passed by looking for Fleur. "I told you. He is sick."

"Leofwine is always sick." Godfrew held out his hand and pulled the shaven-headed young man to his feet. "If you keep putting ale in like he does, it is bound to come out again. The quicker it goes in, the quicker it comes back ... especially that weasel's piss that the French dare to call ale."

"Yeah, we know that, Master Wulf," chimed in Swein. "But he really is sick. Come and see."

Godfrew followed the youngster at his own slow pace toward the threadbare tent that Leofwine called home, though he seemed to spend most of his time sleeping in a drunken stupor under one of the wagons. On the way, Magnus could not resist finding some more horse dung and throwing it at Swein. The two battled it out until they arrived at Leofwine's tent. Even then, they only stopped out of deference to Godfrew.

"See, Master Wulf. He is sick." Swein held the thin tent flap open. Inside, lying in his own vomit, was Leofwine. Bits of undigested food were stuck in his hair. Already, the flies had covered his face and head in search of something tasty to eat. Godfrew kicked Leofwine's foot and the man responded by gurgling and letting his fingers jerk up and down in the sick.

"Dear God, Leofwine, just what have you been drinking. You stink, man." Godfrew stood back from the tent to get some fresh air.

Swein let the flap go. "That's the thing. Master Wulf. He hasn't been drinking."

"Leofwine? Not drinking?"

"Not this morning, anyway." Magnus put his arm around Swein's neck.

"No," Swein added. "That's how we found him. He was supposed to come with us to bring some more ale back for the lads from the commissary's store. But he didn't arrive."

"At first we thought he was skiving off."

"But when we found him, he was like this."

"And it wasn't from getting legless last night, either. He went to bed early, as he said he felt unwell."

"Yes, Magnus." Godfrew lifted the tent flap again and surveyed the prostrate man lying on the floor, liquid excrement starting to ooze through the thin linen of his britches. "Yes, he is unwell, all right. See if you can find Puta. He likes looking after people ... though even he might not want to tend someone this sick."

The following day others became ill and even more the next. By the week's end, most in the camp had succumbed, including Godfrew.

* * *

Godfrew stood in the swirl of the Wandle's woe waters, the water striking his back and almost pushing him over. "To me, boy. Come to me." He held out his hand to the struggling child Elfgifu had pushed toward him through the flood. Despite his father's encouragement, the little boy turned away and floated downstream. Godfrew looked across to the bank where he had put his three eldest sons, but they had wandered off, taking the strange little red-haired girl with them. "Elfgifu! Elfgifu!" His wife stood on the opposite bank and waved to him with another son under her arm. "Wait till I can get to you. Don't put the boy in the water. I keep losing them." Elfgifu stood by the flooded river and prepared to put the child in. "Elfgifu, in the name of your God, don't do that. I have lost the last five. I can't get to them in time. Elfgifu!" His wife smiled and pushed her son into the water toward Godfrew.

"What did he say, Giselle? You understand English better than I." Eleanor bathed Godfrew's sweat-covered brow.

"Something about a river and his sons. I thought he had only three boys, but he is calling out about more sons!" Fleur pulled the blanket back over Godfrew's fevered body as Puta had told her to do before he himself had taken ill with the bloody flux.

"Well, he has more wrong with him than the others." Eleanor sat back and looked at the agitated Godfrew. "This is something other than flux."

The Revenge

"Puta said that Papa was like this when they were in a place called 'The Fens', in England." Fleur leaned across to pull the rag from the bucket of cold water and wring it out. Forming it into a pad, she dabbed Godfrew's forehead. Shock sat at his master's feet, his head on his paws, watching.

Eleanor put a hand on the girl's arm. "I don't want to frighten you, little one, but he is very sick ... your 'Papa'... he may even die. Maybe I should find a priest to shrive him."

"He will not die." Fleur refused to cry and blinked back her tears. "Help me, Eleanor. Don't let him die."

"I will help you keep him alive. Not for his sake, but for yours." Eleanor gave a wry smile, "I tried to kill him once."

"Don't kill him." Fleur started to panic.

"No, that was before he saved you. Perhaps I deserved what he did to me."

"Oi, woman." Clunn shoved his way into the covered wagon—stepping on Shock as he did so, sending the yelping hound to run for cover at the other end and making him step on the moaning Godfrew as he fled. "Get out here now, woman. I have customers waiting."

"You want I come?" Eleanor's English was hesitant and heavily accented.

"Yes, yes, you daft whore." Clunn caught hold of the silver chain around his woman's neck and gave it a tug. "Outside, now. I have two Gascons wanting to sample your flesh."

"Please, not long. I help look after sick wolf."

"No, you won't be long. They want to both have you at the same time. Here ..." he gave the woman a jar ... "take this grease. You'll need it. Now, out." As the woman passed through the flap, Clunn grabbed hold of the blue ribbon hanging down from under her skirt. "Hold it." The woman stopped, still stooped. Clunn pulled the ribbon tight and used its tautness to lift her skirt. He moved his head around as he examined her genital region. "No spots, yet. Good." He let go of the ribbon and smote the woman's backside "Off you go now ... and keep your voice down if they get a bit enthusiastic."

"One day, evil one ... one day ..." The flap closed behind the woman and the accompanying Clunn.

Godfrew felt the fingers of his ninth son slip through his own and he watched helplessly as the child spun down the swollen flood.

* * *

A still weak Godfrew lay on a pallet by the side of the wagon. An awning made of looted crimson cloth provided him with shade. Sitting in front of him was the wolf pack. All were low in spirit, having just had to bury Leofwine. The dirt still stuck to their hands and boots.

"So, Tosti, the Normans and the Frogs have struck a deal." Godfrew took a sip of the boiled honey water Fleur held to his lips. "What else?"

"The Le Man folk got a good deal, from what I can gather." Tosti, his complexion even whiter than usual, ran his left wrist down the side of his still sore stomach. "I wonder if our army being hit by the sickness made the Norman king let them off the hook."

"If they had tried to make a fight of it, the Bastard should have let them invade the camp. Then they would really have been in the shit!" The hair on Magnus' head had already started to grow again. It looked like a field of stubbled wheat after harvesting.

"Spare us the humour, Magnus the Sailor." Godfrew carefully swallowed before continuing, "What else Tosti the Sharp Eared?"

"The King's Captains are going around the camp trying to recruit men for the next campaign ... something to do with one of the king's men ... John Fletcher, I think. He is being bashed around a bit by someone called Fulk the Avenger. They are offering good money to those who will stay on in France."

"I will take a vote on it, gentlemen, but as for myself, I have had enough. Forty days for the Earl, forty days as king's men. I would rather go back home than sign up for another stint." Godfrew leaned back and let his head rest on his French maid's lap.

* * *

The Revenge

It was not until they had reached Alençon that Godfrew ate some solid food. All of the wolf pack, together with the rest of the returning English, rested outside that town and gathered their strength before making their way through the passes into the Orne river valley and heading to Caen where they were to be discharged. Alençon surprised them, for they had expected the prices to rise dramatically on their arrival. Such was the reputation and fear of the English, that prices remained normal and the townsfolk forwent their right to haggle.

The journey back became a blur as the men's thoughts became fixed only on getting home and making it back without losing their plunder. Even Caen held no attractions for them. They longed to get moving on, ever anxious to reach their port of departure.

All except Clunn. Whenever they halted, he had continued to increase his personal wealth at the expense of his woman's body. It was only when the wolves arrived in Cherbourg that they relaxed and began to unwind. The days spent waiting for a ship back to England became an alcohol induced haze. On the arrival of the Silver Goose, the wolves stopped their carousing and set out with heart to dismantle their wagons.

Godfrew wiped his greasy hands down his torn shirt and went back to help swing the bed of the wagon over the ship's side. As the cranes lifted the wagon up, Godfrew and his wolves helped push it out away from the wharf and guide it into the hold. "Well, that's that. I just hope we can get those horses aboard tomorrow without all the fuss we had when we came here."

"Master Wulf." Tosti tugged at Godfrew's sleeve, obviously very agitated.

"Tosti, you lazy little bugger. Where have you been?"

"Yeah, we needed you. I almost strained my thing helping move that whatsit." Duncan put his hands on his hips, hung his head and took deep breaths.

"Did you see the faces of those Frog dockers as they pulled on the ropes to get the wagon bed up?" Magnus slapped Duncan's back, "If only they knew what booty was hidden under the false floor!"

"Shut up!" Swein grabbed Magnus' head and put it under his arm, a hand over his mouth. The two friends began a strange dance as Magnus struggled to free himself.

"For once, your four whiskered friend is right, Magnus. Shut up." Godfrew pried Swein's fingers away from Magnus. "Now both of you stop clowning around and go and check the horses. I don't like leaving Fleur and Clunn's woman alone with them, just in case something goes wrong."

"Master Wulf!" Tosti forcibly grabbed Godfrew.

"Hey, steady on, Tosti, I hadn't forgotten you." Godfrew studied the young warrior's face with an amused look, "What on earth has rattled you?"

"Clunn."

"Yes, well, Clunn rattles all of us at some time or another." Godfrew used the tattered edge of his shirt to clean the grease away from between his fingers.

"I can't find him! You sent me to get him to help with loading the wagons, but he has disappeared." Tosti started to look about along the wharf side, still seeking his long-time friend. "I can't find him anywhere ... and his woman has gone, too."

Godfrew caught hold of Swein and Magnus who were trying to see who could throw stones the furthest into the harbour. "Quick, you two, get down to the horses. Fleur has been left on her own. Hurry!" He went back to Tosti. "I expect he has found more customers for his woman. He has done well with her here. It seems that they haven't come across such a skilled whore with such diverse talents before."

"I know ... and she has taught me a few new tricks ... though I wish Clunn wouldn't insist on being there all the time ... shouting out instructions and criticising my performance." Tosti ran his fingers through his hair. "But I don't think he has gone to hire her out ... at least, I'm not sure."

"Why? It has happened before ... in almost every town and village we have stopped in on the way back." Godfrew looked and caught Puta's eye. He signalled to him to come over. "I'm only peeved that he has dodged out of doing some work."

"No, something is not right." Tosti waited until Puta joined them before continuing, "When I couldn't find him, I went to see if his woman and Fleur knew where he was. The woman had gone too. Fleur said that a while back the woman just

The Revenge

kissed her and went ... she didn't say a word ... just kissed her and went."

"No Clunn?" asked Puta.

"No Clunn," confirmed Tosti. "First Clunn and now his woman ... both gone."

"All right." Godfrew gave a resigned sigh. "You and Puta go into the town and check all his usual hangouts." He held out his hand "Yes, I know you have been there already, Tosti, but try them again. He may have passed down the street whilst you were inside somewhere, or he may have been out in the back of an alehouse taking care of business. I will go down and get the other two and we will search the docks. We will all meet back at the horses. If he still hasn't turned up by mid-afternoon, I will see if the Captain can spare some of his crew to help in the search."

"That will be fun ... working with sailors who you can't understand properly." Tosti glanced toward the Silver Goose.

"Oh, I don't know. I seem to get on well with the sailor boys." Puta joined Tosti in looking at the ship which nudged and rubbed against the wooden protectors of the stone harbour wall. Puta sighed longingly. "But where are you, Clunn? I know you have been a wretched friend ... always disappointing me ... but where are you, Clunn? Where are you?"

They searched all day and into the night. When the ship sailed the next day on the early morning tide it was without Clunn Crop Ears.

Whilst the wolves had not been able to find Clunn, the rats had—despite his being buried in the middle of the midden heap at the back of The Sporting Cock alehouse. Knotted around Clunn's blackened and swollen neck was a long blue ribbon.

Woden's Wolf

The Parting

On his return, Godfrew gave his wife Elfgifu her gifts from the plunder he had gained whilst serving the king in France. Although she was delighted with the beautiful, solid gold crucifix that he had gained at Beaumont, she was not quite sure what to make of the daughter he had also gained there. Oakleaf found much delight in the pearl necklace she was given. She soon found Fleur to be a delight as well. Godfrew gave his boys jewel-encrusted daggers, but Elfgifu took them, telling Godfrew that she would hide them until they were older. The wolves took their treasure and did with it what they saw best. As they had stayed on in France, Godfrew sent the house carl brothers and Gogmagog's share to their wives, the sisters who ran the Twisted Thorn alehouse.

Earl Ralf took his fourth and used it to speed up the completion of his new church. With little or no trouble from the Earl's tenants, Godfrew poured all his energy into getting the building completed—for Ralf of East Anglia seemed to be in an inordinate hurry to get it all finished. For almost a year—in all types of weather—Godfrew chased, harried, bullied and persuaded the tradesmen to make their best effort. Soon after the hay mowing, when men felt they could at last sit back and gather their strength for harvest time, Earl Ralf demanded that—despite the fact that the wall paintings had not been finished and the wooden furnishings not all completed—the church be prepared for its consecration by the Bishop of Norwich.

On that auspicious day, Godfrew stood in a place of honour with his family. Elfgifu was on her knees with her head bowed muttering a constant flow of prayers. Fleur was unsure what to do and looked to Godfrew for clues. Oakleaf struggled to keep the unruly boys in order, out from under the feet of dignitaries and away from the Earl's guests.

Godfrew stood too long. He wished the service complete and moved his weight from one leg to another as his back started to set. Out of the corner of his eye, he could see the master carpenter, Athelmere, and his men. They were pointing and worrying about the congregation leaning on and fingering the temporarily stacked wooden furnishings that awaited staining and waxing. He looked back at the altar. The shining beauty of the Bishop's cope and vestments contrasted with the roughly drawn, partially completed wall decorations. The scent from the swung censors mingled and clashed with the smell of paint, drying whitewash and still raw mortar.

The piled furniture gave a groan. A group of carpenters rushed in to prevent a disaster. The congregation became flustered and started to mill around, much as a flock of sheep that had been disturbed by a strange dog. The Bishop, disquieted by what was happening, finished his lines in triple time. He gave a curt blessing and got out quickly with his attendants.

Earl Ralf came up to Godfrew smiling, his normally unreadable eyes for once twinkling. "Excellent, Geri. That is out of the way and, with its endowments included, has bought the church's favour." He watched, amused, as the congregation fought past the carpenters and made their way out of the church. "Now, finishing the place off. You have someone else who can oversee it?"

"My Lord?" Godfrew let go of Fleur's hand and grabbed his son Jaul, who was about to get a hand on the Earl's sword.

"You always seem to have things well organised, so I assume you have someone who can complete the church." Ralf twirled an end of his dark moustache.

"Tosti. He can read and write. He has a reputation amongst the workmen. I would need to speak to them all first, but ...yes, he could see the job done."

"Good." The earl smiled disarmingly. "I am getting married."

"Congratulations, my Lord," said Godfrew, unsure what Earl Ralf meant the announcement to indicate. Jaul gave up trying to break away from his father to get at the sword, so he began to pry the small iron nails from the hands of Christ on Fleur's crucifix.

"I am marrying young Roger of Hereford's sister, Emma."

"I pray that you will be happy, my Lord." Elfgifu grabbed Jaul's hand, bobbed her head and left, taking Fleur with her.

Earl Ralf inclined his head in thanks and then gave his attention back to Godfrew: "Naturally, there is to be a banquet ... all that sort of thing."

The Parting

"Naturally, my Lord."

"So, I want you to organise getting hold of the necessary and shipping it up to ..." Ralf turned his head, "Connan, where is it that I am getting married? Waltheof offered the place to me."

"Exnig ... I think he called it ... it's somewhere in the shire of Cambridge." The Breton Steward had recently returned from France and looked tired. His face was now marred with a scar that split his left eyebrow in twain and scored his cheek.

"Yes, ship it up to Exnig in Cambridgeshire. Connan will get the butler to work out what is wanted. You will have to pick it all up and make sure that it arrives in time."

"My Lord." Already Godfrew's mind was calculating the arrangements he would have to make.

"One thing though, I know the English custom is to celebrate at weddings by drinking special ales fortified by honey. Someone once mentioned that you would know where to get it."

"My Lord. My uncle is renowned as a brewer. I trust that there will be enough time to get some from him."

"Time? I'm not sure. Connan will tell you when the wedding is. I have so much on my mind at the moment." Earl Ralf started to leave, but had a second thought and turned back, his finger to his lip. "Another thing ... the wine. Find me a new supplier for my wine. That last lot, the stuff you brought to me in Scotland ... it tasted decidedly off ... almost like sheep's piss smells."

* * *

Godfrew stood in the shadows directing and controlling the supplies of honey-ale and wine, ensuring that the best went to the top table and the sober. The ale and wines of lower quality went to those whose pallets were past appreciating fine quality. The light from the hall dimmed for a moment. Godfrew glanced over to see two men walking down the passage, unaware of his presence. The lead man was solid and bear-like in build. The other was tall and thin, walking with the help of a staff. He waited until they had passed and he was sure of their identity before he stood out in the passageway and called quietly after them: "My Lord Waltheof."

The thin man, despite his obvious physical infirmities, pushed Earl Waltheof against the wall and stood protectively in front of him, his staff grasped and held like a quarter-staff, ready to strike.

"Steady, Red. I think I recognise that voice and that stance." Waltheof moved alongside the ancient warrior and peered at the darkened figure before him. "Step closer to the light here." The figure moved. "Ah, so it is you, young thane. Ralf mentioned that he had a man with an elf smitten eye working for him. I guessed it was you."

"I knew it was you. Ralf mentioned you when Waltheof spoke to him about the quality of the ale. He said that you had got it. An eye like that? I knew it must be you, even if every time someone talks about you they give you a different name," added Red.

"My Lord. I wish to have a word with you about what is happening here."

"The wedding? Don't worry. The ale is excellent." The Earl tapped old Red on the shoulder, "Relax, Red." Red changed back from the alert warrior to an old man and leaned hard on his staff. "Now," Waltheof said to Godfrew, "a word with you, young Gareth, my forester."

"Gareth ... yes, a very helpful young man. Now my Lord ..."

"What have you done with him ... Gareth."

"Done my Lord?" Vague memories of the evil deeds of the wolf pack on the return to its lair at Lydbury flicked through Godfrew's mind. "He ... we ... did no more than we had to do, my Lord Waltheof."

"Not with Gareth ... to Gareth." The three men moved to one side to let pages pass by. They carried fully-feathered boiled swans stuffed with bread and chestnuts, the trays garnished with aromatic lovell, so that the swans gave the illusion of swimming through water weeds. The Earl waited until they had entered the hall before continuing to question Godfrew: "Come now, young thane ... Gareth."

"Gareth left us in the foot hills of the Pennines. We struck south and he headed for Chester. Why, my Lord?" Godfrew looked around, uncomfortable that the conversation was not yet over, unwilling to be seen talking with Earl Waltheof.

The Parting

"He never got there. At least his mother never saw him ... and he never came back to me." Waltheof gave a grim smile. "I would hate to think that his loss was on your account."

"Without Gareth, we would never had made it home. I would never have let any harm come to him. Now, my Lord, I must ..."

"Very fond of young Gareth, weren't you, Waltheof?" Red shuffled into the light, the scar around his head that he had collected at the Stamford Bridge fight was now puckered and white. There were small lumps in the scar tissue where fragments of bone were still working their way to the surface.

"My Lord, please ..."

"How are you enjoying your settled life with Ralf, young thane. Much quieter than your time with old Edric the Wild, eh?"

"It has had its moments, Lord Waltheof, but this is my last job for the Earl. My uncle at Battersea has been struck by the palsy, leaving him unable to use his right side ...and his wife is dying, so I asked to be released from service. Earl Ralf has kindly agreed. But please, my Lord ..."

"Battersea? Hardly the hub of the kingdom! What are you going to do with yourself there?"

"Brew ale, my Lord, but ...."

"And sampling it, too, no doubt!"

Old Red smacked his lips. "A good drop of stuff young Ralf got in for the bride-ale. From your uncle's?"

"Yes, he is renowned for it." Godfrew turned back to Waltheof. " My Lord ..."

"Excellent ale! Let me know when you get yourself set up. I'll have some of that ale for myself."

"My Lord." Godfrew's voice became strident, "Please, my Lord. I have something important to say to you."

Waltheof laughed. "Sorry, young thane. Yes, what is it."

Godfrew looked around and came close to the Earl. "My Lord, there are things that are being talked about here. Things that perhaps should be kept quiet?"

"No!" The Earl turned to his foster father, "Red? Have you heard anything?"

The old warrior shrugged his shoulders. "No."

"There will be, my Lord." Godfrew waited for the returning pages to go past and enter the kitchen before speaking again. "Earl Ralf's new wife."

"Lovely bit of stuff," commented Red, poking his tongue through the gap where his front teeth should have been. "Wouldn't mind a bit of it myself. Mind of her own though, I shouldn't wonder. Spice on the meat, that!" He cackled with pleasure at the thought.

"Surprisingly enough, Ralf seems enamoured of her," Waltheof commented to Red. "I thought that it was the usual family alliance thing, but he seems to be under her spell."

"I wouldn't mind being under her, Waltheof." Again Red cackled.

"My Lord," Godfrew interrupted. "It may be that the king does not approve of the union."

"Maybe?"

"I cannot possibly comment, my Lord, but it may be of great importance to you to clarify the matter with Earl Ralf." Godfrew wrung his hands "There are other things afoot, my Lord." He dared to touch the earl's cuff. "Please, be careful. A web is being spun and it would be risky to get caught in it."

"Ralf is the spider?"

"His wife's brother fits the role better, my Lord. I fear for Earl Ralf in the matter. I think he is already ensnared, tempted by the Earl Roger's using his sister as the bait."

"How do you know these things, young thane?" Waltheof asked.

Red stuck his face next to Waltheof's ear and whispered into it. "Your young thane was Edric's wandering wolf ... and, from what I understand, he may have fulfilled the same task for young Ralf, too."

"Ah, yes, Red is right. You have spent many years gathering information, both for your masters and for yourself. Just because you are working in Ralf's household doesn't mean that you have got out of the habit. So," Waltheof gave Godfrew a long quizzical look, "why are you telling me all this?"

"I owe you my life, Earl Waltheof of Northampton. In return, I would try and save yours."

"So the plot—if indeed there is a plot—is not of your liking?"

The Parting

"It is not right ... not properly prepared? Timing wrong? Out of balance? Not thought through? I don't know, my Lord. I just don't like the feel of it."

"It doesn't feel right?" Waltheof's voice was edged with humour.

Again, the three men had to make way for pages to pass through, laded with dishes—this time cut rounds of cheeses of all types. The lead dish included a large white cheese covered with yellow slime as the centre piece. Hard, crumbling cheese streaked with blue sat around it in a decorative pattern.

"My Lord, it doesn't smell right."

* * *

Edwin kissed Elfgifu on the forehead. "Welcome ... I suppose I should now call you niece rather than Elfgifu ... but welcome. I am so glad to see you all. Look, three little boys and a girl. Now where did she get that red hair from? Not our side, I'm sure. And another maid .. a cousin, I think. My nephew told me you had a cousin staying with you to help with the children. You with four children ... who would have thought ... it seems only yesterday." Edwin the brewer of Battersea, shook his plump head from side to side. For the first time, Elfgifu noticed his useless arm and the drooped mouth that added the slur to his voice. "That was a shock when my nephew told me ... as if seeing him after so many years was not shock enough. To think that my ale was so famous that the Earl of East Anglia himself asked for it to be used as his bridal ale. I was telling my old friend Aldred ... well boasting really ...."

"Uncle Edwin." Godfrew joined the gathering in front of the inn's door. "Perhaps if we could finish the greetings inside. Elfgifu, my wife, wishes to see your wife, my aunt."

"Oh, yes, of course. Silly me. I have got myself so excited about you all being here. Come in, come in." Edwin turned on his left leg and led the way indoors, dragging his useless right leg behind him. "There is such a mess here at the moment. What with my wife, your aunt, being so ill and us with no maid at present. And the problems I am having with the brewing at the moment. Well, nephew, I can't do much these day except supervise ... and the kids they send me to help make the brew ... well, they are little more than useless. Now, when you were here, I had Stain the Mute's boys most of the time. He could never afford to keep them, so I knew that if they were here helping me, at least they would get one meal a day in their bellies. Now Stain's boys were good. They soon learned how to make real ale. Why ..."

"Uncle Edwin. May I call you that?" Elfgifu undid her light travelling cloak and passed it to Oakleaf.

"Of course, my dear. I have already said so. Why to think that I and my wife ... your aunt now ...why, we brought you two together. After my nephew came to order the honey ale, I said to my wife, your aunt, 'Just to think that all unsuspecting, we made a marriage here in our own little house' ... not that it is a house, of course, for really it is a ..."

Godfrew broke in on behalf of his wife, "Uncle Edwin, please, where is your wife, my aunt?"

"Oh, yes. Yes, of course. I know that she will be overwhelmed to see you. I was only saying to her ..."

Elfgifu followed Edwin through to the back rooms. Godfrew looked around until he saw Oakleaf. Grabbing Jaul as he raced past, he tucked him under his arm, then he took Fleur's hand and headed back outside. "Come on, Oakleaf, we will go and see if the old lean-to is standing. You and the children can sleep in there."

* * *

Godfrew sat on the stool by the bedside and looked at his wife as she finished her prayers over the sleeping form of Uncle Edwin's wife. "Will she live?"

"Not for long, I'm afraid." Elfgifu pulled the bed covers back and looked over the woman's body. "To think that she was once so big ... and now look at her ... all skin and bones."

"Is she starving to death?"

"No, I am sure that this lump on her breast has something to do with it. It is unnatural ... see, it is hard whilst a breast should be soft."

"Now how should I know about that, Elfgifu?" Godfrew gave a rueful grin. "It is so long since I felt yours that I have forgotten what a nice plump breast feels like."

"You never change, do you ... and you have never grown up." Elfgifu pulled the bed clothes over Edwin's wife and tucked them in. "In fact, none of you men ever seem to grow up ... and those who would play at being warriors are the worst. It is only us women who have to grow up. We have to bear children, keep homes and look after the affairs of the family while you men ... you men just carry on as you did when you were kids."

"You are tired." Godfrew stood. "Oakleaf is busy washing the boys, but I could get Fleur in and she could keep watch whilst you rest."

"That's another thing, Wulf. Why did you bring her back? I'm sure that the poor child would have been better off if you had left her in France where she belongs." Elfgifu brushed past Godfrew and started to get a pillow and a spare blanket out of the wooden chest at the foot of the bed for her own use.

"I could never have left her in France. You didn't see what we did in France ... to France." He sat down again and hung his head between his knees. When he spoke again, his voice was thick and muffled. "You say that we warriors never grow up. To be honest, we durst not." He took a breath, then sat up and looked at his wife. "We ... rather I ... have seen ... done ... or caused to be done ... things that you would curse me for." He took another deep breath. "When there is trouble, the women cry: 'Where are the men who should be protecting us? Where are the brave warriors?' ... but if they knew ... if they saw what we had to do to protect them, then they would ..." He shook his head. "I don't know what they would do ... but one thing I do know ... they wouldn't want to soil themselves by associating with the men they sent out to do the dirty work."

Elfgifu came and put her arm around her husband's shoulder, "I hadn't thought ... I didn't know."

"Didn't you?" Godfrew looked up into her face, "I thought that was why you stopped sleeping with me."

"Silly." Elfgifu stroked Godfrew's bald head. "We never stopped sleeping together."

"You know what I mean." Godfrew took his wife's hand and kissed it. "I supposed that you didn't want anymore children, but there must have been other ways of not having anymore."

"Silly, Wulf." Elfgifu pulled Godfrew's head against her tummy and cradled his head in her hands. "It wasn't that I didn't want to have any more. I couldn't. When I gave birth to Njal, I tore apart. I couldn't have any more sons for you ... no more than I could 'sleep' with you. Then, with me thinking you dead, I took a vow of chastity. I did not want another man and—with the thought of their getting their hands on your rumoured treasure hoard—there would have been many would- be husbands. I wanted none of that. I have had no other man but you ... and I have never desired it any other way."

Godfrew slowly unwrapped his wife's fingers and look at her sadly. "Why did you not explain? If I had known about what having Njal had done to you, I would have found things easier to bear. If only I had known!"

"If you had know, you would have wanted to try, just in case I was wrong." She bent and kissed Godfrew. "I know you only too well, Wulf, the young man!" Edwin's wife moaned and turned onto her side. Elfgifu readjusted the bed clothes to keep the woman covered. "They have had a good marriage. I wonder what Uncle Edwin will do without her?" Elfgifu came back to Godfrew and sat on his lap, her head resting on his. "Don't ever leave me again, Wulf. I knowen not if I could ever live withouten thee."

"Nor I without you, Cariad."

* * *

For two weeks after Edwin's wife died, Elfgifu fasted and kept a prayer vigil in the church of Saint Mary. Godfrew was working in the shed, mashing the barley grain when the priest came to him and told him that Elfgifu had been taken ill and could he come and collect her. Now she lay in the same bed as Edwin's wife had lain.

Godfrew mopped her brow as she muttered what sounded like a prayer. At first she kept coming back to reality and asking for a little food, or a drink, but the time between bouts of delirium became shorter. As the day turned to night, her mutterings became noiseless—her lips moving and

The Parting

mouthing words, but without a sound issuing forth except a deep rattling from her chest. During the bouts of fever, Elfgifu's grip was strong and almost broke Godfrew's fingers as he held her hand, but when the fever left, her hands went limp and her fingers fluttered like butterflies around the flowers in spring.

When Elfgifu's fingers stopped fluttering and her chest stopped rattling, Godfrew held her limp hand to his face and started to chant a half-forgotten poem that his mother had taught him as a boy, from The Last Judgment.

> At the day of Doom
> The blessed shall be
> In the glorious sweet life
> Assigned to all Saints
> In the heavenly kingdom
> That is ever their home.
> For time never ending
> Lasting for all time
> The purest of heart
> Shall all praise the Lord,
> Dear guardian of life
> In light encompassed
> Honoured with grace
> Endeared unto God.
> Now always for ever
> With bright angel band
> Oh wonderful gold one
> Precious in this life
> Now shining with glory
> Joy in worship of God
> Who now will embrace you
> In his host of the holy.

* * *

"Oh, nephew ... such news I have just heard from some peddlers in the bar. That Earl you served ... Ralf ... he and the Earl of Hereford have revolted against the king. You really did the right thing in getting out of there when you did ... there will be hell to pay. The king has already started to land a big army, so they tell me. They also said that the local Fyrd has blocked ..." Edwin stopped suddenly, startled at the scene before him. At the end of the room sat Fleur with the three boys and Shock, all cuddled together like pups in a litter. Sitting at Elfgifu's feet on the end of the bed was Oakleaf ... and with his head resting on her generous soft breast was Godfrew, crying for the first time since he was a small child.

THE OLD MAN

Sad he with no lord,
No comfort of warm hearth,
Seeking he always
For that now gone
Talks he to shadows
Stares he at bright sky
Looking for one lord
Who will give him home.

The Seeking

The old man rolled along

the road at a stiff gait. He held the bridle of the horse, encouraging it through the muddy pot-holes in the road and through the Sussex Weald. His chest heaved and rattled with the physical effort. The horse gave a strong pull and the cart lurched forward, its load of sacks filled with charcoal crunching as they readjusted themselves. He let go of the bridle, walked alongside the horse and took off his broad-rimmed hat.

As he pulled out a dirty rag from his sleeve and wiped his sweat-covered bald head, he looked at the damp rag, then ran it over his face—the material catching on the sparse white whiskers that covered his chin like a light hoar frost.

The old man hawked and spat, then turned to check that his black hound was following. Ahead of him rumbled another cart with a figure walking alongside the horse. The other man was shorter than the old man, but more powerfully built and strode along with the vigour of youth.

"It's no good you rushing, Moithar. We will not get back home today. Why all the hurry?" Godfrew coughed up another piece of phlegm and spat it out. Shuck Shockson ran alongside his master and leered up at him, tongue lolling out of his gaping mouth. Fresh blood stained his flanks. Godfrew touched the hound's head with his hand. "Not you, too? Why is everyone in such a hurry these days?"

Shuck quickly moved away and faced the road from whence they had come and gave a sharp bark. Godfrew had just enough time to flatten himself against the cart to prevent himself from being trampled under foot by a pony being ridden hard. The rider had his hair cut short, but hanging on behind him was a young boy with his hair long in the English style. The pony overtook Moithar's cart and then swung around as the rider hauled on the reins.

"HALT! HALT!" The rider held out his hand." I said stop! STOP!"

Moithar called to his horse and it gladly stopped, pleased for the chance to rest.

"Who are you and what are you doing here? Who you, why here?" demanded the rider, sliding down from his saddle.

"We are the brewers. We are taking charcoal back." Moithar ran his hands down the back of his horse, causing it to shiver and stamp its back hooves.

"What these?" the rider picked hold of two blood-covered animals hanging from the cart's rail.

"Short-legged hares. The hound caught them back there. We are going to have them for supper." Moithar started to undo the animals. "Why? Do you want one?"

"Not hares." The rider took the proffered animal and examined it. "These rabbits."

"Rabbits? What are rabbits?" Moithar turned and called back to Godfrew. "Dad, what are rabbits?" [1]

Godfrew came up and stood on the other side of the rider, leaning on an scarred old wooden staff. "Rabbits? No idea, son."

The rider screwed up his face in disgust at such ignorance. "Rabbits, these belong to lord. They kept only for him. You no take."

"If they belong to the Lord, then we can take them," Godfrew answered aggressively. "For does not scripture say that God told Noah after the flood that man can take all creatures for his own use?"

The rider turned his attention away from Moithar and gave it to Godfrew. "Not God-type Lord, dummy! Manor Lord."

Godfrew leaned more heavily on the staff he held in his hand. "This is common land. Even if these funny hares are called "rabbits" by you French, this is common land. No one holds the right of exclusive hunting here. We have held that right since the land was wrested from the Welsh. Generation after generation of English have hunted here without let or

---

[21] Rabbits were introduced to England by the Normans as a semi-domesticated source of game.

hindrance ... so don't tell me, Frenchman, what we can or can't do in our own land."

"Look, old fool, things different now. This land common, but you no hunt."

"Piss off, Frog."

"Dad!" Moithar called out in desperation.

"Old man, I take you back. We go Manor court. You in trouble."

"Me? In trouble? I think not." Godfrew edged back his old white wool cloak to reveal that the staff he held was attached to the head of his axe, Neckbiter.

"Dad, no!" Moithar's loud call disturbed his cart horse and he grabbed hold of its bridle to calm it.

The rider ignored what was happening behind him and kept his attention on Godfrew. "You silly old fool. What you think you do with that?"

Godfrew shucked the cloak off of his shoulder and took up a fighting stance.

"Dear God save me from imbeciles such as this!" The rider threw back his head and laughed. "You look very stupid, old man," he laughed again.

"Dad, don't."

Godfrew lifted the axe as far as his damaged shoulder would let him. There was a sound of ripping linen as the shoulder muscle tore and freed itself. Neckbiter arced through the air and the Frenchman's laughter changed to a cry of fear, then stopped altogether.

* * *

Moithar threw a blood-soaked shirt onto the fire. "Why the boy, dad? Why the boy?"

"He would have got us hanged as well as an adult. Besides," he picked up a stick and poked the smouldering fire into life again, "if you kill the vixen you must kill the cubs also, or they too will grow to raid your chickens."

"It was all so unnecessary, Dad. The Frenchman may well have been happy to have just taken the funny hares from us."

"Or he may have taken our hands from us." Satisfied that the fire was burning well, Godfrew moved back to the carts and the shelter provided by the canvas strung between them. Shuck walked behind, almost tripping him up, hoping for some more rabbit stew.

Moithar followed him. "Even our hands would have been better than our lives. They will hang us, you know, if they find out."

"They won't. They may find something, but they won't connect it with us." Godfrew eased his aching bones down onto the ground and propped himself up against the cart's wheel. Shuck came and sat alongside him and rested his head on his master's leg.

"They must find out." Moithar's voice trembled. "They must find the bodies. Even if we get away with it, the local folk will have to pay the Murdrum fine." [1]

"No doubt, in the fullness of time, they will find the bodies." Godfrew played with his hound's ears, appreciating the silkiness. "They won't find anything to trace back to us. Nor should they even consider foul play ... I mean, there won't be much left of them after the wild sow and her tribe have eaten their fill!"

"Trust you to know of such things. Knowing how to make murder look like an accident by setting the bodies up so that it looks as if they have been attacked and eaten by wild boar ... like that poor French priest who was travelling from Clapham to ... Dear God it wasn't ..."

"He was just a stroppy old git. Thought he owned the road."

"And his two companions?"

"In the wrong place at the wrong time. Besides, they were Bretons. I don't like Bretons."

"At least you weren't involved in the death of that falconer from Landoc who was at the Halfarthing manor. He got killed by wolves."

---

[22] Because of the high rate of homicide being suffered by the Normans and their French allies, King William I legislated that all Frenchmen who settled in England after the invasion were to be in the king's peace and, therefore, he was their protector in an alien land. Its introduction was recognised at the time as being necessary due to the hatred of the Normans by the English and their attacks on them. The fine was a high one of 46 Marks. The sum was to be paid by the lord of the dead man to the Crown if the perpetrator was not hastily caught. If the killer could not reimburse the victim's lord, then the Hundred where the crime had been committed had to.

The Seeking

"In Surrey? Wolves? More like Hasse's deer hounds. He always lets them run loose in the woods around the Wandsworth Common." Godfrew coughed and waited to get his breath back before continuing. "It was my bloody pigeon anyway. Arrogant little shit seemed to think that hounds couldn't catch pigeons. At least, I think that's what I think he was trying to say ... I mean, even the other Frenchmen couldn't seem to understand what he said, so what chance did I have of understanding him. Arrogant little git ... always poking his finger on your chest to make his point. I made a point with him that day."

"Shit." Moithar sat down by the other cart, deliberately avoiding any physical contact with his father. "And now this poor sod." Suddenly he stood up, agitated. "What about the horse?"

"We will wait till the morning. I will take her deep into the woods. She may return home, she may not. If someone finds her, they may wonder about the blood, but then if they have found the remains of the corpses after the boars have gnawed them they will only assume that the Frenchman got hurt and tried to ride for help before succumbing to his injuries."

"Which is why you dumped their bodies near the dens of two different sows?"

"You are learning." Godfrew allowed himself to slip down and began to settle himself for the night.

"But why the boy, Dad?"

"Why worry? He was French."

"So is my wife. And that makes your grandsons half-French."

"That, Moithar, is different."

"Is it? I don't think so." Moithar gathered his cloak and headed for a clump of bushes where he could sleep alone. "To be honest, you have become a liability." He took some steps and then stopped. "First it was insulting any of our customers who wouldn't or couldn't speak English. Then you stopped selling to people with French names ... now this. I can't even take you out without you getting stuck into any French people you come across. The older you get, the worse you have become." He strode off. "What am I to do with you, Dad?" he asked himself.

* * *

Moithar came into the back of the kitchen wiping his naked torso with an old rag and called out to his wife: "Fleur, do me a favour. I have tried to wash all the charcoal off, but you know how it gets everywhere. Check to see if I have got my back clean."

"Husband, come here."

"Where my love?" Moithar wiped the rag around his neck and inspected it for dirt.

"In our bedroom." Fleur's voice, for all her years of speaking English was still tinged with a French accent.

Moithar went into the room. "What's up?"

"This." Fleur pointed to the bed. Spread on the cover was a small pile of broken gold jewellery and a thin dented arm band. At the front of the pile was a beautiful unmarked gold arm band in the shape of a dragon—its eyes made of ruby—its teeth and claws small diamonds. Beside it was a red-gold ring engraved with Runes.

"That's Dad's arm band that King Harold gave him and that beautiful dragon one is the band that Earl Edric gave him." Moithar picked up the finger ring. "This is Mum's ring."

"I remember Papa taking it from Oakleaf's finger the day she died giving birth to her sixth still-born son." Fleur took the ring from her husband and held it reverently in her fingers. "Why has he left them here?"

"The silly old fool." Moithar rushed out and headed for the lean-to where his father slept. When he came back his face was white. "He's gone!"

"How do you know?" Fleur got up off the bed and took her husband's hand "How?"

"The cloak. The tatty old wolf-skin thing he always wore. It's gone ... and so is his axe."

"Yes, but he may have just gone to split wood or something."

"And leave the gold?" Moithar glanced toward the open door. "No, he has gone. He also left this." He held a piece of dirty paper in his hand. "You read it. You know that I am not too good with letters."

The Seeking

Fleur took the paper and slowly read it, mouthing the words as she did so. "Oh, dear God, he has gone!" She sat down on the bed again, shocked. "He says that the gold is for me ... Jaul got his share when he married the second cousin and went to inherit the family farm near Wallbedding ... you got your share to buy the land around the inn ... Njal got his when he left to go to Greekland and fight in the Guard for the Emperor ... this is for me. He says that he is sorry for hurting me." She touched the bits of gold. When she looked back at Moithar, she had tears in her eyes. "I don't want the gold. I want him! Oh, Moithar, what is to become of my Papa?"

* * *

The smoke from the central fire filled the inside of the alehouse with biting smoke and helped hide the group of five youths huddled in the far corner. Disdaining to open the shuttered window over their table, they kept their heads together whispering plans and plots, ceasing only when the serving wench came on one of her occasional futile missions to see if they wanted to buy more ale. The apparent leader scratched at one of the many spots on his face. "Look you can all go on as much as yer like, but if we are to get to Windsor and join up with Red William's [1] army, then we will have to get 'old of some money. Despite what Dag 'ere says you can't just turn up and expect them to feed you ... not until you are signed up anyway."

"Bollocks, Addle. We can steal it!" clarified Dag. His face sported a soft, brown down through which stray pimples poked like mountains capped by yellow snow.

"Steal it, Dag? Get caught stealing vrom ver king's army and you'll get yer balls cut orf." The speaker stopped to pick his nose. "Yer will. Get yer bollocks cut orf."

"Yours ain't dropped yet, so 'ows vey gonna find 'em, eh?" Dag checked his empty cup for the twelfth time, still hoping to find a drop to drink.

"Look, you furry-faced ass!" the young man brought his face close to Dag's, his finger still picking his nose.

---

[23] William II, or William Rufus as he was known. There is debate as to whether the nickname came from him having red hair or from the fact that he tended to flush.

"Leave it aht! You are bowf right." Addle looked around before continuing. He peered through the smoke that hung to the low ceiling. It ran down the end wall where they sat, then flowed across the floor to rejoin the smouldering log from whence it had come. "As Rowan here says," Addle inclined his head to the nose-exploring youth by his side, "if yer gets caught fieving from the king, yer gets bits removed from yer body. The more you've nicked, the more important the bits."

"Well, that ain't his bollocks, that's for sure. 'e still don't knows wot 'e's got 'em for." A good-looking boy with a long nose and sparkling teeth chimed in.

"Knock it off," Addle whispered. "Now, w'ere Dag is right is in the fact that the only way we is goin' ter get any money is ter," he took a quick glance around the room, "nick it."

"That's wot I said, init?"

"No, Dag ... bollock brains ... it ain't. You were on about nicking food from the army. I'm on about nicking silver so that we can buy food from the army, or whoever." Addle smiled revealing that his two front teeth were chipped from the outside edges, forming a "V."

"Where do we nick it from, clever clogs?" asked the lad with the long nose. His clear blue eyes ran from the smoke.

"Hush, keep it down." Addle stood up for a short moment to check that they were not being overheard. His height ensured that he kept his head bowed so as not to hit the ceiling. "'Where from,' did you say? Well, not from any of our masters, that's for sure. We will need to stay with our jobs until we 'ave got enough money."

"The army may have gorn by ven. I 'ear Red William don't 'ang abaht." Rowan finally found what he was looking for and wiped the boogy on the underneath of the scratched and dented wooden table they were seated around.

"So we've got ter start now."

"Now, Addle?"

"Now, Hode," Addle informed the lad with the long nose.

"W'ere?" asked Rowan as he started to dig into his other nostril.

"Not w'ere, rather 'o," Addle dipped his finger into a small puddle of spilt ale and then licked it.

The Seeking

"Yes, 'o?" Hode pushed closer into the huddle, "'O, Addle? Got anyone in mind?"

"Well, I'm not sure yet. It would 'ave to be someone who din't know us. Maybe someone 'o was an easy target ... yer know ... a push over." Addle scratched his face for inspiration, "Someone like that bent old man we saw down the alley ... 'im with the skinny black dog. He 'ad a purse, I 'eard it jingle."

"He wouldn't like it," commented the fifth member of the group.

"Wouldn't 'e, Stumph?" commented Dag, sarcastically.

"No, he wouldn't," asserted the old man.

Addle swallowed slowly and looked down at the saxe blade resting against his windpipe. He gently turned to try and see his assailant, but the old man grabbed his hair and yanked his head back. "Sorry, mister, sorry!" Addle flicked his eyes around, looking to his mates for help, but they had all backed off and stood against the wall.

"I don't know if 'sorry' will be enough, young spotty." The saxe moved gently across Addle's throat leaving a thin tracery of blood in its wake.

"Please, mister, we didn't mean no 'arm. Honest." Dag started to move slowly along the wall hoping to find a way out of the ale-house.

"Stay where you are, pimple face ... and you others, sit down on the bench," the old man commanded. "So, you young fools are not only incompetent plotters ... you are also hopeless liars. What shall I do with you?" The old man pulled on Addle's hair and made him stand. The tall youth's forehead kissed the ceiling.

Shuck strutted over, cocked his leg and piddled down Addle's leg.

"I think that you should show some manners and give up your seat for your elders and betters. The rest of you ... sit where I can see you." Using Addle's hair to control him, Godfrew sat down at the table and made the spotty-faced youth kneel alongside him. "That's better." Godfrew pulled the hair and made Addle look at him, "Now are we going to behave ourself?" Godfrew compelled Addle to nod 'yes.' "Oh good, 'cos my poor old back is starting to ache, having to

Woden's Wolf

bend across and keep this blade against that pockmarked throat of yours."

Godfrew removed the saxe and Addle felt its sting as it went across his flesh. "Find your mate a seat now. Come on, move up on the bench and make room for him." The youths bum-shuffled to make way for Addle who was trying to stop his neck from bleeding by dabbing it with the cuff of his filthy shirt.

"Right, gentlemen, a drink?" They stared at him. "I assume that you will indulge." Godfrew tapped the table with the hilt of his saxe to get the serving wench's attention: "A large jug of ale please ... your best ... and bring an extra cup for me. Thank you." He beamed at his audience, "So, you want to join the Norman king's army, do you? What on earth makes you think he will have you? No training, no armour." He took a silver penny out from his purse and flicked its edge with his thumb, making it spin in the air. The coin landed on the table and spun before slowly running out of energy and coming to a ringing halt. "And no money!"

Stumph, the quiet one, broke the silence. "We wasn't thinking of joining the army. We had hoped to join the camp followers, driving carts and the like ... working in the supply train."

Godfrew waited till the wench brought the ale before replying. "Supply train, eh? Think it is easy work, eh?" He tapped the side of his nose. "Easy money!"

Addle looked up from attending to his neck, "Can't be that 'ard, jus' driving a cart or loading wagons."

"Oh, yes, in home territory it is quite easy ... picking things up from here ... dropping them there. Easy work." Godfrew poured himself a cup of ale and pushed the jug toward the boys. "Easy work, but poorly paid, especially if you are serving Fyrd duty."

"This ain't Fyrd. The King, Red William, 'e don't like the Fyrd they say, prefers to 'ire men wot's willin' ter stay wiv 'im till ver fightin' is done." Dag cautiously took the jug and filled his clay cup—all the time watching Godfrew—waiting to see if it was a trap.

"Poorly paid work ... and boring ... no better than the work you are doing now."

The Seeking

"We ain't got good jobs." Rowan spat out as he wrenched the jug from Dag and slopped foaming ale into his cup.

"I have." Hode picked up the jug and poured for himself and Stumph, then pushed it over to Addle.

Addle filled his cup carefully to the brim, then took a sip from it whilst it was still on the table. He looked sideways at Hode, "Call looking after Drang One-Arm's swine a good job? Them that 'e lets roam the streets feeding from midden heaps? I'd rather 'ave no job than 'ave that one."

"So, no decent jobs ... no money ... no training ..." Godfrew sipped his ale and screwed his eyes up at the taste, "...and I would suggest—no hope."

"We can 'andle 'orses and load carts." Addle picked his still full cup carefully up and sucked the foam off of the top. "We don't need no trainin', mister."

"As I said earlier, working the supply train is easy work—in home territory. But things change when you move into your enemy's land. Then it is not easy work, but it can pay rich dividends for those who know what to do." Godfrew poured the rest of his ale back into the jug. The boys downed their ale and rushed to refill their cups. Godfrew watched them with amusement. He waited till they had finished their second ale before talking to them again. "You wanted to rob me to get the money to get to ... where was it? Windsor?"

"Windsor." Stumph confirmed.

"To get to Windsor you would have needed to rob me and how many others? I may have the silver to buy you a drink, but I do not have enough to keep and feed five hungry young men for a week or more until they get—or maybe even don't get—a job with the Norman army that is setting off to make war in ..."

"Northumberland. The King is to attack Earl Robert of Northumbria."

"Robert?" Godfrew shook his head. "Even the earls these days are all French."

"Not like in your day, eh, Grandad?" jested Dag. Godfrew's saxe slammed into the table top a hair's breadth from Dag's fingers. The youth went white and returned to his drink.

"Spotty," Godfrew looked at Addle and the others nudged him to answer.

"Addle. Me name is Addle, mister."

"Very well then ... Addle. Now, Addle, you need money and training. Now I can give you that. I have a venture in mind that will be advantageous to all of us."

* * *

Godfrew leaned against the trunk of the stunted tree and squinted down the hill toward the river valley. "Well, Spotty, what do you see?"

The youth was as tall as Godfrew. When he turned around, he looked Godfrew straight in the eye. "Look, old man, me name is Addle! Get it? Addle!"

"All right, young Addle. What do you see, down there?"

"Wots ver mattah? Can'ts yer sees fer yerself?" Addle's irritation was being egged on by the persistent attention of the gnats that were taking an intense interest in the fluid being expelled by his festering pimples.

Godfrew grabbed the boy by the throat and jammed him against the tree. "Never mind what I can see. I know what is down there. You don't. You are the one who is being taught a lesson." He let go of Addle, who straightened his clothes and brushed down his hair.

"Awright, awright. No need ter get so excited."

"What do you see?"

"Grass, an' a river, an' some 'ills in ver distance."

Godfrew waved the other youths to join them. "Did you hear that? That is what we call 'The Broad View.' Nothing wrong with it. Now we need to look closer. Hode ... or whatever your name is ... give me some of the details."

"Right." Hode leaned his body into the tree and panned the scene in front of him. "There is a 'ouse or farm in ver valley some way from ver river. It's got a 'edge rahnd it. Ahtside are some cahs, well I fink vey are cahs ... 'cos vey may be bulls."

"Anyone else?"

The others poked and nudged Dag till he moved up and took in the view before him. "Ver's a road dahn ver. Look, it runs along ver side of ver river, or near enough. An ver's some birds by ver river. Geese?"

The Seeking

"Nothing else?" asked Godfrew. Dag looked again and shook his head. "Now, you —with your finger permanently stuck up your nose—come here."

"Oi, Rowan, 'e means you," clarified Dag gleefully before giving his own nose a small pick.

Godfrew beckoned Rowan over. "I once knew someone else who was fond of digging around in his nose and he came to a very sticky end." Rowan stood by Godfrew's side. "Right, Rowan. Look along the river." The youth obliged. "Now can you see anything ... a building perhaps?"

"Oh, yeah! Yeah, a building."

"A mill?" prompted Godfrew.

"Yeah, yeah. A mill. I can see the water stirred up, so it must be a mill." Having done his job, Rowan went over to stand with his mates—well pleased with himself. He celebrated with a sly dig and scrape of his left nostril.

"Come on, Stumph." Godfrew collected the last of the gang and made him look at the scene. "Look and tell me what you see ... anything that may be of interest or use. Remember, you are part of an army's supply train in a hostile land. You are going to have to get supplies from this place and they will not want to give them to you."

Stumph watched. He took so long that Addle went to poke him, but Godfrew stopped him. Eventually Stumph said, "People ... there are people down there."

"Very good, Stumph," Godfrew said, encouraging the boy. "What are they doing? These people—what are they doing?"

"There are two people with the cows ... probably a man and a boy. There is another man sitting outside the farm. He is working on something, possibly a scythe, as the sun glinted on some metal. There are some half a dozen women down by the river ... washing, I think. In the farm there are, I think, three or four men moving about." Stumph the Silent glanced at Godfrew, hoping that his information was sufficient.

"Very good. Now let us sit down and consider what to do." Godfrew led his band back into the trees that covered the crown of the hill. He found a small clearing that was near enough to the road for them to hear any approaching people, sat down and made a fuss with his hound while the boys picked their spot and made themselves comfortable. "Now we know the basic layout and roughly what to expect. The farm is the target. It lies off the valley road by a way. It is also set back from the track that runs from the common woods to the valley. It has a hedge around it. It runs cattle in addition to the usual crops. More importantly, it runs geese."

"Geese, mister?" interrupted Addle. "We ain't after no geese. Wot we gonna do wiv geese?"

"Avoid frightening them, I hope!" Godfrew allowed himself a slight smile. "Geese frighten easily and they will raise the alarm if you are not careful. Now what else have we? Ah, yes, there is a mill. It is near enough to the farm to be of concern, but far enough away for them not to see what is happening there. People? Well, Stumph saw ... say thirteen. Allowing for a goose girl and others being indoors, there could be twenty folk there." He kicked the foot of Dag who was sprawled opposite him. "Fungus face, what do we need to do now?"

"I ain't gonna charge in and try and nick ver goods, not against vat many."

"Very wise. You would be spotted long before you got there, especially if you had carts or wagons with you. So what have we got to do now?" No one said anything. Addle and Dag gave attention to their pimples and Rowan, his nose. Hode stared at his feet and Stumph looked at Godfrew. "Well, Stumph? What do we have to do now?"

"Get more information."

"Right! Now, if this were a foreign land, it would be a bit difficult and it could take a couple of days. However, this is England—so it is easier. The fact that I already know the lie of the land makes it even easier still." Godfrew eased his back, disturbing Shuck, who had gone to sleep with his head across his master's knees. "This is what we will do. Addle and I will go down the track past the farm. We will do no more than glance at it, but we will note things about it ... the ground, whether it is soft or hard ... the trees or bushes ... where the goose pens are. We will turn right when we get to the lane and go to Wandsworth before heading up the hill again, then we will come back here. Rowan and Hodge will go back along the common land and come down the hill at Halfarthing. They will come along the lane and then go to the mill. They will talk to the miller and ask permission to cross the river over his weir bridge so that they may make

The Seeking

their way to Merton. Whilst there, they will ask if he has any fish he can sell them. He is not supposed to sell them, but I am sure he will. They will use this as a chance to talk to him about this and that ... and the farm ... nothing too specific. Afterwards, they will come back here by way of Upper Tooting. Later this afternoon, Stumph and Dag will go down the path and stop at the farm and ask for directions to Tooting. Like Addle and I, they will be looking around and observing, but nothing to arouse suspicion. Their information will mainly come from any conversations they have with the folk at the farm. Now I will talk to you in pairs to make certain that you fully understand what you have to do and where you have to go. We will all meet back here. Once we have all returned and talked, I will give you the plan for taking the farm ... that fair holding of Garrat."

* * *

Addle sat back contentedly and picked his teeth with a trout's rib bone. "Very tasty that. I 'ad wondered if it weren't gonna be orf, seein' as it's turned warm."

"Smoked, see?" Rowan licked his fingers and then held them out for Shuck to finish cleaning. "Smoked fish lasts better."

"Yes, Hodge." Godfrew wiped his greasy fingers on the long grass by his side. "Good thinking to buy the smoked fish from the miller. I wouldn't have allowed a fire, so without the smoked trout we would have had only apples and cheese. Well done. It shows that you are starting to think." Godfrew got up slowly and stood with his back to a tree. "Pay attention, because it's lesson time."

"We don't want no lessons, we want ter get on wiv it," Dag protested, shying his apple core into the bushes.

"You need the lesson and you will get it whether you like it or not. Men have died to provide this knowledge. If you don't learn from it, you may join them quicker than you think." Godfrew looked directly at Dag, "Now get the apple core back."

"Eh?"

"It will attract the swine. Wherever the swine wander, the swineherd goes. After we have gone, it doesn't matter, but meantime, bring it back here. I don't want any nosy swineherds poking their snouts in on our little talk." Dag muttered at Godfrew and retrieved the core. Godfrew waited for him to sit down again before continuing. "When you are sent out by your unit to gather food, you have to look at all your options before deciding what to do. Now, the size of your target will depend on how many men you have and whether those men are 'hangers-on' like yourselves, or mounted warriors."

"'angers on?" Addle protested, cleaning his ear out with a small twig.

"Yes," confirmed Godfrew, "hangers on. That is how the soldiers will see you, even if their stomachs are dependent on the supplies you are gathering and transporting. They will only see you as 'hangers-on.' Nothing else." Godfrew carefully bent and picked up a stick. With it, he drew a circle and some lines. "Here is a farm, village, town, whatever. Now, one thing you must remember is that you never take on a walled town. That is for the army or a special group to tackle. You are looking for places that are either undefended or only lightly defended. You are after supplies, not a fight." He scribed another circle—this one outside the imaginary target. "If you have to go in during daytime you should only go in if you have horsemen with you. The horsemen should gallop around and around the target making lots of noise and creating as much confusion as possible. Then, when the rest of you have arrived, they should charge up and down the streets —making a big show of it—confusing the locals as to just how many of them there are whilst you move from door to door checking the houses. Don't let the horsemen get involved in any fighting. They won't win in the confined streets. Their job is to create illusions that will prevent the locals from standing still long enough to start working out just what is happening. Now the key thing here is to leave the residents a way out. You want them to flee. You do not want a fight, because if they stood and made a go of it, they could well beat you. They will usually outnumber you. Remember that even a rat will attack if it is cornered. Let the folk think only of saving their lives ... and let them want to do that by running away." Godfrew scrubbed the dust drawing out with his foot. "Dawn attacks are the best. Go in at first light, before anyone is up. Use all available cover and go in on foot.

The Seeking

Pick your target houses and all strike at once on a given signal. Again, use noise and confusion to make the locals think that there are lots of you—and, again, leave them a bolt hole. If a house has two entrances, only attack one of them. If there is only one, make sure that they have a window they can get out of. Fire can be very useful here if your own army controls the countryside. If it doesn't, avoid using fire as it will only bring the enemy soldiers down on you."

"Is this 'ow we're gonna take Garrat, old man?" Dag passed the unwanted apple core to Shuck, who grabbed it and ran under a tree to eat.

"No. This is a lesson only. It is for use in enemy territory. Garrat is a different proposition. Before I start on the plan to take the place, let me tell you how you can use the experience of tonight's attack later on."

"Tonight? Gawd, I was 'opin' to get some kip." Rowan leaned forward took off his shoes and began massaging his feet. "I've walked bleedin' miles today, I 'ave."

"Tonight ... before the information you have gathered becomes stale." Shuck came and stretched himself up Godfrew's leg, hooking his claws into his master's belt. Godfrew let his hand drop to stroke the hound's head. "Now, the lesson. Night attacks should only be done in special circumstances."

"An' this is one, old man?" asked Addle. He dug the fish bone deep into a crevasse in his teeth, then spat out a piece of fish.

"This is one," Godfrew confirmed. "Normally, as part of the supply train, you would only get involved in a night attack if the army was really desperate for supplies and you had been compelled to strike out deep into your foe's land. However, you may show a talent for raiding and reeving. If you do, your Captain may send you out on special missions. Often, the special missions could involve getting into and out of a place at night without arousing the neighbourhood. The main thing with a night attack is to have as much information as you can get, then make sure that you know where things are. It is very easy to get lost at night, even in a house. Now, like the dawn attack, you should use the natural cover to get as close as possible. Go in pairs ... if someone comes near ... freeze. If you try and hide or fall to the ground, you are more likely to be seen than if you just stand still. Now, if you are spearheading a major attack, you resort to fire and the other 'confusion' tactics we have already discussed."

"Discussed?" queried Rowan, wiping a boogy on the legs of his britches.

Godfrew gave the boy a hard look. "Listen ... if you want to live." He ran his eye over the other youths and checked that they were listening before carrying on. "Often—and this job tonight is a case in hand—the need is to do the business without others knowing. Here we will try and get in and out with the minimum disturbance. Right?" Godfrew lifted Shuck off of his belt and eased his back by taking a couple of steps. "Let's find out what information you have gathered for me so that I can plan tonight's foray."

"At last, old man, we get to the plan for the rape and pillage," said Dag with a leer.

Godfrew looked at the boy with disdain. "Rape and pillage? What would you know of such things? Pillage you may get—though on this job it will be more like 'thieving.' Rape you will not get."

"I always fought ..."

"Never mind what you thought, Dag. Even during war, rape is not to be encouraged." The youngster looked confused. "When you have your head down and your arse up, you cannot see the man standing behind you with the pitchfork," Godfrew explained, "and the worst thing is to rape a woman in front of her man—be he husband or father—he will be sure to want revenge. Now ... information please."

"Yeah, well ..." Addle started.

"No," Godfrew cut him short, "I think we will hear from Stumph first seeing as he went into the holding itself."

Stumph shyly got up and came to stand in front of Godfrew, "The most important thing, mister, is that tomorrow night the man who holds the place ... Robert Spencer ... he is going away for the night to London and taking his wife and some of the men with him."

"Well done!" Godfrew patted Stumph on the shoulder. "In that case, gentlemen, we go in tomorrow night."

Addle got to his feet with Dag at his side. "I fought we was gonna do it ternight. You said when we wanted ter go in termorrah, vat we 'ad ter go in ternight!"

The Seeking

"My dearly beloved spotty ones, if we wait till tomorrow our chances of success improve to no end. Remember, a good plan is a flexible plan." He gestured to them to sit. "Now, let us get on with pooling our knowledge about Garrat."

* * *

In the deep velvet night, Godfrew and Addle crouched in the bushes and watched the shadows move. "Well, Addle, what can you see?"

"Trainin', right?"

"Right, Addle, training. Now, what can you see? Are the others in place?"

"Yeah. Rowan and Hodge are in vose bushes over vere where you told 'em to go. I saw Dag and Stumph move rahnd the ahver side, so vey must be in place by nah."

"Good. Now the action begins." Godfrew held a ball of smelly cheese in front of Shuck's nose. The hound licked it. Before he could bite the cheese, Godfrew pulled it back and the hound strained against the short leash that Addle held him on. "Ready, Addle? Good. Now when I throw the cheese, let the hound go." Godfrew stepped out of the bushes and hefted the ball of cheese into the goose pen and Shuck streaked out after it, leaping the fence and landing in amongst its feathered occupants who started making a horrible honking row.

Doors opened and the men came out whilst their women hung back and watched from the doorway.

"What's going on, Alf?"

"Something has upset the geese."

"I know that, stupid. I can hear them too!"

"Where's Master Reynard?"

"I here. What problem?"

"The geese. I'll go and look. Alf, get that billhook and stay with me, just in case."

"Can you see anything?"

"Something moved." There was the sound of a stone being thrown followed by a yelp. "Fox!"

"Better go after it, Stan."

"You want I come?" asked the French voice.

"No, Master Reynard. I won't even need old Alf here. It's headed for those bushes. There is an old badger's set there ... been empty for some time, but that'll be where the fox is headed. I'll get the Master's old hunting spear, if you don't mind, and then I'll go and get the bugger."

Godfrew caught Shuck as he came running back to the bushes and made a fuss of him. "Put the leash back on him, Addle, and tie him to the bush by that badger's hole. Then watch and wait for the man to come here."

It took a while before the man came out from the farm, but when he did, he headed straight for where Shuck was tied up. In addition to a spear, the man had a spade and he used this to clear the bushes in front of him. Nearing the old set, he quietly laid the spade down and approached the hole with the spear held ready ... just in case the fox was daft enough to be outside. "I can see you, you little thief," he whispered to himself. "What? You're not a fox you're a ...." Godfrew hit the man behind the back of the ear with his saxe and he went down hard.

"You've bleedin' killed 'im, old man."

"No, I haven't, but if you don't help me gag and tie him, he may wake up and kill you!" Godfrew unwound some coarse rope from around his waist and commenced to bind the man. Once satisfied, he led Addle to the farm hedge. In his time, the hedge around Garrat had been thick enough to keep stock in and people out. Now, it was purely decorative with fencing being used to restrain the animals. Waiting for them by the hedge, were the others.

"All clear, mister," confirmed Stumph. "Only the geese are still honking."

"Right." Godfrew glanced inside the farmyard. "You know what to do. I will see you at the main house. Just don't knock anything over. Your movements will be masked by the disturbed geese, but if you knock things over, the game will be up." He glanced in the yard again. "Right, go!"

In pairs, the raiders moved through the gaps in the hawthorn hedge and into the yard. Whilst Godfrew and Addle made their way to the big house and checked it out, the others moved around the smaller dwellings and jammed the doors shut with poles cut from the fencing, then stuck wedges in the window shutters. By the time all the houses

The Seeking

had been locked up, Godfrew had pried open a window shutter on the big house and had cut out the membrane window made of uncured leather

"Stumph, you are the smallest. Get in there and remove the bar on the front door. You went into this room when you scrounged milk the other day, so you shouldn't bump into anything." Godfrew indicated to Rowan and Dag to help the youth up and through the window while he rested against the wall, his chest heaving with the night's exertions.

Without a sound, the front door opened and Stumph beckoned them all in. Godfrew removed his broad-rimmed hat and hung it from his belt. He pulled the hood of his wolf-skin cloak over his head and adjusted the eye holes in the mask so that he could see better. "Right," he whispered, "you work your way through the rooms. Gag and tie up anyone you find. There shouldn't be many, as most went with the man and woman this morning."

"Plunder?" asked Addle quietly, a gleam of avarice in his eye.

"Plunder," Godfrew confirmed. "But only after you have secured the building. There is bound to be a big upstairs room. Pay particular attention to it. Leave any smaller rooms upstairs to me. I have things other than treasure to seek. Whilst you seek treasure, I seek French pups."

"Treasure, eh!"

"Treasure, my spotty Addle. However, don't get too carried away. Take coins in preference, then jewellery. Nothing too bulky. In the upstairs room, check any wood paneling and listen for hollow sounds in the floor. If you open any chests, remember that any treasure is likely to be under a false bottom rather than amongst the contents of the chest." Godfrew put his right hand under his cloak and released the leather thong that held his axe, Neckbiter, in place across his back.

Rowan stopped picking his nose and stared. "Blimey, mister. Where did vat come from?"

"It has always been there. I will attend to my business. You attend to yours. Just don't take too long. We have to be out of here fast. Now go!" Godfrew hissed.

Godfrew left the others and crept up the stairs. As he suspected, there was short passage with a door at the end. Ig-

Woden's Wolf

noring that, he checked the side of the passage and found that there were two doors, one either side. The first room proved to be empty of anything other than an unslept child's bed. He moved across the narrow passage to the second door.

The door opened silently and the wolf crept in. A fat old woman lay asleep on the floor at the foot of the bed. In the bed lay two brown-haired boys, the smaller with his thumb in his mouth. The wolf lifted his axe. Just as he took aim, the elder boy woke and screamed. The wolf swung the axe, but before blade could bite, the boy had rolled off the bed taking his brother with him.

The old woman woke and scrambled to her feet. The boys ran to her and hid behind her skirt. She looked like a bantam with her chicks. The wolf paced toward her and raised his axe. A stray moon beam, passing through the open window, lit his face. "Move out of the way, woman. I want those French cubs you're hiding."

"They are but children. Leave them alone!" The woman pulled the boys closer to her side.

"They may be children, but the sins of the fathers will be vested on their children. Now get out of the way!"

"Nanny, Nanny don't let the big bad wolf hurt us, please!"

"He speaks English!" spat out the wolf.

"Of course he speaks English. He speaks better English than he speaks his mother and father's French." The woman rummaged around her voluminous waist and produced her eating knife, which she held at arm's length toward the wolf.

The wolf hesitated for a moment, then lowered the axe a fraction. "Why does he speak English?"

"Who do you think is bringing the boys up? Madam with her airs and graces and her expensive tastes? No! Nanny is bringing them up. They suckled at my breasts. They grew their bodies on my English milk. As I am English, so will any child I raise be English!"

The wolf lifted the axe again. "I will not be deprived of my vengeance. As the Frenchmen deprived me of those that I loved, so will I deprive them of their loved ones. Get out of the way, woman!"

Nanny slashed in the air with her knife and then pulled back, "I know who you are. You are no wolf. You are Godfrew Alfredson, the Longshanks. That eye!" The woman smiled

The Seeking

and her voice became very bold. "You don't frighten me, Master Godfrew. I remember you, all right ... a proper little mummy's boy with your nose in a book or hanging around your mother's skirts learning to sew." She smirked. "You don't remember me though, do you? I'm Heth, Ake Swineherd's daughter. Not that you, with your fine manners, would remember my name."

The wolf looked hard at the fat woman with her crossed eyes. "Yes, I do remember now. You have your father's eyes."

"Well, you don't frighten me with your wolf's head. Leave my boys alone."

The younger boy poked his head from behind Heth's skirt, "Nanny, is this one of the wicked Normans that burnt the house down when you were a little girl? Has he come back to kill us all, as he killed everyone then?"

There was a noise in the passage as the gang made their way upstairs in search of plunder. Godfrew looked at the young boys, then glanced at the door. He let Neckbiter drop to his waist.

"Don't worry about me raising the alarm. For the sake of your father, I wouldn't see you hang. But leave the boys alone." As she spoke, tears started to well in Heth's crossed eyes, but her voice was still strong and she still presented her knife at Godfrew.

Godfrew left the room and closed the door behind him. As he turned, he bumped into Addle.

"Is ver any of ver French in vere?"

Godfrew shook his head. "No, only English. They will not betray us." He looked for the others. "Have you found enough loot? We need to get out of here."

"Plenty. We was waitin' fer you," the spotty youth replied, then led the way down the tight stairs. The others were gathered by the door and Godfrew led them out.

There, in the yard, barring the gateway, was Reynard the Reeve, holding a billhook in his hand. Godfrew stepped toward him. "You no go." Reynard raised his weapon, "You put back what you have ..."

Godfrew misjudged the blow and instead of cleaving the Frenchman in twain, he succeeded only in opening up the man's belly and spilling his guts. Reynard dropped to his knees looking despondently at the intestines running through his fingers. Godfrew took another step forward. This time, Neckbiter lived up to its name and took off the reeve's head.

"Wot yer do that for?" Addle went white and then sunk to his knees and vomited.

"Would you rather I had let him live so that he could have us all hanged? If you can't deal with a small thing like this, then you had better forget about serving in the army."

"Are you coming with us, mister?" asked Stumph, a small bag of plunder at his feet.

"No." Godfrew bent carefully and wiped the blade of his axe clean on Reynard's shirt. "You must go on your own now. You guide the others. Just keep them moving and don't let them spend too much at once." He took deep breaths to steady his beating heart. "Just keep moving till you reach the safety of the army."

"We got what we came for, mister, did you?"

"No, Stumph. No, I did not." Godfrew got up again and looked at the lad. "Now move out whilst you may. You have places to go and so have I."

* * *

A tired old grey wolf snuck into the graveyard of the newly expanded priory at Upper Totting. For a while, he moved around in the darkness till he found what he was looking for. The wolf then dug a hole at the foot of the grave where Godfrew's father lay. He buried Neckbiter in it.

The Grace of God

The young monk stood in the lamp lit cell and waited for the man kneeling on the stone floor to finish his prayers. At the "amen," the young monk bent and helped the older man to his feet.

"Thank you, Brother Wulfstan. I'm sure that the older you get, the harder the floor becomes." The older monk brushed his habit where his knees had gathered dust from the flagstones. "Now what can I do for you?"

"Brother Guthric, we have a new 'guest'. I have him in the infirmary at present." Wulfstan smiled and shrugged. "I need a second opinion."

"So us old ones still have our uses, eh?" Guthric opened the door of the cell. "Now whilst we walk to see this 'guest' of ours, perhaps you had better tell me more about him. A beggar, I assume?"

"I don't think that he is your usual beggar. The villagers brought him in. Apparently, he has been seen wandering around the Thornton Heath for days. The relevant point is that he has his eyes bandaged and uses a stick as a guide, but he couldn't have been blind long, as he keeps banging into things." Wulfstan opened the door of the Infirmary and continued walking toward the guest cells. "They didn't want to approach him, as whenever they got near him he took to them with a big knife. And, of course, there was also his skinny dog. I told you he had a half-starved dog?"

"No, Brother, but carry on."

"Anyway, whenever they went near him, he attacked them. And the dog went for them, too. Eventually, he collapsed. I think the villagers would have left him to die, but the dog kept on running up to them—whimpering and trying to get them to follow him back to his master. The villagers took this to be a sign from God. They picked him up and brought him here." Wulfstan stopped outside a cell door. "He is in here. I had better warn you that it looks as if he and the dog have spent the winter sleeping rough. I doubt that if, during that time, either of them have had any water near their bodies except rain." He opened the door and the two monks went in.

The old man sat on a stool jammed into the corner of the cell. His body was shaking. His clothes were ragged and torn. The animal-skin cloak he wore had large patches as bald as his head. What fur remained on the tattered cloak was matted with filth and clogged with burrs and grass seed. The man's bald head was burnt and blistered in places. Thorns lay buried and festering under the skin. When he moved, his left shoulder dropped low and sat at an awkward angle. One of his grime-encrusted hands rested in his lap with its black broken nails shining like ebony in the flickering lamp light. The other hand sat on the head of an equally filthy and skinny black hound. At the sound of the monks coming into the guest cell, the old man let his hound be and fiddled around at his back searching for something.

"If you are looking for that evil-looking knife of yours, old man, you won't find it. I have put it somewhere safe until you are ready to leave us." Wulfstan sat on the bed watching the hound warily. Guthric looked at him quizzically and the younger monk lifted the hem of his habit to reveal a set of bright red hound's-tooth marks on the calf of his leg.

Brother Guthric approached the old man and his hound. He dug in his pocket and found a small piece of stale bread which he proffered to the dog. Shuck took it and dived under the bed to devour his prize. "Now, my friend, you are at the Archbishop of Canterbury's palace at Croydon. I am Brother Guthric, the Almoner, and my young colleague is Brother Wulfstan. We are here to help you."

Godfrew nodded his head. "Croydon? I have been here before."

"Good. It is always pleasant to return to a place we know." Guthric stood at Godfrew's side and looked him over. "Well, my friend, you have a bad fever which we will have to try and bring down, but you also have something wrong with your eyes. May I?" He put his hand to the bandage that encompassed Godfrew's head. "Thank you." The monk started to unwind the filthy rag.

"Light ... I can't stand the light."

The Grace of God

"The light hurts his right eye," explained Brother Wulfstan. "His left has a cataract on it. The cataract is well established, so it has been there for a long time."

"From birth." Shuck returned to his master's side and nudged up Godfrew's hand to be patted and fussed.

"I have the bandage off now. I will get Brother Wulfstan to shield the light, but I will need enough to see by. Please remember that we are trying to help you." Guthric gently pried open Godfrew's gummed up right eye. Apart from the pupil, it was blood red, like raw liver. Godfrew flinched and fought to close it again. "My, that is bad." Guthric turned to the other monk, "I assume that you have looked for foreign objects in it?" Wulfstan nodded. "Then it is beyond me. We will need someone more experienced than I to look at it. Meantime, we should get both our guest and his hound bathed." Brother Guthric replaced the bandage. "What worries me, young Wulfstan, is that the only one who might know what is wrong is old Brother Marcus at Lewisham. Perhaps even he won't know what to do. Getting Brother Marcus here will take three days or so. I hope the old man lasts that long. I don't like the look of that fever. We must try and get his temperature down. If we are not careful, the fever will kill him off before we can get his eye looked at!"

Godfrew patted his lap and Shuck jumped up and settled down, his head resting in the crook of Godfrew's arm. "Many have tried to kill me and they have all failed. Do you think that you can do any better than they?"

"Latin! You were right, Brother Wulfstan. He is not your usual beggar!"

* * *

Godfrew stood in the full flood of the Wandle's woe waters, his back against the current. Elfgifu stood on the bank and pushed the last of his nine sons toward him. The child became caught in the swirling water and was swept away. Cold water surged over Godfrew's shoulders as he fought to make his way toward his wife.

"Stay, Elfgifu! Stay!"

His wife smiled at him and stepped into the river. She, too, was caught and swept off. Her hands flailed and raised foam on the water's surface. When Godfrew looked back at the river bank, Elfgifu was still there.

"Stay, Elfgifu! Stay!"

His wife smiled at him and stepped into the river again, only to loose her footing and disappear under the surging waters.

The force of the river's flow slackened and Godfrew could not feel it crashing over his back anymore. He turned and looked upstream. There, heading toward him, were boats. As he watched, they floated around the front of him in a semi-circle. He stared at the people sitting in the small boats and he gasped as he recognised them. In the first boat sat his hand-fast wife Eve and her two Norman friends. In the next was Drogo of Wimbledon, then two Norman soldiers who were holding up the severed ear of Teodoric the goldsmith. Godfrew turned and tried to head off downstream, but his path was blocked by two other boats manned by young Rennie and the lover of Clunn's woman, Eleanor. There, was the French priest and his travelling companions. There, also, was the falconer from Landoc and with them were the other unfortunate French who had crossed the old man as he had travelled the Sussex Weald and the roads of Surrey. Then came another boat manned by the French warren keeper, his son and Reynard of Garrat. Godfrew saw a gap, only to have to have it filled by Addle, Dag, and Rowan with the hangman's rope still around their broken necks. A church bell sounded and Godfrew looked to the far bank and saw the burnt church at Beaumont. Its slaughtered congregation were all filing toward the Wandle and wading in toward him. Coming downstream were barges filled with war dead, all beating a slow march on their shields with their swords, urged on by an old man in a wolf-skin cloak and slouch hat riding a six-legged black horse[1] through the waters. There was only one way left, the nearer bank. Godfrew turned and there stood a man with a beard and long flowing hair. He seemed to be bathed in light and his pure white clothes shone.

---

24 Woden's horse, Slepnir, was said to have had six legs, which accounted for the animal's speed.

The Grace of God

The man held his arms out at right angles. Godfrew saw the nail marks on his hands and fell to his knees in the receding woe waters.

Jesus smiled gently. When he spoke, it was with a voice of strong rich honey:

> Peace is my own gift
> I give freely to all.
> The world has no gift
> The likeness of this.
> I went away once
> But I will return soon.
> As I died for one,
> So did I die for all.
> In me, trust you only,
> Then saved you shall be.
> Take gift of all life;
> Take gift of all grace.
> As King of all kings,
> As Lord of all lords,
> All gifts are mine
> To give as I will give.
> Put aside arm bands,
> Rings of pure gold.
> Accept as my gift
> Forgiveness of all.
> Salvation is mine,
> So says the Father.
> As I reign in high heaven,
> Come reign then with me.[1]

Godfrew stood and started to walk toward Jesus, but his dead accusers left their boats and stood between him and the shore. Desperately he cried out, "Lord, Lord, how can I come to you? You see all, you know my past deeds. How can I ever overcome what lies between us?"

Jesus brought his hands together as if in prayer.

> Pray come now and join me

---

[25] After John 14 v 27-28.

> In blessed realms of truth,
> Damned not by conscience,
> Though you stand guilty.
> God's love is greater
> Than all of your dark sins.
> Tempted by foul fiend,
> The flesh of men weaken,
> But I bought your soul
> On the gore stained rood.
> Now none condemn you,
> For all is forgiven.
> Grace gift of the Father
> Through the blood of his Son.[1]

As he spoke, Jesus parted his hands and Godfrew's victims moved aside and let him through. As he stood before the Lord, Godfrew wept, then Jesus took him in his arms and embraced him. As the embrace continued, Godfrew felt the peace of God fill him and act as balm to all his wounds.

* * *

Brothers Wulfstan and Guthric came into the cell and, hesitantly walking between them, his arms around their shoulders, was a bowed and ancient monk. At the sight of the hard bed, he inclined his head toward it and then accepted the help of the younger monks to sit on its edge.

"This is the old man with the bad eyes then?" The voice was broken and crackled.

Wulfstan stood by the old monk's elbow and shouted in his ear, "Yes, Brother Marcus."

"Wake him up and get the bandages off so that I can have a look. Hurry now. I am a very old man. If you take too long, I may be dead before you have finished." While he waited, Brother Marcus' bent and arthritic fingers played with his rosary beads.

"I am awake." Godfrew struggled to get up and the disturbed Shuck came out from under the threadbare cloak and stretched. The hound's tongue curled as he yawned.

---

[26] After 1 John 3 v 29-22.

The Grace of God

Carefully, Guthric removed the bandages and let Marcus examine Godfrew's eyes. The old monk sat back and pulled on the end of his nose. "Had a bad back at all?"

"Most of my life."

"Then I think I know what is wrong." Brother Marcus smiled, "I have herbs that will reduce the inflammation and others that will stop your iris opening. I assume you know what your iris is?" Godfrew nodded. "Good. At the moment, your iris is trying to rip itself away from the rest of your eye. In God's time—and with help from the right herbs that His hands have provided—it will cease doing that. It will take time. You will need to stay in the dark, perhaps forever, perhaps just for a while. That is in God's hand." He leaned forward again, lifted the lid on Godfrew's left eye and studied the cataract. "You know, I have a thought running around the back of my head." He tapped his nose. "That eye of yours is unusual. Many years ago I treated a young man here for a bad back. He, too, had the white eye and he spoke Latin, as you do. Now what was his name? Badger? Fox? No ... no ... I have it: Wulf! Are you Wulf?"

"No, Brother, I am not Wulf. I am Godfrew ... God's Peace."

* * *

The monk bent forward and kissed the nun gently on the lips. They touched hands, then parted: she to continue along the cloister and he to enter the library. At a large reading table, an already open book greeted him and he poured over its contents.

"I realise that Scripture tells us to greet each other with the kiss of peace, but I had not realised that you also had to do it on departure as well!"

The monk stopped reading and peered short-sightedly at the darkened corner from whence the voice had come. "Is there someone there, or am I being tempted by a devil as Saint Anthony was in the desert?"

"Don't panic, Brother. You won't have to seek the Exorcist to cleanse the room before resuming your labours."

The monk got off of his stool and walked toward the voice. "Ah, there you are, Father."

"I am not a priest, so you needn't call me Father."

"Oh, sorry, Brother. I saw the tonsure, so I thought you had been consecrated." The monk put his hands inside his sleeves and studied the old man who sat on the floor in the dark corner.

"Sorry, Brother, but you are wrong again. I am not a Brother either. This tonsure is direct from God, not a Bishop." Godfrew ran his right hand over his bald pate.

The monk spread his hand and clicked his tongue on his pallet. "Hallelujah, a miracle!" His sparkling eyes betrayed the statement as a jest.

"One that was spread over many years and seemed to have been caused more by shock and horror than by divine blessing." Godfrew laid aside the book he was reading and levered himself upright by pressing against the smooth dressed stone of the wall. Shuck moved near the monk and sniffed the hem of his habit.

"A man who has lived in the world appreciates God's blessings more than one who has shut himself away. The apostle Paul has much to say on the subject." The monk turned and looked longingly at his seat. "Come, join me on the long stool. I find all this standing too much ... one of the reasons I ducked out of mainstream monastic life. All those hours spent standing muttering prayers from rote without even thinking about what is being said. You know, of course, that the Lord Jesus himself condemned that sort of practice? Yes, a practice that is bad for both the back and the soul. A good reason for opting out."

"One of many, I think, Brother. But, no, I must stay in the dark. My eye hurts in the light."

"Ah, the beggar that speaks Latin!" the monk smiled, his teeth showing in the brown and silver of his close-cropped beard. "I saw the habit and the head and thought you ..." He shrugged and smiled again.

"The habit is borrowed and the tonsure natural. As in my past, I am not what I seem." Godfrew snapped his fingers to get his hound back at his side. He could see that the monk was uncomfortable about Shuck's cold, wet nose exploring his legs. "But, back to the kiss."

"That was my wife, Balthild."

"Your wife? Is that allowed?"

The Grace of God

"Look, do you mind if we sit down? Even if it is only on the floor. My back, you see." The monk pulled out his hands from his sleeves and gestured to the wall.

"I am happy to do so, for my back causes me problems as well." Godfrew pressed against the wall and slid down onto the floor.

The monk gently edged himself down to sit alongside Godfrew. "Is being married allowed? Now that is an interesting one. Whilst our Lord Jesus remained unwed, many of his disciples were married—including Peter, of whom the Pope claims to be his successor and imitator. Paul remained single and recommended it to others, but recognised that it did not suit everyone."

"But monks aren't supposed to be married. In fact, many say that all the religious should be celibate." Godfrew could see that the monk was unhappy about the attention Shuck was giving his master, so he discouraged the hound from licking his ear and made him sit on his lap instead.

"If that were so, then why did Paul spend so much time telling Timothy that church officials—Bishops and the like—should only be selected from those who had control of their children and who were married to sober wives."

"But monks?"

"It is not liked." The monk examined his fingernails in detail.

"From what I have just read in this book of rules, it is forbidden. Is that right, Brother ..."

"Job ... Brother Job. Forbidden? Yes ... well ... once you have joined orders it is forbidden to get married—not by Scripture of course ... only by the church. But Balthild and me ... well ... we have been married for many years now—long before we decided that we would serve the Lord full time. Celibate we can be ... but out of love with each other ... Never!" He smiled and shrugged expressively. "You do understand?"

"Perhaps I do ..." Godfrew turned to Job with a wicked smile. "... but does the Burgandian Anslem ... the Archbishop of Canterbury ... does he understand?"

Job looked up from his preoccupation with his beautifully manicured nails. "Who knows, seeing as he has only just come back from exile. But I doubt it. From all accounts he is a strict follower of the Benedictine order and very rigorous in his observance."

"So why are you here at his palace? Awaiting sentence?" Godfrew ran his fingers over both of Shuck's silken ears.

"Keeping out of his way, really. Apparently he hates being Archbishop and would like nothing better than to return to being a monk back at the Abbey of Bec in Normandy. I don't think that my superiors expect him to make any use of his summer palace at Croydon, so they sent me here."

"And they let your wife come with you? How considerate!"

"How corrupt, really. For although we have renounced all our worldly goods, our sons and daughters haven't and they are quite happy to spend a little silver to ensure that their parents continue to live in happiness together." Job turned to Godfrew and lowered his voice to a whisper. "It is silver that buys my superior's tolerance of some of my other foibles as well ... that and the fact that I have skills useful to them."

"Have you, indeed? They must be very desirable skills, Brother Job."

"They think so. Myself, I think that anyone could do what I do if they had the training." Job pushed away Shuck as he returned to continue his cold-nosed investigation of the monk's legs. "I oversee building projects. At the moment, I am building a new Chapel here, but it is taking a lot longer than it should have. Up till now, I have always been victorious over the trials and travails of completing complex tasks on time and to budget, but this job has problems. One major problem actually."

"I once oversaw the building of a church ... in Norwich, it was."

"Did you, indeed? I assume that you have nowhere to go at present. Why don't you earn your keep by helping me?"

"Perhaps I could. I am enjoying the peace that I have found here and would like to stay. I wouldn't become a monk as, like David, I am a warlike man and my hands are stained with blood. But to stay here, I need a job ... yes ... why not."

"Then it is settled, brother. You know my name, but I do not know yours."

"Godfrew."

The Grace of God

"Then, Brother Godfrew ... for you do indeed look like one of the brethren ... then, Brother Godfrew let us go forth on the road to victory together."

* * *

"Well, Brother, what do you think?" Job walked alongside Godfrew as they looked at the paintings in the new chapel.

"My honest opinion, Brother?" Godfrew ran his hand over his head and then over his face. "Honestly?"

"Honestly." They stopped and Job and Godfrew looked around the completed chancel and the brilliantly coloured paintings on its walls. "Well?"

"A bit complex for my taste," Godfrew confessed, as he pulled the broad rim of his borrowed straw hat further over his face to reduce the amount of light getting into his still sore eye.

"What is your taste then, Brother?" Brother Job stepped closer to the wall and examined the brush work of the painting.

"Honestly? Yes, sorry ... you said that you wanted my honest opinion." Godfrew took another look at the art works. "Well, my taste is for nothing more than whitewashed walls to show the purity of God." He glanced at Job who continued to examine the quality of the workmanship. "However, having said that, I understand the need for pictures to educate those who can't read, or are simple-minded and all that. But ..."

" ... but, Brother Godfrew?" Job turned around and looked at Godfrew from under his lowered brow. "Speak honestly, remember!"

"But these are so complex that I cannot understand what they are trying to depict." Godfrew expected some reaction from the monk, but he got none. "Now, I know that my knowledge of Scripture is somewhat lacking, though I am trying to make up for lost time but I don't recognise any of the scenes ... and those that I might recognise are muddled."

"An interesting statement." Brother Job stood back from the wall and looked all around the chancel. "Quite right, of course, Brother. It is excessively muddled. Now ..." he turned around and opened his hands to encompass the whole of the chapel " ... now tell me what you think of the rest of the job."

Godfrew cautiously peered under his brim at the work site. He coughed and after clearing his throat, he smiled gently at Job. "I'm not sure how to put this, Brother Job—particularly as you, by your own confession, have been overseeing the building of churches and the like for some time ... and I only did it once, but ..." Godfrew took in a deep breath before continuing, " ... but, Brother, why have you had the chancel fully completed and yet have left the rest of the building unfinished? I mean, most of the other walls are little more than chest high."

The monk clicked his tongue on his pallet and threw his hands open wide. "Ah, you have noticed the fatal flaw to the job!"

"It does seem somewhat strange, Brother."

"It is somewhat strange. So strange that it is driving me close to the sin of anger. We spend more time each day covering and uncovering the chancel and its hideous and garish paintings than we do on getting the rest of the work done. It is not as if I can leave the chancel uncovered. If I did that, I would spend my nights in fear of mildew appearing on the paintings." Job shook his head in disbelief and walked slowly over to a small table and its two attendant chairs.

Godfrew and Shuck followed the monk. Job sat down with a sigh of relief and opened a ledger book that sat on the table. Godfrew moved his stool so that he was out of the light and sat down with Shuck at his feet. "I'm sorry, Brother, but I can't understand why you have built the chapel this way when you yourself are unhappy with the way it is being done."

"I know you can read Latin and, as you have done this type of work yourself, you must be familiar with bookkeeping. Take a look at this one. Meanwhile, I will go and get us some honey and water to drink."

"Mead?"

"Sorry, no. This honey and water will be unfermented. I may not stick to all the rules, but unnecessary drinking of alcoholic beverages is a vice I do not indulge in."

"Didn't Paul tell Timothy to stop drinking only water and for the sake of his health to take some wine instead?"

The Grace of God

Job eased himself up off the stool. "But, my friend, this isn't water. It is hot water with honey dissolved in it!" he chuckled. "Now, read the book, if you please. I would like your comments on it before I am prepared to discuss the method of construction being employed at this building site."

Godfrew poured over the book, checking costs and material. When Brother Job still hadn't returned, he started looking at the time schedule. He had just pushed the ledger to one side and closed his aching eye when the monk reappeared with two steaming pottery mugs in his hand.

"Sorry to have taken so long, Brother Godfrew, but it was the noon-tide service ... 'Sext' ... and I got roped in." He put the mugs down carefully on the table, together with two crusty wheaten rolls. "Seeing as I was not able to provide you with the mead you asked for, I thought I would compensate with some food, courtesy of my wife, who works in the buttery."

"Thank you, Brother. My guts were just starting to ache as much as my eye. It is all very well spending my time with monks. I just wish I didn't have to eat like them as well." Shuck came and sat alongside his master and rested his head on his lap. Soon, Godfrew's borrowed habit acquired a dark, damp spot from his hound's drooling.

Job tucked into his roll with relish and crumbs of crust stuck to his clipped beard. "Oh, I almost forgot." He rummaged in his hood and produced a couple of small turnips. "I'm sure that the Lord will bless us for sampling the bounty of the earth and appreciating the delicate flavours thereof."

Godfrew accepted the proffered vegetable and wiped off the loose, gritty soil on his sleeve. Shuck's head adopted the same movements as his master's hand as it stropped the turnip on the coarse cloth. Godfrew took a bite and chewed. Whilst he held the vegetable in his lap, Shuck took the opportunity to take an exploratory lick. Finding the taste not suited to his palate, he went off to seek bread crumbs from around Brother Job instead.

After finishing his meal, Job settled on his stool, rested his hands on his stomach and closed his eyes. "So, Brother Godfrew, what did the book tell you?"

Godfrew tossed the rest of his roll to Shuck and cleaned his mouth with a mouthful of the now lukewarm honey water. He glanced at Job, who appeared to be asleep in the multicoloured spring sunlight that was filtering through the small panes of coloured glass above the dusty altar. "What did the book tell me?"

"Honestly now, Brother, remember that this is the Lord's work we are about, or so I am frequently told." Job's lips moved, but he still seemed to be asleep. Shuck very gently removed a large flake of crust from the monk's lap without him noticing.

"Well," Godfrew began reluctantly, "I must first say that I have been away from this type of work for some time and I don't know what the current prices for transport, labour and materials are."

"However."

"However, Brother, I think that you are paying good prices for what you are getting done. What I can't understand though ... and please forgive me for saying this ... but what I can't understand is why you keep getting so far completed and then pulling most of the structure down again!"

"Christomo," muttered Job.

"Pardon, Brother?" Godfrew put his little finger in his ear and cleaned it. "My ears. Sorry, they frequently ring and hiss, so I don't always hear properly."

"Christomo," muttered Job.

"You did say Christomo!" Godfrew sat back, happy that he had heard clearly what had been said. After he had thought about it for a while he frowned. "Christomo?" he asked, puzzled.

"Christomo," confirmed Job.

"And what, pray, is 'Christomo'?"

Brother Job opened an eye and raised an eyebrow, "Christomo is the fatal flaw in the job that I mentioned earlier."

"You still haven't told me what 'Christomo' is Brother!"

Job chuckled, opened his eyes and sat up. "Not 'what', but 'who'. Christomo is the name of the Sacrist."

Godfrew shuffled his seat nearer Job, being careful to ensure that any direct light did not fall in his sore eye. "Brother Job, you know my ignorance so please, what is a Sacrist?"

"And I thought that you were a man of the world!" Job enjoyed another chuckle at Godfrew's expense. "A Sacrist, my

The Grace of God

friend, is the monk responsible for the protection and maintenance of sacred things and the buildings that contain them. The famous—or perhaps I should say 'infamous'—Christomo is the Sacrist for Canterbury. This, being the Archbishop's summer palace, he is responsible for the construction of the new chapel."

"And he is the fatal flaw?"

"And he is the fatal flaw," confirmed Job. "A nice enough man in himself, but ..."

"Not the man for the job?"

"Not the man for the job. Every time we get so far, he comes along and changes his mind. We go back to ground level ... literally. It is a minor miracle that he has left the chancel alone, though at times I wish he had got that pulled down as well. The only real blessing is that our blessed Archbishop still thinks of himself as a monk and tends to shun things and places that might be thought of as ostentatious, such as a summer palace."

"This Christomo, has he given thought to the costs he is running up? There must have been an awful lot of widow's mites wasted in all this construction and demolition."

"Costs? What have costs got to do with it? Ask Christomo when you see him!"

"Which is when?"

"Which is tomorrow."

"Hence, you priming me?"

"My, my, Brother Godfrew, how quickly you catch on!" Brother Job stood up scattering a cloud of crust crumbs. Shuck gave a yelp of delight and dived at them, almost knocking the monk over.

* * *

Job, Godfrew and Shuck waited outside the incomplete chapel and let the sound of the workmen drift past them. The object of their observations was a slim monk of average height who was trying to hold a meaningful discussion with two other monks, both under a vow of silence. They were trying to get by with sign language.

"Christomo?" Godfrew asked from inside his hooded black habit.

"The very same." Job confirmed, as he twiddled his thumbs.

"Why is he trying to have such a long discussion with people who cannot give him clear answers back?"

"With Father Christomo, talking is the important part, not listening." Job clicked his tongue and smiled at Godfrew's hidden face. "Why? If he listened, he may have to consider someone else's opinion! Now, that wouldn't do at all, would it?" Job went back to watching the other monks. "I hope your Latin is up to scratch, because our Christomo is Irish, so Latin will be the means of communication."

Godfrew grunted, "It is not the best, but I have not had too many problems to date." Shuck took to rubbing himself on Godfrew's leg, adding more jet black hair to that which was already woven into the faded black fabric of his master's habit.

"Not had any problems so far?" Again Brother Job clicked his tongue. "Father Christomo will soon fix that. Ah, at last he has finished ear bashing poor old Theodore and Jude."

As Christomo got nearer, Godfrew saw that he was, in fact, quite dishevelled. Large splodges of spilt food graced his habit, which had faded from black to almost grey. His tonsure had almost disappeared. In fact, Godfrew had not been sure that he had a tonsure at first, but assumed that the monk did have one from the fact that the hair on the back and sides of his head was quite long and scraggly. Black whiskers poked hither and thither from the man's face and there was heavy griming in its creases.

"A bit tatty, isn't he? I thought that being an official of the Cathedral priory, he would have made an effort to look a bit smarter."

"Oh, Brother Godfrew, you must realise that Father Christomo is far too busy to worry about things such as appearance. Mind, he is a bit more 'worse-for-wear' than I expected. He must have missed the Easter bath and shave ... probably too busy."

"Were you too busy as well, Brother?"

"I bathed! In fact, I often sneak in extra baths. I find the order's thrice a year bathing routine does not fit well with my skin's tendency to develop rashes." Job stopped twiddling his

The Grace of God

thumbs and quickly examined his immaculate fingernails before hiding them in his sleeves.

As Christomo got nearer, Godfrew dropped his voice to a whisper. "I'm not talking about bathing, Brother. I'm talking about shaving."

"I'm not a priest. I haven't been consecrated. I'm not required to have a tonsure." Job hissed back.

"It was your face I was thinking about."

"Look, baby-fluff face, I was far too busy." Job stopped whispering as he realised that he had used Christomo's usual excuse for not doing something. "I will talk to you later about YOUR sins." Job threw back his hood and took a step toward the monk, hurrying toward him. When he spoke, his voice was full of good will and warmth. "Father Christomo. How nice to see you again. I trust that the Lord has been blessing you?"

"Yes, yes. Lots to do, of course. Always busy, always busy." Christomo touched the corners of his mouth, one at a time, with his tongue. "I see the work is expanding at a prodigious rate—well within the situational time frame agreed to by all parties at our last information exchange. Good man, good man." After tonguing the corners of his mouth again, he strode onto the building site. "Now I know, Brother Job, that you will accept this not as a criticism of your self or, indeed, of your excellent expenders of manual labour, but the windows do seem to be a trifle wide spread thus having the potential to increase the feeling of spatial insulation."

Job glanced at the partially completed chapel walls before commenting to the Sacrist, who was prodding still wet mortar with a small stick: "Father Christomo, you approved the plans."

"Yes, well, it could be said that I may, or indeed may not, for both options are perfectly reasonable ... that I may have let my bottom line parameters fail to vertically integrate with the phase two maxim paradigm while implementing real-time multi-functional simulations resulting in a non-viable utilisation strategy vis-a-vis projected outcomes. However, I would be perfectly happy—indeed delighted—to discuss and debate, in a non-threatening manner, the whole or any part of that suggestion. Indeed, I would be prepared to stand by any decision made as a result of said exchange of ideas should ... and it need not be that way, of course ... but should it be decided that a firm ... and that, too, could be subject to negotiation ... that a firm statement be issued on the matter." Christomo took a quick lick at his mouth and then resumed. "However, be that as it may, all ideas and all ideas and plans, especially if they are intended to bring about an epochal coalescence of optics and spatial illusion within a very limited ... and I repeat, very limited area ... must, by the very nature of the thing, be subject to and influenced by the need to ensure that they are indeed 'living' in all senses of the word—and therefore subject to alterations, amendments, and modifications. To summarise: all things are negotiable."

Godfrew waited for the Sacrist to wander off and continue inspecting the work on the windows. "Brother Job." His companion waited for him to catch up, "What did he say?"

Job raised his eyebrows and sighed. "He said that he may have made a mistake and that we are going to have to change it all again."

Christomo stood with his back to the chancel and surveyed the chapel, making a square of his hands and framing aspects of the various views. "Now, Brother Job, I am at present convinced—though should you wish to participate in further dialogue of the meaningful variety, you are more than welcome ... nay, very welcome ... to submit modifications and variations to the proposals —and that is all they are at this point in time. So, please interrupt if you wish to make a verbal contribution. Now, as I was saying, I am convinced that -—with only minor modifications—we can construct here a place of worship that will display an equipoise of semiotic deigraphical eminence." The monk licked the corners of his lips.

Job walked slowly over to where the Sacrist stood. "Father Christomo, I hate to say this, but we are supposed to be building a simple chapel for a very simple man. It is not supposed to be a cathedral."

Christomo gave a shocked look to Brother Job. "Sorry? Did you suggest that we should not valorise the deity by utilising all our full skill set and attributes to the maximum in displaying a hagiography and an angiography of extraor-

The Grace of God

dinary beatitude in such a manner as to give Him the greatest glory?"

"The cost, Father Christomo, the cost." Job started wringing his hands. "We are well over budget now!"

"Brother Job, this is for the glory of God, not an outhouse for serfs!" Christomo shook his head in disbelief and a flea leaped across to Brother Job. "The matter of costs do not come into it. It is no good, you bringing your secular ideas ... and having said that, I would not like you to think that I hold the aforesaid secular ideas in ridicule, but secular ideas do not fit in with the requisites of Mother Church when it comes to constructing ... nay 'creating' ... a place of worship—albeit a private chapel—to ensure that the private and no doubt powerful ... though that is not to say that God does not listen to yours and, indeed, my prayers any less than that of someone as highly exalted as the Archbishop ... but powerful prayers they undoubtedly are, but none-the-less private prayers of the country's leading official of Mother Church."

"You will obtain the extra money then, Father Christomo?"

"The money will be provided—in the fullness of time and when the circumstances dictate—in total payment for the outlay in manual and physical expenditure." Christomo licked his lips again. "Of this I have full, indeed, overwhelming confidence." The Sacrist moved on to the chancel. "Remember that when it comes to glorifying God, money is not a consideration."

"He says that no matter what, he is changing the plans yet again despite the fact that he has no money." Job translated for Godfrew as they followed in the other's wake.

Christomo walked around the only completed part of the chapel, prodding and poking wherever he went. Finally, he faced Brother Job. "Hmm." He cupped his chin and thought for a while before continuing. "Brother Job, I wonder if we have done the right thing here. I am becoming more and more convinced that we need to replace the existing window with one of a more annular shape, fitted with multicoloured and multi-faceted glass to give an anodyne effect to the scenes of purgatory and hell portrayed on the walls."

Godfrew gasped, "So that's what the pictures are! I never would have guessed."

"He is?" Christomo asked Job.

"Brother Godfrew, my assistant."

"He is right, of course. The pictorial portrayal of such involved and complex theological concepts cannot be—though here, of course, others may disagree with me ... and they, of course, are perfectly entitled to their opinion—even if I do feel that any debate organised on the matter would be won by those of a similar mind set as myself. No, the concepts cannot be portrayed in such a simplistic manner if they are to be totally heuristic and display a total taxonomy of the subject. There are so many other possible ideas and thoughts on the matter that have been omitted." He turned to the hooded Godfrew. "Thank you, Brother for pointing the fault out to me. I shall immediately take steps to have the error rectified."

"Father Christomo," Job ran after the fast disappearing Sacrist. "May I please ask you when you will confirm the alterations and the arrangements for paying for the work?"

Christomo stopped and looked at Job in a strange way. "But we have agreed on the salient and necessary points."

"Please, Father?"

"If you insist, I will send a written and detailed confirmation of the verbal dialogue and interchange that we have had today. Then, should you feel it essential, I will arrange a discussion regarding the feasibility of some more meaningful interpersonal dialogue leading to the possibility of organising an ongoing verbal conversation on the continuation and potential modification of the plans and designs for the chapel. Good day, Brother."

"Good day, Father."

Godfrew came and stood at Job's side. "I know my hearing is shot and that I would have missed most of what was said, but I assume that he is going to pull the whole thing down again. If we make the changes, will that be it?"

Job gave a big sigh and shook his head. "I'm sorry to say it, but Father Christomo's decisions are always different to what you thought. Even when I get the written instructions giving me his final decision, it will only be valid for the day on which it was written. I suppose it is not his fault that he is the way he is. He was an oblate monk, given by his family as a child to the church, he has never known anything other than the cloister. The real world means nothing to him."

* * *

For three years the building and rebuilding of the chapel went on. Every time it seemed as if they were nearing completion, Father Christomo would make a 'progress' inspection and major alterations would then result. There was, however, eventually progress leading to the completion of the job. By now, Godfrew had well settled into the routine and life at Croydon—with its small priory and never-used Archbishop's palace. His previous life seemed as if it had belonged to someone else. With the chapel complete and only awaiting dedication, Godfrew and Job even managed to find time for some quiet fishing in the artificial fish ponds that had been formed by damming the river Wandle as it flowed through the grounds of the palace.

Brother Job removed the trout from his line and mercifully broke its neck, muttering a prayer of thanks as he did so. He laid it alongside the morning's catch and rebaited his hook. "What a pleasant pastime fishing is ... and productive, too. I will get these gracious gifts of God along to my wife later and no doubt we shall see them at evening meal. I am so glad that we have returned to the winter schedule and get fed again in the evenings."

"It's all right for you, Brother, but I have yet to catch anything." Godfrew wriggled his numbing buttocks, disturbing his hound Shuck in the process. The dog got up, shook, and then settled himself down again, this time with his head in his master's lap. "But, I agree with you. Fishing is a pleasant pastime. It gives you a chance to enjoy the beauty of God's handiwork, indulge in contemplation and—in your case anyway—catch something to eat ... and all at the same time. Far better than spending all our time on the chapel ... putting up and taking down."

"Yes, Brother Godfrew ... far better. Though I must say that I am surprised at the way things progressed once Father Christomo was taken off of the job. Now that was a strange thing, for it is most unusual for people such as a Sacrist to loose their positions, especially when their new role is little more than being a copy clerk for a prior!"

"One could almost say it was a miracle."

"A miracle that, as I understand it, was brought about by a letter being received by the Archbishop himself, informing him that he should look into the expenses being laid out on his building and maintenance programmes." Job threw his line into the still clear water, raising ever widening ripples. The line floated on the surface and Job watched it drift toward the end of the pond where the river again took shape.

"As I understand it, the Archbishop is a very plain man who takes great interest in how the money in his archdiocese is being spent." Godfrew pulled in his line, the bait still attached and unwanted by the fish. He stood up and made a long cast, putting the line right into the middle of the pond. Shuck, again disturbed, pricked up his ears at something only he could hear and ran off to investigate.

"I know that, Brother, and I can understand his concern at what was happening to the funds that Father Christomo had stewardship of, but how did the letter get straight into his own hands without passing through those of others who might well have been tempted to divert it to the Sacrist instead?"

"The ways of the Lord are mysterious, are they not, Brother Job?"

"I can see, Brother Godfrew, that I am not going to get any further with this line of enquiry, so I shall just pull in the fish I have caught and then head back toward the kitchens with our offerings."

Godfrew pulled in his empty hand line and wound it around his piece of wood. "I doubt if you will see your fish at supper, Brother. I would think that they will be kept back for the function being held after the new chapel's consecration tomorrow." He looked across at Job who was laying out his latest catch alongside the others. "This will be the first time Archbishop Anslem has been here in all the time he has been Archbishop. I wonder if he is making the effort to see just what sort of value he got for Father Christomo's lavish outlay?"

Job glanced lovingly at the bright silver fish laid out before him and then reluctantly bent down and strung them together to make it easier carry them back to the kitchen. "Such beautiful creatures! It is a shame to kill them, but then ... it is such a joy to eat them. Oh, the complexities of life. I'm sure you are right and that we will not get to eat them. Still, it will be an honour if the Archbishop himself gets to have one—lightly broiled in butter and bay leaf. That would be good." Job licked his bewhiskered lips at the thought. "Washed down with a good, dry, white Rhenish wine." He looked over at Godfrew who was casting his eye around for his missing hound. "You are not a wine man yourself are you?"

"Ale or cider, me. Most wine tastes like sheep's piss."

"But you do know where to get it. I heard that you were able to advise the Chamberlain where to go to get the best value for his wines and beers." Job wound his line around his pole. "Now how did you get to know that?"

"A previous life, Brother. I have got to know many things in my past life. Most I want to forget, but there are a few matters that are worth remembering." Godfrew returned to looking around the grounds. "Now, where on earth is Shuck. It is not like him to disappear for so long."

"Come on, Brother, we have to be back soon for service. That hound of yours has a well-developed sense of smell. He will find you when he is ready."

"Did you say that my hound smells?" Godfrew followed Job as he headed off across the flat green lawn.

"Really, Brother, your hearing is getting very bad. It is almost as bad as your eyesight." Job stopped. "Look ... there he is ... over there."

"Where?"

"Honestly ... and I thought I was short sighted!" Job caught hold of Godfrew's elbow and guided him to the rear of the palace and the cellar doors. "Can you see him now?"

"Where?" Godfrew screwed his eye up and squinted hard at the blur in front of him. "I'm not that bad, I know where we are, but he is black and that makes him hard to see in the shadows. Where is he?"

Job turned his companion slightly and pointed. "There ... being made a fuss of by that woman near the cart."

"Dear God!" Godfrew dug his heels in and pulled back from Job's guiding hand.

"What's the matter, Brother? I know that some of the brethren think that all women are from the Devil, but you and I are men of the world and we know better than that." He gave Godfrew's elbow another tug. "Brother, what is it? Who is that woman?"

"Papa? Papa? Is that really you?" Fleur let go of Shuck's silken ears and ran toward the two monks. "Papa?"

"My beloved Fleur!" Godfrew held his arms open wide and embraced his daughter. "God's peace, my child."

Fleur cried and clung to Godfrew "Oh, my Papa, I ... we ... we thought you must be dead." Godfrew stroked Fleur's hair that poked beneath her wimple, the bright copper now mingled with shinning silver. "When that monk came and said that he had been told that we sold the best ale in Surrey, I thought no more of it, till he described the man who had made the recommendation." She pulled back to look at Godfrew's face, tears still welling in her reddened eyes. "I hoped ... no, knew ... that it must be my Papa. I made Moithar bring me when he delivered the ale. Oh, Papa ... how I have missed you."

"You are never far from my thoughts, little one." Godfrew gave her a squeeze. "The children?"

"I left them at home. The journey would have been too much." Fleur felt the coarseness of Godfrew's black habit with the tips of her fingers. She searched his eyes. "Papa? Have you become a monk?"

"Me? A monk?" Godfrew chuckled, then kissed Fleur's head. "Bless you ... no, but I have found a place for myself here."

Fleur's eyes closed and she started crying again, "Then, then you won't be coming home with me—us?"

"My precious, precious one. I have spent many years seeking and seeking, I knew not what. At last I have found it and found it in abundance." He held his daughter close and rocked her. "I have found God's peace. I will always be here. Just come and talk to me whenever you need me."

A bell started tolling. "Brother Godfrew?" Job said quietly, unwilling to break the moment, "it is time for service."

"Think of me, my pretty little flower, as often as I think of you ... and visit me again."

The Grace of God

"I will, Papa. I will ... often." Fleur reluctantly let go of her foster father cum father-in-law. Godfrew kissed her on both cheeks and followed Brother Job toward the small priory.

Moithar came out of the cellar just as Godfrew walked past. "So ... you are still alive then ... you old bugger?"

"I love you too, my son."

* * *

Godfrew, Job and Job's wife sat under a willow tree and watched the autumn sunset. Wisps of mist hung over the fish ponds and gnats hovered, seeking warm flesh. Job sank his hands deeper into his sleeves. The movement was made more difficult by the fact that his right arm was looped through his wife's left. "Your daughter, did you say, Brother? But you have also said that she is your daughter-in-law?"

"Yes, she is." Godfrew closed his eyes and let the vision of his beloved Fleur fill his mind. "It is a long story and one I will not tell you. But she is all I have left that I care to remember."

"What of your sons, Brother?" asked Job's wife, Balthild.

"My eldest left home one harvest to work on the last piece of land remaining to my family in Sussex. He never returned. My second cousin only had daughters and, rather than let the property fall into French hands, he asked Jaul if he wanted to marry his eldest girl and keep the land in the family."

"Is she a nice girl, the one that your Jaul married?" Balthild probed.

"I have never met her. I only found out what had happened by chance. Otherwise, I would have thought that he had been killed. My youngest, Njal, may, in fact, be dead, for all I know. He went to join the Varangian Guard and serve the Greek Emperor. I just pray that he made it. Of my three living sons, just the middle one, Moithar, stayed with me ... and that has been a stormy relationship. Only my Fleur has remained close to me, though in view of the circumstances in which I claimed her, I am never sure why."

"I heard you ask her about the grandchildren," butted in Job. "Do they have the same copper hair as her?"

"The granddaughter has. The boys have the same golden hair as my wife had—not the white colouring of their father."

"Your wife had golden hair? I thought you told me it was ginger?"

"It was, it was. She was very distinctive with that hair and her Herefordshire accent."

Job looked puzzled. "I thought you told me she was from Kent?"

"Yes, she was." Godfrew slipped back into a world of his own and Job and Balthild got up and left him with Shuck and the fading sunset.

The Release

Godfrew sat on the altar steps and watched the final preparations being made for the consecration of the chapel later that day. The horrific paintings on the chancel wall remained, but their visual assault had been softened by arrangements of wild flowers set along the walls. Godfrew looked at the altar itself and sighed with relief that the monstrosity of a cross that had been commissioned by Father Christomo had not been put out. In its place stood the simple wood and silver one from Archbishop Anslem's private chapel at Canterbury. As he sat there, he was joined by the priest of Croydon, Father Ethelwulf.

"Good morning, Godfrew. At last ... your work is complete." The old priest touched Godfrew's shoulder. "Have you thought about what you will do now?"

"Not yet." Godfrew looked at Ethelwulf. The priest's face bore the broken nose and missing front teeth of an old warrior. The man's finger joints were swollen and his joints creaked with the arthritics of an old sailor. "I had hoped to stay here where I feel so at home, but I am not sure that I can. Brother Job is moving on to his next job. Maybe the palace will have a position for me. I don't know."

"If it is the Lord's will, then you will stay. If it is not, then he will show you the way. Though whatever happens, my son, he will be with you."

"Of that I am sure, Father. But it is unsettling." Godfrew screwed his good eye up as a beam of early light came in through the coloured glass behind the altar and made a pool of light around him and the priest. "It was here that Jesus came to me, forgave my sins and gave me peace."

"Talking of which, my son, you have never confessed." Father Ethelwulf watched Godfrew's face for his reaction.

Godfrew went quiet and looked into his lap. "Father, God forgave me for what I had done in my previous life. I confessed to him. Why should I do the same again to you?"

"My ... my ... the time you have spent with our resident rebel, Brother Job, has affected you!" Despite his words, Ethelwulf did not seem put out. "Tell me, my son, when did you last confess ... to a priest of the mother church that is."

"Before the fight at Stamford Bridge. We all did, King Harold insisted." Godfrew gave an ironic snort. "He said that God was on our side and that he wanted his blessing on all that we did in our defense of the realm. I hear that the Normans did the same. No ... wait ... after the taking of Shrewsbury ... on the way home, I stayed at an Abbey whilst my arm healed. I seem to remember that the Abbess insisted that I took Confession. Yes ... I remember now, for the penance was ..." He went red and closed his eyes. "No ... that must have been a dream ... the sort of dream that one has when one has been too long away from one's wife. No ... the last time I confessed was that futile attempt at pleasing God before the fight in Yorkshire. Then there was Senlac—the English, no doubt, praying for one thing and the Normans praying for the opposite."

"Godfrew, Godfrew." The warrior-cum-priest moved closer and leaned across to put his face right in front of Godfrew's. "God judged between Harold and William. Why he chose William, only He knows. God often takes peoples and nations along paths that they don't understand at the time. When our great-great-great grandsons look back, maybe they will see why things happened the way that they did. You were part of an army. In that time you would have done many things that God would class as a sin." Godfrew started to protest, but the priest held his finger to his lips. "I know, you have had his personal assurance that you have been forgiven and I am not going to try and deny that, but although you have been washed clean in the blood of Jesus, you have since continued to walk along the dusty path of life. Even if your body has been cleansed, your feet would have become dirty. Come with me and confess. Let me clean your feet, as Jesus did for his disciples."

"Put it like that, Father, and how can I refuse? But I don't agree with the idea of doing meaningless penances!" Godfrew looked the old priest in the eye and raised his eyebrow.

"Still the fighter, Godfrew?" Ethelwulf's eyes twinkled. "I, too, was a fighter—a ship's man. Now, I only fight for God.

The Release

Regarding the penance, I am obliged to give it to you, but the completion of it will be between you and God. Is that an acceptable thing?"

"Yes, Father." Godfrew suddenly felt very tired and old. His heart started beating hard and his fingers tingled.

"Are you all right?" Ethelwulf looked concerned and his eyes darted over Godfrew's face, seeking information.

Godfrew closed his eyes and rocked till the pain in his chest eased and he felt that he had his heart under control again. "Am I all right?" he took deep breaths and then opened his eyes. "Yes, I am all right. Come, let us get this foot washing done."

"It is not very private here, Godfrew. Perhaps we should retire to the little storage room to the side." Father Ethelwulf helped Godfrew up. "In view of Jesus telling us to pray in a cupboard, I think the storage room will be very appropriate for a plain Christian such as yourself." The two men retired to the small room that already smelled strongly of the candles and packets of incense that were stored there. In the darkness, Godfrew confessed. Knowing Ethelwulf to be a man who had been involved with the foulness of war, he confessed all. The priest put his arms around the penitent's shoulders and comforted him. Godfrew dragged up the past ... laid it out—in the open at last. Knowing that Godfrew had already felt that he had received forgiveness direct from God, Father Ethelwulf laid on Godfrew a penance of prayer that he knew would be acceptable to both Godfrew and God.

As they left the darkened room and stepped into the now bright chapel, Godfrew screwed his eyes up hard and shook his head.

There in front of him was a demon summoned from the pit.

"You, you Saxon dog. At last I have you!"

"Pardon?" Godfrew squinted his eyes to try and see the demon more clearly.

"I wait, God give, you die!" The Breton Captain with the swine's face snorted happily. He turned to the two young soldiers at his side: "Take! Hold! He no escape. And if he does, you adder's offspring, I will have your hides." The soldiers grabbed Godfrew and marched him away.

* * *

Brother Job stood at the barred gate of the wine cellar and peered about, holding his candle high, so as to throw as much light into the place as he could.

At last he saw Godfrew huddled in the corner.

"Let me speak to him." The monk slipped a silver penny into the young soldier's hand.

"Just this once, monk. If my comrade hears about it, he will tell the Captain ... and then I will be joining your friend in there."

"Brother Godfrew!" Job pushed his face against the bars. "What is this all about?"

It took a while for Godfrew to answer. When he did, his voice was muffled by the swelling of his lacerated mouth. "It seems, Brother, that although God has forgiven me my past ... men haven't ... like David, after taking Bathsheba ... I must suffer the consequences of my actions." He coughed. It was some time before he managed to get himself under control and was able to continue. "I owe the Breton his mangled face. I think he wants to dissuade me from continuing such habits." Godfrew tried to laugh, but instead went into another coughing spasm. It took much longer before he could again speak. "This is not the first time I have had the pleasure of being detained by my Breton acquaintance, but I think that this will be the last."

"Never, Brother. He will not kill you. The Prior is going to see him this afternoon, just as soon as the Archbishop has left."

* * *

The Prior, his monks in procession, stood before the Breton Captain bearing bell, book and candle. "That man is one of the brethren. If you do not let him go, I will excommunicate you!" He turned to the monk at his side, "Brother Heluin, you're French, tell him what I said."

Heluin stepped forward. As he did so, he rubbed the star-shaped scar on his cheek that had been made by a stone from an English slingshot as he had charged with the Norman cavalry up the hill at Senlac. "That man is one of the

The Release

brethren. If you do not let him go, I will excommunicate you," he translated.

"Tell that upstart Saxon monk that I don't give a rabid rat's rectum what he says. The prisoner is wanted in four counties for treason and murder. He can do whatever he likes, but the prisoner is mine!" The Breton rubbed his weeping snout with a rag and glared balefully at the Prior with his good eye.

"What did he say?" asked the Prior leaning over Heluin's shoulder.

"He said 'no'."

"Tell him again that the man cannot be tried by any other than the Church, as he is a priest."

"Father?" asked Brother Heluin. "You know that he has not been consecrated. How can I tell this man that Godfrew is a priest?"

The Prior shrugged his shoulders. "Scripturally, all Christians are members of God's Royal Priesthood, but I doubt if our pig-faced friend here wishes to discuss doctrinal and theological niceties. Just tell him what I said and let it be on my conscience."

Heluin coughed into his hand and then readdressed the Breton: "The man you are holding is a priest. He bares a tonsure."

The Captain gave a strange, gurgling laugh. "Him a priest?" He grabbed Heluin's habit and pulled him to a finger length from his fetid face. "He had that tonsure when he murdered my men at Shrewsbury. He had it when he murdered more of them at Huntingdon. I even heard that he had it not so long ago when he murdered the reeve at Garrat. He is no priest. He is just a bald, rabid, old wolf who needs putting down." He let go of Heluin, who staggered back into the arms of the Prior.

"No?" inquired the Prior.

"No," confirmed Heluin.

"Then although I may not be able to help Godfrew, I can and will excommunicate this French excrement."

The Prior and his monks had just finished their act of excommunication when the door opened and a richly-dressed man came in. Although he wore his hair in the long, English style and had drooping moustaches, his dress was French. He waited for the Prior to finish and troop his monks out before going to the Breton Captain.

"What was that all about, Nigel?" asked Rualon. He spoke in Breton.

"Lord Rualon." The Captain dipped his head in salute to the king's councilor and friend. As his head angled down, watery snot fell on the rush-covered floor with a quiet plop. "Nothing important. The Prior was just expressing concern at the fact that I have arrested one of his servants."

"You did what?" Rualon's face went red and he swallowed hard. "You had better have a very good reason for having done so, Nigel, or I will personally see you nailed to the door. The king would be furious if we upset the Archbishop so near to his wedding."

"The man is wanted all over the country for murder and treason. I ... we, rather ... have been seeking him for years. I intend to take him back to Rochester to stand trial." The Captain dabbed his watery eye with the rag and then stuck it under his weeping snout to absorb the drips.

"For years, Nigel? How many years?" Rualon went to the table and poured a watery red wine into the plain wooden goblet that stood by the ewer.

"Since the battle of Hastings when Duke William of Normandy became King William the Conquer of England."

"Oh, no, Nigel. That will not do. The Conqueror's son, King William Rufus, issued an amnesty to those rebels who still stood condemned for their part in the English resistance."

"There is the murder of the reeve at Garrat!" the Captain insisted.

"And that was definitely him? Beyond any reasonable doubt? Enough witnesses to hang him?"

"Perhaps not, Lord Rualon," conceded the Captain, again dabbing his eye.

"Perhaps not! You know not. That place is not even in my jurisdiction. Even arresting him here for trial back in Kent will need some explaining. I suspect that this is a personal matter, Nigel. Is it?" Rualon tasted the wine and found it to his liking, so he quaffed it all and poured himself another.

The Release

The Captain shuffled his feet. "Nothing personal, I assure you. It is just that I have wanted him caught for so long, Lord Rualon."

"Is that so?" Rualon sat on the table edge. "Nigel, you are a thing of the past ... rather like your quarry. Two old men, still fighting the battles of the past. Hah!" He sipped his drink. "Our beloved king, King Henry, is English born. Next week he marries Edith of Scotland, who is of the old English royal family. Their union will at last legitimise the throne. Even those English who still hate the French for the invasion—and all that happened afterwards—will have to agree about that. And you want to stir it all up again? I really think, Nigel, that I will have to have you sent back to Brittany." After another sip of wine, he looked across the rim of the goblet. "Maybe I will recommend to the king that he should have you put in a monastery alongside this prisoner of yours. You could talk about old times together."

"But he is still wanted on existing warrants. I am sure that I can find them when we get back."

"I am sure you will ... warrants with the ink on them still wet, no doubt." Rualon put his now empty goblet down and headed for the door. "I know that you are the Sheriff of Kent's man and not mine, but you will only take this man prisoner at my displeasure. I personally will see King Henry and ask him to pardon the man as part of the benefits he issues on his wedding day. Earlier, you told me that the monks were here only to protest about you arresting one of the servants. You lied! I may not know my Latin as well as I should, but even I could tell that they were excommunicating you. If you ignore what they have done and if you take their servant and put him on trial, I can assure you that they will go to Archbishop 'Holier-Than-Thou' Anslem and cause no end of trouble. There is too much at stake here between King, country and church. With Henry so recent on the throne, I can assure you that I—and all of the King's friends and companions—will not see anyone put everything at risk. Especially, if it is all about a senile old fool who once thought he could reverse history. Rebellions have been caused by less."

The baron strode out.

* * *

What's this all about, Grim?" the freckle-faced young soldier asked his companion as the other man unlocked the gate of the wine cellar.

"Captain Swineface wants to top the old man before we leave, Tok. That's what." The keys jangled as he turned the lock.

"Is that legal?" The gate squealed as it swung on its hinges, breaking fresh spider's webs.

"We are only obeying orders. We are not to reason why—and I, for one, am not willing to risk his wrath." The two young men went over to stir Godfrew as he lay sleeping in the corner. "Come on, old man. Time to go." Godfrew got up slowly and followed the men out into the sunrise.

"You hurry. That oak tree there." The Breton Captain pointed to a lightning struck tree at the rear of the palace of Croydon. In the Captain's mangled hand was a coil of rope with a noose at its end. Shuck stirred himself from the side of the kitchen wall where he had spent the night and ran to sniff Godfrew's hand. The Captain looked gleefully at Godfrew as he stood stoop-shouldered between his guards: "Saxon dog, you are about to get what you deserve," he spat at him in Breton. He struck Godfrew full in the mouth with his good fist, causing him to stagger back. The soldiers caught him and pulled him upright again.

Shuck snarled and barked.

The Captain kicked him. Shuck bit the Captain's leg. "Bastard Saxon dog." The Captain drew his sword and slew the hound—severing him in twain.

As the party marched toward the tree Godfrew began a chant:

> Strong hearts desire
> All of my hope
> Waits on the Cross
> In this world now.
> My powerful friends
> Have all gone before me,
> Leaving earth's trappings,
> The King of Glory to seek.
> Dwelling now with the Father

The Release

>In bright heaven above,
>Abiding in rapture,
>True wonders they see.
>Each day I dream
>Of first seeing the Cross
>And knew then this life
>Is but fleeting, then lost.
>But that token of triumph
>Fair shows me my home
>Where all God's people
>Live established forever
>In joy everlasting
>And praise around the throne.
>There will I live then,
>Abiding in glory,
>True loving bliss,
>With all other saints.
>May the Lord be gracious,
>Who of old trod this earth
>To be nailed on the Cross
>For the sins of all men.
>He redeemed and brought us
>For life everlasting.
>Hope he gives all men
>On this sin-filled globe.
>In that one great deed,
>God's son was triumphant.
>Almighty sole ruler,
>He reigns now with God,
>Bringing his faithful
>To his heavenly bliss
>To join with all saints
>In the splendour of glory,
>When the Lord God Almighty
>Came again to his throne.[1]

"What he say?" asked the Breton, his English still poor despite his many years in the land.

---

[27] Free translation from the Old English of the final verses of *The Dream of the Rood*, circa 800, thought to be by Cynewulf or by someone from his school.

"He is praying," explained Tok.

"Prayer? He need it. He soon dance at rope end."

Godfrew looked up at the sun as it broke above the trees of the palace grounds and dappled the rippling waters of the river Wandle and its ponds. He felt a kick in his chest and his body went numb. As he sank to his knees, he saw Jesus step out of the sun and come toward him with his arms open wide.

Godfrew smiled.

The Breton Captain strode on and then stopped, wondering why he could not hear the others following. "What wrong?" There was no reply, so he turned and saw his men bent over the prostrate body of Godfrew. He stormed back. The soldiers had turned Godfrew over and they were looking at his bluish face. "Dead?"

"Dead, Captain." Grim slipped the sword ring of Earl Edric from Godfrew's finger and dropped it into his pouch.

"Bastard." The Captain took a closer look at the face of his old adversary." You bastard, you are smiling. You won didn't you ... and you know it." He stood back and kicked Godfrew in the face. "Laugh at me, would you!"

* * *

The old woman knelt in prayer by the small flowering thorn bush at the foot of the grave in the churchyard at Croydon. White frost shimmered on the blades of grass. As the woman told her beads and prayed in her French-accented English for the soul of her long dead Papa, her golden-haired sons stood protectively behind her.

And at the side of each young man sat a black hound.

THE END